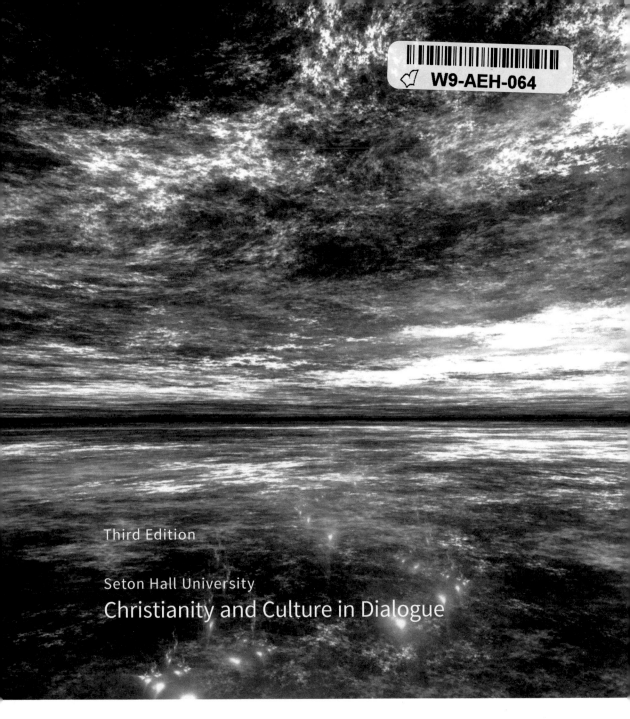

Third Edition

Seton Hall University

Christianity and Culture in Dialogue

macmillan learning
curriculum solutions

Copyright © 2018 by Seton Hall University

Photos provided by Hayden-McNeil, LLC are owned or used under license

Editors: Anthony Sciglitano and Laura Pallitto

Contributors: Richard Liddy, Nancy Enright, Ki Joo Choi, Peter Savastano, John Ranieri, Mary Balkun, Roseanne Mirabella, Robert Pallitto, Colleen Conway, Anthony Sciglitano

Printed in the United States of America

10 9 8 7 6 5 4 3 2 1

ISBN 978-0-7380-9897-5

Macmillan Learning Curriculum Solutions
14903 Pilot Drive
Plymouth, MI 48170
www.macmillanlearning.com

Sciglitano 9897-5 F17

 macmillan learning
curriculum solutions

Sustainability

Hayden-McNeil's standard paper stock uses a minimum of 30% post-consumer waste. We offer higher % options by request, including a 100% recycled stock. Additionally, Hayden-McNeil Custom Digital provides authors with the opportunity to convert print products to a digital format. Hayden-McNeil is part of a larger sustainability initiative through Macmillan Learning. Visit http://sustainability.macmillan.com to learn more.

bedford/st. martin's • hayden-mcneil
w.h. freeman • worth publishers

TABLE OF CONTENTS

ACKNOWLEDGMENTS

The work of this reader represents the labor of many groups and individuals at Seton Hall University who some years ago saw the need to engage the entire campus in an ongoing conversation about the big questions that haunt and animate us as intellectual creatures. Thus began the work resulting in creation of a University Core Curriculum. So we must thank the Administration for their support, especially Monsignor Robert Sheeran and Gabriel Esteban, President and Provost respectively at the beginnings of Core 2101: Christianity and Culture in Dialogue.

The Faculty Senate was instrumental in moving this Core through its various stages of approval, no easy feat in an age of professional specialization.

As many here know, none of this could have happened without the generous work of Drs. Roseanne Mirabella, Peter Ahr, Marian Glenn and Mary Balkun, all of whom have worked tirelessly to develop, staff and continuously improve the University Core.

For this volume specifically, we want to thank the Seton Hall faculty contributors: John Ranieri, Richard Liddy, Nancy Enright, Mary Balkun, Colleen Conway, Roseanne Mirabella, Robert Pallitto, and Ki Joo Choi. Professor Choi is deserving of special gratitude here because he penned so many of the introductions for our Reader.

Finally, we want to thank faculty members who gave valuable advice on specific points of fact in the introductions: Fred Booth from Classics, Vicente Medina from Philosophy, and Alan Brill from Jewish-Christian Studies.

CORE 2101: AN INTRODUCTION TO AN INTELLECTUAL ADVENTURE

CORE 1101 introduced you to a number of classic and pivotal texts of the Western tradition. Many of them are rightfully classified as classics because they continue to speak to us today. In fact, many of the texts you read in the first University Core Course have served as the cultural and conceptual foundations to so many aspects of modern life that we typically take them for granted. For instance, I am sure that you, like myself, rarely take the rime to think about a central aspect of our modern lives—democracy! When was the last time you woke up in the morning and thought about the fact that we live in a political community in which all individuals have the right to vote for president, governor, mayor, and so on? My guess is hardly ever, since we take it for granted. However, can you imagine what it would be like to live in a society other than a democratic society? I sure can't. In fact, I have never lived in a society other than a democratic one—democracy is in my blood as it is for all of you in this course. But the idea of a democratic society did not materialize overnight, or even over a period of weeks or months, or even years. The idea of democratic society as we know it today is a relatively recent development. By "recent development" I mean to emphasize that modern democracy is uniquely "Western," that is, the product of a long history of various ideas about truth, goodness, rationality, belief, power, love, and justice in dialogue with each other within what is typically referred to as the *Western tradition*.

What is so interesting about this obvious but often little discussed "fact of modern life" is that the ideas that have facilitated modern democracy (as well as modern cultural institutions and economic systems [from socialism to capitalism]) are not simply non-theological or "secular" *but also* profoundly theological and religious. Let's think about this for a moment. The claim certainly sounds odd at first because we usually think that it is best to keep religious discussions to ourselves, at the very least, in order to "keep the peace" at the family dinner table. (I don't know about you, but in our family, if you discuss religion [and politics] at Thanksgiving dinner, the pumpkin pie may never end up on the dessert plates, but more likely in someone's face!) The fact is, however, that although we have come to "confine" religious beliefs to our own private reflections, our lives would not be what they are now without the kind of dialogue that has taken place between theological and non-theological beliefs and ideas for the past two and a half millennia.

So, what does this all mean? Let me make one proposal: If we want to better appreciate our world today and, perhaps more importantly, know how we can *advance* those social and political values and institutions we hold dear, then we *must* get to know more passionately and deeply the *intellectual* tradition of the "West."

To some large extent, CORE 1101 introduced you to this proposition. In this course, CORE 2101, we consider this proposition more seriously. In doing so, this course aims to remind us that the Western intellectual tradition—the tradition that is the basis of the values and institutions that make our lives what they are today—is a living, breathing, developing tradition, one that consists in a serious. mutually engaging—though sometimes contentious—dialogue, conversation, or, better yet, *deliberation* between theological voices on the one hand and non-religious voices on the other hand. We can specify this dialogue or conversation as one between the Catholic-Christian intellectual tradition and the non-religious philosophical tradition that begins with the ancient Greek thought of Plato. Therefore, it would be a significant mistake to think that when it comes to the Western intellectual tradition we mean only non-religious or secular thinkers and their ideas and writings. No, we *must* include the voices of Catholic thinkers and, more broadly, Christian theologians and philosophers. The Western tradition of political and social ideas would not be "Western" (or a "tradition") unless we remember that it centers on a sustained dialogue between theology and philosophy or, if you wish, between the broader categories of "faith" and "reason."

We already got a sense of this dialogue between faith and reason at the dawn of the first millennium, just as Christianity was developing as a major force in Western life during the middle-late Roman Empire. For instance, one of the earlier Christian thinkers, Tertullian (A.D. 155–222), in his *Pagan Philosophy the Parent of Heresies*, wrote:

> What indeed has Athens to do with Jerusalem? What concord is there between the Academy and the Church? What between heretics and Christians? . . . Away with all attempts to produce a mottled Christianity of Stoic, Platonic and dialectical composition! We want no curious disputation after possessing Christ Jesus, no inquisition over enjoying the gospel! With our faith, we desire no further belief.

For Tertullian, the categories of faith and reason are cast in terms of the metaphor of Jerusalem and Athens (making reference to both the "birth place" of Christianity and to the home of the great ancient Greek thinkers Plato and Aristotle). Although Tertullian believes that Athens has little relevance to Jerusalem, we see him struggling with the ideas of both Christian and non-Christian beliefs, how they might relate, whether they do relate, and, if so, how his image of Jerusalem and Athens in conflict and dialogue is a very helpful view of the central intellectual question or struggle of the Western tradition.

In another early Christian thinker, Justin Martyr (A.D. 105–165), however, we see a more mutual understanding of faith and reason or Jerusalem and Athens. In his *The First Apology* he writes,

> But the truth shall be told, for the wicked demons from ancient times appeared and defiled women, corrupted boys, and presented such terrifying sights to men that

those who were not guided by reason in judging these diabolical acts were panic-stricken. Seized with fear and unaware that these were evil demons, they called them gods and greeted each by the name each demon had bestowed upon himself. *But when Socrates attempted to make these things known and to draw men away from the demons by true reason and judgment, then these very demons brought it about, through men delighting in evil, that he be put to death as an atheist and impious person, because, they claimed, he introduced new divinities. And now they endeavor to do the very same thing to us. And not only among the Greeks were these things through Socrates condemned by reason [logos], but also among the non-Hellenic peoples by the Logos Himself, who assumed a human form and became man, and was called Jesus Christ.* . . . We have been taught that Christ is the first-born of God, and that He is the Logos of whom every race of men are partakers; and they who lived reasonably are Christians, even though they have been called atheists; as among the Greeks, Socrates, Heraclitus, and men like them. . . . Thus are we even called atheists. We do proclaim ourselves atheists as regards those whom you call gods, but not with respect to the Most True God, who is alien to all evil and is the Father of justice, temperance, and the other virtues.

Note the text that is in italics. In these lines we have a conception of faith and reason that is more complementary, dynamic, and robust. Since we have yet to read the words of Socrates as presented in Plato's *Dialogues*, Justin the Martyr's references may seem a bit opaque at this point. That is fine, however, for now. The larger point to be had at this juncture is to notice that Justin Martyr is willing to concede a kind of intellectual solidarity with non-Christian discourses, specifically those of Socrates. They are reasonable, he claims! More accurately, they are truthful! This is also the case with the claims of Christ, the Christian God. Such beliefs—those of Christian faith—are reasonable as well. They are true! In fact, for Justin Martyr, Socrates's claims are not exactly the same as the claims of Christian faith. Instead, although they are reasonable just as the claims of Christian faith are, the claims of Christian faith *further advance and illuminate* what Socrates endeavored to show to the Athenian authorities.

What is remarkable to consider is that Christian writers in the twentieth century must wrestle with the same kinds of issues as Justin and Tertullian, namely, how Christian faith should relate to the particular cultures in which it finds itself. In fact, the twentieth century has two theologians who nicely represent Justin and Tertullian. The great Catholic theologian, Karl Rahner, S.J. (1904–1984), was persuaded that God's gracious illumination was so present in the world that we are able to find wisdom throughout the world's cultures and religions, even to the point where it might be possible to think of non-Christians as what he called "anonymous Christians," that is, people who through the grace present beyond the Church have come to live lives that reflect the Truth. It was also important to Rahner to understand the roots and reasons for modern atheism, so that he could respond to the questions atheists posed to Christian faith.

Another famous theologian of the twentieth century named Karl Barth (1886–1968), who comes from the Reform Protestant tradition, saw things more like Tertullian. Barth was at the forefront of a movement in 1934 that denounced the rise of Hitler's government for Christian reasons. Like Tertullian, Barth was less persuaded than some of his contemporaries that culture reflected the good things of the Gospel. In contrast to Rahner, Barth's theology stressed the utter difference between the God revealed in the New Testament and the culture of his day.

One of the aims of this course is to help you to better see how major thinkers of the Western tradition wrestled with how faith and reason were related to one another for their particular historical context. Socrates, as Plato suggests to us, needed to discern his calling as a philosopher in the midst of a judgment against him by the very community he loved. Saint Paul believed he found a new meaning for his life that should attune the Christian community, not to the way of the world, but to the form of life revealed through Jesus Christ crucified. But Paul claimed that this life is the most reasonable of all! Saints Augustine and Anselm used ideas derived from Plato to express aspects of Christian faith; Ibn Rushd, the great Islamic philosopher, and Thomas Aquinas employed ideas from ancient Greek philosophy to express Muslim and Christian understandings of the world. All of these thinkers, and the others that you will study, strove to form a coherent view of faith and reason that fosters both a personally rewarding life and a vision of the common good.

The units of this course move chronologically, from the ancient period of Greek thought and early Christianity to the medieval period, the beginning of the modern era, and the height of the modern era, and then to the late nineteenth century and the middle of the twentieth century. In the weeks of each unit, as a way of illuminating the nature of the faith and reason dialogue that constitutes the very foundation of our contemporary Western society, an explicitly Catholic Christian text is paired with a non-Christian text.

Some of the readings are difficult, not only in their writing style but also in the content of their ideas. Do not be discouraged if you find the readings difficult! If everything we read were immediately clear, then we would have no need for study and learning. However, this is a great opportunity to better acquaint ourselves with fascinating texts that not only comprise our common intellectual, cultural, and social heritage, but also give us the intellectual resources that we must understand and study if we are to be serious about knowing who we are and where we should be going as a society. As the great artist Paul Gauguin once mused: "Where do we come from? What are we? Where are we going?" Can we answer these fundamental questions of human life and society without studying the theological and non-religious voices of the Western tradition? It certainly would be difficult without doing so. This is the adventure that awaits us in this course! The faculty of Core 2101 looks forward to taking this adventure with you.

ONE FINAL NOTE: Although some of the texts are difficult to read, pay close attention to the rhetoric—or the writing style—the authors use. Sometimes it is hard not to think that some of the authors can state their argument in one sentence or two—so, why do they spend so much time and spill so much ink writing such lengthy texts?!? One reason is certainly the issue of rhetoric. That is, they recognize the power of narrative, storytelling, or the power of good writing. Try to be aware of, and appreciate the fact that, many of the authors in this course are trying to write in a way that they think *will persuade you* to think they are right about a particular issue. In other words, they do not write in a neutral manner, as if what they write means nothing. They believe what they write, and they are trying to convince you of their verity.

Why does this matter to us? First, it matters because it indicates that there is something at stake in these ideas. These ideas matter and our task is to deliberate together in order to determine whether we agree or not. Second, it matters because their rhetorical strategies and styles remind us that how we express ideas and write about them contribute to the force or power a particular idea might have. It is not sufficient to merely say what we think, but we also need to express our thoughts in intelligent, imaginative, and insightful ways. These are, in part, the goals of good writing and good rhetoric. This is a point well worth remembering as you write your own papers and begin to contribute to this ongoing conversation.

Good luck to all of you!

A
ANCIENT GREEK AND EARLY CHRISTIAN THOUGHT:
GREEK CIVIC PIETY AND CHRISTIAN LOVE

Bible

Introduction to Saint Paul's First Letter to the Corinthians

Ki Joo Choi and Anthony Sciglitano

Many of you may already be familiar with Saint Paul's First Letter to the Corinthians. It is one of the books of the New Testament, the second half of the Christian Bible. (The Old Testament or Hebrew Scriptures [or *Tanakh*, in Hebrew] is the first part of the Christian Bible.) This letter is referred to as a Pauline epistle or letter because it is one of the many letters the Apostle Paul wrote to the several burgeoning Christian communities in the early Roman Empire. The First Letter to the Corinthians was written by Paul to the Christian community in the Greek city of Corinth.

The New Testament book called the Acts of the Apostles (which appears after the Gospel of John and before the Epistle to the Romans) tells the history of Paul, who was a persecutor of Christians for the Roman Empire. While on his way to Damascus, however, he hears the voice of Jesus and converts to Christianity, committing himself to the proclamation of the Gospel (or good news) of Jesus Christ's life, death, and Resurrection.

Newly converted, Paul endeavors to cultivate the many small Christian communities that have formed around the Roman Empire. He also establishes many of these communities himself. The Christian community in Corinth was one of these (see Acts of the Apostles, chapter 18). Paul is often referred to as the "Apostle to the Gentiles." The word *gentile* means non-Jews or people of "the nations." An *apostle* is one who is sent; in this case, sent to preach the *Gospel* or good news of Jesus Christ. In addition to Acts of the Apostles, Paul gives us a sense of how he views himself and his purpose in his Epistle or Letter to the Galatians 1:11–17:

> Now I want you to know, brothers, that the gospel preached by me is not of human origin. For I did not receive it from a human being, nor was I taught it, but it came through a revelation of Jesus Christ. For you heard of my former way of life in Judaism, how I persecuted the church of God beyond measure and tried to destroy it, and progressed in Judaism beyond many of my contemporaries among my race, since I was even more a zealot for my ancestral traditions. But when God, who from my mother's womb had set me apart and called me through his grace, was pleased to reveal his Son to me, so that I might proclaim him to the Gentiles, I did not immediately consult flesh and blood, nor did I go up to Jerusalem to those who were apostles before me; rather, I went into Arabia and then returned to Damascus. (cf. Philippians 3:2–6)

Here, it becomes clear that Paul thinks his mission is to bring the Gospel to gentile or non-Jewish populations. It also becomes clear that Paul, even though a Jewish convert to Christianity, still thinks of himself as a faithful Jew with a new message from God.

As you begin to read Paul's First Letter to the Corinthians, it becomes clear that Paul wrote this letter in response to a number of disputes and controversies that erupted among the Christians in Corinth. In advance of his return to Corinth in order to mediate some of the problems there (see chapter 16, verse 8, of 1 Corinthians, abbreviated as 1 Cor. 16:8), he wrote this letter from the town of Ephesus (see Acts 16). The letter is dated as approximately A.D. 53–57 (thus, about five hundred years after Plato's life).

As you read this letter, pay close attention to Paul's diagnosis of the problems and disputes that the Corinthian Christians are experiencing. His diagnosis rests on their failure to remember and hold true to the Christian profession of "Christ crucified" (see chapter 1, verse 23). Please note that Paul interchanges "Christ crucified" and "the Gospel" in this letter. Also be aware that when Paul invokes the name of the crucified Christ, he also means to remind his readers of the reality that Christ is risen. In other words, Christ crucified is also Christ resurrected!

The significance of Christ resurrected will be discussed in more detail in the following text. For now, it will be helpful to first pay particular attention to the centrality of Christ crucified. Central to the profession and belief in Christ crucified is a vision of how members of the Christian community are to relate to one another, which contrasts with what he refers to as living according to the "foolishness" of the world (see chapters 1 and 2). *To live well in genuine community*, according to Paul, one must strive to embody the kind of *love* that is embodied by Christ himself, in the profession that Jesus Christ was crucified on the cross, and not the foolishness of the world. *Pay particular attention to the motif of love in the letter*. For Paul, *to live well* means embodying "Christ crucified." Moreover, to embody Christ crucified is to love one's brothers and sisters (or fellow members of the community) in a specific way.

Rather importantly, consider whether the kind of love Paul advocates is knowable and realizable <u>apart</u> from knowing, believing, and following Christ crucified. What might be the implication of this Pauline linkage of love and Christ crucified? And, how might this linkage challenge, for instance, the views of love and piety as discussed by Plato in *Euthyphro* and *Crito*?

In order to facilitate our investigation into the kind of love that Christ crucified illumines, pay close attention to Paul's judgment of the sexual immorality described in chapter 5, verses 1–2. Note in particular verse 2. The notion of pride is prominent throughout this letter. In chapter 5:6, he writes, "Your boasting is not good." The kind of love that is embodied in "Christ crucified" is contrary to pride or boasting. Another example of Paul's rejection of pride or boasting is his discussion of whether one can eat food that has been offered to idols—see chapters 8, 9, and 10. What is the problem with pride or boasting? And how does this help us to better understand the kind of love that is underscored by "Christ crucified"? (consider chapters 12 and 13). Moreover, pay particular attention to *why* Paul argues "Christ crucified" embodies the kind of love described in chapters 12 and 13. Why does "Christ crucified" reveal to us that the love described in chapters 12 and 13 is in fact the love we ought to pursue in order to live well?

What is it that God does in Christ that illumines the nature of genuine love? Take a look at chapter 1:26–31 and chapter 12:12–13. Do you see anything similar between the kind of rhetoric or persuasive speech Paul uses in 1 Corinthians 1:17 and 2:1–5 and Socrates's rhetoric against the Sophists?

Remember, Paul thinks that *living well*, as individual persons and as members of a larger community, *depends* on possessing the right understanding of *love*. (Note what Paul states in chapter 16:14: "Let all that you do be done in love.") Make sure to reflect on whether you find Paul's discussion of what love entails insightful, helpful, or compelling. Also, reflect on the kinds of views, practices, or habits that Paul thinks support the right kind of love. Alternatively, consider what kinds of beliefs and practices Paul thinks *disrupt or get in the way of* forming the right kind of love.

If Paul begins his letter with a reflection on the meaning of "Christ crucified" for the kind of love that Christians ought to have for their brothers and sisters, he does not end with the Crucifixion. As we noted earlier, the Gospel of "Christ crucified," for Paul, always implies also "Christ risen," that is, the Resurrection. His letter could be read as moving from the Crucifixion (chapter 1) to the sharing of *Eucharist* or communion (chapter 11) to the Resurrection (chapter 15). Although this is an appropriate way to read the letter, remember what we said earlier, that is, that for Paul "Christ crucified" always includes Christ risen. Indeed, Paul understands that there would be no Christian community apart from the Resurrection. There would only be the death of a person who claimed to be the Messiah.[i] In Luke's Gospel, for instance, the Apostles are portrayed at the Crucifixion as quite fearful and perplexed (see, for example, the story of Peter in Luke 22:54–61). Only after the Resurrection, Jesus's appearances to the Apostles, and the gift of the Spirit does the community truly form (see Acts of the Apostles, chapter 2). For Paul, apart from Jesus's Resurrection, Christian faith is "empty" and "in vain" (1 Cor. 15:14, 17). But Paul's discussion of communion and Resurrection in First Corinthians is related to his concerns for the community and the divisions that have occurred within the community. You can see this if you look at Paul's discussion of the Lord's Supper in 11:17–34. Try to grasp how Paul's discussion of the Lord's Supper relates to his displeasure at the behavior of members of the Corinthian community. How does the meaning of the Lord's Supper, or *communion*, contradict the ways in which they are behaving?

Chapter 15 of Paul's letter addresses the Resurrection of Jesus. This is a very important chapter, for Paul thinks that the Resurrection defeats not only sin and death, but also the fear of death. Are there any practical consequences for the community in overcoming the fear of death? Here, pay special attention to 15:29–34, and also think about Paul's teaching on love in chapter 12. Does the Resurrection support Paul's vision of the Christian community, of the love that he wants them to embody? How might it do so?

---

i   *Messiah*, which comes from Hebrew, and *Christ*, which comes from Greek, mean the same thing, "the anointed one." One is anointed with oil in the Old Testament or Hebrew Bible when chosen by God for a special role in the drama of history. So *Christ* is a title, not a last name.

THE FIRST LETTER TO THE CORINTHIANS

Corinth was located on the isthmus between Attica and the Peloponnesus. Its site, with two harbors, Cenchreae on the Saronian Gulf to the east, Lechaeon on the Gulf of Corinth to the north, assured commercial success. The Romans destroyed it in 146 B.C.E., during their campaign against the Achaean League, but in 44 B.C.E. Julius Caesar refounded it as a Roman colony. It grew quickly to prominence again. In 27 B.C.E. it was made the capital of the province of Achaia, which in 44 C.E. became a proconsular "province of the Roman people." The geographer Strabo, writing at the end of the first century B.C.E., said that the original colonists were mainly freedmen from Italy (*Geog.* 8.6.23), but the commercial opportunities of the new colony soon brought many immigrants of all sorts, including apparently a large community of Jews, although the latter have left little evidence of their existence in either material or literary remains. Thus, while the public face of the colony was Roman in language, government, and architecture, there was a cosmopolitan substructure, revealed for example in the use of Greek that suddenly blossomed in public inscriptions in the time of Hadrian. The circumstances of the refounding, and the prominence of former slaves among the first colonists, made for a kind of social mobility rare in ancient towns. The monuments and inscriptions that stand as markers for the ambitions and successes of the community leaders in Corinth rarely mention ancestors; the top ranks of Corinthian society were newly minted. It is not surprising that questions of status are prominent in Paul's letter.

The church was founded by Paul, probably around 51 C.E. (Acts 18:1–11). After his initial stay there he carried on an extended correspondence with the Corinthian Christians, writing a total of at least four and possibly five, six, or even seven letters to them (1 Cor. 5:9; 2 Cor. 2:3 f.); visited them himself twice more; sent personal representatives more than once; and received delegations and informal reports from them. Our First Corinthians follows up on an earlier letter, lost early on, which had not had the effects Paul wanted (1 Cor. 5:9–11). The extant letter was written near the end of Paul's stay in Ephesus (16:8; cf. Acts 19) in the spring probably of the year 54 or 55. It is a response to reports which have come to Paul by two means: a letter, brought by an official delegation, Stephanas, Fortunatus, and Achaicus (16:1 7; cf. 7:1) and information from "Chloe's household" (1:11), otherwise unknown. Although Timothy is already en route overland to Corinth (Paul expects the letter, presumably carried by the returning Stephanas group, to arrive by sea before he does: 4:17; 16:10f.; cf. Acts 19:22), and Paul himself expects to come soon, the problems are urgent enough to require immediate intervention.

The problems are diverse. Paul has heard that there are "factions" or "quarrels" in the church, which stem from invidious comparisons among apostles, Paul, Apollos, and Peter (1:12), some taking special pride in the apostle who baptized them or in whose name they were baptized (vv. 13–17). The Corinthians prize "wisdom and eloquence"— the displays of rhetoric, often laced with stock topics from popular moral philosophy, that made pop stars of many orators. Some Corinthian Christians challenge Paul's authority—apparently they think him lacking in this "wisdom"—and doubt that this unstable missionary will ever be seen again (4:18f; cf. 16:5–7). There are also less subtle problems. A flagrant case of incest in the congregation (chap. 5) produces "boasting" over this violation of ordinary taboos (5:2, 6). Some Christians are suing one another in pagan courts (6:18). Others defend their patronage of the once-famous Corinthian brothels with a slogan that sounds superficially Pauline (6:9–20). Yet others reject sex altogether (chap. 7). The liberating knowledge, taught by Paul himself, that the pagan gods are not real (cf. 1 Thess. 1:9; Gal. 4:8) leads some to the conviction that they are free to participate in social occasions in pagan shrines or to eat meat "sacrificed to idols"; others are scandalized by this practice (chaps. 8–10). The role of women who prophesy in the assemblies is a matter of contention (11:2–16; 14:34–36), and disorder infects the celebration of the Lord's Supper (11:17–34). Charismatic phenomena—especially ecstatic speech (*glossolalia*)—threaten to divide the community (chaps. 12–14). And some do not believe in the resurrection of the dead (chap. 15).

Modern scholars have sought with great diligence and ingenuity to find some underlying ideology that would explain all the problems Paul takes up in this letter: perhaps a sacramental theology shared with the other initiatory cults that flourished in Corinth as in other eastern cities in the Roman era; or perhaps a kind of proto-Gnosticism, based on myths of creation that inverted the Biblical order of reality and elevated the spiritual in opposition to everything physical; or perhaps a "realized eschatology," radicalizing Paul's own apocalyptic preaching, in which the spirit-endowed initiates could already live "as the angels in heaven," disregarding all social and moral conventions and taboos.

More recently scholars have tended instead to see the problems Paul addresses as the sorts of conflicts that would naturally emerge as a radical messianic sect encountered the ordinary structures of social existence in an eastern Roman colony—the expectations of household order, of social rank and power, of women and men, free persons and slaves, patrons and clients, of differing understandings of power, honor, and social obligation. The theological continuities found in the letter, in this view, are more likely to be Paul's own ad hoc constructions, freely melding biblical examples, personal models from his own and other apostles' lives, Jewish traditions of interpretation, and early Christian formulas, traditions, and ritual practices—all in a framework adapted from Greco-Roman rhetoric and philosophy.

Although the Christian communities in Corinth are several in number, meeting ordinarily in the houses of individual patrons, Paul addresses the letter to the single *"ekklēsia of God that is in Corinth"* (1:2). In everyday speech, *ekklēsia* was a political term (see note 2 on 1 Thess. 1:1), and there are many echoes of political rhetoric in this letter. Paul addresses the "town meeting of God" in Corinth in the way a philosophical speaker might address the assembled voting citizens of a democratic Greek polis. Factions were always the great internal danger to the life of the city, and some of the most treasured speeches from the great orators of Paul's age, like Dio Chrysostom of Prusa, are those that celebrate the concord (*homonoia*) that makes truly civilized life possible and that warn against the discord that factions bring. Paul's letter in its main outlines closely resembles such a speech. It uses some of the favorite metaphors of the orators—the community as a well-founded building, the community as a body in which all the "members" work together in harmony—and many of the typical turns of phrase.

Yet that very "eloquence or human wisdom" (2:5) that Paul uses so adroitly in seeking to address the disorder he hears reported of his Corinthian congregations is, from another angle, a part of the problem, one of the means that served that status-seeking "love of honor" that was so strong in Greco-Roman society and visibly manifest in the daily life of the Corinthian colony. Paul purports to speak of a different kind of wisdom, requiring a different eloquence (2:1–5). So he strives here to find a form of rhetoric, a new range of metaphors that will be adequate to express what he calls "the message of the cross"—in Greek, "the *logos* of the cross," that is, the logic and rational structure not only of an appropriate rhetoric but of a revised sense of reality, of what Paul had called in his Letter to the Galatians "a new creation" (Gal. 6:15; cf. 2 Cor. 5: 17).

The letter opens with a formal prescript, in Paul's usual expansive style (1:1–3), followed by a thanksgiving (1:4–9). There follows immediately an appeal for unity and avoidance of factions (1:10), which serves as the thesis for the argument of the entire letter. Because chapter 7 begins, "Now for the matters you wrote about," some commentators have assumed that in the earlier chapters Paul takes up problems reported by Chloe's household, while treating in the later chapters the matters raised in the letter brought by Stephanas, Fortunatus, and Achaicus, but that is not necessarily the case. Paul chooses the sequence to construct a coherent, if complex, argument. In 1:11–4:21 he reflects on the rivalry between adherents of individual apostles—with himself and Apollos as the primary examples (chaps. 3–4; note esp. 4:6 and the note there)—in the light of what he calls "the *logos* of the cross" (1:18). Chapters 5–7 deal with the purity of the community, beginning with correction of a misunderstanding of his earlier letter, dealing with both sexual matters (5:1–3; 6:12–7:40) and lawsuits (chap. 6). The question of eating meat and its association with pagan sacrifices provokes the larger discussion, in 8:1–11:1, of the difficult balance between freedom—the freedom enjoyed by those possessing knowledge and authority and the unique freedom that is central to

Paul's preaching of the gospel—and responsibility for "building up" the community, including those members of the community who are "weak" in the eyes of the ones who take pride in their knowledge and status. The gatherings of the *ekklēsia* for worship expose several sources of division, treated in 11:2–14:40: the behavior and dress of women who are prophesying (11:2–16); divisions between richer and poorer members at the Lord's Supper (11:17–34); and different kinds of "spiritual gifts" (*charismata*, 12:1–14:40). Chapter 15 discusses the resurrection of the dead. Chapter 16 includes instructions for the collection for Jerusalem (vv. 1–4), travel plans (vv. 5–12), a summary appeal (vv. 13–14) with special commendation for Stephanas and thanks for the delegation he led (vv. 15–18), and epistolary greetings (vv. 19–20), Paul adds a greeting in his own handwriting (v. 21) and concludes with a formal anathema and the Aramaic phrase inviting the Lord's coming, both probably from the eucharistic liturgy, and a benediction (vv. 22–24).

1 Corinthians

(1) Paul, called to be an apostle of Christ Jesus by the will of God, and our brother Sosthenes,[1]

(2) To the church of God in Corinth,[2] to those sanctified in Christ Jesus and called to be his holy people, together with all those everywhere who call on the name of our Lord Jesus Christ—their Lord and ours:

(3) Grace and peace to you from God our Father and the Lord Jesus Christ.

(4) I always thank my God for you because of his grace given you in Christ Jesus. (5) For in him you have been enriched in every way—with all kinds of speech and with all knowledge—(6) God thus confirming our testimony about Christ among you.

(7) Therefore you do not lack any spiritual gift as you eagerly wait for our Lord Jesus Christ to be revealed. (8) He will also keep you firm to the end, so that you will be blameless on the day of our Lord Jesus Christ. (9) God is faithful, who has called you into fellowship with his Son, Jesus Christ our Lord.[3]

---

1   Acts 18:17 mentions a Sosthenes, president of the synagogue in Corinth, who, after opposing Paul before the proconsul, was beaten for his trouble. Some commentators, assuming that Paul is referring to the same man here, have speculated about Sosthenes' conversion, but that is by no means certain.

2   For the political term *ekklēsia*, translated "church," see note on 1 Thess. 1:1. Here it collectively designates several groups of believers who met in the homes of various members (see 1 Cor. 16:19 and note on Rom. 16:5), though perhaps occasionally in one place (Rom. 16:23), Paul's use of the singular (contrast the plural in Gal. 1:2) may be significant in view of the central theme of the letter (see the introduction above).

3   The thanksgiving (vv 4–9), brief as it is, nevertheless alludes to a number of the themes of the letter: "enriched" (v. 5) is used sarcastically in 4:8; *logos* and *gnōsis* (v. 5) are the subject of chaps. 1–4; also 8:1, 7, 10, 11; cf. 12:8; 13:2; "spiritual gifts" (*charismata*, v. 7): chaps. 12–14; cf. 7:7; the eschatological emphasis (v. 7), and especially the implication that the "Day of our Lord" (v. 8) will render present human judgments invalid, forms the underlying tension of the entire letter, explicitly 3:10–17; 4:1–5, reaching its climax in chap. 15; "fellowship" (*koinōnia*, v. 9) suggests Paul's emphasis on the harmony and unity of the community.

(10) I appeal to you,[4] brothers and sisters, in the name of our Lord Jesus Christ, that all of you agree with one another in what you say and that there be no divisions[5] among you, but that you be perfectly united in mind and thought. (11) My brothers and sisters, some from Chloe's household[6] have informed me that there are quarrels[7] among you. (12) What I mean is this: One of you says, "I follow Paul"; another, "I follow Apollos"; another, "I follow Cephas"; still another, "I follow Christ."[8]

(13) Is Christ divided?[9] Was Paul crucified for you? Were you baptized into the name of Paul? (14) I thank God that I did not baptize any of you except Crispus and Gaius, (15) so no one can say that you were baptized into my name. (16) (Yes, I also baptized the household of Stephanas;[10] beyond that, I don't remember if I baptized anyone else.) (17) For Christ did not send me to baptize, but to preach the gospel—not with wisdom and eloquence,[11] lest the cross of Christ be emptied of its power.

(18) For the message of the cross is foolishness to those who are perishing, but to us who are being saved it is the power of God. (19) For it is written:

> "I will destroy the wisdom of the wise; the intelligence of the intelligent I will frustrate."[12]

(20) Where are the wise? Where is the teacher of the law? Where is the philosopher of

---

4   This verse states the thesis of the entire letter. The form, "I appeal to you," was commonly used in friendly letters of moral admonition (*parainesis*; see the introduction to 1 Thessalonians), but also in official letters in which commands, e.g., by a Hellenistic ruler to a subject city, could thus be stated with deliberate courtesy (cf. Phlm. 8–10). It occurs frequently in NT letters: see esp. 1 Thess. 4: 10; 5: 14; Rom. 12:1; 15:30; 16:17. The content of the present appeal uses stock phrases of deliberative speeches urging concord (see introduction above): "to say the same thing," "no factions," "the same mind," "the same thought."

5   The "divisions" (*schismata*, from the Greek verb "to tear or split") are not likely organized "parties," as some commentators since the nineteenth century have thought.

6   Chloe is otherwise unknown. Her household, most likely in Corinth, would include slaves and freedpersons (former slaves, now clients), who may be traveling on some business of their mistress or patroness. They are evidently Christians, and the household obviously known to the other Christians of Corinth, but Chloe herself may or may not be a Christian (see the note on Rom. 16:11).

7   "Quarrels" may be too weak a translation; the Greek *eris* is the opposite of *homonoia*, "concord," and in Homer and Hesiod even the name of a goddess who provokes people to war and domestic strife.

8   There is no need to assume that the factions in the Corinthian house churches actually use the slogans Paul attributes to them here, or even that there are precisely four factions. Paul may be using the common rhetorical ploy of speech-in-character to satirize the implication of their dissensions. In the remainder of the first section of the letter (chaps. 1–4) only the rivalry between adherents of Paul and Apollos figures.

9   By suggesting that the dissensions among his addressees are "dividing" Christ Paul may hint of the trope he will use in chap. 12, the community as Christ's body.

10   Stephanas, one of the delegates from Corinth, was present in Ephesus as Paul wrote (16:15–18); did he remind Paul of the omission while the latter was dictating?

11   "Wisdom and eloquence" (lit. "wisdom of speech" or "rhetorical wisdom," *sophia logou* are highly valued in Greco-Roman society, signs of sophistication and superior status. Here Paul begin his ironic, even sarcastic, inversion of those values by insisting that the gospel he was commissioned to preach entails a different *logos* and a different wisdom (1:18–4:21).

12   Isa. 29:14.

this age? Has not God made foolish the wisdom of the world? (21) For since in the wisdom of God the world through its wisdom did not know him, God was pleased through the foolishness of what was preached to save those who believe. (22) Jews demand signs and Greeks look for wisdom, (23) but we preach Christ crucified: a stumbling block to Jews and foolishness to Gentiles, (24) but to those whom God has called, both Jews and Greeks, Christ the power of God and the wisdom of God. (25) For the foolishness of God is wiser than human wisdom, and the weakness of God is stronger than human strength.[13]

(26) Brothers and sisters, think of what you were when you were called. Not many of you were wise by human standards; not many were influential; not many were of noble birth. (27) But God chose the foolish things of the world to shame the wise; God chose the weak things of the world to shame the strong. (28) God chose the lowly things of this world and the despised things—and the things that are not—to nullify the things that are, (29) so that no one may boast before him. (30) It is because of him that you are in Christ Jesus, who has become for us wisdom from God—that is, our righteousness, holiness and redemption. (31) Therefore, as it is written: "Let those who boast boast in the Lord."[14]

(2) And so it was with me, brothers and sisters. When I came to you, I did not come with eloquence or human wisdom as I proclaimed to you the testimony[15] about God. (2) For I resolved to know nothing while I was with you except Jesus Christ and him crucified. (3) I came to you in weakness with great fear and trembling. (4) My message and my preaching were not with wise and persuasive words, but with a demonstration of the Spirit's power,[16] (5) so that your faith might not rest on human wisdom, but on God's power.

---

13   Vv 18–25 are highly rhetorical; note the antithetic parallelism (18. 22–25) and the climactic series of four questions (20). The antithesis between Jews and Greeks—a frequent pairing in Paul's letters—set both on the side of those who are unable to penetrate the oxymoron of God's "foolish" wisdom and "weak" power, over against "those whom God has called," transcending these ethnic identities (23 f.) by a new identity. "Calling" has been emphasized already in 1:1, 2, and now will be treated with some irony in Paul's following reminders of how that "calling" took place (1:26–4:21). See also 7:17–24.

14   Vv. 26–29 are a superb example of Paul's fondness of parallelism. The whole section vv. 26–31 satirizes the status-seeking that Paul discerns behind the church's factionalism. The quotation is from Jer. 9:24

15   "Testimony" (*martyrion*); "mystery" or "secret" (*mysterion*) is also very strongly attested; cf. v. 7. Having reminded the Corinthian status-seekers that they were "nothing" in the world's eyes before God "called" them, Paul now uses his own "weakness" and lack of "eloquence or human wisdom" as an example of the paradox of God's power.

16   How God's Spirit and power were demonstrable is one of the points of contention between Paul and those Corinthian Christians who prided themselves in their "spiritual gifts"; here, however, he speaks quite conventionally and may think of the miracles by which apostles and other "divine men" won attention (2 Cor 12:12; Rom. 15:19; cf. 1 Thess. 1:5)

(6) We do, however, speak a message of wisdom among the mature,[17] but not the wisdom of this age or of the rulers of this age,[18] who are coming to nothing. (7) No, we declare God's wisdom, a mystery that has been hidden and that God destined for our glory before time began.[19] (8) None of the rulers of this age understood it, for if they had, they would not have crucified the Lord of glory. (9) However, as it is written:

> "What no eye has seen,
>   what no ear has heard,
>   and what no human mind has conceived—
>   these things God has prepared for those who
>   love him"—[20]

(10) for God has revealed them to us by his Spirit.

The Spirit searches all things, even the deep things of God. (11) For who knows a person's thoughts except that person's own spirit within? In the same way no one knows the thoughts of God except the Spirit of God. (12) We have not received the spirit of the world but the Spirit who is from God, that we may understand what God has freely given us. (13) This is what we speak, not in words taught us by human wisdom but in words taught by the Spirit, explaining spiritual realities with Spirit-taught words. (14) The person without the Spirit[21] does not accept the things that come from the Spirit of God but considers them foolishness, and cannot understand them because they are discerned only through the Spirit. (15) The person with the Spirit makes judgments about all things, but such a person is not subject to merely human judgments, (16) for,

> "Who has known the mind of the Lord
>   so as to instruct him?"[22]
>   But we have the mind of Christ.

---

17   Or, "perfect." The word (*teleios*) could refer to one who had been "initiated" in the mysteries; also metaphorically for one who was "initiated" into the higher speculations of philosophy. For Philo, for example, the "sage" who had won virtue by self-discipline, mastered the rational means of acquiring truth, and gone on to ecstatic vision became *teleios*, "neither God nor man, but … on the borderline between" the two (*On Dreams*, ii. 234). The primary meaning of the word for Paul here, however, is simply "adult," because he wants to show the people he is admonishing that their behavior reveals them not as "perfected" "spirituals," but as quite "fleshly" "babies" (3:1–4).

18   Commentators have disagreed whether the "rulers of this age" should be understood as political rulers or as demonic powers: the context speaks for the latter; cf. the "god of this age" (2 Cor. 4: 4).

19   The pattern "formerly hidden/now revealed" was evidently a regular form of preaching in the Pauline school; cf. Rom. 16:25 f.; Col.1:26 f.; Eph. 3:4 f., 9 f.: similarly 2 Tim. 1:9 f., Tit. 1:2 f.; 1 Pet. 1:20 f.

20   The source of this quotation cannot be identified; Origen found it in an "Apocalypse of Elijah" which has not survived.

21   "Person without the Spirit"; *psychikos*, i.e., having (only) "soul," *psychē*. Three classes of persons are distinguished: the "spirituals" (*pneumatikoi*), the "souled" (*psychikoi*), and the "fleshly" (*sarkikoi, sarkinoi*, translated here "worldly"). The "spirituals" are identical with the "perfect." The same division appears in some later Christian Gnostic systems, perhaps dependent on this passage; Paul uses it here sarcastically.

22   Isa. 40:13, LXX.

(3) Brothers and sisters, I could not address you as spiritual but as worldly—mere infants in Christ. (2) I gave you milk, not solid food, for you were not yet ready for it. Indeed, you are still not ready. (3) You are still worldly. For since there is jealousy and quarreling among you, are you not worldly? Are you not acting like mere human beings?[23] (4) For when one says, "I follow Paul," and another, "I follow Apollos," are you not mere human beings?

(5) What, after all, is Apollos?[24] And what is Paul? Only servants, through whom you came to believe—as the Lord has assigned to each his task. (6) I planted the seed, Apollos watered it, but God has been making it grow. (7) So neither the one who plants nor the one who waters is anything, but only God, who makes things grow. (8) The one who plants and the one who waters have one purpose, and they will each be rewarded according to their own labor. (9) For we are God's co-workers, you are God's field, God's building.

(10) By the grace God has given me, I laid a foundation as a wise builder, and someone else is building on it. But each one should build with care. (11) For no one can lay any foundation other than the one already laid, which is Jesus Christ. (12) If anyone builds on this foundation using gold, silver, costly stones, wood, hay or straw, (13) their work will be shown for what it is, because the Day[25] will bring it to light. It will be revealed with fire, and the fire will test the quality of each person's work. (14) If what has been built survives, the builder will receive a reward. (15) If it is burned up, the builder will suffer loss but yet will be saved—even though only as one escaping through the flames.

(16) Don't you know that you yourselves are God's temple[26] and that God's Spirit dwells in your midst? (17) If anyone destroys God's temple, God will destroy that person;[27] for God's temple is sacred, and you together are that temple.

---

23   The simple word "human beings" (*anthrōpoi*) mocks the elitism expressed in the spiritual/souled/fleshly divisions. 3:1–4 forms a classic example of Paul's satire. In 2:6–16 Paul seems to accept the position of the "spirituals," that an apostle is one who imparts an esoteric "wisdom," accessible only to "the perfect." But for him that "hidden" wisdom is identical with the public proclamation, "Christ and him crucified." Therefore the mundane fact of their divisions and arguments shows that they are not "spirituals" but only "people of flesh," not "perfect" (i.e., "adults"), but only "babes."

24   On Apollos' mission to Corinth see Acts 18:24–28. Note that of the factions mentioned in 1:12 only that of Apollos is singled out here, and that not in a hostile fashion. It is doubtful whether Cephas = Peter ever actually visited Corinth.

25   I.e., "the day of the Lord," see 1:8. A biblical notion (e.g. Amos 5:18–20; Joel 2:11; Zeph. 1:7–2:3; Isa. 13:6; Ezek. 13:5; 30:2–3), often transferred by early Christians to Jesus, confessed as "Lord," in his capacity as judge at the end-time.

26   In Hellenistic popular philosophy the notion that the individual person is a shrine within which a divine being, i.e., the rational self, dwells is a commonplace (e.g., Epictetus, *Diss.* 2.8.14); Philo applies this cliché to the boy Moses (*Mos.* 1.27) For Paul, however, it is not the individual but the community that is the new temple—an idea that was important also in the sect of the Dead Sea Scrolls. The metaphor of the building (vv. 10–15) is thus particularized into a challenge to the addressees ("don't you know") to act like that sacred edifice which they have been called to be.

27   Sayings in this form ("if any one does x, x will be done to him") occur several places in early Christian literature (e.g., 1 Cor. 14:38; 2 Cor. 9:6; Rom. 2:12; Matt. 5:19; 6:14 f.; 10:32 f.; Mark 4:24 f.; 8:38; Rev. 22:18). The style is that of ancient sacral law (cf. Gen. 9:6; Deut. 28:1. 15; Aeschylus, *Choephoroe* 312 f.), with an eschatological setting.

(18) Do not deceive yourselves. If any of you think you are wise by the standards of this age, you should become "fools" so that you may become wise. (19) For the wisdom of this world is foolishness in God's sight. As it is written: "He catches the wise in their craftiness"[28]; (20) and again, "The Lord knows that the thoughts of the wise are futile."[29] (21) So then, no more boasting about human leaders! All things are yours, (22) whether Paul or Apollos or Cephas or the world or life or death or the present or the future—all are yours, (23) and you are of Christ, and Christ is of God.[30]

(4) This, then, is how you ought to regard us: as servants of Christ and as those entrusted with the mysteries God has revealed.[31] (2) Now it is required that those who have been given a trust must prove faithful. (3) I care very little if I am judged by you or by any human court; indeed, I do not even judge myself. (4) My conscience is clear, but that does not make me innocent. It is the Lord who judges me. (5) Therefore judge nothing before the appointed time; wait till the Lord comes. He will bring to light what is hidden in darkness and will expose the motives of people's hearts. At that time each will receive their praise from God.

(6) Now, brothers and sisters, I have applied these things to myself and Apollos for your benefit,[32] so that you may learn from us the meaning of the saying, "Do not go beyond what is written."[33] Then you will not be puffed up in being a follower of one of us over against the other. (7) For who makes you different from anyone else? What do you have that you did not receive? And if you did receive it, why do you boast as though you did not?

---

28   Job 5:13.

29   Ps. 94:11.

30   Vv. 18–23 are a reprise of the themes introduced in 1:10–25; thus chaps. 1–3 form a rhetorical "circle" or ringcomposition. Note also the carefully stylized ending, vv. 21–23. Chap. 4 pointedly draws out the lessons for the addressees before Paul turns, in chap. 5, to the first of the special issues in Corinth.

31   The words *hypēretēs* and *oikonomos*, translated "servants" and "those entrusted," are common titles in civil, cultic, and business bureaucracies, often rendered "assistant" or "secretary" and "manager."

32   The verb translated "applied" normally means "to transform," perhaps "to speak figuratively." In rhetoric, it pointed to the figure called "covert allusion" by which orators masked their sharp criticisms through irony and metaphor in order to avoid offence or to appeal to shame rather than fear. By explicitly naming what he has been doing—something rhetoricians warn against—Paul makes his argument transparent and puts the addressees, especially the proud lovers of rhetoric, on the spot.

33   A proverb from the way children were taught to write, following carefully an outline traced by their teachers. A modern parallel, in a non-progressive preschool, would be "Don't color outside the lines." Paul is continuing to satirize the childishness of his audience while urging that they follow the real example of chose apostles they claim to idolize.

(8) Already you have all you want! Already you have become rich! You have begun to reign[34]—and that without us! How I wish that you really had begun to reign so that we also might reign with you! (9) For it seems to me that God has put us apostles on display at the end of the procession, like those condemned to die in the arena. We have been made a spectacle to the whole universe, to angels as well as to human beings. (10) We are fools for Christ, but you are so wise in Christ! We are weak, but you are strong! You are honored, we are dishonored! (11) To this very hour we go hungry and thirsty, we are in rags, we are brutally treated, we are homeless. (12) We work hard with our own hands. When we are cursed, we bless; when we are persecuted, we endure it; (13) when we are slandered, we answer kindly. We have become the scum of the earth, the garbage of the world—right up to this moment.

(14) I am writing this not to shame you but to warn you as my dear children.[35] (15) Even if you had ten thousand guardians in Christ, you do not have many fathers, for in Christ Jesus I became your father through the gospel. (16) Therefore I urge you to imitate me. (17) For this reason I have sent to you Timothy, my son whom I love, who is faithful in the Lord. He will remind you of my way of life in Christ Jesus, which agrees with what I teach everywhere in every church.

(18) Some of you have become arrogant, as if I were not coming to you. (19) But I will come to you very soon, if the Lord is willing, and then I will find out not only how these arrogant people are talking, but what power they have. (20) For the kingdom of God is not a matter of talk but of power. (21) What do you prefer? Shall I come to you with a rod of discipline, or shall I come in love and with a gentle spirit.

(5) It is actually reported that there is sexual immorality among you, and of a kind that even pagans do not tolerate: A man has his father's wife.[36] (2) And you are proud! Shouldn't you rather have gone into mourning and have put out of your fellowship the man who has been doing this? (3) For my part, even though I am not physically present, I am with you in spirit. As one who is present with you in this way, I have already passed

---

34   It was a commonplace in popular philosophy, especially in Stoicism, that "only the wise person is truly a king." True wealth, also, was only attained by the wise. With his repeated "already," Paul not only exposes the absence of moral progress in these would-be sages who yet remain children, but also signals their failure to understand the importance of the future fulfillment that Christians must await. This leads to the rhetorical climax in which Paul sarcastically contrasts their exalted self-image (vv. 7f) with the facts of the apostle's life (vv. 9–13). The latter verses are in the form of a "catalogue of circumstances," which appears very often in ancient rhetoric in depictions of the ideal sage. Circumstances, usually hardships, as here, were thought to test the virtue of a person, exposing sham wisdom. Often philosophers attribute their ability to stand firm in the face of hardships to the power of the divine which they served, and so does Paul, though of course his concept of God's power, as he has emphasized in 1:18–25, is quite different from that common in popular philosophy. Paul makes frequent use of this rhetorical pattern: see also 2 Cor. 4:8–9; 6:4–10; 11:23–28; 12:10; Rom. 8:35–39; Phil. 4:11 f.

35   Paul's too-transparent denial that he is "writing ... to shame you," when obviously that is exactly what he is doing, permits him now to turn the childhood metaphor back to the relation of tender affection that is typical of friendly admonitions in ancient moral discourse, as we have seen at length in 1 Thessalonians.

36   I.e., his stepmother; even if the father is dead, the relationship is forbidden by both Roman and Jewish law (see Lev. 18:8).

judgment in the name of our Lord Jesus on the one who has been doing this. (4) So when you are assembled and I am with you in spirit, and the power of our Lord Jesus is present, (5) hand this man over to Satan for the destruction of the sinful nature so that his spirit may be saved on the day of the Lord.[37]

(6) Your boasting is not good. Don't you know that a little yeast leavens the whole batch of dough? (7) Get rid of the old yeast, so that you may be a new unleavened batch—as you really are. For Christ, our Passover lamb, has been sacrificed.[38] (8) Therefore let us keep the Festival, not with the old bread leavened with malice and wickedness, but with the unleavened bread of sincerity and truth.

(9) I wrote to you in my letter[39] not to associate with sexually immoral people—(10) not at all meaning the people of this world who are immoral, or the greedy and swindlers, or idolaters. In that case you would have to leave this world. (11) But now I am writing to you that you must not associate with any who claim to be fellow believers[40] but are sexually immoral or greedy, idolaters or slanderers, drunkards or swindlers. With such persons do not even eat.

(12) What business is it of mine to judge those outside the church? Are you not to judge those inside? (13) God will judge those outside. "Expel the wicked person from among you."[41]

(6) If any of you has a dispute with another, do you dare to take it before the ungodly[42] for judgment instead of before the Lord's people? (2) Or do you not know that the Lord's people will judge the world?[43] And if you are to judge the world, are you not competent to judge trivial cases? (3) Do you not know that we will judge angels? How much more the things of this life! (4) Therefore, if you have disputes about such matters, do you ask for a ruling from those whose way of life is scorned in the church? (5) I say this to shame you. Is it possible that there is nobody among you wise enough to judge a dispute between believers? But instead, one brother goes to law against another—and this in front of unbelievers!

---

37   We cannot be sure what exactly is meant by "destruction of the sinful nature [lit., flesh]," but the most obvious meaning would be the death of the offender. It is not likely that this is the same man mentioned in 2 Cor. 2:5–11.

38   The metaphor is drawn from the Jewish custom that the household must be purged of every trace of leaven before Passover. Although Jesus can be metaphorically identified with a sacrificial lamb elsewhere in the NT (Rev. 5:6, 12; 1 Pet. 1:19), only here is he explicitly called "our Passover lamb" (*pascha*), though that identification may be implied by the chronology of the passion narrative in the Fourth Gospel.

39   This letter is lost; attempts to identify part of it with 2 Cor. 6: 14–7:1 are not persuasive.

40   Lit., "anyone calling himself a brother." The following list of vices is conventional, intended to embrace typical faults, not specific problems in Corinth.

41   Deut. 17:7; 22:21, 24; 24:7; cf 13:5.

42   I.e., in pagan courts; "ungodly" (more accurately, "unjust") here means no more than "unbelievers."

43   The notion comes from Jewish apocalypticism, e.g., in the Dead Sea Scrolls 1QpHab. 5:4 f.; cf Dan. 7:22, Wisd. 3:8; Matt. 19:28; Luke 22:30.

(7) The very fact that you have lawsuits among you means you have been completely defeated already. Why not rather be wronged? Why not rather be cheated? (8) Instead, you yourselves cheat and do wrong, and you do this to your brothers and sisters.[44] (9) Or do you not know that wrongdoers will not inherit the kingdom of God? Do not be deceived: Neither the sexually immoral nor idolaters nor adulterers nor male prostitutes nor practicing homosexuals (10) nor thieves nor the greedy nor drunkards nor slanderers nor swindlers will inherit the kingdom of God. (11) And that is what some of you were. But you were washed, you were sanctified, you were justified in the name of the Lord Jesus Christ and by the Spirit of our God.[45]

(12) "I have the right to do anything,"[46] you say—but not everything is beneficial. "I have the right to do anything"—but I will not be mastered by anything.[47] (13) You say, "Food for the stomach and the stomach for food, and God will destroy them both."[48] The body, however, is not meant for sexual immorality but for the Lord, and the Lord for the body. (14) By his power God raised the Lord from the dead, and he will raise us also. (15) Do you not know that your bodies are members of Christ himself? Shall I then take the members of Christ and unite them with a prostitute? Never! (16) Do you not know that he who unites himself with a prostitute is one with her in body? For it is said, "The two will become one flesh."[49] (17) But whoever is united with the Lord is one with him in spirit.

(18) Flee from sexual immorality. All other sins people commit are outside their bodies, but those who sin sexually sin against their own bodies. (19) Do you not know that your bodies are temples of the Holy Spirit, who is in you, whom you have received from God?[50] You are not your own; (20) you were bought at a price. Therefore honor God with your bodies.

---

44   The form of vv. 6 and 8 is parallel, creating a climactic effect.

45   The "once/now" pattern was a regular form of early Christian preaching; cf. Gal. 4:3 f.; 4:8 f.; Rom. 6:17–22; 7:5 f.; 11:30; Col. 1:21 f.; 3:5–10; Eph. 2:1–10, 11–22; Tit. 3:3–7; 1 Pet. 2:10; 4:3f. When linked, as here, with a catalogue of vices (see note 40 above and the note on Gal. 5:21), it may echo traditional warnings at baptism, which would give more force to Paul's "Do you not know . . . ?" in v. 9.

46   Evidently a slogan of the Corinthian "spirituals"; they may well believe that they are expressing the freedom they learned from Paul (cf. 3:21). Similar phrases are found in the rhetoric of the time to express the absolute freedom of "the divine," of a king, and—in line with the Stoic slogan mentioned above at 4:8—of the truly wise man. The verb (*exestin*) is cognate with the noun *exousia*, "authority," important in chaps. 8–10. Cf. 10:23. Paul's reply is also in the common idiom of political rhetoric; freedom is limited by what is "beneficial" (*sympheron*), i.e., to the community. The slogan, with the same limit, appears again in 10:23.

47   Paul's pun, *exestin/exousiasthēsomai*, can hardly be imitated in English.

48   Whereas the NIV and NRSV make "God will destroy them both" a part of Paul's response to the preceding Corinthian slogan, the TNIV correctly treats these words as part of the slogan, where they support the spiritualists' argument that the body, like the food it consumes, is morally irrelevant. Paul's retort is that God's resurrection of the body (v. 14) proves its moral relevance. Similarly, v. 18b ("every sin a person commits is apart from the body") is perhaps another Corinthian slogan, with v. 18c ("but sexually immoral people sin against their own bodies") a Pauline counter-slogan.

49   Gen. 2:24.

50   A reprise of 3:16, but here focusing on the individual.

(7) Now for the matters you wrote about: "It is good for a man not to have sexual relations with a woman." (2) But since sexual immorality is occurring, each man should have sexual relations with his own wife, and each woman with her own husband. (3) The husband should fulfill his marital duty to his wife, and likewise the wife to her husband. (4) The wife does not have authority over her own body but yields it to her husband. In the same way, the husband does not have authority over his own body but yields it to his wife.[51] (5) Do not deprive each other except perhaps by mutual consent and for a time, so that you may devote yourselves to prayer. Then come together again so that Satan will not tempt you because of your lack of self-control. (6) I say this as a concession, not as a command. (7) I wish that all of you were as I am. But each of you has your own gift from God; one has this gift, another has that.

(8) Now to the unmarried and the widows I say: It is good for them to stay unmarried, as I do. (9) But if they cannot control themselves, they should marry, for it is better to marry than to burn with passion.

(10) To the married I give this command (not I, but the Lord): A wife must not separate from her husband. (11) But if she does, she must remain unmarried or else be reconciled to her husband. And a husband must not divorce his wife.[52]

(12) To the rest I say this (I, not the Lord): If any brother has a wife who is not a believer and she is willing to live with him, he must not divorce her. (13) And if a woman has a husband who is not a believer and he is willing to live with her, she must not divorce him. (14) For the unbelieving husband has been sanctified through his wife, and the unbelieving wife has been sanctified through her believing husband. Otherwise your children would be unclean, but as it is, they are holy.

(15) But if the unbeliever leaves, let it be so. The brother or sister is not bound in such circumstances; God has called us to live in peace. (16) How do you know, wife, whether you will save your husband? Or, how do you know, husband, whether you will save your wife?

(17) Nevertheless, each of you should live as a believer in whatever situation the Lord has assigned to you, just as God has called you.[53] This is the rule I lay down in all the churches. (18) Was a man already circumcised when he was called? He should not become uncircumcised. Was a man uncircumcised when he was called? He should not be circumcised. (19) Circumcision is nothing and uncircumcision is nothing.[54] Keeping

---

51 The carefully balanced clauses about men and women respectively stand in sharp contrast to the traditional, and highly patriarchal, directive that Paul quotes in 1 Thess. 4:3–4, of which this must be a modification.

52 Cf. Matt. 5:32; 19:9; Mark 10:11 f.; Luke 16:18. One of Paul's very rare allusions to a saying of Jesus.

53 Vv. 17–24 comprise another short ring-composition, this one on the subject of "calling" which has appeared earlier in 1:1, 2, 9, 24, 26; 7:15.

54 Compare and contrast Gal. 5:6; 6:15.

God's commands is what counts. (20) Each of you should remain in the situation you were in when God called you.

(21) Were you a slave when you were called? Don't let it trouble you—although if you can gain your freedom, do so.[55] (22) For those who were slaves when called to faith in the Lord are the Lord's freed people; similarly, those who were free when called are Christ's slaves. (23) You were bought at a price; do not become slaves of human beings. (24) Brothers and sisters, all of you, as responsible to God, should remain in the situation in which God called you.

(25) Now about virgins: I have no command from the Lord, but I give a judgment as one who by the Lord's mercy is trustworthy. (26) Because of the present crisis, I think that it is good for a man to remain as he is (27) Are you pledged to a woman? Do not seek to be released. Are you free from such a commitment? Do not look for a wife. (28) But if you do marry, you have not sinned; and if a virgin marries, she has not sinned. But those who marry will face many troubles in this life, and I want to spare you this.

(29) What I mean, brothers and sisters, is that the time is short. From now on those who are married should live as if they were not; (30) those who mourn, as if they did not; those who are happy, as if they were not; those who buy something, as if it were not theirs to keep; (31) those who use the things of the world, as if not engrossed in them. For this world in its present form is passing away.

(32) I would like you to be free from concern. An unmarried man is concerned about the Lord's affairs—how he can please the Lord. (33) But a married man is concerned about the affairs of this world—how he can please his wife—(34) and his interests are divided. An unmarried woman or virgin is concerned about the Lord's affairs: Her aim is to be devoted to the Lord in both body and spirit. But a married woman is concerned about the affairs of this world—how she can please her husband. (35) I am saying this for your own good, not to restrict you, but that you may live in a right way in undivided devotion to the Lord.

(36) If anyone is worried that he might not be acting honorably toward the virgin he is engaged to,[56] and if she is getting beyond the usual age for marrying and he feels he ought to marry, he should do as he wants. He is not sinning. They should get married. (37) But the man who has settled the matter in his own mind, who is under no compulsion but has control over his own will, and who has made up his mind not to marry the

---

55   This translation is possible, but the elliptical clause could also mean, "Even if you can gain your freedom, rather make use [of your slavery]."

56   Lit., "his virgin," as also in v. 38. One traditional interpretation, which refers the passage to the question whether a father should marry off his daughter, is improbable. The case is either of engaged persons who, misunderstanding the basis of Paul's ascetic practice and recommendations, are afraid that marriage would be a sin, or of an early form of "spiritual marriage," i.e., without sexual relations, which is known from the third century on.

virgin—this man also does the right thing. (38) So then, he who marries the virgin does right, but he who does not marry her does better.

(39) A woman is bound to her husband as long as he lives. But if her husband dies, she is free to marry anyone she wishes, but he must belong to the Lord. (40) In my judgment, she is happier if she stays as she is—and I think that I too have the Spirit of God.

(8) Now about food sacrificed to idols:[57] We know that "We all possess knowledge."[58] But knowledge puffs up while love builds up. (2) Those who think they know something do not yet know as they ought to know. (3) But whoever loves God is known by God.[59]

(4) So then, about eating food sacrificed to idols: We know that "An idol is nothing at all in the world" and that "There is no God but one." (5) For even if there are so-called gods, whether in heaven or on earth (as indeed there are many "gods" and many "lords"), (6) yet for us there is but one God, the Father, from whom all things came and for whom we live; and there is but one Lord, Jesus Christ, through whom all things came and through whom we live.

(7) But not everyone possesses this knowledge. Some people are still so accustomed to idols that when they eat sacrificial food they think of it as having been sacrificed to a god, and since their conscience is weak, it is defiled. (8) But food does not bring us near to God; we are no worse if we do not eat, and no better if we do.

(9) Be careful, however, that the exercise of your rights does not become a stumbling block to the weak. (10) For if anyone with a weak conscience sees you, with all your knowledge, eating in an idol's temple,[60] won't they be emboldened[61] to eat what is sacrificed to idols? (11) So this weak brother or sister, for whom Christ died, is destroyed by your knowledge. (12) When you sin against them in this way and wound their weak conscience, you sin against Christ. (13) Therefore, if what I eat causes my brother or sister to fall into sin, I will never eat meat again, so that I will not cause them to fall.

---

57 Chaps. 8:1–11: I have confused many commentators, who find Paul's position inconsistent and unclear. In fact they are a carefully unified rhetorical composition, with Paul's own personal example as the centerpiece (chap. 9, resumed at 10:23–11:1). The confusion results from Paul's sympathy with both positions and the care with which he tries to restate the concerns of each faction within a fuller context of biblical teachings, tradition, facts of social life in Corinth, and above all the possibility that groups with quite different perspectives and interests within the church can learn to live in mutual responsibility and concord.

58 Another slogan of the Corinthian spiritualists, allowing Paul to reprise his earlier warnings about worldly knowledge (1:18–4:21), summing up with an antithesis between knowledge and love.

59 Cf. 3:18; 10:12; also Gal. 6:9.

60 Meals in the cult shrine were extremely important in the family, social, and civic life of Hellenistic culture; for many participants most such occasions had scarcely any religious significance except in the sense of civic piety.

61 Lit., "built up," the sarcastic reverse of 8:1b.

(9) Am I not free? Am I not an apostle?[62] Have I not seen Jesus our Lord? Are you not the result of my work in the Lord? (2) Even though I may not be an apostle to others, surely I am to you! For you are the seal of my apostleship in the Lord.

(3) This is my defense to those who sit in judgment on me. (4) Don't we have the right to food and drink? (5) Don't we have the right to take a believing wife[63] along with us, as do the other apostles and the Lord's brothers and Cephas? (6) Or is it only I and Barnabas who don't have the right not to work for a living?

(7) Who serves as a soldier at his own expense? Who plants a vineyard and does not eat of its grapes? Who tends a flock and does not drink of the milk? (8) Do I say this merely on human authority? Doesn't the Law say the same thing? (9) For it is written in the Law of Moses: "Do not muzzle an ox while it is treading out the grain."[64] Is it about oxen that God is concerned? (10) Surely he says this for us, doesn't he? Yes, this was written for us, because when farmers plow and thresh, they should be able to do so in the hope of sharing in the harvest. (11) If we have sown spiritual seed among you, is it too much if we reap a material harvest from you? (12) If others have this right of support from you, shouldn't we have it all the more?

But we did not use this right. On the contrary, we put up with anything rather than hinder the gospel of Christ.

(13) Don't you know that those who serve in the temple get their food from the temple, and that those who serve at the altar share in what is offered on the altar? (14) In the same way, the Lord has commanded that those who preach the gospel should receive their living from the gospel.[65]

(15) But I have not used any of these rights.[66] And I am not writing this in the hope that you will do such things for me, for I would rather die than allow anyone to deprive me of this boast. (16) For when I preach the gospel, I cannot boast, since I am compelled to preach. Woe to me if I do not preach the gospel! (17) If I preach voluntarily, I have a reward; if not voluntarily, I am simply discharging the trust committed to me. (18) What then is my reward? Just this: that in preaching the gospel I may offer it free of charge, and so not misuse my rights as a preacher of the gospel.

---

62   While chap. 9 seems to interrupt the argument and has been misidentified by many commentators as a self-defense by Paul (because of the word *apologia* in v.3), actually it is a personal example of the principle being developed: Christian freedom includes the freedom to use or to renounce one's "right," depending on the communal situation. The word *exousia*, "right," its verbal form *exestin* (10:23), and its synonym *eleutheros, -ia*, "free," "freedom" (9:1, 19; 10:29), signal the central theme of these chapters.

63   Lit., "a sister [i.e., a Christian] as wife."

64   Deut. 25:4

65   Another allusion to a saying attributed to Jesus: cf. Luke 10:7; Matt. 10:10; Gal. 6:6; 1 Tim. 5:18.

66   Cf. 1 Thess. 2:9; 2 Cor. 11:7–11.

(19) Though I am free and belong to no one, I have made myself a slave to everyone,[67] to win as many as possible. (20) To the Jews I became like a Jew, to win the Jews. To those under the law I became like one under the law (though I myself am not under the law), so as to win those under the law. (21) To those not having the law I became like one not having the law (though I am not free from God's law but am under Christ's law), so as to win those not having the law. (22) To the weak I became weak, to win the weak. I have become all things to all people so that by all possible means I might save some. (23) I do all this for the sake of the gospel, that I may share in its blessings.

(24) Do you not know that in a race all the runners run, but only one gets the prize? Run in such a way as to get the prize. (25) Everyone who competes in the games goes into strict training. They do it to get a crown that will not last; but we do it to get a crown that will last forever. (26) Therefore I do not run like someone running aimlessly; I do not fight like a boxer beating the air. (27) No, I strike a blow to my body and make it my slave so that after I have preached to others, I myself will not be disqualified for the prize.[68]

(10) For I do not want you to be ignorant of the fact, brothers and sisters, that our ancestors were all under the cloud and that they all passed through the sea.[69] (2) They were all baptized into Moses in the cloud and in the sea. (3) They all ate the same spiritual food (4) and drank the same spiritual drink; for they drank from the spiritual rock that accompanied them, and that rock was Christ.[70] (5) Nevertheless, God was not pleased with most of them; their bodies were scattered in the wilderness.

(6) Now these things occurred as examples to keep us from setting our hearts on evil things as they did. (7) Do not be idolaters, as some of them were; as it is written: "The people sat down to eat and drink and got up to indulge in revelry." (8) We should not commit sexual immorality, as some of them did—and in one day twenty-three thousand of them died.[71] (9) We should not test Christ, as some of them did—and were killed by snakes.[72] (10) And do not grumble, as some of them did—and were killed by the destroying angel.[73]

---

67   "Slave to everyone" in contemporary political debate identifies a populist kind of leadership, i.e., from the point of view of the upper classes (and the ambitions of "those who have knowledge" whom Paul addresses here) the demagogue. Paul dares to apply this phrase to himself in order to challenge the assumptions about freedom and its responsibilities within the community.

68   Metaphors from athletics were favorites in Greek rhetoric of every school; perhaps the popularity of the Isthmian Games held near Corinth would give them special currency here.

69   10:1–13 are a homily or *midrash*, in a style found frequently in Jewish literature, on the key passage quoted in v. 7 from Exod. 32:6. Whether Paul is quoting a homily he or someone else previously composed or is constructing it for the occasion, we cannot be sure.

70   The "spiritual food" is the manna (Ex.16:4–35; Deut. 8:3; Ps. 78:23–25); the "spiritual drink," the water from the rock (Ex. 17:6; Num. 20:2–13). The double account of the water miracle (Ex. 17; Num. 20) led to the legend of a rock that "went up with them to the hills and down to the valleys . . ." (Tosefta, *Sukkah* iii.11 and elsewhere).

71   Num. 25.

72   Num. 21:5 f.

73   Num. 14:2, 36; 16:41–49; Ps.106:25–27.

These things happened to them as examples and were written down as warnings for us, on whom the culmination of the ages has come.[74] (12) So, if you think you are standing firm, be careful that you don't fall! (13) No temptation has overtaken you except what is common to us all. And God is faithful; he will not let you be tempted beyond what you can bear. But when you are tempted, he will also provide a way out so that you can endure it.

(14) Therefore, my dear friends, flee from idolatry. (15) I speak to sensible people; judge for yourselves what I say. (16) Is not the cup of thanksgiving for which we give thanks a participation[75] in the blood of Christ? And is not the bread that we break a participation in the body of Christ? (17) Because there is one loaf, we, who are many, are one body, for we all partake of the one loaf.

(18) Consider the people of Israel:[76] Do not those who eat the sacrifices participate in the altar? (19) Do I mean then that food sacrificed to an idol is anything, or that an idol is anything? (20) No, but the sacrifices of pagans[77] are offered to demons, not to God, and I do not want you to be participants with demons. (21) You cannot drink the cup of the Lord and the cup of demons too; you cannot have a part in both the Lord's table and the table of demons. (22) Are we trying to arouse the Lord's jealousy? Are we stronger than he?

(23) "I have the right to do anything," you say—but not everything is beneficial.[78] "I have the right to do anything"—but not everything is constructive. (24) No one should seek their own good, but the good of others.

(25) Eat anything sold in the meat market[79] without raising questions of conscience, (26) for, "The earth is the Lord's, and everything in it."[80]

(27) If an unbeliever invites you to a meal and you want to go, eat whatever is put before you without raising questions of conscience. (28) But if someone says to you, "This has been offered in sacrifice,"[81] then do not eat it, both for the sake of the one who told you and for the sake of conscience.

---

74   For the notion that biblical prophecies contained hidden messages for "the culmination of the ages." compare 1QpHab 7.1 (among the Dead Sea Scrolls). Treating biblical stories as "types" ("as examples" here translates *typikōs*, cf. v. 6, *typoi*) becomes one of the main interpretive strategies of the ancient church; cf. Rom. 5:14.

75   Or, communion, *koinōnia*.

76   Lit., "Israel according to the flesh."

77   Several important witnesses read "they [Israel] sacrifice." The clause is a quotation from Deut. 32:17, which refers to Israel's apostasy (cf. v.7). In the Hebrew that apostasy is called a rejection of "the Rock," though the LXX translation is "God."

78   Cf. 6:12.

79   Temples were the source of most meat sold in the market; priests were by profession butchers.

80   Ps. 24: 1.

81   Who is this imagined informant, a pagan or one of the "weak" Christians? Use of the common term "sacred sacrifice," *hierothyton* here, rather than the parodistic *eidōlothython*, "idol sacrifice," which Paul has used earlier, might suggest the former, but then how are we to take v. 29?

(29) I am referring to the other person's conscience, not yours. For why is my freedom being judged by another's conscience? (30) If I take part in the meal with thankfulness, why am I denounced because of something I thank God for?

(31) So whether you eat or drink or whatever you do, do it all for the glory of God. (32) Do not cause anyone to stumble, whether Jews, Greeks or the church of God—(33) even as I try to please everyone in every way. For I am not seeking[82] my own good but the good of many, so that they may be saved.

(11) Follow my example, as I follow the example of Christ.

(2) I praise you for remembering me in everything and for holding to the traditions just as I passed them on to you.[83] (3) But I want you to realize that the head of every man is Christ, and the head of the woman is man, and the head of Christ is God. (4) Every man who prays or prophesies with his head covered[84] dishonors his head. (5) But every woman who prays or prophesies with her head uncovered dishonors her head[85]—it is the same as having her head shaved. (6) For if a woman does not cover her head, she might as well have her hair cut off; but if it is a disgrace for a woman to have her hair cut off or her head shaved, then she should cover her head.

(7) A man ought not to cover his head, since he is the image and glory of God; but woman is the glory of man. (8) For man did not come from woman, but woman from man;[86] (9) neither was man created for woman, but woman for man. (10) It is for this reason that a woman ought to have authority over her own head, because of the angels.[87] (11) Nevertheless, in the Lord woman is not independent of man, nor is man independent of woman. (12) For as woman came from man, so also man is born of woman. But everything comes from God.

---

82   See 4:16; 1 Thess. 1:6.

83   Vv. 2–16 are one of the most obscure passages in the Pauline letters. Only a few points are relatively clear: (1) The issue is raised by the prophetic movement that flourished briefly, practiced by both men and women, in the early church, and was regarded as a gift of the Spirit and a sign that Christians belonged already to the end of days. (2) One of the "traditions" that Paul "passed on" was the baptismal formula that "in Christ" there is "no 'male and, female'" (Gal. 3:28); in Corinth at least one of the factions tried to find practical applications of such statements in the present life of the community (see above on chap. 7). (3) Paul, though "praising" this fundamental position, wishes to limit the enthusiasm that threatens to lapse into fantasy. His rather awkward argument is based on widespread custom (a woman with loose or uncovered hair dishonors her husband) and speculations based on Gen. 1–2.

84   "With his head covered": the opposite "uncovered" in v. 5 seems to require this translation, but both grammar and Jewish custom speak against it. The Greek would normally mean, "having (something: long hair?) hanging down from the head." Perhaps, then, the requirement suggested for the female prophets refers not to veils or head scarves but to having their hair bound up or braided, to avoid the disheveled locks associated with the frenzy of women participating in Dionysiac or other ecstatic cults.

85   "Head" in vv. 4, 5 must be a double entendre (v. 3), alluding to God and the husband, respectively.

86   Gen. 2:21–23.

87   No one knows what this means, though many guesses have been offered. To ward off the demonic powers (cf. Gen. 6:2 and note 2 Cor. 11:3, 14)? Because angels guard the created order? Because angels share in the community's worship (suggested by comparison with the Dead Sea Scrolls)? Because angels transmit prophecy? None of these is convincing.

(13) Judge for yourselves: Is it proper for a woman to pray to God with her head uncovered? (14) Does not the very nature of things teach you that if a man has long hair, it is a disgrace to him, (15) but that if a woman has long hair, it is her glory? For long hair is given to her as a covering.[88] (16) If anyone wants to be contentious about this, we have no other practice—nor do the churches of God.

(17) In the following directives I have no praise for you, for your meetings do more harm than good.[89] (18) In the first place, I hear that when you come together as a church, there are divisions among you, and to some extent I believe it. (19) No doubt there have to be differences among you to show which of you have God's approval. (20) So then, when you come together, it is not the Lord's Supper you eat, (21) for when you are eating, some of you go ahead with your own private suppers. As a result, one person remains hungry and another gets drunk. (22) Don't you have homes to eat and drink in? Or do you despise the church of God by humiliating those who have nothing? What shall I say to you? Shall I praise you? Certainly not in this matter!

(23) For I received from the Lord what I also passed on to you:[90] The Lord Jesus, on the night he was betrayed, took bread, (24) and when he had given thanks, he broke it and said, "This is my body, which is for[91] you; do this in remembrance of me." (25) In this same way, after supper he took the cup, saying, "This cup is the new covenant in my blood; do this, whenever you drink it, in remembrance of me" (26) For whenever you eat this bread and drink this cup, you proclaim the Lord's death until he comes.

(27) So then, whoever eats the bread or drinks the cup of the Lord in an unworthy manner will be guilty of sinning against the body and blood of the Lord. (28) Everyone ought to examine themselves before they eat of the bread and drink of the cup. (29) For those who eat and drink without discerning the body of Christ[92] eat and drink judgment on themselves. (30) That is why many among you are weak and sick, and a number of you have fallen asleep. (31) But if we were more discerning with regard to ourselves, we would not come under such judgment. (32) Nevertheless, when we are judged in this way by the Lord, we are being disciplined so that we will not be finally condemned with the world.

---

88   Paul was not the first nor the last to confuse custom with "nature" (*physis*). Similar statements are found in pagan and Jewish moralists of this period; e.g., Pseudo-Phocylides, 210–12.

89   Lit., "It is not for the better but for the worse that you come together." Paul ironically plays the literal meaning of "come together" against its extended meaning, "to unite." Thus v. 18 reiterates the theme of the whole letter, the warning against "divisions" (1:10). That the divisions here have their roots in socioeconomic differences is clear, though neither the details of the situation nor of Paul's remedy are certain.

90   "Received," "passed on" are technical terms for transmission of tradition; hence "from the Lord" here (contrast Gal. 1:11 f.) obviously includes, not excludes, human mediation. To the tradition itself, compare Matt. 26:26–28; Mark 14:22–24; Luke 22:17–19. See also the essay by H.J. Klauck in Part IX.

91   Some texts read "broken for," a few, "given for."

92   "Of Christ" is not in the Greek, but many manuscripts add "of the Lord."

(33) So then, my brothers and sisters, when you gather to eat, you should all eat together. (34) Those who are hungry should eat something at home, so that when you meet together it may not result in judgment.

And when I come I will give further directions. (12) Now about the gifts of the Spirit,[93] brothers and sisters, I do not want you to be uninformed. (2) You know that when you were pagans, somehow or other you were influenced and led astray to mute idols. (3) Therefore I want you to know that no one who is speaking by the Spirit of God says, "Jesus be cursed,"[94] and no one can say, "Jesus is Lord," except by the Holy Spirit.

(4) There are different kinds of gifts, but the same Spirit distributes them. (5) There are different kinds of service, but the same Lord. (6) There are different kinds of working, but in all of them and in everyone it is the same God at work.

(7) Now to each one the manifestation of the Spirit is given for the common good. (8) To one there is given through the Spirit a message of wisdom, to another a message of knowledge by means of the same Spirit, (9) to another faith by the same Spirit, to another gifts of healing by that one Spirit, (10) to another miraculous powers, to another prophecy, to another distinguishing between spirits, to another speaking in different kinds of tongues, and to still another the interpretation of tongues. (11) All these are the work of one and the same Spirit, and he distributes them to each one, just as he determines.

(12) Just as a body, though one, has many parts, but all its many parts form one body,[95] so it is with Christ. (13) For we were all baptized by one Spirit so as to form one body—whether Jews or Gentiles, slave or free—and we were all given the one Spirit to drink.[96] (14) Even so the body is not made up of one part but of many.

(15) Now if the foot should say, "Because I am not a hand, I do not belong to the body," it would not for that reason cease to be part of the body. (16) And if the ear should say, "Because I am not an eye, I do not belong to the body," it would not for that reason cease to be part of the body. (17) If the whole body were an eye, where would the sense

---

93 This theme, apparently answering another question of the Corinthians' letter, occupies chaps. 12–14, and continues the discussion of factions that appear when the believers "come together."

94 Various explanations are offered for this startling formula: (1) an allusion to the occasional requirement (attested from the second century) by Roman officers that recanting Christians curse Christ and acclaim Caesar as "Lord" to escape persecution—but nothing in 1 Cor. speaks of persecution; (2) an ecstatic cry by Corinthian "spirituals" or "Gnostics," assumed to distinguish between the physical "Jesus" and the spiritual "Christ"; (3) supposed Jewish curses of the crucified (Deut. 21:23)—but this would have no connection with the context. More likely, it is merely Paul's hyperbole, formulated as a hypothetical opposite of the normal confession "Jesus is Lord."

95 The metaphor of body and limbs to describe a society was ancient and very widespread; the fable of Menenius Agrippa, in which hands, mouth, and teeth rebel against the belly, was especially often quoted (Livy 2:32. 12–33. 1), but many variations were used in political speeches that warned against factions and urged concord. Paul's only innovation is in linking the body metaphor to the baptismal language about "putting on Christ" (v. 13).

96 Cf. Gal. 3:27 f.; Col. 3:11.

of hearing be? If the whole body were an ear, where would the sense of smell be? (18) But in fact God has placed the parts in the body, every one of them, just as he wanted them to be. (19) If they were all one part, where would the body be? (20) As it is, there are many parts, but one body.

(21) The eye cannot say to the hand, "I don't need you!" And the head cannot say to the feet, "I don't need you!" (22) On the contrary those parts of the body that seem to be weaker are indispensable, (23) and the parts that we think are less honorable we treat with special honor. And the parts that are unpresentable are treated with special modesty, (24) while our presentable parts need no special treatment. But God has put the body together, giving greater honor to the parts that lacked it; (25) so that there should be no division in the body, but that its parts should have equal concern for each other. (26) If one part suffers, every part suffers with it; if one part is honored, every part rejoices with it.

(27) Now you are the body of Christ, and each one of you is a part of it. (28) And God has placed in the church first of all apostles, second prophets, third teachers, then miracles, then gifts of healing, of helping, of guidance, and of different kinds of tongues. (29) Are all apostles? Are all prophets? Are all teachers? Do all work miracles? (30) Do all have gifts of healing? Do all speak in tongues? Do all interpret? (31) Now eagerly desire the greater gifts.

And yet I will show you the most excellent way.[97] (13) If I speak in human or angelic tongues, but do not have love, I am only a resounding gong or a clanging cymbal. (2) If I have the gift of prophecy and can fathom all mysteries and all knowledge, and if I have a faith that can move mountains, but do not have love, I am nothing. (3) If I give all I possess to the poor and give over my body [to hardship] that I may boast,[98] but do not have love, I gain nothing.

(4) Love is patient, love is kind. It does not envy, it does not boast, it is not proud. It does not dishonor others, it is not self-seeking, it is not easily angered, it keeps no record of wrongs. (6) Love does not delight in evil but rejoices with the truth. (7) It always protects, always trusts, always hopes, always perseveres.[99]

---

97   Some commentators have taken chap. 13 to be a separate composition, inserted here by Paul himself or a later editor (note the repetition of v. 12:3 la in 14:1a). It is composed in the style of an encomium on a virtue, a form quite familiar in Greek literature: the praises of Eros in Plato's *Symposium* are the most famous; for a Jewish example, see 1 Esd. 4:33–41. It is very carefully constructed, and Paul might well have written it for some earlier occasion, but it sums up themes that have been important throughout the letter. For Paul as for many Greco-Roman moral philosophers, love is the best cure for discord: "knowledge puffs up while love builds up" (8:1).

98   Ancient texts are divided between *kauthēsōmai*, "to be burned," and *kauchēsōmai*, "that I may boast." In either case the allusion is to martyrdom; cf. Dan. 3:28.

99   The list of what love is *not* corresponds rather precisely to Paul's description of the factionalism of the Corinthian Christians: they are jealous (3:3), boast and are "puffed up" (1:29, 31, 3:21; 4:6, 7, 18, 19; 5:2), count up evil and are quick to judge (4:1–5; 6:1–11), and lack the hope promised by the preaching of resurrection (chap. 15), Above all, they are childish (see notes on chaps. 1–4 above and v. 11 below).

(8) Love never fails. But where there are prophecies, they will cease; where there are tongues, they will be stilled; where there is knowledge, it will pass away. (9) For we know in part and we prophesy in part, (10) but when completeness comes, what is in part disappears. (11) When I was a child, I talked like a child, I thought like a child, I reasoned like a child. When I became a man, I put the ways of childhood behind me. (12) For now we see only a reflection as in mirror;[100] then we shall see face to face. Now I know in part; then I shall know fully; even as I am fully known.

(13) And now these three remain: faith, hope and love.[101] But the greatest of these is love.

(14) Follow the way of love and eagerly desire spiritual gifts, especially the gift of prophecy. (2) For those who speak in a tongue[102] do not speak to other people but to God. Indeed, no one understands them; they utter mysteries by the Spirit. (3) But those who prophesy speak to people for their strengthening, encouragement and comfort. (4) Those who speak in a tongue edify themselves, but those who prophesy edify[103] the church. (5) I would like every one of you to speak in tongues, but I would rather have you prophesy. Those who prophesy are greater than those who speak in tongues, unless they interpret, so that the church may be edified.

(6) Now, brothers and sisters, if I come to you and speak in tongues, what good will I be to you, unless I bring you some revelation or knowledge or prophecy or word of instruction? (7) Even in the case of lifeless things that make sounds, such as the pipe or harp, how will anyone know what tune is being played unless there is a distinction in the notes? (8) Again, if the trumpet does not sound a clear call, who will get ready for battle? (9) So it is with you. Unless you speak intelligible words with your tongue, how will anyone know what you are saying? You will just be speaking into the air. (10) Undoubtedly there are all sorts of languages in the world, yet none of them is without meaning. (11) If then I do not grasp the meaning of what someone is saying, I am a foreigner to the speaker, and the speaker is a foreigner to me. (12) So it is with you. Since you are eager for gifts of the Spirit, try to excel in those that build up the church.

(13) For this reason those who speak in a tongue should pray that they may interpret what they say. (14) For if I pray in a tongue, my spirit prays, but my mind is unfruitful. (15) So what shall I do? I will pray with my spirit, but I will also pray with my understanding; I will sing with my spirit, but I will also sing with my understanding.

---

100   The mirror metaphor is used in many ways by ancient authors; here it merely emphasizes the indirectness and incompleteness of knowledge in the present world. On knowing vs. being known (by God), cf. 8:3 and Gal. 4:9.

101   For the triad faith, hope, love, cf. 1 Thess. 1:3; 5:8; Rom 5:1–5; Col. 1:4 f.

102   Cf. 13:1. "To speak in a tongue" was, we assume, similar to the ecstatic phenomenon which we know in some modern religious movements and which we call, after the Greek in the NT, "glossolalia." It consists in involuntary utterance of rapid sequences of inarticulate sounds, perhaps in a chanting cadence. In the early church it was interpreted as a "gift of the Spirit," 12:10, 28, 30; 13:1, 8; Acts 2:4–13 (where the author interprets the phenomenon in a more "rational," miraculous, and symbolic way); 10:46; 19:6; elsewhere in early Christian literature only in the spurious ending of Mark, 16:17.

103   "Edify," i.e., "build up," vv. 4, 5, 12, 17, 26; an important metaphor for Paul: 8:1; 10:23; 1 Thess. 5:11.

(16) Otherwise when you are praising God in the Spirit, how can the others, who are now put in the same situation as an inquirer,[104] say "Amen" to your thanksgiving, since they do not know what you are saying? (17) You are giving thanks well enough, but the others are not edified.

(18) I thank God that I speak in tongues more than all of you. (19) But in the church I would rather speak five intelligible words to instruct others than ten thousand words in a tongue.

(20) Brothers and sisters, stop thinking like children. In regard to evil be infants, but in your thinking be adults.[105] (21) In the Law it is written:

> "With other tongues
> and through the lips of foreigners
> I will speak to this people,
> but even then they will not listen to me,
> says the Lord"[106]

(22) Tongues, then, are a sign, not for believers but for unbelievers; prophecy, however, is not for unbelievers but for believers. (23) So if the whole church comes together and everyone speaks in tongues, and inquirers or unbelievers come in, will they not say that you are out of your mind? (24) But if an unbeliever or an inquirer comes in while everyone is prophesying they are convicted of sin and are brought under judgment by all, (25) as the secrets of their hearts are laid bare. So they will fall down and worship God, exclaiming, "God is really among you!"

(26) What then shall we say, brothers and sisters? When you come together, each of you has a hymn, or a word of instruction, a revelation, a tongue or an interpretation. Everything must be done so that the church may be built up. (27) If anyone speaks in a tongue, two—or at the most three—should speak, one at a time, and someone must interpret. (28) If there is no interpreter, the speaker should keep quiet in the church; let them speak to themselves and to God.

(29) Two or three prophets should speak, and the others should weigh carefully what is said. (30) And if a revelation comes to someone who is sitting down, the first speaker should stop. (31) For you can all prophesy in turn so that everyone may be instructed and encouraged. (32) The spirits of prophets are subject to the control of prophets. (33) For God is not a God of disorder but of peace—as in all the congregations of the Lord's people.

---

104   Lit., "One who fills the place of the outsider [Greek *idiōtes*]."
105   See note on 2:6; Paul may be playing on the various connotations of the word to say that glossolalia is not a sure sign of spiritual "perfection" or "initiation," but may rather, when it produces pride and factiousness, indicate childishness.
106   Isa. 28:11–12.

(34) Women should remain silent in the churches. They are not allowed to speak, but must be in submission, as the law says.[107] (35) If they want to inquire about something, they should ask their own husbands at home; for it is disgraceful for a woman to speak in the church.

(36) Or did the word of God originate with you? Or are you the only people it has reached? (37) If any think they are prophets or otherwise gifted by the Spirit, let them acknowledge that what I am writing to you is the Lord's command. (38) Those who ignore this will themselves be ignored.[108]

(39) Therefore, my brothers and sisters, be eager to prophesy, and do not forbid speaking in tongues. (40) But everything should be done in a fitting and orderly way.

(15) Now, brothers and sisters, I want to remind you of the gospel I preached to you, which you received and on which you have taken your stand. (2) By this gospel you are saved, if you hold firmly to the word I preached to you. Otherwise, you have believed in vain.

(3) For what I received I passed on to you[109] as of first importance: that Christ died for our sins according to the Scriptures, (4) that he was buried, that he was raised on the third day according to the Scriptures, (5) and that he appeared to Cephas, and then to the Twelve. (6) After that, he appeared to more than five hundred of the brothers and sisters at the same time, most of whom are still living, though some have fallen asleep. (7) Then he appeared to James, then to all the apostles, (8) and last of all he appeared to me also, as to one abnormally born.[110]

(9) For I am the least of the apostles and do not even deserve to be called an apostle, because I persecuted the church of God. (10) But by the grace of God I am what I am, and his grace to me was not without effect. No, I worked harder than all of them—yet

---

107   This statement seems flatly to contradict 11:2–16, which presupposes that women are free to prophesy in the church. If 14:33b–35 is taken to refer only to non-ecstatic discussion in the assembly, as v. 35 suggests, then it is not clear why the passage stands in the context of a chapter dealing with ecstasy. Translating "wives" instead of "women," which is perfectly possible, would encounter the same difficulty. Some manuscripts place these verses after v. 10. Some modern commentators regard them as an interpolation by some later, conservative Paulinist; cf. 1 Tim. 2:11 f.

108   On the form of v.38, see note 3:17.

109   On the technical designation of tradition, see notes on 11:23 and Gal. 1:12. The tradition is carefully formulated:
that Christ died for our sins
    according to the scriptures
    and that he was buried
    that he was raised on the third day
    according to the scriptures
    and that he appeared
    to Cephas, then to the Twelve.
Where it ends is not certain, since Paul adds other reports that are also, in a looser sense, tradition.

110   "One abnormally born": lit. an "abortion" or "miscarriage," perhaps a term of abuse used by Paul's opponents; v. 9 can be regarded as interpreting the term.

not I, but the grace of God that was with me. (11) Whether, then, it is I or they, this is what we preach, and this is what you believed.

(12) But if it is preached that Christ has been raised from the dead, how can some of you say that there is no resurrection of the dead?[111] (13) If there is no resurrection of the dead, then not even Christ has been raised.

(14) And if Christ has not been raised, our preaching is useless and so is your faith. (15) More than that, we are then found to be false witnesses about God, for we have testified about God that he raised Christ from the dead. But he did not raise him if in fact the dead are not raised. (16) For if the dead are not raised, then Christ has not been raised either. (17) And if Christ has not been raised, your faith is futile; you are still in your sins. (18) Then those also who have fallen asleep[112] in Christ are lost. (19) If only for this life we have hope in Christ, we are to be pitied more than all others.

(20) But Christ has indeed been raised from the dead, the firstfruits of those who have fallen asleep. (21) For since death came through a human being, the resurrection of the dead comes also through a human being. (22) For as in Adam all die, so in Christ all will be made alive. (23) But in this order: Christ, the firstfruits; then, when he comes, those who belong to him. (24) Then the end will come, when he hands over the kingdom to God the Father after he has destroyed all dominion, authority and power. (25) For he must reign until he has put all his enemies under his[113] feet. (26) The last enemy to be destroyed is death. (27) For he "has put everything under his feet." Now when it says that "everything" has been put under him, it is clear that this does not include God himself, who put everything under Christ. (28) When he has done this, then the Son himself will be made subject to him who put everything under him, so that God may be all in all.[114]

---

111   Paul's question, intended to show the logical absurdity of the position held by "some" of the Corinthian believers, also baffles modern interpreters. If this group accepts the basic statement of "the gospel," which Paul has just outlined and of which Christ's resurrection is an essential element, then how *can* they "say that there is no resurrection of the dead"? Some commentators, pointing out that Paul emphasizes the phrase "from the dead," think he confronts Christians like those he addresses in 1 Thess. 4:13–18, who think of resurrection as an exaltation to heaven and fear that those who have already died will be left out. Others point out the emphasis throughout 1 Corinthians on the phenomena of spirit possession and suggest that "some" believe they have already been "spiritually" resurrected in baptism (cf. the second-century *Gos. Phil.* 79, and the position-attributed to Hymenaeus and Philatus in 2 Tim. 2:18). It would be possible to read some of the extravagant language of the early baptismal liturgy in such a way: see Col. 2:11 f.; Eph. 2:4–7, which speak of the resurrection of the baptized in the past tense, in contrast to Paul's future tenses in Rom. 6:4 f.

112   "Fallen asleep" is a common euphemism for death.

113   Ps. 110:1, with "all" added from Ps. 8:7.

114   Christ's own ultimate submission to God, at the moment of his triumph, is Paul's ultimate example of exercising "rights" for concord rather than discord. Each of Paul's rare uses of language about kingship in this letter makes the same point: 4:8, 20; 15:50.

(29) Now if there is no resurrection, what will those do who are baptized for the dead?[115] If the dead are not raised at all, why are people baptized for them? (30) And as for us, why do we endanger ourselves every hour? (31) I face death every day—yes, just as surely as I boast about you in Christ Jesus our Lord. (32) If I fought wild beasts in Ephesus[116] with no more than human hopes, what have I gained? If the dead are not raised,

> *"Let us eat and drink,*
> *for tomorrow we die."*[117]

(33) Do not be misled: "Bad company corrupts good character."[118] (34) Come back to your senses as you ought, and stop sinning; for there are some who are ignorant of God—I say this to your shame.

(35) But someone will ask, "How are the dead raised? With what kind of body will they come?" (36) How foolish! What you sow does not come to life unless it dies. (37) When you sow, you do not plant the body that will be, but just a seed, perhaps of wheat or of something else. (38) But God gives it a body as he has determined, and to each kind of seed he gives its own body. (39) All flesh is not the same: Human beings have one kind of flesh, animals have another, birds another and fish another. (40) There are also heavenly bodies and there are earthly bodies; but the splendor of the heavenly bodies is one kind, and the splendor of the earthly bodies is another. (41) The sun has one kind of splendor, the moon another and the stars another; and star differs from star in splendor.

(42) So will it be with the resurrection of the dead. The body that is sown is perishable, it is raised imperishable; (43) it is sown in dishonor, it is raised in glory; it is sown in weakness, it is raised in power; (44) it is sown a natural[119] body, it is raised a spiritual body.

If there is a natural body, there is also a spiritual body. (45) So it is written: "The first Adam became a living being"[120]; the last Adam, a life-giving spirit. (46) The spiritual did not come first, but the natural, and after that the spiritual. (47) The first man was of the dust of the earth; the second man is of heaven. (48) As was the earthly man, so are those who are of the earth; and as is the heavenly man, so also are those who are of

---

115   Nothing further is known about the practice of vicarious baptism, though church fathers report similar practices later by Marcionites, Montanists, and Cerinthians (schismatic groups of the second to the fourth centuries).

116   In the diatribe style of the philosophical schools, which pervades this passage, the figure of "fighting beasts" frequently refers to the wise person's struggle against passion or pleasure, but also occasionally against opponents who are hedonists, as the Epicureans were commonly said to be, Paul faces "many opponents" in Ephesus (16:9); If his struggle were merely human (see 3:3f. for a similar use of *kata anthropōn*), i.e., without hope of the future resurrection, his example would be of no significance.

117   Isa. 22:13.

118   Menander, *Thais,* frg. 218.

119   "Natural" in this verse and the next translates *psychikon*; see the note on 2:14.

120   Gen. 2:7. Paul is apparently alluding to and rejecting (v. 46) a tradition, attested by Philo and certain later Gnostic texts, that distinguished the "heavenly man" of Gen. 1:26 ff. from the "earthly man" of Gen. 2.

heaven. (49) And just as we have borne the image of the earthly man, so shall we bear the image of the heavenly man.

(50) I declare to you, brothers and sisters, that flesh and blood cannot inherit the kingdom of God, nor does the perishable inherit the imperishable. Listen, I tell you a mystery:[121] We will not all sleep, but we will all be changed—(52) in a flash, in the twinkling of an eye, at the last trumpet. For the trumpet will sound, the dead will be raised imperishable, and we will be changed. (53) For the perishable must clothe itself with the imperishable, and the mortal with immortality. (54) When the perishable has been clothed with the imperishable, and the mortal with immortality, then the saying that is written will come true: "Death has been swallowed up in victory."

> "Where, O death, is your victory?
> Where, O death, is your sting?"[122]

(56) The sting of death is sin, and the power of sin is the law. (57) But thanks be to God! He gives us the victory through our Lord Jesus Christ.

(58) Therefore, my dear brothers and sisters, stand firm. Let nothing move you. Always give yourselves fully to the work of the Lord, because you know that your labor in the Lord is not in vain.

(16) Now about the collection for the Lord's people.[123] Do what I told the Galatian churches to do. (2) On the first day of every week, each one of you should set aside a sum of money in keeping with your income, saving it up, so that when I come no collections will have to be made. (3) Then, when I arrive, I will give letters of introduction to the men you approve and send them with your gift to Jerusalem. (4) If it seems advisable for me to go also, they will accompany me.

(5) After I go through Macedonia, I will come to you—for I will be going through Macedonia. (6) Perhaps I will stay with you for a while, or even spend the winter, so that you can help me on my journey, wherever I go. (7) For I do not want to see you now and make only a passing visit; I hope to spend some time with you, if the Lord permits. (8) But I will stay on at Ephesus until Pentecost,[124] (9) because a great door for effective work has opened to me, and there are many who oppose me.

(10) When Timothy comes, see to it that he has nothing to fear while he is with you, for he is carrying on the work of the Lord, just as I am. (11) No one, then, should treat him

---

121   Cf. 1 Thess. 4:13–18.

122   The quotation is composite: Isa. 25:8; Hos. 13:14.

123   Cf. 2 Cor. 8, 9; Rom. 15:25–31; Gal. 2:10.

124   Note that Paul can write to the predominantly Gentile congregation off-handedly of the Jewish festival Pentecost-Shavnot; cf. 5:7 f.

with contempt. Send him on his way in peace so that he may return to me. I am expecting him along with the brothers.

(12) Now about our brother Apollos: I strongly urged him to go to you with the brothers. He was quite unwilling[125] to go now, but he will go when he has the opportunity.

(13) Be on your guard; stand firm in the faith; be courageous; be strong. (14) Do everything in love.

(15) You know that the household of Stephanas were the first converts[126] in Achaia, and they have devoted themselves to the service of the Lord's people. I urge you, brothers and sisters, (16) to submit to such as these and to everyone who joins in the work and labors at it. (17) I was glad when Stephanas, Fortunatus and Achaicus arrived, because they have supplied what was lacking from you. (18) For they refreshed my spirit and yours also. Such men deserve recognition.

(19) The churches in the province of Asia send you greetings. Aquila and Priscilla[127] greet you warmly in the Lord, and so does the church that meets at their house. (20) All the brothers and sisters here send you greetings. Greet one another with a holy kiss.[128]

(21) I, Paul, write this greeting in my own hand.

(22) If anyone does not love the Lord, let that person be cursed! Come, Lord![129]

(23) The grace of the Lord Jesus be with you.

(24) My love to all of you in Christ Jesus. Amen.

---

125 Or possibly, "It was not at all God's will for him."

126 Lit. "firstfruits"; for a similar use of the metaphor, see Rom. 16:5.

127 See Acts 18:2, 18, 26; Rom. 16:3. Paul, here as elsewhere, calls the wife Prisca, not Priscilla.

128 Cf. 1 Thess 5:26; 2 Cor. 13:12; Rom. 16:16. In ancient cities only family members usually kissed each other; the exchange of kisses by members of the Christian groups was thus a powerful symbol of their being a new family.

129 The Greek transliterates the Aramaic *marana tha*; probably both this and the preceding anathema belong to the early eucharistic liturgy. Cf. Rev. 22:20.

Introduction to the First Letter of John
Colleen Conway

The New Testament writing known as First John is commonly grouped with two other New Testament writings—Second John and Third John. Together, these three are known as the "Johannine Epistles." They share this designation even though the writings are anonymous and First John actually is not written in the form of a letter. The writings were given the name "John" because they have language and ideas similar to the Gospel of John, which traditionally is understood to be written by John, a disciple of Jesus—although this Gospel, too, is written anonymously.

Because of a number of differences evident between the Gospel of John and First John, most scholars think that the two texts were written by different authors. Nevertheless, it is clear that the author of First John certainly knew the Gospel well. For this reason, most New Testament scholars think that First John was written after the Gospel of John, or at least at a late stage in the development of the Gospel as it now stands, perhaps around 100–110 CE.

Why was First John written? Taking clues from the writing itself, it appears that there was a break in the community to whom the author is writing. This schism is addressed explicitly in First John 2:19—"They went out from us"—which, according to the author, indicates that "they did not belong to us." If you have ever been part of a close group that split because of a disagreement or an argument, you might have an idea of how those who remained in the group might have felt. The author is aware that the remaining believers need encouragement and reassurance about their identity and core belief. He also wants clear lines to be drawn between the two groups.

A close reading of First John suggests that disagreements with this other group concerned belief about Jesus as the Messiah and incarnate Son of God. Notice the author's repeated assertions about the centrality of belief in Jesus (1 John 2:22; 3:23; 4:2; 5:1, 5, 10). Some scholars think that especially the reference in 1 John 4:2 to belief that Jesus "has come in the flesh" indicates a docetic tendency in the opponents—a belief that Jesus did not become fully human but merely "seemed" to be human (the term "docetic" is derived from the Greek verb *dokein*, "to seem"). Others think that this was a group that had returned to the synagogue and no longer confessed a belief in Jesus as the Jewish messiah. In any case, 1 John is written to bolster the confidence and faith of those remaining in the community, to encourage them to abide in Christ and to love one another. It also is written to caution the community against those who would deceive and mislead them (1 John 2:26; 3:7; 4:1–3).

It is in the light of immediate crisis in the author's community that we should consider the language of opposition that runs through the work. The author shares the worldview of the Gospel of John, seeing human existence in starkly dualistic terms. Indeed, this writing extends the oppositional language even farther than the Gospel, introducing the idea of the anti-Christ, a term that appears three times in First John, once in Second John, but nowhere else in the New Testament. This is just one of many oppositional terms introduced in the writing, though. As you read the text, look carefully to determine how the author establishes members of the community from members outside of the community. What do you think about a worldview that divides everyone into "us" versus "them"? How is the "world" regarded in this text, and what is the relationship of the community to this world?

You also might direct particular attention to the many statements about sin. This is clearly a subject of interest to the author. Perhaps it was another point of contention with the defectors. Notice how the author struggles with the concept of sin, shifting, for example, between the idea of believers who deceive themselves if they say they have no sin (1 John 1:8) and those who claim that those born of God do not sin and, in fact, *cannot* sin (1 John 3:8). Scholars have long struggled to make sense of these and other conflicting statements. Why do you suppose that this is such a difficult topic to sort out?

Perhaps one of the most troubling aspects regarding the teachings about sin is the author's instructions not to pray for sin that is "to death" (translated "mortal sin" in the New Revised Standard Version). In the Johannine worldview, sin that is to death is the sign of unbelief (see 1 John 8:21, 24). In 1 John 5:16–17, the author distinguishes between praying for believers, which he encourages, and praying for nonbelievers, which he instructs them not to do. Such a harsh position, not reflected in other parts of the New Testament, again suggests a situation of hurt and hostile feelings resulting from the break in this community.

At the heart of the writing is an affirmation of abiding love between God, the Son, and members of the community. *Agape*, a Greek word for love, appears thirty-eight times in this brief text. Indeed, the author asserts that the central command for the community is that those who love God also must love one another and actually lay down their lives for one another (1 John 3:16, 23; compare with 1 John 15:12–13). If members of the community love one another, God's love is perfected, or fulfilled in them (1 John 4:12). This powerful message of God's love and the absolute necessity of love for one another is what is reinforced at a time of crisis and pain in the community.

THE FIRST LETTER OF JOHN

New Oxford Annotated Bible with Apocrypha, Third Edition edited by Michael D. Coogan (2001): "The First Letter of John"—introduction and footnotes (c. 2,600 words) pp. 406–412. © 2001 by Oxford University Press. By permission of Oxford University Press USA.

Though it lacks the formal features of an ancient letter—such as the opening greeting, designation of recipients and sender, reference to local persons, sender's plans, and concluding greeting (see 2 and 3 John)—1 John presents itself as an authoritative, written communication between the sender and its audience (1.4; 2.1, 7–8, 12–14, 21, 26). The opening (1.1–4) echoes the prologue of the Fourth Gospel (Jn 1.1–18), including the testimony of a communal "we" to its belief in Jesus Christ (1.1; Jn 1.14). Where the Gospel emphasized the presence of the eternal Word of God in Jesus, the epistle focuses on the physical reality of the word of life.

The "we" of a group of authorized teachers provides a formal backdrop for the individual who writes these instructions to the community. In the rest of the letter, the author uses "we" to indicate the common faith that he shares with the readers (for example, 3.23–24). First John is the work of a single teacher, writing in the Johannine tradition. The opening "we" suggests that he belongs to a school of such teachers.

By the end of the second century, the author of 1 John had been identified with John, the evangelist (Eusebius, *Historia ecclesiastica* iii.39.17; *Muratorian Canon*, lines 26–31; *Irenaeus, Adversus Haereses* 3.16.5). Eventually, the Elder, author of 2 and 3 John, was also identified with John, the evangelist. Both theology and language, however, suggest that the Johannine letters were written ca. 100 CE by one or more teachers who are heirs to the evangelist's teaching, rather than by the evangelist himself.

First John often echoes phrases that remind readers of the Fourth Gospel. Yet such expressions also differ from the evangelist. Where the Gospel consistently speaks of Jesus as the light of the world (for example, Jn 1.4–5,7; 9.5; 12.46), in 1 John, "light" refers to God (1.5). "Walking in light" refers to belief in Jesus as revelation of God in the Gospel (Jn 8.12; 12.46) but to ethical conduct of life in 1 John 1.5–7. This ethical meaning for the image occurs in Jewish and other early Christian texts; 1 John often seems closer to those materials than to the Gospel's perspective that Jesus is the unique revelation of God. In the Gospel, belief in Jesus' relationship to the Father determines an individual's salvation (for example, Jn 3.35–36). The hostile confrontation with Jews over the Christian claims for Jesus, which dominates the ministry of Jesus in the Gospel (for instance, Jn 8.13–59), never appears in 1 John. Interpreters who conclude that 1 John reflects an earlier form of the Johannine tradition therefore have to account for the general lack of Jewish concerns in 1 John. In fact, only unbelieving pagans (1 Jn 5.21) and dissident Christians who have broken communion with the Johannine churches (2.18–21) threaten the faith of 1 John's readers.

The writer accuses the dissidents of denying that Jesus is the messiah, that is, denying the Father and Son (2.22–23). Early Christian sayings warn that those who deny Jesus will be rejected in the judgment (see, for instance, Mt 10.32–33 and its parallel at Lk 12.8–9). In the Gospel, denying the divinity of the Son is equivalent to denying the Father (for example, Jn 5.20–23). Since the author of 1 John writes to ensure that its readers will not be deceived by the doctrine of opposing teachers (2.26–27), it would hardly have been the case that the secessionists denied the Christian belief that Jesus is the messiah or the Johannine insight that Jesus is identical with the Father. The link between christological belief and salvation is central to the Johannine tradition (5.1; Jn 1.12). The false teaching must have been one that introduced a subtle change into the tradition. First John 4.1–3 provides a clue: The opponents do not confess that Jesus has come "in the flesh." Combined with the opening stress on testimony to the physical reality of the word of life (1 .1–4), this phrase suggests that their dispute concerned the humanity of Jesus.

Since 1 John does not argue against opposing views directly, interpreters often turn to other reports about dissident teachers in early Christianity. A close similarity to the views rejected in 1 John appears in references to the Gnostic heretic, Cerinthus (ca. 100 CE). He argued that the divine Christ descended upon the righteous man, Jesus, at his baptism. This gift of the Spirit enabled Jesus to work miracles and reveal the unknown Father—God, who is above the Jewish creator. Since the divine cannot suffer, the Christ separated from Jesus prior to his death on the cross (see Irenaeus, *Adversus Haereses* 1.26.1). First John hints that the dissidents taught that Jesus Christ came in water only, not in water and blood (5.6). They apparently denied any saving significance to the death of Jesus on the cross. Though the clues in 1 John suggest that the opponents held some views in common with Cerinthus, the evidence is not decisive. There are no traces of the typical Gnostic teaching about a Father God beyond the creator or hostility to the God of Genesis in 1 John. Perhaps the secessionists derived their views of Jesus—and the Spirit from the portrayal of Jesus in the Gospel of John.

Since the Gospel highlights the unity of believers with Jesus and through him with God (for example, Jn 15.1–10; 17.6–19), schism threatened the promise of salvation at the heart of Johannine Christianity. First John charges the dissidents with breaking the commandment of love by which Jesus and the Father dwell with the community (2.9–11, 20–21; 4.7–12; cf. Jn 14.15,21; 15.9–10). The appearance of such schismatics fulfills the prediction that false prophets and messiahs will attempt to deceive God's faithful (2.22; 4.1; cf. Mk 13.22). Because 1 John is so indirect in speaking about dissident teachers, one cannot determine whether all of the exhortation concerns them. Certainly questions concerning sin, judgment, mutual love among Christians, and confidence in prayer and in the redemptive death of Christ arose in other early Christian churches. Much of 1 John may reflect the ordinary style of preaching in the circle of Johannine teachers (for instance, 5.13–21). First John remains confident that the Spirit's presence in the community will enable readers to recognize this work as an expression of the truth revealed in Jesus (2.27; 4.6, 13).

1. We declare to you what was from the beginning, what we have heard, what we have seen with our eyes, what we have looked at and touched with our hands, concerning the word of life—²this life was revealed, and we have seen it and testify to it, and declare to you the eternal life that was with the Father and was revealed to us—³we declare to you what we have seen and heard so that you also may have fellowship with us; and truly our fellowship is with the Father and with his Son Jesus Christ. ⁴We are writing these things so that our[a] joy may be complete.

⁵ This is the message we have heard from him and proclaim to you, that God is light and in him there is no darkness at all. ⁶If we say that we have fellowship with him while we are walking in darkness, we lie and do not do what is true; ⁷but if we walk in the light as he himself is in the light, we have fellowship with one another, and the blood of Jesus his Son cleanses us from all sin. ⁸If we say that we have no sin, we deceive ourselves, and the truth is not in us. ⁹If we confess our sins, he who is faithful and just will forgive us our sins and cleanse us from all unrighteousness. ¹⁰If we say that we have not sinned, we make him a liar, and his word is not in us.

2. My little children, I am writing these things to you so that you may not sin. But if anyone does sin, we have an advocate with the Father, Jesus Christ the righteous; ²and he is the atoning sacrifice for our sins, and not for ours only but also for the sins of the whole world.

---

a   Other ancient authorities read *your*

1.1–4: Introduction. 1–2: *From the beginning* echoes the opening of John's Gospel (Jn 1.1–18) in which Jesus is the Word, life and light made flesh. Here, the phrase refers to the beginning of Christian faith. *We*, teachers in the Johannine community, charged with handing on the tradition. *Heard, seen, looked at, touched* insist on the human reality of the Son against false teachers (see Introduction). **3–4:** Fellowship with the Father and Son and abiding joy are two signs of genuine Christian community in the Johannine tradition (Jn 15.11; 17.13).

1.5–10: Holiness in the community. 5. Light is a common symbol for the holiness and perfection of God (Ps 4.6; Isa 60.1–2). God's light is a guide for the righteous (Ps 27.1). **6–7:** No one can claim fellowship with God who does not follow God's commands (Jn 3.19; 1 Jn 2.11). Christians do not claim to be perfect. They receive forgiveness thanks to Jesus' death on the cross (cf. Rev. 1.5; 5.9). **8–10:** The false teachers, who reject the saving death of Jesus (see Introduction), may have claimed that true believers did not sin. Such teaching makes God a liar (v. 10). False views about God and sin are typical of the wicked (Ps 53).

2.1–6: Christ, our advocate. 1–2: A similar image of the risen Christ interceding for Christians describes Christ as high priest in Heb 4.14–5.4. Here Christ is *the advocate*, one who defends the faithful in the divine court (for the Holy Spirit as *advocate* see Jn 14.15–16). **3–5:** Knowledge of God requires obedience to God's commandments (cf. Ezek 36.26–27). **6:** Jesus exemplifies the love which is God's commandment (Jn 13.1; 15.11–13).

³Now by this we may be sure that we know him, if we obey his commandments. ⁴Whoever says, "I have come to know him," but does not obey his commandments, is *a* liar, and in such a person the truth does not exist; ⁵but whoever obeys his word, truly in this person the love of God has reached perfection. By this we may be sure that we are in him: ⁶whoever says, "I abide in him," ought to walk just as he walked.

⁷Beloved, I am writing you no new commandment, but an old commandment that you have had from the beginning; the old commandment is the word that you have heard. ⁸Yet I am writing you a new commandment that is true in him and in you, becauseᵃ the darkness is passing away and the true light is already shining. ⁹Whoever says, "I am in the light," while hating a brother or sister,ᵇ is shrill in the darkness. ¹⁰Whoever loves a brother or sisterᶜ lives in the light, and in such a personᵈ there is no cause for stumbling. ¹¹But whoever hates another believerᵉ is in the darkness, walks in the darkness, and does not know the way to go, because the darkness has brought on blindness.

¹²I am writing to you, little children,
        because your sins are forgiven on
                account of his name.

¹³I am writing to you, fathers,
        because you know him who is from
                the beginning.
I am writing to you, young people,
        because you have conquered
                the evil one.

¹⁴I write to you, children,
        because you know the Father.
I write to you, fathers,
        because you know him who is from
                the beginning.

---

a   Or *that*
b   Gk *hating a brother*
c   Gk *loves a brother*
d   Or *in it*
e   Gk *hates a brother*

2.7–11: The love commandment. 7: *I am writing you* repeats 2.1. Fidelity to Christ's *new commandment* to love one another (Jn 13.34) is freedom from sin and darkness. **8:** *The true light is already shining* picks up the portrayal of Jesus as light of the world from the Gospel (Jn 8.12; 9.5; 12.35–36).

2.12–17: Victory over evil. 12–14: A rhythmic series of phrases reminds all in the community from the youngest or newest members to the most senior (*little children . . . fathers . . . young people*) that they share Christ's victory over the world and its ruling power, *the evil one* (see Jn 12.31; 16.11,33b).

I write to you, young people,
> because you are strong
> > and the word of God abides in you,
> > > and you have overcome the
> > > > evil one.

[15]Do not love the world or the things in the world. The love of the Father is not in those who love the world; [16]for all that is in the world—the desire of the flesh, the desire of the eyes, the pride in riches—comes not from the Father but from the world. [17]And the world and its desire[a] are passing away, but those who do the will of God live forever.

[18]Children, it is the last hour! As you have heard that antichrist is coming, so now many antichrists have come. From this we know that it is the last hour. [19]They went out from us, but they did not belong to us; for if they had belonged to us, they would have remained with us. But by going out they made it plain that none of them belongs to us. [20]But you have been anointed by the Holy One, and all of you have knowledge.[b] [21]I write to you, not because you do not know the truth, but because you know it, and you know that no lie comes from the truth. [22]Who is the liar but the one who denies that Jesus is the Christ.[c]

This is the antichrist, the one who denies the Father and the Son. [23]No one who denies the Son has the Father; everyone who confesses the Son has the Father also. [24]Let what you heard from the beginning abide in you. If what you heard from the beginning abides in you, then you will abide in the Son and in the Father. [25]And this is what he has promised us,[d] eternal life.

[26]I write these things to you concerning those who would deceive you. [27]As for you, the anointing that you received from him abides in you, and so you do not need anyone to

---

a   Or *the desire for it*

b   Other ancient authorities

c   Or *the Messiah*

d   Other ancient authorities read *you*

2.15–17: *Though* Jesus came to save the world (1 Jn 2.2), the world also represents the false love for wealth or honor and the passions that separate people from God and one another 13.17).

2.18–29: Victory over false teaching. 18–23: Since the secessionists are agents of the evil one, *anti-christs* who are trying to deceive God's people, (v. 18; 4.1–3), a victory over evil means holding fast the true teaching (see Introduction). The appearance of false teachers who are able to deceive God's people signals the end of days, *the last hour* in apocalyptic texts (Mc 24.4–5,24; CD 5.20; T. *Moses* 7.4; Rev 20.10). The term *antichrist* only occurs in the Johannine letters. It appears to be a variant of the "false messiah" ("pseudochristos") in the Synoptic apocalypse (Mk 13.32; Mt 24.24). The figure of an opponent to God who arises in the last days combines the mythical chaos monster defeated by God's creative power (Isa 27.1; 51.9; Ps 74.13; Job 26.12), **the** figure of Satan as an angelic adversary (Job 1.6; Zech 3.1; Dan *MA, Jubilees* 1.20; I QS 1.18; 3.20–211, a human ruler who embodies evil (Dan 8.25; Ezek 38.1; 39.6;: Mace 9.12; 2 Esd 5.6–13), and the false prophet (Deut 13.2–6; 18.20). **24–27:** The presence of the Holy Spirit within the community enables Christians to distinguish true faith from lies about Jesus (cf. Jn 14.26; 16.13).

teach you. But as his anointing teaches you about all things, and is true and is not a lie, and just as it has taught you, abide in him.[e]

²⁸And now, little children, abide in him, so that when he is revealed we may have confidence and not be put to shame before him at his coming.

²⁹If you know that he is righteous, you may be sure that everyone who does right has been born of him.

3. ¹See what love the Father has given us, that we should be called children of God; and that is what we are. The reason the world does not know us is that it did not know him. ²Beloved, we are God's children now; what we will be has not yet been revealed. What we do know is this: when he[a] is revealed, we will be like him, for we will see him as he is. ³And all who have this hope in him purify themselves, just as he is pure.

⁴Everyone who commits sin is guilty of lawlessness; sin is lawlessness. ⁵You know that he was revealed to take away sins, and in him there is no sin. ⁶No one who abides in him sins; no one who sins has either seen him or known him. ⁷Little children, let no one deceive you. Everyone who does what is right is righteous, just as he is righteous. ⁸Everyone who commits sin is a child of the devil; for the devil has been sinning from the beginning. The Son of God was revealed for this purpose, to destroy the works of the devil. ⁹Those who have been born of God do not sin, because God's seed abides in them;[b] they cannot sin, because they have been born of God. ¹⁰The children of God and the children of the devil are revealed in this way: all who do not do what is right are not from God, nor are those who do not love their brothers and sisters.[c]

¹¹For this is the message you have heard from the beginning, that we should love one another. ¹²We must not be like Cain who was from the evil one and murdered his brother. And why did he murder him? Because his own deeds were evil and his brother's righteous. ¹³Do not be astonished, brothers and sisters,[d] that the world hates you. ¹⁴We know that we have passed from death to life because we love one another. Whoever does

---

e   Or *it*

a   Or *the desire for it*

b   Or *because the children of God abide in him*

c   Gk *his brother*

d   Gk *brothers*

2. 28–29: *At his coming* refers to Christ coming **in** judgment. Those who remain true to their faith in Jesus have nothing to fear (cf. Jn 3.36).

3.1–10: God's children are holy. 1–3; As God's children Christians become like Christ (Jn 1.12–13; I '3.15–16; 17.16–19). **4–6:** Jesus' coming has taken away the sin of those who remain faithful (1.5–2.2). **7–8:** Christians must take care not to be deceived about sin (2.1). **9–10:** *God's seed*, probably the Holy Spirit (2.26–27), and love for one another (Jn 13.35) distinguish God's children from others.

3.11–17: Moral examples. 11: See 2.7. **12:** Cain shows that hating a brother leads to murder (Gen 4–8) **13–14:** Even though they are righteous, like Abel, Christians can expect to be hated by the world 15.18–19) not love abides in death. [15]All who hate a brother or sister are murderers, and you know that murderers do not have eternal life abiding in them. [16]We know love by this, that he laid down his life for us—and we ought to lay down our lives for one another. [17]How does God's love abide in anyone who has the world's goods and sees a brother or sister in need and yet refuses help?

[18]Little children, let us love, not in word or speech, but in truth and action. [19]And by this we will know that we are from the truth and will reassure our hearts before him [20]whenever our hearts condemn us; for God is greater than our hearts, and he knows everything. [21]Beloved, if our hearts do not condemn us, we have boldness before God; [22]and we receive from him whatever we ask, because we obey his commandments and do what pleases him.

[23]And this is his commandment, that we should believe in the name of his Son Jesus Christ and love one another, just as he has commanded us. [24]All who obey *his* commandments abide in him, and he abides in them. And by this we know that he abides in us, by the Spirit that he has given us.

4. Beloved, do not believe every spirit, but test the spirits to see whether they are from God; for many false prophets have gone out into the world. [2]By this you know the Spirit of God: every spirit that confesses that Jesus Christ has come in the flesh is from God and every spirit that does not confess Jesus[a] is not from God. And this is the spirit of the antichrist, of which you have heard that it is coming; and now it is already in the world. [4]Little children, you are from God, and have conquered them; for the one who is in you is greater than the one who is in the world. [5]They are from the world; therefore what they say is from the world, and the world listens to them. [6]We are from God. Whoever knows God listens to us, and whoever is not from God does not listen to us. From this we know the spirit of truth and the spirit of error.

---

a   Other ancient authorities read *does away with Jesus* (Gk *dissolves Jesus*)

3.15: The phrase, *do not have eternal life abiding in them*, invites readers to apply this lesson to the secessionists. Though they claim to have faith, this break with the community is equivalent to murdering a brother (4.5; cf. Mt 5.21–22). **16–18:** Jesus' death is the supreme example of love (Jn 13, 15.9,13).

3.19–24: Love as confidence before God, 19–20: Love is the basis for God's judgment even if the false teachers have sown seeds of doubt (2.28). **21–22:** Jesus promised that God would answer his disciples' prayer (Jn 16.23–24). **23–24:** Belief in the Son and love establish a permanent relationship between believers and God Jn 16.26–27).

4.1–6: Testing spirits. **1–3:** Since false teachers can appear genuine (cf. Mc 7. 15–23), Christians must test such claims by their belief in Jesus (cf. 1 Cor 12.1–3). The secessionists have modified the tradition. **by** denying that the Christ *has come* in the flesh. **4–6:** The Holy Spirit verifies that 1 John is witness to authentic tradition (Jn 16.13–141.5: *The world listens* may imply that the secessionist gospel enjoys greater success than the truth (cf. Jn 15.19).

[7]Beloved, let us love one another, because love is from God; everyone who loves is born of God and knows God. [8]Whoever does not love does not know God, for God is love. [9]God's love was revealed among us this way: God sent his only Son into the world so that we might live through him. [10]In this is love, not that we loved God but that he loved us and sent his Son to be the atoning sacrifice for our sins. [11]Beloved, Since God loved us so much, we also ought to love one another. [12]No one has ever seen God; if we love one another, God lives in us and his love is perfected in us.

[13] By this we know that we abide in him and he in us, because he has given us of his spirit. [14]And we have seen and do testify that the Father has sent his Son as the Savior of the world. [15]God abides in those who confess that Jesus is the Son of God, and they abide in God. [16]So we have known and believe the love that God has for us.

God is love, and those who abide in love abide in God, and God abides in them. [17]Love has been perfected among us in this: that we may have boldness on the day of judgment, because as he is, so are we in this world. [18]There is no fear in love, but perfect love casts out fear; for fear has to do with punishment, and whoever fears has not reached perfection in love. [19]We love[b] because he first loved us. [20]Those who say, "I love God," and hate their brothers or sisters,[c] are liars; for those who do not love a brother or sister[d] whom they have seen, cannot love God whom they have not seen. [21]The commandment we have from him is this: those who love God must love their brothers and sisters also.

5. Everyone who believes that Jesus is the Christ[e] has been born of God, and everyone who loves the parent loves the child. [2]By this we know that we love the children of God, when we love God and obey his commandments. [3]For the love of God is this, that we obey his commandments. And his commandments are not burdensome, [4]for whatever is born of God conquers the world. And this is the victory that conquers the world, our faith. [5]Who is it that conquers the world but the one who believes that Jesus is the Son of God?

---

b   Other ancient authorities add *him*; others add *God*

c   Gk *brothers*

d   Gk *brother*

e   Or *the Messiah*

4.7–21: God's love as the basis of salvation. 7–9: True Christians imitate the love that God has shown in sending the Son to give life to the world (3.16–22; Jn 3.16). **10–12:** God's love has been shown in the death of Jesus (Jn 13.1). It is the basis for the command to love others (Jn 15.12–13). 12: See Jn 1.18: 46, **13–16a:** See 3.23–24. **14:** See Jn 4.42. **16b–18:** *God is love* (cf.Rom 8.32,39; 1 Cor 13.11). When Christian life corresponds to the nature of God (1 Jn 1.5–7), there is no reason to fear God's judgment (2–1–6,28; 3.18–20). **19:** 1 Jn 4.7,1 1. **20:** Love for others is the true evidence of our knowledge and love of God (2.3–11; 3.23–24). **21:** *Those who love God must love their brothers and sisters* represents the double commandment, to love God and neighbor (Mt 22.34–40, quoting Deut 6.5 and Lev 19.18) in the language of the Johannine tradition.

5.1–13: Concluding appeal to keep the true faith. 1–3: Belief in Jesus as the Christ (4.2–3; Jn 1.12–13; 20.31) and love for fellow believers (4.20–21; Jn 13.35) are the hallmarks of Johannine Christianity. **2:** *we know that we love the children of God. when we love God* appears to contradict 4.12. It serves as a polemic against the false teachers. Schism implies hating God's children (3.11–16). **4–5:** See 2.12–14; 4.4.

⁶This is the one who came by water and blood, Jesus Christ, not with the water only but with the water and the blood. And the Spirit is the one that testifies, for the Spirit is the truth. ⁷There are three that testify:ª ⁸the Spirit and the water and the blood, and these three agree. ⁹If we receive human testimony, the testimony of God is greater; for this is the testimony of God that he has testified to his Son. ¹⁰Those who believe in the Son of God have the testimony in their hearts. Those who do not believe in Godᵇ have made him a liar by not believing in the testimony that God has given concerning his Son. ¹¹And his is the testimony: God gave us eternal life, and this life is in his Son. ¹²Whoever has the Son has life; whoever does not have the Son of God does not have life.

¹³I write these things to you who believe in the name of the Son of God, so that you may know that you have eternal life.

¹⁴And this is the boldness we have in him, that if we ask anything according to his will, he hears us. ¹⁵And if we know that he hears us in whatever we ask, we know that we have obtained the requests made of him. ¹⁶If you see your brother or sisterᶜ committing what is not a mortal sin, you will ask, and Godᵈ will give life to such a one—to those whose sin is not mortal. There is sin that is mortal; I do not say that you should pray about that. ¹⁷All wrongdoing is sin, but there is sin that is not mortal.

¹⁸We know that those who are born of God do not sin, but the one who was born of God protects them, and the evil one does not touch them. ¹⁹We know that we are God's children, and that the whole world lies under the power of the evil one. ²⁰And we know that the Son of God has come and has given us understanding so that we may know him who is true;ᵉ and we are in him who is true, in his Son Jesus Christ. He is the true God and eternal life.

²¹Little children, keep yourselves from idols.ᶠ

---

a   A few other authorities read (with variations) ⁷*There are three that testify in heaven, the Father, the Word, and the Holy Spirit, and these three are one.*

b   Other ancient authorities read *in the Son*

c   Gk your *brothers*

d   Gk *he*

e.   Other ancient authorities read *know the true God*

f.   Other ancient authorities add *Amen*

5.6–8: *One who came by water and blood* refers to the death of Jesus as atonement for sin 11.7; 2.2; 4.10; Jn 1.29). The witnesses, *water, blood,* and *Spirit,* are evident in John's account of Jesus' death (Jn 19.34–35; for the water as Spirit, see Jn 7.38–39). **9–12:** The true faith is based not only on human testimony (1.1–4; Jn 1.7–8) but God's testimony as well (cf. Jn 5.31–38). **13:** *I write … that you have eternal life* echoes the ending in Jn 20.31.

5.14–21: Epilogue. Sin and forgiveness in the community. 14–15: God's children can be certain that God will hear their prayers (3.21–22; Jn 14.14–16; 15.16; 16.23–24; Mt 18.19–20). **16–17:** Communal prayer can elicit God's forgiveness and restore sinners (2.1–2; Mt 18.15–20; Jas 5.15b, 19–20). To *those whose sin is not mortal* distinguishes a category of sin that cannot be forgiven. Elsewhere such sin is denying that God's Spirit is at work in Jesus (Mk 3.28–30) or apostasy from Christian faith (Heb 6.4–6) Here, the expression probably refers to the secessionists. Their break with the community means that they no longer dwell with God to have the Spirit (2.19–25). **18:** See 3.8–10. **19:** See 2.12–15; 5.4–5. **20:** *Him who is true* probably refers to knowledge of the true God as other manuscripts propose (Jn 1.18: 14.7,9–10). Knowledge of the *true God* (Father and Son) confers *eternal life* (Jn 17.3). **21:** In a general sense, *keep yourselves from idols* probably refers to the false gods of non–Christian neighbors (1 Cor. 10.14). Traveling missionaries were to reject non-Christian hospitality (3 Jn 7). In this context, the phrase may refer to association with the secessionists and their teaching (2 Jn 7–9).

Plato

Introduction

Ki Joo Choi and Anthony Sciglitano

Plato, born in Athens approximately five hundred years before the birth of Jesus Christ (Plato born c. 428–427 B.C.), is the author of many well known philosophical treatises and dialogues that have served as the basis of so much of Western ideas about citizenship, justice, truth, and goodness. His teacher was Socrates (one of the primary voices in Plato's writings). Plato is also known for being Aristotle's teacher. Aristotle (384–322 B.C.) is often referred to as the "other" great thinker of ancient Greece, alongside Plato. Later in life, Aristotle was teacher to Alexander the Great, who many of you may know as one of the great conquerors of the ancient world, before the rise of the Roman Empire.

Plato wrote at a time of great cultural upheaval in Athens, and in part his philosophy seeks to respond to the challenges of his period. Several things had occurred in Greek society prior to Plato's writing that deeply affected his concerns and his ideas. One event was the breakup of an older mythology and, with it, a view of the social order. We can call this view *Homeric*. We do not have a definite date for when Homer's poems, *The Iliad* and *The Odyssey*, were written, but historians think it was around 700 B.C. It is also important to understand that Homer's texts had the status in Greek society akin to a sacred scripture or the Bible. In fact, they were even read aloud at public ceremonies.

Under what we are calling a Homeric view, Athenians saw themselves as good or virtuous to the extent that they lived appropriately. That meant terms such as *good* (*agathos*) and *bad* (*kakos*) were defined by how well an Athenian fulfilled her social and class roles. The broad notion of a *good person,* therefore, made little sense to Athenians. There were only good or bad kings, good husbands, good wives, good sons and daughters, good servants, good or bad laborers—but no generic good or bad person. So, from a Homeric standpoint, one would not ask "Is Jennifer a good person?"—that did not have much meaning. Instead, one would ask "Is Jennifer a good teacher?", "Is Jennifer a good wife?", "Is Jennifer a good sister?", and so on.

We have some records that indicate the Homeric worldview underwent some changes in the sixth century B.C. It seems that words like *good* (*agathos*) and *bad* (*kakos*) began, at this time, to take on some independence from social roles, so that a poor person could be considered good or with virtue (*arête*) and a rich person could be considered bad. In other words, one's social role or place in society does not completely define moral ideas such as *good, bad, just,* and their opposites. Why? What was going on at this time to change the longstanding Homeric worldview? In the early fifth century B.C., Greek (Homeric) culture became involved in several things that accelerated cultural change and instability. The Persian wars (c. 499–449 B.C.), and later the Peloponnesian wars (c. 431–404 B.C.)—a major inspiration behind Plato's writing of *The Republic*—brought Athenian culture into communication with cultural views that were very different from their own. At times this even meant being ruled by foreign powers. In addition, increased trade and travel brought home to the Athenians the notion that cultures differ rather markedly. This idea of cultural difference and pluralism set up some of the problems that Athenian thinkers such as Plato, Aristotle, and the Sophists addressed in different ways. We will focus here on the Sophists and on Plato.

One way to understand how Plato and the Sophists addressed this problem of cultural pluralism is to think about two important terms: *nature* (*physis*) and *custom* (*nomos*). Here, *nature* indicates cosmic and moral law, the way things are universally, and thus how we should behave in relation to the way things are. If we are human, and thus have a human nature, we ought to behave in ways proper to human beings (and not like slugs, for instance). *Custom* indicates social conventions, including but not limited to laws (*nomoi*) of our particular, and largely accidental, place of residence. We have all heard the phrase, "When in Rome, do as the Romans!" This saying suggests that Romans do some things differently from other places, and when we visit, it is proper to observe local custom. But what if the Romans eat their young? Should we share in this rather upsetting practice as well? I suspect this might damage the tourism industry!

Broadly speaking, we can talk about a Sophist solution to this problem of cultural pluralism and a Platonic solution to this problem. We should note that there was no one Sophist school. Rather, this term is used to designate a family resemblance among a variety of teachers who actually differed significantly. Let's look at a Sophist solution first. Many Sophists looked at cultural differences, and concluded that what philosophy should do is to help people succeed as citizens in whatever place they find themselves. To do this, they reasoned, is *not* to come to eternally true ideas of what The Good, The True, and The Just are, but rather to teach people the art of rhetoric, that is, how to speak persuasively and pleasingly to different kinds of audiences. This strategy would put off deciding what seemed interminable disputes regarding truth, and instead focus on what can lead to success in the courts of law and in government. Therefore, the Sophist emphasis was on custom (*nomos*) rather than nature (*physis*). They felt that this emphasis was better suited to a pluralistic culture that held many different views on the moral good.[i]

In short, many Sophists thought that what one must learn is how to be persuasive, not how to discover and articulate what is indeed true and good. Socrates challenged the Sophists' position. Consider for instance *The Apology*, which you read in *Journey of Transformation*. In the beginning of *The Apology*, Socrates speaks before the Athenian Jury in his own defense (remember, by this time, Socrates is on trial for what we might call today treason). Socrates's opening

---

i. Much of this discussion is taken from Alasdair MacIntyre's *A Short History of Ethics: A History of Moral Philosophy from the Homeric Age to the Twentieth Century* (Great Britain: Routledge Books, 1998), pp. 4–11. Also see the same author's *After Virtue: A Study in Moral Theory*, Second Edition (South Bend, IN: University of Notre Dame Press, 1984), pp. 121–146.

words of his own defense outlines the Sophists' position and then his rebuttal of that position:

> I do not know, men of Athens, how my accusers affected you; as for me, I was almost carried away in spite of myself, so persuasively did they speak. And yet, hardly anything of what they said was true. Of the many lies they told, one in particular surprised me, namely that you should be careful not to be deceived by an accomplished speaker like me. That they were not ashamed to be immediately proved wrong by the facts, when I show myself not to be an accomplished speaker at all, that I thought was most shameless on their part—unless indeed they call an accomplished speaker the man who speaks the truth . . . From me you will hear the whole truth, though not, by Zeus, gentlemen, expressed in embroidered and stylized phrases like theirs, but things spoken at random and expressed in the first words that come to mind, for I put my trust in the justice of what I say, and let none of you expect anything else. *(Apology 17a–c)*[ii]

A little later, Socrates tells us that the excellence of a "speaker lies in telling the truth" (18.a). This is a direct rejection of the Sophists' position that only rhetorical persuasion matters and not the articulation of what is actually true in itself. So, if the Sophists address their situation of cultural diversity by recommending expertise in speech and learning foreign customs for success (and this is the training that Saint Augustine will receive, incidentally), Socrates (at least as presented by Plato, his student) recommends using reason to discover the truth of things. This presumes, of course, that it is possible to find the truth of things. Not only does Socrates believe this is the case, he bets his life on it![iii] For Socrates, then, the way to address our differences about *morality, justice, good,* and *bad* is to reason together.

Of course, Plato must provide an account as to how we can know the truth, and also why it is that so many are ignorant of it. Indeed, it would not be too much to say that for Plato ignorance is the primary cause of evil and knowledge is a form of salvation. Salvation here is not Christian salvation. Remember, the arrival of Jesus is 400 years in the future. Salvation, here, means moving from a place of untruth to a place of truth, from ignorance to wisdom, from evil to good. This is clear from the cave allegory that you read in *Journey of Transformation.* The people looking at shadows mistook them for reality. Plato is not concerned with whether these people think they are right. Plato thinks

---

ii.   Of course, Socrates too is using rhetoric to persuade. He is contrasting his plain, simple speech to the ornate speech of his adversaries. This is his way of saying, "You may have heard I am a pompous philosopher, but I am really just like the regular people, trying to tell the truth in plain terms." What he does not accept is the idea that philosophy is reducible to the different forms of communication.

iii.   Please note that we are reading Socrates through the mind of his student, Plato. Like Jesus, Socrates left us no writings of his own. Plato asserts what appear to be his own, systematic views in his middle and later periods where scholars will place writings such as Phaedo and Republic (middle) and Laws (late). The Apology and Euthyphro (early writings) will more nearly show Socrates demonstrating the lack of wisdom evident in his opponents, whereas writings such as *The Republic,* thought to be much more representative of Plato than Socrates, will develop a coherent view of justice and governance.

there is such a thing as genuine knowledge. He thinks they were wrong, really wrong, and that they only think they know reality because they live in darkness chained by ignorance. Rise up, ascend from the Cave into the light, and true knowledge of the Good becomes, with intellectual struggle, possible. What one comes to know, and even participate in, is what Plato calls the **Form of the Good.** And participation in or knowledge of the *forms* is Plato's answer to how we can know the truth.

What are these *forms?* Plato thinks there is a spiritual realm of goodness, truth, and beauty that lies beneath or perhaps above the surfaces of things. This realm of forms contains patterns of perfect, never-changing, standards for things like goodness or justice. Anytime we act justly, we do so by way of participating in these perfect and unchanging forms of justice. Coming to know these forms or standards allows us to make judgments about attempts at justice in our own society. This may sound odd, but it is actually based upon a fairly basic intuition. To understand this, you might think back to when you were younger, playing with your siblings, and one of them stole your toy and stomped it into dust. Now you probably felt bad about this, but more than that, you perhaps claimed to your parents that this was "unfair." When you say "unfair," you are implying that you have knowledge of what fairness is, and your sibling's actions do not measure up to that idea of fairness. In other words, you appear to know the "form of fairness" not from the way people behave in the world, and not by looking outside of yourself, but by recollecting something already within your mind. Indeed, Plato thinks that within our soul, we know what things like goodness are, but we forget this due to our existence in bodies and the sense world. We become more interested in filling our bellies than in truth. And so we remain ignorant and lack virtue. To learn the truth, and thus to come to be virtuous (just, good, etc.), we must remember or recollect what we have forgotten, namely, the truth of the spiritual realities called forms (for instance, the form of justice). Aside from death, and thus the shedding of the body, Plato thinks that philosophy is the way to help us recollect what we knew before our souls descended into a body. Philosophy will teach us to think rigorously about our thinking, so that we come to know ourselves, and thus also to know The Good, The True, and The Just. For Plato, philosophy is a kind of therapy meant to cure us from forgetting, ignorance, and vice. Philosophy is a love of wisdom that begets genuine piety and justice.

The foregoing discussion of Socrates's position on knowledge of the truth and thus knowledge of genuine piety and justice is important to keep in mind when reading the following text from Plato, *Crito.* This reading concerns itself with issues of the nature of piety and justice. As you read *Euthyphro,* focus on the notion of piety from Euthyphro's and Socrates's points of view. Note how the notion of piety for both is not simply a "religious" notion and thus only applicable to those who consider themselves, rather obviously, "religious." Rather, piety pertains to how all members of the city, or polis, of Athens are to live in society. Piety, therefore, pertains to justice. Thus, these two dialogues show how critical the notion of piety is—*one cannot live well in society unless one knows what piety ought to mean.* Euthyphro, reflecting the general attitude of Athens, expresses a certain notion of piety. Note that piety pertains to the gods, specifically the nature of the gods and how we ought to regard them. Socrates is trying to bet-ter understand Euthyphro's position on piety and thus what the polis of Athens proposes as the nature of piety. Understand that Euthyphro is putting forward a view of piety based on social roles (i.e., the old Homeric view, as discussed earlier). By questioning Euthyphro's view of piety, Socrates is questioning, by extension, Athens' conception of the social order and thus the old Homeric view of goodness and truth.

In the *Crito*, Socrates makes his own proposal as to the proper view of piety, and Plato contrasts the concerns of Socrates with those of Crito, his visitor in prison. Crito's concerns are rooted in what he sees as the proper role of friends, a father, and a husband. But Socrates poses some difficult questions, and again calls into question this functional or role-based view of the person and morality. For instance, what should we do if our views or loves conflict with the loves of our community? How should we respond to a community that rejects our piety, even if our piety appears more nearly true or authentic? Can you find any hints that Socrates's view might be a threat to democracy?

As you read, focus on the meaning of piety: What does piety mean for Euthy-phro (and thus Athens), and what does it mean for Socrates? What is the central feature of piety for both of them? *Pay particular attention to how the notion of love figures into their conceptions of piety.* This feature of piety is subtle and can easily be missed, but do your best to see how the idea of love is central to their discussions of piety. As you investigate the nature of piety in these two dialogues, do not forget to ask if you agree or disagree with Euthyphro (and Ath-ens) or Socrates. Which account of piety do you find compelling? If you disagree with both, why?

CRITO

Five Dialogues by Plato, translated by G. M. A. Grube and revised by John M. Cooper. Copyright © 2002 Hackett Publishing Company. Reprinted by permission of Hacket Publishing Company, Inc. All rights reserved.

About the time of Socrates' trial, a state galley had set out on an annual religious mission to the small Aegean island of Delos, sacred to Apollo, and while it was away, no execution was allowed to take place. So it was that Socrates was kept in prison for a month after the trial. The ship has now arrived at Cape Sunium in Attica and is thus expected at the Piraeus, Athens' port, momentarily. So Socrates' old and faithful friend, Crito, makes one last effort to persuade him to escape into exile, and all arrangements for this plan have been made. It is this conversation between the two old friends that Plato professes to report in this dialogue. It is, as Crito plainly tells him, his last chance, but Socrates will not take it, and he gives his reasons for his refusal. Whether this conversation took place at this particular time is not important, for there is every reason to believe that Socrates' friends tried to plan his escape and that he refused. Plato more than hints that the authorities would not have minded much, as long as he left the country.

G.M.A.G.

43   **SOCRATES:** Why have you come so early, Crito? Or is it not still early?

CRITO: It certainly is.

SOCRATES: How early?

CRITO: Early dawn.

SOCRATES: I am surprised that the warder was willing to listen to you.

CRITO: He is quite friendly to me by now, Socrates. I have been here often and I have given him something.

SOCRATES: Have you just come, or have you been here for some time?

CRITO: A fair time.

SOCRATES: Then why did you not wake me right away but sit there in silence?

CRITO: By Zeus no, Socrates. I would not myself want to be in distress and awake so long. I have been surprised to see you so peacefully asleep. It was on purpose that I did not wake you, so that you should spend your time most agreeably. Often in the past throughout my life. I have considered the way you live happy, and especially so now that you bear your present misfortune so easily and lightly.

SOCRATES: It would not be fitting at my age to resent the fact that I must die now.

c

CRITO: Other men of your age are caught in such misfortunes, but their age does not prevent them resenting their fate.

SOCRATES: That is so. Why have you come so early?

CRITO: I bring bad news, Socrates, not for you, apparently, but for me and all your friends the news is bad and hard to bear. Indeed, I would count it among the hardest.

SOCRATES: What is it? Or has the ship arrived from Delos, at the arrival of which I must die?

d

CRITO: It has not arrived yet, but it will, I believe, arrive today, according to a message some men brought from Sunium, where they left it. This makes it obvious that it will come today, and that your life must end tomorrow.

SOCRATES: May it be for the best. If it so please the gods, so be it. However, I do not think it will arrive today.

44

CRITO: What indication have you of this?

SOCRATES: I will tell you. I must die the day after the ship arrives.

CRITO: That is what those in authority say.

SOCRATES: Then I do not think it will arrive on this coming day, but on the next. I take to witness of this a dream I had a little earlier during this night. It looks as if it was the right time for you not to wake me.

CRITO: What was your dream?

b

SOCRATES: I thought that a beautiful and comely woman dressed in white approached me. She called me and said: "Socrates, may you arrive at fertile Phthia[1] on the third day."

CRITO: A strange dream, Socrates.

SOCRATES: But it seems clear enough to me, Crito.

c

CRITO: Too clear it seems, my dear Socrates, but listen to me even now and be saved. If you die, it will not be a single misfortune for me. Not only will I be deprived of a friend, the like of whom I shall never find again, but many people who do not know you or me very well will think that I could have saved you if I were willing to spend money, but that I did not care to do so. Surely there can be no worse reputation than to be thought to value money more highly than one's friends, for the majority will not believe that you yourself were not willing to leave prison while we were eager for you to do so.

---

1   A quotation from the ninth book of the *Iliad* (363). Achilles has rejected all the presents of Agamemnon for him to return to the battle and threatens to go home. He says his ships will sail in the morning, and with good weather he might arrive on the third day "in fertile Phthia" (which is his home). Socrates takes the dream to mean that he will die, and his soul will find its home, on the third day. As always, counting the first member of a series, the third day is the day after tomorrow.

SOCRATES: My good Crito, why should we care so much for what the majority think? The most reasonable people, to whom one should pay more attention, will believe that things were done as they were done.

d   **CRITO:** You see, Socrates, that one must also pay attention to the opinion of the majority. Your present situation makes clear that the majority can inflict not the least but pretty well the greatest evils if one is slandered among them.

SOCRATES: Would that the majority could inflict the greatest evils, for they would then be capable of the greatest good, and that would be fine, but now they cannot do either. They cannot make a man either wise or foolish, but they inflict things haphazardly.

e   **CRITO:** That may be so. But tell me this, Socrates, are you anticipating that I and your other friends would have trouble with the informers if you escape from here, as having stolen you away, and that we should be compelled to lose all our property or pay heavy fines and suffer other punishment besides? If you have any such fear, forget it. We would

45   be justified in running this risk to save you, and worse, if necessary. Do follow my advice, and do not act differently.

SOCRATES: I do have these things in mind, Crito, and also many others.

CRITO: Have no such fear. It is not much money that some people require to save you and get you out of here. Further, do you not see that those informers are cheap, and that

b   not much money would be needed to deal with them? My money is available and is, I think, sufficient. If, because of your affection for me, you feel you should not spend any of mine, there are those strangers here ready to spend money. One of them, Simmias the Theban, has brought enough for this very purpose. Cebes, too, and a good many others. So, as I say, do not let this fear make you hesitate to save yourself, nor let what you said in court trouble you, that you would not know what to do with yourself if you left Athens,

c   for you would be welcomed in many places to which you might go. If you want to go to Thessaly, I have friends there who will greatly appreciate you and keep you safe, so that no one in Thessaly will harm you.

Besides, Socrates, I do not think that what you are doing is just, to give up your life when you can save it, and to hasten your fate as your enemies would hasten it, and in-

d   deed have hastened it in their wish to destroy you. Moreover, I think you are betraying your sons by going away and leaving them, when you could bring them up and educate them. You thus show no concern for what their fate may be. They will probably have the usual fate of orphans. Either one should not have children, or one should share with them to the end the toil of upbringing and education. You seem to me to choose the easiest path, whereas one should choose the path a good and courageous man would choose, particularly when one claims throughout one's life to care for virtue.

e   I feel ashamed on your behalf and on behalf of us, your friends, lest all that has happened to you be thought due to cowardice on our part: the fact that your trial came to court when it need not have done so, the handling of the trial itself, and now this absurd ending which will be thought to have got beyond our control through some cowardice

46   and unmanliness on our part, since we did not save you, or you save yourself, when it was possible and could be done if we had been of the slightest use. Consider, Socrates, whether this is not only evil, but shameful, both for you and for us. Take counsel with yourself, or rather the time for counsel is past and the decision should have been taken, and there is no further opportunity, for this whole business must be ended tonight. If we delay now, then it will no longer be possible; it will be too late. Let me persuade you on every count, Socrates, and do not act otherwise.

b   **SOCRATES:** My dear Crito, your eagerness is worth much if it should have some right aim; if not, then the greater your keenness the more difficult it is to deal with. We must therefore examine whether we should act in this way or not, as not only now but at all times I am the kind of man who listens to nothing within me but the argument that on reflection seems best to me. I cannot, now that this fate has come upon me, discard the

e   arguments I used; they seem to me much the same. I value and respect the same principles as before, and if we have no better arguments to bring up at this moment, be sure that I shall not agree with you, not even if the power of the majority were to frighten us with more bogeys, as if we were children, with threats of incarcerations and executions and confiscation of property. How should we examine this matter most reasonably?

d   Would it be by taking up first your argument about the opinions of men, whether it is sound in every case that one should pay attention to some opinions, but not to others? Or was that well-spoken before the necessity to die came upon me, but now it is clear that this was said in vain for the sake of argument, that it was in truth play and nonsense? I am eager to examine together with you, Crito, whether this argument will appear in any way different to me in my present circumstances, or whether it remains the same, whether we are to abandon it or believe it. It was said on every occasion by

e   those who thought they were speaking sensibly, as I have just now been speaking, that one should greatly value some people's opinions, but not others. Does that seem to you a sound statement?

You, as far as a human being can tell, are exempt from the likelihood of dying tomor-
47   row, so the present misfortune is not likely to lead you astray. Consider then, do you not think it a sound statement that one must not value all the opinions of men, but some and not others, nor the opinions of all men, but those of some and not of others? What do you say? Is this not well said?

CRITO: It is.

SOCRATES: One should value the good opinions, and not the bad ones?

CRITO: Yes.

SOCRATES: The good opinions are those of wise men, the bad ones those of foolish men?

CRITO: Of course.

b   **SOCRATES:** Come then, what of statements such as this: Should a man professionally engaged in physical training pay attention to the praise and blame and opinion of any man, or to those of one man only, namely a doctor or trainer?

CRITO: To those of one only.

SOCRATES: He should therefore fear the blame and welcome the praise of that one man, and not those of the many?

CRITO: Obviously.

SOCRATES: He must then act and exercise, eat and drink in the way the one, the trainer and the one who knows, thinks right, not all the others?

CRITO: That is so.

c   **SOCRATES:** Very well. And if he disobeys the one, disregards his opinion and his praises while valuing those of the many who have no knowledge, will he not suffer harm?

CRITO: Of course.

SOCRATES: What is that harm, where does it tend, and what part of the man who disobeys does it affect?

CRITO: Obviously the harm is to his body, which it ruins.

SOCRATES: Well said. So with other matters, not to enumerate them all, and certainly with actions just and unjust, shameful and beautiful, good and bad, about which
d   we are now deliberating, should we follow the opinion of the many and fear it, or that of the one, if there is one who has knowledge of these things and before whom we feel fear and shame more than before all the others? If we do not follow his directions, we shall harm and corrupt that part of ourselves that is improved by just actions and destroyed by unjust actions. Or is there nothing in this?

CRITO: I think there certainly is, Socrates.

e   **SOCRATES:** Come now, if we ruin that which is improved by health and corrupted by disease by not following the opinions of those who know, is life worth living for us when that is ruined? And that is the body, is it not?

CRITO: Yes.

SOCRATES: And is life worth living with a body that is corrupted and in bad condition?

CRITO: In no way.

SOCRATES: And is life worth living for us with that part of us corrupted that unjust action harms and just action benefits? Or do we think that part of us, whatever it is, that is concerned with justice and injustice, is inferior to the body?

CRITO: Not at all.

SOCRATES: It is more valuable?

CRITO: Much more.

SOCRATES: We should not then think so much of what the majority will say about us, but what he will say who understands justice and injustice, the one, that is, and the truth itself. So that, in the first place, you were wrong to believe that we should care for the opinion of the many about what is just, beautiful, good, and their opposites. "But," someone might say, "the many are able to put us to death."

CRITO: That too is obvious, Socrates, and someone might well say so.

SOCRATES: And, my admirable friend, that argument that we have gone through remains, I think, as before. Examine the following statement in turn as to whether it stays the same or not, that the most important thing is not life, but the good life.

CRITO: It stays the same.

SOCRATES: And that the good life, the beautiful life, and the just life are the same; does that still hold, or not?

CRITO: It does hold.

SOCRATES: As we have agreed so far, we must examine next whether it is just for me to try to get out of here when the Athenians have not acquitted me. If it is seen to be just, we will try to do so; if it is not, we will abandon the idea. As for those questions you raise about money, reputation, the upbringing of children, Crito, those considerations in truth belong to those people who easily put men to death and would bring them to life again if they could, without thinking; I mean the majority of men. For us, however, since our argument leads to this, the only valid consideration, as we were saying just now, is whether we should be acting rightly in giving money and gratitude to those who will lead me out of here, and ourselves helping with the escape, or whether in truth we shall do wrong in doing all this. If it appears that we shall be acting unjustly, then we have no need at all to take into account whether we shall have to die if we stay here and keep quiet, or suffer in another way, rather than do wrong.

CRITO: I think you put that beautifully, Socrates, but see what we should do.

e

SOCRATES: Let us examine the question together, my dear friend, and if you can make any objection while I am speaking, make it and I will listen to you, but if you have no objection to make, my dear Crito, then stop now from saying the same thing so often, that I must leave here against the will of the Athenians. I think it important to persuade you before I act, and not to act against your wishes. See whether the start

49

of our inquiry is adequately stated, and try to answer what I ask you in the way you think best.

CRITO: I shall try.

SOCRATES: Do we say that one must never in any way do wrong willingly, or must one do wrong in one way and not in another? Is to do wrong never good or admirable, as we have agreed in the past, or have all these former agreements been washed out during

b

the last few days? Have we at our age failed to notice for some time that in our serious discussions we were no different from children? Above all, is the truth such as we used to say it was, whether the majority agree or not, and whether we must still suffer worse things than we do now, or will be treated more gently, that, nonetheless, wrongdoing or injustice is in every way harmful and shameful to the wrongdoer? Do we say so or not?

CRITO: We do.

SOCRATES: So one must never do wrong.

CRITO: Certainly not.

SOCRATES: Nor must one, when wronged, inflict wrong in return, as the majority believe, since one must never do wrong.

c

CRITO: That seems to be the case.

SOCRATES: Come now, should one do harm to anyone or not, Crito?

CRITO: One must never do so.

SOCRATES: Well then, if one is oneself done harm, is it right, as the majority say, to do harm in return, or is it not?

CRITO: It is never right.

SOCRATES: Doing people harm is no different from wrongdoing.

CRITO: That is true.

SOCRATES: One should never do wrong in return, nor do any man harm, no matter

d

what he may have done to you. And Crito, see that you do not agree to this, contrary to your belief. For I know that only a few people hold this view or will hold it, and there is no common ground between those who hold this view and those who do not, but they inevitably despise each other's views. So then consider very carefully whether we have this view in common, and whether you agree, and let this be the basis of our deliberation, that neither to do wrong nor to return a wrong is ever correct, nor is doing harm in return for harm done. Or do you disagree and do not share this view as a basis for discussion? I have held it for a long time and still hold it now, but if you think otherwise, tell me now. If, however, you stick to our former opinion, then listen to the next point.

CRITO: I stick to it and agree with you. So say on.

SOCRATES: Then I state the next point, or rather I ask you: when one has come to an agreement that is just with someone, should one fulfill it or cheat on it?

CRITO: One should fulfill it.

SOCRATES: See what follows from this: if we leave here without the city's permission, are we harming people whom we should least do harm to? And are we sticking to a just agreement, or not?

CRITO: I cannot answer your question, Socrates. I do not know.

SOCRATES: Look at it this way. If, as we were planning to run away from here, or whatever one should call it, the laws and the state came and confronted us and asked: "Tell me, Socrates, what are you intending to do? Do you not by this action you are attempting intend to destroy us, the laws, and indeed the whole city, as far as you are concerned? Or do you think it possible for a city not to be destroyed if the verdicts of its courts have no force but are nullified and set at naught by private individuals?" What shall we answer to this and other such arguments? For many things could be said, especially by an orator on behalf of this law we are destroying, which orders that the judgments of the courts shall be carried out. Shall we say in answer, "The city wronged me, and its decision was not right." Shall we say that, or what?

CRITO: Yes, by Zeus, Socrates, that is our answer.

SOCRATES: Then what if the laws said: "Was that the agreement between us, Socrates, or was it to respect the judgments that the city came to?" And if we wondered at their words, they would perhaps add: "Socrates, do not wonder at what we say but answer, since you are accustomed to proceed by question and answer. Come now, what accusation do you bring against us and the city, that you should try to destroy us? Did we not, first, bring you to birth, and was it not through us that your father married your mother and begat you? Tell us, do you find anything to criticize in those of us who are concerned with marriage?" And I would say that I do not criticize them. "Or in those of us concerned with the nurture of babies and the education that you too received? Were those assigned to that subject not right to instruct your father to educate you in the arts and in physical culture?" And I would say that they were right. "Very well," they would continue, "and after you were born and nurtured and educated, could you, in the first place, deny that you are our offspring and servant, both you and your forefathers? If this is so, do you think that we are on an equal footing as regards the right, and that whatever we do to you it is right for you to do to us? You were not on an equal footing with your father as regards the right, nor with your master if you had one, so as to retaliate for anything they did to you, to revile them if they reviled you, to beat them if they beat you, and so with many other things. Do you think you have this right to retaliation against your country and its laws? That if we undertake to destroy you and think it right to do so, you can undertake to destroy us, as far as you can, in return? And will you say that you are right to do so, you who truly care for virtue? Is your wisdom such as not to realize that your country is to be honored more than your mother, your father, and all your ancestors, that it is more to be revered and more sacred, and that it counts for more among the gods and sensible men, that you must worship it, yield to it, and placate its anger more than your father's? You must either persuade it or obey its orders, and endure in silence whatever it instructs you to endure, whether blows or bonds, and if it leads you into war to be wounded or killed, you must obey. To do so is right, and one must not give way or retreat or leave one's post, but both in war and in courts and everywhere else, one must obey the commands of one's city and country, or persuade it as to the nature of justice. It is impious to bring violence to bear against your mother or father; it is much more so to use it against your country." What shall we say in reply, Crito, that the laws speak the truth, or not?

CRITO: I think they do.

SOCRATES: "Reflect now, Socrates," the laws might say, "that if what we say is true, you are not treating us rightly by planning to do what you are planning. We have given you birth, nurtured you, educated you; we have given you and all other citizens a share of all the good things we could. Even so, by giving every Athenian the opportunity, once arrived at voting age and having observed the affairs of the city and us the laws, we proclaim that if we do not please him, he can take his possessions and go wherever he pleases. Not one of our laws raises any obstacle or forbids him, if he is not satisfied with us or the city, if one of you wants to go and live in a colony or wants to go anywhere else, and keep his property. We say, however, that whoever of you remains, when he sees how we conduct our trials and manage the city in other ways, has in fact come to an agreement with us to obey our instructions. We say that the one who disobeys does wrong in three ways, first because in us he disobeys his parents, also those who brought him up, and because, in spite of his agreement, he neither obeys us nor, if we do something wrong, does he try to persuade us to do better. Yet we only propose things, we do not issue savage commands to do whatever we order; we give two alternatives, either to persuade us or to do what we say. He does neither. We do say that you too, Socrates, are open to those charges if you do what you have in mind; you would be among, not the least, but the most guilty of the Athenians." And if I should say "Why so?" they might well be right to upbraid me and say that I am among the Athenians who most definitely came to that agreement with them. They might well say: "Socrates, we have convincing proofs that we and the city were congenial to you. You would not have dwelt here most consistently of all the Athenians if the city had not been exceedingly pleasing to you. You have never left the city, even to see a festival, nor for any other reason except military service; you have never gone to stay in any other city, as people do; you have had no desire to know another city or other laws; we and our city satisfied you.

"So decisively did you choose us and agree to be a citizen under us. Also, you have had children in this city, thus showing that it was congenial to you. Then at your trial you could have assessed your penalty at exile if you wished, and you are now attempting to do against the city's wishes what you could then have done with her consent. Then you prided yourself that you did not resent death, but you chose, as you said, death in preference to exile. Now, however, those words do not make you ashamed, and you pay no heed to us, the laws, as you plan to destroy us, and you act like the meanest type of slave by trying to run away, contrary to your commitments and your agreement to live as a citizen under us. First then, answer us on this very point, whether we speak the truth when we say that you agreed, not only in words but by your deeds, to live in accordance with us." What are we to say to that, Crito? Must we not agree?

CRITO: We must, Socrates.

SOCRATES: "Surely," they might say, "you are breaking the commitments and agreements that you made with us without compulsion or deceit, and under no pressure of time for deliberation. You have had seventy years during which you could have gone away if you did not like us, and if you thought our agreements unjust. You did not choose to go to Sparta or to Crete, which you are always saying are well governed, nor to any other city, Greek or foreign. You have been away from Athens less than the lame or the blind or other handicapped people. It is clear that the city has been outstandingly more congenial to you than to other Athenians, and so have we, the laws, for what city can please without laws? Will you then not now stick to our agreements? You will, Socrates, if we can persuade you, and not make yourself a laughingstock by leaving the city.

"For consider what good you will do yourself or your friends by breaking our agreements and committing such a wrong. It is pretty obvious that your friends will themselves be in danger of exile, disfranchisement, and loss of property. As for yourself, if you go to one of the nearby cities—Thebes or Megara, both are well governed—you will arrive as an enemy to their government; all who care for their city will look on you with suspicion, as a destroyer of the laws. You will also strengthen the conviction of the jury that they passed the right sentence on you, for anyone who destroys the laws could easily be thought to corrupt the young and the ignorant. Or will you avoid cities that are well governed and men who are civilized? If you do this, will your life be worth living? Will you have social intercourse with them and not be ashamed to talk to them? And what will you say? The same as you did here, that virtue and justice are man's most precious possession, along with lawful behavior and the laws? Do you not think that Socrates would appear to be an unseemly kind of person? One must think so. Or will you leave those places and go to Crito's friends in Thessaly? There you will find the greatest license and disorder, and they may enjoy hearing from you how absurdly you escaped from prison in some disguise, in a leather jerkin or some other things in which escapees wrap themselves, thus altering your appearance. Will there be no one to say that you, likely to live but a short time more, were so greedy for life that you transgressed the most important laws? Possibly, Socrates, if you do not annoy anyone, but if you do, many disgraceful things will be said about you.

"You will spend your time ingratiating yourself with all men, and be at their beck and call. What will you do in Thessaly but feast, as if you had gone to a banquet in Thessaly? As for those conversations of yours about justice and the rest of virtue, where will they be? You say you want to live for the sake of your children, that you may bring them up and educate them. How so? Will you bring them up and educate them by taking them to Thessaly and making strangers of them, that they may enjoy that too? Or not so, but they will be better brought up and educated here, while you are alive, though absent? Yes, your friends will look after them. Will they look after them if you go and live in Thessaly, but not if you go away to the underworld? If those who profess themselves your friends are any good at all, one must assume that they will.

"Be persuaded by us who have brought you up, Socrates. Do not value either your children or your life or anything else more than goodness, in order that when you arrive in Hades you may have all this as your defense before the rulers there. If you do this deed, you will not think it better or more just or more pious here, nor will any one of your friends, nor will it be better for you when you arrive yonder. As it is, you depart, if you depart, after being wronged not by us, the laws, but by men; but if you depart, after shamefully returning wrong for wrong and mistreatment for mistreatment, after breaking your agreements and commitments with us, after mistreating those you should mistreat least—yourself, your friends, your country, and us—we shall be angry with you while you are still alive, and our brothers, the laws of the underworld, will not receive you kindly, knowing that you tried to destroy us as far as you could. Do not let Crito persuade you, rather than us, to do what he says."

Crito, my dear friend, be assured that these are the words I seem to hear, as the Corybants seem to hear the music of their flutes, and the echo of these words resounds in me, and makes it impossible for me to hear anything else. As far as my present beliefs go, if you speak in opposition to them, you will speak in vain. However, if you think you can accomplish anything, speak.

CRITO: I have nothing to say, Socrates.

e   **SOCRATES:** Let it be then, Crito, and let us act in this way, since this is the way the god is leading us.

The Passion of Perpetua and Felicity

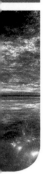

Introduction
Nancy Enright

The *Journal of Perpetua* has been an important text for many centuries. As a record of a martyrdom, told mainly through the words of a martyr and then through an eye-witness account of her death, it is historically important and religiously significant. The first known writing of a Christian woman, it also is important in terms of gender studies and the role of women in the church.

J. Quasten (in *Patrology*, Vol. 1) includes an excellent summary of the text and its significance:

> The Passion of Perpetua and Felicitas gives an account of the martyrdom of three catechumens Saturus, Saturninus and Revocatus, and two young women, Vibia Perpetua, 22 years of age, "well born, liberally educated, honorably married, having father and mother and two brothers, one like herself a catechumen, and an infant son at the breast," and her slave Felicitas, who was pregnant at the time of her arrest and gave birth to a girl shortly before her death in the arena. They suffered martyrdom on March 7, 202, at Carthage.
>
> The account is one of the most beautiful pieces of ancient Christian literature. It is unique as far as its authorship is concerned. The largest part of the account (ch. 3–10) is Perpetua's own diary: "The whole story of her martyrdom is from this point onwards told by herself as she left it written by her own hand and with her own mind" (ch. 2). Chapters 11 and 13 were written by Saturus.
>
> There is reason to believe that the author of the other chapters and the editor of the entire Passion was no less a person than Tertullian, the contemporary of Perpetua and the greatest writer of the African Church at that time. The resemblance in phrase and syntax and in words and ideas between Tertullian's works *Ad Martyres* and *De Patientia* and the Passion of Perpetua and Felicitas is striking. At St. Augustine's time, the Acts were still held in such esteem that he has to warn his listeners not to put them on a level with the canonical Scriptures (*De anima et eius origine*, I, 10, 12). (p. 181)

As you read the *Journal of Perpetua* and the subsequent account of her own and the other believers' martyrdom, one thing that you should look at is the difference in your own response to reading about an actual martyrdom of real people, recorded graphically and personally, with your response to reading about the idea of martyrdom. The concept of dying for the faith is found in many of the early Christian writings. Tertullian, who may be (as Quasten mentions above) the editor of the *Journal of Perpetua*, writes about the subject of martyrdom, as does Justin. Also, in many of his letters, St. Paul alludes to the idea of dying for one's faith. This piece, however, gives us a nearly day-to-day account of what it was like to be in a prison for one's faith, how it impacted one personally (as in Perpetua's reference to her pain at not having her nursing baby with her and her relief once he was brought to the prison), and even the complications of dealing with family members (such as Perpetua's father) who did not understand.

Another issue to consider is the role of women in the early church. Clearly, the *Journal of Perpetua* shows that women were accorded a role of importance among the early Christians. In the Roman world of the early third century, women were entirely second-class citizens. The Christian faith attracted women, in part, because it welcomed them as equally children of God, sisters in Christ, and as such, co-heirs of the grace of God (as Paul also referred to gentile believers). Though the early Christians inherited some patriarchal practices from the world surrounding them, Christianity offered much more, not less, freedom and status to women, as this text clearly shows. You might look for instances in the text that show Perpetua's sense of her identity as a Christian and as a woman in her interaction with her father (who, as a Roman, would have been the "paterfamilias" and still very much in authority over even his grown daughter), her visions, and her courageous death.

Finally, an interesting issue to explore in this text is the nature of the relationships among the early believers. Try to find as many references as you can to Perpetua's sense of oneness with her other believers, a unity that went much deeper than family ties (as we see in her interactions with her father and even her child). Notice how the slave woman, Felicitas, who was arrested with Perpetua, became a sister to the young noblewoman. The transcending of class was a significant concern in the early church. We see this in Paul's rebuking of the Corinthians when they neglected the unity of the Lord's table, with the rich people not sharing their meals with the poor believers. We see a similar concern in James' letter (not in this text, but in James chapters 2 and 5 if you want to read further on this subject).

As we read the *Journal of Perpetua,* the question remains: Was her death a triumph or a tragedy? Her father clearly saw it as a tragedy. No doubt many of the bystanders felt the same, seeing the death of a twenty-two year-old woman with everything to live for as a senseless waste. Or we might see it as she herself and her fellow believers did—as a culmination of giving over of oneself, which is required of all believers in Christ, and as a triumph over the forces that sought to destroy her faith and her spiritual identity. The text does everything in its power to convince the reader of the latter. You, as a reader, will have to decide if you agree.

THE PASSION OF PERPETUA AND FELICITY

The Passion of Perpetua and Felicity by Thomas J. Heffernan (2012): pp. 125–134. By permission of Oxford University Press USA.

I

[1]If the old examples of the faith, which testify to the grace of God and lead to the edification of men, were written down so that by reading them God should be honored and man comforted—as if through a reexamination of those deeds—should we not set down new acts that serve each purpose equally? [2]For these too will some day also be venerable and compelling for future generations, even if at the present time they are judged to be of lesser importance, due to the respect naturally afforded the past. [3]But let those who would restrict the singular power of the one spirit to certain times understand this: that newer events are necessarily greater because they are more recent, because of the overflow of grace promised for the end of time. [4]In the last days, says the Lord, "I will pour out my Spirit on all flesh; and their sons and daughters shall prophesy; and I will pour out my Spirit on my servants and handmaidens; and your young men shall see visions and your old men shall dream dreams." [5]And we, who also acknowledge and honor the new prophecies and new visions as well, according to the promise, and regard the other virtues of the Holy Spirit as intended for the instruction of the church (to which church the same spirit was sent distributing all gifts to all, just as the Lord grants to each one); therefore, out of necessity we both proclaim and celebrate them in reading for the glory of God, lest any person who is weak or despairing in their faith should think that only the ancients received divine grace (either in the favor of martyrdom or of revelations), since God always grants what he has promised, as a proof to the unbelievers and as a kindness to believers. [6]And so we also announce to you, our brothers and little sons, that which we have heard and touched, so that you who were present may be reminded of the glory of the Lord, and that you who know it now through hearing may have a sharing with the holy martyrs, and through them with our Lord Jesus Christ, to whom be glory and honor for ever and ever. Amen.

II

[1]Some young catechumens were arrested: Revocatus and Felicity, his fellow slave; Saturninus; and Secundulus. And among these was also Vibia Perpetua—a woman well born, liberally educated, and honorably married, [2]who had a father, mother, and two brothers, one of whom was also a catechumen. She had an infant son still at the breast [3]and was about twenty-two years of age. From this point there follows a complete account of her martyrdom, as she left it, written in her own hand and in accordance with her own understanding.

III

[1]"While, she said," we were still with the prosecutors, my father, because of his love for me, wanted to change my mind and shake my resolve. 'Father,' I said, 'do you see this vase lying here, for example, this small water pitcher or whatever?' 'I see it,' he said. [2]And I said to him: 'Can it be called by another name other than what it is?' And he said: 'No.' 'In the same way, I am unable to call myself other than what I am, a Christian.' [3]Then my father, angered by this name, threw himself at me, in order to gouge out my eyes. But he only alarmed me and he left defeated, along with the arguments of the devil. [4]Then for a few days, freed from my father, I gave thanks to the Lord and was refreshed by my father's absence. [5]In the space of a few days we were baptized. The Spirit told me that nothing else should be sought from the water other than the endurance of the body. After a few days we were taken into the prison. I was terrified because I had never before known such darkness. [6]Oh cruel day! The crowding of the mob made the heat stifling; and there was the extortion of the soldiers. Last of all, I was consumed with worry for my infant in that dungeon. [7]Then Tertius and Pomponius, the blessed deacons who ministered to us, arranged by a bribe that we should be released for a few hours to revive ourselves in a better part of the prison. [8]Then all left the prison and sought some time for themselves. I nursed my baby, who was now weak from hunger. In my worry for him, I spoke to my mother concerning the baby and comforted my brother. I entrusted my son to them. I suffered grievously when I saw how they suffered for me. [9]I endured such worry for many days, and I arranged for my baby to stay in prison with me. Immediately I grew stronger, and I was relieved of the anxiety and worry I had for my baby. Suddenly the prison became my palace, so that I wanted to be there rather than anywhere else.

IV

[1]"Then my brother said to me: 'Lady my sister, you are now greatly esteemed, so much so that you might ask for a vision, and it may be shown to you whether there will be suffering or freedom.' [2]And I, who knew that I was able to speak with the Lord, whose great benefits I had known, confidently promised him, saying: 'Tomorrow, I will tell you.' And I asked, and this was shown to me. [3]I see a bronze ladder of great length, reaching up to heaven, but so narrow that people could only climb up one at a time. And on the sides of the ladder, iron implements of every kind were attached. There were swords, lances, hooks, knives, and daggers, so that if anyone climbed up carelessly, or not looking upwards, he was torn to pieces and his flesh clung to the iron weapons. [4]And there was a serpent of great size lying at the foot of the ladder, which would lie in wait for those who climbed and deterred them from climbing. [5]And the first to go up was Saturus. (Because he had been our teacher and because he had not been present when we were seized, he later voluntarily handed himself over for our sake.) [6] And he

reached the top of the ladder and he turned back to me and said: 'Perpetua, I am waiting for you, but be careful that the serpent does not bite you.' And I said: 'In the name of Jesus Christ, he will not hurt me.' [7]And from beneath the ladder itself, the serpent slowly stuck out its head, as if it feared me, and I stepped on its head and climbed up, as if it were the first step. [8]And I saw an enormous garden and a white-haired man sitting in the middle of it dressed in shepherd's clothes, a big man, milking sheep. And standing around were many thousands dressed in white. [9]And he raised his head, looked at me, and said: 'You are welcome here, child.' And he called me, and from the cheese that he had milked he gave me as it were a mouthful. And I received it in my cupped hands and ate it. And all those standing around said: 'Amen.' [10]And I woke up at the sound of their voice, still eating some unknown sweet. And at once I told this to my brother. And we knew we would suffer, and we ceased to have any hope in this world.

V

[1]"A few days later, a rumor circulated that we were to be given a hearing. My father arrived from the city, worn with worry; he climbed up to me, in order to change my mind, saying: [2]'My daughter, have pity on my gray hair, have pity on your father, if I am worthy to be called father by you, if with these hands I have raised you to this flower of youth, if I have preferred you to all your brothers, do not shame me among men. [3]Think about your brothers, think about your mother and your mother's sister, think about your son who will not be able to live without you. [4]Give up your pride; do not destroy us all. For, if you are punished, none of us will be able to speak freely again: [5]My father said these things to me, as a father would, out of his love for me, kissing my hands and throwing himself at my feet. Weeping, he no longer called me daughter, but lady. [6]And I grieved for my father's anguish, because he alone of all my family would not rejoice in my suffering. And I tried to comfort him saying: 'What God has willed shall be done in the prisoner's platform. Know that we are no longer in our own power but in God's.'" And in great sadness he left me.

VI

[1]"On another day, while we were eating lunch, we were suddenly rushed off for a hearing. We arrived at the forum and immediately a rumor circulated throughout the neighborhood surrounding the forum, and a huge crowd had gathered. [2]We climbed the platform. The others, having been questioned, confessed. Then they came to me. And my father appeared in that very place with my son and dragged me from the step saying: 'Offer the sacrifice. Have pity on your baby.' [3]And Hilarianus, the procurator, who at that time had received the right of the sword on the death of proconsul Minucius Timinianus, said: 'Spare the gray hair of your father, spare your infant son. Offer the sacrifice for the health of the emperors.' [4]'I will not,' I answered. Hilarianus then said:

'Are you a Christian?' 'I am a Christian,' I replied. [5]And when my father persisted in his efforts to change my mind, Hilarianus ordered him to be thrown to the ground and beaten with a rod. My father's suffering made me sad, almost as if I had been beaten. I grieved for his pitiable old age. [6]Then Hilarianus pronounced sentence on us all and condemned us to the beasts. And we descended the platform and returned cheerfully to prison. [7]But because my baby had become accustomed to nurse at my breasts and to stay with me in prison, I immediately sent Pomponius, the deacon, to ask my father for the child. [8]But my father would not give him back. And as God willed, the baby no longer desired my breasts, nor did they ache and become inflamed, so that I might not be tormented by worry for my child or by the pain in my breasts.

VII

[1]"A few days later while we were all praying, suddenly, in the midst of our prayer a voice came to me, and I cried out the name of Dinocrates. I was shocked because never before then had his name entered my mind, and I grieved as I remembered his fate. [2]And I knew at once that I was worthy and that I ought to pray for him. And I began to pray intensely for him and groan before the Lord. [3]Immediately, on that very night this vision was shown to me. [4]I saw Dinocrates coming out of a dark place where there were many others; he was very hot, thirsting, and his face was covered with dirt and his skin was pale. And he had that wound on his face which was there when he died. [5]This Dinocrates was my brother in the flesh, who died horribly at the age of seven from a cancer of the face. All men who saw it loathed the manner of his death. [6]Therefore I prayed for him. But between him and me there was a great gulf so that we were not able to get close to each other. [7]Moreover, in that place where Dinocrates was, there was a pool full of water with a rim that was higher than the height of the boy. And Dinocrates stretched himself up as if to drink. [8]I was saddened because, although the pool had water in it, he was not able to drink because of the height of the rim. [9]And I awakened, and I knew that my brother was suffering. But I trusted that I could help him in his suffering. And I prayed for him every day until we were transferred to the military prison, for we were to fight in the military games; it was on the birthday of Geta Caesar. [10]And I prayed day and night for my brother with groans and tears so that this gift might be given to me.

VIII

[1]"On the day on which we were kept in the stocks, this vision was shown to me. I saw that place which I had seen before, but now there was Dinocrates, his body clean, well dressed and refreshed, and where the wound was, I saw a scar. [2]And that pool which I had seen earlier, I now saw with its rim lowered to the boy's navel, and he drew water from it without ceasing. [3]And above the rim there was a golden cup full of water. And Dinocrates began to drink from it, but the cup never emptied. [4]And when his thirst

was quenched, he began to play in the water, rejoicing in the manner of children. And I woke up. I knew then that he was freed from his suffering.

IX

[1]"Then after a few days, Pudens, the military adjutant, who was in charge of the prison, began to show us considerable respect, recognizing that there was some great power in us. He allowed many to visit us so that we were able to comfort one another. [2]Now when the day of the games drew near, my father, devastated with worry, came to visit me, and he began to tear out his beard and to throw it on the ground. He then threw himself on his face and, cursing his years, spoke such words to me as might move creation itself. [3]I grieved for his unhappy old age.

X

[1]"On the day before we were to fight, I saw this in a vision: Pomponius, the deacon, had come to the door of the prison, and was knocking loudly. [2]And I went out and opened the door for him. He was wearing a white unbelted robe, and multilaced sandals. [3]And he said to me: 'Perpetua, we are awaiting you: come.' And he took me by the hand and we began to walk through places that were rugged and winding. [4]And finally, after great difficulty, we arrived at the amphitheatre, all out of breath, and he led me into the middle of the arena, and he said to me 'Don't be afraid: I am here with you, and I will struggle with you.' And he went away. [5]And I saw many people who were astonished; and, because I knew that I had been condemned to the beasts, I was puzzled that the beasts were not being turned loose on me. [6]And a certain Egyptian, foul in appearance and intending to fight with me, came out against me, surrounded by his helpers. Handsome young men came to me as my helpers and supporters. [7]And I was stripped naked, and I became a man. And my supporters began to rub me with oil, as they are accustomed to do for a match. And I saw that Egyptian on the other side rolling in the dust. [8]Next there came out a man of such great size that he exceeded the height of the amphitheatre. He was wearing an unbelted robe, a purple garment with two stripes running down the middle of his chest, and decorated shoes made of gold and silver, and carrying a rod or wand as if a gladiator trainer, and a green branch on which there were golden apples. [9]And he asked for silence and said: 'This Egyptian, if he defeats this woman, will kill her with the sword, but if she defeats him, she shall receive this branch.' And he departed. [10]And we drew near to each other and began to throw punches at each other. He kept trying to grab hold of my feet while I kept kicking him in his face with my heels. [11]And I was raised up into the air, and I began to strike him stepping on his face, as though I were unable to step on the ground. But when I saw that there was a hesitation, I joined my hands so that my fingers were knit together and I grabbed hold of his head. And he fell on his face and I stepped on his head. [12]And the crowd began

to shout and my supporters began to sing hymns. And I went to the gladiator trainer, and I took the branch. [13]And he kissed me and he said to me: 'Daughter, peace be with you.' And I began to walk in triumph to the Gate of Life. [14]And then I woke up. And I knew that I was going to fight with the devil and not with the beasts; but I knew that victory was to be mine. [15]This is the story of what I did the day before the final conflict. But concerning the outcome of that contest, let whoever wishes to write about it, do so."

XI

[1]But blessed Saturus made known his own vision, which he himself wrote. [2]"We had suffered," he said, "and we departed from the flesh and we began to be carried towards the east by four angels, whose hands were not touching us. [3]But we were moving, not on our backs facing upwards, but as if we were climbing a gentle hill. [4]And when we were freed from this world, we saw a great light, and I said to Perpetua (for she was at my side): 'This is what the Lord promised us: we have received the promise.' [5]And while we were being carried by the four angels, a great space appeared before us, which was like a formal garden, having rose trees and flowers of all sorts. [6]The height of the trees was like that of cypress trees, and their leaves were falling without ceasing. [7]There in the garden were four other angels more radiant than the others. When they saw us, they gave us honor, and they said with admiration to the other angels: 'Look, they are here, they are here.' And those four angels who were carrying us became fearful and put us down. [8]And on foot we crossed the park by a broad path. [9]There we found Jocundus and Saturninus and Artaxius, who were burned alive in the same persecution, and Quintus, who had died as a martyr in prison. And we asked of them where the rest were. [10]And the angels said to us: 'First come, enter and greet the Lord.'

XII

[1]"And we came near a place whose walls seemed to be made of light; and in front of the door of that place stood four angels, who clothed those who entered in white robes. [2]And we entered in, and we heard a choir of voices chanting continually: 'Holy, Holy, Holy.' [3]And we saw sitting in the same place what appeared to be an aged man. He had white hair and a youthful face, but we could not see his feet. [4]And on his right and on his left were four elders, and behind them were standing many other elders. [5]And entering in a spirit of wonder we stood before the throne, and four angels lifted us up, and we kissed him. And he stroked our faces with his hand. [6]And the other elders said to us: 'Let us stand'; and we stood and offered each other the sign of peace. And the elders said to us: 'Go and play.' [7]And I said to Perpetua: 'You have what you want.' And she said to me: 'Thanks be to God, because just as I was happy in the flesh, I am even happier here now.'

XIII

[1]"And we went out and we saw in front of the gates Optatus the bishop on the right-hand side and Aspasius the priest and teacher on the left, separated and sorrowful. [2]And they threw themselves at our feet and said: 'Make peace between us, for you have gone away and left us in this state: [3]And we said to them: 'Are you not our father and our priest? How can you throw yourselves at our feet?' And we were greatly moved and embraced them. [4]And Perpetua began to speak to them in Greek, and we led them into a park under a rose tree. [5]And while we were speaking with them, the angels said to them: 'Let them rest; and if you have any disagreements among yourselves, forgive one another: [6]And the angels admonished them and said to Optatus: 'Rebuke your people, because they are gathering around you, just as if they were returning from the chariot races, arguing about the different teams: [7]And it seemed to us as if they wanted to shut the gates. [8]And we began to recognize there many of our brothers, and martyrs also. We were all nourished by an indescribable fragrance that satisfied us. Then, rejoicing, I awoke.'

XIV

[1]These were the extraordinary visions of the most blessed martyrs Saturus and Perpetua, which they themselves wrote. [2]As for Secundulus, God called him from this world while still in prison, and by his earlier death, one not without favor, so that he might escape the fight with the beasts. [3]Yet his flesh, if not his soul, knew the sword.

XV

[1]As for Felicity, the Lord's favor touched her in this way. [2]She was now in her eighth month (for she was pregnant when she was arrested). As the day of the games drew near, she was in agony, fearing that her pregnancy would spare her (since it was not permitted to punish pregnant women in public), and that she would pour forth her holy and innocent blood afterwards, along with common criminals. [3]But also her fellow martyrs were deeply saddened that they might leave behind so good a friend, their companion, to travel alone on the road to their shared hope. [4]And so, two days before the games, they joined together in one united supplication, groaning, and poured forth their prayer to the Lord. [5]Immediately after their prayer her labor pains came upon her. And when—because of the natural difficulty associated with an eighth-month delivery—she suffered in her labor, one of the assistant jailers said to her: "If you are suffering so much now, what will you do when you are thrown to the beasts which you scorned when you refused to sacrifice?" [6]And she replied "Now I alone suffer what I am suffering, but then there will be another inside me, who will suffer for me, because I am going to suffer for him." [7]And she gave birth to a baby girl, whom a certain sister brought up as her own daughter.

XVI

[1]Therefore, since the Holy Spirit has given permission that the narrative of this contest be written down, and by such permission has willed it, although we are unworthy to add to the description of such great glory, nevertheless we shall carry out the command of the most holy Perpetua, or rather her sacred trust, adding one further example of her resolve and sublimity of spirit. [2]The tribune treated them with great cruelty because of the warnings of the most devious of men. He feared that they would be carried off from prison through magical incantations. Perpetua said directly to his face: [3]"Why do you not permit us to refresh ourselves—we, the most noble of the condemned belonging to Caesar, who are to fight on his birthday? Would it not be to your credit, if we were brought forth well fed?" [4]The Tribune was horrified and flushed; and he ordered them to be treated more humanely, so that her brothers, and the others, might be granted the chance to visit and be refreshed with the prisoners, for now even the adjutant in charge of the prison was a believer.

XVII

[1]And then on the day before the games, when at that last meal which they call "free," they partook, as far as it was possible, not of a "free meal" but a "love-feast." They boldly flung their words at the mob, threatening them with the judgment of God, bearing witness to the happiness they found in their suffering and mocking the curiosity of those who jostled to see them. Saturus said: [2]"Will not tomorrow be enough for you? Why do you long to see that which you hate? Today our friends, tomorrow our enemies. But take a good look at our faces, so that you will be able to recognize us on that day." [3]And so the crowd left the prison stunned, and many of them became believers.

XVIII

[1]The day of their victory dawned, and they marched from the prison to the amphitheatre, joyously, as if going to heaven, their faces radiant; and if by chance they trembled, it was from joy and not from fear. [2]Perpetua followed, with a shining face and a calm step, as a wife of Christ and darling of God, and the intensity of her stare caused the spectators to look away. [3]Likewise Felicity rejoiced that she had given birth safely, so that she might fight with the beasts—advancing from blood to blood, from the midwife to a net-bearing gladiator—now to be washed after childbirth in a second baptism. [4]And when they were led to the gate, they were forced to put on costumes; the men, those of the priests of Saturn, and the women, those of the priestesses of Ceres. But that noble-minded woman fiercely resisted this to the end. [5]She said: "We came here freely, so that our freedom might not be violated, and we handed over our lives so that we would not be forced to do anything like this. We had this agreement with you."

[6]Injustice recognized justice. The tribune agreed that they should be brought in dressed simply as they were. [7]Perpetua was singing a hymn, already trampling on the head of the Egyptian. Revocatus, Saturninus, and Saturus were threatening the spectators. [8]Then, when they passed under the gaze of Hilarianus, they began to say to him through gestures and nods: "You [judge] us but God will [judge] you." [9]The crowd, angered by this, demanded that they be whipped along a line of beast-hunting gladiators. And they gave thanks that they had obtained some share in the Lord's sufferings.

XIX

[1]But he who said: "Ask and you shall receive" gave to those who asked the death that each desired. [2]For whenever they spoke among themselves concerning their desire for martyrdom, Saturninus declared that he wished to be thrown to all the different kinds of beasts so that he might wear a more glorious crown. [3]And so at the beginning of the spectacle, he and Revocatus were attacked by a leopard, and then while on the platform, they were charged by a bear. [4]Saturus hated nothing more than a bear, and now he was confident that he would die from one bite of a leopard. [5]However, he was offered to a wild boar. Yet it was the hunter who had tied him to the wild boar who was gored by the same beast, and died a few days after the games. Saturus himself was only dragged. [6]And when he was tied on the bridge awaiting the bear, the bear refused to leave its cage. And so Saturus, unhurt, was called back for the second time.

XX

[1]For the young women, however, the devil prepared a wild cow—not a traditional practice—matching their sex with that of the beast. [2]And so stripped naked and covered only with nets, they were brought out again. The crowd shuddered, seeing that one was a delicate young girl and that the other had recently given birth, as her breasts still dripping with milk. [3]So they were called back and dressed in unbelted robes. Perpetua was thrown down first and fell on her loins. [4]Then sitting up, she noticed that her tunic was ripped on the side, and so she drew it up to cover her thigh, more mindful of her modesty than her suffering. [5]Then she requested a pin and she tied up her tousled hair; for it was not right for a martyr to suffer with disheveled hair, since it might appear that she was grieving in her moment of glory. [6]Then she got up; and when she saw Felicity crushed to the ground, she went over to her, gave her her hand and helped her up. [7]And the two stood side by side. The cruelty of the crowd now being sated, they were called back to the Gate of Life. [8]There Perpetua was received by a certain Rusticus, also a catechumen, who clung to her side. She awakened, as if from a sleep—she was so deep in the spirit and in ecstasy—and looked about her, and said, to the amazement of all: "When are we to be thrown to the mad cow; or whatever it is?" [9]And when she heard that it had already happened, she refused at first to believe it until she noticed certain marks of

physical violence on her body and her clothing. ¹⁰Then after calling her brother and the catechumen, she spoke to them, saying: "Stand fast in faith and love one another, and do not lose heart because of our sufferings."

XXI

¹At another gate, Saturus was exhorting the soldier Pudens, saying: "It is exactly," he said, "as I imagined and predicted. Until now no beast has touched me. And now you must believe this with all your heart: See, I will go in there and be killed by one bite from a leopard." ²And immediately at the end of the game, a leopard rushed out and bit Saturus. He was so covered with blood from one bite that as he was returning, the crowd roared in witness to his second baptism: "A saving bath, a saving bath." ³For truly one was saved who had bathed in such manner. ⁴Then he said to the soldier Pudens: "Farewell, remember the faith and me; and do not let these things trouble you but strengthen you." ⁵At the same time he asked Pudens for the small ring from his finger, and dipping it into his wound, he returned it to him as a legacy, leaving it to him as a pledge and a memorial of his blood. ⁶Then, being now unconscious, he was thrown with the others in the accustomed place to have his throat cut. ⁷But the crowd demanded that they be brought back to the middle of the arena, so that as the sword penetrated the bodies of the martyrs their eyes might be accomplices to the murder. The martyrs got up unaided and moved to where the crowd wished them to be. First they kissed each other so that the ritual of peace would seal their martyrdom. ⁸The others, in silence and without moving, received the sword's thrust, and particularly Saturus, who had first climbed up the ladder, was the first to give up his spirit. For once again he was waiting for Perpetua. ⁹Perpetua, however—so that she might taste something of the pain—screamed out in agony as she was pierced between the bones. And when the right hand of the novice gladiator wavered, she herself guided it to her throat. ¹⁰Perhaps such a woman, feared as she was by the unclean spirit, could not have been killed unless she herself had willed it.

¹¹O bravest and most blessed martyrs! O truly called and chosen for the glory of our Lord Jesus Christ! Anyone who praises, honors, and adores his glory surely should read these deeds, which are no less worthy than the old ones for building up the church. For these new deeds of courage too may witness that one and the same Holy Spirit is always working among us even now, along with God, the Father almighty, and his Son, our Lord, Jesus Christ, to whom is glory and endless power for ever and ever. Amen.

Saint Augustine

Introduction
Ki Joo Choi

All of you are familiar with Saint Augustine from CORE 1101 from his great spiritual autobiography *The Confessions* (written between A.D. 397–398). Upon his conversion to Christianity, Augustine rose quickly through the ranks of the Church, becoming Bishop of Hippo (in Northern Africa, now Annaba, Algeria, the major African city in the Roman Empire; note that Augustine was African, born in Thagaste in A.D. 354, which is present day Souk Ahras, Algeria).

As you are familiar with from *The Confessions*, Augustine spent much effort defending Christianity from various heresies, such as Manicheanism, Pelagianism, and so forth. He also defended the Church from political authorities within the Roman Empire. This is the motivation for his expansive treatise *The City of God*, or in Latin, *De Civitate Dei*.

The text was completed in A.D. 426 and began shortly after the sacking of Rome by the Visigoths in A.D. 410 (the Visigoths, or the "Northern Barbarians" as the Romans regarded them, were people of eastern Germanic tribes). As Rome was invaded, and the Roman Empire appeared to be in decline, many Roman elites blamed the ascendency of Christianity in the Roman Empire as a significant cause of Rome's decline. Only if Rome kept faithful to its pagan gods rather than allow its citizens to increasingly convert to Christianity, they believed, would Rome have been strong enough to be spared such a humiliating defeat at the hands of "barbarians" from northern Europe. Some of these elites fled Rome and found refuge in North Africa. There, they continued the teaching that Christianity was to blame for Roman decline. Augustine rejected this thesis. In order to do so he, in *The City of God*, explores the notion of what constitutes a true republic. This is the subject matter of our reading, Book 19 of *The City of God*.

In exploring the true meaning of a republic, Augustine is not only trying to defend Christianity from the criticisms of Rome, but is also trying to explore how people in general, whether Roman pagan or Roman Christian, should live if they are to live well. Thus, in exploring the notion of a republic, Augustine is trying to do the same thing as Plato (in his discussion of piety) and Paul (in his discussion of what it means to embody Christ crucified). Augustine, somewhat obviously, resonates with many themes from the Apostle Paul (they are both Christian), but develops Paul's themes in important and distinct ways and with much more specific attention to contrary views. Pay close attention to how Augustine does so.

For Augustine, *to live well requires that we know what it means to live in a genuine republic for a genuine community*. Read chapters 21–24 of Book XIX *first*. Here you will see that Augustine turns to the famous Roman thinker Cicero's definition of a republic, "a fellowship of a multitude united through a consensus concerning right and a sharing of advantage" (chapter 21). Augustine does not necessarily disagree with Cicero's definition of a republic, but as you read chapters 21–24 of Book XIX, it becomes clear that he thinks Cicero's definition is better revised along the following lines: "a fellowship of a multitude of rational beings united through sharing in agreement about what it loves" (chapter 24). For Augustine, Cicero is right that a community cannot be a republic unless there is an agreement on the "right" or justice. But Augustine thinks that we cannot possess genuine justice unless we love correctly.

Pay attention to why Augustine thinks that God must be the only proper object of our love (in other words, pay attention to why Augustine thinks that we must love God above all else if we are to live justly and, therefore, as a community describable as a genuine republic).

In order to better understand why Augustine thinks that we must love God above all else if we are to live well as a genuine republic, go back to the beginning of Book XIX and read chapters 1–19 *after* you have read chapters 21–24. In chapters 1–19 you will see Augustine endeavoring to evaluate the Roman philosopher Varro's exploration of the final end or good of human life (i.e., the source of human happiness—see the second paragraph of chapter 1). Note in chapter 2 that, according to Varro, "When anyone attains the final good, he is forthwith made happy." In response, Augustine argues that the final or ultimate end or good of human life cannot be natural or of the body. He then goes on to argue that the final good of the human person cannot be in social life. In these discussions, Augustine offers an eloquent discussion on the moral limits of the human person (another way of putting this is that Augustine offers a powerful picture of human anthropology or the nature of the human person). Pay close attention to what Augustine thinks are the moral limits of the human person (e.g., note how he thinks that the reality of the human body and necessity of virtue speak to our moral fragility and corruption—see chapter 4). And pay close attention to how this picture of the human person helps him to explain why the ultimate good of the human person cannot be located in the natural or in social living.

If the source of human happiness cannot be located in the natural or in social living, then, according to Augustine, we must admit that the ultimate good of the human person is located in God—the supreme, *immutable, incorruptible,* perfect good. If we recognize this, Augustine thinks that we will have a proper understanding of how to approach and use the *mutable* goods of temporal, earthly existence. Notice how Augustine uses the image of the traveler (chapter 17) to discuss this point. The one who genuinely *loves God* is one who uses material, earthly goods for the sake of reaching the goal of perfection (or life in the heavenly city). This goal can only come in "hope," says Augustine, for it is something that is realizable fully only by God's power (see the last two paragraphs of chapter 4). Our task in this world is to pursue health, virtue, justice, peace, and communal order and harmony as vital earthly goods that *aid* or *support* our pilgrimage or journey toward the heavenly city (or the source of our true happiness—fellowship with God—the incorruptible, immutable good!).

As you explore Augustine's notion of a true republic, challenge yourself to think about how he might respond to Paul, Socrates, and Euthyphro (or Athens). Augustine thinks that in order to live well *one must love properly.* This is also the case for Paul, and also the case for Socrates and Euthyphro. Try to compare and contrast their conceptions of love (and *what* each thinks we ought to love) and, correlatively, their conceptions of what one must do to live well. Which conception do you find most interesting, most insightful, or most compelling?

THE CITY OF GOD, BOOK XIX

Introduction

Book XVIII marks the end of the section of The City of God *devoted to the progress or development of the two cities. With Book XIX, Augustine turns to their respective ends. He initiates the discussion with a consideration of Varro's enumeration of the manifold and diverse views held by the philosophers on the subject of the end of human life (Chs. 1–2). In a key chapter, he rejects all such views because they overestimate the ability of either natural goods or virtue to secure happiness (Ch. 4). Among other things, the philosophers recommend pursuing a social and political life, but our author points out that such a life necessarily involves many evils. In the selections included here, he laments the predicaments in which human judges often find themselves (Ch. 6) as well as the problems posed by the diversity of languages and the miseries of war (Ch. 7). The next section of the book contains the city of God's answer to the question about the supreme good. This leads Augustine into his famous meditations on the nature of peace in Chapters 12 and 13. He then turns to a series of reflections on temporal existence in light of that notion of peace. Included here are important comments on slavery (Ch. 15), the household (Chs. 16–17), and the relative merits of the active and contemplative lives (Ch. 19). In Chapter 21, Augustine returns to the discussion of Cicero's* Republic *that he had begun in Book II, Chapter 21. Now, however, he argues that if the implications of Cicero's arguments are spelled out completely, then one must admit that the Romans never really were a people. In the end, the only true people, the only true city, is the city of God.*

Chapter 1

Because I see that I must next discuss the proper ends of the two cities—namely, the earthy and the heavenly—I must first explain, insofar as the limits imposed by the plan of this work allow, the arguments by which mortals have struggled to make themselves happy in the misery of this life. This is necessary in order to clarify the difference between their futilities and our hope, which God has given us, and its object, namely true happiness, which God will give us. This will be done not only through divine authority, but also, for the sake of unbelievers, through reason.

Concerning the ends of goods and evils, philosophers have engaged in many and varied disputes among themselves; but the question they have pursued with the greatest effort, turning it over in their minds, is, What makes man happy? Indeed, our final good is that for the sake of which other things are desired, but which is itself desired for its own sake; and the final evil is that on account of which other things are avoided, but which is avoided on its own account. Hence, we now call the "final good" not that through which good is destroyed, and so ceases to exist, but that through which it is perfected, and so exists fully; and we call the "final evil" not that through which evil ceases to be, but that through which it produces its greatest harm. Thus, these ends are the supreme good and the supreme evil.

As I said, many who have professed the study of wisdom in the futility of this age have worked hard to discover these ends, as well as to obtain the supreme good and to avoid the supreme evil in this life. Although they wandered off in different directions, nevertheless the limit of nature did not permit them to deviate from the path of truth so far that they failed to place the final good and final evil in the soul, in the body, or in both. To this tripartite division of schools Marcus Varro,[1] in his book *On Philosophy,* directed his attention, diligently and subtly scrutinizing a large number of different teachings. By applying certain distinctions he easily arrived at 288 possible—though not necessarily actual—schools.[2] . . .

Chapter 2

Then there are those three kinds of life: the first is the leisurely—but not slothful—life, devoted to contemplating or seeking the truth; the second is the busy life devoted to conducting human affairs; and the third is the life which mixes both of these kinds. When it is asked which of these three ought to be chosen, the final good is not being disputed. What is considered by that question is which of these three brings difficulty or assistance for seeking or preserving the final good. When anyone attains the final good, he is forthwith made happy. However, the life devoted to learned leisure, to public business, or to performing both alternately does not necessarily make one happy. Certainly, many are able to live in one or another of these three ways, but err with respect to desiring the final good by which man is made happy.

Therefore, it is one thing to ask about the final good and the final evil, and the answer to that question distinguishes every single one of the philosophical schools. It is quite another thing to ask questions about the social life, the hesitation of the Academics, the dress and diet of the Cynics, and the three kinds of life—the leisurely, the active, and the combined. The final good and evil are not disputed in any of these questions.

---

1   On Varro, see the note on III. 9.

2   Varro's book *On Philosophy,* like most of his other works, is not extant. In an omitted section, Augustine explains that Varro arrived at the figure of 288 in the following way: he reasoned that there are four things which human beings seek (pleasure, repose, a combination of the two, or the primary goods of nature). These four things may be desired for the sake of virtue, or virtue may be desired for their sake, or both might be desired for their own sakes. There are also two possible positions concerning whether one seeks the good only for oneself or for one's fellows as well. Next, one could hold his position as certain or, like the New Academics, as probable. Then, one could accept the traditional dress of philosophers as appropriate or follow the view of the Cynics on dress. Finally, one could hold that the life of leisure is best, or that the active life is best, or that a combination of the two is best. Multiplying $4 \times 3 \times 2 \times 2 \times 2 \times 3$, Varro arrived at no fewer than 288 possible philosophical schools.

By using these four distinctions—that is, the distinctions derived from the social life, the new Academics, the Cynics, and the three kinds of life—Marcus Varro reaches 288 schools. If there are other distinctions, they could be added in the same way. By removing all of those four distinctions, because they do not bear upon the question of pursuing the supreme good and thus do not give rise to what can properly be called "schools," he returns to those twelve in which it is asked. What is the good of man, the pursuit of which makes man happy? From these twelve, he shows that one is true and the rest false.[3] . . .

To Varro, it seemed proper that these three schools be treated carefully. He asked, Which ought to be chosen? True reason does not permit more than one to be true, whether it is among these three or—as we will see later on—somewhere else.[4] In the meantime, we will examine, as briefly and clearly as we can, how Varro chooses one of these three. Certainly, these three schools arise as follows: either the primary goods of nature[5] are chosen for the sake of virtue, or virtue is chosen for the sake of the primary goods of nature, or both—that is, both virtue and the primary goods of nature—are chosen for their own sakes.[6]

Chapter 4

If, then, we are asked what the city of God would reply to each of these questions, and, most importantly, what it thinks about the final good and final evil, it will reply that eternal life is the supreme good and eternal death the supreme evil, and that in order to attain the one and avoid the other, we must live rightly. That is why it is written, "The just man lives by faith" (Gal 3:11), for we do not at present see our good and thus must seek it through believing, nor does our living rightly derive from ourselves, except insofar as he, who gave the very faith through which we believe ourselves to be in need of help from him, helps us in our believing and praying.

Those, however, who have held that the final good and evil are in this life, whether they place the supreme good in the body, in the soul, or in both—and indeed, to express it more explicitly, whether they place it in pleasure or in virtue or both; whether in rest or virtue or in both; whether in pleasure and rest simultaneously or in virtue or in all

---

3   Varro reduces the twelve to three in the following way: pleasure, repose, and the combination of the two are all included in what the Stoic philosophers call the "primary goods of nature." Hence, those four possible positions are reduced to one. The three possible positions left are that virtue is to be desired for the sake of the primary goods of nature, that the primary goods of nature are to be desired for the sake of virtue, and that both should be desired for their own sakes.

4   In Chapter 4, it will become evident that Augustine thinks the supreme good lies in none of these three positions of the philosophers but somewhere else.

5   This phrase was used by the Stoic philosophers to refer to the basic goods of both mind and body, such as health, strength, beauty, perception, understanding, and so forth.

6   In an omitted section, Varro chooses the latter position, since it properly aimed at both what is good for the soul and for the body. As will become clear, in Chapter 4 Augustine attacks the idea that the primary goods of nature could contribute to the final good and then ridicules the idea that moral virtue could do so.

these; whether in the primary things of nature or in virtue or in all these—they wanted to be happy here and now and, through an astonishing vanity, they wanted to be made happy by their own actions. The Truth ridiculed them through the prophet, saying, "The Lord knows the thoughts of men" (Ps 94:11), or, as the apostle Paul puts this testimony, "The Lord knows the thoughts of the wise, that they are vain" (1 Cor 3:20).

Indeed, who is able, however great the flood of his eloquence, to expound the miseries of this life? Cicero lamented them, as well as he was able, in the *Consolation* on the death of his daughter,[7] but how much was he able to do? In truth, when, where, and in what way can those things called the primary goods of nature be so well possessed in this life that they are not tossed about under the sway of unforeseen accidents? What pain contrary to pleasure, what restlessness contrary to rest, could not befall the body of a wise man? Certainly, the amputation or the debility of a man's limbs destroys his soundness, deformity his beauty, feebleness his health, exhaustion his strength, numbness or slowness his mobility. Which of these is it that cannot overcome the flesh of a wise person? The postures and movements of the body, when they are fitting and harmonious, are likewise numbered among the primary goods of nature. Yet what if some state of ill health causes the limbs to shake and tremble? What if the spine is so curved that the hands are forced to touch the ground, making the man a sort of quadruped? Is not every type of posture and movement of the body distorted?

What about the primary things of the mind itself, which are called goods? Sense and intellect are placed first since on account of them perception and comprehension of the truth are possible. Yet what sort of and how much sensation remains if, to say nothing of other things, a man becomes deaf and blind? Indeed, if reason and intelligence recede from someone rendered insane by some illness, where would those faculties slumber? The mad, when they speak or act, do many absurd things, for the most part unrelated—indeed, even opposed—to their own good intentions and inclinations. When we either reflect on or observe what they say and do, if we consider them properly, we are barely—if at all—able to contain our tears. What shall I say of those who suffer the assault of demons? Where is their own intelligence hidden or buried when an evil spirit uses both their soul and their body according to its own will? Who is confident that this evil cannot befall a wise man in this life? Next, how well and to what extent do we perceive truth in this flesh, when, as we read in the true book of Wisdom, "The corruptible body weighs down the soul and the earthly dwelling oppresses the intelligence as it considers many things" (Wis 9:15)? An "impulse" or "appetite for action," if in this way Latin rightly names that which the Greeks call *hormé*, is counted as one of the primary goods of nature. Yet is it not precisely this which also produces those miserable motions and deeds of the insane which horrify us when sense is distorted and reason is put to sleep?

---

7   Cicero composed this work after the death of his daughter Tullia in 45 B.C. Unfortunately, it survives only in fragments.

Further, virtue itself, which is not among the primary goods of nature because it is added afterward through education, claims to be the highest of human goods, and yet what does it do except conduct perpetual wars with vices, not external but internal ones, not those of others but our very own? Is this not the particular struggle of that virtue which in Greek is named *sóphrosyné*, in Latin "temperance," by which the carnal passions are curbed so that they do not drag the mind into consenting to every sort of shameful action? Vice is never absent when, in the words of the apostle, "The flesh desires in opposition to the spirit." To this vice there is contrary virtue, when, as the same apostle says: "The spirit desires in opposition to the flesh. For these," he says, "are at war with each other, so that what you will is not what you do" (Gal 5:17). What, however, do we will to do when we will to be perfected by the supreme good? It can only be that the flesh not desire in opposition to the spirit and that this vice opposed to what the spirit desires not be in us. We are not strong enough to do this in this life, however much we will, but with the help of God, let us at least not surrender the spirit and so yield to the flesh warring against the spirit, and be dragged into sinning by our own consent. Therefore, let us not believe that, as long as we are in this internal war, we have already attained our happiness, which we will to attain by conquering the flesh. And who is so utterly wise as to have no conflict at all with his lusts?

What about the virtue called prudence? Does not its total vigilance consist in distinguishing goods from evils, so that in seeking the former and avoiding the latter no error sneaks in? Yet in this way does not prudence itself give evidence that we are among evils or that evils are within us? Prudence teaches that evil is consenting to the desire to sin and that good is withholding consent to that desire. Nevertheless, that evil, to which prudence teaches us not to consent, and to which temperance enables us not to consent, is not removed from this life by either prudence or temperance.

What about justice, whose function is to render to each his due, thereby establishing in man a certain just order of nature, so that the soul is subordinated to God, and the flesh to the soul, and consequently the flesh and the soul to God? Does it not demonstrate in performing this function that it is still laboring at its task instead of resting in the completion of its goal? Surely, the less the soul keeps God in its own thoughts, the less it is subordinated to him; and the more the flesh desires in opposition to the spirit, the less is it subordinated to the soul. Therefore, as long as there is in us this weakness, this plague, this weariness, how shall we dare to say that we are already made well? If we are not yet made well, how shall we dare to say that we are already happy in the attainment of final happiness?

As for the virtue called courage, no matter how wise one may be, it bears the clearest witness to human evils, which it is forced to endure patiently. I am astonished to see with what boldness the Stoic philosophers contend that such evils are not evils, yet they allow that if evils become so great that a wise man cannot or ought not endure them, he may be driven to bring about his own death and leave this life.[8] So great is the stupid pride of these men that, while holding that the final good is found in this life and that they are made happy by their own efforts, their wise man (that is, the man whom they describe with an amazing inanity) is one who—even if he is made blind, deaf, dumb, and lame, even if he is tormented by pain and assailed by any other such evils that could be spoken or thought, so that he is driven to bring about his own death—is still not ashamed to call this life so composed of evils "happy"!

O happy life, which seeks the help of death in order to be ended! If it is happy, he should remain in it. In what way are those things not evils? They conquer the good of courage and not only compel the same courage to yield to themselves, but also to rave, so that it both calls the same life happy and persuades one to flee it! Who is so blind that he does not see that if it is happy, one ought not flee it? In saying that such life must be fled, they openly admit the weakness of their position. The neck of their pride having been broken, why they do not also admit that such a life is miserable? I ask, did Cato kill himself because of endurance or lack of endurance? He would not have done it, except that he could not bear to endure the victory of Ceasar.[9] Where is the courage here? Truly, it yielded; truly, it surrendered; truly, it was so completely overcome that it abandoned, deserted, and fled the happy life. Or was it not then happy? Clearly, it was miserable. In what sense, then, were there no evils which made life miserable and something necessary to flee? . . .

If virtues are true—and true virtues cannot exist except in those who possess true piety—they do not profess to be able to protect the men who have them from suffering miseries. True virtues are not such liars as to profess this. They do, however, profess that human life, which is compelled by the great number and magnitude of evils in this world to be miserable, is happy through hope in a future world, and in the same way made well. Indeed, how can it be happy until it is made well? And thus the apostle Paul, speaking not of imprudent, impatient, intemperate, and unjust men, but of men living according to true piety and thereby having true virtues, says: "By hope we are made well. However, hope that is seen is not hope, for how can one hope for what one sees? However, if we hope for what we do not see, we look forward to it with patience" (Rom 8:24–25).

Therefore, as we are made well by hope, so we are made happy by hope, and as we do not presently possess well-being, but look forward to it in the future "with patience," so it is with happiness. This is because we are now among evils, which we must endure patiently, until we arrive at those goods in which we will find only indescribable delight

---

8   The Stoics argued that suicide was appropriate, at least under some conditions. On the Stoics, see the note on V. 9.

9   Rather than endure what he considered to be the tyranny of Caesar, Cato of Utica killed himself in 46 B.C. The Stoics considered Cato to be a hero for this.

and none of the things which we must now endure. Such well-being, which we will find in the future world, will itself be final happiness. Because they do not see this happiness, the philosophers refuse to believe in it, but struggle to fabricate for themselves in this life an utterly false happiness through a virtue as dishonest as it is proud.

Chapter 6

What about the legal judgments of men concerning other men? No matter how much peace abides in cities, they cannot be eliminated. How wretched, how sad we think they are! Those judging are unable to discern the consciences of those whom they judge. Consequently, they are frequently compelled to investigate the truth by torturing innocent witnesses concerning a case that is not even their own.[10] What about when someone whose own case is at stake is tortured? He is asked whether he is guilty while he is being tortured. Even an innocent person, then, pays a most certain penalty for an uncertain crime, and not because it is discovered that he committed it, but because it is not known that he did not commit it. Thus, the ignorance of the judge is frequently the calamity of the innocent.

What is much more intolerable, what must be lamented and washed, if it were possible, by fountains of tears, is this: a judge, on account of ignorance, tortures an accused in order not to execute an innocent person mistakenly, yet it happens that the judge does execute, through wretched ignorance, one who is both innocent and tortured, one whom the judge had tortured in order that he might not execute an innocent person. If, following the "wise," the accused has chosen to flee this life rather than endure the tortures any longer, he says he has committed what he did not commit. Though he is condemned and executed, the judge still does not know whether the person he tortured in order that he might not mistakenly execute an innocent person was innocent or not. Thus, he both tortures an innocent man in order to know and kills him though he does not know.

In this darkness of the social life, will a judge who is "wise" sit in judgment or not?[11] Certainly he will, for human society, which he considers it a crime to desert, binds him and drags him to this duty. These things he does not consider to be crimes: that innocent witnesses are tortured in the cases of others; that the innocent who are accused are frequently overcome by the power of pain when they are tortured, and are then punished on account of falsely confessing; that, although not punished by death, they frequently die while being tortured or as a result of being tortured; or that sometimes the accusers, perhaps desiring to be beneficial to human society by seeing to it that no crimes go unpunished, are unable to prove the charges even though they are true, since

---

10   Torture was an accepted and even required practice for Roman judges.

11   Augustine is chiding the philosophers who hold that the happy life is a social life. His point is that social life can never truly be happy in this world.

the witnesses lie and the defendant himself fiercely endures the torture without confessing, and are themselves mistakenly condemned by a judge. This great number and magnitude of evils he does not consider to be sins, for a wise judge does not do them because of a will to harm, but because of the necessity imposed by not knowing, and also because of the necessity of judging imposed by human society.

Accordingly, even if they are not the malice of the wise, these evils are certainly what we call the misery of man. If indeed it is through the necessity of not knowing and of judging that he tortures and punishes the guiltless, is it not enough for him that we do not hold him to be guilty? Must we call him "happy" besides? How much more thoughtful and appropriate it is for man to recognize misery in this necessity, and to hate himself because of it, and if he is wise in the manner of the pious, to cry out to God, "Deliver me from my necessities!" (Ps 25:17)

Chapter 7

After the city or municipality comes the world, which they regard as the third level of human society. Beginning with the household, they progress to the city and then to the world. Like converging waters, as the world is larger, so is it more dangerous. In the first place, the diversity of languages in the world alienates one man from another. Imagine that two people meet and are compelled by some necessity not to pass by but to remain together. If neither knows the language of the other, although they are both human beings, speechless animals—even if they are of different species—will associate with each other more easily. When human beings realize that they cannot communicate between themselves solely because of the difference of language, nothing promotes their association despite their similarity of nature. A man would rather be with his own dog than a foreigner.

Yet it might be said that, by taming peoples through the peace of society, the imperial city attempts to impose not only its yoke but also its language, so that there is no lack of interpreters, but indeed a great abundance. This is true. Yet how does it compensate for the numerous and immense wars, the great slaughter of men, the tremendous effusion of human blood? Even though those evils are now settled, the misery of them is not yet finished. Although bordering, hostile nations have never been and are not presently lacking, and although wars always have been and continue to be waged against them, nevertheless the very size of the empire has given rise to wars of a worse kind; namely, social and civil wars. The human race is shaken by these more miserable wars, either when they are waged so that there might eventually be calm, or when a fresh outbreak of them is feared. If I wanted to speak appropriately of these evils, great and immense destructions, and hard and dire necessities, even though I could by no means do so as the subject demands, where would this lengthy discussion end?

They say, however, that the wise man will wage only just wars—as if, mindful that he is human, he would not much rather lament that he is subject to the necessity of waging just wars.[12] If they were not just, he would not be required to wage them, and thus he would be free of the necessity of war. It is the iniquity on the part of the adversary that forces a just war upon the wise man. Even if it did not give rise to the necessity of war, such iniquity must certainly be lamented by a human being since it belongs to human beings. Therefore, let anyone who reflects with sorrow upon these evils so great, so horrid, and so savage, confess that he is miserable. Anyone, however, who either permits or considers these things without sorrow in mind is certainly much more miserable, since he thinks himself happy because he has lost human feeling.

Chapter 11

Because the name "peace" is also frequently used with respect to things which are subject to death, where there certainly is no eternal life, we prefer to call the end of this city, where its highest good will be, "eternal life" rather than "peace." Of this end the apostle says, "Now, indeed, having been liberated from sin and having become servants of God, you will have your reward in sanctification, your true end in eternal life" (Rom 6:22).

On the other hand, "eternal life" could be taken by those who are not familiar with the Sacred Scriptures to include also the life of the wicked. One might think this either because certain philosophers profess the immortality of the soul, or also because our faith professes the unending punishment of the impious, who certainly could not be eternally tormented unless they also lived eternally.

So that it can be understood more easily by all, it must be said that the end of this city, in which it will have its highest good, is either "peace in eternal life" or "eternal life in peace." Peace is such a great good that even with respect to earthly and mortal things, nothing is heard with greater pleasure, nothing desired more longingly, and in the end, nothing better can be found. If I wish to speak of it somewhat longer I will not, I think, be burdensome to readers, both because my subject is the end of this city and because of the very sweetness of peace, which is dear to all.

Chapter 12

Anyone who pays any attention to human affairs and our common human nature, recognizes as I do that just as there is no one who does not wish to be joyful, so there is no one who does not wish to have peace. Indeed, even those who want war want nothing other than to achieve victory; by warring, therefore, they desire to attain a glorious peace. What else is victory, unless triumphing over the opposition? When this has happened, there will be peace. Therefore, even those who are eager to exercise the military virtues by commanding or fighting wage war with the intention of peace. Consequently,

---

12   For Augustine's views on war, see the section on "War."

the desired end of war is peace, for everyone seeks peace, even by waging war, but no one seeks war by making peace.

Even those who want the peace they now have to be disturbed do not hate peace, but they desire to change the peace according to their own wishes. Thus, they are not unwilling that there be peace, but they want it on their own terms. Furthermore, even if they have separated themselves from others through sedition, when they conspire or plot amongst themselves they do not achieve what they intend unless they have some sort of peace. Likewise, robbers themselves want to have peace with their partners, so that they might more violently and safely attack to the peace of others. Perhaps one person is so strong and so wary of conspiring with others that he does not ally himself to any partners. Waiting in ambush and prevailing alone, he gains plunder by crushing and annihilating whom he can. Still, with those whom he cannot kill and from whom he wants to hide what he does, he certainly has some sort of a shadow of peace.

In his home, with his wife and children and anyone else who might be there, he surely strives to be at peace. Their complying with his command is no doubt pleasing. If they do not do so, he is enraged; he rebukes and punishes them. He establishes peace in his own home, if it is necessary, even by brutality. He thinks that peace is not possible unless the rest of the household is subject to a ruler, and in his own home he himself is that ruler. That is why, if the service of a great multitude, or of cities, or peoples is offered to him, so that they would serve him in the same manner as he wanted to be served in his own household, then he would no longer conceal himself like a bandit in a hideout, but raise himself up like a visible king, although the same desire and malice would abide in him. Thus, all desire to have peace with their own associates, whom they want to live according to their own decree. Indeed, they want, if they are able, to make even those against whom they wage war into their own associates, and to impose on them, when conquered, the laws of their own peace.

Let us imagine someone of the sort sung about in poetry and myth, someone whom, perhaps because of his unsociability and savageness, they have preferred to call "semihuman" rather than "human." His kingdom was the solitude of his horrible cave. So extraordinary was his malice that a name was invented from it, for in the Greek language evil is called *kakos*, which is what he was named.[13] He had no wife with whom to carry on endearing conversation, no little children to play with, no older children to give orders to, no friends with whom to enjoy speaking. He did not even enjoy the society of his father Vulcan, compared to whom he was happier simply because he had not generated such a monster as himself. He gave nothing to anyone, but took from whomever he could whatever and whenever he wanted.

---

13   The story of Cacus is related by Virgil in *Aeneid* VIII. 184–305.

Nevertheless, in the very solitude of his own cave, in which, as is said, "the ground was always reeking with fresh carnage,"[14] he wanted nothing other than peace—a peace in which no one would molest him, in which the quiet was not disturbed by the violence of anyone or the fear of it. Further, he desired to be at peace with his body, and to the extent that he was at peace with it, all was well with him. When he commanded, the limbs of his body submitted. Yet, his own mortality rebelled against him out of need and stirred up sedition through hunger, aiming to dissociate and exclude the soul from the body. In order to make peace with that mortality as quickly as possible, he plundered, he killed, and he devoured. Though monstrous and savage, he was nevertheless monstrously and savagely providing for the peace of his own life and well-being. Moreover, if he had been willing to make peace with others while he was striving to make peace in his cave and in himself, he would not have been called evil or a monster or semihuman. Also, if the appearance of his body and his breathing horrible fire frightened human society, possibly he was not so much savage because of a desire for harming but because of the necessity of his staying alive.

He might not, however, have even existed, or, what is more believable, he might not have been the same as the description given by the vanity of poetry, for if Cacus were not blamed too much, Hercules would be praised too little.[15] Therefore, it is better, as I have said, to believe that a human or semihuman of that sort never existed, as is the case with many of the imaginings of the poets.

Even the most savage wild animals, from whom Cacus got part of his wildness (for he was even said to be half-wild), care for their own species by means of a certain peace. They do this by associating, begetting, bearing, cherishing, and nourishing the offspring, even though they are for the most part insociable and solitary. I do not mean those animals such as sheep, deer, doves, starlings, and bees, but those such as lions, wolves, foxes, eagles, and owls. Indeed, what tigress, pacifying her wildness, does not gently purr and caress her young? What kite, however much it circles its prey alone, does not unite with a mate, put together a nest, warm the eggs, nourish the young birds, and as if with the mother of his family, keep peace in his domestic society as much as he can? How much more is man brought by the laws of his nature, as it were, to enter into society and keep peace with all men to the extent that he is able?

After all, even the evil wage war for the sake of the peace of their own associates, and they would want to make everyone their own, if they could, so that everyone and everything would be enslaved to one individual. How would that happen if they did not consent to his peace, either through love or fear? In this manner, pride imitates God in a distorted way. It hates equality with partners under God, but wants to impose its own

---

14   *Aeneid* VIII. 195.
15   Cacus was eventually slain by Hercules.

domination upon its partners in place of God. Consequently, it hates the just peace of God and loves its own iniquitous peace. Nevertheless, it is not able not to love some sort of peace. Truly, there is no defect so contrary to nature that it wipes away even the last vestiges of nature. Accordingly, he who knows to prefer the upright to the deformed, and the ordered to the distorted, sees that the peace of the iniquitous, in comparison to the peace of the just, should not be called "peace" at all. However, it is necessary that even what is distorted be at peace in some way with a part of the things in which it exists or from which it is established. Otherwise, it would not exist at all.

This is just like if someone were to hang with his head downward. The position of the body and the order of the limbs would certainly be distorted, because what nature demands to be above is below, and what it wants to be below is above. This distortion disturbs the peace of the flesh and for that reason is painful. It is nevertheless true that the soul is at peace with the body and is busy struggling for its well-being, and thus there is someone suffering. If the soul departs, having been driven out by the pain, as long as the structure of the limbs remains, so does a certain amount of peace, and thus there is still something hanging there. Because the earthly body tends toward the earth and is resisted by the chain by which it is suspended, it tends to the order of its own peace and requests in a weighty voice, as it were, a place where it might rest. Now lifeless and without any sense, nevertheless it does not depart from the peace of its own natural order, either when it has it or when it reaches toward it.

If embalming potions and treatments are applied, which do not allow the form of the cadaver to break up and dissolve, a sort of peace still unites certain parts to other parts and connects the whole mass in its suitable and therefore peaceful place in the earth. If no one applies the treatment for burying, however, then the cadaver disintegrates in the course of nature. It is in a state of disturbance due to dissenting vapors which are disagreeable to our senses (for this is what is smelled in putrefaction), until it is assimilated to the elements of the world and gradually, little by little, separates into their peace. Nevertheless, in no way is anything withdrawn from the laws of the supreme creator and governor by whom the peace of the universe is administered, for even if tiny animals are born from the cadaver of a greater animal, by the same law of the creator each little body serves its own little soul in the well-being of peace. Even if the flesh of the dead is devoured by other animals, wherever it is carried, whatever the things to which it is joined, whatever the things into which it is changed and altered, it finds those same laws diffused throughout all things for the well-being of every mortal species, making peace by harmonizing suitable elements.

Chapter 13
Thus, the peace of the body is the ordered proportion of its parts. The peace of the irrational soul is the ordered repose of the appetites. The peace of the rational soul is the

ordered agreement of knowledge and action. The peace of the body and the soul is the ordered life and well-being of a living thing. The peace between a mortal man and God is an ordered obedience, in faith, under the eternal law.

The peace among human beings is ordered concord. The peace of the household is an ordered concord concerning commanding and obeying among those who dwell together. The peace of the city is an ordered concord concerning commanding and obeying among the citizens. The peace of the heavenly city is a fellowship perfectly ordered and harmonious, enjoying God and each other in God. The peace of all things is the tranquility of order.

Order is the arrangement of things equal and unequal, allotting to each its own position. Hence, the miserable indeed lack the tranquility of order in which there is no disturbance, since insofar as they are miserable, they certainly are not at peace. Nevertheless, since they are deservedly and justly miserable, they are not, in their very own misery, able to be outside that order. They are surely not united to the happy, but, by the law of order, are separated from them. When they are free from disturbance, they are adjusted to the circumstances in which they find themselves by a harmony of some degree. Thus, some tranquility of order belongs to them, and so some peace. Therefore, the reason they are miserable is because, even if they have some freedom from concern and are not suffering, they are still not in a position where they ought to be exempt from concern and suffering. They are more miserable, however, if they are not at peace with the very law by which the order of nature is administered.

Moreover, when they suffer, they suffer in that part in which a disturbance of peace occurs, but there is still peace in that part not disturbed by suffering and in the structure itself, which is not dissolved. As, therefore, there is a kind of life without suffering, but suffering cannot exist without some life, so there is a kind of peace without any war, but war cannot exist without some peace. This does not follow because of what war itself is, but because it is waged by those or in those who are natural beings in some way. They would not exist at all, unless they remained in a peace of some sort.

Accordingly, there is a nature in which there is no evil, or even in which there can be no evil, but there cannot be a nature in which there is no good. Thus, not even the nature of the devil himself, insofar as it is a nature, is evil. Rather, it is the distortion of that nature that makes it evil. Hence, he did not stand firm in the truth, but he did not escape the judgment of the truth. He did not remain in the tranquility of order, but he nevertheless did not avoid the power of the one who orders. The goodness of God, which is in the devil's nature, does not remove him from the justice of God, which orders by punishing him. God did not then reproach the good that he created, but the evil that the devil has committed. Neither does God take away all that he gave to the devil's nature, but some he takes and some he leaves, so that there might be something to suffer the loss of what was taken away. That very suffering is a witness to the good taken away and the good left behind, for unless good were left behind, the devil could not suffer because of the good lost. . . .

Therefore, God, who founded all natures most wisely and ordered them most justly, who established the mortal human race as the greatest embellishment of the earth, gave to mankind certain goods suitable for this life. These goods include a temporal peace proportional to the short span of a mortal life, a peace involving health, preservation, and the society of one's own kind. They also include the things necessary for guarding or recovering this peace (such as what is appropriately and fittingly present to the senses: light, sound, breathable air, drinkable water, and whatever is suitable for feeding, covering, healing, and adorning the body). All this was given through the most equitable stipulation, that he who uses such mortal goods rightly, adapting them to the peace of mortals, would receive more and better goods; namely, the peace of immortality and the glory and honor suitable to it, in an eternal life which is for enjoying God and one's neighbor in God. He, however, who uses mortal goods wrongly, would lose them and would not receive eternal ones.

Chapter 15

God said, "Let him have dominion over the fish of the sea and the winged things of the heavens and all the crawling things which crawl upon the earth" (Gn 1:26). He did not will that the rational being, having been made according to his own image, dominate any except the irrational beings; he did not will that man dominate man, but that man dominate the beasts. Therefore, the first just men were established as shepherds of beasts rather than as kings of men, so that even in this way God might suggest what the order of creatures requires and what the reward of sinners drives away. Surely it is understood that the condition of slavery is rightly imposed on the sinner. Accordingly, nowhere in the scripture do we read the word "slave" before the just Noah punished the sin of his son with this word. Thus, he earned the name through fault, not through nature. . . .

The first cause of slavery, then, is sin, with the result that man is placed under man by the bondage of this condition. This does not happen except through the judgment of God, in whom there is no iniquity, and who knows how to distribute the various punishments according to the merits of the delinquent. Yet, as the Lord above says, "Anyone who sins is a slave of sin" (Jn 8:34), and thus indeed many religious people enslaved to iniquitous masters are nevertheless not enslaved to the free: "For by whatever one has been conquered, to that one has also been made a slave" (2 Pt 2:19). And it is certainly a happier condition to be enslaved to a man than to a lust, since the very lust for dominating—not to mention others—ravishes the hearts of mortals by a most savage mastery. In that order of peace by which some are subordinated to others, humility is as beneficial to the enslaved as pride is harmful to the dominating.

Nevertheless, by the nature in which God first established man, no one is a slave of man or of sin. It is also true that penal slavery is ordained by that law which commands the preservation and prohibits the disturbance of the natural order, because if nothing had been done contrary to that law, there would have been nothing requiring the restraint of penal slavery. That is why the apostle also warns slaves to be subject to their masters and to serve with good will and from the heart (Eph 6:5), so that if they are not able to be freed by their masters, they might make their slavery in a certain sense free, by serving not with the cunning of fear, but with the faithfulness of affection, until iniquity is transformed and all human rule and power are made void, and God is all in all (1 Cor 15:24, 28).

Chapter 16

... Those who are true "fathers of their families" are concerned that all in their family—the slaves as well as the children—should worship and be reconciled to God.[16] Such fathers desire and long to come to the heavenly household, where the duty of ruling mortals is not necessary because the duty of being concerned for the welfare of those already happy in that immortality will no longer be necessary. Until that home is reached, fathers ought to endure more because they rule than slaves do because they serve.

If, however, anyone in the household opposes the domestic peace through disobedience, he is disciplined by word or by whip or by any other kind of just and legitimate punishment, to the extent that human society allows. Such discipline is for the profit of the one being disciplined, so that he is readjusted to the peace from which he had departed. After all, just as it is not kindness to help someone when it would cause him to lose a greater good, so it is not innocence to spare punishment and permit someone to fall more grievously into wickedness.[17] Therefore, in order to be innocent, duty demands not only that one not bring evil to anyone, but also that one restrain another from sin or punish his sin, so that either the person who is punished might be set straight by the experience or others frightened by his example.

Hence, because the human household ought to be the beginning or the building block of the city, and because every beginning is directed to some end of its own kind and every part to the integrity of the whole whose part it is, the consequence is clearly that domestic peace is directed to civic peace. That is to say, the ordered concord concerning commanding and obeying of those dwelling together is directed to the ordered concord concerning commanding and obeying of the citizens. Accordingly, the father of the family should obtain the precepts by which he rules his household from the laws of the city, so that his household might be adapted to the peace of the city.

---

16   The phrase "fathers of their families" refers to the Roman institution of the *paterfamilias*.

17   This passage should be compared with the selection from *Letter 93* in the section on "The Use of Persecution."

Chapter 17

The household of those who do not live by faith chases an earthly peace consisting of the affairs and advantages of this temporal life. The household of human beings living by faith, on the other hand, looks forward to the future, to those things which are promised as eternal, and makes use of temporal and earthly things like a traveller. Those things do not seize such a person and turn him away from the path to God. They do not increase the burdens of "the corruptible body which weighs down the soul" (Wis 9:15), but sustain him for more easily enduring them. Consequently, both sorts of men and both sorts of households use the things necessary for this mortal life, but the end of such use is unique to each and varies greatly. So also the earthly city, which does not live by faith, desires earthly peace and it secures the concord concerning commanding and obeying of the citizens, so that there might be a certain orderly arrangement of human wills concerning the things pertaining to mortal life. The heavenly city, however, or rather the part of it which journeys in this mortal life and lives by faith, necessarily uses this peace, too, until the very mortality which makes such a peace necessary might pass away.

Because of this, so long as it leads the life of a captive, as it were, journeying within the earthly city, already having received a promise of redemption and a spiritual gift as a pledge of it, the heavenly city has no doubts about conforming to the laws of the earthly city which administer the things required for the sustenance of the mortal life. Because mortality itself is common to both of the cities, concord between them is preserved with respect to those things pertaining to the mortal life. . . .

So long as this heavenly city journeys on the earth, it calls forth citizens from all peoples and gathers a society of foreigners speaking all languages. It is not troubled at all about differences in customs, laws, and institutions by which the earthly peace is either sought or maintained. So long as they do not impede the religion which teaches the worship of the one, supreme, and true God, the heavenly city abrogates or destroys none of them, but indeed observes and follows them, for whatever the diversities of different nations, they nevertheless strive toward the one and the same end of earthly peace.

Hence, even the heavenly city uses the earthly peace on its journey, and it is concerned about and desires the orderly arrangement of human wills concerning the things pertaining to mortal human nature, insofar as it is agreeable to sound piety and religion. It directs the earthly peace to the heavenly peace, which is so truly peace that it must be held and said that the only peace, at least of rational creatures, is the most ordered and most harmonious society enjoying God and each other in God. When that peace comes, there will not be mortal life, but a whole and certain life; not the ensouled body weighing down the soul in its corruption (Wis 9:15), but a spiritual body with no wants and with every part subordinated to the will. While it journeys, the heavenly city possesses this peace in faith, and out of this faith it lives justly when it directs to the attainment of that peace whatever good actions it performs toward God, and also those performed toward the neighbor, since the life of this city is certainly social.

Chapter 19

The style of dress or manner of living in which anyone follows the faith that leads to God does not matter to the heavenly city, so long as these are not in contradiction with the divine precepts. Thus, even philosophers, when they become Christians, are not required to change their style of dress or eating customs, which do not impede religion, though they are required to change their false teachings. Accordingly, that city does not care at all about the distinction that Varro made concerning the Cynics,[18] so long as nothing is done basely or intemperately.

With respect to those three kinds of life, the leisurely, the active, and the combination of the two, although every one, through sound faith, can lead his life according to any one of them and attain the everlasting reward, what one holds through the love of truth and what one expends through the duty of charity are nevertheless important. Thus, no one ought to be so leisurely that he does not, in his leisure, consider the advantage of his neighbor; neither should anyone be so active that he does not consider the contemplation of God to be necessary.

In leisure, one ought not delight in slothful idleness, but in either the investigation or discovery of truth, so that everyone advances in it and does not withhold his discoveries from others. In action, no one ought to love honor or power in this life, because all is vanity under the sun (Eccl 1:2–3). Rather, the work itself that is done through the same honor or power should be loved, if it is done rightly and profitably. That is to say, it should be loved if it advances the well-being of the subjects, which is according to God, as we have argued earlier.

Because of this the apostle said, "He who desires the episcopacy desires a good work" (1 Tm 3:1). He wanted to explain that the name "episcopacy" is the name of a work not of an honor. Indeed, the word is Greek, and it comes from the fact that he who is set over others "superintends" them; that is, he exercises care for them. Indeed, the Greek word *skopos* means intention; therefore, for *episkopein* we can say, if we want, "superintend." Consequently, he who desires to be over others rather than to benefit others should understand that he is not a bishop.

Thus, no one is prohibited from zealousness for knowledge of the truth, because the life of learned leisure pertains to what is praiseworthy. On the other hand, to desire high position, without which a people cannot be ruled, is indecent, even if the position is held and administered in a decent manner. Because of this, charity for truth seeks holy leisure, while the requirements of charity accept just activity. If this latter burden is not

---

18   The Cynics were a school of philosophers who adopted a distinctively shabby style of dress.

imposed, one is free to grasp for and to contemplate truth. If, however, the burden is imposed, accepting it is on account of the requirements of charity. Even in this instance, however, delight in the truth is not abandoned completely, otherwise that sweetness might be lost and these requirements crush us.

Chapter 21

It is at this place that I will explain, as briefly and clearly as I can, what in the second book of this work I promised that I would demonstrate; namely, that, according to the definition that Scipio uses in the *Republic* of Cicero, there never was a Roman republic.[19] He succinctly defines a "republic" as "the affair of a people." If this definition is true, there never was a Roman republic, because Rome never was the affair of a people, which is Scipio's definition of a republic.

The reason for this is that he defined "a people" as "a fellowship of a multitude united through a consensus concerning right and a sharing of advantage." What he calls "a consensus concerning right" he explains in the dialogue by making it clear that it is not possible for a republic to be managed without justice. Therefore, where there is no true justice, there can be no right. What is done by right is indeed done justly; what is done unjustly, however, cannot be done by right. The iniquitous institutions of human beings must not be said or thought to exist by right, because even those institutions say that right flows from the fountain of justice, and that what is customarily said by those who do not understand right correctly—i.e. that right is the advantage of the strongest—is false.[20]

Accordingly, where there is no true justice, there can be no fellowship of men united through a consensus concerning right, and therefore there can be no people according to the definition of Scipio or Cicero. Moreover, if there is no people, neither can there be an affair of a people, but only of some sort of a multitude which is not worthy of the name of "a people." Consequently, if a republic is "the affair of a people," and there is no people which is not "united by means of a consensus concerning right," and there is no right where there is no justice, without doubt it must be concluded that where there is no justice, there is no republic.

Furthermore, justice is that virtue which distributes to everyone his due. What sort of justice is it, then, that takes a man away from the true God and subjects him to unclean demons? Is *this* to distribute to each his due? Or, is he who takes the ground purchased by someone and gives it to another who has no right to it unjust, but he who takes himself away from the dominion of the God who made him and enslaves himself to malicious spirits just?

19   See II. 21.
20   In Book 1 of Plato's *Republic*, Thrasymachus defines justice as "the advantage of the strongest."

Certainly, the cause of justice against injustice is argued very energetically and forceful-ly in that very same book, *The Republic*. Earlier, the case of injustice against justice was considered and it was said that the republic could not stand firm or be managed except through injustice. It was set down as the most powerful part of the argument that it was unjust for men to serve other men as their masters, but that unless the imperial city to whom the great republic belongs follows such injustice it is not able to rule its provinces. The response from the side of justice was that this rule over the inhabitants of the prov-inces is just because servitude is advantageous for such men and is done for their benefit when it is done correctly—that is, when the license for wrongdoing is taken away from the wicked. Also, it was argued that they will be in a better condition as a result of hav-ing been subdued, because they were in a worse condition before being subdued.

In order to strengthen this reasoning, a famous example was stated as though it was bor-rowed from nature: "Why, then, does God rule man, the soul rule the body, the reason rule lust and the rest of the corrupt parts of the soul?"[21] Plainly, this example teaches well that servitude is advantageous to some and that serving God is indeed advanta-geous to all. In serving God, the soul correctly rules the body, and the reason in the soul subordinated to the Lord God correctly rules lust and the rest of the corrupt parts of the soul. Thus, when a man does not serve God, what in him can be reckoned to belong to justice? Indeed, when not serving God, the soul can in no way justly rule the body, or human reason the vices. Furthermore, if there is not any justice in such a man, without doubt neither is there any in a fellowship of human beings which consists of such men. Therefore, this is not that "consensus concerning right" which makes a multitude of human beings a "people," whose affair is called a "republic."

What shall I say concerning that "advantage," the sharing of which also unites a fel-lowship of men so that it is named "a people," as stipulated by the definition? If you carefully direct your attention, you will see that there is no advantage to any who live impiously, as do all who do not serve God but serve the demons who, the more impi-ous they are, the more they want to receive sacrifice as gods, even though they are the most unclean spirits of all. Yet, what we have said about the consensus concerning right I think is sufficient to make it apparent that, according to this definition, there is no people which might be said to be a republic in which there is no justice.

If our enemies say that the Romans have not served unclean spirits but good and holy gods in their republic, must what we have already said sufficiently, indeed more than sufficiently, be repeated yet again? Who, except the excessively stupid or the shamelessly contentious, having arrived at this point after reading the earlier books of this work, finds it possible to doubt but that the Romans have up to this point served evil and impure demons? Nevertheless, in order to say no more about the sort of gods they are

---

21 *Republic* III.25

worshipping with sacrifices, I instead cite what is written in the law of the true God: "Anyone sacrificing to the gods, except only to the Lord, will be eradicated" (Ex 22:20). Thus, he who admonishes with such a threat did not want either good gods or evil ones to receive sacrifice.

Chapter 23

. . . We ourselves—his city—are the best and most radiant sacrifice. We celebrate this mystery through our offerings, which are known to the faithful, as we have argued in the preceding books.[22] Indeed, through the Hebrew prophets the divine oracles thundered that the offering of sacrificial victims by the Jews, a foreshadowing of the future, would cease, and that peoples from the rising of the sun to its setting would offer one sacrifice, as we see happening now.[23] From these oracles we have taken as much as seemed sufficient and have already sprinkled them throughout this work.

Thus, justice exists when the one and supreme God rules his obedient city according to his grace, so that it does not sacrifice to any whatsoever except Him alone. As a result, in everyone belonging to that same city and obeying God, the soul faithfully commands the body, and reason the corrupt parts of the soul, in accord with the lawful order. Consequently, just like a single just man, a fellowship and a people of just men lives by faith, which works through love, by which man loves God as God ought to be loved, and his neighbor as himself. Where that justice does not exist, truly there is no "fellowship of men united through a consensus concerning right and a sharing of advantage." If this justice does not exist, then a people does not exist, if this is the true definition of a people. Therefore, neither does a republic exist, for there is no affair of a people where there is no people.

Chapter 24

If, however, a people is not defined in that way, but in another—if, for example, it is said that a people is "a fellowship of a multitude of rational beings united through sharing in an agreement about what it loves"—then truly, in order to see the character of a people, what it loves must be considered. If it is not fellowship of a multitude of beasts, but of rational creatures, and is united through sharing in an agreement about what it loves, then, no matter what it loves, it is not unreasonable to call it "a people." It is a better people if it agrees in loving better things; a worse one if it agrees in loving worse things. According to this definition, the Roman people is a people, and its affair is without doubt a republic. However, history gives witness to what that people loved originally and subsequently, and by what morals it arrived at the bloodiest revolutions and then at social and civil wars, utterly shattering and annihilating concord itself, which is, in

---

22   Augustine treats this especially in X. 6, which is not included in this volume.
23   Augustine may have in mind Malachi 1:11.

a certain sense, the well being of a people. Of this we have said much in the preceding books. . . .

Justin Martyr

Editor's Introduction
Anthony Sciglitano

Justin Martyr (d. 163) was a second century Christian writer who came to Christian faith through his study of philosophy. Christianity, for Justin, was not a *religion* as opposed to *philosophy*, but rather was the True Philosophy. By his own account, Justin did not become Christian lightly. He studied a variety of philosophies: Stoic, Aristotelian, Platonic, and Pythagorean. After he became Christian, Justin wandered over the Roman Empire and taught Christianity. Justin was also one of the early martyrs of Christianity. *Martyr* literally means witness, but the title is reserved for those who die for their beliefs. After Christianity split off from Judaism late in the first century, Christianity became an illegal religion. This did not always mean they were persecuted, but they could find themselves forced to renounce their faith or suffer torture, maiming, and/or death. Some persecutions were locally ordered, whereas others were ordered for the Empire as a whole. One of the earliest records we possess of this process is a letter from a governor named Pliny addressed to the Emperor Trajan around A.D. 110. You can find this letter in your Course Documents folder in Blackboard. We also have a record of the martyrdom of Perpetua and Felicity in A.D. 203. This can be found in your reader.

Justin was also classed as an *apologist*. As you will see from the reading, Justin is not *apologetic* in our common use of the term. Rather, *apologist* here means someone who offers a defense of Christian faith against misunderstandings and distortions. Justin offers what he calls his *Apology* (#1) by arguing that Christianity is not only reasonable, but the most reasonable and moral of all belief systems. In this way, he tries to persuade the elite of Rome that Christianity should be supported rather than persecuted in the Empire. In fact, you will see that much of Justin's way of arguing is familiar from earlier materials you have read. Like Paul and Plato, for instance, Justin is concerned with true piety (#2) or love of God, how this piety relates to truth and reason (#2), and what this piety means for the way people should act toward and live with one another, that is, with morality (#10, #17). Piety is also referenced under its opposite, *impiety* (#36). You will also notice that the term *atheist* comes up several times in the letter (#6, #10, #16).

Justin begins in #2 by asserting that the truly pious recognize truth as holding the place of highest honor in humanity's affections. He then goes on to relate truth to justice. Piety, truth, and justice are all related in this paragraph. Perhaps it is not surprising that Justin is concerned with justice. After all, he is attempting to convince the Emperor that the way Christians are being treated is contrary to justice and to reason (see #7). Focus here on #2 and try to articulate how Justin thinks piety, truth, and justice are related. Does he sound like Socrates to you? In this same paragraph, Justin discusses a variety of human behaviors and cares that get in the way of true justice. Describe the kinds of behavior and the kinds of care that get in the way of true and just judgment.

Now Justin thinks that true piety leads to certain kinds of behavior. We have seen this already in that he thinks true piety, and thus love of truth, ought to lead to just behavior. But in #10 and #17 we hear from Justin what being Christian means to the way in which he thinks people ought to live or the kind of person one ought to be. Notice that Justin is contrasting what he understands as a Christian view of life and community to the non-Christian culture around him, and also to the way he thought he should live prior to becoming Christian. Notice the kinds of changes that Justin lists here. What does he think becoming Christian means for morality, for relations to others in the community, and also for one's approach to those with whom one has a disagreement? Justin claims in #10 that "God persuades only, and draws us gently in our regeneration, by co-operating freely with those rational powers He has bestowed upon us." Reflect upon how this view relates to what Justin says in #17 regarding how Christians respond to those who hate them. Here, Justin speaks of Christ. Can you see any relation between what Justin says here and Paul's view that Christians ought to embody "Christ crucified"?

There is one important theme running through Justin's *Apology* that we have yet to touch upon. This theme is what theologians call his **"Logos doctrine."** *Doctrine* means teaching. *Logos* is more difficult to define because it has a number of meanings. Here, it means "word," "truth," and "wisdom." However, when Justin speaks of the *Logos*, he means both the Word of God and also the Wisdom of God. He thinks that this Wisdom was given to the prophets in the Old Testament and became flesh in Jesus Christ. So, for Justin, Jesus is the embodiment in time of God's eternal Word, Wisdom, Truth, or Reason. Justin is taking this idea from two places. The first is the Gospel of John, especially John 1:1–5, 14, and 17. John's Gospel says that the Word (*Logos*) was with God in the beginning and that the Word (*Logos*) "became flesh." Justin is also using ideas from Greek philosophy where *Logos* means the rationality of what is real. Plato's *Forms*, for instance, are the height of rationality and are also what is most real according to Plato. So Justin is putting together Greek "reason" with Christian "revelation" of the Truth.

Now, a question arises as to which holds priority for Justin, Christian *revelation*, that is, what is found in the Gospels, or Greek *reason*, that is, what can be known simply by reasoning as Plato does. To gain more clarity on our question, let's examine two opposed ways to read what Justin is saying:

1. The first way to read Justin says that Jesus shows us what is truly reasonable, and thus calls us to reform our reasoning and our lives to attune them to the Wisdom presented through his life, teaching, death, and resurrection. To the extent that non-Christian ideas and forms of life of philosophers, playwrights, poets, and so on, exhibit a likeness to the Wisdom shown through Jesus's life, teaching, death, and resurrection, they should be considered truly reasonable, and thus true. To the extent that they contradict the meaning and way of life portrayed through Jesus's life, teaching, death, and resurrection, they should be considered untrue or unreasonable.

2. A second way to read Justin suggests that he favors philosophical reasoning to such an extent that the Gospel no longer serves as the primary
criterion for truth. On this view, Justin seems to be saying that whenever
people use their reason well, they are participating in the Truth. This view
would hold that Justin thinks we can come to philosophical truth apart
from reading the Gospel, and that if we think something is true, then the
Gospel *must* also affirm that teaching. The question here becomes whether
Justin accommodates his culture too much. We will see later that Tertullian, another early Christian writer, opposes all accommodation with the
surrounding culture.

Where does Justin speak of the *Logos* in your reading? The relevant passages for
us are #31, #44, #46, and #57. Because #46 is quite important to our discussion,
and because it is oddly paraphrased in your reading, we include a fuller form of
the same paragraph here:

> But the truth shall be told, for the wicked demons from ancient times
> appeared and defiled women, corrupted boys, and presented such ter-
> rifying sights to men that those who were not guided by reason in judging
> these diabolical acts were panic-stricken. Seized with fear and unaware
> that these were evil demons, they called them gods and greeted each by
> the name each demon had bestowed upon himself. **But when Socrates**
> **attempted to make these things known and to draw men away from the**
> **demons by true reason and judgment**, then these very demons brought it
> about, through men delighting in evil, that he be put to death as **an atheist**
> **and impious person**, because, they claimed, he introduced new divinities.
>
> And now they endeavor to do the very same thing to us. And not only
> among the Greeks were these things through Socrates condemned by rea-
> son [logos], but also among the non-Hellenic peoples by **the Logos Himself,**
> **who assumed a human form and became man, and was called Jesus Christ.**
> **. . . We have been taught that Christ is the first-born of God, and that He**
> **is the Logos of whom every race of men are partakers; and they who lived**
> **reasonably are Christians, even though they have been called atheists; as**
> **among the Greeks, Socrates, Heraclitus and. . . . Abraham men like them.**
> **. . . Thus are we even called atheists. We do proclaim ourselves atheists as**
> **regards those whom you call gods, but not with respect to the Most True**
> **God, who is alien to all evil and is the Father of justice, temperance, and the**
> **other virtues.** (Justin Martyr, c. A.D. 105–163, the *First Apology*) [I have put
> in bold those elements that are most relevant for our discussion.]

Paragraph #57 hides *Logos* in "seeds of Truth," *Logos Spermatikos* in Greek.
Here, Justin is suggesting that "seeds of Truth" can be found throughout the
world, but only in a partial and often contradictory fashion.

Try to make an argument as to whether reading #1 or reading #2 above presents
the better interpretation of Justin's ideas. Or, perhaps you have a different
interpretation altogether!

Good luck to you!

JUSTIN MARTYR

From *Readings in Christian Humanism*, edited by Shaw, et al. Reprinted by permission of Augsburg Fortress Publishers.

Justin, known as the martyr, was born early in the second century and met a martyr's death in A.D. 163. Little is known of his life except what can be gleaned from his writings. He was born in Palestine of pagan parents and was educated in turn in contemporary pagan philosophies: first that of the Stoics, then that of the Peripatetics, and finally that of the Pythagoreans. Each of the philosophies left him unconvinced and dissatisfied; he claimed that none of them provided him with the truth. The quest for truth led him to Christianity, which he embraced with enthusiasm and heroic courage. He traveled about the Roman Empire as a teacher of Christianity and came to Rome during the reign of the emperor Antoninus Pius (A.D. 138–161). Justin lectured on the Christian faith while at Rome and founded a school there. During the reign of Marcus Aurelius (A.D. 161–180), he was brought to trial, an account of which fortunately has survived, found guilty, and martyred along with a group of companions in A.D. 163.

The writings of Justin Martyr have a special place in early Christian literature. They are classified with the writings of the apologists who worked on the frontier of the church and the world and sought to defend the Christian faith from misrepresentation and attack. The apologists also sought to commend Christianity to the interested inquirer and to demonstrate the falsity of polytheism. Most of the surviving apologies are in the form of legal documents petitioning the Roman authorities to investigate what Christianity was really about. The apologists took pains to challenge current calumnies and were particularly eager to answer the charge that the Christian church endangered the Roman state. They insisted that the Christian faith was a force for the maintenance and welfare of the world.

Evidently Justin was a rather prolific writer, although only three of his works have survived. There are two *Apologies* against the pagans (Romans) and a *Dialogue with the Jew Trypho*, the oldest Christian apology against the Jews. These works are written in Greek and lack literary grace or style. They possess, however, compelling power. Justin suggests that the Roman authorities err under Roman law when punishment is imposed although a defendant is not actually convicted of a crime. The first section of the *First Apology* demonstrates the folly of the official Roman attitude toward the Christians. The second section provides a justification of the Christian religion and gives a detailed description of the church's doctrine and worship.

From Justin Martyr, First Apology

1. To the Emperor Titus Aelius Adrianus Antoninus Pius Augustus Caesar, and to his son Verissimus the philosopher, and to Lucius the philosopher, the natural son

of Caesar, but the adopted of Pius, the lover of learning; and to the sacred senate, and to all the people of Rome, in the behalf of men of all ranks and nations unjustly loaded with public odium and oppression, I, Justin, the son of Priscus, and grandson of Bacchius, Natives of Flavia Neapolis of Palestine, Syria, I, who am one of this suffering multitude, humbly offer this Apology.

2. It is the voice of reason, and ever attended to by men truly pious and worthy the name of philosopher, that truth alone is the thing to be had in the highest honour, and to hold the first place in our affections, and the ancients to be followed not one step further than they are followers of truth. ~~The same right reason dictates also that we are not only to strike in with any sect of men, unjust either in practice or principle; but, moreover, that a lover of the truth must by all means, and before life itself, and in defiance of all the menaces of death, choose to square his words and actions by the rules of justice whatever it cost him.~~ And whereas you wear the glorious titles of pious and philosophers, and guardians of justice and lovers of learning, though these, I say, are the darling characters you affect to be distinguished by everywhere, yet whether you make them good or no shall be seen by the following discourse; for we come not here with a design to flatter or ingratiate by the power of fine words, but we come in plain terms to demand judgment according to the strictest and exactest rules of justice, that neither prejudice nor the vanity of getting into the good graces of superstitious men, nor blind passion, or a scandalous report which has so long prepossessed you, might any longer prevail with you to pass sentence against yourselves by condemning the innocent; ~~for it is a maxim among us Christians that we cannot possibly suffer any real hurt, if we cannot be convicted of doing any real evil: "You may kill indeed, but you cannot hurt us."~~

6. And thus far we frankly confess the charge, that with respect to the gods in worship among you we are atheists; but far otherwise in respect of the most true God, the Father of righteousness, purity, and every virtue, a God infinitely removed from the least mixture or spot of evil: Him and His only-begotten Son (Who has instructed us in what I just now mentioned concerning these evil spirits, and likewise acquainted us with another host of good and godlike ministering spirits), both these, I say, together with the Spirit Who spake by the prophets, ~~we worship and adore; and our way of worshipping is in spirit and truth; and as we have been taught, so are we ready to communicate the same freely to every one that is willing to learn.~~

7. But perhaps it will be objected that some Christians have been taken up and convicted as evildoers. Well, I might grant the objection and more; not only that some, but many, and at many times, have been thus duly convicted upon a fair trial; but then I must tell you again that you condemned not the persons aforesaid as criminals, but as Christians. Moreover, we confess that as all the sects in general among

the Greeks went under the common name of philosopher, though extremely different in opinions, so truly among the barbarians the professors of this new wisdom, whether in reality or appearance only, go all by the same title, and are denominated Christians; wherefore we pray that all those who are indicted by the name of Christian may be examined as to their actions, and that every person may suffer as an evil-doer, and not as a Christian; and if he be found not guilty, that he may be discharged as a Christian who has done nothing worthy of punishment. And as to our false accusers, far be it from us to desire you to punish—their own painful wickedness, and utter ignorance of all that is good and amiable, is punishment in abundance.

8. I could wish you would take this also into consideration, that what we say is really for your own good; for it is in our power at any time to escape your torments, by denying the faith when you question us about it. ~~But we scorn to purchase life at the expense of a lie; for our souls are winged with a desire of a life of eternal duration and purity, of an immediate conversation with God the Father and Maker of all things; we are in haste to be confessing and finishing our faith, being fully persuaded that we shall arrive at this beatific state if we approve ourselves to God by our works, and express our passion by our obedience for that divine life which is never interrupted by any clashing evil.~~ But to lay before you, in short, what we expect, and what we have learned from Christ, and what we teach the world, take it as follows: Plato and we are both alike agreed as to a future judgment, but differ about the judges—Rhadamanthus and Minos are his judges, Christ ours. And moreover we say that the souls of the wicked, being reunited to the same bodies, shall be consigned over to eternal torments, and not, as Plato will have it, to the period of a thousand years only. But if you will affirm this to be incredible or impossible, there is no help but you must fall from error to error, till the day of judgment convinces you we are in the right.

9. But we cannot vouchsafe to worship with numerous victims, and garlands of flowers, the work of men's hands,—what you must help into the temple, and being so placed think fit to dub them gods; for we know them to be senseless, inanimate idols, and in nothing resembling the form of God (for we cannot conceive God to be anywise like what is drawn to represent and honour Him by), but in imitation only of those evil spirits who have imposed upon the world under such titles and apparitions. But what need I mention to such knowing persons as you are how the artists manage the subject-matter of their gods, how they hack and hew it, and cast it and hammer it, and not seldom form vessels of dishonour; by changing their figure only, and giving them another turn by the help of art, out comes a worshipful set of things you call gods. This we look upon not only as the highest flight of human folly, but as the most injurious affront to the true God, Who is a God of

glory and form ineffable, thus to transfer His incommunicable Name upon such corruptible and helpless things as wood and stone. Besides, the artificers of what you worship are the lewdest of men, and, not to mention particulars, practised in all sorts of wickedness, as you yourselves are very sensible of; men who debauch the girls while they are helping them to make your gods. Oh! stupidity of men as thunderstruck! that ever you should let such beasts have a hand in making your gods, and put them and the temples which hold them under the protection of such villains, never reflecting what an execrable crime it is, either to think or say, that men have the care and keeping of the gods!

10. And while we look upon God as the Giver of all good things, we can never think He stands in need of the material and gross oblations of men; but we are taught, and most firmly believe and know, that they only are the acceptable worshippers of God who form their minds by the mind eternal, and express it in temperance, justice, humanity, and such other virtues as are the essential excellence of the Divine Nature, or the more proper inmost perfections of Him Who is a God unnameable; and this Almighty Being, so good in Himself, made all things in the beginning for the good of man out of a chaos of rude ill-favoured matter; and they who walk according to His will, and demonstrate their worthiness by their works, we are sure will be admitted into the Divine presence, there to reign with Him, where corruption and suffering never come. For as He created us at first, when we were not, so by the same power will He restore us to begin again, and crown with the immortal enjoyment of Himself such as have made it their choice to please their Maker; for though we had no choice in our creation, yet in our regeneration we have; for God persuades only, and draws us gently in our regeneration, by co-operating freely with those rational powers He has bestowed upon us. And we are verily of opinion that it would be for the interest of all men living not only to tolerate the learning of the Christian faith, but to give it all the public encouragement possible; for that inward conscientious discharge of our several duties, which human laws can never reach, the wisdom which is from above would bring about effectually, were it not for those false and atheistical accusations which are sowed about the world by diabolical spirits, who take advantage to strike in with that original sin and proneness to all evil that reigns in our nature, and which is sure to enter into confederacy with them; but of all their accusations we are entirely innocent.

11. But upon the first word you hear of our expectations of a kingdom, you rashly conclude it must needs to be a kingdom upon earth, notwithstanding all we can say that it is one in Heaven, and though you have such an experimental proof to the contrary from our professing ourselves Christians upon examination, when we know death to be the certain consequence of such a profession. But were our thoughts fixed upon a kingdom of this world, we would surely deny our religion for

the safety of our lives, and have recourse to all the methods of concealment to secure us in a whole skin against that good day we expect. But since our hopes do not fasten upon things present, the preservation of our lives is the least of our concern, because we know our murderers can cut us short but a few days; for all must die.

16. In the first place, then, it is certain we cannot justly be branded for atheists, we who worship the Creator of the universe, not with blood, libations, and incense (which we are sufficiently taught He stands in no need of); but we exalt Him to the best of our power with the rational service of prayers and praises, in all the oblations we make unto Him; believing this to be the only honour worthy of Him; not to consume the creatures which He has given us for our use, and the comfort of those that want, in the fire by sacrifice, but to approve ourselves thankful to Him, and to express this gratitude in the rational pomp of the most solemn hymns at the altar in acknowledgment of our creation, preservation, and all the blessings of variety in things and seasons; and also for the hopes of a resurrection to a life incorruptible, which we are sure to have for asking, provided we ask in faith. Who that knows anything of us will not confess this to be our way of worshipping? And who can stigmatize such worshippers for atheists? The Master Who instructed us in this kind of worship, and Who was born for this very purpose, and crucified under Pontius Pilate, procurator of Judea, in the reign of Tiberius Caesar, is Jesus Christ, Whom we know to be the Son of the true God, and therefore hold Him the second in order, and the Prophetic Spirit the third; and that we have good reason for worshipping in this subordination, I shall show hereafter. For here they look upon it as downright madness to assign to a crucified man the next place to the immutable, eternal God, Parent of all things, being entirely in the dark as to the mystery of this order; and therefore I advise you to give diligent attention while I expound it to you.

17. But first I am to caution you against those spirits, which I have already accused for practising upon you, that they do not delude and pervert you from reading and understanding what I am now proposing to your consideration; for to hold you in slavery and bondage is the prize they contend for, and sometimes by visions in sleep, sometimes by magical imposture they make sure of all such as are little concerned about their salvation. I could wish you would follow our example, who by the persuasions of the Logos have revolted from these spiritual wickednesses, and come over to the obedience of the only begotten God, through His Son Jesus Christ. We, who heretofore gave ourselves a loose to women, now strictly contain within the bounds of chastity; we, who devoted ourselves to magic arts, now consecrate ourselves entirely to the good unbegotten God; we, who loved nothing like our possessions, now produce all we have in common, and spread our whole stock before our indigent brethren; we, who were pointed with mutual hatred and

destruction, and would not so much as warm ourselves of the same fire with those of a different tribe upon the account of different institutions now since the coming of Christ co-habit and diet together, and pray for our enemies; and all our returns for evil are but the gentlest persuasives to convert those who unjustly hate us, that by living up to the same virtuous precepts of Christ they might be filled with the same comfortable hopes of obtaining the like happiness with ourselves, from that God Who is the Lord of all things.

30. As to the Son of God called Jesus, should we allow Him to be nothing more than man, yet the title of the Son of God is very justifiable upon the account of His wisdom; for is not God styled by your own writers, Father of Gods and Men? But now if we say that the Logos of God is properly the begotten of God, by a generation quite different from that of men, as I have already mentioned, yet even this I say is no more than what you might very well tolerate, considering you have your Mercury in worship under the title of the Word and Messenger of God. As to the objection of our Jesus being crucified, I say that suffering was common to all the fore-mentioned sons of Jove, but only they suffered another kind of death; so that Christ does not seem at all inferior to them upon the score of the difference of His suffering, but much superior even in this very respect of His passion, as I shall prove in the following discourse, or rather indeed have proved already; for the excellence of every one is to be judged of by the nature and end of his actions. As to His being born of a Virgin, you have your Perseus to balance that; as to His curing the lame and the paralytic, and such as were cripples from their birth, this is little more than what you say of your Aesculapius.

31. But in order to make it more plain that whatever we have declared from Christ and His preceding prophets is true and older than any of your writers, and that we desire to be believed, not because we deliver many the same things with them, but because we deliver the truth, and nothing but the truth, and that Jesus alone is properly the Son of God, as being the Logos, and First-begotten, and Power of God, and by His counsel was made man, and taught these doctrines for the conversion and restoration of mankind, before Whose coming in our flesh these same evil spirits, by their instruments, the poets, dressed up fables to represent these things as already past and over, on purpose to defeat the good designs of His coming; just such another pack of scandalous wicked lies they have at present invented to render Christians odious, for which they cannot produce one witness, nor anything like proof, as I shall presently make appear.

36. But we who are truly Christians are so far from maintaining any unjust or ungodly opinions, that exposing of infants, which is so much in practice among you, we teach to be a very wicked practice; first, because we see that such children, both girls and boys, are generally all trained up for the service of lust; for as the ancients

bred up these foundlings to feed cows, or goats, or sheep, or grasshorses, so now-a-days such boys are brought up only to be abused against nature; and accordingly you have a herd of these women and effeminate men, standing prostitute for sale in every nation; and you traffic with such kind of cattle, and take toll and custom for their wickedness, when all such monstrous practices ought to be quite and clean rooted out of the world. And besides, whoever has to do with such wicked creatures, not only defiles himself with a mixture repugnant to all the laws of religion and temperance, but it is a great chance that the sinner does not pollute himself with some of his own children or nearest relations. Some there are who prostitute their own wives and children, and others are cut publicly for pathic obscenity, and their instruments made a sacrifice to the mother of the gods. And of all the established deities among you, a painted serpent is the greatest symbol and mystery. And such actions as you commit in the face of the sun, and are creditable vices among you, as if you had not one spark of divine light left, those you charge upon us; though this charge will do no harm to us, who are entire strangers to such sins, but to the doers of them only, and to such as falsely lay them to the charge of Christians. But the ringleader and prince of evil spirits is by us called the serpent, and Satan, and false accuser, as you may easily find from our Scriptures, who together with all his host of angels, and men like himself, shall be thrust into fire, there to be tormented, world without end, as our Christ has foretold; and the reason why God has not done this already is out of mercy to such of mankind as He foresees will repent and be saved; some of which are now in being, and others as yet unborn. And from the beginning He made mankind intelligent and free creatures, fit for the choice and practice of truth and goodness, so that every sinner should be without excuse before God; for we are endued with reason, and formed for contemplation. If any one, therefore, shall disbelieve the providence of God, or shall deny His existence, notwithstanding the evidence of His world, or assert Him to be a Being delighted with wickedness, or as unactive as a stone, and that vice and virtue are nothing in themselves, and depend only upon the opinions of men; this, I say, is a consummate piece of impiety and injustice. And another reason against exposing infants is, that we are afraid they should perish for want of being taken up, and so bring us under the guilt of murder.

44. That the prophets were inspired by nothing but the Divine Wisdom of Logos, Who would forsee things at such a distance, is what I believe you yourselves will grant me; but where this Logos was to be born, hear what Micah, another prophet, says, and thus it stands: "And thou, Bethlehem, in the land of Judah, art not the least among the princes of Judah; for out of thee shall come a Governor that shall rule My people Israel." Now this Bethlehem, where Christ Jesus was born, is a certain village in Judaea, about thirty-five furlongs from Jerusalem, as you may see in the censual tables of Cyrenius, the first Prefect of Judaea; and how Christ after He

was born lived in obscurity, and how this obscurity of life was foretold likewise, we have our prophets to show, for thus they speak;_____.

46. We have been taught that Christ is the first-begotten of God, and . . . He is the Reason of which every race of man partakes. Those who lived in accordance with Reason are Christians . . . such as . . . Socrates, Heraclitus and . . . Abraham . . . those who lived without Reason were ungracious and enemies to Christ. . . . But those who lived by Reason, and those who so live now are Christians. . . .

56. Moreover, the Holy prophetic Spirit has instructed us in the doctrine of free-will by Moses, who introduces God, speaking to the new-made man in this manner: "Behold good and evil is before you; choose the good." And again, by another prophet, Isaiah, He speaks to the same effect in the person of God, the Father and Lord of the universe: "Wash ye, make you clean, put away the evil of your doings, learn to do well, judge the fatherless, and plead for the widow. Come now, and let us reason together, saith the Lord: Though your sins be as scarlet, they shall be as white as snow; though they be red like crimson, they shall be as wool. If ye be willing and obedient, ye shall eat the good of the land: But if ye refuse and rebel, the sword shall feed upon you; for the mouth of the Lord hath spoken it" (Isa. i. 16–20). And whereas it is said that the "sword shall feed upon you," and not that the disobedient shall be cut off by swords, I must tell you, by the by, that the "sword of God" is fire, which shall prey upon those who have made wickedness their choice, and therefore He says, "The sword shall feed upon you; the mouth of the Lord hath spoken it." Whereas had He spoken of a common sword which cuts off, and despatches in a moment, He would not have used the word "feeding upon," which intimates a gradual destruction.

57. When Plato therefore said "that the blame lies at his door who wills the sin, but God wills no evil," he borrowed the saying from Moses; for Moses is older than any of your Greek writers; and as to all their notions about the immortality of the soul, and punishments after death, and their divine theories, and such-like doctrines, the philosophers and poets plainly took their hints from the prophets, which they consulted and built upon, and by this means the seeds of truth seem to be scattered about the world; but it is evident they understood them not as they should do, from the manifold contradictions amongst them.

58. By maintaining, therefore, that future events have been foretold by the prophets, we do not maintain that the things foretold came to pass by any necessity, but from that divine prescience which foresees all the actions of men, without necessitating them to act. And since a just retribution of rewards and punishments is a current opinion in the world, God has been pleased to second this motion by the prophetic Spirit, the more to awaken mankind and to print a future judgment perpetually

upon their minds, and withal to show that His providence is concerned about us, and observes all our actions.

66. Since therefore we thus demonstrably prove that the things now come to pass were proclaimed by the prophets long before the events, how can we withhold from believing that the prophecies as yet unfulfilled will as verily be accomplished in their season as those we now see verified with our own eyes? For as these were once foretold and disbelieved, and yet came to pass, so the remainder will be brought to as certain an issue, in spite of ignorance and infidelity; for the very same prophets have foretold a twofold Advent of Christ, one wherein He was to come in the guise of an inglorious suffering mortal, and this is over; the other, wherein He shall come in His own form, encircled with celestial glory, and His host of angels, when He shall raise from the dead all the men that ever had a being, and shall invest the righteous with bodies incorruptible, and make the ungodly, together with these wicked spirits, feel His vengeance in fire everlasting.

68. I have a great many other prophecies in store, but I forbear, concluding what has been produced to be enough in reason for the conviction of such as have ears that will admit them to a fair hearing, and understandings prepared for truth. I can hardly persuade myself that you can take us for such romancers as those who dress up stories about the factitious progeny of Jove, mighty talkers, but able to prove nothing. For what motive could ever possibly have persuaded us to believe a crucified man to be the First-begotten of the Unbegotten God, and that He should come to be the judge of all the world, had we not met with those prophetic testimonies of Him proclaimed so long before His incarnation? Were we not eye-witnesses to the fulfilling of them? Did we not see the desolation of Judaea, and men out of all nations proselyted to the faith by His apostles, and renouncing the ancient errors they were brought up in? Did we not find the prophecies made good in ourselves, and see Christians in greater number and in greater sincerity from among the Gentiles than from the Jews and Samaritans? For all sorts of people are by the prophetic Spirit styled Gentiles; but the Jews and Samaritans stand distinguished by the name of the house of Israel and Jacob.

70. So many, therefore, and such mighty proofs as your own eyes are witnesses to cannot fail, methinks, of generating a firm and rational faith in the minds of those who are lovers of truth, and not carried away with opiniatrety and passion; but the instructors of your youth, who read them lectures out of the fables of the poets, never let them into the ground of these fictions. And that they are the work of devilcraft only, the better to delude mankind and hold them in darkness, I shall now prove. For these devilish spirits no sooner understood by the prophets that Christ was to come, and the ungodly to be punished with fire, but they trumped up that crew of Jove's sons abovesaid, imagining by this forgery to debauch the world into

an opinion, that these prophecies concerning Christ were just such another pack of lies as the fables of the poets; and these stories they divulged among the Greeks and all the Gentiles, when they learned from the prophets that these were the people that should mostly come over to the Christian faith; but not diving far enough into the sense of the prophets, they attempted to copy after them, and, like men in the dark, blundered in their imitation, as I shall now show you.

90. And so far as these things shall appear agreeable to truth and reason, so far we desire you would respect them accordingly, but if they seem trifling, despise them as trifles; however, do not proceed against the professors of them, who are people of the most inoffensive lives, as severely as against your professed enemies; for, tell you I must, that if you persist in this course of iniquity, you shall not escape the vengeance of God in the other world.

Tertullian

Editor's Introduction
Anthony Sciglitano

If Justin is generally thought to utter a giant "Yes!" to the philosophical traditions of Greco-Roman culture, Tertullian is generally thought to utter a giant
"No!" Now the story, as you have most likely realized from your reading of
Justin, is more complicated than these generalities would suggest. Justin will
be insistent that Jesus Christ is the measure of all truth, and Tertullian will be
a more sophisticated user of philosophical discourse than might be suspected
from the previous statement.

Tertullian comes from Carthage, a rather large metropolis in North Africa (where
Saint Augustine travels in Bk. III of his *Confessions*). He is known to have written elegant Latin, and is perhaps responsible for the early development of the
Church's Latin. Upon converting to Christianity, a conversion he considered
moral every bit as much as intellectual, Tertullian wanted little to do with the
legal and cultural systems of the Roman Empire. Tertullian was a more rigorous
opponent of bringing philosophical ideas into Christianity than Justin.

It is important to understand that Tertullian rarely focuses on the processes or
rigorous methods of reason that we often associate with philosophy. Instead,
he focuses on the content of particular philosophical schools, that is, *what*
they teach rather than *how* they teach one to think. It becomes clear that he
has read quite a lot of philosophy, even if he does not think these philosophers
have much to offer Christian thought and practice. Tertullian will spill much ink
contradicting the views of philosophers and also of heretics, that is, people who
claim to be Christian, but alter or distort Christian teaching. *Hairesis*, the root
word for heresy, means selection or choice. In using this term, early Christians
suggested that heretics "selected" out those aspects of the truth they found
objectionable and thus constructed their own "mottled Christianity" out of a
variety of philosophical influences.

In the selections you will read from the course, Tertullian addresses several
philosophical views and contrasts them with Christian views. He will abbrevi-
ate or symbolize the contrast between philosophy and Christian truth using the
twin cities of Athens (Philosophy) and Jerusalem (Christianity) (sometimes he
uses *Judaea*). He also contrasts what he considers *orthodox* (right views) to the
heretical teaching of Marcion. I will discuss Marcion in the following text.

We will see the opposition between philosophical views and Christian revelation running through the Tertullian readings in several ways: (1) Tertullian will
oppose Judaea or Jerusalem to Athens, that is, Christian revelation to Greek
philosophy (chapters III and VII); (2) Tertullian thinks that the Christian view
of the soul is quite different from Greek views of the soul in terms of the soul's
origin and its nature (chapters IV, V, and XXII); (3) Tertullian rejects the idea that
the body is the source of evil, and contends that the soul is more nearly the

source of human evildoing (chapter XL); (4) Against Marcion, Tertullian will argue that the Creator and the Redeemer are One God. This last point is a difficult one, and so requires some explanation of Marcion's views.

Marcion is something of a shadowy figure from the second century. We only know of his ideas through the writings of his early Christian opponents, and they are numerous! But of course it is always precarious to read someone's thought through the eyes of their enemies. So most of what I say here must be understood as probable rather than certain knowledge. As far as we can tell, Marcion was a fairly wealthy shipping magnate from Sinope who came to Rome in approximately A.D. 140. He brought with him a sizeable donation for the Roman Christian community and was welcomed there. However, he was also soon sent packing, along with his money. Why?

According to early Christian writers, Marcion thought that the God represented in the Old Testament could not possibly be the same God who is the Father of Jesus Christ in the New Testament. So, Marcion advocated eliminating the Old Testament from Christianity and preserving only the letters of Paul and parts of the Gospel of Luke. There seem to be a number of reasons he held this view, although some of this is also historically murky. One version has it that Marcion saw in the Old Testament a God of law, justice, and vengeance. He thought that this God is utterly opposed to the God of love, mercy, and *not* law that one finds in the parts of the New Testament that he approved. So, on the difficult issue of how to reconcile justice and mercy, Marcion decided to jettison justice. Our story now gets a little more complicated. I am using terms such as *Old* and *New Testament* as if Marcion found a Bible whole and entire which he then edited or cut down. This is not quite the case. The formation of the Bible as we know it took another two hundred years or so to occur. But certainly most early Christians took the Old Testament to be an authoritative source of truth, and Christian contemporaries, such as Justin Martyr, accepted the four gospels, but official lists were not yet promulgated as far as we know. In any event, Marcion's view was rejected, and Christians for the most part brought together the texts of the Old Testament with the texts of what became the New Testament.

Picking up our main story, Marcion thought that the God of Creation and the God of Israel could not be the same God as Jesus's Father. This view, of course, disconnected Jesus's Father from the act of Creation and from forming an ongoing relationship with Israel through covenants. For Marcion, the pious of Israel were actually the villains in the story because they clung to the God who created a malformed, evil world of matter. God, the Father of Jesus, on the other hand, is a God of pure Spirit who will rescue us not from our own fault, but rather from the God of Israel and Creation. This anti-creation stance has effects on how one reads, or even edits, the books of the Bible. For instance, Marcion appears to have denied a genuine human birth to Jesus. The teaching that Jesus only "seemed" to be human, and was not truly human, was called *docetism* in the early Church and was considered a heresy. The reasons for these denials are not difficult to grasp. If the material world is considered evil, it makes sense to deny that God became a part of it as the Christian teaching on Jesus states. Jesus became part of the material world by being "born of woman." So, Marcion denies this birth. In addition, the Gospels of Matthew and Luke both include genealogies that connect Jesus's human birth with the history of Israel's faithful (Abraham, Moses, Isaiah, David, etc.). This provides another reason for Marcion to deny the birth stories of the New Testament. Perhaps oddly, however, Marcion does not deny Jesus's death. He appears to have thought that his death purchased salvation from the God of Creation.

Near the beginning of his *Against Marcion*, Tertullian writes that "It is the God of the Jews whom men's souls call God" (Tertullian *Against Marcion* I.X). In contrast to Marcion, Tertullian believed there was a fundamental continuity between the Old and New Testaments. He felt that Marcion cut out whatever he didn't like from God's revealed truth, and that this could not be justified. Tertullian felt that the God of the Jews was a just God, and that Jesus did not eliminate justice when he also showed the depths of God's mercy and love. Nor did the Old Testament, according to Tertullian, lack for examples of God's love and mercy. Moreover, on Tertullian's view, the material world is a remarkable gift of the Creator, not something to be despised. As you read Tertullian, compare his views to those of Justin. Does he seem to agree with Justin on major points? Is his tone different from that of Justin? Are his emphases the same as what you find in Justin's writing?

TERTULLIAN

From *Readings in Christian Humanism*, edited by Shaw, et al. Reprinted by permission of Augsburg Fortress Publishers.

Tertullian (c. 160–230) is in many ways an ambiguous and elusive character. When he was born and when he died are not known with any degree of precision. He seems to have burst into prominence amid the controversy he loved so well and then faded out of sight. His activity as a writer seems to be confined to the quarter-century from 195–220. Tertullian was associated with the flourishing church in north Africa and is often considered to have been its first real star. His birthplace seems to have been Carthage, and off and on he was associated with that city. On the authority of Jerome it is suggested that he was a presbyter. He himself reveals the fact that he had been a pagan and was converted to Christianity; he may have been a jurist, and if so, he attained some eminence in that field as witness the citations in Justinian's *Corpus Juris Civilis*. What he did as presbyter remains shadowy, and most of what is known about him and his work emerges through his writings, of which a number of important products remain.

Tertullian has been called the creator of ecclesiastical Latin, and many, indeed most, commentators agree that this is an accurate assessment. His Latin is fluent and stylish; he seems to have had to create religious terminology in Latin because little or none had existed before. What he created became the foundation for continued discussion in Latin and came to be regarded as the proper theological vocabulary of the West. Tertullian's sentences are short and crisp and clearly influenced by the knowledge of good Latin style. The passion of his rhetoric is something that clearly distinguishes Tertullian. He loved to attack an opponent and then proceed to demolish him. His opponents were always wholly in the wrong; there seems to have been no room for compromise in his temperament. Tertullian believed himself to have been morally reborn through Christianity. Thus he defended his faith with all the passion he could muster. He hated the persecutors of Christianity violently; he seems always to have sought moral rigor. Frequently he attacks the moral laxness of his opponents. Any form of Christianity that seemed to be an ally of philosophy was Tertullian's enemy. Tertullian did not hide his feelings or prejudices; they are everywhere in his work!

From Tertullian, On Prescription Against Heretics

Chapter III

The Soul's Origin Defined Out of the Simple Words of Scripture. Would to God that no "heresies had been ever necessary, in order that they which are approved may be made manifest!" We should then never be required to try our strength in contests about the soul with philosophers, those patriarchs of heretics, as they may be fairly called. The apostle, so far back as his own time, foresaw, indeed, that philosophy would do violent injury to the truth. This admonition *about false philosophy* he was induced to offer after he had been at Athens, had become acquainted with that *loquacious* city, and had there had a taste of its huckstering wiseacres and talkers. In like manner is the treatment of the soul according to the sophistical doctrines of men which "mix their wine with water." Some of them deny the immortality of the soul; others affirm that it is immortal, and something more. Some raise disputes about its substance; others about its form; others, again, respecting each of its several faculties. One school of philosophers derives its state from various sources, while another ascribes its departure to different destinations. *The various schools reflect the character of their masters,* according as they have received their impressions from the dignity of Plato, or the vigour of Zeno, or the equanimity of Aristotle, or the stupidity of Epicurus, or the sadness of Heraclitus, or the madness of Empedocles. The fault, I suppose, of the divine doctrine lies in its springing from Judaea rather than from Greece. Christ made a mistake, too, in sending forth fishermen to preach, rather than the sophist. Whatever noxious vapours, accordingly, exhaled from philosophy, obscure the clear and wholesome atmosphere of truth, it will be for Christians to clear away, both by shattering to pieces the arguments which are drawn from the principles of things—I mean those of the philosophers—and by opposing to them the maxims of heavenly wisdom—that is, such as are revealed by the Lord; in order that both the pitfalls wherewith philosophy captivates the heathen may be removed, and the means employed by heresy to shake the faith of Christians may be repressed. We have already decided one point in our controversy with Hermogenes, as we said at the beginning of this treatise, when we claimed the soul to be formed by the breathing of God, and not out of matter. We relied even there on the clear direction of the inspired statement which informs us how that "the lord God breathed on man's face the breath of life, so that man became a living soul"—by that inspiration of God, of course. On this point, therefore, nothing further need be investigated or advanced by us. It has its own treatise, and its own heretic. I shall regard it as my introduction to the other branches of the subject.

Chapter IV

In Opposition to Plato, the Soul Was Created and Originated at Birth

After seeding the origin of the soul, its condition or state comes up next. For when we acknowledge that the soul originates in the breath of God, it follows that we attribute a beginning to it. This Plato, indeed, refuses to assign to it, for he will have the soul to be unborn and unmade. We, however, from the very fact of its having had a beginning, as well as from the nature thereof, teach that it had both birth and creation. And when we ascribe both birth and creation to it, we have made no mistake: for being *born*, indeed, is one thing, and being made is another,—the former being the term which is best suited to living beings. When distinctions, however, have places and times of their own, they occasionally possess also reciprocity of application among themselves. Thus, the being made admits of being taken in the sense of being brought forth; inasmuch as everything which receives *being* or *existence*, in any way whatever, is in fact generated. For the maker may really be called the parent of the thing that is made: in this sense Plato also uses the phraseology. So far, therefore, as concerns our belief in the souls being made or born, the opinion of the philosopher is overthrown by the authority of prophecy even.

Chapter V
Probable View of the Stoics, that the Soul Has a Corporeal Nature

Suppose one summons a Fubulus to his assistance, and a Critolaus, and a Zenocrates, and on this occasion Plato's friend Aristotle. They may very possibly hold themselves ready for stripping the soul of its corporeity, unless they happen to see other philosophers opposed to them in their purpose—and this, too, in greater numbers—asserting for the soul a corporeal nature. Now I am not referring merely to those who mould the soul out of manifest bodily substances, as Hipparchus and Heraclitus [do] out of fire; as Hippon and Thales [do] out of water; as Empedocles and Critias [do] out of blood; as Epicurus [does] out of atoms, since even atoms by their coherence form corporeal masses; as Cricolaus and his Peripatetics [do] out of certain indescribable *quintessence*, if that may be called a body which rather includes and embraces bodily substances—but I call on the Stoics also to help me, who, while declaring almost in our own terms that the soul is a spiritual essence (inasmuch as breath and spirit are in their nature very near akin to each other), will yet have no difficulty in persuading (us) that the soul is a corporeal substance. Indeed, Zeno, defining the soul to be a spirit generated with [the body], constructs his argument in this way: That substance which by its departure causes the living being to die is a corporeal one. Now it is by the departure of the spirit, which is generated with [the body], that the living being dies; therefore the spirit which is generated with [the body] is a corporeal substance. But this spirit which is generated with [the body] is the soul: it follows, then, that the soul is a corporeal substance. Cleanthes, too, will have it that family likeness passes from parents to their children not merely in bodily features, but in characteristics of the soul, as if it were out of a mirror of a [a man's] manners, and faculties, and affections, that bodily likeness and unlikeness are caught and reflected by the soul also. It is therefore as being corporeal that it is susceptible of likeness and unlikeness. Again, there is nothing in common between things corporeal and things incorporeal as to their susceptibility. But the soul certainly sympathizes with the body, and shares in its pain, whenever it is injured by bruises, and wounds, and sores: the body, too, suffers with the soul, and is united with it (whenever it is afflicted with anxiety, distress, or love) in the loss of vigour which its companion sustains, whose shame and fear it testifies by its own blushes and paleness. The soul, therefore, is [proved to be] corporeal from this inter-communion of susceptibility. Chrysippus also joins hands in fellowship with Cleanthes, when he lays it down that it is not at all possible for things which are endued with body to be separated from things which have not body; because they have no such relation as mutual contact or coherence. Accordingly Lucretius says:

"Tangere enim et tangi nisi corpus nulla potest res."

"For nothing but body is capable of touching or of being touched."

(Such severance, however, is quite natural between the soul and the body); for when the body is deserted by the soul, it is overcome by death. The soul, therefore, is endued with a body; for if it were not corporeal, it could not desert the body.

Chapter VII
Pagan Philosophy the Parent of Heresies. The Connection Between Deflections from Christian Faith and the Old Systems of Pagan Philosophy

These are "the doctrines" of men and "of demons" produced for itching ears of the spirit of this world's wisdom: this the Lord called "foolishness," and "chose the foolish things of the world" to confound even philosophy itself. For [philosophy] it is which is the material of the world's wisdom, the rash interpreter of the nature and the dispensation of God. Indeed heresies are themselves instigated by philosophy. From this source come the Aeons, and I know not what infinite forms, and the trinity of man in the system of Valentinus, who was of Plato's school. From the same source came Marcion's better god, with all his tranquillity; he came of the Stoics. Then, again, the opinion that the soul dies is held by the Epicureans; while the denial of the restoration of the body is taken from the aggregate school of all the philosophers; also, when matter is made equal to God, then you have the teaching of Zeno; and when any doctrine is alleged touching a god of fire, then Heraclitus comes in. The same subject-matter is discussed over and over again by the heretics and the philosophers; the same arguments are involved. Whence comes evil? Why is it permitted? What is the origin of man? and in what way does he come? Besides the question which Valentinus has very lately proposed—Whence comes God? Which he settles with the answer: From *enthymesis* and *ectroma.* Unhappy Aristotle! who invented for these men dialectics, the art of building up and pulling down; an art so evasive in its propositions, so farfetched in its conjectures, so harsh in its arguments, so productive of contentions—embarrassing even to itself, retracting everything, and really treating of nothing! Whence spring those "fables and endless genealogies," and "unprofitable questions," and "words which spread like a cancer?" From all these, when the apostle would restrain us, he expressly names *philosophy* as that which he would have us be on our guard against. Writing to the Colossians, he says "See that no one beguile you through philosophy and vain deceit, after the tradition of men, and contrary to the wisdom of the Holy Ghost." He had been at Athens, and had in his interview [with its philosophers] become acquainted with that human wisdom which pretends to know the truth, whilst it only corrupts it, and is itself divided into its own manifold heresies, by the variety of its mutually repugnant sects. What indeed has Athens to do with Jerusalem? What concord is there between the Academy and the Church? What between heretics and Christians? Our instruction comes from "the porch of Solomon," who had himself taught that "the Lord should be sought in simplicity of heart." Away with all attempts to produce a mottled Christianity of Stoic, Platonic, and dialectic composition! We wane no curious disputation after possessing Christ Jesus, no inquisition after enjoying the gospel! With our faith, we desire no further belief. For this is our palmary faith, that there is nothing which we ought to believe besides.

Chapter XXII
Recapitulation, Definition of the Soul

Hermogenes has already heard from us what are the other natural faculties of the soul, as well as their vindication and proof; whence it may be seen that the soul is rather the offspring of God than of matter. The names of these faculties shall here be simply repeated, that they may not seem to be forgotten and passed out of sight. We have assigned, then, to the soul both that freedom of the will which we just now mentioned, and its dominion over the works of nature, and its occasional gift of divination, independently of that endowment of prophecy which accrues to it expressly from the grace of God. We shall therefore now quit this subject of the soul's disposition, in order to set out fully in order its various qualities. The soul, then, we define to be sprung from the breath of God, immortal, possessing in its own nature, developing its power in various ways, free in its determinations, subject to the changes of accident, in its faculties mutable, rational, supreme, endued out of one [archetypal soul]. It remains for us now to consider how it is developed out of this one original source; in other words, whence, and when, and how it is produced.

Chapter XL
The Body of Man Only Ancillary to the Soul in the Commission of Evil

Every soul, then, by reason of its birth, has its nature in Adam until it is born again in Christ; moreover, it is unclean all the while that it remains without this regeneration; and because unclean, it is actively sinful, and suffuses even the flesh (by reason of their conjunction) with its own shame. Now although the flesh is sinful, and we are forbidden to walk in accordance with it, and its works are condemned as lusting against the spirit, and men on its account are censured as carnal, yet the flesh has not such ignominy on its own account. For it is not of itself that it thinks anything or feels anything for the purpose of advising or commanding sin. How should it, indeed? It is only a ministering thing, and its ministration is not like that of a servant or familiar friend—animated and human beings; but rather that of a vessel, or something of that kind: it is body, not soul. Now a cup may minister to a thirsty man; and yet, if the thirsty man will not apply the cup to his mouth, the cup will yield no ministering service. Therefore the *differentia*, or distinguishing property, of man by no means lies in his earthy element; nor is the flesh of the human person, as being some faculty of his soul, and a personal quality; but it is a thing of quite a different substance and different condition, although annexed to the soul as a chattel or as an instrument for the offices of life. Accordingly the flesh is blamed in the Scriptures, because nothing is done by the soul without the flesh in operations of concupiscence, appetite, drunkenness, cruelty, idolatry, and other works of the flesh,—operations, I mean, which are not confined to sensations, but result in effects. The emotions of sin, indeed, when not resulting in effects, are usually imputed to the soul: "Whosoever looketh on a woman to lust after, hath already in his heart committed adultery with her." But what has the flesh alone, without the soul, ever done in operations of virtue, righteousness, endurance, or chastity? What absurdity, however, it is to attribute sin and crime to that substance to which you do not assign any good actions or character of its own! Now the party which aids in the commission of a crime is brought to trial, only in such a way that the principal offender who actually committed the crime may bear the weight of the penalty, although the abettor too does not escape indictment. Greater is the odium which falls on the principal, when his officials are punished through his fault. He is beaten with mote stripes who instigates and orders the crime, whilst at the same time he who obeys such an evil command is not acquitted.

Chapter XLI

Notwithstanding the Depravity of Man's Soul by Original Sin, There Is Yet Left a Basis Whereon Divine Grace Can Work for Its Recovery by Spiritual Regeneration.

There is, then, besides the evil which supervenes on the soul from the intervention of the evil spirit, an antecedent, and in a certain sense natural, evil which arises from its corrupt origin. For, as we have said before, the corruption of our nature is another nature having a god and father of its own, namely the author of [that] corruption. Still there is a portion of good in the soul, of that original, divine, and genuine good, which is its proper nature. For that which is derived from God is rather obscured than extinguished. It can be obscured, indeed, because it is not God; extinguished, however, it cannot be, because it comes from God. As therefore light, when intercepted by an opaque body, still remains, although it is not apparent, by reason of the interposition of so dense a body; so likewise the good in the soul, being weighed down by the evil, is, owing to the obscuring character thereof, either not seen at all, its light being wholly hidden, or else only a stray beam is there visible where it struggles through by an accidental outlet. Thus some men are very bad, and some very good; but yet the souls of all form but one genus: even in the worst there is something good, and in the best there is something bad. For God alone is without sin; and the only man without sin is

Christ, since Christ is also God. Thus the divinity of the soul bursts forth in prophetic forecasts in consequence of its primeval good; and being conscious of its origin, it bears testimony to God (its author) in exclamations such as: *Good God! God knows! Good-bye!* Just as no soul is without sin, so neither is any soul without seeds of good.

Therefore, when the soul embraces the faith, being renewed in its second birth by water and the power from above, then the veil of its former corruption being taken away, it beholds the light in all its brightness. It is also taken up (in its second birth) by the Holy Spirit, just as in its first birth it is embraced by the unholy spirit. The flesh follows the soul now wedded to the Spirit, as a part of the bridal portion—no longer the servant of the soul, but of the Spirit. O happy marriage, if in it there is committed no violation of the nuptial vow.

From Tertullian, Against Praxeas

Chapter IV

God's Honour in the Incarnation of His Son
Vindicated, Marcion's Disparagement of
Human Flesh Inconsistent as Well as Impious.
Christ Has Cleansed the Flesh. The Foolishness
of God Is Most Wise.

Since, therefore, you do not reject the assumption of a body as impossible or as hazardous to the character of God, it remains for you to repudiate and censure it as unworthy of Him. Come now, beginning from the nativity itself, declaim against the uncleanness of the generative elements within the womb, the filthy concretion of fluid and blood, of the growth of the flesh for nine months long out of that very mire. Describe the womb as it enlarges from day to day,—heavy, troublesome, restless even in sleep, changeful in its feelings of dislike and desire. Inveigh now likewise against the shame itself of a woman in travail, which, however, ought rather to be honoured in consideration of that peril, or to be held sacred in respect of [the mystery of] nature. Of course you are horrified also at the infant, which is shed into life with the embarrassments which accompany it from the womb; you likewise, of course, loathe it even after it is washed, when it is dressed out in its swaddling-clothes, graced with repeated anointing, smiled on with nurse's fawns. This reverend course of nature, you, O Marcion, [are pleased to] spit upon; and yet, in what way were you born? You detest a human being at his birth; then after what fashion do you love anybody? Yourself, of course, you had no love of, when you departed from the Church and the faith of Christ. But never mind, if you are not on good terms with yourself or even if you were born in a way different from other people. Christ, at any rate, has loved even that man who was condensed in his mother's womb amidst all its uncleannesses, even that man who was brought into life out of the said womb, even that man who was nursed amidst the nurse's simpers. For his sake He came down [from heaven], for his sake He preached, for his sake "He humbled Himself even unto death—the death of the cross." He loved, of course, the being whom He redeemed at so great a cost. If Christ is the Creator's *Son*, it was with justice that He loved His own [creature]; if He comes from another god, His love was excessive, since He redeemed a being who belonged to another. Well, then, loving man He loved his nativity also, and his flesh as well. Nothing can be loved apart from that through which whatever exists has its existence. Either take away nativity, and then show us *your* man; or else withdraw the flesh, and then present to our view the being whom God has redeemed—since it is these very conditions which constitute the man whom God has redeemed. And are *you* for turning these conditions into occasions of blushing to the very creature whom He has redeemed, [censuring them], too, as unworthy of Him who certainly would not have redeemed them had He not loved them? Our birth He reforms from death by a second birth from heaven; our flesh He restores from every harassing malady; when leprous, He cleanses it of the stain; when blind, He rekindles its light; when palsied, He renews its strength; when possessed with devils, He exorcises it; when dead, He reanimates it,—then shall *we* blush to own it? If, to be sure, He had chosen to be born of a mere animal, and were to preach the kingdom of heaven invested with the body of a beast either wild or tame, your censure (I imagine) would have instantly met Him with this demurrer: "This is disgraceful for God, and this is unworthy of the Son of God, and simply foolish." For no other reason than because one thus judges. It is of course, foolish, if we are to judge God by our own conceptions. But, Marcion, consider well this Scripture, if indeed you have not erased it: "God hath chosen the foolish things of the world, to confound the wise." Now what are those foolish things? Are they the conversion of men to the worship of the true God, the rejection of error, the whole training in righteousness, chastity, mercy, patience, and innocence? These things certainly are not "foolish." Inquire again, then, of what things he spoke, and when you imagine that you have discovered what they are will you find anything to be so "foolish" as believing in a God that has been born, and that of a virgin, and of a fleshly nature too, who wallowed in all the before-mentioned humiliations of nature? But someone may say, "These are not the foolish things; they must be other things which God has chosen to confound the wisdom of the world." And yet, according to the world's wisdom, it is more easy to believe that Jupiter became a bull or a swan, if we listen to Marcion, than that Christ really became a man.

Chapter V

Christ Truly Lived and Died in Human Flesh. Incidents of His Human Life on Earth, and Refutation of Marcion's Docetic Parody of the Same.

There are, to be sure, other things also quite as foolish [as the birth of Christ], which have reference to the humiliations and sufferings of God. Or else, let them call a crucified

God "wisdom." But Marcion will apply the knife to this *doctrine* also, and even with greater reason. For which is more unworthy of God, which is more likely to raise a blush of shame that *God* should be born, or that He should die? that He should bear the flesh, or the cross? be circumcised, or be crucified? be cradled, or be coffined? be laid in a manger, or in a tomb? *Talk of "wisdom!"* You will show more of *that* if you refuse to believe this also. But, after all, you will not be "wise" unless you become a "fool" to the world, by believing "the foolish things of God." Have you, then, cut away all sufferings from Christ, on the ground that, as a mere phantom, He was incapable of experiencing them? We have said above that He might possibly have undergone the unreal mockeries of an imaginary birth and infancy. But answer me at once, you that murder truth: Was not God really crucified? And, having been really crucified, did He not really die? And, having indeed really died, did He not really rise again? Falsely did Paul "determine to know nothing amongst us but Jesus and Him crucified." Falsely has he impressed upon us that He was buried; falsely inculcated that He rose again. False, therefore, is our faith also. And all that we hope for from Christ will be a phantom. O thou most infamous of men, who aquitest of all guilt the murderers of God! For nothing did Christ suffer from them, if He really suffered nothing at all. Spare the whole world's one only hope, thou who are destroying the indispensable dishonour of our faith. Whatsoever is unworthy of God, is of gain to me. I am safe, if I am not ashamed of my Lord. "Whosoever," says He, "shall be ashamed of me, of him will I also be ashamed." Other matters for shame find I none which can prove me to be shameless in good sense, and foolish in a happy one, by my own contempt of shame. The Son of God was crucified; I am not ashamed because men must needs be ashamed *of it*. And the Son of God died; it is by all means to be believed, because it is absurd. And He was buried, and rose again; the fact is certain, because it is impossible. But how will all this be true in Him, if He was not Himself true—if He really had not in Himself that which might be crucified, might die, might be buried, and might rise again? *I mean* this flesh suffused with blood, built up with bones, interwoven with nerves, entwined with veins, *a flesh* which knew how to be born, and how to die, human without doubt, as born of a human being. It will therefore be mortal in Christ, because Christ is man and the Son of man. Else why is Christ man and the Son of man, if he has nothing of man, and nothing from man? Unless it be either that man is anything else than flesh, or man's flesh comes from any other source than man, or Mary is anything else than a human being, or Marcion's man is *as* Marcion's god. Otherwise Christ could not be described as being man without flesh, nor the Son of man without any human parent; just as He is not God without the Spirit of God, nor the Son of God without having God for His father. Thus the nature of the two substances displayed Him as man and God—in one respect born, in the other unborn, in one respect fleshly, in the other spiritual; in one sense weak, in the other exceeding strong; in one sense dying, in the other living. This property of the two states—the divine and the human—is distinctly asserted with equal truth of both natures alike, with the same belief both in respect of the spirit and of the flesh. The powers of the Spirit, proved Him to be God, His sufferings attested the flesh of man. If His powers were not without the Spirit in like manner, were not His sufferings without the flesh. If His flesh with its sufferings was fictitious, for the same reason was the Spirit false with all its powers. Wherefore halve Christ with a lie? He was wholly the truth. Believe me, He chose rather to be born, than in any part to pretend—and that indeed to His own detriment—that He was bearing about a flesh hardened without bones, solid without muscles, bloody without blood, clothed without the tunic *of skin,* hungry without appetite, eating without teeth, speaking without a tongue, so that His word was a phantom to the ears through an imaginary voice. A phantom, too, it was of course after the resurrection, when, showing His hands and His feet for the disciple to examine, He said, "Behold and see that it is I myself, for a spirit hath not flesh and bones, as ye see me have"; without doubt, hands, and feet, and bones are not what a spirit possesses, but only the flesh. How do you interpret this statement, Marcion, you who tell us that Jesus comes only from the most excellent God, who is both simple and good? See how He *rather* cheats, and deceives, and juggles the eyes of all, and the senses of all, as well as their access to and contact with Him! You ought rather to have brought Christ down, not from heaven, but from some troop of mountebanks, not as God besides man, but simply as a man, a magician; not as the High Priest of our salvation, but as the conjurer in a show; not as the raiser of the dead, but as the misleader of the living,—except that, if He were a magician, He must have had a nativity!

THE CREEDS

Creeds such as the Apostles' Creed and the Nicene Creed can be described as terse summaries of the essentials of Christian belief. It is known that such summaries of belief existed in New Testament times. It is also most likely that there was no fixed wording for such summaries until the middle of the second century. Early references to what may be described as creeds emphasize an oral tradition known as the "rule of faith." The earliest use of creeds by Christians is recorded in connection with baptism, where they served as interrogatory statements of faith. What began as interrogatory statements about the faith eventually became declaratory statements used to instruct those preparing for baptism. From the surviving evidence it does not seem that the creeds originated as a defense of the faith, though they did indeed come to serve that purpose. From early Christian times to the present these creeds have served as statements of what it is essential that a Christian must believe. For many Christians the recital of the creed has become part of the Eucharistic liturgy.

The Apostles' Creed is so-called because Rufinus, in the early, fifth century, recorded the tradition that the twelve apostles around the time of Pentecost composed a uniform statement of belief which all would teach as they went about their missionary work. A later account of the composition of the Apostles' Creed embroidered on the account furnished by Rufinus by adding the point that each apostle contributed one of the twelve clauses. This account of the composition of the Apostles' Creed and the formula that had been preserved were not questioned until the fifteenth century when doubts were raised at the church council held at Ferrara-Florence in 1438–39. Soon after the Council it was demonstrated that the wording of the Apostles' Creed could not have been apostolic in origin. It was agreed, however, that the Apostles' Creed did represent the teaching of the apostles. In the form in which it has survived to the present day, the wording of the Apostles' Creed is no older than the eighth century.

The Nicene Creed came into being as part of an effort to combat heresy in the early Christian church. In the fourth century the Arian heresy, involving the relationship of the Father and the Son in the Trinity, threatened to split the church irreparably. Consequently the Roman emperor Constantine, in an effort to pacify the warring factions, called the first Ecumenical Council at Nicea in 325. The council promulgated a creed meant to exclude Arianism, although the formula arrived at, the insertion of the key word *homoousios* did not settle the controversy. It was only after the Arians were subdued that a universally acceptable formula was set forth. This formula, or statement of the creed, is referred to as the Nicene Creed and was approved and issued by the second Ecumenical Council at Constantinople in 381.

Apostles' Creed

I believe in God the Father Almighty, creator of heaven and earth.

I believe in Jesus Christ, His only Son, our Lord. He was conceived by the power of the Holy Spirit, and born of the virgin Mary. He suffered under Pontius Pilate, was crucified, died, and was buried.

He descended into hell. On the third day he rose again.

He ascended into heaven, and is seated at the right hand of the Father. He will come again to judge the living and the dead.

I believe in the Holy Spirit, the holy catholic Church, the communion of saints, the forgiveness of sins, the resurrection of the body, and the life everlasting. Amen.

Nicene Creed

We believe in one God, the Father, the Almighty, maker of heaven and earth,
of all that is, seen and unseen.
We believe in one Lord, Jesus Christ, the only Son of God, eternally begotten of the
Father, God from God, Light from Light, true God from true God,
begotten, not made, of one Being with the Father. Through him all
things were made. For us and for our salvation he came down from heaven;
by the power of the Holy Spirit he became incarnate from the Virgin Mary,
and was made man.
For our sake he was crucified under Pontius Pilate; he suffered death and was buried.
On the third day he rose again in accordance with the Scriptures;
he ascended into heaven and is seated at the right hand of the Father.
He will come again in glory to judge the living
and the dead, and his kingdom will have no end.
We believe in the Holy Spirit, the Lord, the giver of life, who proceeds from
the Father and the Son With the Father and the Son he is worshiped
and glorified. He has spoken through the prophets. We believe in one
holy catholic and apostolic Church. We acknowledge one Baptism
for the forgiveness of sins.
We look for the resurrection of the dead, and the life of the world to come. Amen.

B
MEDIEVAL PERSPECTIVES

Saint Thomas Aquinas

Introduction

Ki Joo Choi and Anthony Sciglitano

Thomas Aquinas was born in Roccasecca in the Kingdom of Naples in A.D. 1225 and died there in A.D. 1274. He is often considered the first among the great medieval Christian thinkers. He, along with Augustine, is referred to in Catholicism as a *Doctor of the Church,* a title given to those whose teachings and writings are regarded as highly respected. Despite his family's disapproval, Thomas joined the Dominican religious order, studied theology at the University of Paris (the Ivy League of its time), and then was given the opportunity to teach theology there.

Thomas is most well-known for his magisterial *Summa Theologica*, completed in A.D. 1274. As the "summary of theology" it represents Thomas's most systematic articulation of Christian belief and practice and was intended as a textbook or a kind of manual for students studying theology. The *Summa contra Gentiles*, completed in A.D. 1264, was written before the *Summa Theologica*, shortly after Thomas left the University of Paris for Naples and Umbria, Italy.

The title *Summa contra Gentiles* ("summary contrary to the gentiles") suggests that Thomas rejects the validity of non-revelatory (or, for the sake of simplicity, non-biblical) knowledge of God. Thomas, however, is in fact emphasizing the compatibility of knowledge of God known through biblical revelation *and* natural reason.

As you read the required text for this week, pay close attention to Thomas's rationale for the possibility of knowing God through the light of natural reason. This rationale is offered at the beginning of the text, in which the notion of truth (Truth!) as the final or ultimate end (or *telos* [in Greek]) of the universe plays a central part. Then as you read on, pay close attention to the role human sense experience plays in the work of natural reason with respect to apprehending truth, specifically the truth of God's existence and his nature.

Although Thomas makes clear that there is "natural, rational" knowledge of God, note that Thomas is not willing to say that knowledge of God as divinely revealed is irrelevant. Far from it. Pay particular attention to the reasons Thomas provides for the abiding relevance of divine revelation.

Note particularly that Thomas thinks that natural reason can only go so far in discerning the truths about God. Yet, Thomas is resolute in his stance that it is appropriate for us to use natural reason to attempt to discern these truths, even if some of these truths may be beyond the capacities of human reason. Try to discern why he thinks so. Moreover, he claims that it is reasonable to believe those truths about God that we cannot ultimately know through natural reason. Again, try to understand why he thinks this is reasonable.

At the end of the text, Thomas returns to the notion of the deep relatedness of divine revelation and the truths knowable through natural reason. What are his concluding reasons, and how do they reflect and build upon the reasons provided earlier in the text?

Finally, as you go through the text and consider the questions that have just been delineated, consider Thomas's conception of human knowing or nature of knowledge, specifically with respect to truth. Thomas clearly believes that a true understanding of the world is possible. But how do we gain such understanding? What is Thomas's proposal? Is truthful knowledge of the world—us and God—possible through the use of mere human, natural reason? Are not scripture and divine revelation also critical for Thomas? If so, then what is the implication of this for the nature of knowledge, for the nature of how we know truth, or for the form of human knowing? Is truthful knowledge a function of *a kind of* inductive reasoning? Or can truthful knowledge be attained through abstract deduction? How does Thomas's approach compare to that of Ibn Rushd? To that of Anselm? Maimonides?

You also have included in your readings a selection from Thomas's *Summa Theologica Part I, Question 1, Articles 1–2 (ST 1.1.1–2)*. To read this selection, you must first know something about the form of Thomas's work here. Thomas's *Summa Theologica* is similar to the form that a typical disputation or argument would take in the medieval university. Thomas formulates a question or thesis, gives answers to the questions that *are not* Thomas's answers, cites an authority that contradicts the original answers, and then makes his own argument regarding the original question. Finally, he responds directly to the original answers to the question, also titled objections. So, there are five parts to each "article":

1. Thesis or Question (i.e., Whether it can be proven that God exists);

2. Objections to the Thesis (i.e., it cannot be proven that God exists; these are indicated by the numbers in bold);

3. A position contrary to the Objections is asserted, but not yet argued (i.e., a quote from Saint Augustine to the effect that the existence of God can be proven; this position is indicated by the bold "On the contrary");

4. Thomas's own argument of the Thesis (this argument is indicated by the bold "I answer");

5. Thomas's demonstrative or argumentative responses to the Objections (these are indicated by the bold "Reply to 1, Reply to 2").

What is interesting about this form of argument is its rigor and its forthrightness. Objections to one's own position are put forth clearly and require a direct response. In other words, Thomas does not believe it is acceptable to ignore the reasoning or views of others when engaging in philosophical or theological discourse. Of course, this is a demanding way to think that rejects shortcuts and opts for careful thought. You might run an experiment by reading an editorial in a contemporary newspaper and asking whether the argument provided there includes the five elements of a Thomistic article. Does the author state her thesis? Does she do justice to the position of the opposition? Does she provide her own, full answer to the question? Does she respond directly to the contrary position? You might also use this as a criterion for your own arguments in your papers for this class.

The two questions you will read here ask whether theology is necessary and whether theology is a form of knowledge (*scientia*). What do you think of Thomas's view that theology is a form of knowledge? Does this agree with what you generally think about faith and religious belief, or is his view surprising? Do you find it compelling? Why or why not? Does Thomas's answer to this question suggest anything about the study of theology in a university?

SUMMA CONTRA GENTILES
Book 1, Chapters 1–8

Chapter 1

The Office of the Wise Man

"My mouth shall meditate truth, and my lips shall hate impiety" (Prov. 8:7).

[1] The usage of the multitude, which according to the Philosopher is to be followed in giving names to things,[1] has commonly held that they are to be called *wise* who order things rightly and govern them well. Hence, among other things that men have conceived about the wise man, the Philosopher includes the notion that "it belongs to the wise man to order."[2] Now, the rule of government and order for all things directed to an end must be taken from the end. For, since the end of each thing is its good, a thing is then best disposed when it is fittingly ordered to its end. And so we see among the arts that one functions as the governor and the ruler of another because it controls its end. Thus, the art of medicine rules and orders the art of the chemist because health, with which medicine is concerned, is the end of all the medications prepared by the art of the chemist. A similar situation obtains in the art of ship navigation in relation to shipbuilding, and in the military art with respect to the equestrian art and the equipment of war. The arts that rule other arts are called architectonic, as being the ruling arts. That is why the artisans devoted to these arts, who are called master artisans, appropriate to themselves the name of wise men. But, since these artisans are concerned, in each case, with the ends of certain particular things, they do not reach to the universal end of all things. They are therefore said to be wise with respect to this or that thing; in which sense it is said that "as a wise architect, I have laid the foundation" (I Cor. 3:10). The name of the absolutely wise man, however, is reserved for him whose consideration is directed to the end of the universe, which is also the origin of the universe. That is why, according to the Philosopher, it belongs to the wise man to consider the highest causes.[3]

---

1   Aristotle, *Topics*, II, 1 (102a 30).
2   Aristotle, *Metaphysics*, I, 2 (982a 18).
3   Aristotle, *Metaphysics*, I, 1 (981b 28).

[**2**] Now, the end of each thing is that which is intended by its first author or mover. But the first author and mover of the universe is an intellect, as will be later shown.[4] The ultimate end of the universe must, therefore, be the good of an intellect. This good is truth. Truth must consequently be the ultimate end of the whole universe, and the consideration of the wise man aims principally at truth. So it is that, according to His own statement, divine Wisdom testifies that He has assumed flesh and come into the world in order to make the truth known: "For this was I born, and for this came I into the world, that I should give testimony to the truth" (John 18:37). The Philosopher himself establishes that first philosophy is the science of truth, not of any truth, but of that truth which is the origin of all truth, namely, which belongs to the first principle whereby all things are. The truth belonging to such a principle is, clearly, the source of all truth; for things have the same disposition in truth as in being. [5]

[3] It belongs to one and the same science, however, both to pursue one of two contraries and to oppose the other. Medicine, for example, seeks to effect health and to eliminate illness. Hence, just as it belongs to the wise man to meditate especially on the truth belonging to first principle and to teach it to others, so it belongs to him to refute the opposing falsehood.

[4] Appropriately, therefore, is the twofold office of the wise man shown from the mouth of Wisdom in our opening words: to meditate and speak forth of the divine truth, which is truth in person (Wisdom touches on this in the words *my mouth shall meditate truth*), and to refute the opposing error (which Wisdom touches on in the words *and my lips shall hate impiety*). By *impiety* is here meant falsehood against the divine truth. This falsehood is contrary to religion, which is likewise named *piety*. Hence, the falsehood contrary to it is called *impiety*.[6]

Chapter 2

The Author's Intention in The Present Work

[1] Among all human pursuits, the pursuit of wisdom is more perfect, more noble, more useful, and more full of joy.

It is more perfect because, in so far as a man gives himself to the pursuit of wisdom, so far does he even now have some share in true beatitude. And so a wise man has said: "Blessed is the man that shall continue in wisdom" (Ecclus. 14:22).

It is more noble because through this pursuit man especially approaches to a likeness to God Who "made all things in wisdom" (Ps. 103:24). And since likeness is the cause of

---

4   See also *SCG*, II, ch. 24

5   Aristotle, *Metaphysics*, Ia, 1. (993b 30).

6   In the present chapter, I have changed *wickedness* in the Douay text to *impiety*, since this is demanded by the sense.

love, the pursuit of wisdom especially joins man to God in friendship. That is why it is said of wisdom that "she is an infinite treasure to men! which they that use become the friends of God" (Wis. 7:14).

It is more useful because through wisdom we arrive at the kingdom of immortality. For "the desire of wisdom bringeth to the everlasting kingdom" (Wis. 6:21).

It is more full of joy because "her conversation hath no bitterness, nor her company any tediousness, but joy and gladness" (Wis. 7:16).

[2] And so, in the name of the divine Mercy, I have the confidence to embark upon the work of a wise man, even though this may surpass my powers, and I have set myself the task of making known, as far as my limited powers will allow, the truth that the Catholic faith professes, and of setting aside the errors that are opposed to it. To use the words of Hilary: "I am aware that I owe this to God as the chief duty of my life, that my every word and sense may speak of Him."[7]

[3] To proceed against individual errors, however, is a difficult business, and this for two reasons. In the first place, it is difficult because the sacrilegious remarks of individual men who have erred are not so well known to us so that we may use what they say as the basis of proceeding to a refutation of their errors. This is, indeed, the method that the ancient Doctors of the Church used in the refutation of the errors of the Gentiles. For they could know the positions taken by the Gentiles since they themselves had been Gentiles, or at least had lived among the Gentiles and had been instructed in their teaching. In the second place, it is difficult because some of them, such as the Mohammedans and the pagans, do not agree with us in accepting the authority of any Scripture, by which they may be convinced of their error. Thus, against the Jews we are able to argue by means of the Old Testament, while against heretics we are able to argue by means of the New Testament. But the Mohammedans and the pagans accept neither the one nor the other. We must, therefore, have recourse to the natural reason, to which all men are forced to give their assent. However, it is true, in divine matters the natural reason has its failings.

[4] Now, while we are investigating some given truth, we shall also show what errors are set aside by it; and we shall likewise show how the truth that we come to know by demonstration is in accord with the Christian religion.

---

7   St. Hilary, *De Trinitate*, I, 37 (*PL*, 10, 48).

Chapter 3

On the Way in Which Divine Truth Is to Be Made Known

[1] The way of making truth known is not always the same, and, as the Philosopher has very well said, "it belongs to an educated man to seek such certitude in each thing as the nature of that thing allows."[8] The remark is also introduced by Boethius.[9] But, since such is the case, we must first show what way is open to us in order that we may make known the truth which is our object.

[2] There is a twofold mode of truth in what we profess about God. Some truths about God exceed all the ability of the human reason. Such is the truth that God is triune. But there are some truths which the natural reason also is able to reach. Such are that God exists, that He is one, and the like. In fact, such truths about God have been proved demonstratively by the philosophers, guided by the light of the natural reason.

[3] That there are certain truths about God that totally surpass man's ability appears with the greatest evidence. Since, indeed, the principle of all knowledge that the reason perceives about some thing is the understanding of the very substance of that being (for according to Aristotle "what a thing is" is the principle of demonstration),[10] it is necessary that the way in which we understand the substance of a thing determines the way in which we know what belongs to it. Hence, if the human intellect comprehends the substance of some thing, for example, that of a stone or of a triangle, no intelligible characteristic belonging to that thing surpasses the grasp of the human reason. But this does not happen to us in the case of God. For the human intellect is not able to reach a comprehension of the divine substance through its natural power. For, according to its manner of knowing in the present life, the intellect depends on the sense for the origin of knowledge; and so those things that do not fall under the senses cannot be grasped by the human intellect except in so far as the knowledge of them is gathered from sensible things. Now, sensible things cannot lead the human intellect to the point of seeing in them the nature of the divine substance; for sensible things are effects that fall short of the power of their cause. Yet, beginning with sensible things, our intellect is led to the point of knowing about God that He exists, and other such characteristics that must be attributed to the First Principle. There are, consequently, some intelligible truths about God that are open to the human reason; but there are others that absolutely surpass its power.

[4] We may easily see the same point from the gradation of intellects. Consider the case of two persons of whom one has a more penetrating grasp of a thing by his intellect

---

8   Aristotle, *Nicomachean Ethics*, I, 3 (1094b 24).
9   Boethius, *De Trinitate*, II (PL, 64, col. 1250).
10   Aristotle, *Posterior Analytics*, II, 3 (90b 31).

than does the other. He who has the superior intellect understands many things that the other cannot grasp at all. Such is the case with a very simple person who cannot at all grasp the subtle speculations of philosophy. But the intellect of an angel surpasses the human intellect much more than the intellect of the greatest philosopher surpasses the intellect of the most uncultivated simple person; for the distance between the best philosopher and a simple person is contained within the limits of the human species, which the angelic intellect surpasses. For the angel knows God on the basis of a more noble effect than does man; and this by as much as the substance of an angel, through which the angel in his natural knowledge is led to the knowledge of God, is nobler than sensible things and even than the soul itself, through which the human intellect mounts to the knowledge of God. The divine intellect surpasses the angelic intellect much more than the angelic surpasses the human. For the divine intellect is in its capacity equal to its substance, and therefore it understands fully what it is, including all its intelligible attributes. But by his natural knowledge the angel does not know what God is, since the substance itself of the angel, through which he is led to the knowledge of God, is an effect that is not equal to the power of its cause. Hence, the angel is not able, by means of his natural knowledge, to grasp all the things that God understands in Himself; nor is the human reason sufficient to grasp all the things that the angel understands through his own natural power. Just as, therefore, it would be the height of folly for a simple person to assert that what a philosopher proposes is false on the ground that he himself cannot understand it, so (and even more so) it is the acme of stupidity for a man to suspect as false what is divinely revealed through the ministry of the angels simply because it cannot be investigated by reason.

[5] The same thing, moreover, appears quite clearly from the defect that we experience every day in our knowledge of things. We do not know a great many of the properties of sensible things, and in most cases we are not able to discover fully the natures of those properties that we apprehend by the sense. Much more is it the case, therefore, that the human reason is not equal to the task of investigating all the intelligible characteristics of that most excellent substance.

[6] The remark of Aristotle likewise agrees with this conclusion. He says that "our intellect is related to the prime beings, which are most evident in their nature, as the eye of an owl is related to the sun."[11]

[7] Sacred Scripture also gives testimony to this truth. We read in Job: "Peradventure thou wilt comprehend the steps of God, and wilt find out the Almighty perfectly?" (11:7). And again: "Behold, God is great, exceeding our knowledge" (Job 36:26). And St. Paul: "We know in part" (1 Cor. 13:9).

---

11   Aristotle, Metaphysics, Ia, 1 (993b 9).

[8] We should not, therefore, immediately reject as false, following the opinion of the Manicheans and many unbelievers, everything that is said about God even though it cannot be investigated by reason.

Chapter 4

That the Truth about God to Which the Natural Reason Reaches Is Fittingly Proposed to Men for Belief

[1] Since, therefore, there exists a twofold truth concerning the divine being, one to which the inquiry of the reason can reach, the other which surpasses the whole ability of the human reason, it is fitting that both of these truths be proposed to man divinely for belief. This point must first be shown concerning the truth that is open to the inquiry of the reason; otherwise, it might perhaps seem to someone that, since such a truth can be known by the reason, it was uselessly given to men through a supernatural inspiration as an object of belief.

[2] Yet, if this truth were left solely as a matter of inquiry for the human reason, three awkward consequences would follow.

[3] The first is that few men would possess the knowledge of God. For there are three reasons why most men are cut off from the fruit of diligent inquiry which is the discovery of truth. Some do not have the physical disposition for such work. As a result, there are many who are naturally not fitted to pursue knowledge; and so, however much they tried, they would be unable to reach the highest level of human knowledge which consists in knowing God. Others are cut off from pursuing this truth by the necessities imposed upon them by their daily lives. For some men must devote themselves to taking care of temporal matters. Such men would not be able to give so much time to the leisure of contemplative inquiry as to reach the highest peak at which human investigation can arrive, namely, the knowledge of God. Finally, there are some who are cut off by indolence. In order to know the things that the reason can investigate concerning God, a knowledge of many things must already be possessed. For almost all of philosophy is directed towards the knowledge of God, and that is why metaphysics, which deals with divine things, is the last part of philosophy to be learned. This means that we are able to arrive at the inquiry concerning the aforementioned truth only on the basis of a great deal of labor spent in study. Now, those who wish to undergo such a labor for the mere love of knowledge are few, even though God has inserted into the minds of men a natural appetite for knowledge.

[4] The second awkward effect is that those who would come to discover the above mentioned truth would barely reach it after a great deal of time. The reasons are several. There is the profundity of this truth, which the human intellect is made capable of grasping by natural inquiry only after a long training. Then, there are many things that

must be presupposed, as we have said. There is also the fact that, in youth, when the soul is swayed by the various movements of the passions, it is not in a suitable state for the knowledge of such lofty truth. On the contrary, "one becomes wise and knowing in repose," as it is said in the *Physics*.[12] The result is this. If the only way open to us for the knowledge of God were solely that of the reason, the human race would remain in the blackest shadows of ignorance. For then the knowledge of God, which especially renders men perfect and good, would come to be possessed only by a few, and these few would require a great deal of time in order to reach it.

[5] The third awkward effect is this. The investigation of the human reason for the most part has falsity present within it, and this is due partly to the weakness of our intellect in judgment, and partly to the admixture of images. The result is that many, remaining ignorant of the power of demonstration, would hold in doubt those things that have been most truly demonstrated. This would be particularly the case since they see that, among those who are reputed to be wise men, each one teaches his own brand of doctrine. Furthermore, with the many truths that are demonstrated, there sometimes is mingled something that is false, which is not demonstrated but rather asserted on the basis of some probable or sophistical argument, which yet has the credit of being a demonstration. That is why it was necessary that the unshakeable certitude and pure truth concerning divine things should be presented to men by way of faith.[13]

[6] Beneficially, therefore, did the divine Mercy provide that it should instruct us to hold by faith even those truths that the human reason is able to investigate. In this way, all men would easily be able to have a share in the knowledge of God, and this without uncertainty and error.

[7] Hence it is written: "Henceforward you walk not as also the Gentiles walk in the vanity of their mind, having their understanding darkened" (Eph. 4:17–18). And again: "All thy children shall be taught of the Lord" (Isa. 54:13).

Chapter 5

That the Truths the Human Reason Is Not Able to Investigate Are Fittingly Proposed to Men for Belief

[1] Now, perhaps some will think that men should not be asked to believe what the reason is not adequate to investigate, since the divine Wisdom provides in the case of

---

12   Aristotle, *Physics*, VII, 3 (247b 9).

13   Although St. Thomas does not name Maimonides or his *Guide for the Perplexed (Dux neutrorum),* there are evident points of contact between the Catholic and the Jewish theologian. On the reasons for revelation given here, on our knowledge of God, on creation and the eternity of the world, and on Aristotelianism in general, St. Thomas has Maimonides in mind both to agree and to disagree with him. By way of background for SCG, I, the reader can usefully consult the references to Maimonides in E. Gilson, *History of Christian Philosophy in the Middle Ages* (New York, 1955), pp. 649–651.

each thing according to the mode of its nature. We must therefore prove that it is necessary for man to receive from God as objects of belief even those truths that are above the human reason.

[**2**] No one tends with desire and zeal towards something that is not already known to him. But, as we shall examine later on in this work, men are ordained by the divine Providence towards a higher good than human fragility can experience in the present life.[14] That is why it was necessary for the human mind to be called to something higher than the human reason here and now can reach, so that it would thus learn to desire something and with zeal tend towards something that surpasses the whole state of the present life. This belongs especially to the Christian religion, which in a unique way promises spiritual and eternal goods. And so there are many things proposed to men in it that transcend human sense. The Old Law, on the other hand, whose promises were of a temporal character, contained very few proposals that transcended the inquiry of the human reason. Following this same direction, the philosophers themselves, in order that they might lead men from the pleasure of sensible things to virtue, were concerned to show that there were in existence other goods of a higher nature than these things of sense, and that those who gave themselves to the active or contemplative virtues would find much sweeter enjoyment in the taste of these higher goods.

[3] It is also necessary that such truth be proposed to men for belief so that they may have a truer knowledge of God. For then only do we know God truly when we believe Him to be above everything that it is possible for man to think about Him; for, as we have shown,[15] the divine substance surpasses the natural knowledge of which man is capable. Hence, by the fact that some things about God are proposed to man that surpass his reason, there is strengthened in man the view that God is something above what he can think.

[4] Another benefit that comes from the revelation to men of truths that exceed the reason is the curbing of presumption, which is the mother of error. For there are some who have such a presumptuous opinion of their own ability that they deem themselves able to measure the nature of everything; I mean to say that, in their estimation, everything is true that seems to them so, and everything is false that does not. So that the human mind, therefore, might be freed from this presumption and come to a humble inquiry after truth, it was necessary that some things should be proposed to man by God that would completely surpass his intellect.

[5] A still further benefit may also be seen in what Aristotle says in the *Ethics*.[16] There was a certain Simonides who exhorted people to put aside the knowledge of divine

---

14   *SCG*, III, ch. 48.
15   See above, ch. 3.
16   Aristotle, *Nicomachean* Ethics, X, 7 (1177b 31).

things and to apply their talents to human occupations. He said that "he who is a man should know human things, and he who is mortal, things that are mortal." Against Simonides Aristotle says that "man should draw himself towards what is immortal and divine as much as he can." And so he says in the *De animalibus* that, although what we know of the higher substances is very little, yet that little is loved and desired more than all the knowledge that we have about less noble substances.[17] He also says in the *De caelo et mundo* that when questions about the heavenly bodies can be given even a modest and merely plausible solution, he who hears this experiences intense joy.[18] From all these considerations it is clear that even the most imperfect knowledge about the most noble realities brings the greatest perfection to the soul. Therefore, although the human reason cannot grasp fully the truths that are above it, yet, if it somehow holds these truths at least by faith, it acquires great perfection for itself.

[**6**] Therefore it is written: "For many things are shown to thee above the understanding of men" (Ecclus. 3:25). Again: "So the things that are of God no man knoweth but the Spirit of God. But to us God hath revealed them by His Spirit" (I Cor. 2:11, 10).

Chapter 6

That to Give Assent to the Truths of Faith Is Not Foolishness Even Though They Are Above Reason

[1] Those who place their faith in this truth, however, "for which the human reason offers no experimental evidence,"[19] do not believe foolishly, as though "following artificial fables" (II Peter 1:16). For these "secrets of divine Wisdom" (Job 11:6) the divine Wisdom itself, which knows all things to the full, has deigned to reveal to men. It reveals its own presence, as well as the truth of its teaching and inspiration, by fitting arguments; and in order to confirm those truths that exceed natural knowledge, it gives visible manifestation to works that surpass the ability of all nature. Thus, there are the wonderful cures of illnesses, there is the raising of the dead, and the wonderful immutation in the heavenly bodies; and what is more wonderful, there is the inspiration given to human minds, so that simple and untutored persons, filled with the gift of the Holy Spirit, come to possess instantaneously the highest wisdom and the readiest eloquence. When these arguments were examined, through the efficacy of the above mentioned proof, and not the violent assault of arms or the promise of pleasures, and (what is most wonderful of all) in the midst of the tyranny of the persecutors, an innumerable throng of people, both simple and most learned, flocked to the Christian faith. In this faith there are truths preached that surpass every human intellect; the pleasures of the flesh

---

17   Aristotle, *De partibus animalium*, I, 5 (644b 32).
18   Aristotle, *De caelo et mundo*, II, 12 (291b 26).
19   St. Gregory, *Homiliae in evangelia*, II, hom. 26, i (*PL*, 76, col. 1197).

are curbed; it is taught that the things of the world should be spurned. Now, for the minds of mortal men to assent to these things is the greatest of miracles, just as it is a manifest work of divine inspiration that, spurning visible things, men should seek only what is invisible. Now, that this has happened neither without preparation nor by chance, but as a result of the disposition of God is clear from the fact that through many pronouncements of the ancient prophets God had foretold that He would do this. The books of these prophets are held in veneration among us Christians, since they give witness to our faith.

[2] The manner of this confirmation is touched on by St. Paul: "Which," that is, human salvation, "having begun to be declared by the Lord, was confirmed unto us by them that hear Him: God also bearing them witness of signs, and wonders, and divers miracles, and distributions of the Holy Ghost" (Heb. 2:3–4).

[3] This wonderful conversion of the world to the Christian faith is the clearest witness of the signs given in the past; so that it is not necessary that they should be further repeated, since they appear most clearly in their effect. For it would be truly more wonderful than all signs if the world had been led by simple and humble men to believe such lofty truths, to accomplish such difficult actions, and to have such high hopes. Yet it is also a fact that, even in our own time, God does not cease to work miracles through His saints for the confirmation of the faith.

[4] On the other hand, those who founded sects committed to erroneous doctrines proceeded in a way that is opposite to this. The point is clear in the case of Mohammed He seduced the people by promises of carnal pleasure to which the concupisence of the flesh goads us. His teaching also contained precepts that were in conformity with his promises, and he gave free rein to carnal pleasure. In all this, as is not unexpected, he was obeyed by carnal men. As for proofs of the truth of his doctrine, he brought forward only such as could be grasped by the natural ability of anyone with a very modest wisdom. Indeed, the truths that he taught he mingled with many fables and with doctrines of the greatest falsity. He did not bring forth any signs produced in a supernatural way, which alone fittingly gives witness to divine inspiration; for a visible action that can be only divine reveals an invisibly inspired teacher of truth. On the contrary, Mohammed said that he was sent in the power of his arms—which are signs not lacking even to robbers and tyrants. What is more, no wise men, men trained in things divine and human, believed in him from the beginning. Those who believed in him were brutal men and desert wanderers, utterly ignorant of all divine teaching, through whose numbers Mohammed forced others to become his followers by the violence of his arms. Nor do divine pronouncements on the part of preceding prophets offer him any witness. On the contrary, he perverts almost all the testimonies of the Old and New Testaments by making them into fabrications of his own, as can be seen by anyone who examines his law. It was, therefore, a shrewd decision on his part to forbid his followers

to read the Old and New Testaments, lest these books convict him of falsity. It is thus clear that those who place any faith in his words believe foolishly.

Chapter 7

That the Truth of Reason Is Not Opposed to the Truth of the Christian Faith

[1] Now, although the truth of the Christian faith which we have discussed surpasses the capacity of the reason, nevertheless that truth that the human reason is naturally endowed to know cannot be opposed to the truth of the Christian faith. For that with which the human reason is naturally endowed is clearly most true; so much so, that it is impossible for us to think of such truths as false. Nor is it permissible to believe as false that which we hold by faith, since this is confirmed in a way that is so clearly divine. Since, therefore, only the false is opposed to the true, as is clearly evident from an examination of their definitions, it is impossible that the truth of faith should be opposed to those principles that the human reason knows naturally.

[2] Furthermore, that which is introduced into the soul of the student by the teacher is contained in the knowledge of the teacher—unless his teaching is fictitious, which it is improper to say of God. Now, the knowledge of the principles that are known to us naturally has been implanted in us by God; for God is the Author of our nature. These principles, therefore, are also contained by the divine Wisdom. Hence, whatever is opposed to them is opposed to the divine Wisdom and, therefore, cannot come from God. That which we hold by faith as divinely revealed, therefore, cannot be contrary to our natural knowledge.

[3] Again. In the presence of contrary arguments our intellect is chained, so that it cannot proceed to the knowledge of the truth. If, therefore, contrary knowledges were implanted in us by God, our intellect would be hindered from knowing truth by this very fate. Now, such an effect cannot come from God.

[4] And again. What is natural cannot change as long as nature does not. Now, it is impossible that contrary opinions should exist in the same knowing subject at the same time. No opinion or belief, therefore, is implanted in man by God which is contrary to man's natural knowledge.

[5] Therefore, the Apostle says: "The word is nigh thee, even in thy mouth and in thy heart. This is the word of faith, which we preach" (Rom. 10:8). But because it overcomes reason, there are some who think that it is opposed to it: which is impossible.

[6] The authority of St. Augustine also agrees with this. He writes as follows: "That which truth will reveal cannot in any way be opposed to the sacred books of the Old and the New Testament."[20]

[7] From this we evidently gather the following conclusion: whatever arguments are brought forward against the doctrines of faith are conclusions incorrectly derived from the first and self-evident principles imbedded in nature. Such conclusions do not have the force of demonstration; they are arguments that are either probable or sophistical. And so, there exists the possibility to answer them.

Chapter 8

How the Human Reason Is Related to the Truth of Faith

[1] There is also a further consideration. Sensible things, from which the human reason takes the origin of its knowledge, retain within themselves some sort of trace of a likeness to God. This is so imperfect, however, that it is absolutely inadequate to manifest the substance of God. For effects bear within themselves, in their own way, the likeness of their causes, since an agent produces its like; yet an effect does not always reach to the full likeness of its cause. Now, the human reason is related to the knowledge of the truth of faith (a truth which can be most evident only to those who see the divine substance) in such a way that it can gather certain likenesses of it, which are yet not sufficient so that the truth of faith may be comprehended as being understood demonstratively or through itself. Yet it is useful for the human reason to exercise itself in such arguments, however weak they may be, provided only that there be present no presumption to comprehend or to demonstrate. For to be able to see something of the loftiest realities, however thin and weak the sight may be, is, as our previous remarks indicate, a cause of the greatest joy.

[2] The testimony of Hilary agrees with this. Speaking of this same truth, he writes as follows in his *De Trinitate*: "Enter these truths by believing, press forward, persevere. And though I may know that you will not arrive at an end, yet I will congratulate you in your progress. For, though he who pursues the infinite with reverence will never finally reach the end, yet he will always progress by pressing onward. But do not intrude yourself into the divine secret, do not, presuming to comprehend the sum total of intelligence, plunge yourself into the mystery of the unending nativity; rather, understand that these things are incomprehensible."[21]

---

20   St. Augustine, *De genesi ad litteram*, II, c. 18 (*PL*, 34, col. 280).
21   St. Hilary, *De Trinitate*, II, 10, ii (*PL*, 10, coll. 58–59).

SUMMA THEOLOGIAE
Part 1, Question 1, Articles 1.1.1–2

The Nature of Holy Teaching

"Question 1: The Nature of Holy Teaching," by St. Thomas Aquinas, reprinted from Holy Teaching: Introducing the Summa Theologiae of St. Thomas Aquinas (2005) by Frederick Christian Bauerschmidt, by permission of Brazos, a division of Baker Publishing Group.

1.1.1

Whether, Besides Philosophical Studies, Any Further Teaching Is Required?

It seems that, besides philosophical studies [*philosophicas disciplinas*], we have no need of any further teaching [*doctrinam*].[22]

1. A human being should not seek to know what is above reason; according to Sirach 3:22, "Seek not the things that are too high for you." But whatever is not above reason is fully treated of in philosophical studies. Therefore any other teaching besides philosophical studies is superfluous.

2. Teaching can be concerned only with being, for nothing can be known, except what is true; and all that is, is true.[23] But everything that is, is treated of in philosophical disciplines—even God himself, so that there is a part of philosophy called "theology," or "the divine science," as the Philosopher has proved in his *Metaphysics* (bk. 6, chap. I, 1026a).[24] Therefore, besides philosophical disciplines, there is no need of any further knowledge.

---

22 *Philosophicae disciplinae* might also be translated as "the philosophical disciplines," referring to such areas of philosophy as logic or ethics or metaphysics. However, I have translated it as "philosophical studies" in order to include both the activity of accomplished philosophers and that of students of philosophy. *Doctrina* does not refer primarily to a proposition that one is expected to believe (what we today normally mean by a "doctrine") but to an activity: the activity of teaching. This is significant because Thomas is not asking about the legitimacy of some set of propositions but rather about the legitimacy of a particular kind of teaching activity. Thus Aquinas's question is whether there is a need for a teaching other than the teaching associated with philosophy—in other words, why do we need theology or, as Aquinas calls it, *sacra doctrina* (holy teaching)?

23 Like virtually all medieval philosophers, Aquinas presumes what in technical language is called "the convertibility of the transcendentals," which refers to those perfections that necessarily accompany existence, such as goodness, truth, and unity. So inasmuch as something exists, it is good, true, and one, And the more perfectly the existence of something is realized, the better, truer, and more unified it is. The point of the objection is that because being and truth are "convertible," philosophy, which in metaphysics deals with "being," is all you need for truth.

24 The point of the objection here is that philosophers *also* inquire after God's existence and nature, therefore philosophical inquiry is sufficient for understanding God.

On the contrary: It is written in 2 Timothy 3:16, "All Scripture inspired of God is useful to teach, to reprove, to correct, to instruct in justice." But Scripture inspired of God is not part of the philosophical disciplines, which are acquired through human reason. Therefore it is useful that besides philosophical studies, there should be other knowledge, namely, that which is inspired of God.

I answer: It was necessary for human salvation that there should be a teaching revealed by God, besides the philosophical studies investigated by human reason. First, because humanity is directed to God as to an end that surpasses the grasp of its reason.[25] According to Isaiah 66:4, "eye has not seen, O God, without you, what things you have prepared for those that love you."[26] But the end must first be known by people who are to direct their thoughts and actions to the end.[27] Therefore it was necessary for the well-being [*ad salutem*] of humanity that certain truths that exceed human reason should be made known by divine revelation.[28]

Even regarding those truths about God that human reason *could* have discovered, it was necessary that human beings should be taught by a divine revelation; because the truth about God such as reason could discover, would be known only by a few, and that after a long time, and with the mixing in of many errors.[29] But humanity's whole well-being,

---

25   This is a basic principle of Aquinas's thought (and, indeed, of all Christian, Jewish, and Muslim theology), namely, that God is the goal or purpose (i.e., the "end") of our existence.

26   Thomas is here conflating Isaiah 64:4, which reads "those who wait upon you," with l Corinthians 2:9, which reads "those who love him."

27   That is, you cannot be said to be acting to obtain a particular goal unless you have at least *some* knowledge of the goal. If I went to college but did not know that the college gave out diplomas upon successful completion of the course of study, then one would not normally say that obtaining a degree was the goal of my going to college.

28   How one interprets *ad salutem* here affects how one understands the overall shape of Thomas's thinking on the question of faith and reason. The Latin *salus* has a wider range of meanings than the English word "salvation." The root meaning of *salus* is "health" or "well-being," and although it certainly can, and in this specific case probably does, refer to the ultimate well-being of eternal life with God, it is not restricted to this meaning. If one takes *salus* in the more restricted sense of eternal life with God, then Thomas can be understood to be saying that human reason is sufficient to secure this-worldly well-being, but that we need a truth beyond what reason can give us—the special teaching by God known as revelation—in order to attain eternal life. Put differently, he would be saying that reason suffices for natural fulfillment, but revelation is necessary for *supernatural* fulfillment. However, if one takes *salus* in the broader sense of human well-being or flourishing, then Thomas would seem to be saying that a knowledge of divine truths beyond reason contributes to flourishing in all areas of human life, not simply in our religious or spiritual lives. This interpretation would lead to the conclusion that even in the "natural" realms of family and politics and the market there are potentials that are unrealized apart from divine truth. Thus one might say that in the last analysis human beings have no purely "natural" fulfillment, but only a "*supernatural*" one. Human beings are fulfilled as *humans* only in going beyond what it means to be human. Evidence for both interpretations can be found in the writings of Aquinas. Many debates over the proper interpretations of Aquinas, especially in the last century, have centered around this and related questions. Of particular relevance is the question of the relationship between divine grace and human nature.

29   Aquinas does believe that we can know *some* things about God by simply using our human reason, but he also thinks that such knowledge is quite minimal, and that it can be had only by very smart people who have a lot of time for thinking. And even when they have arrived at some genuine truths about God (e.g., that God exists), they will still be wrong about many other things about God (e.g., that he requires human sacrifices).

which is in God, depends upon the knowledge of this truth. Therefore, in order that the salvation of human beings might be brought about more fittingly and more surely, it was necessary that they should be taught divine truths by divine revelation.[30]

It was therefore necessary that, besides philosophical studies investigated through reason, there should be a holy teaching learned through revelation.

Reply to 1: Even if things that are too lofty for human knowledge may not be sought for by a person through reason, nevertheless, once they are revealed by God, they must be accepted by faith.[31] Therefore the text continues, "For many things are shown to you above human understanding" (Sirach 3:25). And in this, holy teaching consists.

Reply to 2: Disciplines are differentiated according to the various means through which knowledge is obtained. The astronomer and the physicist both may prove the same conclusion, that the earth, for instance, is round:[32] the astronomer by means of mathematics (i.e., leaving aside matter), but the physicist by means of matter itself. Therefore there is no reason why those things that may be learned from philosophical studies, so far as they can be known by natural reason, may not also be taught us by another discipline, so far as they fall within revelation. Therefore, the theology included in holy teaching differs in kind from that theology that is part of philosophy.[33]

---

30 It is worth noting here that when Thomas says revelation is "necessary," he does not mean that God is in any way obliged to reveal himself to human beings. Rather, he means that given the divine purpose of saving humanity—and not simply the clever and leisured, but also the dull and busy—it was fitting that God teach human beings. On this use of "necessary," see Thomas's discussion in 3.46.1.

31   In response to the first objection Aquinas points out that the discipline of theology is based not on what *we* think about God, but on what God has revealed about himself. At the same time, the human response of faith *is* an intellectual act.

32   Contrary to current popular opinion, educated medieval people knew that the world was round. As early as the sixth century BC the Greek philosopher Pythagoras argued for a round earth, and almost no educated person after this thought that the earth was flat. The widespread belief that Christopher Columbus was the first to "prove" the roundness of the earth apparently originated in the nineteenth century.

33   What makes one kind of knowledge different from another is not so much the knowledge itself as it is the *means* by which the knowledge is obtained. Aquinas's point is that philosophy and theology might lead us to the same bit of knowledge (e.g., that there exists a first mover of the universe), but they are still distinct ways of pursuing knowledge, since in the case of philosophy we believe something because human reason tells us, whereas in the case of theology we believe something because God tells us.

1.1.2

Whether Holy Teaching Is Scientia?[34]

It seems that holy teaching is not *scientia*.

1. Every *scientia* proceeds from self-evident premises.[35] But holy teaching proceeds from articles of faith that are not self-evident, since their truth is not admitted by all; as 2 Thessalonians 3:2 says, "For not all have faith." Therefore holy teaching is not *scientia*.

2. No *scientia* deals with individual facts.[36] But holy teaching treats of individual faces, such as the deeds of Abraham, Isaac, and Jacob and similar cases. Therefore holy teaching is not *scientia*.

On the contrary: Augustine says in *De Trinitate* (bk. 14, chap. 1, no. 3), "To this *scientia* alone belongs that by which saving faith is begotten, nourished, protected, and strengthened." But this can be said of no *scientia* except holy teaching. Therefore holy teaching is *scientia*.

---

34   I have chosen to leave the word *scientia* untranslated in order to remind readers that in medieval usage the word *scientia* meant something quite different from its modern English cognate "science." In one way, *scientia* is something much broader than our modern conception of "science." Loosely translated, it simply means "knowledge," in contrast to "opinion" or "faith." More precisely, however, *scientia* names the result of a process by which unknown things are deduced from known things; as Aquinas says, "The nature of *scientia* consists in this, that from things already known conclusions about other matters follow of necessity" (*Exposition on Boethius's "De Trinitate"* 2.2). Normally *scientia* proceeds from premises or "first principles" to certain conclusions; probably the best model for us to think of is how a proof in geometry works (see note 35, below). One can see how *scientia* differs from our modern notion of science, in which knowledge is based on experimentation, not on deduction.
        It is also important to note that in order to have true *scientia* of something, it is not enough to accept it as true; one must also grasp *why* it is true. Thus, to use an example from geometry, in order to have *scientia* of the Pythagorean theorem it is not enough to memorize it; one must also be able to grasp how the proof works. Aquinas contrasts *scientia* in its normal sense with both faith and opinion. Unlike opinion, it is certain of what it holds true (because its conclusions "follow of necessity"), and unlike faith it involves a process in which reason gives assent to something that it "sees"—as when, after struggling to understand the Pythagorean theorem, one says, "Ah, *now* I see!"
        In addition to referring to the knowledge that one possesses, *scientia* can also have the sense of a body of knowledge, or what we today might call a "discipline." This is the primary meaning it has in 1.1.8.
35   The objection is that if *scientia* is to be taken as certain knowledge, then it must begin from certain truths that no one could deny (what Aquinas calls premises or "first principles"). Thus, in geometry we might begin from the truth that a whole is always bigger than its part (which is self-evident to anyone who knows the meaning of "whole" and "part"); and in philosophy we might begin with the truth that the same statement cannot at the same time be both true and not true (which is self-evident to anyone who knows the meaning of "true" and "false"). If someone will not grant these premises, then they have no access to geometric or philosophical truth. The objection here is that in theology there are no premises that everyone accepts, as is evidenced by the fact that not everyone has faith.
36   The objection expresses the common medieval view that genuine knowledge is first and foremost a knowledge of universals (such as "humanity" or "circularity") and not of concrete particulars ("this human being" or "this circle").

I answer: Holy teaching is *scientia*. We must bear in mind that there are two kinds of *scientiae*.[37]

There are some that proceed from premises known by the natural light of intelligence, such as arithmetic and geometry and the like. There are some that proceed from premises known by the light of a higher *scientia*: thus the *scientia* of optics proceeds from premises established by geometry, and music from premises established by arithmetic. And it is in this way that holy teaching is *scientia*, because it proceeds from premises established by the light of a higher *scientia*, namely, the *scientia* of God and the blessed.[38] Therefore, just as the musician accepts on authority the premises taught to him by the mathematician, so holy teaching is established on premises revealed by God.

Reply to 1: The premises of any *scientia* are either in themselves self-evident, or can be traced back to the conclusions of a higher *scientia*, and such, as we have said, are the premises of holy teaching.

Reply to 2: Individual facts are dealt with in holy teaching, not because it is concerned with them principally, but rather they are introduced both as examples to be followed in our lives (as in moral *scientiae*) and in order to establish the authority of those through whom the divine revelation, on which Holy Scripture or teaching is based, has come down to us.[39]

---

37 Here Aquinas makes a move that you will see him make again and again: he points out that we use the word *scientia* in at least two ways and that the answer to this question lies in properly distinguishing them. Aquinas pays close attention to our use of language and frequently resolves questions by sorting out linguistic confusions. For example, he distinguishes various ways in which we use terms like "necessity," "comprehension," and "temptation."

38 Aquinas points out that not all forms of inquiry proceed from self-evident premises. Some forms (like geometry and mathematics) do, but others (such as optics and music) begin from premises established by a "higher" (i.e., logically prior) *scientia* (cf. the reply to objection 1). Thomas calls the latter forms of inquiry "subaltern" *scientiae*. So, for example, although music is based on premises derived from mathematics, a musician may be a perfectly fine musician without having a firm grasp of (i.e., *scientia*) the premises of mathematics. What Aquinas is saying is that theology is based on premises that are self-evident only to God and the blessed (those who behold God face to face in heaven). Just as the subaltern *scientia* of music must "borrow" knowledge from mathematics, so too the *scientia* of theology "borrows" knowledge from God's own self-knowledge. One point to note here is that the higher *scientia* acts as an "authority" for the lower.

Thus from the perspective of God and the blessed, *sacra doctrina* is *scientia* in the normal sense (see note 13, above); for human beings in this life it is *scientia* only in the sense of a subaltern *scientia*.

39 Here Aquinas accepts the objections' presumption that *scientia* is concerned with the eternal and unchanging, not the contingent and historical. Thus that with which the *scientia* of holy teaching is primarily concerned is God, who is eternal and unchanging. However, in a secondary sense the *scientia* of holy teaching *also* knows those historical events by which the identity of God has been revealed in the world—such as the deeds of Abraham, Isaac, and Jacob; as Thomas goes on to argue in 1.1.4, theology is a practical inquiry (i.e., concerned with human action) as well as a speculative inquiry (i.e., concerned with truth). One might also add, though Aquinas does not argue this here, that Abraham, Isaac, and Jacob can be the object of *scientia* because they are known by God in an eternal and unchanging manner (since God exists outside of time).

Ibn Rushd

Introduction
Ki Joo Choi

You may have noticed that the reading for this week is slightly different from the readings of the previous weeks. Ibn Rushd is an Islamic thinker who was born in present day Spain (A.D. 1126) and died in Marrakesh, now Morocco (A.D. 1 198). To some large extent, his commentaries on Aristotle, among other ancient Greeks, was the occasion for the reintroduction or revival of Aristotelian thought to many medieval Christian thinkers. For Ibn Rushd, Aristotle's thought allowed him to articulate Islamic beliefs and practices more deeply and with greater sophistication.

As an Islamic text of philosophy and theology, elements of what Ibn Rushd argues in *The Decisive Treatise Determining the Nature of the Connection Between Religion and Philosophy* may seem unfamiliar to many of you. For instance, his references to the Law are another way of speaking of the study of the revelation of the Quran (the words of God or Allah recited by the Prophet Muhammad). Yet, although Islamic, this text offers much to both Christians and non-Christians alike—specifically views on the nature of knowing.

As you read the text, pay specific attention to why Ibn Rushd thinks that philosophical reasoning is legitimate and necessary. What is striking in Ibn Rushd's text is the premise that philosophical reasoning can correlate with the truths of the Quran. In fact, he thinks that such a premise is articulated in the Quran itself. To help show how this might be the case, consider, as a short exercise, the following Quranic passage (from Sura or "chapter" 10 of the Quran, titled "Jonah"):

[10:0] In the name of God, Most Gracious, Most Merciful

[10:1] A.LR.* These (letters) are the proofs of this book of wisdom.

[10:2] Is it too much of a wonder for the people that we inspired a man like them? He (was inspired to say), "You shall warn the people, and give good news to those who believe that they have attained a position of prominence at their Lord." The disbelievers said, "This is a clever magician!"

[10:3] Your only Lord is GOD; the One who created the heavens and the earth in six days, then assumed all authority. He controls all matters. There is no intercessor, except in accordance with His will. Such is GOD your Lord. You shall worship Him. Would you not take heed?

[10:4] To Him is your ultimate return, all of you. This is GOD's truthful promise. He initiates the creation, then repeats it, in order to reward those who believe and lead a righteous life, equitably. As for those who disbelieve, they incur hellish drinks, and a painful retribution for their disbelieving.

[10:5] He is the One who rendered the sun radiant, and the moon a light, and He designed its phases that you may learn to count the years and to calculate. GOD did not create all this, except for a specific purpose. He explains the revelations for people who know.

[10:6] Surely, in the alternation of night and day, and what GOD created in the heavens and the earth, there are proofs for people who are righteous.

Note that this Sura claims that, along with his own self-revelation, Allah also provides "natural" means of verifying the veracity of this self-revelation—they are "proofs" (verse 6).

To that extent, Ibn Rushd believes that philosophical inquiry about the truths of the Quran is merited and welcome, perhaps even required. But note that philosophical reasoning or inquiry is referred to as demonstration or demonstrative reasoning. As you read this week's text, pay close attention to what Ibn Rushd means by demonstrative reasoning. Demonstrative reasoning cannot mean simply philosophical reasoning or knowing—for why would he bother to delineate philosophical reasoning as demonstrative reasoning?!? By referring to demonstrative reasoning he is trying to articulate the form of philosophical reasoning that is most appropriate. But what exactly is demonstrative reasoning? Read this text with that question in mind.

One feature of demonstrative reasoning not to be missed is the extent to which it requires consulting and conversing with past highly regarded non-Islamic philosophical thinkers and traditions as well as leading Islamic thinkers and schools of thought. Also note the analogy he draws between demonstrative reasoning and the kind of reasoning that is characteristic of the sciences, such as mathematics and astronomy. Consider what significance might be inferred from this feature of demonstrative reasoning.

By demonstrative reasoning, does Ibn Rushd mean that we can "demonstrate" the truths of the Quran or derive the truths of the Quran *without* ever consulting or even knowing about the Quran, and *without* ever consulting those thinkers in the past who have exemplified demonstrative thinking? Is demonstrative reasoning, therefore, a "pure" or "independent" form of rational inquiry?

What are we to make of the fact that, for Ibn Rushd, demonstrative reasoning is something motivated by the Quran itself, and that demonstrative reasoning *requires* consulting with prominent and authoritative thinkers of the Islamic community *as well as* those philosophers who *preceded* Islam? What does this say about the nature of demonstrative thinking? (Again, refer to the analogy Ibn Rushd draws between demonstrative reasoning in philosophy and the kind of reasoning that is characteristic of the mathematical sciences!) More broadly, what does this say about the nature of philosophical or rational thinking itself? Can we in fact know what is true (True!) or real (or the reality of the world) "on our own" apart from consulting sacred texts and the various traditions of learning that we are inheritors and members of? If not, then is demonstrative reasoning a form of deductive reasoning, similar to Anselm's? Or is he providing a more inductive form of knowing, one that infers conceptual conclusions from more particular, concrete social and cultural experiences? In considering this question, consider whether such an inductive approach can in fact lead to truthful knowledge. Alternatively, do you think that a more deductive approach is persuasive or compelling?

Lastly, note the interesting question that Ibn Rushd raises toward the end of the text: the possibility that demonstrative reasoning may lead to conclusions that on the surface contradict Quranic revelation. How does he respond to such a question or possible problem? What is the solution he proposes? And how does this solution further reflect the nature of demonstrative reasoning he articulates in *The Decisive Treatise?*

THE DECISIVE TREATISE DETERMINING THE NATURE OF THE CONNECTION BETWEEN RELIGION AND PHILOSOPHY

"The Decisive Treatise Determining the Nature of the Connection Between Religion and Philosophy," by Ibn Rushd, translated by G. F. Hourani, reprinted from Averroes on the Harmony of Religion and Philosophy, G. F. Hourani, Trans. Luzac & Co., Ltd., London, 1961. Reprinted by permission of E.J.W. Gibb Memorial Trust.

What is the attitude of the Law to philosophy?

Thus spoke the lawyer, imām, judge, and unique scholar, Abul Walīd Muhammad Ibn Ahmad Ibn Rushd:

Praise be to God with all due praise, and a prayer for Muhammad His chosen servant and apostle. The purpose of this treatise is to examine, from the standpoint of the study of the Law, whether the study of philosophy and logic is allowed by the Law, or prohibited, or commanded—either by way of recommendation or as obligatory.

Chapter One

The Law Makes Philosophic Studies Obligatory

If teleological study of the world is philosophy, and if the Law commands such a study, then the Law commands philosophy.

We say: If the activity of 'philosophy' is nothing more than study of existing beings and reflection on them as indications of the Artisan, i.e. inasmuch as they are products of art (for beings only indicate the Artisan through our knowledge of the art in them, and the more perfect this knowledge is, the more perfect the knowledge of the Artisan becomes), and if the Law has encouraged and urged reflection on beings, then it is clear that what this name signifies is either obligatory or recommended by the Law.

The Law commands such a study.

That the Law summons to reflection on beings, and the pursuit of knowledge about them, by the intellect is clear from several verses of the Book of God, Blessed and Exalted, such as the saying of the Exalted, 'Reflect, you have vision' (Qur'an, LIX, 2): this is textual authority for the obligation to use intellectual reasoning, or a combination of intellectual and legal reasoning (VII, 185). Another example is His saying, 'Have they not studied the kingdom of the heavens and the earth, and whatever things God has created?': this is a text urging the study of the totality of beings. Again, God the Exalted has taught that one of those whom He singularly honoured by this knowledge was Abraham, peace on him, for the Exalted said (VI, 75), 'So we made Abraham see the kingdom of the heavens and the earth, that he might be' [and so on to the end of the verse]. The Exalted also said (LXXXVIII, 17–18), 'Do they not observe the camels, how they have been created, and the sky, how it has been raised up?' and He said (III, 191), 'and they give thought to the creation of the heavens and the earth', and so on in countless other verses.

This study must be conducted in the best manner, by demonstrative reasoning.

Since it has now been established that the Law has rendered obligatory the study of beings by the intellect, and reflection on them, and since reflection is nothing more than inference and drawing out of the unknown from the known, and since this is reasoning or at any rate done by reasoning, therefore we are under an obligation to carry on our study of beings by intellectual reasoning. It is further evident that this manner of study, to which the Law summons and urges, is the most perfect kind of study using the most perfect kind of reasoning; and this is the kind called 'demonstration'.

To master this instrument the religious thinker must make a preliminary study of logic, just as the lawyer must study legal reasoning. This is no more heretical in the one case than in the other. And logic must be learned from the ancient masters, regardless of the fact that they were not Muslims.

The Law, then, has urged us to have demonstrative knowledge of God the Exalted and all the beings of His creation. But it is preferable and even necessary for anyone, who wants to understand God the Exalted and the other beings demonstratively, to have first understood the kinds of demonstration and their conditions [of validity], and in what respects demonstrative reasoning differs from dialectical, rhetorical and fallacious reasoning. But this is not possible unless he has previously learned what reasoning as such is, and how many kinds it has, and which of them are valid and which invalid. This in turn is not possible unless he has previously learned the parts of reasoning, of which it is composed, i.e. the premises and their kinds. Therefore he who believes in the Law, and obeys its command to study beings, ought prior to his study to gain a knowledge of these things, which have the same place in theoretical studies as instruments have in practical activities.

For just as the lawyer infers from the Divine command to him to acquire knowledge of the legal categories that he is under obligation to know the various kinds of legal syllogisms, and which are valid and which invalid, in the same way he who would know [God] ought to infer from the command to study beings that he is under obligation to acquire a knowledge of intellectual reasoning and its kinds. Indeed it is more fitting for him to do so, for if the lawyer infers from the saying of the Exalted, 'Reflect, you who have vision', the obligation to acquire a knowledge of legal reasoning, how much more fitting and proper that he who would know God should infer from it the obligation to acquire a knowledge of intellectual reasoning!

It cannot be objected: 'This kind of study of intellectual reasoning is a heretical innovation since it did not exist among the first believers.' For the study of legal reasoning and its kinds is also something which has been discovered since the first believers, yet it is not considered to be a heretical innovation. So the objector should believe the same about the study of intellectual reasoning. (For this there is a reason, which it is not the place to mention here.) But most [masters] of this religion support intellectual reasoning, except a small group of gross literalists, who can be refuted by [sacred] texts.

Since it has now been established that there is an obligation of the Law to study intellectual reasoning and its kinds, just as there is an obligation to study legal reasoning, it is clear that, if none of our predecessors had formerly examined intellectual reasoning and its kinds, we should be obliged to undertake such an examination from the beginning, and that each succeeding scholar would have to seek help in that task from his predecessor in order that knowledge of the subject might be completed. For it is difficult or impossible for one man to find out by himself and from the beginning all that he needs of that subject, as it is difficult for one man to discover all the knowledge that he needs of the kinds of legal reasoning; indeed this is even truer of knowledge of intellectual reasoning.

But if someone other than ourselves has already examined that subject, it is clear that we ought to seek help towards our goal from what has been said by such a predecessor on the subject, regardless of whether this other one shares our religion or not. For when a valid sacrifice is performed with a certain instrument, no account is taken, in judging the validity of the sacrifice, of whether the instrument belongs to one who shares our religion or to one who does not, so long as it fufills the conditions for validity. By 'those who do not share our religion' I refer to those ancients who studied these matters before Islam. So if such is the case, and everything that is required in the study of the subject of intellectual syllogisms has already been examined in the most perfect manner by the ancients, presumably we ought to lay hands on their books in order to study what they said about that subject; and if it is all correct we should accept it from them, while if there is anything incorrect in it, we should draw attention to that.

After logic we must proceed to philosophy proper. Here too we have to learn from our predecessors, just as in mathematics and law. Thus it is wrong to forbid the study of ancient philosophy. Harm from it is accidental, like harm from taking medicine, drinking water, or studying law.

When we have finished with this sort of study and acquired the instruments by whose aid we are able to reflect on beings and the indications of art in them (for he who does not understand the art does not understand the product of art, and he who does not understand the product of art does not understand the Artisan), then we ought to begin the examination of beings in the order and manner we have learned from the art of demonstrative syllogisms.

And again it is clear that in the study of beings this aim can be fulfilled by us perfectly only through successive examinations of them by one man after another, the later ones seeking the help of the earlier in that task, on the model of what has happened in the mathematical sciences. For if we suppose that the art of geometry did not exist in this age of ours, and likewise the art of astronomy, and a single person wanted to ascertain by himself the sizes of the heavenly bodies, their shapes, and their distances from each other, that would not be possible for him—e.g. to know the proportion of the sun to the earth or other facts about the sizes of the stars—even though he were the most intelligent of men by nature, unless by a revelation or something resembling revelation. Indeed if he were told that the sun is about 150 or 160 times as great as the earth, he would think this statement madness on the part of the speaker, although this is a fact which has been demonstrated in astronomy so surely that no one who has mastered that science doubts it.

But what calls even more strongly for comparison with the art of mathematics in this respect is the art of the principles of law; and the study of law itself was completed only over a long period of time. And if someone today wanted to find out by himself all the arguments which have been discovered by the theorists of the legal schools on controversial questions, about which debate has taken place between them in most countries of Islam (except the West), he would deserve to be ridiculed, because such a task is impossible for him, apart from the fact that the work has been done already. Moreover, this is a situation that is self-evident not in the scientific arts alone but also in the practical arts; for there is not one of them which a single man can construct by himself. Then how can he do it with the art of arts, philosophy? If this is so, then whenever we find in the works of our predecessors of former nations a theory about beings and a reflection on them conforming to what the conditions of demonstration require, we ought to study what they said about the matter and what they affirmed in their books. And we should accept from them gladly and gracefully whatever in these books accords with the truth, and draw attention to and warn against what does not accord with the truth, at the same time excusing them.

From this it is evident that the study of the books of the ancients is obligatory by Law, since their aim and purpose in their books is just the purpose to which the Law has urged us, and that whoever forbids the study of them to anyone who is fit to study them, i.e. anyone who unites two qualities, (1) natural intelligence and (2) religious integrity and moral virtue, is blocking people from the door by which the Law summons them to knowledge of God, the door of theoretical study which leads to the truest knowledge of Him; and such an act is the extreme of ignorance and estrangement from God the Exalted.

And if someone errs or stumbles in the study of these books owing to a deficiency in his natural capacity, or bad organization of his study of them, or being dominated by his passions, or not finding a teacher to guide him to an understanding of their contents, or a combination of all or more than one of these causes, it does not follow that one should forbid them to anyone who is qualified to study them. For this manner of harm which arises owing to them is something that is attached to them by accident, not by essence; and when a thing is beneficial by its nature and essence, it ought not to be shunned because of something harmful contained in it by accident. This was the thought of the Prophet, peace on him, on the occasion when he ordered a man to give his brother honey to drink for his diarrhea, and the diarrhea increased after he had given him the honey: when the man complained to him about it, he said, 'God spoke the truth; it was your brother's stomach that lied.' We can even say that a man who prevents a qualified person from studying books of philosophy, because some of the most vicious people may be thought to have gone astray through their study of them, is like a man who prevents a thirsty person from drinking cool, fresh water until he dies of thirst, because some people have choked to death on it. For death from water by choking is an accidental matter, but death by thirst is essential and necessary.

Moreover, this accidental effect of this art is a thing which may also occur accidentally from the other arts. To how many lawyers has law been a cause of lack of piety and immersion in this world! Indeed we find most lawyers in this state, although their art by its essence calls for nothing but practical virtue. Thus it is not strange if the same thing that occurs accidentally in the art which calls for practical virtue should occur accidentally in the art which calls for intellectual virtue.

For every Muslim the Law has provided a way to truth suitable to his nature, through demonstrative, dialectical or rhetorical methods.

Since all this is now established, and since we, the Muslim community, hold that this divine religion of ours is true, and that it is this religion which incites and summons us to the happiness that consists in the knowledge of God, Mighty and Majestic, and of His creation, that [end] is appointed for every Muslim by the method of assent which his temperament and nature require. For the natures of men are on different levels with respect to [their paths to] assent. One of them comes to assent through demonstration; another comes to assent through dialectical arguments, just as firmly as the demonstrative man through demonstration, since his nature does not contain any greater capacity; while another comes to assent through rhetorical arguments, again just as firmly as the demonstrative man through demonstrative arguments.

Thus since this divine religion of ours has summoned people by these three methods, assent to it has extended to everyone, except him who stubbornly denies it with his tongue or him for whom no method of summons to God the Exalted has been appointed in religion owing to his own neglect of such matters. It was for this purpose that the Prophet, peace on him, was sent with a special mission to 'the white man and the black man' alike; I mean because his religion embraces all the methods of summons to God the Exalted. This is clearly expressed in the saying of God the Exalted (XVI, 125), 'Summon to the way of your Lord by wisdom and by good preaching, and debate with them in the most effective manner'.

Chapter Two

Philosophy Contains Nothing Opposed to Islam

Demonstrative truth and scriptural truth cannot conflict.

Now since this religion is true and summons to the study which leads to knowledge of the Truth, we the Muslim community know definitely that demonstrative study does not lead to [conclusions] conflicting with what Scripture has given us; for truth does not oppose truth but accords with it and bears witness to it.

If the apparent meaning of Scripture conflicts with demonstrative conclusions it must be interpreted allegorically, i.e. metaphorically.

This being so, whenever demonstrative study leads to any manner of knowledge about any being, that being is inevitably either unmentioned or mentioned in Scripture. If it is unmentioned there is no contradiction, and it is in the same case as an act whose category is unmentioned, so that the lawyer has to infer it by reasoning from Scripture. If Scripture speaks about it, the apparent meaning of the words inevitably either accords or conflicts with the conclusions of demonstration about it. If this [apparent meaning] accords there is no argument. If it conflicts there is a call for allegorical interpretation of it. The meaning of 'allegorical interpretation' is: extension of the significance of an expression from real to metaphorical significance, without forsaking therein the standard metaphorical practices of Arabic, such as calling a thing by the name of something resembling it or a cause or consequence or accompaniment of it, or other things such as are enumerated in accounts of the kinds of metaphorical speech.

If the lawyer can do this, the religious thinker certainly can. Indeed these allegorical interpretations always receive confirmation from the apparent meaning of other passages of Scripture.

Now if the lawyer does this in many decisions of religious law, with how much more right is it done by the possessor of demonstrative knowledge! For the lawyer has at his disposition only reasoning based on opinion, while he who would know [God] [has at his disposition] reasoning based on certainty. So we affirm definitely that whenever the conclusion of a demonstration is in conflict with the apparent meaning of Scripture, that apparent meaning admits of allegorical interpretation according to the rules for such interpretation in Arabic. This proposition is questioned by no Muslim and doubted by no believer. But its certainty is immensely increased for those who have had close dealings with this idea and put it to the test, and made it their aim to reconcile the assertions of intellect and tradition. Indeed we may say that whenever a statement in Scripture conflicts in its apparent meaning with a conclusion of demonstration, if Scripture is considered carefully, and the rest of its contents searched page by page, there will invariably be found among the expressions of Scripture something which in its apparent meaning bears witness to that allegorical interpretation or comes close to bearing witness.

All Muslims accept the principle of allegorical interpretation; they only disagree about the extent of its application.

In the light of this idea the Muslims are unanimous in holding that it is not obligatory either to take all the expressions of Scripture in their apparent meaning or to extend them all from their apparent meaning by allegorical interpretation. They disagree [only] over which of them should and which should not be so interpreted: the Ash'arites for instance give an allegorical interpretation to the verse about God's directing Himself and the Tradition about His descent, while the Hanbalites take them in their apparent meaning.

The double meaning has been given to suit people's diverse intelligence. The apparent contradictions are meant to stimulate the learned to deeper study.

The reason why we have received a Scripture with both an apparent and an inner meaning lies in the diversity of people's natural capacities and the difference of their innate dispositions with regard to assent. The reason why we have received in Scripture texts whose apparent meanings contradict each other is in order to draw the attention of those who are well grounded in science to the interpretation which reconciles them. This is the idea referred to in the words received from the Exalted (III, 7), 'He it is who has sent down to you the Book, containing certain verses clear and definite' [and so on] down to the words 'those who are well grounded in science'.

In interpreting texts allegorically we must never violate Islamic consensus, when it is certain. But to establish it with certainty with regard to theoretical texts is impossible, because there have always been scholars who would not divulge their interpretation of such texts.

It may be objected: 'There are some things in Scripture which the Muslims have unanimously agreed to take in their apparent meaning, others [which they have agreed] to interpret allegorically, and others about which they have disagreed; is it permissible, then, that demonstration should lead to interpreting allegorically what they have agreed to take in its apparent meaning, or to taking in its apparent meaning what they have agreed to interpret allegorically?' We reply: If unanimous agreement is established by a method which is certain, such [a result] is not sound; but if [the existence of] agreement on those things is a matter of opinion, then it may be sound. This is why Abū Hāmid,

Abul-Ma'ālī, and other leaders of thought said that no one should be definitely called an unbeliever for violating unanimity on a point of interpretation in matters like these.

That unanimity on theoretical matters is never determined with certainty, as it can be on practical matters, may be shown to you by the fact that it is not possible for unanimity to be determined on any question at any period unless that period is strictly limited by us, and all the scholars existing in that period are known to us (i.e. known as individuals and in their total number), and the doctrine of each of them on the question has been handed down to us on unassailable authority, and, in addition to all this, unless we are sure that the scholars existing at the time were in agreement that there is not both an apparent and an inner meaning in Scripture, that knowledge of any question ought not to be kept secret from any-one, and that there is only one way for people to understand Scripture. But it is recorded in Tradition that many of the first believers used to hold that Scripture has both an apparent and an inner meaning, and that the inner meaning ought not to be learned by anyone who is not a man of learning in this field and who is incapable of understanding it. Thus, for example, Bukhari reports a saying of 'Alī Ibn Abī Tālib, may God be pleased with him, 'Speak to people about what they know. Do you want God and His Prophet to be accused of lying?' Other examples of the same kind are reported about a group of early believers. So how can it possibly be conceived that a unanimous agreement can have been handed down to us about a single theoretical question, when we know definitely that not a single period has been without scholars who held that there are things in Scripture whose true meaning should not be learned by all people?

The situation is different in practical matters: everyone holds that the truth about these should be disclosed to all people alike, and to establish the occurrence of unanimity about them we consider it sufficient that the question [at issue] should have been widely discussed and that no report of controversy about it should have been handed down to us. This is enough to establish the occurrence of unanimity on matters of practice, but on matters of doctrine the case is different.

Ghazāīlī's charge of unbelief against Fārābī and Ibn Sīnā, for asserting the world's eternity and God's ignorance of particulars and denying bodily resurrection, is only tentative, not definite.

You may object: 'If we ought not to call a man an unbeliever for violating unanimity in cases of allegorical interpretation, because no unanimity is conceivable in such cases, what do you say about the Muslim philosophers, like Abū Nasr and Ibn Sīnā? For Abū Hāmid called them both definitely unbelievers in the book of his known as *The disintegration [The incoherence of the Philosophers]*, on three counts: their assertions of the pre-eternity of the world and the God the Exalted does not know particulars' (may He be Exalted far above that (ignorance]!), 'and their allegorical interpretation of the passages concerning the resurrection of bodies and states of existence in the next life.'

We answer: It is apparent from what he said on the subject that his calling them both unbelievers on these counts was not definite, since he made it clear in *The book of distinction* that calling people unbelievers for violating unanimity can only be tentative.

Such a charge cannot be definite, because there has never been a consensus against allegorical interpretation. The Qur'an itself indicates that it has inner meanings which it is the special function of the demonstrative class to understand.

Moreover, it is evident from what we have said that a unanimous agreement cannot be established in questions of this kind, because of the reports that many of the early believers of the first generation, as well as others, have said that there are allegorical interpretations which ought not to be expressed to those who are qualified to receive allegories. These are 'those who are well grounded in science'; for we prefer to place the stop after the words of God the Exalted (III, 7) 'and those who are well grounded in science,' because if the scholars did not understand allegorical interpretation, there would be no superiority in their assent which would oblige them to a belief in Him not found among the unlearned. God has described them as those who believe in Him, and this can only be taken to refer to the belief which is based on demonstration; and this [belief] only occurs together with the science of allegorical interpretation. For the unlearned believers are those whose belief in Him is not based on demonstration, and if this belief which God has attributed to the scholars is peculiar to them, it must come through demonstration, and if it comes through demonstration it only occurs together with the science of allegorical interpretation. For God the Exalted has informed us that those [verses] have an allegorical interpretation which is the truth, and demonstration can only be of the truth. That being the case, it is not possible for general unanimity to be established about allegorical interpretations, which God has made peculiar to scholars. This is self-evident to any fair-minded person.

Besides, Ghazālī was mistaken in ascribing to the Peripatetics the opinion that God does not know particulars. Their view is that His knowledge of both particulars and universals differs from ours, in being the cause, not an effect, of the object known. They even hold that God sends premonitions in dreams of particular events.

In addition to all this we hold that Abu Hāmid was mistaken about the Peripatetic philosophers, in ascribing to them the assertion that God, Holy and Exalted, does not know particulars at all. In reality they hold that God the Exalted knows them in a way which is not of the same kind as our way of knowing them. For our knowledge of them is an effect of the object known, originated when it comes into existence and changing when it changes; whereas Glorious God's Knowledge of existence is the opposite of this: it is the cause of the object known, which is existent being. Thus to suppose the kinds of knowledge similar to each other is to identify the essences and properties of opposite things, and that is the extreme of ignorance. And if the name of 'knowledge' is predicated of both originated and eternal knowledge, it is predicated by sheer homonymy, as many names are predicated of opposite things: e.g. *jalal* of great and small, *sarīm* of light and darkness. Thus there exists no definition embracing both kinds of knowledge at once, as the theologians of our time imagine. We have devoted a separate essay to this question, impelled by one of our friends.

But how can anyone imagine that the Peripatetics say that God the Glorious does not know particulars with His eternal Knowledge, when they hold that true visions include premonitions of particular events due to occur in future time, and that this warning foreknowledge comes to people in their sleep from the eternal Knowledge which orders and rules the universe? Moreover, it is not only particulars which they say God does not know in the manner in which we know them, but universals as well; for the universals known to us are also effects of the nature of existent being, while with His Knowledge the universals known to us are also effects of the nature of existent being, while His Knowledge the reverse is true. Thus the conclusion to which demonstration leads is that His Knowledge transcends qualification as 'universal' or 'particular'. Consequently there is no point in disputing about this question, i.e. whether to call them unbelievers or not.

Moses Maimonides

Editor's Introduction
Anthony Sciglitano

Moses Maimonides, born in Spain in the twelfth century, is probably the most influential Jewish thinker in history. Maimonides was also a prolific writer, having written a code summarizing Jewish Law, a set of thirteen principles of Jewish faith, a massive commentary on the *Mishnah*[i], the philosophical text from which you will read called *The Guide for the Perplexed,* and assorted other treatises on topics such as happiness and resurrection. In addition to his writing, Maimonides served in a demanding role as physician to the Sultan in Cairo, Egypt and as leader for the Jewish community there. Maimonides was a medieval figure, but just as Thomas Aquinas is a central thinker for Catholicism today, so Maimonides remains a central thinker in contemporary Jewish thought. Indeed, there is a Jewish saying that gives some indication of his importance: "From Moses [the Prophet] to Moses [Maimonides], there was none like Moses."

Like Thomas Aquinas (A.D. 1225–1274) and Ibn Rushd (A.D. 1126–1198), Maimonides was philosophically influenced by the writings of Aristotle. Also like Thomas Aquinas and Ibn Rushd, Maimonides needed to work out how God's revealed truth relates to philosophical or "natural" reason. For a medieval Jewish thinker, this meant addressing the relationship between Jewish belief in the truth of God's Word found in the Jewish Scriptures (or Tanakh[ii]) and the truth discovered through the light of Aristotle's philosophy. This is one of the tasks he set for himself in *The Guide for the Perplexed.* Indeed, the "perplexity" that Maimonides wants to address derives from the difficulty of interpreting certain biblical statements, especially about God, when their literal meaning appears absurd. For instance, when the Bible speaks of the "finger of God," are we to believe that God really has fingers?[iii] Or, when the Bible says that man and woman were created in the "image and likeness of God," are we to think that we look like God in some physical sense? Maimonides thought such views were irresponsible and that God is not to be thought of in physical terms. God, he argues, is incorporeal (i.e., without bodily form).

Much of *The Guide for the Perplexed* is taken up with analysis of biblical passages and terms and how they should be read apart from a strictly literalistic reading. Here, Maimonides will try to establish ways of reading perplexing or difficult passages. In addition, Maimonides is concerned for issues of what are called predication.

---

i   The *Mishnah* is the written compilation of what is called "oral Torah," or the Pharisaic and the Rabbinic commentary on Jewish writings codified in the 3rd Century. The *Mishnah* is divided into 6 parts, and each part is divided into between seven and twelve treatises on a wide variety of subjects related to Jewish life. For instance, the *Mishnah* treats of agriculture, marital relations and divorce, the status of non-Jews in God's plan of salvation. It is joined with later Rabbinic commentary on the *Mishnah* to form the Talmud. The Rabbis are the teachers of Judaism.

ii   The *TaNaKh* is the Jewish acronym for *Torah* (Teachings or Law), *Nevi'im* (Prophets), *Ketuvim* (Writings), the three parts of the Jewish Bible.

iii Thomas Aquinas finds it necessary to address the same kind of issue in *ST* 1.1.9–10 when he addresses whether scripture appropriately uses metaphors and whether words in scripture may have more than one meaning.

What is predication? When we speak of God, we often say things that we think are quite unproblematic. We might say, for instance, that "God is good. "In this sentence, "good" is the predicate of God just as in the sentence "The apple is good," "good" is predicated of "the apple." Now, on the face of it, "goodness" sounds like a predicate any person who believes in God would use. Yet, the fact that we also predicate "goodness" of apples, cars, pets, and people should give us pause. How, we might ask, is the goodness of God different from the goodness of all these other things that are confined to our world? Three kinds of answers to this question are at least thinkable: univocal, equivocal, and analogical.

1. *Univocal Predication.* Univocal predication would presume that God's goodness and human or worldly goodness are of the same kind. One might say, for instance, "God's goodness is greater than the goodness we find in the things of this world," but "greater" simply means more of the goodness that we already comprehend. In other words, the same idea or category of goodness encompasses both God and creatures. On this understanding, the difference between God and creatures is one of degree, but not of kind, a quantitative and not a qualitative difference. This is what medieval thinkers such as Moses Maimonides and Thomas Aquinas called *univocal* predication. Neither Maimonides nor Thomas thought our predication of God could be univocal.

2. *Equivocal Predication.* Maimonides argues that predicates for God are *equivocal.* In other words, words such as "good" or "true" or "wise" cannot refer to God properly, but can only represent human concepts. They do not affirm anything of God's actual essence. For Maimonides, the most that can be said about our predications is that they deny the opposite. So, "God is Good," may be appropriately translated as "God is not *not-*Good." We might represent equivocal predication by saying that "God's goodness is utterly unlike any goodness we find in the things of the world." This kind of predication is quite different from univocal predication, and seeks to keep God from being understood as another limited thing or even more than one thing. In theological terms, Maimonides is protecting against idolatry and polytheism. Now, Maimonides has several reasons for his judgment that our attempts to say something about God inevitably fail. We can explore two here.

    For Maimonides, all of our statements about things in this world have two parts: a subject and a predicate: "The table is red," "The clock is slow," "The board is green." Even were we to speak of human beings, we would say that "Roberto is slim," "Janice is wise," and so on. Notice that we assume that none of these predicates are necessary. Roberto need not be slim and it is not assumed that Janice will *necessarily* be wise simply because she is human. She could also be foolish. In other words, Janice's existence is not the same as her essence. Janice is a human being. That is her essence. But she may exist as a wise human being or a foolish human being. So, our predication is complex. We cannot simply say "Janice" and have everyone assume that she is wise. In the case of human beings, we must specify. This

is also the case with non-human objects in our world. A sofa can be green or red, soft or firm, in the study or in the kitchen. So, our way of knowing and speaking about our world assumes that there is "space" or logical difference between *what* something is (human, couch) and *how* it is (wise or foolish, soft or firm). In a sense, then, our knowing is always an act of putting together things that we know first through our senses and then in our minds. Things in our world, then, appear to be composed of parts.

For Maimonides, however, Scripture tells us that God is One. In medieval philosophy, this meant that there is no space between God's essence and God's existence. God's goodness, power, wisdom, and justice are utterly identical with God's nature. Yet our predication is always complex, always putting together aspects of something that do not necessarily go together. So, our complex predication misleads us when we predicate of a perfectly simple being. We appear to make God like the things we encounter in the world, that is, like things that are complex. Take, for instance, the sentence, "God is just." If we can also say that "Janice is just," and when we say this we know that Janice could be unjust, it begins to sound like God is merely another being like Janice who could be just or unjust. This would suggest that God's "justice" is not necessary to his very essence. But for Maimonides this cannot be the case for God. *How* God is differs not at all from *what* God is. So, our form of predication is misleading when speaking of the divine.

In addition, Maimonides takes it that God is Spirit and not matter. Yet our way of knowing depends upon knowing through our senses first. For Maimonides there is no way around this. We are corporeal or bodily beings and must use our senses to know. This is quite different from Plato's view of knowledge and much more like that of Aristotle. However, it presents a problem for predication. Knowing through the senses is fine for knowing and speaking of material reality, that is, things with bodies or physical form. But it is not adequate at all for knowing a God who is pure spirit. Again, for Maimonides, predication of God based upon knowledge of material reality would suggest that God is like things we find in this world.

So, according to Maimonides, our predication of God is "*equivocal*" predication. In other words, he thought that our statements about God's characteristics or attributes do not refer to what these attributes are like in God's nature. Instead, Maimonides thought that a statement such as "God is good" can only work *to deny* the opposite statement, so that its real meaning is "God is not *not*-Good." In other words, Maimonides thought our ability to say something true about God's nature is extremely limited. Our positive statements about God (i.e., God is Good, God is wise, God is strong) only serve *to deny* that God's nature is evil, unwise, or weak.

One other, very important point still needs to be made. If Maimonides did not think that our affirmative predications of God's *nature* were meaningful, he did think that some predicates were rightly said of God's *actions*. This is important because Scripture clearly does say that God is, for instance, righteous and merciful. Indeed, Maimonides focuses on three terms: *chesed* ("loving-kindness"), *mishpat* ("judgment"), and *tzedakah* ("righteousness"). God is called kind or loving, judge, and righteous based on particular actions or kinds of actions that God has performed. Maimonides writes, "He [God] is called *chasid*, "kind," because He created the Universe; *tzaddik*, "righteous," on account of His mercy with the weak, in providing for every living being according to its powers; and *shofet*, "judge," on account of the relative good and the great relative evils that are decreed by God's justice as directed by His wisdom."[iv]

Actions, according to Maimonides, presuppose that there is an actor, but do not tell us anything specific about that actor's nature. In other words, speaking of action does not assume that the actor, in this case God, is complex by separating out essence from existence. It is normal to think of one actor doing many different kinds of action. Now it is crucial to be able to speak of God's actions because otherwise it would be difficult to see how we might live in God's image as loving, righteously merciful, and just otherwise.

3. *Analogical Predication.* Thomas Aquinas argues that our predication for God is neither *univocal* nor *equivocal*, but *analogical*. Having read Maimonides, Thomas Aquinas tries to integrate his insights into his own view. He certainly agrees with Maimonides in rejecting univocal predication. He also agrees with Maimonides that human predication of the divine can never fully comprehend God's essence. Yet Thomas holds that we can affirm certain things of God's nature if we understand that we mean them analogically. For instance, we can note that God's goodness has some similarity to the goodness of things found in this world, but only because God grants any goodness that we find in those things. According to Thomas Aquinas, the things of this world tell us something about their creator in the way that an effect says something about its cause, a book reveals something about its author, or a work of art tells us something about the artist. For instance, we might notice the Grand Canyon and think that the One who made all of this must be both wise and powerful. Nevertheless, Thomas agrees with Maimonides that such predicates as "powerful" and "wise" cannot be limited to *our* conceptions of them. So, Thomas thinks we must negate or remove the limits of *our* concepts and understand that God's "power" and "wisdom" have a fullness and richness beyond our comprehension. Our predications are true, but also profoundly inadequate. This idea that our statements about God are both true and yet profoundly inadequate is what we mean by *analogical* predication.

As you can see, medieval thought was rather complex, and we are just tapping the surface of issues surrounding predication here. Maimonides, like many of the Christian (as well as Islamic) medieval thinkers, grappled with

---

iv   Maimonides, *The Guide for the Perplexed*, Part III, Chapter 53, p. 393, trans. by M. Friedlander (New York: Dover, 1956).

the question of divine predication. In some ways he agreed with Christian medieval thinkers such as Thomas Aquinas on the question of predication, and disagreed strongly in other ways. In his Introduction to The Guide for the Perplexed, Maimonides's main aim is to prepare his readers to think seriously and intelligently about perplexing biblical passages and the meaning of divine predication. It is a fascinating piece because it begins to address issues of biblical interpretation that are still with us. Certainly religious people today, whether Jewish, Christian, or Muslim, find some of their own scriptural passages difficult or even troubling. Maimonides seeks to help his community address just this issue. There are a number of important things to think about in this reading:

1. What is the intended audience for Maimonides' *Guide for the Perplexed*? What does he expect someone who is reading this text to know and to believe?

2. Does Maimonides think that religious belief and reason are contradictory? Why or why not?

3. Does Maimonides think that "perplexity" is a good or bad thing? Should one be perplexed when reading Scripture? What are the reasons someone might not be perplexed? Why might someone be perplexed?

4. Why do you think Maimonides uses the image of a "lightning flash" when speaking of truth? Do you think this image relates to his idea of equivocal predication? Do you find this a helpful image?

THE GUIDE FOR THE PERPLEXED
Epistle Dedicatory

In the name of the Lord, God of the World[1]

My honored pupil *Rabbi Joseph*,[2] *may the Rock guard you, son of Rabbi Judah, may his repose be in Paradise.* When you came to me, having conceived the intention of journeying from the country farthest away in order to read texts under my guidance, I had a high opinion of you because of your strong desire for inquiry and because of what I had observed in your poems of your powerful longing for speculative matters. This was the case since your letters and compositions in rhymed prose came to me from Alexandria, before your grasp was put to the test. I said however: perhaps his longing is stronger than his grasp. When thereupon you read under my guidance texts dealing with the science of astronomy and prior to that texts dealing with mathematics, which is necessary as an introduction to astronomy, my joy in you increased because of the excellence of your mind and the quickness of your grasp. I saw that your longing for mathematics was great, and hence I let you train yourself in that science, knowing where you would end. When thereupon you read under my guidance texts dealing with the art of logic, my hopes fastened upon you, and I saw that you are one worthy to have the secrets of the prophetic books revealed to you so that you would consider in them that which perfect men ought to consider. Thereupon I began to let you see certain flashes and to give you certain indications. Then I saw that you demanded of me additional knowledge and asked me to make clear to you certain things pertaining to divine matters, to inform you of the intentions of the Mutakallimūn in this respect, and to let you know whether their methods were demonstrative and, if not, to what art they belonged. As I also saw, you had already acquired some smattering of this subject from people other than myself; you were perplexed, as stupefaction had come over you; your noble soul demanded of you to *find out acceptable words.*[3] Yet I did not cease dissuading you from this and enjoining upon you to approach matters in an orderly manner. My purpose in this was that the truth should be established in your mind according to the proper methods and that certainty should not come to you by accident. Whenever during your association with me a [biblical] *verse* or some text of the *Sages* was mentioned in which there was a pointer to some strange notion, I did not refrain from explaining it to you. Then when God decreed our separation and you betook yourself elsewhere, these meetings aroused in me a resolution that had slackened. Your absence moved me to compose this Treatise,

---

1   Gen. 2 :33. The correct sense of that Hebrew invocation is "God of Eternity." However, in current Hebrew the words mean "God of the World"; this seems to have been the meaning that Maimonides had in mind.

2   As Maimonides states in this Epistle, the *Guide* was written for the benefit of this disciple and for those like him. For that reason, some importance should be attached to the description, given in the text, of the intellectual attainment of Joseph, son of Judah.

3   Eccles. 12:10.

which I have composed for you and for those like you, however few they are. I have set it down in dispersed chapters. All of them that are written down will reach you where you are, one after the other. Be in good health.

Introduction to the First Part

"Introduction to the First Part," by Moses Maimonides, translated by Shlomo Pines. Reprinted from *The Guide of the Perplexed*, vol. 1, translated by Shlomo Pines. Copyright © 1963 by the University of Chicago. Reprinted by permission of The University of Chicago Press.

Cause me to know the way wherein I should walk,
   For unto Thee have I lifted my soul.[1]

Unto you, O men, I call,
   And my voice is to the sons of men.[2]

Incline thine ear, and hear the words of the wise,
   And apply thy heart unto my knowledge.[3]

The first purpose of this Treatise is to explain the meanings of certain terms occurring in books of prophecy. Some of these terms are equivocal; hence the ignorant attribute to them only one or some of the meanings in which the term in question is used. Others are derivative terms; hence they attribute to them only the original meaning from which the other meaning is derived. Others are amphibolous terms, so that at times they are believed to be univocal and at other times equivocal. It is not the purpose of this Treatise to make its totality understandable to the vulgar or to beginners in speculation, nor to teach those who have not engaged in any study other than the science of the Law—I mean the legalistic study of the Law. For the purpose of this Treatise and of all those like it is the science of Law in its true sense. Or rather its purpose is to give indications to a religious man for whom the validity of our Law has become established in his soul and has become actual in his belief—such a man being perfect in his religion and character, and having studied the sciences of the philosophers and come to know what they signify. The human intellect having drawn him on and led him to dwell within its province, he must have felt distressed by the externals of the Law and by the meanings of the above-mentioned equivocal, derivative, or amphibolous terms, as he continued to understand them by himself or was made to understand them by others. Hence he would remain in a state of perplexity and confusion as to whether he should follow his intellect, renounce what he knew concerning the terms in question,

---

1   Ps. 143:8.
2   Prov. 8:4.
3   Prov. 22:17.

and consequently consider that he has renounced the foundations of the Law. Or he should hold fast to his understanding of these terms and not let himself be drawn on together with his intellect, rather turning his back on it and moving away from it, while at the same time perceiving that he had brought loss to himself and harm to his religion. He would be left with those imaginary beliefs to which he owes his fear and difficulty and would not cease to suffer from heartache and great perplexity.

This Treatise also has a second purpose: namely, the explanation of very obscure parables occurring in the books of the prophets, but not explicitly identified there as such. Hence an ignorant or heedless individual might think that they possess only an external sense, but no internal one. However, even when one who truly possesses knowledge considers these parables and interprets them according to their external meaning, he too is overtaken by great perplexity. But if we explain these parables to him or if we draw his attention to their being parables, he will take the right road and be delivered from this perplexity. That is why I have called this Treatise "The Guide of the Perplexed."

I do not say that this Treatise will remove all difficulties for those who understand it. I do, however, say that it will remove most of the difficulties, and those of the greatest moment. A sensible man thus should not demand of me or hope that when we mention a subject, we shall make a complete exposition of it, or that when we engage in the explanation of the meaning of one of the parables, we shall set forth exhaustively all that is expressed in that parable. An intelligent man would be unable to do so even by speaking directly to an interlocutor. How then could he put it down in writing without becoming a butt for every ignoramus who, thinking that he has the necessary knowledge, would let fly at him the shafts of his ignorance? We have already explained in our legal compilations some general propositions concerning this subject and have drawn attention to many themes. Thus we have mentioned there that the *Account of the Beginning*[4] is identical with natural science, and the *Account of the Chariot*[5] with divine science; and have explained the rabbinic saying: *The Account of the Chariot ought not to be taught even to one man, except if he be wise and able to understand by himself, in which case only the chapter heading may be transmitted to him.*[6] Hence you should not ask of me here anything beyond the *chapter headings*. And even those are not set down in order or arranged in coherent fashion in this Treatise, but rather are scattered and entangled with other subjects that are to be clarified. For my purpose is that the truths be glimpsed and then again be concealed, so as not to oppose that divine purpose which one cannot possibly oppose and which has concealed from the vulgar among the people those truths especially requisite for His apprehension. As He has said: *The secret of the*

---

4   *ma'aseh bereshith.* Literally: *the Work of the Beginning.*
5   *ma'aseh merkabah.* Literally: *the Work of the Chariot.*
6   Babylonian Talmud (hereafter cited as B.T.), Hagigah, 11b, 13a.

Lord is with them that fear Him.[7] Know that with regard to natural matters as well, it is impossible to give a clear exposition when teaching some of their principles as they are. For you know the saying of [the Sages], *may their memory be blessed: The Account of the Beginning ought not to be taught in the presence of two men.*[8] Now if someone explained all those matters in a book, he in effect would be *teaching* them to thousands of men. Hence these matters too occur in parables in the books of prophecy. *The Sages, may their memory be blessed,* following the trail of these books, likewise have spoken of them in riddles and parables, for there is a close connection between these matters and the divine science, and they too are secrets of that divine science.

You should not think that these great *secrets* are fully and completely known to anyone among us. They are not. But sometimes truth flashes out to us so that we think that it is day, and then matter and habit in their various forms conceal it so that we find ourselves again in an obscure night, almost as we were at first. We are like someone in a very dark night over whom lightning flashes time and time again. Among us there is one[9] for whom the lightning flashes time and time again, so that he is always, as it were, in unceasing light. Thus night appears to him as day. That is the degree of the great one among the prophets, to whom it was said: *But as for thee, stand thou here by Me,*[10] and of whom it was said: *that the skin of his face sent forth beams, and so on.*[11] Among them there is one to whom the lightning flashes only once in the whole of his night; that is the rank of those of whom it is said: *they prophesied, but they did so no more.*[12] There are others between whose lightning flashes there are greater or shorter intervals. Thereafter comes he who does not attain a degree in which his darkness is illumined by any lightning flash. It is illumined, however, by a polished body or something of that kind, stones or something else that give light in the darkness of the night. And even this small light that shines over us is not always there, but flashes and is hidden again, as if it were the *flaming sword which turned every way.*[13] It is in accord with these states that the degrees of the perfect vary. As for those who never even once see a light, but grope about in their night, of them it is said: *They know not, neither do they understand; They go about in darkness.*[14] The truth, in spite of the strength of its manifestation, is entirely hidden from them, as is said of them: *And now men see not the light which is bright in the skies.*[15] They are the vulgar among the people. There is then no occasion to mention them here in this Treatise.

---

7   Ps. 25:14.
8   B.T., Hagigah, 11b.
9   Or: there are those.
10   Deut. 5:28.
11   Exod. 34:29.
12   Num. 11:25.
13   Gen. 3:24.
14   Ps. 82:5.
15   Job 37:21

Know that whenever one of the perfect wishes to mention, either orally or in writing, something that he understands of these *secrets*, according to the degree of his perfection, he is unable to explain with complete clarity and coherence even the portion that he has apprehended, as he could do with the other sciences whose teaching is generally recognized. Rather there will befall him when teaching another that which he had undergone when learning himself. I mean to say that the subject matter will appear, flash, and then be hidden again, as though this were the nature of this subject matter, be there much or little of it. For this reason, all the Sages possessing knowledge of God the Lord,[16] knowers of the truth, when they aimed at teaching something of this subject matter, spoke of it only in parables and riddles. They even multiplied the parables and made them different in species and even in genus. In most cases the subject to be explained was placed in the beginning or in the middle or at the end of the parable; this happened where a parable appropriate for the intended subject from start to finish could not be found. Sometimes the subject intended to be taught to him who was to be instructed was divided—although it was one and the same subject—among many parables remote from one another. Even more obscure is the case of one and the same parable corresponding to several subjects, its beginning fitting one subject and its ending another. Sometimes the whole is a parable referring to two cognate subjects within the particular species of science in question. The situation is such that the exposition of one who wishes to teach without recourse to parables and riddles is so obscure and brief as to make obscurity and brevity serve in place of parables and riddles. The men of knowledge and the sages[17] are drawn, as it were, toward this purpose by the divine will just as they are drawn by their natural circumstances. Do you not see the following fact? God, may His mention be exalted, wished[18] us to be perfected and the state of our societies to be improved by His laws regarding actions. Now this can come about only after the adoption of intellectual beliefs, the first of which being His apprehension, may He be exalted, according to our capacity. This, in its turn, cannot come about except through divine science, and this divine science cannot become actual except after a study of natural science. This is so since natural science borders on divine science, and its study precedes that of divine science in time as has been made clear to whoever has engaged in speculation on these matters. Hence God, may He be exalted, caused His book to open with the *Account of the Beginning*, which, as we have made clear, is natural science. And because of the greatness and importance of the subject and because our capacity falls short of apprehending the greatest of subjects as it really is, we are told[19] about those profound matters—which divine wisdom has deemed necessary to convey to us—in parables and

---

16   In the context this appears to be the meaning of the two adjectives *al-ilāhī al-rabbānī*; the literal meaning of the former is "divine"; the latter is derived from *rabb* signifying "the Lord."

17   *al-hukamā'*. The term often designates the philosophers.

18   In the text: God . . . when He wished. The sentence that follows is anacoluthic.

19   *khūtibnā*. The Arabic word for rhetoric derives from the same verbal form of the root in question.

riddles and in very obscure words. As [the Sages], *may their memory he blessed*, have said: *It is impossible to tell mortals*[20] *of the power of the Account of the Beginning. For this reason Scripture tells you obscurely: In the beginning God created, and so on.*[21] They thus have drawn your attention to the fact that the above-mentioned subjects are *obscure*. You likewise know *Solomon's* saying: *That which is far off, and exceeding deep; who can find it out?*[22] That which is said about all this is in equivocal terms so that the multitude might comprehend them in accord with the capacity of their understanding and the weakness of their representation, whereas the perfect man, who is already informed, will comprehend them otherwise.

We had promised in the Commentary on the *Mishnah* that we would explain strange subjects in the "Book of Prophecy" and in the "Book of Correspondence"—the latter being a book in which we promised to explain all the difficult passages in the *Midrashim*[23] where the external sense manifestly contradicts the truth and departs from the intelligible. They are all parables. However, when, many years ago, we began these books and composed a part of them, our beginning to explain matters in this way did not commend itself to us. For we saw that if we should adhere to parables and to concealment of what ought to be concealed, we would not be deviating from the primary purpose. We would, as it were, have replaced one individual by another of the same species. If, on the other hand, we explained what ought to be explained, it would be unsuitable for the vulgar among the people. Now it was to the vulgar that we wanted to explain the import of the *Midrashim* and the external meanings of prophecy. We also saw that if an ignoramus among the multitude of Rabbanites should engage in speculation on these *Midrashim*, he would find nothing difficult in them, inasmuch as a rash fool, devoid of any knowledge of the nature of being, does not find impossibilities hard to accept. If, however, a perfect man of virtue should engage in speculation on them, he cannot escape one of two courses: either he can take the speeches in question in their external sense and, in so doing, think ill of their author and regard him as an ignoramus—in this there is nothing that would upset the foundations of belief; or he can attribute to them an inner meaning, thereby extricating himself from his predicament and being able to think well of the author whether or not the inner meaning of the saying is clear to him. With regard to the meaning of prophecy, the exposition of its various degrees, and the elucidation of the parables occurring in the prophetic books, another manner of explanation is used in this Treatise. In view of these considerations, we have given up composing these two books in the way in which they were begun. We have confined ourselves to mentioning briefly the foundations of belief and general truths, while dropping hints that approach a clear exposition, just as we have set them forth in the great legal compilation, *Mishneh Torah.*

---

20   Literally: *flesh and blood.*
21   Cf. Midrash Shnei Kerubim, Batei Midrashoth, IV.
22   Eccles. 7:24.
23   Maimonides uses here and subsequently the term *drashoth.*

My speech in the present Treatise is directed, as I have mentioned, to one who has philosophized[24] and has knowledge of the true sciences,[25] but believes at the same time in the matters pertaining to the Law and is perplexed as to their meaning because of the uncertain terms and the parables. We shall include in this Treatise some chapters in which there will be no mention of an equivocal term. Such a chapter will be preparatory for another, or it will hint at one of the meanings of an equivocal term that I might not wish to mention explicitly in that place, or it will explain one of the parables or hint at the fact that a certain story is a parable. Such a chapter may contain strange matters regarding which the contrary of the truth sometimes is believed, either because of the equivocality of the terms or because a parable is taken for the thing being represented or vice versa.

As I have mentioned parables, we shall make the following introductory remarks: Know that the key to the understanding of all that the prophets, peace be on them, have said, and to the knowledge of its truth, is an understanding of the parables, of their import, and of the meaning of the words occurring in them. You know what God, may He be exalted, has said: *And by the ministry of the prophets have I used similitudes.*[26] And you know that He has said: *Put forth a riddle and speak a parable.*[27] You know too that because of the frequent use prophets make of parables, the prophet has said: *They say of me: Is he not a maker of parables?*[28] You know how *Solomon* began his book: *To understand a proverb, and a figure; The words of the wise, and their dark sayings.*[29] And it said in the *Midrash*: *To what were the words of the Torah to be compared before the advent of Solomon? To a well the waters of which are at a great depth and cool, yet no man could drink of them. Now what did one clever man do? He joined cord with cord and rope with rope and drew them up and drank. Thus did Solomon say one parable after another and speak one word after another until he understood the meaning of the words of the Torah.*[30] That is literally what they say. I do not think that anyone possessing an unimpaired capacity imagines that the *words of the Torah* referred to here that one contrives to understand through understanding the meaning of parables are ordinances concerning the building of *tabernacles*, the *lulab*, and the *law of four trustees*. Rather what this text has in view here is, without any doubt, the understanding of obscure matters. About this it has been said: *Our Rabbis say: A man who loses a sela*[31] *or a pearl in his house can*

---

24   Or: has become a philosopher.

25   Translated in accordance with the Ibn Tibbon Hebrew translation, which supposes a very slight graphical alteration of the Arabic text as we have it. The Arabic text could be rendered: and really have knowledge of the sciences. But the sentence is awkward.

26   Hos. 12:11.

27   Ezek. 17:2.

28   Ezek. 21:5.

29   Prov. 1:6.

30   Cf. Midrash on the Song of Songs, 1:1.

31   A silver coin.

find the pearl by lighting a taper worth an issar.[32] *In the same way this parable in itself is worth nothing, but by means of it you can understand the words of the Torah.*[33] This too is literally what they say. Now consider the explicit affirmation of [the Sages], *may their memory be blessed*, that the internal meaning of the *words of the Torah* is a *pearl* whereas the external meaning of all parables *is* worth *nothing*, and their comparison of the concealment of a subject by its parable's external meaning to a man who let drop a pearl in his house, which was dark and full of furniture. Now this pearl is there, but he does not see it and does not know where it is. It is as though it were no longer in his possession, as it is impossible for him to derive any benefit from it until, as has been mentioned, he lights a lamp—an act to which an understanding of the meaning of the parable corresponds. The Sage has said: *A word fitly spoken is like apples of gold in settings [maskiyyoth] of silver.*[34] Hear now an elucidation of the thought that he has set forth. The term *maskiyyoth* denotes filigree traceries; I mean to say traceries in which there are apertures with very small eyelets, like the handiwork of silversmiths. They are so called because a glance penetrates through them; for in the [Aramaic] *translation* of the Bible the Hebrew term *va-yashqeph*—meaning, he glanced—is translated *va-istekhe.*[35] The Sage accordingly said that a saying uttered with a view to two meanings is like an apple of gold overlaid with silver filigree-work having very small holes. Now see how marvellously this dictum describes a well-constructed parable. For he says that in a saying that has two meanings—he means an external and an internal one—the external meaning ought to be as beautiful as silver, while its internal meaning ought to be more beautiful than the external one, the former being in comparison to the latter as gold is to silver. Its external meaning also ought to contain in it something that indicates to someone considering it what is to be found in its internal meaning, as happens in the case of an apple of gold overlaid with silver filigree-work having very small holes. When looked at from a distance or with imperfect attention, it is deemed to be an apple of silver; but when a keen-sighted observer looks at it with full attention, its interior becomes clear to him and he knows that it is of gold. The parables of the prophets, peace be on them, are similar. Their external meaning contains wisdom that is useful in many respects, among which is the welfare of human societies,[36] as is shown by the external meaning of *Proverbs* and of similar sayings. Their internal meaning, on the other hand, contains wisdom that is useful for beliefs concerned with the truth as it is.

Know that the prophetic parables are of two kinds. In some of these parables each word has a meaning, while in others the parable as a whole indicates the whole of the intended meaning. In such a parable very many words are to be found, not every one of

---

32   A coin; ninety-six *issar* were worth a *sela*.

33   Cf. Midrash on the Song of Songs, 1:1.

34   Prov. 25:11.

35   A verbal form deriving from the same root as the word *maskiyyoth*. Gen. 26:8.

36   Literally: the weal of the circumstances of the human societies.

which adds something to the intended meaning. They serve rather to embellish the parable and to render it more coherent or to conceal further the intended meaning; hence the speech proceeds in such a way as to accord with everything required by the parable's external meaning. Understand this well.

An example of the first kind of prophetic parable is the following text: *And behold a ladder set up on the earth, and so on.*[37] In this text, the word *ladder* indicates one subject; the words *set up on the earth* indicate a second subject; the words *and the top of it reached to heaven* indicate a third subject; the words *and behold the angels of God* indicate a fourth subject; the word *ascending* indicates a fifth subject; the words *and descending* indicate a sixth subject; and the words *And behold the Lord stood above it* indicate a seventh subject. Thus every word occurring in this parable refers to an additional subject in the complex of subjects represented by the parable as a whole.

An example of the second kind of prophetic parable is the following text: *For at the window of my house I looked forth through my lattice; And I beheld among the thoughtless ones, I discerned among the youths, A young man void of understanding, Passing through the street near her corner, And he went the way to her house; In the twilight, in the evening of the day, In the blackness of night and the darkness. And, behold, there met him a woman With the attire of a harlot, and wily of heart. She is riotous and rebellious, and so on.*[38] *Now she is in the streets, now in the broad places, and so on.*[39] *So she caught him, and so on.*[40] *Sacrifices of peace-offerings were due from me, and so on.*[41] *Therefore came I forth to meet thee, and so on.*[42] *I have decked with coverlets, and so on.*[43] *I have perfumed my bed, and so on.*[44] *Come, let us take our fill of love, and so on.*[45] *For my husband is not at home, and so on.*[46] *The bag of money, and so on.*[47] *With her much fair speech she causeth him to yield. With the blandishment of her lips she enticeth him away.*[48] The outcome of all this is a warning against the pursuit of bodily pleasures and desires. Accordingly he [Solomon] likens matter, which is the cause of all these bodily pleasures, to a *harlot* who is also *a married woman*. In fact his entire book is based on this allegory. And we shall explain in various chapters of this Treatise his wisdom in likening matter *to a married*

---

37   Gen. 28:12–13. After the word *earth*, the verses read: *and the top of it reached to heaven, and behold the angels of God ascending and descending on it. And behold the Lord stood above it.*

38   The omitted words are: *her feet abide not in her house.*

39   The omitted words are: *and lieth in wait at every corner.*

40   The omitted words are: *and kissed him, and with impudent face she said unto him.*

41   The omitted words are: *this day have I paid my vows.*

42   The omitted words are: *diligently to seek thy face, and I have found thee.*

43   The omitted words are: *my bed, with striped cloths of the yarn of Egypt.*

44   The omitted words are: *with myrrh, aloes and cinnamon.*

45   The omitted words are: *until the morning; let us solace ourselves with loves.*

46   The omitted words are: *he is gone a long journey.*

47   The omitted words are: *he has taken with him, and will come home at the full moon.*

48   Prov. 7:6–21.

harlot, and we shall explain how[49] he concluded this book of his with a eulogy of the *woman* who is not a *harlot* but confines herself to attending to the welfare of her household and husband.[50] For all the hindrances keeping man from his ultimate perfection, every deficiency affecting him and every disobedience, come to him from his matter alone, as we shall explain in this Treatise. This is the proposition that can be understood from this parable as a whole. I mean that man should not follow his bestial nature;[51] I mean his matter, for the proximate matter of man is identical with the proximate matter of the other living beings.[52] And as I have explained this to you and disclosed the secret of this parable, you should not hope [to find some signification corresponding to every subject occurring in the parable][53] so that you could say: what can be submitted for the words, *Sacrifices of peace offerings were due from me; this day have I paid my vows?* What subject is indicated by the words, *I have decked my couch with coverlets?* And what subject is added to this general proposition by the words, *For my husband is not at home?* The same holds good for the other details in this *chapter.* For all of them only figure in the consistent development of the parable's external meaning, the circumstances described in it being of a kind typical for adulterers. Also the spoken words and other such details are of a kind typical of words spoken among adulterers. Understand this well from what I have said for it is a great and important principle with regard to matters that I wish to explain.

When, therefore, you find that in some chapter of this Treatise I have explained the meaning of a parable and have drawn your attention to the general proposition signified by it, you should not inquire into all the details occurring in the parable, nor should you wish to find significations corresponding to them. For doing so would lead you into one of two ways: either into turning aside from the parable's intended subject, or into assuming an obligation to interpret things not susceptible of interpretation and that have not been inserted with a view to interpretation. The assumption of such an obligation would result in extravagant fantasies such as are entertained and written about in our time by most of the sects of the world, since each of these sects desires to find certain significations for words whose author in no wise had in mind the significations wished by them. Your purpose, rather, should always be to know, regarding most parables, the whole that was intended to be known. In some matters it will suffice you to gather from my remarks that a given story is a parable, even if we explain nothing more; for once you know it is a parable, it will immediately become clear to you what it is a parable of. My remarking that it is a parable will be like someone's removing a screen from between the eye and a visible thing.

49   A literal translation; perhaps the sense requires "why."
50   Literally: the state of her husband.
51   Literally: his bestiality.
52   Or: the other animals.
53   The words enclosed in brackets appear in Ibn Tibbon's Hebrew translation, but not in the printed Arabic text. There is little doubt that in case Ibn Tibbon's text is more correct.

Instruction with Respect to This Treatise

If you wish to grasp the totality of what this Treatise contains, so that nothing of it will escape you, then you must connect its chapters one with another; and when reading a given chapter, your intention must be not only to understand the totality of the subject of that chapter, but also to grasp each word that occurs in it in the course of the speech, even if that word does not belong to the intention of the chapter. For the diction of this Treatise has not been chosen at haphazard,[54] but with great exactness and exceeding precision, and with care to avoid failing to explain any obscure point. And nothing has been mentioned out of its place, save with a view to explaining some matter in its proper place. You therefore should not let your fantasies elaborate on what is said here, for that would hurt me and be of no use to yourself. You ought rather to learn everything that ought to be learned and constantly study this Treatise. For it then will elucidate for you most of the obscurities of the Law that appear as difficult to every intelligent man. I adjure—by God, may He be exalted!—every reader of this Treatise of mine not to comment upon a single word of it and not to explain to another anything in it save that which has been explained and commented upon in the words of the famous Sages of our Law who preceded me. But whatever he understands from this Treatise of those things that have not been said by any of our famous Sages other than myself should not be explained to another; nor should he hasten to refute me, for that which he understood me to say might be contrary to my intention. He thus would harm me in return for my having wanted to benefit him and would *repay evil for good.*[55] All into whose hands it falls should consider it well; and if it slakes his thirst, though it be on only one point from among the many that are obscure,[56] he should thank God and be content with what he has understood. If, on the other hand, he finds nothing in this Treatise that might be of use to him in any respect, he should think of it as not having been composed at all. If anything in it, according to his way of thinking, appears to be in some way harmful, he should interpret it, even if in a farfetched way, in order to *pass a favorable judgment.*[57] For as we are enjoined to act in this way toward our vulgar ones, all the more should this be so with respect to our erudite ones and Sages of our Law who are trying to help us to the truth as they apprehend it. I know that, among men generally, every beginner will derive benefit from some of the chapters of this Treatise, though he lacks even an inkling of what is involved in speculation. A perfect man, on the other hand, devoted to Law and, as I have mentioned, perplexed, will benefit from all its chapters. How greatly will he rejoice in them and how pleasant will it be to hear them! But those who are confused and whose brains have been polluted by false opinions and misleading ways deemed by them to be true sciences, and who hold themselves to be men of speculation

---

54 Literally: the speech does not fall as it may happen.
55 Cf. Ps. 38:21.
56 Literally: though it were only in a certain matter from among the complex of what is difficult.
57 Cf. Mishnah, Aboth, I 6.

without having any knowledge of anything that can truly be called science,[58] those will flee from many of its chapters. Indeed, these chapters will be very difficult for them to bear because they cannot apprehend their meaning and also because they would be led to recognize the falseness of the counterfeit money in their hands—their treasure and fortune held ready for future calamities. God, may He be exalted, knows that I have never ceased to be exceedingly apprehensive about setting down those things that I wish to set down in this Treatise. For they are concealed things; none of them has been set down in any book—written in the religious community[59] in these times of *Exile*[60]—the books composed in these times being in our hands. How then can I now innovate and set them down? However, I have relied on two premises, the one being [the Sages'] saying in a similar case, *It is time to do something for the Lord, and so on*;[61] the second being their saying, Let all thy acts be for the sake of Heaven.[62] Upon these two premises have I relied when setting down what I have composed in some of the chapters of this Treatise.

To sum up: I am the man who when the concern pressed him and his way was straitened and he could find no other device by which to teach a demonstrated truth other than by giving satisfaction to a single virtuous man while displeasing ten thousand ignoramuses—I am he who prefers to address that single man by himself, and I do not heed the blame of those many creatures. For I claim to liberate that virtuous one from that into which he has sunk, and I shall guide him in his perplexity until he becomes perfect and he finds rest.

Introduction

One of seven causes should account for the contradictory or contrary statements to be found in any book or compilation.

The first cause. The author has collected the remarks of various people with differing opinions, but has omitted citing his authorities and has not attributed each remark to the one who said it. Contradictory or contrary statements can be found in such compilations because one of the two propositions is the opinion of one individual while the other proposition is the opinion of another individual.

The second cause. The author of a particular book has adopted a certain opinion that he later rejects; both his original and later[63] statements are retained in the book.

The third cause. Not all the statements in question are to be taken in their external sense; some are to be taken in their external sense, while some others are parables and

---

58   In this phrase the same Arabic term is translated by two words: "knowledge" and "science."

59   Meaning the Jewish community.

60   The Hebrew word *galuth* is used.

61   The verse continues as follows: *for they have infringed Thy Law.* Ps. 119:126; cf. B.T., Berakhoth, 63.

62   Mishnah, Aboth, II 17.

63   Literally: his first and his second.

hence have an inner content. Alternatively, two apparently contradictory propositions may both be parables and when taken in their external sense may contradict, or be contrary to, one another.

The fourth cause. There is a proviso that, because of a certain necessity, has not been explicitly stated in its proper place; or the two subjects may differ, but one of them has not been explained in its proper place, so that a contradiction appears to have been said, whereas there is no contradiction.

The fifth cause arises from the necessity of teaching and making someone understand. For there may be a certain obscure matter that is difficult to conceive. One has to mention it or to take it as a premise in explaining something that is easy to conceive and that by rights ought to be taught before the former, since one always begins with what is easier. The teacher, accordingly, will have to be lax and, using any means that occur to him or gross speculation, will try to make that first matter somehow understood. He will not undertake to state the matter as it truly is in exact terms, but rather will leave it so in accord with the listener's imagination that the latter will understand only what he now wants him to understand. Afterwards, in the appropriate place, that obscure matter is stated in exact terms and explained as it truly is.

The sixth cause. The contradiction is concealed and becomes evident only after many premises. The greater the number of premises needed to make the contradiction evident, the more concealed it is. It thus may escape the author, who thinks there is no contradiction between his two original propositions. But if each proposition is considered separately—a true premise being joined to it and the necessary conclusion drawn—and this is done to every conclusion—a true premise being joined to it and the necessary conclusion drawn—, after many syllogisms the outcome of the matter will be that the two final conclusions are contradictory or contrary to each other. That is the kind of thing that escapes the attention of scholars who write books. If, however, the two original propositions are evidently contradictory, but the author has simply forgotten the first when writing down the second in another part[64] of his compilation, this is a very great weakness, and that man should not be reckoned among those whose speeches deserve consideration.

The seventh cause. In speaking about very obscure matters it is necessary to conceal some parts and to disclose others. Sometimes in the case of certain dicta this necessity requires that the discussion proceed on the basis of a certain premise, whereas in another place necessity requires that the discussion proceed on the basis of another premise contradicting the first one. In such cases the vulgar must in no way be aware of the contradiction; the author accordingly uses some device to conceal it by all means.

---

64   Literally: place.

The contradictions that are to be found in the *Mishnah* and the *Baraithoth* are due to the first cause. Thus you will find that they constantly ask: *Does not the beginning [of the passage] constitute an objection against its end?* In such cases the answer is: *The beginning is the opinion of a certain rabbi and the end that of another rabbi.* You likewise will find that they say: *Rabbi [Judah ha-Nasi] agreed with the opinion of a certain rabbi in this one matter and therefore cited it anonymously. In that other matter he agreed with the opinion of that other rabbi and therefore cited it anonymously.* You often will find them also saying: *Who is the author of this anonymous passage? Such and such rabbi. Who is the author of that passage of the Mishnah? Such and such rabbi.* Such cases are innumerable. The contradictions or divergences to be found in the *Talmud* are due to the first cause and to the second. Thus you find them constantly saying: *In this matter he agreed with this rabbi and in that with another rabbi.* They likewise say: *He agreed with him on one point and disagreed on another.* They also say: *[The two statements are made by] two Amoraim who disagree as to the opinion of a certain rabbi.* All contradictions of this kind are due to the first cause. Contradictions due to the second cause are referred to when they say: *Rab abandoned this opinion. Raba abandoned that opinion.* In such cases an inquiry is made as to which of the two statements is the later one. This is similar to their saying: *In the first recension [of the Talmud] by Rabbi Ashi, he said one thing, and in the second another.* That some passages in every prophetic book, when taken in their external sense, appear to contradict or to be contrary to one another is due to the third cause and to the fourth. And it was with this in view that this entire introduction was written. You already know how often [the Sages], *may their memory be blessed*, say: *One verse says this and another verse says that.* They straightway establish that there is an apparent contradiction. Thereupon they explain that a proviso is lacking in the statement of the subject or that the two texts have different subjects. Thus they say: *Solomon, is it not enough for you that your words contradict those of your father? They also contradict themselves, and so on.*[65] Cases of this are frequent in the sayings of the *Sages, may their memory be blessed*; however, most of the prophetic statements they refer to concern commandments or precepts regarding conduct. We, on the other hand, propose to draw attention to verses that are apparently contradictory with regard to opinions and beliefs. Part of this will be explained in some of the chapters of this Treatise, for this subject too belongs to *the mysteries of the Torah.* Whether contradictions due to the seventh cause are to be found in the books of the prophets is a matter for speculative study and investigation. Statements about this should not be a matter of conjecture. As for the divergences occurring in the books of the philosophers, or rather of those who know the truth, they are due to the fifth cause. On the other hand, the contradictions occurring in most of the books of authors and commentators other than those we have mentioned are due to the sixth cause. Likewise in the *Midrashim* and the *Haggadah* there is to be found great

---

65   B.T., Shabbath, 30a.

contradiction due to this cause. That is why the Sages have said: *No questions should be asked about difficulties in the Haggadah.* There are also to be found therein contradictions due to the seventh cause. Divergences that are to be found in this Treatise are due to the fifth cause and the seventh. Know this, grasp its true meaning, and remember it very well so as not to become perplexed by some of its chapters.

And after these introductory remarks, I shall begin to mention the terms whose true meaning, as intended in every passage according to its context, must be indicated. This, then, will be a key permitting one to enter places the gates to which were locked. And when these gates are opened and these places are entered into, the souls will find rest therein, the eyes will be delighted, and the bodies will be eased of their toil and of their labor.

Chapters LII–LIV

> *The Guide for the Perplexed, Second Edition*, chapters LII through LIV, pp. 391–397, by Moses Maimonides, and translated by M. Friedlander. Dover Publications, Inc. Reprinted by permission of Dover Publications.

Chapter LII

We do not sit, move, and occupy ourselves when we are alone and at home, in the same manner as we do in the presence of a great king; we speak and open our mouth as we please when we are with the people of our own house-hold and with our relatives, but not so when we are in a royal assembly. If we therefore desire to attain human perfection, and to be truly men of God, we must awake from our sleep, and bear in mind that the great king that is over us, and is always joined to us, is greater than any earthly king, greater than David and Solomon. The king that cleaves to us and embraces us is the Intellect that influences us, and forms the link between us and God. We perceive God by means of that light that He sends down unto us, wherefore the Psalmist says, "In Thy light shall we see light" (Ps. xxxvi. 9): so God looks down upon us through that same light, and is always with us beholding and watching us on account of this light. "Can any hide himself in secret places that I shall not see him?" (Jer. xxiii. 24). Note this particularly.

When the perfect bear this in mind, they will be filled with fear of God, humility, and piety, with true, not apparent, reverence and respect of God, in such a manner that their conduct, even when alone with their wives or in the bath, will be as modest as they are in public intercourse with other people. Thus it is related of our renowned Sages that even in their sexual intercourse with their wives they behaved with great modesty. They also said, Who is modest? He whose conduct in the dark night is the same as in the day. You know also how much they warned us not to walk proudly, since "the fullness of the whole earth is His glory" (Isa. vi. 3). They thought that by these rules the abovementioned idea will be firmly established in the hearts of men, viz., that we are always before God, and it is in the presence of His glory that we go to and fro. The great men among our Sages would not uncover their heads because they believed that God's glory was round them and over them; for the same reason they spoke little. In our Commentary on the Sayings of the Fathers (chap. i.17) we have fully explained how we have to restrict our speech. Comp. "For God is in heaven and thou upon earth, therefore let thy words be few" (Eccles. v. 1).

What I have here pointed out to you is the object of all our religious acts. For by [carrying out] all the details of the prescribed practices, and repeating them continually, some few pious men may attain human perfection. They will be filled with respect and reverence towards God; and bearing in mind who is with them, they will perform their duty. God declares in plain words that it is the object of all religious acts to produce in man fear of God and obedience to His word—to state of mind which we have demonstrated in this chapter for those who desire to know the truth, as being our duty to seek. Comp. "If thou wilt not observe to do all the words of this law that are written in this book, that thou mayest fear this glorious and fearful name, the Lord thy God "(Deut. xxviii. 58). Consider how clearly it is stated here that the only object and aim of "all the words of this law" is to [make man] fear "the glorious and fearful name." That this end is attained by certain acts we learn likewise from the phrase employed in this verse: "If thou wilt not observe *to do* . . . that thou mayest fear." For this phrase clearly shows that fear of God is inculcated [into our hearts] when we act in accordance with the positive and the negative precepts. But the truths which the Law teaches us—the knowledge of God's Existence and Unity—create in us love of God, as we have shown repeatedly. You know how frequently the Law exhorts us to love God. Comp. "And thou shalt love the Lord thy God with all thine heart, and with all thy soul, and with all thy might" (Deut. vi. 5). The two objects, love and fear of God, are acquired by two different means. The love is the result of the truths taught in the Law, including the true knowledge of the Existence of God; whilst fear of God is produced by the practices prescribed in the Law. Note this explanation.

Chapter LIII

This chapter treats of the meaning of three terms which we find necessary to explain, viz., *hesed* ("loving-kindness"), *mishpat* ("judgment"), and *Zedakah* ("righteousness").

In our Commentary on the Sayings of the Fathers (chap. v. 7) we have explained the expression *hesed* as denoting an excess [in some moral quality]. It is especially used of extraordinary kindness. Loving-kindness is practiced in two ways: first, we show kindness to those who have no claim whatever upon us; secondly, we are kind to those to whom it is due, in a greater measure than is due to them. In the inspired writings the term *hesed* occurs mostly in the sense of showing kindness to those who have no claim to it whatever. For this reason the term *hesed* is employed to express the good bestowed upon us by God; "I will mention the loving-kindness of the Lord" (Isa. lxiii. 7). On this account, the very act of the creation is an act of God's loving-kindness. "I have said, The Universe is built up in loving-kindness" (Ps. lxxxix. 3); i.e., the building up of the Universe is an act of loving-kindness. Also, in the enumeration of God's attributes, Scripture says: "And abundant in loving-kindness" (Exod. xxxiv. 6).

The term *zedakah* is derived from zedakah, "righteousness"; it denotes the act of giving everyone his due, and of showing kindness to every being according as it deserves. In Scripture, however, the expression *zedakah* is not used in the first sense, and does not apply to the payment of what we owe to others. When we therefore give the hired labor his wages, or pay a debt, we do not perform an act of *zedakah*. But we do perform an act of *zedakah* when we fulfill those duties towards our fellowmen which our moral conscience imposes upon us; e.g., when we heal the wound of the sufferer. Thus Scripture says, in reference to the returning of the pledge [to the poor debtor]: "And it shall be *zedakah* (righteousness) unto thee" (Deut. xxiv. 11). When we walk in the way-of virtue we act righteously towards our intellectual faculty, and pay what is due unto it; and because every virtue is thus *zedakah*, Scripture applies the term to the virtue of faith in God. Comp. "And he believed in the Lord, and he accounted it to him as righteousness" (Gen. xv. 6); "And it shall be our righteousness" (Deut. vi. 25).

The noun *mishpat*, "judgment" denotes the act of deciding upon a certain action in accordance with justice which may demand either mercy or punishment.

We have thus shown that *hesed* denotes pure charity; *zedekah* kindness, prompted by a certain moral conscience in man, and being a means of attaining perfection for his soul, whilst *mishpat* may in some cases find expression in revenge, in other cases in mercy.

In discussing the impropriety of admitting attributes of God (Part L, chap, liii., *seq*.), we stated that the divine attributes which occur in Scripture are attributes of His actions; thus He is called *hasid*, "kind," because He created the Universe; *zaddik*, "righteous," on account of His mercy with the weak, in providing for every living being according to its powers; and *shofet*, "judge," on account of the relative good and the great relative evils that are decreed by God's justice as directed by His wisdom. These three names occur in the Pentateuch: "Shall not the Judge (*shofet*) of all the earth," etc. (Gen. xviii. 25); "Righteous (*zaddik*) and upright is he" (Deut. xxxii. 4); "Abundant in loving-kindness" (*hased*, Exod. xxxiv. 6).

We intended in explaining these three terms to prepare the reader for the next chapter.

Chapter LIV

The term *hokmah* ("wisdom") in Hebrew is used of four different things: (1) It denotes the knowledge of those truths which lead to the knowledge of God. Comp. "But where shall wisdom be found?" (Job xxviii. 12); "If thou seekest her like silver" (Prov. ii. 4). The word occurs frequently in this sense. (2) The expression *hokmah* denotes also knowledge of any workmanship. Comp. "And every wise-hearted among you shall come and make all that the Lord hath commanded" (Exod. xxxv. 10); "And all the women that were wise-hearted did spin" (*ibid*. ver. 25). (3) It is also used of the acquisition of moral principles. Comp. "And teach his senators wisdom" (Ps. cv. 22); "With the ancient is wisdom" (Job xii. 12); for it is chiefly the disposition for acquiring moral principles that is developed by old age alone. (4) It implies, lastly, the notion of cunning and subtlety; comp. "Come on, let us deal wisely with them" (Exod. i. 10). In the same *sense* the term is used in the following passages: "And fetched thence a wise woman" (2 Sam. xiv. 2); "They are wise to do evil" (Jer. iv. 22). It is possible that the Hebrew *hokmah* ("wisdom") expresses the idea of cunning and planning, which may serve in one case as a means of acquiring intellectual perfection, or good moral principles; but may in another case produce skill in workmanship, or even be employed in establishing bad opinions and principles. The attribute *hakam* ("wise") is therefore given to a person that possesses great intellectual faculties, or good moral principles, or skill in art; but also to persons cunning in evil deeds and principles.

According to this explanation, a person that has a true knowledge of the whole Law is called wise in a double sense; he is wise because the Law instructs him in the highest truths, and secondly, because it teaches him good morals. But as the truths contained in the Law are taught by way of tradition, not by a philosophical method, the knowledge of the Law, and the acquisition of true wisdom, are treated in the books of the Prophets and in the words of our Sages as two different things; real wisdom demonstrates by proof those truths which Scripture teaches us by way of tradition. It is to this kind of wisdom, which proves the truth of the Law that Scripture refers when it extols wisdom, and speaks of the high value of that perfection, and of the consequent paucity of men capable of acquiring it, in sayings like these: "Not many are wise" (Job xxxii. 9); "But where shall wisdom be found" (*ibid*, xxviii. 12)? In the writings of our Sages we notice likewise many passages in which distinction is made between knowledge of the Law and wisdom. They say of Moses, our Teacher, that he was Father in the knowledge of the Law, in wisdom and in prophecy. When Scripture says of Solomon, "And he was wiser than all men" (1 Kings v. 11), our Sages add, "but not greater than Moses"; and the phrase, "than all men," is explained to mean, "than all men of his generation"; for this reason [only] "Heman, Chalcol, and Darda, the sons of Mahol," the renowned wise men of that time, are named. Our Sages further say, that man has first to render account concerning his knowledge of the Law, then concerning the acquisition of wisdom, and at last concerning the lessons derived by logical conclusions from the Law, i.e., the lessons concerning his actions. This is also the right order: we must first learn the truths by tradition, after this we must be taught how to prove them, and then investigate the actions that help to improve man's ways. The idea that man will have to render account concerning these three things in the order described, is expressed by our Sages in the following passage: "When man comes to the trial, he is first asked, 'Hast thou fixed certain seasons for the study of the Law? Hast thou been engaged in the acquisition of wisdom? Hast thou derived from one thing another thing?" This proves that our Sages distinguished between the knowledge of the Law on the one hand, and wisdom on the other, as the means of proving the lessons taught in the Law by correct reasoning.

Hear now what I have to say after having given the above explanation. The ancient and the modern philosophers have shown that man can acquire four kinds of perfection. The first kind, the lowest, in the acquisition of which people spend their days, is perfection as regards property; the possession of money, garments, furniture, servant, land, and the like; the possession of the title of a great king belongs to this class. There is no close connexion between this possession and its possessor; it is a perfectly imaginary relation when on account of the great advantage a person derives from these possessions, he says, This is my house, this is my servant, this is my money, and these are my hosts and armies. For when he examines himself he will find that all these things are external, and their qualities are entirely independent of the possessor. When, therefore, that relation ceases, he that has been a great king may one morning find that there is no difference between him and the lowest person, and yet no change has taken place in the things which were ascribed to him. The philosophers have shown that he whose sole aim in all his exertions and endeavours is the possession of this kind of perfection, only seeks perfectly imaginary and transient things; and even if these remain his property all his lifetime, they do not give him any perfection.

The second kind is more closely related to man's body than the first. It includes the perfection of the shape, constitution, and form of man's body; the utmost evenness of temperaments, and the proper order and strength of his limbs. This kind of perfection must likewise be excluded from forming our chief aim; because it is a perfection of the body, and man does not possess it as man, but as a living being; he has this property besides in common with the lowest animal; and even if a person possesses the greatest possible strength, he could not be as strong as a mule, much less can he be as strong as a lion or an elephant; he, therefore, can at the utmost have strength that might enable him to carry a heavy burden, or break a thick substance, or do similar things, in which there is no great profit for the body. The soul derives no profit whatever from this kind of perfection.

The third kind of perfection is more closely connected with man himself than the second perfection. If includes moral perfection, the highest degree of excellency in man's character. Most of the precepts aim at producing this perfection; but even this kind is only a preparation for another perfection, and is not sought for its own sake. For all moral principles concern the relation of man to his neighbor; the perfection of man's moral principles is, as it were, given to man for the benefit of mankind. Imagine a person being alone, and having no connexion whatever with any other person, all his good moral principles are at rest, they are not required, and give man no perfection whatever. These principles are only necessary and useful when man comes in contact with others.

The fourth kind of perfection is the true perfection of man; the possession of the highest intellectual faculties; the possession of such notions which lead to true metaphysical opinions as regards God. With this perfection man has obtained his final object; it gives him true human perfection; it remains to him alone; it gives him immortality, and on its account he is called man. Examine the first three kinds of perfection, you will find that, if you possess them, they are not your property, but the property of others; according to the ordinary view, however, they belong to you and to others. But the last kind of perfection is exclusively yours; no one else owns any part of it, "They shall be only thine own, and not strangers' with thee" (Prov. v. 17). Your aim must therefore be to attain this [fourth] perfection that is exclusively yours, and you ought not to continue to work and weary yourself for that which belongs to others, whilst neglecting your soul till it has lost entirely its original purity through the dominion of the bodily powers over it. The same idea is expressed in the beginning of those poems, which allegorically represent the state of our soul. "My mother's children were angry with me; they made me the keeper of the vineyards; but mine own vineyard have I not kept" (Song i. 6). Also the following passage refers to the same subject, "Lest thou give thine honour unto others, and thy years unto the cruel" (Prov. v. 9).

The prophets have likewise explained unto us these things, and have expressed the same opinion on them as the philosophers. They say distinctly that perfection in property, in health, or in character, is not a perfection worthy to be sought as a cause of pride and glory for us; that the knowledge of God, i.e., true wisdom, is the only perfection which we should seek, and in which we should glorify ourselves. Jeremiah, referring to these four kinds of perfection, says: "Thus saith the Lord, Let not the wise man glory in his wisdom, neither let the mighty man glory in his might, let not the rich man glory in his riches; but let him that glorieth glory in this, that he understand and knoweth me" (Jer. ix. 22, 23). See how the prophet arranged them according to their estimation in the eyes of the multitude. The rich man occupies the first rank; next is the mighty man; and then the wise man; that is, the man of good moral principles: for in the eyes of the multitude, who are addressed in these words, he is likewise a great man. This is the reason why the three classes are enumerated in this order.

Our Sages have likewise derived from this passage the above-mentioned lessons, and stated the same theory that has been explained in this chapter, viz., that the simple term, *hokmah*, as a rule, denotes the highest aim of man, the knowledge of God; that those properties which man acquires, makes his peculiar treasure, and considers as his perfection, in reality do not include any perfection; and that the religious acts prescribed in the Law, viz., the various kinds of worship and the moral principles which benefit all people in their social intercourse with each other, do not constitute the ultimate aim of man, nor can they be compared to it, for they are but preparations leading to it. Hear the opinion of our Sages on this subject in their own words. The passage occurs in *Bereshit Rabba*, and runs thus, "In one place Scripture says, 'And all things that are desirable (*hafazim*) are not to be compared to her' (Prov. viii. 11); and in another place, 'And all things that thou desirest (*hafazeha*) are not to be compared unto her'" (*ibid.* iii. 15). By "things that are desirable" the performance of Divine precepts and good deeds is to be understood, whilst "things that thou desirest" refer to precious stones and pearls. Both—things that are desirable, and things that thou desirest—cannot be compared to wisdom, but "in this let him that glorieth glory, that he understand and knoweth me." Consider how concise this saying is, and how perfect its author; how nothing is here omitted of all that we have put forth after lengthy explanations and preliminary remarks.

Having stated the sublime ideas contained in that Scriptural passage, and quoted the explanation of our Sages, we will now complete what the remainder of that passage teaches us. The prophet does not content himself with explaining that the knowledge of God is the highest kind of perfection; for if this only had been his intention, he would have said, "But in this let him who glorieth glory, that he understand and knoweth me," and would have stopped there; or he would have said, "that he understand and knoweth me that I am One," or, "that I have not any likeness," or, "that there is none like me," or a similar phrase. He says, however, that man can only glory in the knowledge of God and in the knowledge of His ways and attributes, which are His actions, as we have shown (Part L liv.) in expounding the passage, "Show me now thy ways "(Exod. xxiviii. 13). We are thus told in this passage that the Divine acts which ought to be known, and ought to serve as a guide for our actions, are, *hesed* "loving-kindness," *mishpat*, "judgment," and *zedakah*, "righteousness." Another very important lesson is taught by the additional phrase, "in the earth." It implies a fundamental principle of the Law; it rejects the theory of those who boldly assert that God's providence does not extend below the sphere of the moon, and that the earth with its contents is abandoned, that "the Lord hath forsaken the earth" (Ez. viii. 12). It teaches, as has been taught by the greatest of all wise men in the words, "The earth is the Lord's" (Exod. ix. 29), that His providence extends to the earth in accordance with its nature, in the same manner as it controls the heavens in accordance with their nature. This is expressed in the words, 'That I am the Lord which exercise loving-kindness, judgment, and righteousness in the earth." The prophet thus, in conclusion, says, "For in these things I delight, saith the Lord," i.e., My object [in saying this] is that you shall practice loving-kindness, judgment, and righteousness in the earth. In a similar manner we have shown (Part I. liv.) that the object of the enumeration of God's thirteen attributes is the lesson that we should acquire similar attributes and act accordingly. The object of the above passage is therefore to declare, that the perfection, in which man can truly glory, is attained by him when he has acquired—as far as this is possible for man—the knowledge of God, the knowledge of His Providence, and of the manner in which it influences His creatures in their production and continued existence. Having acquired this knowledge he will then be determined always to seek loving-kindness, judgment, and righteousness, and thus to imitate the ways of God. We have explained this many times in this treatise.

This is all that I thought proper to discuss in this treatise, and which I considered useful for men like you. I hope that, by the help of God, you will, after due reflection, comprehend all the things which I have treated here. May He grant us and all Israel with us to attain what He promised us, "Then the eyes of the blind shall be opened, and the ears of the deaf shall be unstopped" (Isa. xxxv. 5); "The people that walked in darkness have seen a great light; they that dwell in the shadow of death upon them hath the light shined" (ibid. ix. 1).

God is near to all who call Him, if they call Him in truth, and turn to Him. He is found by everyone who seeks Him, if he always goes towards Him, and never goes astray. AMEN.

Julian of Norwich

Introduction
Nancy Enright

The famous British anchorite, Julian of Norwich, lived during the fourteenth century in a small cell attached to the Church of St. Julian in Norwich. Her actual name is unknown. Though she lived in complete simplicity and intentional withdrawal from the world, she became well-known for her wise counsel, welcoming the many pilgrims who came to her cell for her advice. Among these was her fellow mystic, Margery Kempe. Her sixteen revelations—or "shewings," as she called them—extended over a period of only twenty-four hours, though it took her, she says, fifteen years to understand them. The message of these revelations is one of enormous comfort and encouragement, though it is never platitudinous. Rather, the revelations are rooted in a profound understanding of the meaning of Christ's passion and death.

Julian experienced her "shewings" after a mysterious illness that she attributed to being an answer to a prayer. At about thirty years of age, while still living with her family, Julian asked God for the gift of an illness that would seem to bring her close to death. Along with this request for physical suffering, Julian requested two other things: a deep and personal understanding of the passion of Christ and "three wounds" of "true contrition," "genuine compassion," and "sincere longing for God." All of these requests were apparently answered. In the throes of her illness, which seemed to come upon her suddenly, she experienced what it is like to lose sensation in her body and to feel the approach of death. Her intention in seeking this experience was not to have suffering for its own sake, but to deepen her spiritual life and increase her personal holiness. After receiving the "last rites," or Extreme Unction, Julian recovered. It was then that she experienced the first of her revelations.

From this first "shewing," in which she saw Christ crowned with thorns, to the last, the theme of their message is the love of God for His people. Aware in a new way of the intense suffering of Christ and His great willingness to endure it for our sake, Julian also received specific words from Him regarding the depth of His love. In one vision, she saw a hazelnut, and it was revealed to her that it represented "all that is," and the Lord showed her that it exists solely because of his love for it. A recurring phrase in the revelations is "All shall be well," and the sense of grace, the enormity of forgiveness available through Christ's passion and death, is the source of this comforting belief in God's providence. Even sin, the source of Christ's great agony, is rendered powerless through it. Though our sins grieve us, they do not stop God from loving us. Often she speaks of Christ as "our mother," emphasizing the nurturing, gentle, life-giving nature of his love, though never negating the historical reality of Jesus Christ as a human male. Speaking in the tradition of mystical adoration that acknowledges the nature of God as being beyond male and female, Julian echoes such passages in the Bible where God describes his own love as being like a mother's.

In fact, though some scholars would disagree, Julian makes a point of acknowledging that her revelations are not meant to contradict any teaching of the Church. Though it might be argued that she makes this assertion out of fear of reprisals, her character—so transparently revealed in her book—makes such a possibility very unlikely. Julian feared neither death nor suffering. Her gift to the Church of her day and ours is that she reveals to it the true face of orthodoxy—the love underlying the sacramental and hierarchical structure of the Church, rooted in Christ's death and Resurrection and central to all genuine Christian holiness.

REVELATIONS OF DIVINE LOVE (Selections)

Short Text

Chapter i

Here is a vision shown by the goodness of God to a devout woman, and her name is
Julian, who is a recluse at Norwich and still alive, A.D. 1413, in which vision are very
many words of comfort, greatly moving for all those who desire to be Christ's lovers.

I desired three graces by the gift of God. The first was to have recollection of Christ's
Passion. The second was a bodily sickness, and the third was to have, of God's gift, three
wounds. As to the first, it came into my mind with devotion; it seemed to me that I
had great feeling for the Passion of Christ, but still I desired to have more by the grace
of God. I thought that I wished that I had been at that time with Mary Magdalen and
with the others who were Christ's lovers, so that I might have seen with my own eyes our
Lord's Passion which he suffered for me, so that I might have suffered with him as others
did who loved him, even though I believed firmly in all Christ's pains, as Holy Church
shows and teaches, and as paintings of the Crucifixion represent, which are made by
God's grace, according to Holy Church's teaching, to resemble Christ's Passion, so far
as human understanding can attain. But despite all my true faith I desired a bodily
sight, through which I might have more knowledge of our Lord and saviour's bodily
pains, and of the compassion of our Lady and of all his true lovers who were living at
that time and saw his pains[1], for I would have been one of them and have suffered with
them. I never desired any other sight of God or revelation, until my soul would be separated from the body, for I trusted truly that I would be saved. My intention was, because
of that revelation, to have had truer recollection of Christ's Passion. As to the second
grace, there came into my mind with contrition—a free gift from God which I did not
seek—a desire of my will to have by God's gift a bodily sickness, and I wished it to be
so severe that it might seem mortal, so that I should in that sickness receive all the rites
which Holy Church had to give me, whilst I myself should believe that I was dying, and
everyone who saw me would think the same, for I wanted no comfort from any human,
earthly life. In this sickness I wanted to have every kind of pain, bodily and spiritual,
which I should have if I were dying, every fear and assault from devils, and every other
kind of pain except the departure of the spirit, for I hoped that this would be profitable
to me when I should die, because I desired soon to be with my God.

---

1   The short text reads: 'and of all his true lovers who were believing in his pains, at that time and afterwards', but the long
      text here clearly is superior.

I desired these two, concerning the Passion and the sickness, with a condition, because it seemed to me that neither was an ordinary petition, and therefore I said: Lord, you know what I want. If it be your will that I have it, grant it to me, and if it be not your will, good Lord, do not be displeased, for I want nothing which you do not want. When I was young I desired to have that sickness when I was thirty years old. As to the third, I heard a man of Holy Church tell the story of St. Cecilia, and from his explanation I understood that she received three wounds in the neck from a sword, through which she suffered death. Moved by this, I conceived a great desire, and prayed our Lord God that he would grant me in the course of my life three wounds, that is, the wound of contrition, the wound of compassion and the wound of longing with my will for God. Just as I asked for the other two conditionally, so I asked for this third without any condition. The two desires which I mentioned first passed from my mind, and the third remained there continually.

Chapter ii

And when I was thirty and a half years old, God sent me a bodily sickness in which I lay for three days and three nights; and on the fourth night I received all the rites of Holy Church, and did not expect to live until day. But after this I suffered on for two days and two nights, and on the third night I often thought that I was on the point of death; and those who were around me also thought this. But in this I was very sorrowful and reluctant to die, not that there was anything on earth that it pleased me to live for, or anything of which I was afraid, for I trusted in God. But it was because I wanted to go on living to love God better and longer, and living so, obtain grace to know and love God more as he is in the bliss of heaven. For it seemed to me that all the time that I had lived here was very little and short in comparison with the bliss which is everlasting. So I thought: Good Lord, is it no longer to your glory that I am alive? And my reason and my sufferings told me that I should die; and with all the will of my heart I assented wholly to be as was God's will.

So I lasted until day, and by then my body was dead from the middle downwards, it felt to me. Then I was moved to ask to be lifted up and supported, with cloths held to my head, so that my heart might be more free to be at God's will, and so that I could think of him whilst my life would last; and those who were with me sent for the parson, my curate, to be present at my end. He came with a little boy, and brought a cross; and by that time my eyes were fixed, and I could not speak. The parson set the cross before my face and said: Daughter, I have brought you the image of your saviour. Look at it and take comfort from it, in reverence of him who died for you and me. It seemed to me that I was well as I was, for my eyes were set upwards towards heaven, where I trusted that I was going; but nevertheless I agreed to fix my eyes on the face of the crucifix if I could, so as to hold out longer until my end came, for it seemed to me that I could hold out longer with my eyes set in front of me rather than upwards. After this my sight began to fail, and it was all dark around me in the room, dark as night, except that there was ordinary light trained upon the image of the cross, I never knew how. Everything around the cross was ugly to me, as if it were occupied by a great crowd of devils.

After that I felt as if the upper part of my body were beginning to die. My hands fell down on either side, and I was so weak that my head lolled to one side. The greatest pain that I felt was my shortness of breath and the ebbing of my life. Then truly I believed that I was at the point of death. And suddenly in that moment all my pain left me, and I was as sound, particularly in the upper part of my body, as ever I was before or have been since. I was astonished by this change, for it seemed to me that it was by God's secret doing and not natural; and even so, in this ease which I felt, I had no more confidence that I should live, nor was the ease complete, for I thought that I would rather have been delivered of this world, because that was what my heart longed for.

Chapter iii

And suddenly it came into my mind that I ought to wish for the second wound, that our Lord, of his gift and of his grace, would fill my body full with recollection and feeling[2] of his blessed Passion, as I had prayed before, for I wished that his pains might be my pains, with compassion which would lead to longing for God. So it seemed to me that I might with his grace have his wounds, as I had wished before; but in this I never wanted any bodily vision or any kind of revelation from God, but only the compassion which I thought a loving soul could have for our Lord Jesus, who for love was willing to become a mortal man. I desired to suffer with him, living in my mortal body, as God would give me grace. And at this, suddenly I saw the red blood trickling down from under the crown, all hot, flowing freely and copiously, a living stream, just as it seemed to me that it was at the time when the crown of thorns was thrust down upon his blessed head. Just so did he, both God and man, suffer for me. I perceived, truly and powerfully, that it was himself who showed this to me, without any intermediary; and then I said: Blessed be the Lord! This I said with a reverent intention and in a loud voice, and I was greatly astonished by this wonder and marvel, that he would so humbly be[3] with a sinful creature living in this wretched flesh. I accepted it that at that time our Lord Jesus wanted, out of his courteous love, to show me comfort before my temptations began; for it seemed to me that I might well be tempted by devils, by God's permission and with his protection, before I died. With this sight of his blessed Passion and with his divinity, of which I speak as I understand[4] I saw that this was strength enough for me, yes, and for all living creatures who will be protected from all the devils of hell and from all their spiritual enemies.

---

2   So the long text, which is superior to the short text's 'recollection of feeling'.

3   Or 'would be so familiar'; cf. the long text.

4   Or 'which I saw in my understanding'.

Chapter iv

And at the same time as I saw this corporeal sight, our Lord showed me a spiritual sight of his familiar love. I saw that he is to us everything which is good and comforting for our help. He is our clothing, for he is that love which wraps and enfolds us, embraces us and guides us, surrounds us for his love, which is so tender that he may never desert us. And so in this sight I saw truly that he is everything which is good, as I understand.

And in this he showed me something small, no bigger than a hazelnut, lying in the palm of my hand, and I perceived that it was as round as any ball. I looked at it and thought: What can this be? And I was given this general answer: It is everything which is made. I was amazed that it could last, for I thought that it was so little that it could suddenly fall into nothing. And I was answered in my understanding: It lasts and always will, because God loves it; and thus everything has being through the love of God.

In this little thing I saw three properties.[5] The first is that God made it, the second is that he loves it, the third is that God preserves it. But what is that to me? It is that God is the creator and the lover and protector. For until I am substantially united to him, I can never have love or rest or true happiness; until, that is, I am so attached to him that there can be no created thing between my God and me. And who will do this deed? Truly, he himself, by his mercy and his grace, for he has made me for this and has blessedly restored me.

In this God brought our Lady to my understanding. I saw her spiritually in her bodily likeness, a simple, humble maiden, young in years, of the stature which she had when she conceived. Also God showed me part of the wisdom and truth of her soul, and in this I understood the reverent contemplation with which she beheld her God, marveling with great reverence that he was willing to be born of her who was a simple creature created by him[6]. And this wisdom and truth[7], this knowledge of her creator's greatness and of her own created littleness, made her say meekly to the angel Gabriel: Behold me here, God's handmaiden. In this sight I saw truly that she is greater, more worthy and more fulfilled, than everything else which God has created, and which is inferior to her. Above her is no created thing, except the blessed humanity of Christ. This little thing which is created and is inferior to our Lady, St. Mary—God showed it to me as if it had been a hazelnut—seemed to me as if it could have perished because it is so little.

In this blessed revelation God showed me three nothings, of which nothings this is the first that was shown to me. Every man and woman who wishes to live contemplatively needs to know of this, so that it may be pleasing to them to despise as nothing everything created, so as to have the love of uncreated God. For this is the reason why those

---

5   'Properties' (cf. the long text) is more probable than the short text's 'parts'.

6   This corrects a scribal error found in both texts. See *Showings*, I, 213.

7   So the long text, which is superior to the short text's 'wisdom of truth'.

who deliberately occupy themselves with earthly business, constantly seeking worldly well-being, have not God's rest[8] in their hearts and souls; for they love and seek their rest in this thing which is so little and in which there is no rest, and do not know God who is almighty, all wise and all good, for he is true rest. God wishes to be known, and it pleases him that we should rest in him; for all things which are beneath him are not sufficient for us. And this is the reason why no soul has rest until it has despised as nothing all which is created. When the soul has become nothing for love, so as to have him who is all that is good, then is it able to receive spiritual rest.

Chapter v

And during the time that our Lord showed me this spiritual vision which I have now described, I saw the bodily vision of the copious bleeding of the head persist, and as long as I saw it I said, many times: Blessed be the Lord! In this first revelation of our Lord I saw in my understanding six things. The first is the tokens of his blessed Passion, and the plentiful shedding of his precious blood. The second is the virgin who is his beloved mother. The third is the blessed divinity, that always was and is and ever shall be, almighty, all wisdom and all love. The fourth is everything which he has made; it is great and lovely and bountiful and good. But the reason why it seemed to my eyes so little was because I saw it in the presence of him who is the Creator. For to a soul who sees the Creator of all things, all that is created seems very little. The fifth is that he has made everything which is made for love, and through the same love is it preserved, and always will be without end, as has been said already. The sixth is that God is everything which is good, and the goodness which everything has is God.

This everything God showed me in the first vision, and he gave me space and time to contemplate it. And then the bodily vision ceased, and the spiritual vision persisted in my understanding, and I waited with reverent fear, rejoicing in what I saw and wishing, as much as I dared, to see more, if that were God's will, or to see for a longer time what I had already seen.

Chapter vi

Everything that I say[9] about myself I mean to apply to all my fellow Christians, for I am taught that this is what our Lord intends in this spiritual revelation. And therefore I pray you all for God's sake, and I counsel you for your own profit, that you disregard the wretched worm, the sinful creature to whom it was shown, and that mightily, wisely, lovingly and meekly you contemplate God, who out of his courteous love and his endless goodness was willing to show this vision generally, to the comfort of us all. And you who hear and see this vision and this teaching, which is from Jesus Christ for the

---

8   The short text is corrupt, and this is the reading of the long text. But Julian may have written 'are not his heirs'; cf. *Showings*, I, 215.

9   'Say' is here more probable than 'saw'. See *Showings*, I, 219 and II, 219–20

edification of your souls, it is God's will and my wish that you accept it with as much joy and delight as if Jesus had shown it to you as he did to me. I am not good because of the revelation, but only if I love God better, and so can and so should every man do who sees it and hears it with good will and proper intention. And so it is my desire that it should be to every man the same profit that I asked for myself, and was moved to in the first moment when I saw it; for it is common and general, just as we are all one; and I am sure that I saw it for the profit of many others. For truly it was not revealed to me because God loves me better than the humblest soul who is in a state of grace. For I am sure that there are very many who never had revelations or visions, but only the common teaching of Holy Church, who love God better than I. If I pay special attention to myself, I am nothing at all; but in general I am in the unity of love with all my fellow Christians. For it is in this unity of love that the life consists of all men who will be saved. For God is everything that is good, and God has made everything that is made, and God loves everything that he has made, and if any man or woman withdraws his love from any of his fellow Christians, he does not love at all, because he has not love towards all. And so in such times he is in danger, because he is not at peace; and anyone who has general love for his fellow Christians has love towards everything which is. For in mankind which will be saved is comprehended all, that is, all that is made and the maker of all; for God is in man, and so in man is all. And he who thus generally loves all his fellow Christians loves all, and he who loves thus is safe. And thus will I love, and thus do I love, and thus I am safe—I write as the representative of my fellow Christians—and the more that I love in this way whilst I am here, the more I am like the joy that I shall have in heaven without end, that joy which is the God who out of his endless love willed to become our brother and suffer for us. And I am sure that anyone who sees it so will be taught the truth and be greatly comforted, if he have need of comfort. But God forbid that you should say or assume that I am a teacher, for that is not and never was my intention; for I am a woman, ignorant, weak and frail. But I know very well that what I am saying I have received by the revelation of him who is the sovereign teacher. But it is truly love which moves me to tell it to you, for I want God to be known and my fellow Christians to prosper, as I hope to prosper myself, by hating sin more and loving God more. But because I am a woman, ought I therefore to believe that I should not tell you of the goodness of God, when I saw at that same time that it is his will that it be known? You will see this clearly in what follows, if it be well and truly accepted. Then will you soon forget me who am a wretch, and do this, so that I am no hindrance to you, and you will contemplate Jesus, who is every man's teacher. I speak of those who will be saved, for at this time God showed me no one else; but in everything I believe as Holy Church teaches, for I beheld the whole of this blessed revelation of our Lord as unified in God's sight, and I never understood anything from it which bewilders me or keeps me from the true doctrine of Holy Church.

Chapter xv

And so our good Lord answered to all the questions and doubts which I could raise, saying most comfortingly in this fashion: I will make all things well, I shall make all things well, I may make all things well and I can make all things well; and you will see that yourself, that all things will be well. When he says that he 'may', I understand this to apply to the Father; and when he says that he 'can', I understand this for the Son; and when he says 'I will', I understand this for the Holy Spirit; and when he says 'I shall', I understand this for the unity of the blessed Trinity, three persons in one truth; and when he says 'You will see yourself', I understand this for the union of all men who will be saved in the blessed Trinity.

And in these five words[10] God wishes to be enclosed in rest and in peace. And so Christ's spiritual thirst has an end. For his spiritual thirst is his longing in love, and that persists and always will until we see him on the day of judgment; for we who shall be saved and shall be Christ's joy and bliss are still here, and shall be until that day. Therefore his thirst is this incompleteness of his joy, that he does not now possess us in himself as wholly as he then will.

All this was shown to me as a revelation of his compassion, for on the day of judgment it will cease. So he has pity and compassion on us and he longs to possess us, but his wisdom and his love do not permit the end to come until the best time. And in these same five words[11] said before: 'I may make all things well', I understand powerful consolation from all the deeds of our Lord which are still to be performed; for just as the blessed Trinity created everything from nothing, just so the same blessed Trinity will make well all things which are not well. It is God's will that we pay great heed to all the deeds which he has performed, for he wishes us to know from them all which he will do; and he revealed that to me by those words which he said: And you will see yourself that every kind of thing will be well. I understand this in two ways: One is that I am well content that I do not know it; and the other is that I am glad and joyful because I shall know it. It is God's will that we should know in general that all will be well, but it is not God's will that we should know it now except as it applies to us for the present, and that is the teaching of Holy Church.

Long Text

Chapter 29

But in this I stood[12] contemplating it generally, darkly and mournfully, saying in intention to our Lord with very great fear: Ah, good Lord, how could all things be well,

---

10   'May', 'can', 'will', 'shall', 'you will see . . . '

11   This seems to refer to 'I may make all things well'. See *Showings*, I, 250.

12   Correspondence with the short text resumes

because of the great harm which has come through sin to your creatures? And here I wished, so far as I dared, for some plainer explanation through which I might be at ease about this matter. And to this our blessed Lord answered, very meekly and with a most loving manner, and he showed that Adam's sin was the greatest harm ever done or ever to be done until the end of the world. And he also showed me that this is plainly known to all Holy Church upon earth.

Furthermore, he taught that I should contemplate the glorious atonement, for this atoning is more pleasing to the blessed divinity and more honourable for man's salvation, without comparison, than ever Adam's sin was harmful. So then this is our blessed Lord's intention, and in this teaching we should pay heed to this: For since I have set right the greatest of harms, then it is my will that you should know through this that I shall set right everything which is less.

Chapter 30

He gave understanding of two portions. One portion is our saviour and our salvation. This blessed portion is open, clear, fair and bright and plentiful, for all men who are of good will are comprehended in this portion. We are bound[13] to this by God, and drawn and counselled and taught, inwardly by the Holy Spirit, and outwardly through the same grace by Holy Church. Our Lord wants us to be occupied in this, rejoicing in him, for he rejoices in us. And the more plentifully we accept from this with reverence and humility, the more do we deserve thanks from him, and the more profit do we win for ourselves. And so we may see and rejoice that our portion is our Lord.

The other portion is hidden from us and closed, that is to say all which is additional to our salvation; for this is our Lord's privy counsel, and it is fitting to God's royal dominion to keep his privy counsel in peace, and it is fitting to his servants out of obedience and respect not to wish to know his counsel.

Chapter 32

On one occasion our good Lord said: Every kind of thing will be well[14]; and on another occasion he said: You will see yourself that every kind of thing will be well[15]. And from these two the soul gained different kinds of understanding. One was this: that he wants us to know that he takes heed not only of things which are noble and great, but also of those which are little and small, of humble men and simple, of this man and that man. And this is what he means when he says: Every kind of thing will be well. For he wants us to know that the smallest thing will not be forgotten. Another understanding is this: that there are many deeds which in our eyes are so evilly done and lead to such great

---

13　The short text has 'bidden'.
14　See p. 225.
15　See p. 229.

harms that it seems to us impossible that any good result could ever come of them. And we contemplate this and sorrow and mourn for it so that we cannot rest in the blessed contemplation of God as we ought to do. And the cause is this: that the reason which we use is now so blind, so abject and so stupid that we cannot recognize God's exalted, wonderful wisdom, or the power and the goodness of the blessed Trinity. And this is his intention when he says: You will see yourself that every kind of thing will be well, as if he said: Accept it now in faith and trust, and in the very end you will see truly, in fulness of joy.

And so[16] in the same five words said before: I may make all things well[17], I understand a powerful comfort from all the works of our Lord God which are still to come. There is a deed[18] which the blessed Trinity will perform on the last day, as I see it, and what the deed will be and how it will be performed is unknown to every creature who is inferior to Christ, and it will be until the deed is done. The goodness and the love of our Lord God want us to know that this will be, and his power and his wisdom, through the same love, want to conceal it and hide it from us, what it will be and how it will be done. And the cause why he wants us to know it like this is because he wants us to be at ease in our souls and at peace in love, disregarding every disturbance which could hinder our true rejoicing in him.

This is the great deed ordained by our Lord God from without beginning, treasured and hidden in his blessed breast, known only to himself, through which deed he will make all things well. For just as the blessed Trinity created all things from nothing, just so will the same blessed Trinity make everything well which is not well. And I marvelled greatly at this sight, and contemplated our faith, with this in my mind: Our faith is founded on God's word, and it belongs to our faith that we believe that God's word will be preserved in all things. And one article of our faith is that many creatures will be damned, such as the angels who fell out of heaven because of pride, who now are devils, and many men upon earth who die out of the faith of Holy Church, that is to say those who are pagans and many who have received baptism and who live unchristian lives and so die out of God's love. All these will be eternally condemned to hell, as Holy Church teaches me to believe.

And all this being so, it seemed to me that it was impossible that every kind of thing should be well, as our Lord revealed at this time. And to this I had no other answer as a revelation from our Lord except this: What is impossible to you is not impossible to me. I shall preserve my word in everything, and I shall make everything well. And in this I was taught by the grace of God that I ought to keep myself steadfastly in the faith, as I

---

16   This paragraph corresponds with the short text.

17   See p. 229

18   The rest of this chapter, and the first two paragraphs of chapter 33, are not in the short text.

had understood before, and that at the same time I should stand firm and believe firmly that every kind of thing will be well, as our Lord revealed at that same time. For this is the great deed which our Lord will do, and in this deed he will preserve his word in everything. And he will make well all which is not well. But what the deed will be and how it will be done, there is no creature who is inferior to Christ who knows it, or will know it until it has been done, according to the understanding which I received of our Lord's meaning at this time.

Chapter 82

But here our courteous Lord revealed the moaning and the mourning of our soul, with this meaning: I know well that you wish to live for my love, joyfully and gladly suffering all the penance which may come to you; but since you do not live without sin, you are depressed and sorrowful, and if you could live without sin, you would suffer for my love all the woe which might come to you, and it is true. But do not be too much aggrieved by the sin which comes to you against your will.

And here I understood that the lord looked on the servant with pity and not with blame; for this passing life does not require us to live wholly without sin. He loves us endlessly, and we sin customarily, and he reveals it to us most gently. And then we sorrow and moan discreetly, turning to contemplate his mercy, cleaving to his love and to his goodness, seeing that his is our medicine, knowing that we only sin.

And so by the meekness which we obtain in seeing our sin, faithfully recognizing his everlasting love, thanking him and praising him, we please him. I love you and you love me, and our love will never be divided in two; and it is for your profit that I suffer. And all this was revealed in spiritual understanding, he saying these blessed words: I protect you very safely[19].

And by the great desire which I saw in our blessed Lord that we shall live in this way, that is to say in longing and rejoicing, as all this lesson of love shows, I understood that all which is opposed to this is not from him, but it is from enmity. And he wants us to know it by the sweet light of grace of his substantial and natural love.

If there be any such liver[20] on earth, who is continually protected from falling, I do not know, for it was not revealed to me. But this was revealed, that in falling and in rising we are always preciously protected in one[21] love. For we do not fall in the sight of God, and we do not stand in our own sight; and both these are true, as I see it, but the contemplating of our Lord God is the higher truth. So we are much indebted to him, that he will in this way of life reveal to us this high truth, and I understood that while we

---

19   See p. 154.
20   SS: 'lover'.
21   So SS; P, C: 'our'.

are in this way, it is most profitable to us that we see these both together. For the higher contemplation keeps us in spiritual joy and true delight in God; the other, which is the lower contemplation, keeps us in fear, and makes us ashamed of ourselves.

But our good Lord always wants us to remain much more in the contemplation of the higher, and not to forsake the knowledge of the lower, until the time that we are brought up above, where we shall have our Lord Jesus for our reward, and be filled full of joy and bliss without end.

Chapter 85

And I marvelled greatly at this vision, for despite our foolish living and our blindness here, still endlessly our courteous Lord regards us, rejoicing in this work. And we can please him best of all by wisely and truly believing it, and rejoicing with him and in him. For as truly as we shall be in the bliss of God without end, praising and thanking him, so truly have we been in God's prevision loved and known in his endless purpose from without beginning. In this love without beginning he created us; and in the same love he protects us, and never allows us to be hurt, by which our bliss might be decreased. And therefore when the judgment is given, and we are all brought up above, we shall then clearly see in God the mysteries which are now hidden from us. And then shall none of us be moved to say in any matter: Lord, if it had been so, it would have been well. But we shall all say with one voice: Lord, blessed may you be, because it is so, it is well; and now we see truly that everything is done as it was ordained by you before anything was made.

Chapter 86

This book is begun by God's gift and his grace, but it is not yet performed, as I see it. For charity, let us all join with God's working in prayer, thanking, trusting, rejoicing, for so will our good Lord be entreated, by the understanding which I took in all his own intention, and in the sweet words where he says most happily[22]: I am the foundation of your beseeching. For truly I saw and understood in our Lord's meaning that he revealed it because he wants to have it better known than it is. In which knowledge he wants to give us grace to love him and to cleave to him, for he beholds his heavenly treasure with so great love on earth that he will give us more light[23] and solace in heavenly joy, by drawing our hearts from the sorrow and the darkness which we are in.

And from the time that it was revealed, I desired many times to know in what was our Lord's meaning. And fifteen years after and more, I was answered in spiritual understanding, and it was said: What, do you wish to know your Lord's meaning in this thing? Know it well, love was his meaning. Who reveals it to you? Love. What did he

---

22   See p. 157.
23   'With so great … more light; from SS; P, C omit.

reveal to you? Love[24]. Why does he reveal it to you? For love. Remain in this, and you will know more of the same. But you will never know different, without end.

So I was taught that love is our Lord's meaning. And I saw very certainly in this and in everything that before God made us he loved us, which love was never abated and never will be. And in this love he has done all his works, and in this love he has made all things profitable to us, and in this love our life is everlasting. In our creation we had beginning, but the love in which he created us was in him from without beginning. In this love we have our beginning, and all this shall we see in God without end.

> Thanks be to God. Here ends the book of
> revelations of Julian the anchorite of Norwich, on
> whose soul may God have mercy.[25]

May Jesus grant us this. Amen. So ends the revelation of love of the blessed Trinity, shown by our saviour Jesus Christ for our endless comfort and solace, and also that we may rejoice in him in the passing journey of this life. Amen. Jesus. Amen. I pray almighty God that this book may not come except into the hands of those who wish to be his faithful lovers, and those who will submit themselves to the faith of Holy Church and obey the wholesome understanding and teaching of men who are of virtuous life, settled age and profound learning; for this revelation is exalted divinity and wisdom, and therefore it cannot remain with him who is a slave to sin and to the devil. And beware that you do not accept one thing which is according to your pleasure and liking, and reject another, for that is the disposition of heretics. But accept it all together, and understand it truly; it all agrees with Holy Scripture, and is founded upon it, and Jesus, our true love and light and truth, will show this to all pure souls who meekly and perseveringly ask this wisdom from him. And you to whom this book will come, give our saviour Christ Jesus great and hearty thanks that he made these showings and revelations for you and to you out of his endless love, mercy and goodness, for a safe guide and conduct for you and us to everlasting bliss, which may Jesus grant us. Amen. Here end the sublime and wonderful revelations of the unutterable love of God, in Jesus Christ vouchsafed to a dear lover of his, and in her to all his dear friends and lovers whose hearts like hers do flame in the love of our dearest Jesus.

---

24 'What did . . . Love' from SS; P, C omit.
25 What follows is the colophon found only in S1 and S2, plainly the work of some devout seventeenth-century scribe-editor.

Hildegard of Bingen

Introduction

Nancy Enright

Born in Germany in 1098, Hildegard of Bingen lived a long and fruitful life (d. 1179). A sickly child, she began having visions from a very young age. At the age of eight she was sent to live with a young woman named Jutta, who lived as an anchorite in a cell attached to the church at Disibodenberg. As other young women joined them, they established a Benedictine convent. At thirty-eight, after Jutta's death, Hildegard became superior of this convent. She lived the life of a Benedictine nun until her death at age eighty-one. However, her responsibilities as abbess of a convent did not stop her from writing a wide array of religious texts, including poetry/songs, works on nature and medicine, at least one play, letters to political figures—including kings and popes—and, most importantly, her mystical writings.[i]

Hildegard received a new and profound vision in 1141 when she was forty-two years old. She describes the experience in her introduction to her first major written work, *Scivias* (Know the Ways): "… a fiery light, flashing intensely, came from the open vault of heaven and poured through my whole brain. Like a flame that is hot without burning it kindled all my heart and all my breast, just as the sun warms anything on which its rays fall." The result of the vision was a new experience of knowledge of the Scriptures, but Hildegard kept the visions mostly to herself until she was prompted by God to record them. Eventually, she received twenty-six visions, recorded in the three books of *Scivias*, which Hildegard says took ten years to complete.

She also is the author of two other major, visionary works. *Liber Vitae Meritorum* (Book of Life's Merits), inspired by six visions, offers wise advice about how to live. For example, she warns against the sin of mistrusting God in the face of misfortune, a mistrust that can lead to a belief that one is "fated to be unhappy." Her advice for those falling into this spiritual pitfall is to "turn and place all their trust in God's mercy." A third visionary book, *De Operatione Dei* (Book of Divine Works), grew out of a powerful visionary experience (ten visions together) that came to Hildegard at the age of sixty-five. In one vision she saw "the Fountain of Life," with three figures in a stone fountain, identified as Love, Humility, and Peace. Hildegard wrote, "Everything that God has effected, he has perfected in Love, Humility, and Peace." In this work's Epilogue she connects her physical sufferings on Earth with being filled with the Holy Spirit, who offers her "the cool dew of consolation" and enables her to be of continued service.

Besides the visionary works, Hildegard's poetry and music are enjoying a resurgence that began late in the twentieth century. Recordings of her music are available on Amazon.com and on YouTube, with the latter sometimes accompanied by visuals of medieval illustrations. Her letters offer a remarkable

---

i   The text used for this introduction is *Hildegard of Bingen Mystical Writings*, edited and introduced by Fiona Bowie and Oliver Davies. Crossroad, New York: Spiritual Classics, 1990.

and complex view of a woman who referred to herself in terms like *poor little creature* but also found the courage to rebuke some of the most powerful rulers of her time. For instance, in Hildegard's letter to King Henry II of England, who had Saint Thomas Becket famously murdered in Canterbury, she rebukes him for supporting the "anti-pope" who challenged Pope Alexander. Shortly before her death she wrote a letter to the prefects of Mainz arguing her case and that of her convent for burying a young man, once excommunicated but restored to the Church prior to his death through the last sacraments, basing her argument on a deep respect for the healing power of the sacraments, warning the prelates of the danger of being ensnared, as Satan was, into urging disobedience to God. (She and her sisters had been forbidden to sing the Divine Office as a penalty; she argued that singing is commanded in Scripture.) With this issue resolved and her convent in full peace with the Church, Hildegard died an old woman.

THE BOOK OF DIVINE WORKS
Part I, Vision 1

"The Book of Divine Works," Foreword and Vision One, sections 1–3, from http://
www.academia.edu/3597758/Hildegard_of_Bingen_Book_of_Divine_Works_
Part_I_Vision_1. Introduction and translation by Nathaniel M. Campbell is
under copyright of The Catholic University of America Press.

Hildegard's final and greatest visionary work was the *Liber Divinorum Operum* ("The
Book of Divine Works"), written between 1163 and 1172, with final revisions completed by 1174. In an autobiographical passage included in the *Life of St. Hildegard*
(II.16), the Visionary Doctor describes the genesis of the work in her meditations on
the Prologue to the Gospel of John: "For it was the Word, which before all created
things had no beginning, and after them shall have no end, which summoned all created things into being. (...) Therefore man is the work of God along with every creature.
But man is also said to be the worker of the Divinity and a shadow of his mysteries, and
should in all things reveal the Holy Trinity, for *God made him in his image and likeness*
(Gn 1:26)."

The figure of *Caritas* or Divine Love is the central character in the opening vision
below, the most prominent of the work's allegorical theophanies. Drawing inspiration
from the declaration of the First Letter of John (4:8) that "God is love," Hildegard connects several biblical images—the Ancient of Days, the woman clothed with the sun
(Apocalypse 12:1), the Lamb of God, the wings of the seraph—to describe, in a whirl
of symbols and ideas, the cosmic drama of creation and salvation. At center-stage of this
drama is this figure of *Caritas*—Divine Love, the "supreme and fiery force" that both
sparked and sustains creation, and at the same time reflects and sets alight the body,
soul, and mind of each human being. The scope of Hildegard's visionary theology is
both cosmic and close—reflections of God's loving revelation of himself to humanity
are both grand and utterly intimate, as the Work of God reaches from the very heart of
infinity down into every smallest detail of the created world.

1. *And I saw as it were in the middle of the southern sky an image, beautiful and wonderful in the mystery of God, like a human in form. Her face was of such beauty and
   radiance that I could easier look at the sun than at her; and a great circlet of golden
   color surrounded her head. Above that head, moreover, in the same circlet appeared
   another face like an old man, whose chin and beard touched the crown of the [lower]
   head. And from each side of the figure's neck a single wing came forth, which rose up
   to join together above the aforementioned circlet. At the tip of the arc where the right
   wing curves back, I saw as it were the head of an eagle, which had eyes of fire, in which
   appeared the brilliance of the angels as in a mirror. But at the tip of the arc where
   the left wing curves back there was as it were a human face, which shined like the
   brilliance of the stars. And these faces were turned towards the east. Furthermore,*

from each shoulder of this image, a single wing stretched forth down to her knees. She was clothed with a tunic like the brilliance of the sun, and in her hands she held a lamb, shining like the light of day. Moreover, she was treading with her feet a monster, dreadful in appearance and venomous and black in color, and also a serpent that had fixed his mouth upon the right ear of the monster and, wrapping the rest of its body around the monster's head, had stretched its tail along the monster's left side all the way to its feet.

2.   And this image spoke: "I am the supreme and fiery force, who sets all living sparks alight and breathes forth no mortal things, but judges them as they are. Flying around the circling circle with my upper wings—with wisdom—I have ordered all things rightly.[1] But I am also the fiery life of the essence of divinity—I flame above the beauty of the fields and I shine in the waters and I burn in the sun, the moon, and the stars. With the airy wind I rouse to life all things with some invisible life, which sustains all things. For the air lives in viridity[2] and in the flowers, the waters flow as if they are alive, and the sun lives in its own light. When the moon has waned, it is rekindled by the light of the sun so that it might as it were live anew, and the stars shine bright by living as it were in their own light. I have also established the pillars that contain the whole circle of the earth—the winds. The stronger winds have wings set below them, which are the lighter winds, and these uphold the stronger winds with their lightness, lest they dangerously unleash themselves; in the same way the body covers and contains the soul, lest it should expire. Likewise, as the breath of the soul binds together the body by strengthening it so that it does not weaken, so the stronger winds also animate those subject to them, so that they can fulfil their duties appropriately.

"Therefore I, the fiery force, lie hidden in these things, and they burn because of me, just as breath continually moves a human being and a flickering flame exists within the fire.[3] All of these things live in their essences and were not found in death, because I am life. I am also rationality, possessing the wind of the resounding Word, through which every created thing was made; and in all these things I blow, so that none of them might be mortal in its nature, because I am life.

---

1   Cf. Hildegard's antiphon *O virtus Sapientie*: "O Wisdom's energy! Whirling you encircle and everything embrace in the single way of life."

2   "viridity": *viriditas*. This key term in Hildegard's symbolic vocabulary literally means, "greenness," but its depth of meaning, however, extends beyond a simple color to encompass notions of freshness, fertility, and fruitfulness. For Hildegard, viridity was the fundamental marker of the abundant, fecund, holy life that creation, the "work of God," receives from its Creator. It often makes an appearance in her organic analogies for the Trinity, especially in connection with the Holy Spirit, denoting God's creative fertility, the maternal goodness that gives birth to and nurtures the whole world. In the LDO, the term plays a particularly fruitful role in the symbiosis between the fertility of the physical world and that of the virtuous soul—physical viridity is a vehicle of the divine power that bursts spiritual viridity into bud, while spiritual aridity dries out the physical world around it in some of Hildegard's most celebrated ecological passages depicting the impact of human sin on the environment.

3   These are Trinitarian images: cf. *Explanatio Symboli Sancti Athanasii*, ed. C. P. Evans, in CCCM 226, pp. 116–7.

"For I am life, pure and whole, which was not hewn from stones, neither blossomed from branches nor took root from man's sexual power;[4] but every living thing has taken root in me. For reason is the root, and the resounding Word flourishes within it.

"Therefore, because God is rational, how could it possibly be that he would not actively work, since his every work flourishes through humankind, whom he made in his image and likeness and in whom he marked out all created things according to their measure? For it was always determined from eternity that God would will his work—humankind—to come into being; and when he perfected this work, he gave all creation to humankind so that humans might do their work with it, in the same way that God himself had made his work, that is, humankind.

"But I also fulfill my duty, since all living things are set ablaze from me; and I am uniform life in eternity, which neither begins nor ends. God is this life, working and moving itself, and yet this life is one in three forces. Therefore Eternity is called the Father, the Word is called the Son, and the breath connecting these two is called the Holy Spirit, just as God is signified in human beings, in whom are body, soul, and rationality.[5] Moreover, because 'I flame above the beauty of the fields,' this signifies the earth, which is that material from which God made human beings. And because 'I shine in the waters,' this accords with the soul, since, just as water floods the whole earth, so the soul permeates the whole body. But because 'I burn in the sun and in the moon,' this signifies rationality, and the stars are the countless words of rationality. And when 'with the airy wind I rouse to life all things with some invisible life, which sustains all things,' this is because by the air and wind subsist those living things that grow, moved out of nothingness into existence."

3. And again I heard a voice from heaven saying to me: God, who created all things, made humankind in his image and likeness (Gen. 1:26), and in humankind he signified both the higher and the lower creatures. He held humankind in such loving affection, that he destined them for that place from which the falling angel was cast out, and he ordained them for the glory and honor in blessedness that the fallen angel had lost.[6] This is what this vision that you have seen demonstrates.

---

4   "from man's sexual power": *de uirili ui*; cf. Hildegard, Explanatio Symboli Sancti Athanasii: Christ "is indeed fully God in the wholeness of eternity, and fully human with a rational soul and pure flesh and without the male sexual commingling of human nature" (*Ipse etenim plenus Deus est in integritate eternitatis plenusque homo cum racionali anima et carne munda et absque ulla uirili commixtione humane nature*; in CCCM 226, p. 125).

5   Cf. Hildegard, *Explanatio Symboli Sancti Athanasii*, pp. 120–6.

6   This refers to the notion that redeemed humanity shall refill the tenth choir of angels that had been emptied by the fall of Lucifer and his companions; cf. c. 9 below, and *Scivias* III.2.19.

For when you see *as it were in the middle of the southern sky an image, beautiful and wonderful in the mystery of God, like a human in form*, this is because Divine Love is beautiful because of her election in the strength of unfailing divinity, and wonderful in the gifts of the heavenly Father's mysteries: and thus Divine Love reveals humankind. For when the Son of God put on flesh, he redeemed fallen humankind through the service of Love. Thus *her face is of such beauty and radiance that you could easier look at the sun than at her*: for the abundance of Love is of so great an excellence in the flashing gleam of her gifts, that she surpasses all human understanding and the faculty of knowledge by which humans are able to understand various things in the soul. This transcendence is so great that humans cannot in any way grasp Love with the senses. But this shows symbolically that through her, he is recognized in faith who is not seen visibly with the visible eyes.

4. *And a great circlet of golden color surrounds her head*, because the catholic faith, spread throughout the whole world and rising in the first dawn of exceptional brilliance, embraces the excellence of true Love's abundance with every devotion, as when God redeemed humankind in the humanity of His Son and strengthened them through the pouring out of the Holy Spirit.[7] Thus is one God understood in Trinity, who without temporal beginning before the ages was God in divinity. And when *above that head in the same circlet appears another face like an old man*, this means that the all-surpassing goodness of divinity, which is without beginning and end, brings aid and comfort to the faithful, so that *this face's chin and beard touch the crown of the [lower] head*. For divinity holds fast the lofty reaches of supreme Love by arranging and protecting all things, as when the Son of God in his humanity led lost humankind back to heavenly things.

And from each side of the figure's neck a single wing comes forth, which rise up to join together above the aforementioned circlet. For love of God and love of neighbor are not to be separated from each other, for they proceed through the power of Divine Love in the unity of faith and embrace that faith between them through supreme desire.[8] For holy divinity keeps the countless splendor of its glory hidden from humanity, so long as they dwell in the shadow of death, devoid of the heavenly robe that they lost because of Adam.[9]

---

7   "the first dawn": *prima aurora*; this is one of Hildegard's favorite metaphors for the apostolic church. More broadly, she uses the image of the dawn to signify the irruption of divinity into time; in her liturgical poetry, she associates the dawn light most closely with the Virgin's womb. See Nathaniel M. Campbell, "*Imago expandit splendorem suum*: Hildegard of Bingen's Visio-Theological Designs in the Rupertsberg *Scivias* Manuscript," *Eikón/Imago* 4 (2013, Vol. 2, No. 2), pp. 1–68, esp. pp. 51–5.

8   "love of God and love of neighbor": *dilectio Dei et proximi*; "through the power of Divine Love": *per virtutem caritatis*.

9   On this "heavenly robe," cf. cc. 14 and 15 below.

5. *At the tip of the arc where the right wing curves back, you see as it were the head of an
    eagle, which has eyes of fire, in which appear the multitude of the angels as in a mirror.*
    For when in the soaring heights of triumphant submission, someone makes them-
    self subject to God and overcomes the Devil, they are made lofty in the blessedness
    of divine protection.[10] And when, set on fire by the Holy Spirit, they lift up their
    mind and fix their attention on God, the blessed spirits shall clearly appear in it and
    offer to God the devotion of that person's heart. For in the eagle are signified those
    spiritual people who, with every devotion of the heart and in contemplation, gaze
    often upon God like the angels. For this reason the blessed spirits, gazing intently
    upon God, rejoice because of the good works of the just and show forth these works
    in themselves, and so they continue in their praise of God and never grow weary,
    for they can never reach the end of his praise. For truly, who can count the num-
    berless wonders that God does in the power of his ability? No one. Indeed, there
    is present to the angels a many-mirrored flash in which they see that none can act
    and none has such power as God: there is none like him, for he has no temporality.

6. Indeed, all things that God has worked, he held in his foreknowledge before the
    beginning of time. For in the pure and holy divinity, all things visible and invisible
    appeared without movement and outside of time, before the ages, just as trees or
    other creatures near water are seen in the water, for although they are not physically
    in it, their every shape appears in it.[11] For when God said, "Let there be..." (Gen.
    1:3 etc.), immediately they were clothed with form, as his foreknowledge saw them
    before the ages when they did not yet have physical bodies. For as all things shine
    in the mirror before which they stand, so in the holy divinity all his works appeared
    outside of the passage of time. And how could God lack the work he foreknew,
    since his every work, after it is clothed with a body, fulfills the task appointed for it,
    because the holy divinity foreknew how to be present in knowing, understanding,
    and serving? For just as a ray of light reveals the particular shape of a created thing
    through its shadow, so God's pure foreknowledge looked upon the form of every
    created thing before it was embodied. For the work that God would make gleamed
    in his foreknowledge according to its likeness before it was embodied, just as a per-
    son sees the splendor of the sun before they are able to look upon its substance. And
    as the splendor of the sun points to the sun itself, so also the angels reveal God by
    their praising; and as it is not possible for the sun to be without its light, so neither
    can the Divinity be without the angels' praise. God's foreknowledge both preceded
    and followed his work; and if God's foreknowledge had not existed first, his work

---

10   "someone...themself": Note on translation: Hildegard makes nearly constant use of the generic term *homo* to signify a
      representative "human person," of either gender; when she speaks specifically of a man or woman, she uses specifically
      gendered Latin terms (e.g. *vir* or *femina*). In order to maintain this generic vs. gendered distinction, I have chosen to adopt
      in English the use of the third-person plural pronoun in the non-gendered singular.

11   Cf. LDO III.3.1.

would not have appeared. For if a person's face cannot be seen, their body cannot be recognized; but when a person's face is seen, their body can be praised. Thus God's foreknowledge and his work exist in him.

7. There was, however, a numberless multitude of angels who wished to exist on their own, for when they saw their own radiance, great and glorious in its flashing brilliance, they forgot their Creator. And even before they began to praise him, they were calculating among themselves that their honor's brilliance was so great that none could resist it—this is also why they wished to vilify God. For when they saw that they could never reach the end of his wonders, they hated him; and though they ought to have praised him, with a foolish thought they declared that in their great splendor they would choose another god. Thus they fell into darkness, reduced to such impotence that they could do nothing to any creature except inasmuch as it was permitted to them by their Creator. For because God had adorned the first angel, who was called Lucifer, with all of the ornaments of creation that he would give to every created thing, so that the whole rank [of angels] received its splendor from him, so, when he set himself against [God], he was made more horrifying than every horror, for the holy divinity in its zeal cast him out into the place that is without light.

8. *But at the tip of the arc where the left wing curves back there is as it were a human face, which shines like the brilliance of the stars.* This means that in the summit of conquering humiliation, when humans crush with humility the earthly circumstances that stand in their way—on the left, as it were—and turn themselves to the defense of their Creator, they shall come to possess their human countenance, for it is not according to herd animals but according to that which human nature teaches them that they begin to live in moral integrity.[12] Thus, in their righteous works, too, they show that the good intention of their hearts shines like an outstanding splendor.

9. For when God said, "Let there be light!" (Gen. 1:3), a rational light arose—the angels, both those who remained with God in truth and those who fell into the outer darkness without any light, because they denied that the True Light (John 1:9), which existed in brilliance without beginning before the ages, was God, and because they wanted to be like him in a way that was not possible.[13] Then God caused another life, which he contained within a body, to arise, and this is humankind. To them he gave the place and the glory of the lost angel, so that they might in the praise of God complete that which he had refused to do. Moreover, in that human face is signified those people who, though given to the world in body, yet serve God continually in spirit and do not, on account of this body that remains in and of the

---

12   Cf. Hildegard, *Explanatio Symboli Sancti Athanasii*, pp. 127–8.

13   "a rational light—the angels": cf. Augustine, *De Civ. Dei,* 11.9 (on Gen. 1:3); "the outer darkness": cf. Matt. 25:30.

world, forget the things which are of the spirit in the service of God. *And these faces are turned towards the east,* because both spiritual and secular people who desire to serve God and keep their souls in life, ought to convert themselves to the dawn of a holy way of life and blessedness.

10. *Furthermore, from each shoulder of this image, a single wing stretches forth down to her knees,* because in the strength of Divine Love the Son of God brought to himself the righteous and the sinners and lifted them both by the shoulders, because they had lived rightly, and by the knees, because he had recalled them from the way of injustice; and he made them consorts of the citizens of heaven. Likewise, a person lifts those things that they carry with both the knees and the shoulders. For in the knowledge of Love, humankind has been led in soul and body to the fullness of pure integrity, though they are very often moved away from an upright and steadfast posture. When the gifts of the Holy Spirit pour forth from above upon humankind in pure and holy abundance, they teach them many things about heavenly and spiritual matters. They also instruct humankind in a different way about earthly concerns for the necessary use of the body; nevertheless, humans understand in these matters that they are weak and infirm and mortal, although they are defended by these manifold gifts.

11. Because *she is clothed with a tunic like the brilliance of the sun,* this means that in Love, the Son of God put on a human body without any spot of sin, in the likeness of the sun's beauty. For as the sun shines before the rest of creation at so great a height that no person can touch it, so also no human knowledge is able to grasp the humanity of the Son of God and how it came to be except by believing. *And in her hands she holds a lamb, shining like the light of day,* because in the works of the Son of God, Love offered the gentleness of true faith, shining above all things, when he chose from among the tax collectors and sinners his martyrs, confessors, and penitents, and when out of the wicked he made the righteous, as when he made Paul from Saul, so that they might fly upon the wings of the winds (Ps. 17:11[18:20]), that is, upon the heavenly harmony. Thus, Love completed her work deliberately, one small and distinct piece at a time, so that in it there would be no weakness but rather every fullness. Humans cannot do this, for when they have even the slightest potential of doing something, they can barely keep at it long enough to bring it to completion so that others can see it. A person should think upon these things within themself, for the little bird, when it first hatches from the egg and does not yet have feathers, does not hurry to fly; but after it has received its feathers, it flies to the place it sees as most fitting for itself.

12. *Moreover, she is treading with her feet a monster, dreadful in appearance and venomous and black in color, and also a serpent.* This means that true Love, through the footsteps of the Son of God, bruises discord's injury, which is misshapen by its

excessive vices and horrifying because of its many perversities, and poisonous in deception and black in perdition. Likewise, she bruises the ancient serpent as he lays traps for the faithful, for upon the Cross the Son of God brought him to nothing. *The serpent has fixed his mouth upon the right ear of the monster and, wrapping the rest of its body around the monster's head, stretches its tail along the monster's left side all the way to its feet.* For the devil, while pretending to act benignly, sows his deceit and discord, and lightly littering every type of vice here and there at their beginning, in their end he shows himself to possess the perversity of discord's worst fulfillment. For the serpent, who in his trickery is more cunning than other worms (Gen. 3:1), destroys in that cunning everything he can and turns it to himself in the worst possible way, which is signified by the various colors of his skin. Satan, too, acted this way, for when he recognized his own beauty, he wished that he could be like his Creator. This is also what he whispered to humankind through the head of the serpent, as it were, and he shall not stop doing so until the end of time, as signified by his tail.

13. And so Love is in the wheel of eternity outside of time, just as heat is in fire.[14] For God foreknew in eternity all of his created beings, which he brought forth in the fullness of Love so that humans would lack no refreshment or service in them, for he joined them to humankind as flames are to fire. Moreover, God established the first angel with very many adornments, as was said above, but when the latter saw himself, he looked upon his Lord with hatred and wished himself to be lord. But God cast him down into the well of the abyss. Then that transgressor introduced his evil plan to humankind, and humankind consented to it.

14. For when God created humankind, he clothed them with heavenly clothing, so that they might shine in great radiance. But the devil, seeing the woman, recognized that she would be the mother of a great world, and with the same malice by which he fell from God, he undertook to overcome God by the latter's own work—so he turned the work of God, which is humankind, into his own ally. Then the woman, sensing that in tasting of the fruit she had become something different, gave the fruit to her husband; and so both lost their heavenly clothing.

15. But when God then said, "Adam, where are you?" (Gen. 3:9), he signified by this that Adam should remember that God had made him in his own image and likeness (Gen. 1:26), and that God wished that he would return to him. When God sent Adam into exile, God's own desire to serve compelled him to cover up Adam's nudity, so that in place of the shining vesture, he received an animal skin, just as he exchanged paradise for exile. Indeed, God joined woman to man by the oath of fidelity, so that this fidelity between them might never be destroyed, but that

---

14   Cf. LDO III.5.

they should come together as one in mind, just as God joined them together into one, body and soul. Therefore, whoever should destroy this fidelity and should thus remain impenitent and without correction, shall be cast into the land of Babylon, into the land of confusion and drought, which shall so remain without the beautiful viridity of the field, that is, of the blessing of God. And the vengeance of God shall fall upon him, even to the last line of descendents proceeding from his hot blood, because this sin has touched that man.[15]

16. And as Adam is the father of the whole human race, so also through the Son of God, who was incarnate in virgin nature, has come forth a spiritual people, who shall ascend as God promised to Abraham through the angel, that his seed should be as the stars of heaven, as it is written: "'Look up to heaven and number the stars, if you can.' And he said to him: 'So shall your seed be.' Abraham believed God, and it was reckoned to him as righteousness." (Gen. 15:5-6) The meaning of this should be understood thus: You, who worship and venerate God with a good will, look upon the secrets of God and examine the reward of their merits who shine before God day and night—if this is even possible for a human being, who is burdened by the weight of the body. For as long as humans taste of those things that are of the flesh, they will not be able to fully grasp those that are of the spirit. And in true revelation it is said to that person who labors to worship God with the upright sighs of their heart: "In this way shall the seed of your heart be multiplied and enlightened, that what you have sown on good ground has been watered by the grace of the Holy Spirit. It shall rise up and shine many times over in blessed virtues before God Most High, just as the stars twinkle in the firmament." Therefore, whoever should faithfully believe the divine promise and hold the lofty height of true faith in God, so that they despise all earthly things and reach out towards the heavenly, shall be accounted righteous among the children of God, for they have loved the truth and have had no guile in their hearts.

17. For God also recognized that Abraham's spirit was without the serpent's guile, for he did his works to the injury of none. Thus God chose from his stock that sleeping earth that had no knowledge at all of the taste of that by which the ancient serpent deceived the first woman. This earth was prefigured by the staff of Aaron (Num. 17:8) to be the Virgin Mary, who in her great humility was the enclosed bedchamber of the King. For when she received from the throne the message that the Highest King wished to live in her enclosure, she looked upon that earth from which she was created and replied that she was the handmaid of God (Luke 1:38). The woman who was first deceived did not do this, since she desired to have that which she ought not to have had.[16] But the obedience of Abraham, in which God

---

15   Here Hildegard censures the adulterer, whose "hot blood" withers the holy viridity of the sacrament of marriage.

16   "The woman": sc. Eve.

proved Abraham's faith when he showed him the ram caught in the thorns (Gen. 22:13), prefigured the obedience of the Blessed Virgin, who, believing the word of God's messenger, wished that it should be done unto her according to that messenger's word (Luke 1:38). Thus, the Son of God, whom the ram hanging in the thorn-bushes had prefigured, put on flesh in her. Furthermore, when God said that the race of Abraham would be multiplied according to the stars of heaven, he foresaw that this race should be reckoned as the full number of the celestial court. And since Abraham trusted faithfully in God in all things, so he is called the father of those who shall be the heirs of the Kingdom of Heaven.

And so every person who fears and loves God should lay open the devotion of their heart to these words and know that they have been offered for the saving of humans in body and soul, not indeed by a human being but by me, the one who am (Ex. 3:14).[17]

---

17   This formulaic exhortation closes each of Part I's four visions; the single vision of Part II has its own unique closing, while the five visions of Part III share a similar, though modified, exhortation to Part I. Hildegard employed similar exhortations at the close of each vision in *Scivias* and *Liber Vite Meritorum*, as well.

Saint Anselm

Introduction
Ki Joo Choi

Anselm (d. A.D. 1109) was born in Burgundy, France, in A.D. 1033. In A.D. 1078, he entered the Benedictine order in Normandy, where he became abbot of a Benedictine abbey in the town of Bec, Normandy. Rising in reputation and influence in church and state in Europe, Anselm was appointed Archbishop of Canterbury, England, in A.D. 1093. While Archbishop, Anselm wrote some of his better known theological texts such as *Cur Deus Homo*, or *Why God Became Man* (A.D. 1095– 1098). This text is well-known for the kind of atonement theory that it proposes (that is to say, why Jesus, the Son of God, suffered and died on the cross). Anselm's atonement theory, in many ways, served as a central marker for future theological discussions on the Incarnation, Crucifixion, and Resurrection of Jesus.

The reading that we have from Saint Anselm comes from a more philosophical text he wrote while abbot in Normandy, the *Proslogium*. While the reading is a very short excerpt from the *Proslogium*, it offers clear insight into Anselm's argument for God's reality. Pay close attention to how Anselm begins his argument. From the very outset he writes, "For I do not seek to understand that I may believe, but I believe in order to understand." This is often referred to as Anselm's "faith seeking understanding" (or in Latin, *fides quaerens intellectum*) formulation.

Beginning an argument for the existence of God with this kind of claim may appear strange to many readers, for it can sound as if he is saying that he is attempting to prove what he already believes to be true. To modern ears, this does not sound very "rational" or "scientific." For that reason, it is important that we understand what Anselm is up to. Although the significance of Anselm's *fides quaerens intellectum* is wide ranging, at least one point is worth emphasizing for our purposes in this course. Anselm's "proof" of God's existence operates on the premise that there is such a notion as Truth (truth with a capital "T"!) and that this Truth is knowable through human intellect, reasoning, or understanding. Again, from a modern standpoint, this sounds rather odd, for we are often encouraged to doubt everything until it can be "rationally" verified. However, does it not make sense to believe that there is something in fact to be verified before we engage in rational investigation and inquiry? It is interesting to note that the modern notion of doubting everything until it can be rationally verified has often led many modern thinkers to argue that there is no reality as such or that Truth does not exist—that what is real, therefore, is socially constructed, "all the way down." But that would make little conceptual sense to someone like Anselm.

With that in mind, as you read Anselm's argument for the existence of God, note the form his argument or reasoning takes. It is a deductive argument, one that begins with conceptual premises, and then deduces or infers conclusions from them. Accordingly, note that Anselm begins by articulating the nature of the concept of God. Pay close attention to this: What does the concept of God mean, according to Anselm? Then, pay close attention to how Anselm proceeds to the next step of his argument. He thinks that once we can conceive the fundamental nature of the concept of God, then God must exist in both the human understanding—intellect or mind—*and* in reality. The question is why? The key is to understand Anselm's articulation of the nature of the concept of God, and why the concept of God cannot mean anything *less* than this articulation. Otherwise, he thinks, we would be contradicting the very fundamental nature of the concept of God, which would then, erroneously, prove God's non-existence.

PROSLOGIUM:
OR DISCOURSE ON THE EXISTENCE OF GOD
Chapters 1–19

Preface

In this brief work the author aims at proving in a single argument the existence of God, and whatsoever we believe of God.—The difficulty of the task.—The author writes in the person of one who contemplates God, and seeks to understand what he believes. To this work he had given this title: Faith Seeking Understanding. He finally named it Proslogium,—that is, A Discourse.

After I had published, at the solicitous entreaties of certain brethren, a brief work (the *Monologium*) as an example of meditation on the grounds of faith, in the person of one who investigates, in a course of silent reasoning with himself, matters of which he is ignorant; considering that this book was knit together by the linking of many arguments, I began to ask myself whether there might be found a single argument which would require no other for its proof than itself alone; and alone would suffice to demonstrate that God truly exists, and that there is a supreme good requiring nothing else, which all other things require for their existence and well-being; and whatever we believe regarding the divine Being.

Although I often and earnestly directed my thought to this end, and at some times that which I sought seemed to be just within my reach, while again it wholly evaded my mental vision, at last in despair I was about to cease, as if from the search for a thing which could not be found. But when I wished to exclude this thought altogether, lest, by busying my mind to no purpose, it should keep me from other thoughts, in which I might be successful; then more and more, though I was unwilling and shunned it, it began to force itself upon me, with a kind of importunity. So, one day, when I was exceedingly wearied with resisting its importunity, in the very conflict of my thoughts, the proof of which I had despaired offered itself, so that I eagerly embraced the thoughts which I was strenuously repelling.

Thinking, therefore, that what I rejoiced to have found, would, if put in writing, be welcome to some readers, of this very matter, and of some others, I have written the following treatise, in the person of one who strives to lift his mind to the contemplation of God, and seeks to understand what he believes. In my judgment, neither this work nor the other, which I mentioned above, deserved to be called a book, or to bear the name of an author; and yet I thought they ought not to be sent forth without some title by which they might, in some sort, invite one into whose hands they fell to their perusal. I accordingly gave each a title, that the first might be known as, An Example of Meditation on the Grounds of Faith, and its sequel as, Faith Seeking Understanding. But, after both had been copied by many under these titles, many urged me, and especially Hugo, the reverend Archbishop of Lyons, who discharges the apostolic office in Gaul, who instructed me to this effect on his apostolic authority—to prefix my name to these writings. And that this might be done more fitly, I named the first, *Monologium*, that is, A Soliloquy; but the second, *Proslogium,* that is, A Discourse.

Chapter I

Exhortation of the mind to the contemplation of God.—It casts aside cares, and excludes all thoughts save that of God, that it may seek Him. Man was created to see God. Man by sin lost the blessedness for which he was made, and found the misery for which he was not made. He did not keep this good when he could keep it easily. Without God it is ill with us. Our labors and attempts are in vain without God. Man cannot seek God, unless God himself teaches him; nor find him, unless he reveals himself God created man in his image, that he might be mindful of him, think of him, and love him. The believer does not seek to understand, that he may believe, but he believes that he may understand: for unless he believed he would not understand.

Up now, slight man! flee, for a little while, Thy occupations; hide thyself, for a time, from Thy disturbing thoughts. Cast aside, now, Thy burdensome cares, and put away Thy toilsome business. Yield room for some little time to God; and rest for a little time in him. Enter the inner chamber of Thy mind; shut out all thoughts save that of God, and such as can aid thee in seeking him; close Thy door and seek him. Speak now, my whole heart! Speak now to God, saying, I seek Thy face; Thy face, Lord, will I seek (Psalms xxvii. 8). And come thou now, O Lord my God, teach my heart where and how it may seek thee, where and how it may find thee.

Lord, if thou art not here, where shall I seek thee, being absent? But if thou art everywhere, why do I not see thee present? Truly thou dwellest in unapproachable light. But where is unapproachable light, or how shall I come to it? Or who shall lead me to that light and into it, that I may see thee in it? Again, by what marks, under what form, shall I seek thee? I have never seen thee, O Lord, my God; I do not know Thy form. What, O most high Lord, shall this man do, an exile far from thee? What shall Thy servant do, anxious in his love of thee, and cast out afar from Thy face? He pants to see thee, and Thy face is too far from him. He longs to come to thee, and Thy dwelling-place is inaccessible. He is eager to find thee, and knows not Thy place. He desires to seek thee, and does not know Thy face. Lord, thou art my God, and thou are my Lord, and never have

I seen thee. It is thou that hast made me, and hast made me anew, and hast bestowed upon me all the blessings I enjoy; and not yet do I know thee. Finally, I was created to see thee, and not yet have I done that for which I was made.

O wretched lot of man, when he hath lost that for which he was made! O hard and terrible fate! Alas, what has he lost, and what has he found? What has departed, and what remains? He has lost the blessedness for which he was made, and has found the misery for which he was not made. That has departed without which nothing is happy, and that remains which, in itself, is only miserable. Man once did eat the bread of angels, for which he hungers now; he eateth now the bread of sorrows, of which he knew not then. Alas! for the mourning of all mankind, for the universal lamentation of the sons of Hades! He choked with satiety, we sigh with hunger. He bounded, we beg. He possessed in happiness, and miserably forsook his possession; we suffer want in unhappiness, and feel a miserable longing, and alas! we remain empty.

Why did he not keep for us, when he could so easily, that whose lack we should feel so heavily? Why did he shut us away from the light, and cover us over with darkness? With what purpose did he rob us of life, and inflict death upon us? Wretches that we are, whence have we been driven out; whither are we driven on? Whence hurled? Whither consigned to ruin? From a native country into exile, from the vision of God into our present blindness, from the joy of immortality into the bitterness and horror of death. Miserable exchange of how great a good, for how great an evil! Heavy loss, heavy grief heavy all our fate!

But alas! wretched that I am, one of the sons of Eve, far removed from God! What have I undertaken? What have I accomplished? Whither was I striving? How far have I come? To what did I aspire? Amid what thoughts am I sighing? I sought blessings, and lo! confusion. I strove toward God, and I stumbled on myself. I sought calm in privacy, and I found tribulation and grief, in my inmost thoughts. I wished to smile in the joy of my mind, and I am compelled to frown by the sorrow of my heart. Gladness was hoped for, and lo! a source of frequent sighs!

And thou too, O Lord, how long? How long, O Lord, dost thou forget us; how long dost thou turn Thy face from us? When wilt thou look upon us, and hear us? When wilt thou enlighten our eyes, and show us Thy face? When wilt thou restore thyself to us? Look upon us, Lord; hear us, enlighten us, reveal thyself to us. Restore thyself to us, that it may be well with us,—thyself, without whom it is so ill with us. Pity our toilings and strivings toward thee, since we can do nothing without thee. Thou dost invite us; do thou help us. I beseech thee, O Lord, that I may not lose hope in sighs, but may breathe anew in hope. Lord, my heart is made bitter by its desolation; sweeten thou it, I beseech thee, with Thy consolation. Lord, in hunger I began to seek thee; I beseech thee that I may not cease to hunger for thee. In hunger I have come to thee; let me not go unfed.

I have come in poverty to the Rich, in misery to the Compassionate; let me not return empty and despised. And if, before I eat, I sigh, grant, even after sighs, that which I may eat. Lord, I am bowed down and can only look downward; raise me up that I may look upward. My iniquities have gone over my head; they overwhelm me; and, like a heavy load, they weigh me down. Free me from them; unburden me, that the pit of iniquities may not close over me.

Be it mine to look up to Thy light, even from afar, even from the depths. Teach me to seek thee, and reveal thyself to me, when I seek thee, for I cannot seek thee, except thou teach me, nor find thee, except thou reveal thyself. Let me seek thee in longing, let me long for thee in seeking; let me find thee in love, and love thee in finding. Lord, I acknowledge and I thank thee that thou hast created me in this thine image, in order that I may be mindful of thee, may conceive of thee, and love thee; but that image has been so consumed and wasted away by vices, and obscured by the smoke of wrong-doing, that it cannot achieve that for which it was made, except thou renew it, and create it anew. I do not endeavor, O Lord, to penetrate Thy sublimity, for in no wise do I compare my understanding with that; but I long to understand in some degree Thy truth, which my heart believes and loves. For I do not seek to understand that I may believe, but I believe in order to understand. For this also I believe,—that unless I believed, I should not understand.

Chapter II

Truly there is a God, although the fool hath said in his heart, There is no God.

And so, Lord, do thou, who dost give understanding to faith, give me, so far as thou knowest it to be profitable, to understand that thou art as we believe; and that thou art that which we believe. And, indeed, we believe that thou art a being than which nothing greater can be conceived. Or is there no such nature, since the fool hath said in his heart, there is no God? (Psalms xiv. I). But, at any rate, this very fool, when he hears of this being of which I speak—a being than which nothing greater can be conceived—understands what he hears, and what he understands is in his understanding; although he does not understand it to exist.

For, it is one thing for an object to be in the understanding, and another to understand that the object exists. When a painter first conceives of what he will afterwards perform, he has it in his understanding, but he does not yet understand it to be, because he has not yet performed it. But after he has made the painting, he both has it in his understanding, and he understands that it exists, because he has made it.

Hence, even the fool is convinced that something exists in the understanding, at least, than which nothing greater can be conceived. For, when he hears of this, he understands it. And whatever is understood, exists in the understanding. And assuredly that, than which nothing greater can be conceived, cannot exist in the understanding alone. For, suppose it exists in the understanding alone: then it can be conceived to exist in reality; which is greater.

Therefore, if that, than which nothing greater can be conceived, exists in the understanding alone, the very being, than which nothing greater can be conceived, is one, than which a greater can be conceived. But obviously this is impossible. Hence, there is no doubt that there exists a being, than which nothing greater can be conceived, and it exists both in the understanding and in reality.

Chapter III

God cannot be conceived not to exist.—God is that, than which nothing greater can be conceived.—That which can be conceived not to exist is not God.

And it assuredly exists so truly, that it cannot be conceived not to exist. For, it is possible to conceive of a being which cannot be conceived not to exist; and this is greater than one which can be conceived not to exist. Hence, if that, than which nothing greater can be conceived, can be conceived not to exist, it is not that, than which nothing greater can be conceived. But this is an irreconcilable contradiction. There is, then, so truly a being than which nothing greater can be conceived to exist, that it cannot even be conceived not to exist; and this being thou art, O Lord, our God.

So truly, therefore, dost thou exist, O Lord, my God, that thou canst not be conceived not to exist; and rightly. For, if a mind could conceive of a being better than thee, the creature would rise above the Creator; and this is most absurd. And, indeed, whatever else there is, except thee alone, can be conceived not to exist. To thee alone, therefore, it belongs to exist more truly than all other beings, and hence in a higher degree than all others. For, whatever else exists does not exist so truly, and hence in a less degree it belongs to it to exist. Why, then, has the fool said in his heart, there is no God (Psalms xiv. I), since it is so evident, to a rational mind, that thou dost exist in the highest degree of all? Why, except that he is dull and a fool?

Chapter IV

How the fool has said in his heart what cannot be conceived.—A thing may be conceived in two ways: (1) when the word signifying it is conceived; (2) when the thing itself is understood. As far as the word goes, God can be conceived not to exist; in reality he cannot.

But how has the fool said in his heart what he could not conceive; or how is it that he could not conceive what he said in his heart? since it is the same to say in the heart, and to conceive.

But, if really, nay, since really, he both conceived, because he said in his heart; and did not say in his heart, because he could not conceive; there is more than one way in which a thing is said in the heart or conceived. For, in one sense, an object is conceived, when the word signifying it is conceived; and in another, when the very entity, which the object is, is understood.

In the former sense, then, God can be conceived not to exist; but in the latter, not at all. For no one who understands what fire and water are can conceive fire to be water, in accordance with the nature of the facts themselves, although this is possible according to the words. So, then, no one who understands what God is can conceive that God does not exist; although he says these words in his heart, either without any or with some foreign, signification. For, God is that than which a greater cannot be conceived. And he who thoroughly understands this, assuredly understands that this being so truly exists, that not even in concept can it be non-existent. Therefore, he who understands that God so exists, cannot conceive that he does not exist.

I thank thee, gracious Lord, I thank thee; because what I formerly believed by Thy bounty, I now so understand by thine illumination, that if I were unwilling to believe that thou dost exist, I should not be able not to understand this to be true.

Chapter V

God is whatever it is better to be than not to be; and he, as the only self-existent being, creates all things from nothing.

What art thou, then, Lord God, than whom nothing greater can be conceived? But what art thou, except that which, as the highest of all beings, alone exists through itself, and creates all other things from nothing? For, whatever is not this is less than a thing which can be conceived of. But this cannot be conceived of thee. What good, therefore, does the supreme Good lack, through which every good is? Therefore, thou art just, truthful, blessed, and whatever it is better to be than not to be. For it is better to be just than not just; better to be blessed than not blessed.

Chapter VI

How God is sensible (*sensibilis*) athough he is not a body.—God is sensible, omnipotent, compassionate, passionless; for it is better to be these than not be. He who in any way knows, is not improperly said in some sort to feel.

But, although it is better for thee to be sensible, omnipotent, compassionate, passionless, than not to be these things; how art thou sensible, if thou art not a body; or omnipotent, if thou hast not all powers; or at once compassionate and passionless? For, if only corporeal things are sensible, since the senses encompass a body and are in a body, how art thou sensible, although thou art not a body, but a supreme Spirit, who is superior to body? But, if feeling is only cognition, or for the sake of cognition,—for he who feels obtains knowledge in accordance with the proper functions of his senses; as through sight, of colors; through taste, of flavors,—whatever in any way cognises is not inappropriately said, in some sort, to feel.

Therefore, O Lord, although thou art not a body, yet thou art truly sensible in the highest degree in respect of this, that thou dost cognise all things in the highest degree; and not as an animal cognises, through a corporeal sense.

Chapter VII

How he is omnipotent, although there are many things of which he is not capable.—To be capable of being corrupted, or of lying, is not power, but impotence. God can do nothing by virtue of impotence, and nothing has power against him.

But how art thou omnipotent, if thou art not capable of all things? Or, if thou canst not be corrupted, and canst not lie, nor make what is true, false—as, for example, if thou shouldst make what has been done not to have been done, and the like—how art thou capable of all things? Or else to be capable of these things is not power, but impotence. For, he who is capable of these things is capable of what is not for his good, and of what he ought not to do; and the more capable of them he is, the more power have adversity and perversity against him; and the less has he himself against these.

He, then, who is thus capable is so not by power, but by impotence. For, he is not said to be able because he is able of himself, but because his impotence gives something else power over him. Or, by a figure of speech, just as many words are improperly applied, as when we use "to be" for "not to be," and "to do" for what is really "not to do," or "to do nothing." For, often we say to a man who denies the existence of something: "It is as you say it to be," though it might seem more proper to say, "It is not, as you say it is not." In the same way, we say: "This man sits just as that man does," or, "This man rests just as that man does"; although to sit is not to do anything, and to rest is to do nothing.

So, then, when one is said to have the power of doing or experiencing what is not for his good, or what he ought not to do, impotence is understood in the word power. For, the more he possesses this power, the more powerful are adversity and perversity against him, and the more powerless is he against them.

Therefore, O Lord, our God, the more truly art thou omnipotent, since thou art capable of nothing through impotence, and nothing has power against thee.

Chapter VIII

How he is compassionate and passionless. God is compassionate, in terms of our experience, because we experience the effect of compassion. God is not compassionate, in terms of his own being, because he does not experience the feeling (*affectus*) of compassion.

But how art thou compassionate, and, at the same time, passionless? For, if thou art passionless, thou dost not feel sympathy; and if thou dost not feel sympathy, Thy heart is not wretched from sympathy for the wretched; but this it is to be compassionate. But if thou art not compassionate, whence cometh so great consolation to the wretched? How, then, are thou compassionate and not compassionate, O Lord, unless because thou art compassionate in terms of our experience, and not compassionate in terms of Thy being.

Truly, thou art so in terms of our experience, but thou art not so in terms of thine own. For, when thou beholdest us in our wretchedness, we experience the effect of compassion, but thou dost not experience the feeling. Therefore, thou art both compassionate, because thou dost save the wretched, and spare those who sin against thee; and not compassionate, because thou art affected by no sympathy for wretchedness.

Chapter IX

How the all-just and supremely just God spares the wicked, and justly pities the wicked. He is better who is good to the righteous and the wicked than he who is good to the righteous alone. Although God is supremely just, the source of his compassion is hidden. God is supremely compassionate, because he is supremely just. He saveth the just, because justice goes with them; he frees sinners by the authority of justice. God spares the wicked out of justice; for it is just that God, than whom none is better or more powerful, should be good even to the wicked, and should make the wicked good. If God ought not to pity, he pities unjustly. But this it is impious to suppose. Therefore, God justly pities.

But how dost thou spare the wicked, if thou art all just and supremely just? For how, being all just and supremely just, dost thou aught that is not just? Or, what justice is that to give him who merits eternal death everlasting life? How, then, gracious Lord, good to the righteous and the wicked, canst thou save the wicked, if this is not just, and thou dost not aught that is not just? Or, since Thy goodness is incomprehensible, is this hidden in the unapproachable light wherein thou dwellest? Truly, in the deepest and most secret parts of Thy goodness is hidden the fountain whence the stream of Thy compassion flows.

For thou art all just and supremely just, yet thou art kind even to the wicked, even because thou art all supremely good. For thou wouldst be less good if thou wert not kind to any wicked being. For, he who is good, both to the righteous and the wicked, is better than he who is good to the good alone; and he who is good to the wicked, both by punishing and sparing them, is better than he who is good by punishing them alone. Therefore, thou art compassionate, because thou art all supremely good. And, although it appears why thou dost reward the good with goods and the evil with evils; yet this, at least, is most wonderful, why thou, the all and supremely just, who lackest nothing, bestowest goods on the wicked and on those who are guilty toward thee.

The depth of Thy goodness, O God! The source of Thy compassion appears, and yet is not clearly seen! We see whence the river flows, but the spring whence it arises is not seen. For, it is from the abundance of Thy goodness that thou art good to those who sin against thee; and in the depth of Thy goodness is hidden the reason for this kindness.

For, although thou dost reward the good with goods and the evil with evils, out of goodness, yet this the concept of justice seems to demand. But, when thou dost bestow goods on the evil, and it is known that the supremely Good hath willed to do this, we wonder why the supremely Just has been able to will this.

O compassion, from what abundant sweetness and what sweet abundance dost thou well forth to us! O boundless goodness of God, how passionately should sinners love thee! For thou savest the just, because justice goeth with them; but sinners thou dost free by the authority of justice. Those by the help of their deserts; these, although their deserts oppose. Those by acknowledging the goods thou hast granted; these by pardoning the evils thou hatest. O boundless goodness, which dost so exceed all understanding, let that compassion come upon me, which proceeds from Thy so great abundance! Let it flow upon me, for it wells forth from thee. Spare, in mercy; avenge not, in justice.

For, though it is hard to understand how Thy compassion is not inconsistent with Thy justice; yet we must believe that it does not oppose justice at all, because it flows from goodness, which is no goodness without justice; nay, that it is in true harmony with justice. For, if thou art compassionate only because thou art supremely good, and supremely good only because thou art supremely just, truly thou art compassionate even because thou art supremely just. Help me, just and compassionate God, whose light I seek; help me to understand what I say.

Truly, then, thou art compassionate even because thou art just. Is, then, Thy compassion born of Thy justice? And dost thou spare the wicked, therefore, out of justice? If this is true, my Lord, if this is true, teach me how it is. Is it because it is just, that thou shouldst be so good that thou canst not be conceived better; and that thou shouldst work so powerfully that thou canst not be conceived more powerful? For what can be more just than this? Assuredly it could not be that thou shouldst be good only by requiting (*retribuendo*) and not by sparing, and that thou shouldst make good only those who are not good, and not the wicked also. In this way, therefore, it is just that thou shouldst spare the wicked, and make good souls of evil.

Finally, what is not done justly ought not to be done; and what ought not to be done is done unjustly. If, then, thou dost not justly pity the wicked, thou oughtest not to pity them. And, if thou oughtest not to pity them, thou pityest them unjustly. And if it is impious to suppose this, it is right to believe that thou justly pityest the wicked.

Chapter X

How he justly punishes and justly spares the wicked.—God, in sparing the wicked, is just, according to his own nature, because he does what is consistent with his goodness; but he is not just, according to our nature, because he does not inflict the punishment deserved.

But it is also just that thou shouldst punish the wicked. For what is more just than that the good should receive goods, and the evil, evils? How, then, is it just that thou shouldst punish the wicked, and, at the same time, spare the wicked? Or, in one way, dost thou justly punish, and, in another, justly spare them? For, when thou punishest the wicked, it is just, because it is consistent with their deserts; and when, on the other hand, thou sparest the wicked, it is just, not because it is compatible with their deserts, but because it is compatible with Thy goodness.

For, in sparing the wicked, thou art as just, according to Thy nature, but not according to ours, as thou art compassionate, according to our nature, and not according to thine; seeing that, as in saving us, whom it would be just for thee to destroy, thou art compassionate, not because thou feelest an affection (*affectum*), but because we feel the effect (*effectum*); so thou art just, not because thou requitest us as we deserve, but because thou dost that which becomes thee as the supremely good Being. In this way, therefore, without contradiction thou dost justly punish and justly spare.

Chapter XI

How all the ways of God are compassion and truth; and yet God is just in all his ways.—We cannot comprehend why, of the wicked, he saves these rather than those, through his supreme goodness; and condemns those rather than these, through his supreme justice.

But, is there any reason why it is not also just, according to Thy nature, O Lord, that thou shouldst punish the wicked? Surely it is just that thou shouldst be so just that thou canst not be conceived more just; and this thou wouldst in no wise be if thou didst only render goods to the good, and not evils to the evil. For, he who requiteth both good and evil according to their deserts is more just than he who so requites the good alone. It is, therefore, just, according to Thy nature, O just and gracious God, both when thou dost punish and when thou sparest.

Truly, then, all the paths of the Lord are mercy and truth (Psalms xxv. 10); and yet the Lord is righteous in all his ways (Psalms cxlv. 17). And assuredly without inconsistency: For, it is not just that those whom thou dost will to punish should be saved, and that those whom thou dost will to spare should be condemned. For that alone is just which thou dost will; and that alone unjust which thou dost not will. So, then, Thy compassion is born of Thy justice.

For it is just that thou shouldst be so good that thou art good in sparing also; and this may be the reason why the supremely Just can will goods for the evil. But if it can be comprehended in any way why thou canst will to save the wicked, yet by no consideration can we comprehend why, of those who are alike wicked, thou savest some rather than others, through supreme goodness; and why thou dost condemn the latter rather than the former, through supreme justice.

So, then, thou art truly sensible (*sensibilis*), omnipotent, compassionate, and passionless, as thou art living, wise, good, blessed, eternal: and whatever it is better to be than not to be.

Chapter XII

God is the very life whereby he lives; and so of other like attributes.

But undoubtedly, whatever thou art, thou art through nothing else than thyself. Therefore, thou art the very life whereby thou livest; and the wisdom wherewith thou art wise; and the very goodness whereby thou art good to the righteous and the wicked; and so of other like attributes.

Chapter XIII

How he alone is uncircumscribed and eternal, although other spirits are uncircumscribed and eternal.—No place and time contain God. But he is himself everywhere and always. He alone not only does not cease to be, but also does not begin to be.

But everything that is in any way bounded by place or time is less than that which no law of place or time limits. Since, then, nothing is greater than thou, no place or time contains thee; but thou art everywhere and always. And since this can be said of thee alone, thou alone art uncircumscribed and eternal. How is it, then, that other spirits also are said to be uncircumscribed and eternal?

Assuredly thou art alone eternal; for thou alone among all beings not only dost not cease to be, but also dost not begin to be.

But how art thou alone uncircumscribed? Is it that a created spirit, when compared with thee, is circumscribed, but when compared with matter, uncircumscribed? For altogether circumscribed is that which, when it is wholly in one place, cannot at the same time be in another. And this is seen to be true of corporeal things alone. But uncircumscribed is that which is, as a whole, at the same time everywhere. And this is understood to be true of thee alone. But circumscribed, and, at the same time, uncircumscribed is that which, when it is anywhere as a whole, can at the same time be somewhere else as a whole, and yet not everywhere. And this is recognised as true of created spirits. For, if the soul were not as a whole in the separate members of the body, it would not feel as a whole in the separate members.

Therefore, thou, Lord, art peculiarly uncircumscribed and eternal; and yet other spirits also are uncircumscribed and eternal.

Chapter XIV

How and why God is seen and yet not seen by those who seek him.

Hast thou found what thou didst seek, my soul? Thou didst seek God. Thou hast found him to be a being which is the highest of all beings, a being than which nothing better can be conceived; that this being is life itself, light, wisdom, goodness, eternal blessedness and blessed eternity; and that it is everywhere and always.

For, if thou hast not found Thy God, how is he this being which thou hast found, and which thou hast conceived him to be, with so certain truth and so true certainty? But, if thou hast found him, why is it that thou dost not feel thou hast found him? Why, O Lord, our God, does not my soul feel thee, if it hath found thee? Or, has it not found him whom it found to be light and truth? For how did it understand this, except by seeing light and truth? Or, could it understand anything at all of thee, except through Thy light and Thy truth?

Hence, if it has seen light and truth, it has seen thee; if it has not seen thee, it has not seen light and truth. Or, is what it has seen both light and truth; and still it has not yet seen thee, because it has seen thee only in part, but has not seen thee as thou art? Lord my God, my creator and renewer, speak to the desire of my soul, what thou art other than it hath seen, that it may clearly see what it desires. It strains to see thee more; and sees nothing beyond this which it hath seen, except darkness. Nay, it does not see darkness, of which there is none in thee; but it sees that it cannot see farther, because of its own darkness.

Why is this, Lord, why is this? Is the eye of the soul darkened by its infirmity, or dazzled by Thy glory? Surely it is both darkened in itself, and dazzled by thee. Doubtless it is both obscured by its own insignificance, and overwhelmed by Thy infinity. Truly, it is both contracted by its own narrowness and overcome by Thy greatness.

For how great is that light from which shines every truth that gives light to the rational mind? How great is that truth in which is everything that is true, and outside which is only nothingness and the false? How boundless is the truth which sees at one glance whatsoever has been made, and by whom, and through whom, and how it has been made from nothing? What purity, what certainty, what splendor where it is? Assuredly more than a creature can conceive.

Chapter XV

He is greater than can be conceived.

Therefore, O Lord, thou art not only that than which a greater cannot be conceived, but thou art a being greater than can be conceived. For, since it can be conceived that there is such a being, if thou art not this very being, a greater than thou can be conceived. But this is impossible.

Chapter XVI

This is the unapproachable light wherein he dwells.

Truly, O Lord, this is the unapproachable light in which thou dwellest; for truly there is nothing else which can penetrate this light, that it may see thee there. Truly, I see it not, because it is too bright for me. And yet, whatsoever I see, I see through it, as the weak eye sees what it sees through the light of the sun, which in the sun itself it cannot look upon. My understanding cannot reach that light, for it shines too bright. It does not comprehend it, nor does the eye of my soul endure to gaze upon it long. It is dazzled by the brightness, it is overcome by the greatness, it is overwhelmed by the infinity, it is dazed by the largeness, of the light.

O supreme and unapproachable light! O whole and blessed truth, how far art thou from me, who am so near to thee! How far removed art thou from my vision, though I am so near to thine! Everywhere thou art wholly present, and I see thee not. In thee I move, and in thee I have my being; and I cannot come to thee. Thou art within me, and about me, and I feel thee not.

Chapter XVII

In God is harmony, fragrance, sweetness, pleasantness to the touch, beauty, after his ineffable manner.

Still thou art hidden, O Lord, from my soul in Thy light and thy blessedness; and therefore my soul still walks in its darkness and wretchedness. For it looks, and does not see Thy beauty. It hearkens, and does not hear Thy harmony. It smells, and does not perceive Thy fragrance. It tastes, and does not recognise Thy sweetness. It touches, and does not feel Thy pleasantness. For thou hast these attributes in thyself, Lord God, after thine ineffable manner, who hast given them to objects created by thee, after their sensible manner; but the sinful senses of my soul have grown rigid and dull, and have been obstructed by their long listlessness.

Chapter XVIII

God is life, wisdom, eternity, and every true good.—Whatever is composed of parts is not wholly one; it is capable, either in fact or in concept, of dissolution. In God wisdom, eternity, etc., are not parts, but one, and the very whole which God is, or unity itself, not even in concept divisible.

And lo, again confusion; lo, again grief and mourning meet him who seeks for joy and gladness. My soul now hoped for satisfaction; and lo, again it is overwhelmed with need. I desired now to feast, and lo, I hunger more. I tried to rise to the light of God, and I have fallen back into my darkness. Nay, not only have I fallen into it, but I feel that I am enveloped in it. I fell before my mother conceived me. Truly, in darkness I was conceived, and in the cover of darkness I was born. Truly, in him we all fell, in whom we all sinned. In him we all lost, who kept easily, and wickedly lost to himself and to us that which when we wish to seek it, we do not know; when we seek it, we do not find; when we find, it is not that which we seek.

Do thou help me for Thy goodness' sake! Lord, I sought Thy face; Thy face, Lord, will I seek; hide not Thy face far from me (Psalms xxvii. 8). Free me from myself toward thee. Cleanse, heal, sharpen, enlighten the eye of my mind, that it may behold thee. Let my soul recover its strength, and with all its understanding let it strive toward thee, O Lord. What art thou, Lord, what art thou? What shall my heart conceive thee to be?

Assuredly thou art life, thou art wisdom, thou art truth, thou art goodness, thou art blessedness, thou art eternity, and thou art every true good. Many are these attributes: my straitened understanding cannot see so many at one view, that it may be gladdened by all at once. How, then, O Lord, art thou all these things? Are they parts of thee, or is each one of these rather the whole, which thou art? For, whatever is composed of parts is not altogether one, but is in some sort plural, and diverse from itself; and either in fact or in concept is capable of dissolution.

But these things are alien to thee, than whom nothing better can be conceived of. Hence, there are no parts in thee, Lord, nor art thou more than one. But thou art so truly a unitary being, and so identical with thyself, that in no respect art thou unlike thyself; rather thou art unity itself, indivisible by any conception. Therefore, life and wisdom and the rest are not parts of thee, but all are one; and each of these is the whole, which thou art, and which all the rest are.

In this way, then, it appears that thou hast no parts, and that Thy eternity, which thou art, is nowhere and never a part of thee or of Thy eternity. But everywhere thou art as a whole, and Thy eternity exists as a whole forever.

Chapter XIX

He does not exist in place or time, but all things exist in him.

But if through thine eternity thou hast been, and art, and wilt be; and to have been is not to be destined to be; and to be is not to have been, or to be destined to be; how does thine eternity exist as a whole forever? Or is it true that nothing of Thy eternity passes away, so that it is not now; and that nothing of it is destined to be, as if it were not yet?

Thou wast not, then, yesterday, nor wilt thou be tomorrow; but yesterday and today and tomorrow thou art; or, rather, neither yesterday nor today or tomorrow thou art; but simply, thou art, outside all time. For yesterday and today and tomorrow have no existence, except in time; but thou, although nothing exists without thee, nevertheless dost not exist in space or time, but all things exist in thee. For nothing contains thee, but thou containest all.

C
THE TURN OF MODERNITY

Galileo Galilei and Genesis 1–11

Introduction
Ki Joo Choi

It is hard not to underestimate the historical (and, correlatively, the intellectual) importance of the Galileo controversy. Thanks to a telescope Galileo (b. A.D. 1564–d. A.D. 1642) "reinvented" in A.D. 1609 by making a more powerful version of the Dutch "spyglass," Galileo was able to confirm Nicolaus Copernicus's (1473–1543) heliocentric model of the solar system made in A.D. 1554. Galileo's observation that Earth revolved around the sun was controversial and cataclysmic—simply, revolutionary. It contradicted centuries-old assumptions about the world, first established by the ancient Greek thinkers Ptolemy (90–168) and Aristotle (384–322 B.C.), and then adopted by Christian Europe.

The story of Galileo's astronomical findings and the historical details of the controversy that ensued are complex, dramatic, and fascinating. In the Course: Documents folder of your Blackboard site, you will find some brief, but detailed and fascinating, discussions of Galileo's historical and cultural context. Although these texts are supplementary and not required, they are strongly recommended in order to gain some helpful background for the required readings.

This week's readings begin with Galileo's "Letter to Madame Christina of Lorraine, Grand Duchess of Tuscany." In this letter, Galileo sets out to defend himself against accusations that he is preaching heresy in claiming that the prevailing notion of the sun revolving around Earth is wrong. The accusation more precisely revolves around whether Galileo is contradicting the Christian Bible with his astronomical observations and thus undermining the authority of Christian scripture with respect to knowledge of the truth.

As you read this text, pay particular attention to Galileo's regard for the Bible. Note where he "affirm[s] that the holy Bible can never speak untruth." So it is clear that Galileo does not want to refute the Bible's authority when it comes to knowledge of truth. But that is not the end of the story for Galileo, to be sure. What is interesting to note is that Galileo recommends a better understanding of "the true senses" of biblical passages. With that in mind, as you go through this letter from Galileo, pay close attention to what Galileo thinks is the proper purview of the Bible. That is, what kind of truths does Galileo think the Bible reveals? Galileo wants to make clear that there are two sources of truth, one from what he refers to as "sense experiences and necessary demonstrations" and the other through biblical revelation. The question is, what truths does the Bible reveal and what kind of truths does human observation—sense experience and demonstration—reveal? Correlatively, does Galileo think that the Bible is concerned with the truths that human sense experience is able to discern? Although Galileo claims that God has given us the capacity of the senses, rationality, and the intellect, he is also quite clear on the proposition that the Bible is *not* concerned with the kind of knowledge human sense experience and rationality offers. What is the proper domain of the Bible (or Holy Spirit, as Galileo refers) and what is the proper domain of reason, sense experience, and demonstration?

Although Galileo claims that the Bible reveals certain kinds of truths and that reason and sense experience offer *different kinds* of truths, Galileo admits that some may detect at times what appears to be a contradiction between what the Bible tells us and what scientific reason, observation, and experience might tell us. But he insists that "two truths [i.e., the truths of the Bible and the truths of science] cannot contradict one another." If that is the case, then how does Galileo propose that this seeming contradiction is resolved? Do you see any relation between what Galileo proposes as the relation between revealed truth and truth grasped by way of demonstration and what you find in Thomas Aquinas or in Ibn Rushd?

Finally, we might raise the following questions: If the Bible is concerned with certain kinds of truths, and observation, demonstration, and experience are concerned with different sets of truths, then what does Galileo say ought to be the relationship between theologians and scientists? Do theologians have reason to comment on what scientists do, and vice versa?

After studying this letter, turn next to the second required reading for this week, chapters 1–11 of the book of Genesis in the Hebrew Bible or Old Testament of the Christian Bible. In the beginning of this reading, you will encounter the story of the world's creation (i.e., the story of creation in six days, with a seventh day of rest, the story of the creation of the first human beings, and so forth). Consider some of the questions Galileo raises with respect to these biblical passages. Does Genesis 1–11 strike you as a kind of "science" text? More specifically, do you think portions of Genesis 1–11 can be read literally? Consider the passages on creation, Genesis 1, and note that in this chapter Genesis offers two somewhat different accounts of creation and the first human beings, Adam and Eve (read the beginning to end of Genesis 1 carefully; you will notice the creation story is repeated twice, but with slight variations). What significance might this hold? Does it suggest that the creation accounts of Genesis cannot be interpreted literally?

Assuming that passages in the Bible cannot be read literally, does that mean that the biblical passages are "untrue"? What kind of truths might the Bible offer, if some or many of its passages cannot be understood in a literal fashion? Are these truths similar to the kind Galileo thinks? Are they religious truths? Or moral truths? Or both? Can the truths (whether religious or moral) the Bible offers be discerned *without* the Bible, that is, through scientific inquiry alone? Or does the Bible offer truths to us that no other form of human knowing or inquiry (specifically, in science) can? In order to consider these questions, consider these more specific questions about several passages in Genesis 1–11:

- What do the passages in Genesis regarding creation seem to indicate about the relation between men and women as opposed to the relation between human beings and other living things?

- What are the human consequences of defying God's prohibition in the Garden of Eden? What is the religious and moral significance of these consequences?

- What do you think it means to say that human beings are created in God's image? Given your reading of Genesis 1–11, would you say that creation by God is an accident, a willful and purposeful action, or a necessary action?

- How does Genesis 1–3 characterize the nature of the created world, and how does this characterization differ from the way the created world is described from Genesis 4 onward?

- According to these passages, who is responsible for evil, suffering, and/or sin? Is it God, the serpent, Adam, or Eve?

LETTER TO MADAME CHRISTINA OF LORRAINE, GRAND DUCHESS OF TUSCANY

Concerning the Use of Biblical Quotations in Matters of Science

Galileo Galilei to The Most Serene Grand Duchess Mother:

Some years ago, as Your Serene Highness well knows, I discovered in the heavens many things that had not been seen before our own age. The novelty of these things, as well as some consequences which followed from them in contradiction to the physical notions commonly held among academic philosophers, stirred up against me no small number of professors—as if I had placed these things in the sky with my own hands in order to upset nature and overturn the sciences. They seemed to forget that the increase of known truths stimulates the investigation, establishment, and growth of the arts; not their diminution or destruction.

Showing a greater fondness for their own opinions than for truth, they sought to deny and disprove the new things which, if they had cared to look for themselves, their own senses would have demonstrated to them. To this end they hurled various charges and published numerous writings filled with vain arguments, and they made the grave mistake of sprinkling these with passages taken from places in the Bible which they had failed to understand properly, and which were ill suited to their purposes.

Persisting in their original resolve to destroy me and everything mine by any means they can think of these men are aware of my views in astronomy and philosophy. They know that as to the arrangement of the parts of the universe, I hold the sun to be situated motionless in the center of the revolution of the celestial orbs while the earth rotates on its axis and revolves about the sun. They know also that I support this position not only by refuting the arguments of Ptolemy and Aristotle, but by producing many counter-arguments; in particular, some which relate to physical effects whose causes can perhaps be assigned in no other way. In addition there are astronomical arguments derived from many things in my new celestial discoveries that plainly confute the Ptolemaic system while admirably agreeing with and confirming the contrary hypothesis. . . .

In order to facilitate their designs, they seek so far as possible (at least among the common people) to make this opinion seem new and to belong to me alone. They pretend not to know that its author, or rather its restorer and confirmer, was Nicholas Copernicus; and that he was not only a Catholic, but a priest and a canon. He was in fact so esteemed by the church that when the Lateran Council under Leo X took up the correction of the church calendar, Copernicus was called to Rome from the most remote parts of Germany to undertake its reform. . . . I hope to show that I proceed with much greater piety than they do, when I argue not against condemning this book, but against condemning it in the way they suggest—that is, without understanding it, weighing it, or so much as reading it. For Copernicus never discusses matters of religion or faith, nor does he use arguments that depend in any way upon the authority of sacred writings which he might have interpreted erroneously. He stands always upon physical conclusions pertaining to the celestial motions, and deals with them by astronomical and geometrical demonstrations, founded primarily upon sense experiences and very exact observations. He did not ignore the Bible, but he knew very well that if his doctrine were proved, then it could not contradict the Scriptures when they were rightly understood. . . .

The reason produced for condemning the opinion that the earth moves and the sun stands still is that in many places in the Bible one may read that the sun moves and the earth stands still. Since the Bible cannot err, it follows as a necessary consequence that anyone takes an erroneous and heretical position who maintains that the sun is inherently motionless and the earth movable.

With regard to this argument, I think in the first place that it is very pious to say and prudent to affirm that the holy Bible can never speak untruth—whenever its true meaning is understood. But I believe nobody will deny that it is often very abstruse, and may say things which are quite different from what its bare words signify. Hence in expounding the Bible if one were always to confine oneself to the unadorned grammatical meaning, one might fall into error. Not only contradictions and propositions far from true might thus be made to appear in the Bible, but even grave heresies and follies. Thus it would be necessary to assign to God feet, hands, and eyes, as well as corporeal and human affections, such as anger, repentance, hatred, and sometimes even the forgetting of things past and ignorance of those to come. These propositions uttered by the Holy Ghost were set down in that manner by the sacred scribes in order to accommodate them to the capacities of the common people, who are rude and unlearned. For the sake of those who deserve to be separated from the herd, it is necessary that wise expositors should produce the true senses of such passages, together with the special reasons for which they were set down in these words. This doctrine is so widespread and so definite with all theologians that it would be superfluous to adduce evidence for it.

Hence I think that I may reasonably conclude that whenever the Bible has occasion to speak of any physical conclusion (especially those which are very abstruse and hard to understand), the rule has been observed of avoiding confusion in the minds of the common people which would render them contumacious toward the higher mysteries. Now the Bible, merely to condescend to popular capacity, has not hesitated to obscure some very important pronouncements, attributing to God himself some qualities extremely remote from (and even contrary to) His essence. Who, then, would positively declare that this principle has been set aside, and the Bible has confined itself rigorously to the bare and restricted sense of its words, when speaking but casually of the earth, of water, of the sun, or of any other created thing? Especially in view of the fact that these things in no way concern the primary purpose of the sacred writings, which is the service of God and the salvation of souls—matters infinitely beyond the comprehension of the common people.

This being granted, I think that in discussions of physical problems we ought to begin not from the authority of scriptural passages, but from sense-experiences and necessary demonstrations; for the holy Bible and the phenomena of nature proceed alike from the divine Word, the former as the dictate of the Holy Ghost and the latter as the observant executrix of God's commands. It is necessary for the Bible, in order to be accommodated to the understanding of every man, to speak many things which appear to differ from the absolute truth so far as the bare meaning of the words is concerned. But Nature, on the other hand, is inexorable and immutable; she never transgresses the laws imposed upon her, or cares a whit whether her abstruse reasons and methods of operation are understandable to men. For that reason it appears that nothing physical which sense-experience sets before our eyes or which necessary demonstrations prove to us, ought to be called in question (much less condemned) upon the testimony of biblical passages which may have some different meaning beneath their words. For the Bible is not chained in every expression to conditions as strict as those which govern all physical effects; nor is God any less excellently revealed in Nature's actions than in the sacred statements of the Bible. . . .

From this I do not mean to infer that we need not have an extraordinary esteem for the passages of Holy Scripture. On the contrary, having arrived at any certainties in physics, we ought to utilize these as the most appropriate aids in the true exposition of the Bible and in the investigation of those meanings which are necessarily contained therein, for these must be concordant with demonstrated truths. I should judge that the authority of the Bible was designed to persuade men of those articles and propositions which surpassing all human reasoning, could not be made credible by science, or by any other means than through the very mouth of the Holy Spirit.

Yet even in those propositions which are not matters of faith, this authority ought to be preferred over that of all human writings which are supported only by bare assertions or probable arguments, and not set forth in a demonstrative way. This I hold to be necessary and proper to the same extent that divine wisdom surpasses all human judgment and conjecture.

But I do not feel obliged to believe that that same God who has endowed us with senses, reason, and intellect has intended to forgo their use and by some other means to give us knowledge which we can attain by them. He would not require us to deny sense and reason in physical matters which are set before our eyes and minds by direct experience or necessary demonstrations. This must be especially true in those sciences of which but the faintest trace (and that consisting of conclusions) is to be found in the Bible. Of astronomy, for instance, so little is found that none of the planets except Venus are so much as mentioned, and this only once or twice under the name of "Lucifer." If the sacred scribes had had any intention of teaching people certain arrangements and motions of the heavenly bodies, or had they wished us to derive such knowledge from the Bible, then in my opinion they would not have spoken of these matters so sparingly in comparison with the infinite number of admirable conclusions which are demonstrated in that science. Far from pretending to teach us the constitution and motions of the heavens and the stars, with their shapes, magnitudes, and distances, the authors of the Bible intentionally forebore to speak of these things, though all were quite well known to them. Such is the opinion of the holiest and most learned Fathers, and in St. Augustine we find the following words:

"It is likewise commonly asked what we may believe about the form and shape of the heavens according to the Scriptures, for many contend much about these matters. But with superior prudence our authors have forborne to speak of this, as in no way furthering the student with respect to a blessed life—and, more important still, as taking up much of that time which should be spent in holy exercises. What is it to me whether heaven, like a sphere, surrounds the earth on all sides as a mass balanced in the center of the universe, or whether like a dish it merely covers and overcasts the earth? Belief in Scripture is urged rather for the reason we have often mentioned; that is, in order that no one, through ignorance of divine passages, finding anything in our Bibles or hearing anything cited from them of such a nature as may seem to oppose manifest conclusions, should be induced to suspect their truth when they teach, relate, and deliver more profitable matters. Hence let it be said briefly, touching the form of heaven, that our authors knew the truth but the Holy Spirit did not desire that men should learn things that are useful to no one for salvation." . . .

From these things it follows as a necessary consequence that, since the Holy Ghost did not intend to teach us whether heaven moves or stands still, whether its shape is spherical or like a discus or extended in a plane, nor whether the earth is located at its center or off to one side, then so much the less was it intended to settle for us any other conclusion of the same kind. And the motion or rest of the earth and the sun is so closely linked with the things just named, that without a determination of the one, neither side can be taken in the other matters. Now if the Holy Spirit has purposely neglected to teach us propositions of this sort as irrelevant to the highest goal (that is, to our salvation), how can anyone affirm that it is obligatory to take sides on them, and that one belief is required by faith, while the other side is erroneous? Can an opinion be heretical and yet have no concern with the salvation of souls? Can the Holy Ghost be asserted not to have intended teaching us something that does concern our salvation? I would say here something that was heard from an ecclesiastic of the most eminent degree: "That the intention of the Holy Ghost is to teach us how one goes to heaven, not how heaven goes." . . .

This granted, and it being true that two truths cannot contradict one another, it is the function of wise expositors to seek out the true senses of scriptural texts. These will unquestionably accord with the physical conclusions which manifest sense and necessary demonstrations have previously made certain to us. Now the Bible, as has been remarked, admits in many places expositions that are remote from the signification of the words for reasons we have already given. Moreover, we are unable to affirm that all interpreters of the Bible speak by divine inspiration, for if that were so there would exist no differences between them about the sense of a given passage. Hence I should think it would be the part of prudence not to permit anyone to usurp scriptural texts and force them in some way to maintain any physical conclusion to be true, when at some future time the senses and demonstrative or necessary reasons may show the contrary. Who indeed will set bounds to human ingenuity? Who will assert that everything in the universe capable of being perceived is already discovered and known? Let us rather confess quite truly that "Those truths which we know are very few in comparison with those which we do not know." . . .

I do not wish to place in the number of such lay writers some theologians whom I consider men of profound learning and devout behavior, and who are therefore held by me in great esteem and veneration. Yet I cannot deny that I feel some discomfort which I should like to have removed, when I hear them pretend to the power of constraining others by scriptural authority to follow in a physical dispute that opinion which they think best agrees with the Bible, and then believe themselves not bound to answer the opposing reasons and experiences. In explanation and support of this opinion they say that since theology is queen of all the sciences, she need not bend in any way to accommodate herself to the teachings of less worthy sciences which are subordinate to her; these others must rather be referred to her as to their supreme empress, changing and altering their conclusions according to her statutes and decrees. They add further that if in the inferior sciences any conclusion should be taken as certain in virtue of demonstrations or experiences, while in the Bible another conclusion is found repugnant to this, then the professors of that science should themselves undertake to undo their proofs and discover the fallacies in their own experiences, without bothering the theologians and exegetes. For, they say, it does not become the dignity of theology to stoop to the investigation of fallacies in the subordinate sciences; it is sufficient for her merely to determine the truth of a given conclusion with absolute authority, secure in her inability to err. . . .

First, I question whether there is not some equivocation in failing to specify the virtues which entitle sacred theology to the title of "queen." It might deserve the name by reason of including everything that is learned from all the other sciences and establishing everything by better methods and with profounder learning. It is thus, for example, that the rules for measuring fields and keeping accounts are much more excellently contained in arithmetic and in the geometry of Euclid than in the practices of surveyors and accountants. Or theology might be queen because of being occupied with a subject which excels in dignity all the subjects which compose the other sciences, and because her teachings are divulged in more sublime ways.

That the title and authority of queen belongs to theology in the first sense, I think will not be affirmed by theologians who have any skill in the other sciences. None of these, I think, will say that geometry, astronomy, music, and medicine are much more excellently contained in the Bible than they are in the books of Archimedes, Ptolemy, Boethius, and Galen. Hence it seems likely that regal pre-eminence is given to theology in the second sense; that is, by reason of its subject and the miraculous communication of divine revelation of conclusions which could not be conceived by men in any other way, concerning chiefly the attainment of eternal blessedness.

Let us grant then that theology is conversant with the loftiest divine contemplation, and occupies the regal throne among the sciences by dignity. But acquiring the highest authority in this way, if she does not descend to the lower and humbler speculations of the subordinate sciences and has no regard for them because they are not concerned with blessedness, then her professors should not arrogate to themselves the authority to decide on controversies in professions which they have neither studied nor practiced. Why, this would be as if an absolute despot, being neither a physician or an architect but knowing himself free to command, should undertake to administer medicines and erect buildings according to his whim—at grave peril of his poor patients' lives, and the speedy collapse of his edifices. . . .

If, in order to banish the opinion in question from the world, it were sufficient to stop the mouth of a single man—as perhaps those men persuade themselves who, measuring the minds of others by their own, think it impossible that this doctrine should be able to continue to find adherents—then that would be very easily done. But things stand otherwise. To carry out such a decision it would be necessary not only to prohibit the book of Copernicus and the writings of other authors who follow the same opinion, but to ban the whole science of astronomy. Furthermore, it would be necessary to forbid men to look at the heavens, in order that they might not see Mars and Venus sometimes quite near the earth and sometimes very distant, the variation being so great that Venus is forty times and Mars sixty times as large at one time as another. And it would be necessary to prevent Venus being seen round at one time and forked at another, with very thin horns; as well as many other sensory observations which can never be reconciled with the Ptolemaic system in any way, but are very strong arguments for the Copernican. And to ban Copernicus now that his doctrine is daily reinforced by many new observations and by the learned applying themselves to the reading of his book, after this opinion has been allowed and tolerated for those many years during which it was less followed and less confirmed, would seem in my judgment to be a contravention of truth, and an attempt to hide and suppress her the more as she revealed herself the more clearly and plainly. Not to abolish and censure his whole book, but only to condemn as erroneous this particular proposition, would (if I am not mistaken) be a still greater detriment to the minds of men, since it would afford them occasion to see a proposition proved that it was heresy to believe. And to prohibit the whole science would be but to censure a hundred passages of holy Scripture which teach us that the glory and greatness of Almighty God are marvelously discerned in all his works and divinely read in the open book of heaven. For let no one believe that reading the lofty concepts written in that book leads to nothing further than the mere seeing of the splendor of the sun and the stars and their rising and setting, which is as far as the eyes of brutes and of the vulgar can penetrate. Within its pages are couched mysteries so profound and concepts so sublime that the vigils, labors, and studies of hundreds upon hundreds of the most acute minds have still not pierced them, even after continual investigations for thousands of years.... Likewise, that which presents itself to mere sight is as nothing in comparison with the high marvels that the ingenuity of learned men discovers in the heavens by long and accurate observation....

But finally let us grant to these gentlemen even more than they demand; namely, let us admit that we must subscribe entirely to the opinion of wise theologians. Then, since this particular dispute does not occur among the ancient Fathers, it must be undertaken by the wise men of this age. After first hearing the experiences, observations, arguments, and proofs of philosophers and astronomers on both sides—for the controversy is over physical problems and logical dilemmas, and admits of no third alternative—they will be able to determine the matter positively, in accordance with the dictates of divine inspiration. But as to those men who do not scruple to hazard the majesty and dignity of holy Scripture to uphold the reputation of their own vain fancies, let them not hope that a decision such as this is to be made without minutely airing and discussing all the arguments on both sides. Nor need we fear this from men who will make it their whole business to examine most attentively the very foundations of this doctrine, and who will do so only in a holy zeal for the truth, the Bible, and the majesty, dignity, and authority in which every Christian wants to see these maintained.

Bible

GENESIS 1–11

Genesis 1

1 In the beginning when God created the heavens and the earth, 2 the earth was a formless void and darkness covered the face of the deep, while a wind from God swept over the face of the waters. 3 Then God said, "Let there be light"; and there was light. 4 And God saw that the light was good; and God separated the light from the darkness. 5 God called the light Day, and the darkness he called Night. And there was evening and there was morning, the first day. 6 And God said, "Let there be a dome in the midst of the waters, and let it separate the waters from the waters." 7 So God made the dome and separated the waters that were under the dome from the waters that were above the dome. And it was so. 8 God called the dome Sky. And there was evening and there was morning, the second day. 9 And God said, "Let the waters under the sky be gathered together into one place, and let the dry land appear." And it was so. 10 God called the dry land Earth, and the waters that were gathered together he called Seas. And God saw that it was good. 11 Then God said, "Let the earth put forth vegetation: plants yielding seed, and fruit trees of every kind on earth that bear fruit with the seed in it." And it was so. 12 The earth brought forth vegetation: plants yielding seed of every kind, and trees of every kind bearing fruit with the seed in it. And God saw that it was good. 13 And there was evening and there was morning, the third day. 14 And God said, "Let there be lights in the dome of the sky to separate the day from the night; and let them be for signs and for seasons and for days and years, 15 and let them be lights in the dome of the sky to give light upon the earth." And it was so. 16 God made the two great lights—the greater light to rule the day and the lesser light to rule the night—and the stars. 17 God set them in the dome of the sky to give light upon the earth, 18 to rule over the day and over the night, and to separate the light from the darkness. And God saw that it was good. 19 And there was evening and there was morning, the fourth day. 20 And God said, "Let the waters bring forth swarms of living creatures, and let birds fly above the earth across the dome of the sky." 21 So God created the great sea monsters and every living creature that moves, of every kind, with which the waters swarm, and every winged bird of every kind. And God saw that it was good. 22 God blessed them, saying, "Be fruitful and multiply and fill the waters in the seas, and let birds multiply on the earth." 23 And there was evening and there was morning, the fifth day. 24 And God said, "Let the earth bring forth living creatures of every kind: cattle and creeping things and wild animals of the earth of every kind." And it was so. 25 God made the wild animals of the earth of every kind, and the cattle of every kind, and everything that creeps upon the ground of every kind. And God saw that it was good. 26 Then God said, "Let

us make humankind in our image, according to our likeness; and let them have dominion over the fish of the sea, and over the birds of the air, and over the cattle, and over all the wild animals of the earth, and over every creeping thing that creeps upon the earth." 27 So God created humankind in his image, in the image of God he created them; male and female he created them. 28 God blessed them, and God said to them, "Be fruitful and multiply, and fill the earth and subdue it; and have dominion over the fish of the sea and over the birds of the air and over every living thing that moves upon the earth." 29 God said, "See, I have given you every plant yielding seed that is upon the face of all the earth, and every tree with seed in its fruit; you shall have them for food. 30 And to every beast of the earth, and to every bird of the air, and to everything that creeps on the earth, everything that has the breath of life, I have given every green plant for food." And it was so. 31 God saw everything that he had made, and indeed, it was very good. And there was evening and there was morning, the sixth day.

Genesis 2

Thus the heavens and the earth were finished, and all their multitude. 2 And on the seventh day God finished the work that he had done, and he rested on the seventh day from all the work that he had done. 3 So God blessed the seventh day and hallowed it, because on it God rested from all the work that he had done in creation. 4 These are the generations of the heavens and the earth when they were created. In the day that the Lord God made the earth and the heavens, 5 when no plant of the field was yet in the earth and no herb of the field had yet sprung up—for the Lord God had not caused it to rain upon the earth, and there was no one to till the ground; 6 but a stream would rise from the earth, and water the whole face of the ground—7 then the Lord God formed man from the dust of the ground, and breathed into his nostrils the breath of life; and the man became a living being. 8 And the Lord God planted a garden in Eden, in the east; and there he put the man whom he had formed. 9 Out of the ground the Lord God made to grow every tree that is pleasant to the sight and good for food, the tree of life also in the midst of the garden, and the tree of the knowledge of good and evil. 10 A river flows out of Eden to water the garden, and from there it divides and becomes four branches. 11 The name of the first is Pishon; it is the one that flows around the whole land of Havilah, where there is gold; 12 and the gold of that land is good; bdellium and onyx stone are there. 13 The name of the second river is Gihon; it is the one that flows around the whole land of Cush. 14 The name of the third river is Tigris, which flows east of Assyria. And the fourth river is the Euphrates. 15 The Lord God took the man and put him in the garden of Eden to till it and keep it. 16 And the Lord God commanded the man, "You may freely eat of every tree of the garden; 17 but of the tree of the knowledge of good and evil you shall not eat, for in the day that you eat of it you shall die." 18 Then the Lord God said, "It is not good that the man should be alone; I will make him a helper as his partner." 19 So out of the ground the Lord God formed every animal of the field and every bird of the air, and brought them to the man to see what he would call them; and whatever the man called every living creature, that was its name. 20 The man gave names to all cattle, and to the birds of the air, and to every animal of the field; but for the man there was not found a helper as his partner. 21 So the Lord God caused a deep sleep to fall upon the man, and he slept; then he took one of his ribs and closed up its place with flesh. 22 And the rib that the Lord God had taken from the man he made into a woman and brought her to the man. 23 Then the man said, 'This at last is bone of my bones and flesh of my flesh; this one shall be called Woman, for out of Man this one was taken." 24 Therefore a man leaves his father and his mother and clings to his wife, and they become one flesh. 25 And the man and his wife were both naked, and were not ashamed.

Genesis 3

1 Now the serpent was more crafty than any other wild animal that the Lord God had made. He said to the woman, "Did God say, "You shall not eat from any tree in the garden'?" 2 The woman said to the serpent, "We may eat of the fruit of the trees in the garden; 3 but God said, "You shall not eat of the fruit of the tree that is in the middle of the garden, nor shall you touch it, or you shall die." 4 But the serpent said to the woman, "You will not die; 5 for God knows that when you eat of it your eyes will be opened, and you will be like God, knowing good and evil." 6 So when the woman saw that the tree was good for food, and that it was a delight to the eyes, and that the tree was to be desired to make one wise, she took of its fruit and ate; and she also gave some to her husband, who was with her, and he ate. 7 Then the eyes of both were opened, and they knew that they were naked; and they sewed fig leaves together and made loincloths for themselves. 8 They heard the sound of the Lord God walking in the garden at the time of the evening breeze, and the man and his wife hid themselves from the presence of the Lord God among the trees of the garden. 9 But the Lord God called to the man, and said to him, "Where are you?" 10 He said, "I heard the sound of you in the garden, and I was afraid, because I was naked; and I hid myself." 11 He said, "Who told you that you were naked? Have you eaten from the tree of which I commanded you not to eat?" 12 The man said, "The woman whom you gave to be with me, she gave me fruit from the tree, and I ate." 13 Then the Lord God said to the woman, "What is this that you have done?" The woman said, "The serpent tricked me, and I ate." 14 The Lord God said to the serpent, "Because you have done this, cursed are you among all animals and among all wild creatures; upon your belly you shall go, and dust you shall eat all the days of your life. 15 I will put enmity between you and the woman, and between your offspring and hers; he will strike your head, and you will strike his heel." 16 To the woman he said, "I will greatly increase your pangs in childbearing; in pain you shall bring forth children, yet your desire shall be for your husband, and he shall rule over you." 17 And to the man he said, "Because you have listened to the voice of your wife, and have eaten of the tree

about which I commanded you, "You shall not eat of it,' cursed is the ground because of you; in toil you shall eat of it all the days of your life; 18 thorns and thistles it shall bring forth for you; and you shall eat the plants of the field. 19 By the sweat of your face you shall eat bread until you return to the ground, for out of it you were taken; you are dust, and to dust you shall return." 20 The man named his wife Eve, because she was the mother of all living. 21 And the Lord God made garments of skins for the man and for his wife, and clothed them. 22 Then the Lord God said, "See, the man has become like one of us, knowing good and evil; and now, he might reach out his hand and take also from the tree of life, and eat, and live forever"—23 therefore the Lord God sent him forth from the garden of Eden, to till the ground from which he was taken. 24 He drove out the man; and at the east of the garden of Eden he placed the cherubim, and a sword flaming and turning to guard the way to the tree of life.

Genesis 4

1 Now the man knew his wife Eve, and she conceived and bore Cain, saying, "I have produced a man with the help of the Lord." 2 Next she bore his brother Abel. Now Abel was a keeper of sheep, and Cain a tiller of the ground. 3 In the course of time Cain brought to the Lord an offering of the fruit of the ground, 4 and Abel for his part brought of the firstlings of his flock, their fat portions. And the Lord had regard for Abel and his offering, 5 but for Cain and his offering he had no regard. So Cain was very angry, and his countenance fell. 6 The Lord said to Cain, "Why are you angry, and why has your countenance fallen? 7 If you do well, will you not be accepted? And if you do not do well, sin is lurking at the door; its desire is for you, but you must master it." 8 Cain said to his brother Abel, "Let us go out to the field." And when they were in the field, Cain rose up against his brother Abel, and killed him. 9 Then the Lord said to Cain, "Where is your brother Abel?" He said, "I do not know; am I my brother's keeper?" 10 And the Lord said, "What have you done? Listen; your brother's blood is crying out to me from the ground! 11 And now you are cursed from the ground, which has opened its mouth to receive your brother's blood from your hand. 12 When you till the ground, it will no longer yield to you its strength; you will be a fugitive and a wanderer on the earth." 13 Cain said to the Lord, "My punishment is greater than I can bear! 14 Today you have driven me away from the soil, and I shall be hidden from your face; I shall be a fugitive and a wanderer on the earth, and anyone who meets me may kill me." 15 Then the Lord said to him, "Not so! Whoever kills Cain will suffer a sevenfold vengeance." And the Lord put a mark on Cain, so that no one who came upon him would kill him. 16 Then Cain went away from the presence of the Lord, and settled in the land of Nod, east of Eden. 17 Cain knew his wife, and she conceived and bore Enoch; and he built a city, and named it Enoch after his son Enoch. 18 To Enoch was born Irad; and Irad was the father of Mehujael and Mehujael the father of Methushael, and Methushael the father of Lamech. 19 Lamech took two wives; the name of the one

was Adah, and the name of the other Zillah. 20 Adah bore Jabal; he was the ancestor of those who live in tents and have livestock. 21 His brother's name was Jubal; he was the ancestor of all those who play the lyre and pipe. 22 Zillah bore Tubal-cain, who made all kinds of bronze and iron tools. The sister of Tubal-cain was Naamah. 23 Lamech said to his wives: "Adah and Zillah, hear my voice; you wives of Lamech, listen to what I say: I have killed a man for wounding me, a young man for striking me. 24 If Cain is avenged sevenfold, truly Lamech seventy-sevenfold." 25 Adam knew his wife again, and she bore a son and named him Seth, for she said, "God has appointed for me another child instead of Abel, because Cain killed him." 26 To Seth also a son was born, and he named him Enosh. At that time people began to invoke the name of the Lord.

Genesis 5

1 This is the list of the descendants of Adam. When God created humankind, he made them in the likeness of God. 2 Male and female he created them, and he blessed them and named them "Humankind" when they were created. 3 When Adam had lived one hundred thirty years, he became the father of a son in his likeness, according to his image, and named him Seth. 4 The days of Adam after he became the father of Seth were eight hundred years; and he had other sons and daughters. 5 Thus all the days that Adam lived were nine hundred thirty years; and he died. 6 When Seth had lived one hundred five years, he became the father of Enosh. 7 Seth lived after the birth of Enosh eight hundred seven years, and had other sons and daughters. 8 Thus all the days of Seth were nine hundred twelve years; and he died. 9 When Enosh had lived ninety years, he became the father of Kenan. 10 Enosh lived after the birth of Kenan eight hundred fifteen years, and had other sons and daughters. 11 Thus all the days of Enosh were nine hundred five years; and he died. 12 When Kenan had lived seventy years, he became the father of Mahalalel. 13 Kenan lived after the birth of Mahalalel eight hundred and forty years, and had other sons and daughters. 14 Thus all the days of Kenan were nine hundred and ten years; and he died. 15 When Mahalalel had lived sixty-five years, he became the father of Jared. 16 Mahalalel lived after the birth of Jared eight hundred thirty years, and had other sons and daughters. 17 Thus all the days of Mahalalel were eight hundred ninety-five years; and he died. 18 When Jared had lived one hundred sixty-two years he became the father of Enoch. 19 Jared lived after the birth of Enoch eight hundred years, and had other sons and daughters. 20 Thus all the days of Jared were nine hundred sixty-two years; and he died. 21 When Enoch had lived sixty-five years, he became the father of Methuselah. 22 Enoch walked with God after the birth of Methuselah three hundred years, and had other sons and daughters. 23 Thus all the days of Enoch were three hundred sixty-five years. 24 Enoch walked with God; then he was no more, because God took him. 25 When Methuselah had lived one hundred eighty-seven years, he became the father of Lamech. 26 Methuselah lived after the birth of Lamech seven hundred eighty-two years, and had other sons and daughters. 27 Thus

all the days of Methuselah were nine hundred sixty-nine years; and he died. 28 When Lamech had lived one hundred eighty-two years, he became the father of a son; 29 he named him Noah, saying, "Out of the ground that the Lord has cursed this one shall bring us relief from our work and from the toil of our hands." 30 Lamech lived after the birth of Noah five hundred ninety-five years, and had other sons and daughters. 31 Thus all the days of Lamech were seven hundred seventy-seven years; and he died. 32 After Noah was five hundred years old, Noah became the father of Shem, Ham, and Japheth.

Genesis 6

1 When people began to multiply on the face of the ground, and daughters were born to them, 2 the sons of God saw that they were fair; and they took wives for themselves of all that they chose. 3 Then the Lord said, "My spirit shall not abide in mortals forever, for they are flesh; their days shall be one hundred twenty years." 4 The Nephilim were on the earth in those days—and also afterward—when the sons of God went in to the daughters of humans, who bore children to them. These were the heroes that were of old, warriors of renown. 5 The Lord saw that the wickedness of humankind was great in the earth, and that every inclination of the thoughts of their hearts was only evil continually. 6 And the Lord was sorry that he had made humankind on the earth, and it grieved him to his heart. 7 So the Lord said, "I will blot out from the earth the human beings I have created—people together with animals and creeping things and birds of the air, for I am sorry that I have made them." 8 But Noah found favor in the sight of the Lord. 9 These are the descendants of Noah. Noah was a righteous man, blameless in his generation; Noah walked with God. 10 And Noah had three sons, Shem, Ham, and Japheth. 11 Now the earth was corrupt in God's sight, and the earth was filled with violence. 12 And God saw that the earth was corrupt; for all flesh had corrupted its ways upon the earth. 13 And God said to Noah, "I have determined to make an end of all flesh, for the earth is filled with violence because of them; now I am going to destroy them along with the earth. 14 Make yourself an ark of cypress wood; make rooms in the ark, and cover it inside and out with pitch. 15 This is how you are to make it: the length of the ark three hundred cubits, its width fifty cubits, and its height thirty cubits. 16 Make a roof for the ark, and finish it to a cubit above; and put the door of the ark in its side; make it with lower, second, and third decks. 17 For my part, I am going to bring a flood of waters on the earth, to destroy from under heaven all flesh in which is the breath of life; everything that is on the earth shall die. 18 But I will establish my covenant with you; and you shall come into the ark, you, your sons, your wife, and your sons' wives with you. 19 And of every living thing, of all flesh, you shall bring two of every kind into the ark, to keep them alive with you; they shall be male and female. 20 Of the birds according to their kinds, and of the animals according to their kinds, of every creeping thing of the ground according to its kind, two of every kind shall come

in to you, to keep them alive. 21 Also take with you every kind of food that is eaten, and store it up; and it shall serve as food for you and for them." 22 Noah did this; he did all that God commanded him.

Genesis 7

1 Then the Lord said to Noah, "Go into the ark, you and all your household, for I have seen that you alone are righteous before me in this generation. 2 Take with you seven pairs of all clean animals, the male and its mate; and a pair of the animals that are not clean, the male and its mate; 3 and seven pairs of the birds of the air also, male and female, to keep their kind alive on the face of all the earth. 4 For in seven days I will send rain on the earth for forty days and forty nights; and every living thing that I have made I will blot out from the face of the ground." 5 And Noah did all that the Lord had commanded him. 6 Noah was six hundred years old when the flood of waters came on the earth. 7 And Noah with his sons and his wife and his sons' wives went into the ark to escape the waters of the flood. 8 Of clean animals, and of animals that are not clean, and of birds, and of everything that creeps on the ground, 9 two and two, male and female, went into the ark with Noah, as God had commanded Noah. 10 And after seven days the waters of the flood came on the earth.

11 In the six hundredth year of Noah's life, in the second month, on the seventeenth day of the month, on that day all the fountains of the great deep burst forth, and the windows of the heavens were opened. 12 The rain fell on the earth forty days and forty nights. 13 On the very same day Noah with his sons, Shem and Ham and Japheth, and Noah's wife and the three wives of his sons entered the ark, 14 they and every wild animal of every kind, and all domestic animals of every kind, and every creeping thing that creeps on the earth, and every bird of every kind—every bird, every winged creature. 15 They went into the ark with Noah, two and two of all flesh in which there was the breath of life. 16 And those that entered, male and female of all flesh, went in as God had commanded him; and the Lord shut him in. 17 The flood continued forty days on the earth; and the waters increased, and bore up the ark, and it rose high above the earth. 18 The waters swelled and increased greatly on the earth; and the ark floated on the face of the waters. 19 The waters swelled so mightily on the earth that all the high mountains under the whole heaven were covered; 20 the waters swelled above the mountains, covering them fifteen cubits deep. 21 And all flesh died that moved on the earth, birds, domestic animals, wild animals, all swarming creatures that swarm on the earth, and all human beings; 22 everything on dry land in whose nostrils was the breath of life died. 23 He blotted out every living thing that was on the face of the ground, human beings and animals and creeping things and birds of the air; they were blotted out from the earth. Only Noah was left, and those that were with him in the ark. 24 And the waters swelled on the earth for one hundred fifty days.

Genesis 8

1 But God remembered Noah and all the wild animals and all the domestic animals that were with him in the ark. And God made a wind blow over the earth, and the waters subsided; 2 the fountains of the deep and the windows of the heavens were closed, the rain from the heavens was restrained, 3 and the waters gradually receded from the earth. At the end of one hundred fifty days the waters had abated; 4 and in the seventh month, on the seventeenth day of the month, the ark came to rest on the mountains of Ararat. 5 The waters continued to abate until the tenth month; in the tenth month, on the first day of the month, the tops of the mountains appeared. 6 At the end of forty days Noah opened the window of the ark that he had made 7 and sent out the raven; and it went to and fro until the waters were dried up from the earth. 8 Then he sent out the dove from him, to see if the waters had subsided from the face of the ground; 9 but the dove found no place to set its foot, and it returned to him to the ark, for the waters were still on the face of the whole earth. So he put out his hand and took it and brought it into the ark with him. 10 He waited another seven days, and again he sent out the dove from the ark; 11 and the dove came back to him in the evening, and there in its beak was a freshly plucked olive leaf; so Noah knew that the waters had subsided from the earth. 12 Then he waited another seven days, and sent out the dove; and it did not return to him anymore. 13 In the six hundred first year, in the first month, on the first day of the month, the waters were dried up from the earth; and Noah removed the covering of the ark, and looked, and saw that the face of the ground was drying. 14 In the second month, on the twenty-seventh day of the month, the earth was dry. 15 Then God said to Noah, 16 "Go out of the ark, you and your wife, and your sons and your sons' wives with you. 17 Bring out with you every living thing that is with you of all flesh—birds and animals and every creeping thing that creeps on the earth—so that they may abound on the earth, and be fruitful and multiply on the earth." 18 So Noah went out with his sons and his wife and his sons' wives. 19 And every animal, every creeping thing, and every bird, everything that moves on the earth, went out of the ark by families. 20 Then Noah built an altar to the Lord, and took of every clean animal and of every clean bird, and offered burnt offerings on the altar. 21 And when the Lord smelled the pleasing odor, the Lord said in his heart, "I will never again curse the ground because of humankind, for the inclination of the human heart is evil from youth; nor will I ever again destroy every living creature as I have done. 22 As long as the earth endures, seedtime and harvest, cold and heat, summer and winter, day and night, shall not cease."

Genesis 9

God blessed Noah and his sons, and said to them, "Be fruitful and multiply, and fill the earth. 2 The fear and dread of you shall rest on every animal of the earth, and on every bird of the air, on everything that creeps on the ground, and on all the fish of the sea; into your hand they are delivered. 3 Every moving thing that lives shall be food for you; and just as I gave you the green plants, I give you everything. 4 Only, you shall not eat flesh with its life, that is, its blood. 5 For your own lifeblood I will surely require a reckoning: from every animal I will require it and from human beings, each one for the blood of another, I will require a reckoning for human life. 6 Whoever sheds the blood of a human, by a human shall that person's blood be shed; for in his own image God made humankind. 7 And you, be fruitful and multiply, abound on the earth and multiply in it." 8 Then God said to Noah and to his sons with him, 9 "As for me, I am establishing my covenant with you and your descendants after you, 10 and with every living creature that is with you, the birds, the domestic animals, and every animal of the earth with you, as many as came out of the ark. 11 I establish my covenant with you, that never again shall all flesh be cut off by the waters of a flood, and never again shall there be a flood to destroy the earth." 12 God said, "This is the sign of the covenant that I make between me and you and every living creature that is with you, for all future generations: 13 I have set my bow in the clouds, and it shall be a sign of the covenant between me and the earth. 14 When I bring clouds over the earth and the bow is seen in the clouds, 15 I will remember my covenant that is between me and you and every living creature of all flesh; and the waters shall never again become a flood to destroy all flesh. 16 When the bow is in the clouds, I will see it and remember the everlasting covenant between God and every living creature of all flesh that is on the earth." 17 God said to Noah, "This is the sign of the covenant that I have established between me and all flesh that is on the earth." 18 The sons of Noah who went out of the ark were Shem, Ham, and Japheth. Ham was the father of Canaan. 19 These three were the sons of Noah; and from these the whole earth was peopled. 20 Noah, a man of the soil, was the first to plant a vineyard. 21 He drank some of the wine and became drunk, and he lay uncovered in his tent. 22 And Ham, the father of Canaan, saw the nakedness of his father, and told his two brothers outside. 23 Then Shem and Japheth took a garment, laid it on both their shoulders, and walked backward and covered the nakedness of their father; their faces were turned away, and they did not see their father's nakedness. 24 When Noah awoke from his wine and knew what his youngest son had done to him, 25 he said, "Cursed be Canaan; lowest of slaves shall he be to his brothers." 26 He also said, "Blessed by the Lord my God be Shem; and let Canaan be his slave. 27 May God make space for Japheth, and let him live in the tents of Shem; and let Canaan be his slave." 28 After the flood Noah lived three hundred fifty years. 29 All the days of Noah were nine hundred fifty years; and he died.

Genesis 10

These are the descendants of Noah's sons, Shem, Ham, and Japheth; children were born to them after the flood. 2 The descendants of Japheth: Gomer, Magog, Madai, Javan, Tubal, Meshech, and Tiras. 3 The descendants of Gomer: Ashkenaz, Riphath, and Togarmah. 4 The descendants of Javan: Elishah, Tarshish, Kittim, and Rodanim. 5 From these the coastland peoples spread. These are the descendants of Japheth in their lands, with their own language, by their families, in their nations. 6 The descendants of Ham: Cush, Egypt, Put, and Canaan. 7 The descendants of Cush: Seba, Havilah, Sabtah, Raamah, and Sabteca. The descendants of Raamah: Sheba and Dedan. 8 Cush became the father of Nimrod; he was the first on earth to become a mighty warrior. 9 He was a mighty hunter before the Lord; therefore it is said, "Like Nimrod a mighty hunter before the Lord." 10 The beginning of his kingdom was Babel, Erech, and Accad, all of them in the land of Shinar. 11 From that land he went into Assyria, and built Nineveh, Rehobothir, Calah, and 12 Resen between Nineveh and Calah; that is the great city. 13 Egypt became the father of Ludim, Anamim, Lehabim, Naphtuhim, 14 Pathrusim, Casluhim, and Caphtorim, from which the Philistines come. 15 Canaan became the father of Sidon his firstborn, and Heth, 16 and the Jebusites, the Amorites, the Girgashites, 17 the Hivites, the Arkites, the Sinites, 18 the Arvadites, the Zemarites, and the Hamathites. Afterward the families of the Canaanites spread abroad. 19 And the territory of the Canaanites extended from Sidon, in the direction of Gerar, as far as Gaza, and in the direction of Sodom, Gomorrah, Admah, and Zeboiim, as far as Lasha. 20 These are the descendants of Ham, by their families, their languages, their lands, and their nations. 21 To Shem also, the father of all the children of Eber, the elder brother of Japheth, children were born. 22 The descendants of Shem: Elam, Asshur, Arpachshad, Lud, and Aram. 23 The descendants of Aram: Uz, Hul, Gether, and Mash. 24 Arpachshad became the father of Shelah: and Shelah became the father of Eber. 25 To Eber were born two sons: the name of the one was Peleg, for in his days the earth was divided, and his brother's name was Joktan. 26 Joktan became the father of Almodad, Sheleph, Hazarmaveth, Jerah, 27 Hadoram, Uzal, Diklah, 28 Obal, Abimael, Sheba, 29 Ophir, Havilah, and Jobab; all these were the descendants of Joktan. 30 The territory in which they lived extended from Mesha in the direction of Sephar, the hill country of the east. 31 These are the descendants of Shem, by their families, their languages, their lands, and their nations; 32 These are the families of Noah's sons, according to their genealogies, in their nations: and from these the nations spread abroad on the earth after the flood.

Genesis 11

1 Now the whole earth had one language and the same words. 2 And as they migrated from the east, they came upon a plain in the land of Shinar and settled there. 3 And they said to one another, "Come, let us make bricks, and burn them thoroughly." And they had brick for stone, and bitumen for mortar. 4 Then they said, "Come, let us build ourselves a city, and a tower with its top in the heavens, and let us make a name for ourselves; otherwise we shall be scattered abroad upon the face of the whole earth." 5 The Lord came down to see the city and the tower, which mortals had built. 6 And the Lord

said, "Look, they are one people, and they have all one language; and this is only the beginning of what they will do; nothing that they propose to do will now be impossible for them. 7 Come, let us go down, and confuse their language there, so that they will not understand one another's speech." 8 So the Lord scattered them abroad from there over the face of all the earth, and they left off building the city. 9 Therefore it was called Babel, because there the Lord confused the language of all the earth; and from there the Lord scattered them abroad over the face of all the earth. 10 These are the descendants of Shem. When Shem was one hundred years old, he became the father of Arpachshad two years after the flood; 11 and Shem lived after the birth of Arpachshad five hundred years, and had other sons and daughters. 12 When Arpachshad had lived thirty-five years, he became the father of Shelah; 13 and Arpachshad lived after the birth of Shelah four hundred three years, and had other sons and daughters. 14 When Shelah had lived thirty years, he became the father of Eber; 15 and Shelah lived after the birth of Eber four hundred three years, and had other sons and daughters. 16 When Eber had lived thirty-four years, he became the father of Peleg; 17 and Eber lived after the birth of Peleg four hundred thirty years, and had other sons and daughters. 18 When Peleg had lived thirty years, he became the father of Reu; 19 and Peleg lived after the birth of Reu two hundred nine years, and had other sons and daughters. 20 When Reu had lived thirty-two years, he became the father of Serug; 21 and Reu lived after the birth of Serug two hundred seven years, and had other sons and daughters. 22 When Serug had lived thirty years, he became the father of Nahor; 23 and Serug lived after the birth of Nahor two hundred years, and had other sons and daughters. 24 When Nahor had lived twenty nine years, he became the father of Terah; 25 and Nahor lived after the birth of Terah one hundred nineteen years, and had other sons and daughters. 26 When Terah had lived seventy years, he became the father of Abram, Nahor, and Haran. 27 Now these are the descendants of Terah. Terah was the father of Abram, Nahor, and Haran; and Haran was the father of Lot. 28 Haran died before his father Terah in the land of his birth, in Ur of the Chaldeans. 29 Abram and Nahor took wives; the name of Abram's wife was Sarai, and the name of Nahor's wife was Milcah. She was the daughter of Haran the father of Milcah and Iscah. 30 Now Sarai was barren; she had no child. 31 Terah took his son Abram and his grandson Lot son of Haran, and his daughter-in-law Sarai, his son Abram's wife, and they went out together from Ur of the Chaldeans to go into the land of Canaan; but when they came to Haran, they settled there. 32 The days of Terah were two hundred five years; and Terah died in Haran.

Charles Darwin

Introduction
Ki Joo Choi

Born in Shrewsbury, England, Darwin (b. 1809–d. 1882) is most famous for the groundbreaking work On the Origin of Species, *published in 1859 (full title:* On the Origin of Species by Means of Natural Selection, or the Preservation of Favored Races in the Struggle for Life). It was an achievement of twenty years of observations of the natural world that began with his five-year journey exploring the coastline on the famed ship HMS *Beagle*, primarily in South America. In this text, he lays out the case, through meticulous observations of various animal and plant species, for evolution, the view that creatures of the natural world change through a process he called natural selection. It is no exaggeration to state that Darwin's evolutionary theory revolutionized modern biology and our conception of—and approach to—the governing principle of the natural world. Indeed, it might not be too much to say that evolution is the leading idea, both scientific and cultural, of the nineteenth and twentieth centuries.

Like Galileo's personal background and the kind of controversy he stirred with his work in astronomy, the story of Darwin's life and work in the natural sciences is surprising, controversial, dramatic, and too important to ignore. In the Course Documents folder of your Blackboard site, please find several readings that will help you grasp both the context and background for Darwin himself, and also the ways in which modern biology have deepened our knowledge of evolution.

In the Darwin reading, we focus on two selections from Darwin's *The Descent of Man, and Selection in Relation to Sex* (1871), which followed his *On the Origin of Species*. To some large extent, *Descent* can be considered a kind of application of his theory of evolution to the human species. As such, he offers interesting observations about religion and the origins and future of human morality.

The first selection from *Descent* is from the Introduction. Pay careful attention to Darwin's goal in this Introduction. He states the goal from the very outset: "The sole object of this work is to consider, firstly, whether man, like every other species, is descended from some preexisting form; secondly, the manner of his development; and thirdly, the value of the differences between the so-called races of man . . . ." In order to pursue these goals, Darwin claims that he will be examining the "homological structure, embryological development, and the rudimentary organs" of the various species, which will confirm, Darwin states, "the principle of gradual evolution."

Pay careful attention to how Darwin, in the Introduction, draws connections between non-human animals and the human species with respect to their homological· structure, embryological development, and rudimentary organs. Then, pay specific attention to his reflections on what evolutionary theory might mean for the seeming racial differences between the human species.

And then focus on the last paragraph of the Introduction, where he makes a judgment about the Bible, particularly the creation stories in Genesis of the Bible. Why does he think that some people believe that human persons were "created" rather than evolved? Does he think that the Bible's story of human creation is true?

As you think about these questions, consider some larger questions that Darwin's discussion in the Introduction raises: Though Darwin suggests that the biblical account of human creation is dubious, must we necessarily conclude that biblical and theological accounts of human creation and existence are irrelevant? Alternatively posited, is Darwin's theory of evolution contrary to theological insights on human existence in some fundamental manner? Can they possibly coexist in a mutually substantive way? Lastly, and perhaps most fundamentally, does Darwin's theory of evolution cast doubt on the existence of God—or, more generally, the existence of the transcendent?

In the second selection from Darwin's *Descent*, from chapter 4, Darwin seeks to show how evolutionary theory can help to explain the origins of human morality. This second selection may seem more "technical" than the first selection (maybe a biologist would be able to understand this text better than the non-biologist!). Nonetheless, do the best you can to persevere through the text, for it offers a provocative analysis of how human morality evolved and continues to evolve. Note his discussion of the interaction between what he calls the "social instincts" (such as sympathy) and the "instincts of self-preservation, hunger, lust, vengeance." Darwin claims that evolutionary theory helps us to better understand how some human persons and communities were able to acquire the social instinct of sympathy, rather than being ruled merely by the "instincts of self-preservation, hunger, lust, vengeance" (he obviously thinks that if these instincts were to prevail, human morality and human society would not be possible). How does Darwin think the social instinct of sympathy was acquired? What was the evolutionary process that led to the development and acquisition of sympathy (and, correlatively, conscience)?

As you read further on, pay close attention to Darwin's proposal that "[a]s man advances" evolutionarily, the social instinct of sympathy will continue to expand, and thus the moral culture of humans will continue to progress. Why does he think this will be the case? Why is he confident that evolutionary theory indicates that human morality will grow—that is, that human persons will become "more" or "increasingly" ethical or moral?

As you study these questions with respect to chapter 4 of Darwin's *Descent*, consider further the following larger questions on the relationship between evolutionary theory, morality, and religion:

1. Is Darwin's discussion of the evolutionary development of human morality adequate? That is, does it fully illuminate the nature of human morality? Can human morality be fully explained through an evolutionary perspective? Are religious perspectives wholly irrelevant to human morality?

2.   Do you think that humans can become "more" ethical; as Darwin's evolutionary theory suggests? Consider whether we are in fact more ethical as a human species today than we were 200, 500, 1,000, or 2,000 years ago. If we are not "more" ethical today, then what does this say about Darwin's evolutionary theory of human morality? What would being "more" ethical mean to you?

3.   What might be some of the social, political, and economic consequences or implications of Darwin's insights on the evolution of human morality? In chapter 4, he suggests that humanity will evolve toward greater political, economic, and social unity. Do you think this is possible through human evolution alone? Is this realistic? What might *the unity of human communities* from a Darwinian perspective mean? What might it look like? What might be the positives and negatives of such a vision of human unity from a Darwinian perspective?

THE DESCENT OF MAN (SELECTIONS)

"The Descent of Man," by Charles Darwin. *The Nature of Life: Readings in Biology*, 2001, Great Books Foundation. Reprinted with questions by permission.

Introduction

In consequence of the views now adopted by most naturalists and which will ultimately, as in every other case, be followed by others who are not scientific, I have been led to put together my notes, so as to see how far the general conclusions arrived at in my former works were applicable to man. This seemed all the more desirable, as I had never deliberately applied these views to a species taken singly. When we confine our attention to any one form, we are deprived of the weighty arguments derived from the nature of the affinities which connect together whole groups of organisms—their geographical distribution in past and present times, and their geological succession. The homological structure, embryological development, and rudimentary organs of a species remain to be considered, whether it be man or any other animal to which our attention may be directed; but these great classes of facts afford, as it appears to me, ample and conclusive evidence in favor of the principle of gradual evolution. The strong support derived from the other arguments should, however, always be kept before the mind.

The sole object of this work is to consider, firstly, whether man, like every other species, is descended from some preexisting form; secondly, the manner of his development; and thirdly, the value, of the differences between the so-called races of man. . . .

This work contains hardly any original facts in regard to man, but as the conclusions at which I arrived, after drawing up a rough draft, appeared to me interesting, I thought that they might interest others. It has often and confidently been asserted that man's origin can never be known, but ignorance more frequently begets confidence than does knowledge: it is those who know little, and not those who know much, who so positively assert that this or that problem will never be solved by science. The conclusion that man is the codescendant with other species of some ancient, lower, and extinct form is not in any degree new. Lamarck long ago came to this conclusion, which has lately been maintained by several eminent naturalists and philosophers. . . .

He who wishes to decide whether man is the modified descendant of some preexisting form would probably first inquire whether man varies, however slightly, in bodily structure and in mental faculties and if so, whether the variations are transmitted to his offspring in accordance with the laws which prevail with the lower animals. Again, are the variations the result, as far as our ignorance permits us to judge, of the same general causes, and are they governed by the same general laws, as in the case of other organisms, for instance, by correlation, the inherited effects of use and disuse, etc.? Is man subject to similar malconformations, the result of arrested development, of reduplication of parts, etc., and does he display in any of his anomalies reversion to some former and ancient type of structure? It might also naturally be inquired whether man, like so many other animals, has given rise to varieties and subraces, differing but slightly from each other, or to races differing so much that they must be classed as doubtful species? How are such races distributed over the world, and how, when crossed, do they react on each other in the first and succeeding generations? And so with many other points.

The inquirer would next come to the important point, whether man tends to increase at so rapid a rate as to lead to occasional severe struggles for existence and consequently to beneficial variations, whether in body or mind, being preserved, and injurious ones eliminated. Do the races or species of men, whichever term may be applied, encroach on and replace one another so that some finally become extinct? We shall see that all these questions, as indeed is obvious in respect to most of them, must be answered in the affirmative, in the same manner as with the lower animals. But the several considerations just referred to may be conveniently deferred for a time, and we will first see how far the bodily structure of man shows traces, more or less plain, of his descent from some lower form. . . .

The Bodily Structure of Man

It is notorious that man is constructed on the same general type or model as other mammals. All the bones in his skeleton can be compared with corresponding bones in a monkey, bat, or seal. So it is with his muscles, nerves, blood vessels, and internal viscera. The brain, the most important of all the organs, follows the same law, as shown by Huxley and other anatomists. Bischoff, who is a hostile witness, admits that every chief fissure and fold in the brain of man has its analogy in that of the orang, but he adds that at no period of development do their brains perfectly agree; nor could perfect agreement be expected, for otherwise their mental powers would have been the same. . . . But it would be superfluous here to give further details on the correspondence between man and the higher mammals in the structure of the brain and all other parts of the body.

It may, however, be worthwhile to specify a few points, not directly or obviously connected with structure, by which this correspondence or relationship is well shown.

Man is liable to receive from the lower animals, and to communicate to them, certain diseases, as hydrophobia, variola, the glanders, syphilis, cholera, herpes, etc., and this fact proves the close similarity[1] of their tissues and blood, both in minute structure and composition, far more plainly than does their comparison under the best microscope or by the aid of the best chemical analysis. Monkeys are liable to many of the same noncontagious diseases as we are; thus Rengger, who carefully observed for a long time the

---

1   A reviewer has criticized ("British Quarterly Review," Oct. 1. 1871, p. 472) what I have here said with much severity and contempt, but as I do not use the term identity, I cannot see that I am greatly in error. There appears to me a strong analogy between the same infection or contagion producing the same result or one closely similar, in two distinct animals, and the testing of two distinct fluids by the same chemical reagent.

Cebus azarae in its native land, found it liable to catarrh, with the usual symptoms, and which, when often recurrent, led to consumption. These monkeys suffered also from apoplexy, inflammation of the bowels, and cataract in the eye. The younger ones when shedding their milk teeth often died from fever. Medicines produced the same effect on them as on us. Many kinds of monkeys have a strong taste for tea, coffee, and spirituous liquors; they will also, as I have myself seen, smoke tobacco with pleasure.[2] Brehm asserts that the natives of northeastern Africa catch the wild baboons by exposing vessels with strong beer, by which they are made drunk. He has seen some of these animals, which he kept in confinement, in this state, and he gives a laughable account of their behavior and strange grimaces. On the following morning they were very cross and dismal; they held their aching heads with both hands and wore a most pitiable expression; when beer or wine was offered them, they turned away with disgust, but relished the juices of lemons. An American monkey, an Ateles, after getting drunk on brandy, would never touch it again and thus, was wiser than many men. These trifling facts prove how similar the nerves of taste must be in monkeys and man, and how similarly their whole nervous system is affected.

Man is infested with internal parasites, sometimes causing fatal effects, and is plagued by external parasites, all of which belong to the same genera or families as those infesting other mammals, and in the case of scabies to the same species. Man is subject, like other mammals, birds, and even insects, to that mysterious law which causes certain normal processes, such as gestation as well as the maturation and duration of various diseases, to follow lunar periods. His wounds are repaired by the same process of healing, and the stumps left after the amputation of his limbs, especially during an embryonic period, occasionally possess some power of regeneration, as in the lowest animals.

The whole process of that most important function, the reproduction of the species, is strikingly the same in all mammals, from the first act of courtship by the male to the birth and nurturing of the young. Monkeys are born in almost as helpless a condition as our own infants, and in certain genera the young differ fully as much in appearance from the adults as do our children from their full-grown parents. It has been urged by some writers as an important distinction that with man the young arrive at maturity at a much later age than with any other animal; but if we look to the races of mankind which inhabit tropical countries, the difference is not great, for the orang is believed not to be adult till the age of from ten to fifteen years. Man differs from woman in size, bodily strength, hairiness etc., as well as in mind, in the same manner as do the two sexes of many mammals. So that the correspondence in general structure, in the minute structure of the tissues, in chemical composition and in constitution, between man and the higher animals, especially the anthropomorphous apes, is extremely close.

---

2   The same tastes are common to some animals much lower in the scale. Mr. A. Nicols informs me that he kept in Queensland, in Australia, three individuals of the *Phaseolarctus cinereus* and that, without having been taught in any way, they acquired a strong taste for rum and for smoking tobacco.

Embryonic Development

Man is developed from an ovule, about a 125th of an inch in diameter, which differs in no respect from the ovules of other animals. The embryo itself at a very early period can hardly be distinguished from that of other members of the vertebrate kingdom. At this period the arteries run in arch-like branches, as if to carry the blood to branchiae which are not present in the higher vertebrate, though the slits on the sides of the neck still remain... marking their former position. At a somewhat later period, when the extremities are developed, "the feet of lizards and mammals," as the illustrious Von Baer remarks, "the wings and feet of birds, no less than the hands and feet of man, all arise from the same fundamental form" It is, says Prof. Huxley, quite in the later stages of development that the young human being presents marked differences from the young ape, while the latter departs as much from the dog in its developments as the man does. Startling as this last assertion may appear to be, it is demonstrably true. . . .

After the foregoing statements made by such high authorities, it would be superfluous on my part to give a number of borrowed details, showing that the embryo of man closely resembles that of other mammals. It may, however, be added, that the human embryo likewise resembles certain low forms when adult in various points of structure. For instance, the heart at first exists as a simple pulsating vessel, the excreta are voided through a cloacal passage, and the os coccyx projects like a true tail, "extending considerably beyond the rudimentary legs." In the embryos of all air-breathing vertebrates, certain glands, called the corpora Wolffiana, correspond with, and act like the kidneys of mature fishes. Even at a later embryonic period, some striking resemblances between man and the lower animals may be observed. Bischoff says "that the convolutions of the brain in a human fetus at the end of the seventh month reach about the same stage of development as in a baboon when adult." The great toe, as Professor Owen remarks, "which forms the fulcrum when standing or walking, is perhaps the most characteristic peculiarity in the human structure," but in an embryo, about an inch in length, Prof. Wyman found "that the great toe was shorter than the others and, instead of being parallel to them, projected at an angle from the side of the foot, thus corresponding with the permanent condition of this part in the quadrumana." I will conclude with a quotation from Huxley, who after asking, Does man originate in a different way from a dog, bird, frog, or fish? says, "The reply is not doubtful for a moment, without question, the mode of origin and the early stages of the development of man are identical with those of the animals immediately below him in the scale: without a doubt in these respects, he is far nearer to apes than the apes are to the dog."

Rudiments

This subject, though not intrinsically more important than the two last, will for several reasons be treated here more fully. Not one of the higher animals can be named which does not bear some part in a rudimentary condition, and man forms no exception to the rule. . . .

Rudiments of various muscles have been observed in many parts of the human body, and not a few muscles which are regularly present in some of the lower animals can occasionally be detected in man in a greatly reduced condition. Everyone must have noticed the power which many animals, especially horses, possess of moving or twitching their skin, and this is effected by the *panniculus carnosus*. Remnants of this muscle in an efficient state are found in various parts of our bodies; for instance, the muscle on the forehead, by which the eyebrows are raised. . . .

Some few persons have the power of contracting the superficial muscles on their scalps, and these muscles are in a variable and partially rudimentary condition. M. A. de Candolle has communicated to me a curious instance of the long-continued persistence or inheritance of this power as well as of its unusual development. He knows a family in which one member, the present head of the family, could, when a youth, pitch several heavy books from his head by the movement of the scalp alone, and he won wagers by performing this feat. His father, uncle, grandfather, and his three children possess the same power to the same unusual degree. . . .

The extrinsic muscles which serve to move the external ear and the intrinsic muscles which move the different parts are in a rudimentary condition in man, and they all belong to the system of the *panniculus*; they are also variable in development, or at least in function. I have seen one man who could draw the whole ear forward; other men can draw it upward; another who could draw it backward, and from what one of these persons told me, it is probable that most of us, by often touching our ears, and thus directing our attention toward them, could recover some power of movement by repeated trials. The power of erecting and directing the shell of the ears to the various points of the compass is no doubt of the highest service to many animals as they thus perceive the direction of danger; but I have never heard, on sufficient evidence, of a man who possessed this power, the one which might be of use to him. . . .

The sense of smell is of the highest importance to the greater number of mammals— to some, as the ruminants, in warning them of danger; to others, as the carnivora, in finding their prey; to others again, as the wild boar, for both purposes combined. But the sense of smell is of extremely slight service, if any, even to the dark-colored races of men, in whom it is much more highly developed than in the white and civilized races.[3] Nevertheless it does not warn them of danger nor guide them to their food, nor does it prevent the Eskimos from sleeping in the most fetid atmosphere nor many savages from eating half-putrid meat. In Europeans the power differs greatly in different individuals as I am assured by an eminent naturalist who possesses this sense highly developed and who has attended to the subject. Those who believe in the principle of gradual evolution will not readily admit that the sense of smell in its present state was originally acquired by man as he now exists. He inherits the power in an enfeebled and so far rudimentary condition from some early progenitor to whom it was highly serviceable and by whom it was continually used. In those animals which have this sense highly developed, such as dogs and horses, the recollection of persons and of places is strongly associated with their odor, and we can thus perhaps understand how it is, as Dr. Maudsley has truly remarked, that the sense of smell in man "is singularly effective in recalling vividly the ideas and images of forgotten scenes and places."

Man differs conspicuously from all the other Primates in being almost naked. But a few short straggling hairs are found over the greater part of the body in the man, and fine down on that of a woman. The different races differ much in hairiness, and in the individuals of the same race the hairs are highly variable, not only in abundance, but likewise in position: thus in some Europeans the shoulders are quite naked, while in others they bear thick tufts of hair. There can be little doubt that the hairs thus scattered over the body are the rudiments of the uniform hairy coat of the lower animals. . . .

It appears as if the posterior molar, or wisdom teeth, were tending to become rudimentary in the more civilized races of man. These teeth are rather smaller than the other molars, as is likewise the case with the corresponding teeth in the chimpanzee and orang, and they have only two separate fangs. They do not cut through the gums till about the seventeenth year, and I have been assured that they are much more liable to decay and are earlier lost than the other teeth; but this is denied by some eminent dentists. They are also much more liable to vary, both in structure and in the period of their development, than the other teeth. . . .

With respect to the alimentary canal, I have met with an account of only a single rudiment, namely the vermiform appendage[4] of the cecum. The cecum is a branch, or diverticulum, of the intestine, ending in a cul-de-sac, and is extremely long in many of the lower vegetable-feeding mammals. In the marsupial koala it is actually more than thrice

---

3   The account given by Humboldt of the power of smell possessed by the natives of South America is well known and has been confirmed by others. M. Houzeau ("Etudes sur les Facultés Mentales," etc., ctom. i., 1872. p. 91) asserts that he repeatedly made experiments and proved that Negroes and Indians could recognize persons in the dark by their odor. Dr W. Ogle has made some curious observations on the connection between the power of smell and the coloring matter of the membrane of the olfactory region as well as of the skin of the body. I have, therefore, spoken in the text of the dark-colored races having a finer sense of smell than the white races....

4   [*veriform appendage:* appnedix.]

as long as the whole body. It is sometimes produced into a long, gradually tapering point and is sometimes constricted in parts. It appears as if, in consequence of changed diet or habits, the cecum had become much shortened in various animals, the vermiform appendage being left as a rudiment of the shortened part. That this appendage is a rudiment we may infer from its small size and from the evidence which Prof. Canestrini has collected of its variability in man. It is occasionally quite absent, or again is largely developed. The passage is sometimes completely closed for half or two-thirds of its length, with the terminal part consisting of a flattened solid expansion. In the orang this appendage is long and convoluted; in man it arises from the end of the short cecum, and is commonly from four to five inches in length, being only about a third of an inch in diameter. Not only is it useless, but it is sometimes the cause of death, of which fact I have lately heard two instances; this is due to small hard bodies, such as seeds, entering the passage and causing inflammation. . . .

In man, the os coccyx, together with certain other vertebrae hereafter to be described, though functionless as a tail, plainly represents this part in other vertebrate animals. At an early embryonic period it is free, and projects beyond the lower extremities; as may be seen in the drawing… of a human embryo. Even after birth it has been known, in certain rare and anomalous cases, to form a small external rudiment of a tail. . . .

The bearing of the three great classes of facts now given is unmistakable. But it would be superfluous fully to recapitulate the line of argument given in detail in my *Origin of Species*. The homological construction of the whole frame in the members of the same class is intelligible if we admit their descent from a common progenitor, together with their subsequent adaptation to diversified conditions. On any other view, the similarity of pattern between the hand of a man or monkey, the foot of a horse, the flipper of a seal, the wing of a bat, etc., is utterly inexplicable. It is no scientific explanation to assert that they have all been formed on the same ideal plan. With respect to development, we can clearly understand, on the principle of variation supervening at a rather late embryonic period and being inherited at a corresponding period, how it is that the embryos of wonderfully different forms should still retain, more or less perfectly, the structure of their common progenitor. No other explanation has ever been given of the marvelous fact that the embryos of a man, dog, seal, bat, reptile, etc., can at first hardly be distinguished from each other. In order to understand the existence of rudimentary organs, we have only to suppose that a former progenitor possessed the parts in question in a perfect state and that under changed habits of life they became greatly reduced, either from simple disuse or through the natural selection of those individuals which were least encumbered with a superfluous part, aided by the other means previously indicated.

Thus we can understand how it has come to pass that man and all other vertebrate animals have been constructed on the same general model, why they pass through the same early stages of development, and why they retain certain rudiments in common. Consequently we ought frankly to admit their community of descent; to take any other view is to admit that our own structure, and that of all the animals around us, is a mere snare laid to entrap our judgment. This conclusion is greatly strengthened if we look to the members of the whole animal series and consider the evidence derived from their affinities or classification, their geographical distribution, and geological succession. It is only our natural prejudice and that arrogance which made our forefathers declare that they were descended from demigods which leads us to demur to this conclusion. But the time will before long come when it will be thought wonderful that naturalists who were well acquainted with the comparative structure and development of man and other mammals should have believed that each was the work of a separate act of creation.

Content Questions

1. What three types of evidence does Darwin emphasize, and what does he assert they will prove?

2. How does Darwin answer the question of whether human races differ only slightly from each other or are so distinct as to be "doubtful species"?

3. According to Darwin, what do the similarities between illnesses and reactions to liquor in monkeys and humans prove?

4. What point is Darwin making when he discusses the ability of the members of a particular family to contract their scalp muscles? Why is this point important to his argument?

5. Why does Darwin believe that the human sense of smell has been inherited in "an enfeebled...condition"?

6. According to Darwin, what does the uselessness of the wisdom teeth and appendix illustrate about humankind's descent from a lower form?

Application Questions

1. Darwin provides many examples of homologous similarities between humans and other animals. What is the definition of a homologous similarity? Explain the difference between homologous and analogous similarities. What are the potential problems that arise for the evolutionary biologist if this distinction is not made correctly?

2. Since the publication of *The Descent of Man*, additional evidence has been collected to support the idea that humans have evolved from an apelike ancestor. Describe some of this evidence.

Discussion Questions

1. In Darwin's view, why is evolution the only tenable scientific explanation for the facts he presents?

2. Darwin states that ignorance is more likely than knowledge to make someone assert that humankind's origin will never be known. Why might this be so?

3. Analyze the conclusion of this excerpt, in which Darwin asserts that evolution is the only intellectually satisfying way to explain the similarities between humans and other animals. How convincing is Darwin's case for this conclusion?

THE DESCENT OF MAN
Chapter 4

Comparison of the Mental Powers of Man and the Lower Animals, cont.

I FULLY subscribe to the judgment of those writers[5] who maintain that of all the differences between man and the lower animals, the moral sense or conscience is by far the most important. This sense, as Mackintosh[6] remarks, "has a rightful supremacy over every other principle of human action"; it is summed up in that short but imperious word ought, so full of high significance. It is the most noble of all the attributes of man, leading him without a moment's hesitation to risk his life for that of a fellow-creature; or after due deliberation, impelled simply by the deep feeling of right or duty, to sacrifice it in some great cause. Immanuel Kant exclaims, "Duty! Wondrous thought, that workest neither by fond insinuation, flattery, nor by any threat, but merely by holding up thy naked law in the soul, and so extorting for thyself always reverence, if not always obedience; before whom all appetites are dumb, however secretly they rebel; whence thy original?"[7]

This great question has been discussed by many writers[8] of consummate ability; and my sole excuse for touching on it, is the impossibility of here passing it over; and because, as far as I know, no one has approached it exclusively from the side of natural history. The investigation possesses, also, some independent interest, as an attempt to see how far the study of the lower animals throws light on one of the highest psychical faculties of man.

The following proposition seems to me in a high degree probable—namely, that any animal whatever, endowed with well-marked social instincts,[9] the parental and filial

---

5   See, for instance, on this subject, Quatrefages, Unite de l'Espece Humaine, 1861, p, 21, &c.

6   Dissertation on Ethical Philosophy, 1837, p. 231, &c.

7   Metaphysics of Ethics translated by J. W. Semple, Edinburgh, 1836, p. 136.

8   Mr. Bain gives a list (Mental and Moral Science, 1868, pp. 543–725) of twenty-six British authors who have written on this subject, and whose names are familiar to every reader; to these, Mr. Bain's own name, and those of Mr. Lecky, Mr. Shadworth Hodgson, Sir J. Lubbock, and others, might be added.

9   Sir B. Brodie, after observing that man is a social animal (Psychological Enquiries, 1854, p. 192), asks the pregnant question, "Ought not this to settle the disputed question as to the existence of a moral sense?" Similar ideas have probably occurred to many persons, as they did long ago to Marcus Aurelius. Mr. J. S. Mill speaks, in his celebrated work, Utilitarianism, pp. 459,460, of the social feelings as a "powerful natural sentiment," and as "the natural basis of sentiment for utilitarian morality." Again he says, "Like the other acquired capacities above referred to, the moral faculty, if not a part of our nature, is a natural out-growth from it; capable, like them, in a certain small degree of springing up spontaneously." But in opposition to all this, he also remarks, "If, as in my own belief, the moral feelings are not innate, but acquired, they are not for that reason less natural." It is with hesitation that I venture to differ at all from so profound a thinker, but it can hardly be disputed that the social feelings are instinctive or innate in the lower animals; and why should they not be so in man? Mr. Bain (see, for instance, The Emotions and the Will, 1865, p. 481) and others believe that the moral sense is acquired by each individual during his lifetime. On the general theory of evolution this is at least extremely improbable. The ignoring of all transmitted mental qualities will, as it seems to me, be hereafter judged as a most serious blemish in the works of Mr. Mill.

affections being here included, would inevitably acquire a moral sense or conscience, as soon as its intellectual powers had become as well, or nearly as well developed, as in man. For, firstly, the social instincts lead an animal to take pleasure in the society of its fellows, to feel a certain amount of sympathy with them, and to perform various services for them. The services may be of a definite and evidently instinctive nature; or there may be only a wish and readiness, as with most of the higher social animals, to aid their fellows in certain general ways. But these feelings and services are by no means extended to all the individuals of the same species, only to those of the same association. Secondly, as soon as the mental faculties had become highly developed, images of all past actions and motives would be incessantly passing through the brain of each individual: and that feeling of dissatisfaction, or even misery, which invariably results, as we shall hereafter see, from any unsatisfied instinct, would arise, as often as it was perceived that the enduring and always present social instinct had yielded to some other instinct, at the time stronger, but neither enduring in its nature, nor leaving behind it a very vivid impression. It is clear that many instinctive desires, such as that of hunger, are in their nature of short duration; and after being satisfied, are not readily or vividly recalled. Thirdly, after the power of language had been acquired, and the wishes of the community could be expressed, the common opinion how each member ought to act for the public good, would naturally become in a paramount degree the guide to action. But it should be borne in mind that however great weight we may attribute to public opinion, our regard for the approbation and disapprobation of our fellows depends on sympathy, which, as we shall see, forms an essential part of the social instinct, and is indeed its foundation-stone. Lastly, habit in the individual would ultimately play a very important part in guiding the conduct of each member, for the social instinct, together with sympathy, is, like any other instinct, greatly strengthened by habit, and so consequently would be obedience to the wishes and judgment of the community. These several subordinate propositions must now be discussed, and some of them at considerable length.

It may be well first to premise that I do not wish to maintain that any strictly social animal, if its intellectual faculties were to become as active and as highly developed as in man, would acquire exactly the same moral sense as ours. In the same manner as various animals have some sense of beauty, though they admire widely-different objects, so they might have a sense of right and wrong, though led by it to follow widely different lines of conduct. If, for instance, to take an extreme case, men were reared under precisely the same conditions as hive-bees, there can hardly be a doubt that our unmarried females would, like the worker-bees, think it a sacred duty to kill their brothers, and mothers would strive to kill their fertile daughters; and no one would think of interfering.[10] Nevertheless, the bee, or any other social animal, would gain in our supposed case, as it appears to me, some feeling of right or wrong, or a conscience. For each individual would have an inward sense of possessing certain stronger or more enduring instincts, and others less strong or enduring; so that there would often be a struggle as to which impulse should be followed; and satisfaction, dissatisfaction, or even misery would be felt, as past impressions were compared during their incessant passage through the mind. In this case an inward monitor would tell the animal that it would have been better to have followed the one impulse rather than the other. The one course ought to have been followed, and the other ought not; the one would have been right and the other wrong; but to these terms I shall recur.

Sociability.—Animals of many kinds are social; we find even distinct species living together; for example, some American monkeys; and united flocks of rooks, jackdaws, and starlings. Man shews the same feeling in his strong love for the dog, which the dog returns with interest. Everyone must have noticed how miserable horses, dogs, sheep, &c., are when separated from their companions, and what strong mutual affection the two former kinds, at least, shew on their reunion. It is curious to speculate on the feelings of a dog, who will rest peacefully for hours in a room with his master or any of the family, without the least notice being taken of him; but if left for a short time by himself, barks or howls dismally. We will confine our attention to the higher social animals; and pass over insects, although some of these are social, and aid one another in many important ways. The most common mutual service in the higher animals is to warn one another of danger by means of the united senses of all. Every sportsman knows, as Dr. Jaeger remarks,[11] how difficult it is to approach animals in a herd or troop. Wild horses and cattle do not, I believe, make any danger-signal; but the attitude of any one of them who first discovers an enemy, warns the others. Rabbits stamp loudly on the ground with their hindfeet as a signal: sheep and chamois do the same with their forefeet, uttering likewise a whistle. Many birds, and some mammals, post sentinels, which in the case of seals are said[12] generally to be the females. The leader of a troop of monkeys acts

---

10   Mr. H. Sidgwick remarks, in an able discussion on this subject (the Academy, June 15, 1872, p. 231), "A superior bee, we may feel sure, would aspire to a milder solution of the popular question." Judging, however, from the habits of many or most savages, man solves the problem by female infanticide, polyandry and promiscuous intercourse; therefore it may well be doubted whether it would be by a milder method. Miss Cobbe, in commenting ("Darwinism in Morals," Theological Review, April, 1872, pp. 188–191) on the same illustration, says, the principles of social duty would be thus reversed; and by this, I presume, she means that the fulfillment of a social duty would tend to the injury of individuals; but she overlooks the fact, which she would doubtless admit, that the instincts of the bee have been acquired for the good of the community. She goes so far as to say that if the theory of ethics advocated in this chapter were ever generally accepted, "I cannot but believe that in the hour of their triumph would be sounded the knell of the virtue of mankind!" It is to be hoped that the belief in the permanence of virtue on this earth is not held by many persons on so weak a tenure.

11   Die Darwin'sche Theorie, s. 101.

12   Mr. R. Brown in Proc. Zoolog. Soc., 1868, p. 409

as the sentinel, and utters cries expressive both of danger and of safety.[13] Social animals perform many little services for each other: horses nibble, and cows lick each other, on any spot which itches: monkeys search each other for external parasites; and Brehm states that after a troop of the Cercopithecus griseoviridis has rushed through a thorny brake, each monkey stretches itself on a branch, and another monkey sitting by, "conscientiously" examines its fur, and extracts every thorn or burr.

Animals also render more important services to one another: thus wolves and some other beasts of prey hunt in packs, and aid one another in attacking their victims. Pelicans fish in concert. The Hamadryas baboons turn over stones to find insects, &c.; and when they come to a large one, as many as can stand round, turn it over together and share the booty. Social animals mutually defend each other. Bull bisons in N. America, when there is danger, drive the cows and calves into the middle of the herd, whilst they defend the outside. I shall also in a future chapter give an account of two young wild bulls at Chillingham attacking an old one in concert, and of two stallions together trying to drive away a third stallion from a troop of mares. In Abyssinia, Brehm encountered a great troop of baboons who were crossing a valley; some had already ascended the opposite mountain, and some were still in the valley; the latter were attacked by the dogs, but the old males immediately hurried down from the rocks, and with mouths widely opened, roared so fearfully, that the dogs quickly drew back. They were again encouraged to the attack; but by this time all the baboons had reascended the heights, excepting a young one, about six months old, who, loudly calling for aid, climbed on a block of rock, and was surrounded. Now one of the largest males, a true hero, came down again from the mountain, slowly went to the young one, coaxed him, and triumphantly led him away—the dogs being too much astonished to make an attack. I cannot resist giving another scene which was witnessed by this same naturalist; an eagle seized a young Cercopithecus, which, by clinging to a branch, was not at once carried off; it cried loudly for assistance, upon which the other members of the troop, with much uproar, rushed to the rescue, surrounded the eagle, and pulled out so many feathers, that he no longer thought of his prey, but only how to escape. This eagle, as Brehm remarks, assuredly would never again attack a single monkey of a troop.[14]

It is certain that associated animals have a feeling of love for each other, which is not felt by nonsocial adult animals. How far in most cases they actually sympathise in the

---

13   Brehm, Illustriertes Thierleben, B. i., 1864, ss. 52, 79. For the case of the monkeys extracting thorns from each other, see s. 54. With respect to the Hamadryas turning over stones, the fact is given (s. 76), on the evidence of Alvarez, whose observations Brehm thinks quite trustworthy. For the cases of the old male baboons attacking the dogs, see s. 79; and with respect to the eagle, s. 56.

14   Mr. Belt gives the case of a spider-monkey (Ateles) in Nicaragua, which was heard screaming for nearly two hours in the forest, and was found with an eagle perched close by it. The bird apparently feared to attack as long as it remained face to face; and Mr. Belt believes, from what he has seen of the habits of these monkeys, that they protect themselves from eagles by keeping two or three together. The Naturalist in Nicaragua, 1874, p. 118.

pains and pleasures of others, is more doubtful, especially with respect to pleasures. Mr. Buxton, however, who had excellent means of observation,[15] states that his macaws, which lived free in Norfolk, took "an extravagant interest" in a pair with a nest; and whenever the female left it, she was surrounded by a troop "screaming horrible acclamations in her honour." It is often difficult to judge whether animals have any feeling for the sufferings of others of their kind. Who can say what cows feel, when they surround and stare intently on a dying or dead companion; apparently, however, as Houzeau remarks, they feel no pity. That animals sometimes are far from feeling any sympathy is too certain; for they will expel a wounded animal from the herd, or gore or worry it to death. This is almost the blackest fact in natural history, unless, indeed, the explanation which has been suggested is true, that their instinct or reason leads them to expel an injured companion, lest beasts of prey, including man, should be tempted to follow the troop. In this case their conduct is not much worse than that of the North American Indians, who leave their feeble comrades to perish on the plains; or the Fijians, who, when their parents get old, or fall ill, bury them alive.[16]

Many animals, however, certainly sympathise with each other's distress or danger. This is the case even with birds. Captain Stansbury[17] found on a salt lake in Utah an old and completely blind pelican, which was very fat, and must have been well fed for a long time by his companions. Mr. Blyth, as he informs me, saw Indian crows feeding two or three of their companions which were blind; and I have heard of an analogous case with the domestic cock. We may, if we choose, call these actions instinctive; but such cases are much too rare for the development of any special instinct.[18] I have myself seen a dog, who never passed a cat who lay sick in a basket, and was a great friend of his, without giving her a few licks with his tongue, the surest sign of kind feeling in a dog.

It must be called sympathy that leads a courageous dog to fly at any one who strikes his master, as he certainly will. I saw a person pretending to beat a lady, who had a very timid little dog on her lap, and the trial had never been made before; the little creature instantly jumped away, but after the pretended beating was over, it was really pathetic to see how perseveringly he tried to lick his mistress's face, and comfort her. Brehm[19] states that when a baboon in confinement was pursued to be punished, the others tried to protect him. It must have been sympathy in the cases above given which led the baboons and Cercopitheci to defend their young comrades from the dogs and the eagle. I will give only one other instance of sympathetic and heroic conduct, in the case of a

---

15   Annals and Magazine of Natural History, November, 1868, p. 382.

16   Sir J. Lubbock, Prehistoric Times, 2nd ed., p. 446.

17   As quoted by Mr. L. H. Morgan, The American Beaver, 1868, p. 272. Capt. Stansbury also gives an interesting account of the manner in which a very young pelican, carried away by a strong stream, was guided and encouraged in its attempts to reach the shore by half a dozen old birds.

18   As Mr. Bain states, "Effective aid to a sufferer springs from sympathy proper": Mental and Moral Science, 1868, p. 245.

19   Illustriertes Thierleben, B.i., s. 85.

little American monkey. Several years ago a keeper at the Zoological Gardens showed me some deep and scarcely healed wounds on the nape of his own neck, inflicted on him, whilst kneeling on the floor, by a fierce baboon. The little American monkey, who was a warm friend of this keeper, lived in the same compartment, and was dreadfully afraid of the great baboon. Nevertheless, as soon as he saw his friend in peril, he rushed to the rescue, and by screams and bites so distracted the baboon that the man was able to escape, after, as the surgeon thought, running great risk of his life.

Besides love and sympathy, animals exhibit other qualities connected with the social instincts, which in us would be called moral; and I agree with Agassiz[20] that dogs possess something very like a conscience.

Dogs possess some power of self-command, and this does not appear to be wholly the result of fear. As Braubach[21] remarks, they will refrain from stealing food in the absence of their master. They have long been accepted as the very type of fidelity and obedience. But the elephant is likewise very faithful to his driver or keeper, and probably considers him as the leader of the herd. Dr. Hooker informs me that an elephant, which he was riding in India, became so deeply bogged that he remained stuck fast until the next day, when he was extricated by men with ropes. Under such circumstances elephants will seize with their trunks any object, dead or alive, to place under their knees, to prevent their sinking deeper in the mud; and the driver was dreadfully afraid lest the animal should have seized Dr. Hooker and crushed him to death. But the driver himself, as Dr. Hooker was assured, ran no risk. This forbearance under an emergency so dreadful for a heavy animal, is a wonderful proof of noble fidelity.[22]

All animals living in a body, which defend themselves or attack their enemies in concert, must indeed be in some degree faithful to one another; and those that follow a leader must be in some degree obedient. When the baboons in Abyssinia[23] plunder a garden, they silently follow their leader; and if an imprudent young animal makes a noise, he receives a slap from the others to teach him silence and obedience. Mr. Galton, who has had excellent opportunities for observing the half-wild cattle in S. Africa, says,[24] that they cannot endure even a momentary separation from the herd. They are essentially slavish, and accept the common determination, seeking no better lot than to be led by any one ox who has enough self-reliance to accept the position. The men who break in these animals for harness, watch assiduously for those who, by grazing apart, shew a self-reliant disposition, and these they train as fore-oxen. Mr. Galton adds that such animals

---

20   De l'Espece et de la Classe, 1869, p. 97

21   Die Darwin'sche Art-Lehre, 1869, s, 54

22   See also Hooker's Himalayan Journals, vol. ii., 1854, p. 333.

23   Brehm, Illustriertes Thierleben, B. i., s. 76

24   See his extremely interesting paper on "Gregariousness in Cattle, and in Man," Macmillan's Magazine, Feb., 1871, p. 353.

are rare and valuable; and if many were born they would soon be eliminated, as lions are always on the look-out for the individuals which wander from the herd.

With respect to the impulse which leads certain animals to associate together, and to aid one another in many ways, we may infer that in most cases they are impelled by the same sense of satisfaction or pleasure which they experience in performing other instinctive actions; or by the same sense of dissatisfaction as when other instinctive actions are checked. We see this in innumerable instances, and it is illustrated in a striking manner by the acquired instincts of our domesticated animals; thus a young shepherd-dog delights in driving and running round a flock of sheep, but not in worrying them; a young fox-hound delights in hunting a fox, whilst some other kinds of dogs, as I have witnessed, utterly disregard foxes. What a strong feeling of inward satisfaction must impel a bird, so full of activity, to brood day after day over her eggs. Migratory birds are quite miserable if stopped from migrating; perhaps they enjoy starting on their long flight; but it is hard to believe that the poor pinioned goose, described by Audubon, which started on foot at the proper time for its journey of probably more than a thousand miles, could have felt any joy in doing so. Some instincts are determined solely by painful feelings, as by fear, which leads to self-preservation, and is in some cases directed towards special enemies. No one, I presume, can analyse the sensations of pleasure or pain. In many instances, however, it is probable that instincts are persistently followed from the mere force of inheritance, without the stimulus of either pleasure or pain. A young pointer, when it first scents game, apparently cannot help pointing. A squirrel in a cage who pats the nuts which it cannot eat, as if to bury them in the ground, can hardly be thought to act thus, either from pleasure or pain. Hence the common assumption that men must be impelled to every action by experiencing some pleasure or pain may be erroneous. Although a habit may be blindly and implicitly followed, independently of any pleasure or pain felt at the moment, yet if it be forcibly and abruptly checked, a vague sense of dissatisfaction is generally experienced.

It has often been assumed that animals were in the first place rendered social, and that they feel as a consequence uncomfortable when separated from each other, and comfortable whilst together; but it is a more probable view that these sensations were first developed; in order that those animals which would profit by living in society, should be induced to live together, in the same manner as the sense of hunger and the pleasure of eating were, no doubt, first acquired in order to induce animals to eat. The feeling of pleasure from society is probably an extension of the parental or filial affections, since the social instinct seems to be developed by the young remaining for a long time with their parents; and this extension may be attributed in part to habit, but chiefly to natural selection. With those animals which were benefited by living in close association, the individuals which took the greatest pleasure in society would best escape various dangers, whilst those that cared least for their comrades, and lived solitary, would perish in greater numbers. With respect to the origin of the parental and filial affections, which apparently lie at the base of the social instincts, we know not the steps by which they have been gained; but we may infer that it has been to a large extent through natural selection. So it has almost certainly been with the unusual and opposite feeling of hatred between the nearest relations, as with the worker-bees which kill their brother drones, and with the queen-bees which kill their daughter-queens; the desire to destroy their nearest relations having been in this case of service to the community. Parental affection, or some feeling which replaces it, has been developed in certain animals extremely low in the scale, for example, in star-fishes and spiders. It is also occasionally present in a few members alone in a whole group of animals, as in the genus Forficula, or earwigs.

The all-important emotion of sympathy is distinct from that of love. A mother may passionately love her sleeping and passive infant, but she can hardly at such times be said to feel sympathy for it. The love of a man for his dog is distinct from sympathy, and so is that of a dog for his master. Adam Smith formerly argued, as has Mr. Bain recently, that the basis of sympathy lies in our strong retentiveness of former states of pain or pleasure. Hence, "the sight of another person enduring hunger, cold, fatigue, revives in us some recollection of these states, which are painful even in idea." We are thus impelled to relieve the sufferings of another, in order that our own painful feelings may be at the same time relieved. In like manner we are led to participate in the pleasures of others.[25] But I cannot see how this view explains the fact that sympathy is excited, in an immeasurably stronger degree, by a beloved, than by an indifferent person. The mere sight of suffering, independently of love, would suffice to call up in us vivid recollections and associations. The explanation may lie in the fact that, with all animals, sympathy is directed solely towards the members of the same community, and therefore cowards known, and more or less beloved members, but not to all the individuals of the same species. This fact is not more surprising than that the fears of many animals should be directed against special enemies. Species which are not social, such as lions and tigers, no doubt feel sympathy for the suffering of their own young, but not for that of any other animal. With mankind, selfishness, experience, and imitation, probably add, as Mr. Bain has shown, to the power of sympathy; for we are led by the hope of receiving good in return to perform acts of sympathetic kindness to others: and sympathy is much strengthened by habit. In however complex a manner this feeling may have originated, as it is one of high importance to all those animals which aid and defend one another, it will have been increased through natural selection; for those communities, which included the

---

25   See the first and striking chapter in Adam Smith's Theory of Moral Sentiments. Also Mr. Bain's Mental and Moral Science, 1868, pp. 244, and 275–282. Mr. Bain states, that, "Sympathy is, indirectly, a source of pleasure to the sympathiser"; and he accounts for this through reciprocity. He remarks that "The person benefited, or others in his stead, may make up, by sympathy and good offices returned, for all the sacrifice." But if, as appears to be the case, sympathy is strictly an instinct, its exercise would give direct pleasure, in the same manner as the exercise, as before remarked, of almost every other instinct.

greatest number of the most sympathetic members, would flourish best, and rear the greatest number of offspring.

It is, however, impossible to decide in many cases whether certain social instincts have been acquired through natural selection, or are the indirect result of other instincts and faculties, such as sympathy, reason, experience, and a tendency to imitation; or again, whether they are simply the result of long-continued habit. So remarkable an instinct as the placing sentinels to warn the community of danger, can hardly have been the indirect result of any of these faculties; it must, therefore, have been directly acquired. On the other hand, the habit followed by the males of some social animals of defending the community, and of attacking their enemies or their prey in concert, may perhaps have originated from mutual sympathy; but courage, and in most cases strength, must have been previously acquired, probably through natural selection.

Of the various instincts and habits, some are much stronger than others; that is, some either give more pleasure in their performance, and more distress in their prevention, than others; or, which is probably quite as important, they are, through inheritance, more persistently followed, without exciting any special feeling of pleasure or pain. We are ourselves conscious that some habits are much more difficult to cure or change than others. Hence a struggle may often be observed in animals between different instincts, or between an instinct and some habitual disposition; as when a dog rushes after a hare, is rebuked, pauses, hesitates, pursues again, or returns ashamed to his master; or as between the love of a female dog for her young puppies and for her master,—for she may be seen to slink away to them, as if half ashamed of not accompanying her master. But the most curious instance known to me of one instinct getting the better of another, is the migratory instinct conquering the maternal instinct. The former is wonderfully strong; a confined bird will at the proper season beat her breast against the wires of her cage, until it is bare and bloody. It causes young salmon to leap out of the fresh water, in which they could continue to exist, and thus unintentionally to commit suicide. Everyone knows how strong the maternal instinct is, leading even timid birds to face great danger, though with hesitation, and in opposition to the instinct of self-preservation. Nevertheless, the migratory instinct is so powerful, that late in the autumn swallows, house-martins, and swifts frequently desert their tender young, leaving them to perish miserably in their nests.[26]

---

26   This fact, the Rev. L. Jenyns states (see his edition of White's Nat. Hist. of Selborne, 1853, p. 204), was first recorded by the illustrious Jenner, in Phil. Transact., 1824, and has since been confirmed by several observers, especially by Mr. Blackwall. This latter careful observer examined, late in the autumn, during two years, thirty-six nests; he found that twelve contained young dead birds, five contained eggs on the point of being hatched, and three, eggs not nearly hatched. Many birds, not yet old enough for a prolonged flight are likewise deserted and left behind. See Blackwall, Researches in Zoology, 1834, pp. 108, 118. For some additional evidence, although this is not wanted, see Leroy, Lettres Phil., 1802, p. 217. For swifts, Gould's Introduction to the Birds of Great Britain, 1823, p. 5. Similar cases have been observed in Canada by Mr. Adams; Pop. Science Review, July, 1873, p. 283

We can perceive that an instinctive impulse, if it be in any way more beneficial to a species than some other or opposed instinct, would be rendered the more potent of the two through natural selection; for the individuals which had it most strongly developed would survive in larger numbers. Whether this is the case with the migratory in comparison with the maternal instinct, may be doubted. The great persistence, or steady action of the former at certain seasons of the year during the whole day, may give it for a time paramount force.

Man a social animal.—Everyone will admit that man is a social being. We see this in his dislike of solitude, and in his wish for society beyond that of his own family. Solitary confinement is one of the severest punishments which can be inflicted. Some authors suppose that man primevally lived in single families; but at the present day, though single families, or only two or three together, roam the solitudes of some savage lands, they always, as far as I can discover, hold friendly relations with other families inhabiting the same district. Such families occasionally meet in council, and unite for their common defence. It is no argument against savage man being a social animal, that the tribes inhabiting adjacent districts are almost always at war with each other; for the social instincts never extend to all the individuals of the same species. Judging from the analogy of the majority of the Quadrumana, it is probable that the early ape-like progenitors of man were likewise social; but this is not of much importance for us. Although man, as he now exists, 'has few special instincts, having lost any which his early progenitors may have possessed, this is no reason why he should not have retained from an extremely remote period some degree of instinctive love and sympathy for his fellows. We are indeed all conscious that we do possess such sympathetic feelings;[27] but our consciousness does not tell us whether they are instinctive, having originated long ago in the same manner as with the lower animals, or whether they have been acquired by each of us during our early years. As man is a social animal, it is almost certain that he would inherit a tendency to be faithful to his comrades, and obedient to the leader of his tribe; for these qualities are common to most social animals. He would consequently possess some capacity for self-command. He would from an inherited tendency be willing to defend, in concert with others, his fellow-men; and would be ready to aid them in any way, which did not too greatly interfere with his own welfare or his own strong desires.

The social animals which stand at the bottom of the scale are guided almost exclusively, and those which stand higher in the scale are largely guided, by special instincts in the aid which they give to the members of the same community; but they are likewise in part impelled by mutual love and sympathy, assisted apparently by some amount of reason. Although man, as just remarked, has no special instincts to tell him how to aid his

---

27   Hume remarks (An Enquiry Concerning the Principles of Morals, ed. of 1751, p. 132), "There seems a necessity for confessing that the happiness and misery of others are not spectacles altogether indifferent to us, but that the view of the former... communicates a secret joy; the appearance of the latter...throws a melancholy damp over the imagination."

fellow-men, he still has the impulse, and with his improved intellectual faculties would naturally be much guided in this respect by reason and experience. Instinctive sympathy would also cause him to value highly the approbation of his fellows; for, as Mr. Bain has clearly shewn,[24] the love of praise and the strong feeling of glory, and the still stronger horror of scorn and infamy, "are due to the workings of sympathy." Consequently man would be influenced in the highest degree by the wishes, approbation, and blame of his fellow-men, as expressed by their gestures and language. Thus the social instincts, which must have been acquired by man in a very rude state, and probably even by his early ape-like progenitors, still give the impulse to some of his best actions; but his actions are in a higher degree determined by the expressed wishes and judgment of his fellow-men, and unfortunately very often by his own strong selfish desires. But as love, sympathy and self-command become strengthened by habit, and as the power of reasoning becomes clearer, so that man can value justly the judgments of his fellows, he will feel himself impelled, apart from any transitory pleasure or pain, to certain lines of conduct. He might then declare—not that any barbarian or uncultivated man could thus think—I am the supreme judge of my own conduct, and in the words of Kant, I will not in my own person violate the dignity of humanity.

The more enduring Social Instincts conquer the less persistent Instincts.—We have not, however, as yet considered the main point, on which, from our present point of view, the whole question of the moral sense turns. Why should a man feel that he ought to obey one instinctive desire rather than another? Why is he bitterly regretful, if he has yielded to a strong sense of self-preservation, and has not risked his life to save that of a fellow-creature? Or why does he regret having stolen food from hunger?

It is evident in the first place, that with mankind the instinctive impulses have different degrees of strength; a savage will risk his own life to save that of a member of the same community, but will be wholly indifferent about a stranger: a young and timid mother urged by the maternal instinct will, without a moment's hesitation, run the greatest danger for her own infant, but not for a mere fellow-creature. Nevertheless many a civilized man, or even boy, who never before risked his life for another, but full of courage and sympathy, has disregarded the instinct of self-preservation, and plunged at once into a torrent to save a drowning man, though a stranger. In this case man is impelled by the same instinctive motive, which made the heroic little American monkey, formerly described, save his keeper, by attacking the great and dreaded baboon. Such actions as the above appear to be the simple result of the greater strength of the social or maternal instincts rather than that of any other instinct or motive; for they are performed too instantaneously for reflection, or for pleasure or pain to be felt at the time; though, if prevented by any cause, distress or even misery might be felt. In a timid man, on the other hand, the instinct of self-preservation, might be so strong, that he would be unable to force himself to run any such risk, perhaps not even for his own child.

I am aware that some persons maintain that actions performed impulsively, as in the above cases, do not come under the dominion of the moral sense, and cannot be called moral. They confine this term to actions done deliberately, after a victory over opposing desires, or when prompted by some exalted motive. But it appears scarcely possible to draw any clear line of distinction of this kind.[28] As far as exalted motives are concerned, many instances have been recorded of savages, destitute of any feeling of general benevolence towards mankind, and not guided by any religious motive, who have deliberately sacrificed their lives as prisoners,[29] rather than betray their comrades; and surely their conduct ought to be considered as moral. As far as deliberation, and the victory over opposing motives are concerned, animals may be seen doubting between opposed instincts, in rescuing their offspring or comrades from danger; yet their actions, though done for the good of others, are not called moral. Moreover, anything performed very often by us, will at last be done without deliberation or hesitation, and can then hardly be distinguished from an instinct; yet surely no one will pretend that such an action ceases to be moral. On the contrary, we all feel that an act cannot be considered as perfect, or as performed in the most noble manner, unless it be done impulsively, without deliberation or effort, in the same manner as by a man in whom the requisite qualities are innate. He who is forced to overcome his fear or want of sympathy before he acts, deserves, however, in one way higher credit than the man whose innate disposition leads him to a good act without effort. As we cannot distinguish between motives, we rank all actions of a certain class as moral, if performed by a moral being. A moral being is one who is capable of comparing his past and future actions or motives, and of approving or disapproving of them. We have no reason to suppose that any of the lower animals have this capacity; therefore, when a Newfoundland dog drags a child out of the water, or a monkey faces danger to rescue its comrade, or takes charge of an orphan monkey, we do not call its conduct moral. But in the case of man, who alone can with certainty be ranked as a moral being, actions of a certain class are called moral, whether performed deliberately, after a struggle with opposing motives, or impulsively through instinct, or from the effects of slowly-gained habit.

But to return to our more immediate subject. Although some instincts are more powerful than others, and thus lead to corresponding actions, yet it is untenable, that in man the social instincts (including the love of praise and fear of blame) possess greater strength, or have, through long habit, acquired greater strength than the instincts of self-preservation, hunger, lust, vengeance, &c. Why then does man regret, even though

---

28   I refer here to the distinction between what has been called material and formal morality. I am glad to find that Professor Huxley (Critiques and Addresses, 1873, p. 287) takes the same view on this subject as I do. Mr. Leslie Stephen remarks (Essays on Free Thinking and Plain Speaking, 1873, p. 83), "The metaphysical distinction between material and formal morality is as irrelevant as other such distinctions."

29   I have given one such case, namely of three Patagonian Indians who preferred being shot, one after the other, to betraying the plans of their companions in war (Journal of Researches, 1845, p. 103).

trying to banish such regret, that he has followed the one natural impulse rather than the other; and why does he further feel that he ought to regret his conduct? Man in this respect differs profoundly from the lower animals. Nevertheless we can, I think, see with some degree of clearness the reason of this difference.

Man, from the activity of his mental faculties, cannot avoid reflection: past impressions and images are incessantly and clearly passing through his mind. Now with those animals which live permanently in a body, the social instincts are ever present and persistent. Such animals are always ready to utter the danger-signal, to defend the community, and to give aid to their fellows in accordance with their habits; they feel at all times, without the stimulus of any special passion or desire, some degree of love and sympathy for them; they are unhappy if long separated from them, and always happy to be again in their company. So it is with ourselves. Even when we are quite alone, how often do we think with pleasure or pain of what others think of us,—of their imagined approbation or disapprobation; and this all follows from sympathy, a fundamental element of the social instincts. A man who possessed no trace of such instincts would be an unnatural monster. On the other hand, the desire to satisfy hunger, or any passion such as vengeance, is in its nature temporary, and can for a time be fully satisfied. Nor is it easy, perhaps hardly possible, to call up with complete vividness the feeling, for instance, of hunger; nor indeed, as has often been remarked, of any suffering. The instinct of self-preservation is not felt except in the presence of danger, and many a coward has thought himself brave until he has met his enemy face to face. The wish for another man's property is perhaps as persistent a desire as any that can be named; but even in this case the satisfaction of actual possession is generally a weaker feeling than the desire: many a thief, if not an habitual one, after success has wondered why he stole some article.[30]

A man cannot prevent past impressions often repassing through his mind; he will thus be driven to make a comparison between the impressions of past hunger, vengeance satisfied, or danger shunned at other men's cost, with the almost ever-present instinct of sympathy, and with his early knowledge of what others consider as praiseworthy or blameable. This knowledge cannot be banished from his mind, and from instinctive

---

30   Enmity or hatred seems also to be a highly persistent feeling, perhaps more so than any other that can be named. Envy is defined as hatred of another for some excellence or success; and Bacon insists (Essay ix.), "Of all other affections envy is the most importune and continual." Dogs are very apt to hate both strange men and strange dogs, especially if they live near at hand, but do not belong to the same family, tribe, or clan; this feeling would thus seem to be innate, and is certainly a most persistent one. It seems to be the complement and converse of the true social instinct. From what we hear of savages, it would appear that something of the same kind holds good with them. If this be so, it would be a small step in any one to transfer such feelings to any member of the same tribe if he had done him an injury and had become his enemy. Nor is it probable that the primitive conscience would reproach a man for injuring his enemy; rather it would reproach him, if he had not revenged himself. To do good in return for evil, to love your enemy, is a height of morality to which it may be doubted whether the social instincts would, by themselves, have ever led us. It is necessary that these instincts, together with sympathy, should have been highly cultivated and extended by the aid of reason, instruction, and the love or fear of God, before any such golden rule would ever be thought of and obeyed.

sympathy is esteemed of great moment. He will then feel as if he had been baulked in following a present instinct or habit, and this with all animals causes dissatisfaction, or even misery.

The above case of the swallow affords an illustration, though of a reversed nature, of a temporary though for the time strongly persistent instinct conquering another instinct, which is usually dominant over all others. At the proper season these birds seem all day long to be impressed with the desire to migrate; their habits change; they become rest-less, are noisy and congregate in flocks. Whilst the mother-bird is feeding, or brooding over her nestlings, the maternal instinct is probably stronger than the migratory; but the instinct which is the more persistent gains the victory, and at last, at a moment when her young ones are not in sight, she takes flight and deserts them. When arrived at the end of her long journey, and the migratory instinct has ceased to act, what an agony of remorse the bird would feel, if, from being endowed with great mental activity, she could not prevent the image constantly passing through her mind, of her young ones perishing in the bleak north from cold and hunger.

At the moment of action, man will no doubt be apt to follow the stronger impulse; and though this may occasionally prompt him to the noblest deeds, it will more commonly lead him to gratify his own desires at the expense of other men. But after their gratifica-tion when past and weaker impressions are judged by the ever-enduring social instinct, and by his deep regard for the good opinion of his fellows, retribution will surely come. He will then feel remorse, repentance, regret, or shame; this later feeling, however, re-lates almost exclusively to the judgment of others. He will consequently resolve more or less firmly to act differently for the future; and this is conscience; for conscience looks backwards, and serves as a guide for the future.

The nature and strength of the feelings which we call regret, shame, repentance or re-morse, depend apparently not only on the strength of the violated instinct, but partly on the strength of the temptation, and often still more on the judgment of our fel-lows. How far each man values the appreciation of others, depends on the strength of his innate or acquired feeling of sympathy; and on his own capacity for reasoning out the remote consequences of his acts. Another element is most important, although not necessary, the reverence or fear of the Gods, or Spirits believed in by each man: and this applies especially in cases of remorse. Several critics have objected that though some slight regret or repentance may be explained by the view advocated in this chapter, it is impossible thus to account for the soul-shaking feeling of remorse. But I can see little force in this objection. My critics do not define what they mean by remorse, and I can find no definition implying more than an overwhelming sense of repentance. Remorse seems to bear the same relation to repentance, as rage does to anger, or agony to pain. It is far from strange that an instinct so strong and so generally admired, as maternal love, should, if disobeyed, lead to the deepest misery, as soon as the impression of the past cause of disobedience is weakened. Even when an action is opposed to no special instinct, merely to know that our friends and equals despise us for it is enough to cause great misery. Who can doubt that the refusal to fight a duel through fear has caused many men an agony of shame? Many a Hindoo, it is said, has been stirred to the bottom of his soul by having partaken of unclean food. Here is another case of what must, I think, be called remorse. Dr. Landor acted as a magistrate in West Australia, and relates[31] that a native on his farm, after losing one of his wives from disease, came and said that, "He was going to a distant tribe to spear a woman, to satisfy his sense of duty to his wife. I told him that if he did so, I would send him to prison for life. He remained about the farm for some months, but got exceedingly thin, and complained that he could not rest or eat, that his wife's spirit was haunting him, because he had not taken a life for hers. I was inexorable, and assured him that nothing should save him if he did." Nevertheless the man disappeared for more than a year, and then returned in high condition; and his other wife told Dr. Landor that her husband had taken the life of a woman belonging to a distant tribe; but it was impossible to obtain legal evidence of the act. The breach of a rule held sacred by the tribe, will thus, as it seems, give rise to the deepest feelings,—and this quite apart from the social instincts, excepting in so far as the rule is grounded on the judgment of the community. How so many strange superstitions have arisen throughout the world we know not; nor can we tell how some real and great crimes, such as incest, have come to be held in an abhorrence (which is not however quite universal) by the lowest savages. It is even doubtful whether in some tribes incest would be looked on with greater horror, than would the marriage of a man with a woman bearing the same name, though not a relation. "To violate this law is a crime which the Australians hold in the greatest abhorrence, in this agreeing exactly with certain tribes of North America. When the question is put in either district, is it worse to kill a girl of a foreign tribe, or to marry a girl of one's own, an answer just opposite to ours would be given without hesitation[32]. We may, therefore, reject the belief, lately insisted on by some writers, that the abhorrence of incest is due to our possessing a special God-implanted conscience. On the whole it is intelligible, that a man urged by so powerful a sentiment as remorse, though arising as above explained, should be led to act in a manner, which he has been taught to believe serves as an expiation, such as delivering himself up to justice.

Man prompted by his conscience, will through long habit acquire such perfect self-command, that his desires and passions will at last yield instantly and without a struggle to his social sympathies and instincts, including his feeling for the judgment of his fellows. The still hungry, or the still revengeful man will not think of stealing food, or of wreaking his vengeance. It is possible, or as we shall hereafter see, even probable, that the habit

---

31   Insanity in Relation to Law, Ontario, United States, 1871, p. 1
32   E. B. Tylor, in Contemporary Review, April, 1873, p. 707

of self-command may, like other habits, be inherited. Thus at last man comes to feel, through acquired and perhaps inherited habit, that it is best for him to obey his more persistent impulses. The imperious word ought seems merely to imply the consciousness of the existence of a rule of conduct, however it may have originated. Formerly it must have been often vehemently urged that an insulted gentleman ought to fight a duel. We even say that a pointer ought to point, and a retriever to retrieve game. If they fail to do so, they fail in their duty and act wrongly.

If any desire or instinct leading to an action opposed to the good of others still appears, when recalled to mind, as strong as, or stronger than, the social instinct, a man will feel no keen regret at having followed it; he will be conscious that if his conduct were known to his fellows, it would meet with their disapprobation; and few are so destitute of sympathy as not to feel discomfort when this is realised. If he has no such sympathy, and if his desires leading to bad actions are at the time strong, and when recalled are not over-mastered by the persistent social instincts, and the judgment of others, then he is essentially a bad man;[33] and the sole restraining motive left is the fear of punishment, and the conviction that in the long run it would be best for his own selfish interests to regard the good of others rather than his own.

It is obvious that every one may with an easy conscience gratify his own desires, if they do not interfere with his social instincts, that is with the good of others; in order to be quite free from self-reproach, or at least of anxiety, it is almost necessary for him to avoid the disapprobation, whether reasonable or not, of his fellow-men. Nor must he break through the fixed habits of his life, especially if these are supported by reason; for if he does, he will assuredly feel dissatisfaction. He must likewise avoid the reprobation of the one God or gods in whom, according to his knowledge or superstition, he may believe; but in this case the additional fear of divine punishment often supervenes.

The strictly Social Virtues at first alone regarded. The above view of the origin and nature of the moral sense, which tells us what we ought to do, and of the conscience which reproves us if we disobey it, accords well with what we see of the early and undeveloped condition of this faculty in mankind. The virtues which must be practised, at least generally, by rude men, so that they may associate in a body, are those which are still recognised as the most important. But they are practised almost exclusively in relation to the men of the same tribe; and their opposites are not regarded as crimes in relation to the men of other tribes. No tribe could hold together if murder, robbery, treachery, &c., were common; consequently such crimes within the limits of the same tribe "are branded with everlasting infamy";[34] but excite no such sentiment beyond these limits. A

---

33 Dr. Prosper Despine, in his Psychologie Naturelle, 1868 (tom. i., p. 243; ctom. ii., p. 169) gives many curious cases of the worst criminals who apparently have been entirely destitute of conscience.

34 See an able article in the North British Review, 1867, p. 395. See also Mr. W. Bagehot's articles on the "Importance of Obedience and Coherence to Primitive Man," in the Fortnightly Review, 1867, p. 529, and 1868, p. 457, &c.

North-American Indian is well pleased with himself. and is honoured by others, when he scalps a man of another tribe; and a Dyak cuts off the head of an unoffending person, and dries it as a trophy. The murder of infants has prevailed on the largest scale throughout the world,[35] and has met with no reproach; but infanticide, especially of females, has been thought to be good for the tribe, or at least not injurious. Suicide during former times was not generally considered as a crime,[36] but rather, from the courage displayed, as an honourable act; and it is still practised by some semi-civilised and savage nations without reproach, for it does not obviously concern others of the tribe. It has been recorded that an Indian Thug conscientiously regretted that he had not robbed and strangled as many travellers as did his father before him. In a rude state of civilisation the robbery of strangers is, indeed, generally considered as honourable.

Slavery, although in some ways beneficial during ancient times,[37] is a great crime; yet it was not so regarded until quite recently, even by the most civilised nations. And this was especially the case, because the slaves belonged in general to a race different from that of their masters. As barbarians do not regard the opinion of their women, wives are commonly treated like slaves. Most savages are utterly indifferent to the sufferings of strangers, or even delight in witnessing them. It is well known that the women and children of the North American Indians aided in torturing their enemies. Some savages take a horrid pleasure in cruelty to animals,[38] and humanity is an unknown virtue. Nevertheless, besides the family affections, kindness is common, especially during sickness, between the members of the same tribe, and is sometimes extended beyond these limits. Mungo Park's touching account of the kindness of the negro women of the interior to him is well known. Many instances could be given of the noble fidelity of savages towards each other, but not to strangers; common experience justifies the maxim of the Spaniard, "Never, never trust an Indian." There cannot be fidelity without truth; and this fundamental virtue is not rare between the members of the same tribe: thus Mungo Park heard the negro women teaching their young children to love the truth. This, again, is one of the virtues which becomes so deeply rooted in the mind, that it is sometimes practised by savages, even at a high cost, towards strangers; but to lie to your enemy has rarely been thought a sin, as the history of modern diplomacy too plainly shews. As soon as a tribe has a recognised leader, disobedience becomes a crime, and even abject submission is looked at as a sacred virtue.

---

35   The fullest account which I have met with is by Dr. Gerland, in his Ober den Aussterben der Naturvolker, 1868: but I shall have to recur to the subject of infanticide in a future chapter.

36   See the very interesting discussion on suicide in Lecky's History of European Morals, vol. i., 1869, p. 223. With respect to savages, Mr. Winwood Reade informs me that the negroes of west Africa often commit suicide. It is well known how common it was amongst the miserable aborigines of South America after the Spanish conquest. For New Zealand, see The Voyage of the Novara, and for the Aleutian Islands, Muller, as quoted by Houzeau, Les Facultes Mentales, &c., tom. ii., p. 136.

37   See Mr. Bagehot, Physics and Policies, 1872, p, 72.

38   See, for instance, Mr. Hamilton's account of the Kaffirs, Anthropological Review, 1870, p. xv.

As during rude times no man can be useful or faithful to his tribe without courage, this quality has universally been placed in the highest rank; and although in civilised countries a good yet timid man may be far more useful to the community than a brave one, we cannot help instinctively honouring the latter above a coward, however benevolent. Prudence, on the other hand, which does not concern the welfare of others, though a very useful virtue, has never been highly esteemed. As no man can practise the virtues necessary for the welfare of his tribe without self-sacrifice, self-command, and the power of endurance, these qualities have been at all times highly and most justly valued. The American savage voluntarily submits to the most horrid tortures without a groan, to prove and strengthen his fortitude and courage; and we cannot help admiring him, or even an Indian Fakir, who, from a foolish religious motive, swings suspended by a hook buried in his flesh.

The other so-called self-regarding virtues, which do not obviously, though they may really, affect the welfare of the tribe, have never been esteemed by savages, though now highly appreciated by civilised nations. The greatest intemperance is no reproach with savages. Utter licentiousness, and unnatural crimes, prevail to an astounding extent.[39] As soon, however, as marriage, whether polygamous, or monogamous, becomes common, jealousy will lead to the inculcation of female virtue; and this, being honoured, will tend to spread to the unmarried females. How slowly it spreads to the male sex, we see at the present day. Chastity eminently requires self-command; therefore, it has been honoured from a very early period in the moral history of civilised man. As a consequence of this, the senseless practice of celibacy has been ranked from a remote period as a virtue.[40] The hatred of indecency, which appears to us so natural as to be thought innate, and which is so valuable an aid to chastity, is a modern virtue, appertaining exclusively, as Sir G. Staunton remarks,[41] to civilised life. This is shewn by the ancient religious rites of various nations, by the drawings on the walls of Pompeii, and by the practices of many savages.

We have now seen that actions are regarded by savages, and were probably so regarded by primeval man, as good or bad, solely as they obviously affect the welfare of the tribe,— not that of the species, nor that of an individual member of the tribe. This conclusion agrees well with the belief that the so-called moral sense is aboriginally derived from the social instincts, for both relate at first exclusively to the community.

The chief causes of the low morality of savages, as judged by our standard, are, firstly, the confinement of sympathy to the same tribe. Secondly, powers of reasoning insufficient to recognise the bearing of many virtues, especially of the selfregarding virtues,

---

39   Mr. M'Lennan has given (Primitive Marriage, 1865, p. 176) a good collection of facts on this head.
40   Lecky, History of European Morals, vol. i., 1869, p. 109
41   Embassy to China, vol. ii., p. 348.

on the general welfare of the tribe. Savages, for instance, fail to trace the multiplied evils consequent on a want of temperance, chastity, &c. And, thirdly, weak power of self-command; for this power has not been strengthened through long-continued, perhaps inherited, habit, instruction and religion.

I have entered into the above details on the immorality of savages,[42] because some authors have recently taken a high view of their moral nature, or have attributed most of their crimes to mistaken benevolence.[43] These authors appear to rest their conclusion on savages possessing those virtues which are serviceable, or even necessary, for the existence of the family and of the tribe,—qualities which they undoubtedly do possess, and often in a high degree.

Concluding Remarks.— It was assumed formerly by philosophers of the derivative[44] school of morals that the foundation of morality lay in a form of Selfishness; but more recently the "Greatest happiness principle" has been brought prominently forward. It is, however, more correct to speak of the latter principle as the standard, and not as the motive of conduct. Nevertheless, all the authors whose works I have consulted, with a few exceptions,[45] write as if there must be a distinct motive for every action, and that this must be associated with some pleasure or displeasure. But man seems often to act impulsively, that is from instinct or long habit, without any consciousness of pleasure, in the same manner as does probably a bee or ant, when it blindly follows its instincts. Under circumstances of extreme peril, as during a fire, when a man endeavours to save a fellow-creature without a moment's hesitation, he can hardly feel pleasure; and still less has he time to reflect on the dissatisfaction which he might subsequently experience if he did not make the attempt. Should he afterwards reflect over his own conduct, he would feel that there lies within him an impulsive power widely different from a search after pleasure or happiness; and this seems to be the deeply planted social instinct.

In the case of the lower animals it seems much more appropriate to speak of their social instincts, as having been developed for the general good rather than for the general

---

42   See on this subject copious evidence in chap. vii. of Sir J. Lubbock, Origin of Civilisation, 1870.

43   For instance Lecky, History of European Morals, vol. i., p. I 24.

44   This term is used in an able article in the Westminster Review, Oct., 1869, p. 498; For the "Greatest happiness principle," see J. S. Mill, Utilitarianism, p. 448

45   Mill recognises (System of Logic, vol. ii., p. 422) in the clearest manner, that actions may be performed through habit without the anticipation of pleasure. Mr. H. Sidgwick also, in his "Essay on Pleasure and Desire" (The Contemporary Review, April, 1872, p. 671), remarks: "To sum up, in contravention of the doctrine that our conscious active impulses are always directed towards the production of agreeable sensations in ourselves, I would maintain that we find everywhere in consciousness extra-regarding impulse, directed towards something that is not pleasure; that in many cases the impulse is so far incompatible with the self-regarding that the two do not easily co-exist in the same moment of consciousness." A dim feeling that our impulses do not by any means always arise from any contemporaneous or anticipated pleasure, has, I cannot but think, been one chief cause of the acceptance of the intuitive theory of morality, and of the rejection of the utilitarian or "Greatest happiness" theory. With respect to the latter theory the standard and the motive of conduct have no doubt often been confused, but they are really in some degree blended.

happiness of the species. The term, general good, may be defined as the rearing of the greatest number of individuals in full vigour and health, with all their faculties perfect, under the conditions to which they are subjected. As the social instincts both of man and the lower animals have no doubt been developed by nearly the same steps, it would be advisable, if found practicable, to use the same definition in both cases, and to take as the standard of morality, the general good or welfare of the community, rather than the general happiness; but this definition would perhaps require some limitation on account of political ethics.

When a man risks his life to save that of a fellow-creature, it seems also more correct to say that he acts for the general good, rather than for the general happiness of mankind. No doubt the welfare and the happiness of the individual usually coincide; and a contented, happy tribe will flourish better than one that is discontented and unhappy. We have seen that even at an early period in the history of man, the expressed wishes of the community will have naturally influenced to a large extent the conduct of each member; and as all wish for happiness, the "greatest happiness principle" will have become a most important secondary guide and object; the social instinct, however, together with sympathy (which leads to our regarding the approbation and disapprobation of others), having served as the primary impulse and guide. Thus the reproach is removed of laying the foundation of the noblest part of our nature in the base principle of selfishness; unless, indeed, the satisfaction which every animal feels, when it follows its proper instincts, and the dissatisfaction felt when prevented, be called selfish.

The wishes and opinions of the members of the same community, expressed at first orally, but later by writing also, either form the sole guides of our conduct, or greatly reinforce the social instincts; such opinions, however, have sometimes a tendency directly opposed to these instincts. This latter fact is well exemplified by the Law of Honour, that is, the law of the opinion of our equals, and not of all our countrymen. The breach of this law, even when the breach is known to be strictly accordant with true morality, has caused many a man more agony than a real crime.

We recognise the same influence in the burning sense of shame which most of us have felt, even after the interval of years, when calling to mind some accidental breach of a trifling, though fixed, rule of etiquette. The judgment of the community will generally be guided by some rude experience of what is best in the long run for all the members; but this judgment will not rarely err from ignorance and weak powers of reasoning. Hence the strangest customs and superstitions, in complete opposition to the true welfare and happiness of mankind, have become all-powerful throughout the world. We see this in the horror felt by a Hindoo who breaks his caste, and in many other such cases. It would be difficult to distinguish between the remorse felt by a Hindoo who has yielded to the temptation of eating unclean food, from that felt after committing a theft; but the former would probably be the more severe.

How so many absurd rules of conduct, as well as so many absurd religious beliefs, have originated, we do not know; nor how it is that they have become, in all quarters of the world, so deeply impressed on the mind of men; but it is worthy of remark that a belief constantly inculcated during the early years of life, whilst the brain is impressible, appears to acquire almost the nature of an instinct; and the very essence of an instinct is that it is followed independently of reason. Neither can we say why certain admirable virtues, such as the love of truth, are much more highly appreciated by some savage tribes than by others;[46] nor, again, why similar differences prevail even amongst highly civilised nations. Knowing how firmly fixed many strange customs and superstitions have become, we need feel no surprise that the self-regarding virtues, supported as they are by reason, should now appear to us so natural as to be thought innate, although they were not valued by man in his early condition.

Not withstanding many sources of doubt, man can generally and readily distinguish between the higher and lower moral rules. The higher are founded on the social instincts, and relate to the welfare of others. They are supported by the approbation of our fellow-men and by reason. The lower rules, though some of them when implying self-sacrifice hardly deserve to be called lower, relate chiefly to self, and arise from public opinion, matured by experience and cultivation; for they are not practised by rude tribes.

As man advances in civilisation, and small tribes are united into larger communities, the simplest reason would tell each individual that he ought to extend his social instincts and sympathies to all the members of the same nation, though personally unknown to him. This point being once reached, there is only an artificial barrier to prevent his sympathies extending to the men of all nations and races. If, indeed, such men are separated from him by great differences in appearance or habits, experience unfortunately shews us how long it is, before we look at them as our fellow-creatures. Sympathy beyond the confines of man, that is, humanity to the lower animals, seems to be one of the latest moral acquisitions. It is apparently unfelt by savages, except towards their pets. How little the old Romans knew of it is shewn by their abhorrent gladiatorial exhibitions. The very idea of humanity, as far as I could observe, was new to most of the Gauchos of the Pampas. This virtue, one of the noblest with which man is endowed, seems to arise incidentally from our sympathies becoming more tender and more widely diffused, until they are extended to all sentient beings. As soon as this virtue is honoured and practised by some few men, it spreads through instruction and example to the young, and eventually becomes incorporated in public opinion.

The highest possible stage in moral culture is when we recognise that we ought to control our thoughts, and "not even in inmost thought to think again the sins that made

---

46   Good instances are given by Mr. Wallace in Scientific Opinion, Sept. 15, 1869; and more fully in his Contributions to the Theory of Natural Selection, 1870, p. 353.

the past so pleasant to us."[47] Whatever makes any bad action familiar to the mind, renders its performance by so much the easier. As Marcus Aurelius long ago said, "Such as are thy habitual thoughts, such also will be the character of thy mind; for the soul is dyed by the thoughts[48]).

Our great philosopher, Herbert Spencer, has recently explained his views on the moral sense. He says, "I believe that the experiences of utility organised and consolidated through all past generations of the human race, have been producing corresponding modifications, which, by continued transmission and accumulation, have become in us certain faculties of moral intuition-certain emotions responding to right and wrong conduct, which have no apparent basis in the individual experiences of utility."[49] There is not the least inherent improbability, as it seems to me, in virtuous tendencies being more or less strongly inherited; for, not to mention the various dispositions and habits transmitted by many of our domestic animals to their offspring. I have heard of authentic cases in which a desire to steal and a tendency to lie appeared to run in families of the upper ranks; and as stealing is a rare crime in the wealthy classes, we can hardly account by accidental coincidence for the tendency occurring in two or three members of the same family. If bad tendencies are transmitted, it is probable that good ones are likewise transmitted. That the state of the body by affecting the brain, has great influence on the moral tendencies is known to most of those who have suffered from chronic derangements of the digestion or liver. The same fact is likewise shewn by the "perversion or destruction of the moral sense being often one of the earliest symptoms of mental derangement";[50] and insanity is notoriously often inherited. Except through the principle of the transmission of moral tendencies, we cannot understand the differences believed to exist in this respect between the various races of mankind.

Even the partial transmission of virtuous tendencies would be an immense assistance to the primary impulse derived directly and indirectly from the social instincts. Admitting for a moment that virtuous tendencies are inherited, it appears probable, at least in such cases as chastity, temperance, humanity to animals, &c., that they become first impressed on the mental organization through habit, instruction and example, continued during several generations in the same family, and in a quite subordinate degree, or not at all, by the individuals possessing such virtues having succeeded best in the struggle for life. My chief source of doubt with respect to any such inheritance, is that senseless customs, superstitions, and tastes, such as the horror of a Hindoo for unclean food, ought on the same principle to be transmitted. I have not met with any evidence in support of the transmission of superstitious customs or senseless habits, although in itself it

---

47   Tennyson, Idylls of the King, p. 244.
48   Marcus Aurelius, Meditations, Bk. V, sect. 16
49   Letter to Mr. Mill in Bain's Mental and Moral Science, 1868, p. 722.
50   Maudsley, Body and Mind, 1870, p. 60.

is perhaps not less probable than that animals should acquire inherited tastes for certain kinds of food or fear of certain foes.

Finally the social instincts, which no doubt were acquired by man as by the lower animals for the good of the community, will from the first have given to him some wish to aid his fellows, some feeling of sympathy, and have compelled him to regard their approbation and disapprobation. Such impulses will have served him at a very early period as a rude rule of right and wrong. But as man gradually advanced in intellectual power, and was enabled to trace the more remote consequences of his actions; as he acquired sufficient knowledge to reject baneful customs and superstitions; as he regarded more and more, not only the welfare, but the happiness of his fellow-men; as from habit, following on beneficial experience, instruction and example, his sympathies became more tender and widely diffused, extending to men of all races, to the imbecile, maimed, and other useless members of society, and finally to the lower animals, so would the standard of his morality rise higher and higher. And it is admitted by moralists of the derivative school and by some institutions, that the standard of morality has risen since an early period in the history of man.[51]

As a struggle may sometimes be seen going on between the various instincts of the lower animals, it is not surprising that there should be a struggle in man between his social instincts, with their derived virtues, and his lower, though momentarily stronger impulses or desires. This, as Mr. Galton[52] has remarked, is all the less surprising, as man has emerged from a state of barbarism within a comparatively recent period. After having yielded to some temptation we feel a sense of dissatisfaction, shame, repentance, or remorse, analogous to the feelings caused by other powerful instincts or desires, when left unsatisfied or baulked. We compare the weakened impression of a past temptation with the ever present social instincts, or with habits, gained in early youth and strengthened during our whole lives, until they have become almost as strong as instincts. If with the temptation still before us we do not yield, it is because either the social instinct or some custom is at the moment predominant, or because we have learnt that it will appear to us hereafter the stronger, when compared with the weakened impression of the temptation, and we realise that its violation would cause us suffering. Looking to future generations, there is no cause to fear that the social instincts will grow weaker, and we may expect that virtuous habits will grow stronger, becoming perhaps fixed by inheritance. In this case the struggle between our higher and lower impulses will be less severe, and virtue will be triumphant.

---

51   A writer in the North British Review (July, 1869, p. 531), well capable of forming a sound judgment, expresses himself strongly in favour of this conclusion. Mr. Lecky (History of Morals, vol. i., p.143) seems to a certain extent to coincide therein.

52   See his remarkable work on Hereditary Genius, 1869, p. 349. The Duke of Argyll (Primeval Man, 1869, p. 188) has some good remarks on the contest in man's nature between right and wrong.

Summary of the last two Chapters.—There can be no doubt that the difference between the mind of the lowest man and that of the highest animal is immense. An anthropomorphous ape, if he could take a dispassionate view of his own case, would admit that though he could form an artful plan to plunder a garden—though he could use stones for fighting or for breaking open nuts, yet that the thought of fashioning a stone into a tool was quite beyond his scope. Still less, as he would admit, could he follow out a train of metaphysical reasoning, or solve a mathematical problem, or reflect on God, or admire a grand natural scene. Some apes, however, would probably declare that they could and did admire the beauty of the coloured skin and fur of their partners in marriage. They would admit, that though they could make other apes understand by cries some of their perceptions and simpler wants, the notion of expressing definite ideas by definite sounds had never crossed their minds. They might insist that they were ready to aid their fellow-apes of the same troop in many ways, to risk their lives for them, and to take charge of their orphans; but they would be forced to acknowledge that disinterested love for all living creatures, the most noble attribute of man, was quite beyond their comprehension.

Nevertheless the difference in mind between man and the higher animals, great as it is, certainly is one of degree and not of kind. We have seen that the senses and intuitions, the various emotions and faculties, such as love, memory, attention, curiosity, imitation, reason, &c., of which man boasts, may be found in an incipient, or even sometimes in a well-developed condition, in the lower animals. They are also capable of some inherited improvement, as we see in the domestic dog compared with the wolf or jackal. If it could be proved that certain high mental powers, such as the formation of general concepts, self-consciousness, &c. were absolutely peculiar to man, which seems extremely doubtful, it is not improbable that these qualities are merely the incidental results of other highly-advanced intellectual faculties; and these again mainly the result of the continued use of a perfect language. At what age does the new-born infant possess the power of abstraction, or become self-conscious, and reflect on its own existence? We cannot answer; nor can we answer in regard to the ascending organic scale. The half-art, half-instinct of language still bears the stamp of its gradual evolution. The ennobling belief in God is not universal with man; and the belief in spiritual agencies naturally follows from other mental powers. The moral sense perhaps affords the best and highest distinction between man and the lower animals; but I need say nothing on this head, as I have so lately endeavoured to shew that the social instincts,—the prime principle of man's moral constitution[53]—with the aid of active intellectual powers and the effects of habit, naturally lead to the golden rule, "As ye would that men should do to you, do ye to them likewise"; and this lies at the foundation of morality.

---

53   Marcus Aurelius, Meditations, Bk. V, sect. 55

In the next chapter I shall make some few remarks on the probable steps and means by which the several mental and moral faculties of man have been gradually evolved. That such evolution is at least possible, ought not to be denied, for we daily see these faculties developing in every infant; and we may trace a perfect gradation from the mind of an utter idiot, lower than that of an animal low in the scale, to the mind of a Newton.

Leo Tolstoy

Introduction
Robert M. Pallitto

Lev Nikolayevich ("Leo") Tolstoy (1828–1910) was a literary writer whose formidable talents and prolific output earned him a place as one of the greatest writers in history. Born into a wealthy and prominent Russian family, Tolstoy held the title of Count. He served in the Russian Imperial Army during the Crimean War and studied at Kazan University but did not complete a degree. As an adult, Tolstoy returned to the family estate, Yasnaya Polyana ("Bright Glade") outside Moscow, and he lived there for the larger portion of his life with his wife and children. He is best known for his literary masterwork *War and Peace*, which was an epic novel set during the Napoleonic era. He also produced a number of other literary works, including *Sevastopol Sketches* and *Anna Karenina*, before turning to didactic (morally instructive) themes in his later life. Over the span of his lifetime he witnessed Russia's imperial expansion, liberation of the serfs, workers' strikes, and a society moving toward the cusp of revolution. Like Prokudin-Gorsky's famous early color photograph of Tolstoy seated on a bench on the grounds of Yasnaya Polyana, Tolstoy's life and work themselves reveal a thinker rooted in the pre-modern world of Old Russia while also looking forward and prefiguring the wrenching changes soon to come.

War and Peace was published in 1869. According to the philosopher and critic Isaiah Berlin, Tolstoy wrote it after becoming "obsessed by the desire to write a historical novel, one of his principal aims being to contrast the 'real' texture of life, both of individuals and communities, with the 'unreal' picture presented by historians" (33). The world-historical events of the Napoleonic wars are told through the stories of five Russian families, and the details of events in those families allow Tolstoy to capture the texture of history that he sought. Berlin saw Tolstoy seeking to depict inner or spiritual events because "it is they—the 'inner' events—that are the most real, the most immediate experience of human beings; they, and only they, are what life, in the last analysis, is made of" (33).

Tolstoy's aim was to "throw light on the fundamental ethical problems which obsessed him as they did every Russian thinker in the nineteenth century. What is to be done? How should one live? Why are we here? What must we be and do?" (Berlin, 30). Tolstoy pursued these matters even more fervently in his *Confessions* as well as in more strictly didactic works. In the *Confessions* he narrates his early life and describes his arrival at a crisis point in middle age as he seeks but does not immediately find answers to his urgent questions about the meaning and purpose of his life. He asks what will remain after he dies. He questions the significance of his literary fame. He embraces Orthodox Christianity with a Russian cultural orientation but remains critical of some aspects of organized religion. In his intense introspection, Tolstoy displays an acute and perceptive understanding of clinical depression and gives voice, eloquently and lucidly, to the existential questions that engage all of us at some point in our lives. He embraced anarchism and pacifism and in fact experimented with communal living at Yasnaya Polyana.

Whether read as a classic of confessional literature, an autobiographical portrait of a brilliant writer, or an eloquent expression of a spiritual response to the existential crisis that all of us eventually face, Tolstoy's *Confessions* more than repay the reader's effort.

Isaiah Berlin, 1979. *Russian Thinkers*. New York: Penguin Books

A CONFESSION

From The Classical Library (http://www.classicallibrary.org/tolstoy/confession/index.htm)

I

I was baptized and brought up in the Orthodox Christian faith. I was taught it in childhood and throughout my boyhood and youth. But when I abandoned the second course of the university at the age of eighteen I no longer believed any of the things I had been taught.

Judging by certain memories, I never seriously believed them, but had merely relied on what I was taught and on what was professed by the grown-up people around me, and that reliance was very unstable.

I remember that before I was eleven a grammar school pupil, Vladimir Milyutin (long since dead), visited us one Sunday and announced as the latest novelty a discovery made at his school. This discovery was that there is no God and that all we are taught about Him is a mere invention (this was in 1838). I remember how interested my elder brothers were in this information. They called me to their council and we all, I remember, became very animated, and accepted it as something very interesting and quite possible.

I remember also that when my elder brother, Dmitriy, who was then at the university, suddenly, in the passionate way natural to him, devoted himself to religion and began to attend all the Church services, to fast and to lead a pure and moral life, we all—even our elders—unceasingly held him up to ridicule and for some unknown reason called him "Noah". I remember that Musin-Pushkin, the then Curator of Kazan University, when inviting us to dance at his home, ironically persuaded my brother (who was declining the invitation) by the argument that even David danced before the Ark. I sympathized with these jokes made by my elders, and drew from them the conclusion that though it is necessary to learn the catechism and go to church, one must not take such things too seriously. I remember also that I read Voltaire when I was very young, and that his raillery, far from shocking me, amused me very much.

My lapse from faith occurred as is usual among people on our level of education. In most cases, I think, it happens thus: a man lives like everybody else, on the basis of principles not merely having nothing in common with religious doctrine, but generally opposed to it; religious doctrine does not play a part in life, in intercourse with others it is never encountered, and in a man's own life he never has to reckon with it. Religious doctrine is professed far away from life and independently of it. If it is encountered, it is only as an external phenomenon disconnected from life.

Then as now, it was and is quite impossible to judge by a man's life and conduct whether he is a believer or not. If there be a difference between a man who publicly professes orthodoxy and one who denies it, the difference is not in favor of the former. Then as now, the public profession and confession of orthodoxy was chiefly met with among people who were dull and cruel and who considered themselves very important. Ability, honesty, reliability, good-nature and moral conduct, were often met with among unbelievers.

The schools teach the catechism and send the pupils to church, and government officials must produce certificates of having received communion. But a man of our circle who has finished his education and is not in the government service may even now (and formerly it was still easier for him to do so) live for ten or twenty years without once remembering that he is living among Christians and is himself reckoned a member of the orthodox Christian Church.

So that, now as formerly, religious doctrine, accepted on trust and supported by external pressure, thaws away gradually under the influence of knowledge and experience of life which conflict with it, and a man very often lives on, imagining that he still holds intact the religious doctrine imparted to him in childhood whereas in fact not a trace of it remains.

S., a clever and truthful man, once told me the story of how he ceased to believe. On a hunting expedition, when he was already twenty-six, he once, at the place where they put up for the night, knelt down in the evening to pray—a habit retained from childhood. His elder brother, who was at the hunt with him, was lying on some hay and watching him. When S. had finished and was settling down for the night, his brother said to him: "So you still do that?"

They said nothing more to one another. But from that day S. ceased to say his prayers or go to church. And now he has not prayed, received communion, or gone to church, for thirty years. And this not because he knows his brother's convictions and has joined him in them, nor because he has decided anything in his own soul, but simply because the word spoken by his brother was like the push of a finger on a wall that was ready to fall by its own weight. The word only showed that where he thought there was faith, in reality there had long been an empty space, and that therefore the utterance of words and the making of signs of the cross and genuflections while praying were quite senseless actions. Becoming conscious of their senselessness he could not continue them.

So it has been and is, I think, with the great majority of people. I am speaking of people of our educational level who are sincere with themselves, and not of those who make the profession of faith a means of attaining worldly aims. (Such people are the most fundamental infidels, for if faith is for them a means of attaining any worldly aims, then certainly it is not faith.) These people of our education are so placed that the light of knowledge and life has caused an artificial erection to melt away, and they have either already noticed this and swept its place clear, or they have not yet noticed it.

The religious doctrine taught me from childhood disappeared in me as in others, but with this difference, that as from the age of fifteen I began to read philosophical works, my rejection of the doctrine became a conscious one at a very early age. From the time I was sixteen I ceased to say my prayers and ceased to go to church or to fast of my own volition. I did not believe what had been taught me in childhood but I believed in something. What it was I believed in I could not at all have said. I believed in a God, or rather I did not deny God—but I could not have said what sort of God. Neither did I deny Christ and his teaching, but what his teaching consisted in I again could not have said.

Looking back on that time, I now see clearly that my faith—my only real faith—that which apart from my animal instincts gave impulse to my life—was a belief in perfecting myself. But in what this perfecting consisted and what its object was, I could not have said. I tried to perfect myself mentally—I studied everything I could, anything life threw in my way; I tried to perfect my will, I drew up rules I tried to follow; I perfected myself physically, cultivating my strength and agility by all sorts of exercises, and accustoming myself to endurance and patience by all kinds of privations. And all this I considered to be the pursuit of perfection, the beginning of it all was of course moral perfection, but that was soon replaced by perfection in general: by the desire to be better not in my own eyes or those of God but in the eyes of other people. And very soon this effort again changed into a desire to be stronger than others: to be more famous, more important and richer than others.

II

Some day I will narrate the touching and instructive history of my life during those ten years of my youth. I think very many people have had a like experience. With all my soul I wished to be good, but I was young, passionate and alone, completely alone when I sought goodness. Every time I tried to express my most sincere desire, which was to be morally good, I met with contempt and ridicule, but as soon as I yielded to low passions I was praised and encouraged.

Ambition, love of power, covetousness, lasciviousness, pride, anger, and revenge—were all respected.

Yielding to those passions I became like the grown-up folk and felt that they approved of me. The kind aunt with whom I lived, herself the purest of beings, always told me that there was nothing she so desired for me as that I should have relations with a married woman: 'Rien ne forme un jeune homme, comme une liaison avec une femme comme il faut'.[1] Another happiness she desired for me was that I should become an aide-de-camp, and if possible aide-de-camp to the Emperor. But the greatest happiness of all would be that I should marry a very rich girl and so become possessed of as many serfs as possible.

---

1   Nothing so forms a young man as an intimacy with a woman of good breeding.

I cannot think of those years without horror, loathing and heartache. I killed men in war and challenged men to duels in order to kill them. I lost at cards, consumed the labor of the peasants, sentenced them to punishments, lived loosely, and deceived people. Lying, robbery, adultery of all kinds, drunkenness, violence, murder—there was no crime I did not commit, and in spite of that people praised my conduct and my contemporaries considered and consider me to be a comparatively moral man.

So I lived for ten years.

During that time I began to write from vanity, covetousness, and pride. In my writings I did the same as in my life, to get fame and money, for the sake of which I wrote, it was necessary to hide the good and to display the evil, and I did so. How often in my writings I contrived to hide under the guise of indifference, or even of banter, those strivings of mine towards goodness which gave meaning to my life! And I succeeded in this and was praised.

At twenty-six years of age[2] I returned to Petersburg after the war, and met the writers. They received me as one of themselves and flattered me. And before I had time to look round I had adopted the views on life of the set of authors I had come among, and these views completely obliterated all my former strivings to improve—they furnished a theory which justified the dissoluteness of my life.

The view of life of these people, my comrades in authorship, consisted in this: that life in general goes on developing, and in this development we—men of thought—have the chief part; and among men of thought it is we—artists and poets—who have the greatest influence. Our vocation is to teach mankind. And lest the simple question should suggest itself: What do I know, and what can I teach? it was explained in this theory that this need not be known, and that the artist and poet teach unconsciously. I was considered an admirable artist and poet, and therefore it was very natural for me to adopt this theory. I, artist and poet, wrote and taught without myself knowing what. For this I was paid money; I had excellent food, lodging, women, and society; and I had fame, which showed that what I taught was very good.

This faith in the meaning of poetry and in the development of life was a religion, and I was one of its priests. To be its priest was very pleasant and profitable. And I lived a considerable time in this faith without doubting its validity. But in the second and still more in the third year of this life I began to doubt the infallibility of this religion and to examine it. My first cause of doubt was that I began to notice that the priests of this religion were not all in accord among themselves. Some said: We are the best and most useful teachers; we teach what is needed, but the others teach wrongly. Others said: No! we are the real teachers, and you teach wrongly, and they disputed, quarrelled, abused,

---

2   He was in fact 27 at the time.

cheated, and tricked one another. There were also many among us who did not care who was right and who was wrong, but were simply bent on attaining their covetous aims by means of this activity of ours. All this obliged me to doubt the validity of our creed.

Moreover, having begun to doubt the truth of the authors' creed itself, I also began to observe its priests more attentively, and I became convinced that almost all the priests of that religion, the writers, were immoral, and for the most part men of bad, worthless character, much inferior to those whom I had met in my former dissipated and military life; but they were self-confident and self-satisfied as only those can be who are quite holy or who do not know what holiness is. These people revolted me, I became revolting to myself, and I realized that that faith was a fraud.

But strange to say, though I understood this fraud and renounced it, yet I did not renounce the rank these people gave me: the rank of artist, poet, and teacher. I naively imagined that I was a poet and artist and could teach everybody without myself knowing what I was teaching, and I acted accordingly.

From my intimacy with these men I acquired a new vice: abnormally developed pride and an insane assurance that it was my vocation to teach men, without knowing what.

To remember that time, and my own state of mind and that of those men (though there are thousands like them today), is sad and terrible and ludicrous, and arouses exactly the feeling one experiences in a lunatic asylum.

We were all then convinced that it was necessary for us to speak, write, and print as quickly as possible and as much as possible, and that it was all wanted for the good of humanity. And thousands of us, contradicting and abusing one another, all printed and wrote—teaching others. And without noticing that we knew nothing, and that to the simplest of life's questions: What is good and what is evil? we did not know how to reply, we all talked at the same time, not listening to one another, sometimes seconding and praising one another in order to be seconded and praised in turn, sometimes getting angry with one another—just as in a lunatic asylum.

Thousands of workmen laboured to the extreme limit of their strength day and night, setting the type and printing millions of words which the post carried all over Russia, and we still went on teaching and could in no way find time to teach enough, and were always angry that sufficient attention was not paid us.

It was terribly strange, but is now quite comprehensible. Our real innermost concern was to get as much money and praise as possible. To gain that end we could do nothing except write books and papers. So we did that. But in order to do such useless work and to feel assured that we were very important people we required a theory justifying our activity. And so among us this theory was devised: "All that exists is reasonable. All that exists develops. And it all develops by means of Culture. And Culture is measured by the circulation of books and newspapers. And we are paid money and are respected because we write books and newspapers, and therefore we are the most useful and the best of men." This theory would have been all very well if we had been unanimous, but as every thought expressed by one of us was always met by a diametrically opposite thought expressed by another, we ought to have been driven to reflection. But we ignored this; people paid us money and those on our side praised us, so each of us considered himself justified.

It is now clear to me that this was just as in a lunatic asylum; but then I only dimly suspected this, and like all lunatics, simply called all men lunatics except myself.

III

So I lived, abandoning myself to this insanity for another six years, till my marriage. During that time I went abroad. Life in Europe and my acquaintance with leading and learned Europeans[3] confirmed me yet more in the faith of striving after perfection in which I believed, for I found the same faith among them. That faith took with me the common form it assumes with the majority of educated people of our day. It was expressed by the word "progress". It then appeared to me that this word meant something. I did not as yet understand that, being tormented (like every vital man) by the question how it is best for me to live, in my answer, "Live in conformity with progress", I was like a man in a boat who when carried along by wind and waves should reply to what for him is the chief and only question, "whither to steer", by saying, "We are being carried somewhere".

I did not then notice this. Only occasionally—not by reason but by instinct—I revolted against this superstition so common in our day, by which people hide from themselves their lack of understanding of life.... So, for instance, during my stay in Paris, the sight of an execution revealed to me the instability of my superstitious belief in progress. When I saw the head part from the body and how they thumped separately into the box, I understood, not with my mind but with my whole being, that no theory of the reasonableness of our present progress could justify this deed; and that though everybody from the creation of the world had held it to be necessary, on whatever theory, I knew it to be unnecessary and bad; and therefore the arbiter of what is good and evil is not what people say and do, nor is it progress, but it is my heart and I. Another instance of a realization that the superstitious belief in progress is insufficient as a guide to life, was my brother's death. Wise, good, serious, he fell ill while still a young man, suffered for more than a year, and died painfully, not understanding why he had lived and still less why he had to die. No theories could give me, or him, any reply to these questions during his slow and painful dying. But these were only rare instances of doubt, and I

---

3   Russians generally make a distinction between Europeans and Russians.—A.M.

actually continued to live professing a faith only in progress. "Everything evolves and I evolve with it: and why it is that I evolve with all things will be known someday." So I ought to have formulated my faith at that time.

On returning from abroad I settled in the country and chanced to occupy myself with peasant schools. This work was particularly to my taste because in it I had not to face the falsity which had become obvious to me and stared me in the face when I tried to teach people by literary means. Here also I acted in the name of progress, but I already regarded progress itself critically. I said to myself: "In some of its developments progress has proceeded wrongly, and with primitive peasant children one must deal in a spirit of perfect freedom, letting them choose what path of progress they please." In reality I was ever revolving round one and the same insoluble problem, which was: How to teach without knowing what to teach. In the higher spheres of literary activity I had realized that one could not teach without knowing what, for I saw that people all taught differently, and by quarrelling among themselves only succeeded in hiding their ignorance from one another. But here, with peasant children, I thought to evade this difficulty by letting them learn what they liked. It amuses me now when I remember how I shuffled in trying to satisfy my desire to teach, while in the depth of my soul I knew very well that I could not teach anything needful for I did not know what was needful. After spending a year at school work I went abroad a second time to discover how to teach others while myself knowing nothing.

And it seemed to me that I had learnt this abroad, and in the year of the peasants' emancipation (1861) I returned to Russia armed with all this wisdom, and having become an Arbiter[4] I began to teach, both the uneducated peasants in schools and the educated classes through a magazine I published. Things appeared to be going well, but I felt I was not quite sound mentally and that matters could not long continue in that way. And I should perhaps then have come to the state of despair I reached fifteen years later had there not been one side of life still unexplored by me which promised me happiness: that was my marriage.

For a year I busied myself with arbitration work, the schools, and the magazine; and I became so worn out—as a result especially of my mental confusion—and so hard was my struggle as Arbiter, so obscure the results of my activity in the schools, so repulsive my shuffling in the magazine (which always amounted to one and the same thing: a desire to teach everybody and to hide the fact that I did not know what to teach), that I fell ill, mentally rather than physically, threw up everything, and went away to the Bashkirs in the steppes, to breathe fresh air, drink kumys[5], and live a merely animal life.

Returning from there I married. The new conditions of happy family life completely

---

4   To keep peace between peasants and owners.—A.M.
5   A fermented drink prepared from mare's milk.—A.M.

diverted me from all search for the general meaning of life. My whole life was centered at that time in my family, wife and children, and therefore in care to increase our means of livelihood. My striving after self-perfection, for which I had already substituted a striving for perfection in general, i.e., progress, was now again replaced by the effort simply to secure the best possible conditions for myself and my family.

So another fifteen years passed.

In spite of the fact that I now regarded authorship as of no importance—the temptation of immense monetary rewards and applause for my insignificant work—and I devoted myself to it as a means of improving my material position and of stifling in my soul all questions as to the meaning of my own life or life in general.

I wrote: teaching what was for me the only truth, namely, that one should live so as to have the best for oneself and one's family.

So I lived; but five years ago something very strange began to happen to me. At first I experienced moments of perplexity and arrest of life, as though I did not know what to do or how to live; and I felt lost and became dejected. But this passed and I went on living as before. Then these moments of perplexity began to recur oftener and oftener, and always in the same form. They were always expressed by the questions: What is it for? What does it lead to?

At first it seemed to me that these were aimless and irrelevant questions. I thought that it was all well known, and that if I should ever wish to deal with the solution it would not cost me much effort; just at present I had no time for it, but when I wanted to I should be able to find the answer. The questions however began to repeat themselves frequently, and to demand replies more and more insistently; and like drops of ink always falling on one place they ran together into one black blot.

Then occurred what happens to everyone sickening with a mortal internal disease. At first trivial signs of indisposition appear to which the sick man pays no attention; then these signs reappear more and more often and merge into one uninterrupted period of suffering. The suffering increases, and before the sick man can look round, what he took for a mere indisposition has already become more important to him than anything else in the world—it is death!

That is what happened to me. I understood that it was no casual indisposition but something very important, and that if these questions constantly repeated themselves they would have to be answered. And I tried to answer them. The questions seemed such stupid, simple, childish ones; but as soon as I touched them and tried to solve them I at once became convinced, first, that they are not childish and stupid but the most important and profound of life's questions; and secondly that, occupying myself with my Samara estate, the education of my son, or the writing of a book, I had to know why I was doing it. As long as I did not know why, I could do nothing and could not live. Amid the thoughts of estate management which greatly occupied me at that time, the question would suddenly occur: "Well, you will have 6,000 desyatin as[6] of land in Samara Government and 300 horses, and what then?" .... And I was quite disconcerted and did not know what to think. Or when considering plans for the education of my children, I would say to myself: "What for?" Or when considering how the peasants might become prosperous, I would suddenly say to myself: "But what does it matter to me?" Or when thinking of the fame my works would bring me, I would say to myself, "Very well; you will be more famous than Gogol or Pushkin or Shakespeare or Moliere, or than all the writers in the world—and what of it?" And I could find no reply at all. The questions would not wait, they had to be answered at once, and if I did not answer them it was impossible to live. But there was no answer.

I felt that what I had been standing on had collapsed and that I had nothing left under my feet. What I had lived on no longer existed, and there was nothing left.

IV

My life came to a standstill. I could breathe, eat, drink, and sleep, and I could not help doing these things; but there was no life, for there were no wishes the fulfillment of which I could consider reasonable. If I desired anything, I knew in advance that whether I satisfied my desire or not, nothing would come of it. Had a fairy come and offered to fulfil my desires I should not have known what to ask. If in moments of intoxication I felt something which, though not a wish, was a habit left by former wishes, in sober moments I knew this to be a delusion and that there was really nothing to wish for. I could not even wish to know the truth, for I guessed of what it consisted. The truth was that life is meaningless. I had as it were lived, lived, and walked, walked, till I had come to a precipice and saw clearly that there was nothing ahead of me but destruction. It was impossible to stop, impossible to go back, and impossible to close my eyes or avoid seeing that there was nothing ahead but suffering and real death—complete annihilation.

It had come to this, that I, a healthy, fortunate man, felt I could no longer live: some irresistible power impelled me to rid myself one way or other of life. I cannot say I wished to kill myself. The power which drew me away from life was stronger, fuller, and more widespread than any mere wish. It was a force similar to the former striving to live, only in a contrary direction. All my strength drew me away from life. The thought of self-destruction now came to me as naturally as thoughts of how to improve my life had come formerly, and it was seductive that I had to be cunning with myself lest I should carry it out too hastily. I did not wish to hurry, because I wanted to use all efforts to disentangle the matter. "If I cannot unravel matters, there will always be time." And it was then that I, a man favoured by fortune, hid a cord from myself lest I should hang

6   The desyatina is about 2.75 acres.—A.M.

myself from the crosspiece of the partition in my room where I undressed alone every evening, and I ceased to go out shooting with a gun lest I should be tempted by so easy a way of ending my life. I did not myself know what I wanted: I feared life, desired to escape from it, yet still hoped something of it.

And all this befell me at a time when all around me I had what is considered complete good fortune. I was not yet fifty; I had a good wife who loved me and whom I loved, good children, and a large estate which without much effort on my part improved and increased. I was respected by my relations and acquaintances more than at any previous time. I was praised by others and without much self-deception could consider that my name was famous. And far from being insane or mentally diseased, I enjoyed on the contrary a strength of mind and body such as I have seldom met with among men of my kind; physically I could keep up with the peasants at mowing, and mentally I could work for eight and ten hours at a stretch without experiencing any ill results from such exertion. And in this situation I came to this—that I could not live, and, fearing death, had to employ cunning with myself to avoid taking my own life.

My mental condition presented itself to me in this way: my life is a stupid and spiteful joke someone has played on me. Though I did not acknowledge a "someone" who created me, yet such a presentation—that someone had played an evil and stupid joke on my by placing me in the world—was the form of expression that suggested itself most naturally to me.

Involuntarily it appeared to me that there, somewhere, was someone who amused himself by watching how I lived for thirty or forty years: learning, developing, maturing in body and mind, and how, having with matured mental powers reached the summit of life from which it all lay before me, I stood on that summit—like an arch-fool—seeing clearly that there is nothing in life, and that there has been and will be nothing. And he was amused. . . .

But whether that "someone" laughing at me existed or not, I was none the better off. I could give no reasonable meaning to any single action or to my whole life. I was only surprised that I could have avoided understanding this from the very beginning—it has been so long known to all. Today or tomorrow sickness and death will come (they had come already) to those I love or to me; nothing will remain but stench and worms. Sooner or later my affairs, whatever they may be, will be forgotten, and I shall not exist. Then why go on making any effort? . . . How can man fail to see this? And how go on living? That is what is surprising! One can only live while one is intoxicated with life; as soon as one is sober it is impossible not to see that it is all a mere fraud and a stupid fraud! That is precisely what it is: there is nothing either amusing or witty about it, it is simply cruel and stupid.

There is an Eastern fable, told long ago, of a traveller overtaken on a plain by an enraged beast. Escaping from the beast he gets into a dry well, but sees at the bottom of the well a dragon that has opened its jaws to swallow him. And the unfortunate man, not daring to climb out lest he should be destroyed by the enraged beast, and not daring to leap to the bottom of the well lest he should be eaten by the dragon, seizes a twig growing in a crack in the well and clings to it. His hands are growing weaker and he feels he will soon have to resign himself to the destruction that awaits him above or below, but still he clings on. Then he sees that two mice, a black one and a white one, go regularly round and round the stem of the twig to which he is clinging and gnaw at it. And soon the twig itself will snap and he will fall into the dragon's jaws. The traveller sees this and knows that he will inevitably perish; but while still hanging he looks around, sees some drops of honey on the leaves of the twig, reaches them with his tongue and licks them. So I too clung to the twig of life, knowing that the dragon of death was inevitably awaiting me, ready to tear me to pieces; and I could not understand why I had fallen into such torment. I tried to lick the honey which formerly consoled me, but the honey no longer gave me pleasure, and the white and black mice of day and night gnawed at the branch by which I hung. I saw the dragon clearly and the honey no longer tasted sweet. I only saw the unescapable dragon and the mice, and I could not tear my gaze from them; and this is not a fable but the real unanswerable truth intelligible to all.

The deception of the joys of life which formerly allayed my terror of the dragon now no longer deceived me. No matter how often I may be told, "You cannot understand the meaning of life so do not think about it, but live," I can no longer do it: I have already done it too long. I cannot now help seeing day and night going round and bringing me to death. That is all I see, for that alone is true. All else is false.

The two drops of honey which diverted my eyes from the cruel truth longer than the rest: my love of family, and of writing—art as I called it—were no longer sweet to me.

"Family" . . . said I to myself. But my family—wife and children—are also human. They are placed just as I am: they must either live in a lie or see the terrible truth. Why should they live? Why should I love them, guard them, bring them up, or watch them? That they may come to the despair that I feel, or else be stupid? Loving them, I cannot hide the truth from them: each step in knowledge leads them to the truth. And the truth is death.

"Art, poetry?" . . . Under the influence of success and the praise of men, I had long assured myself that this was a thing one could do though death was drawing near—death which destroys all things, including my work and its remembrance; but soon I saw that that too was a fraud. It was plain to me that art is an adornment of life, an allurement to life. But life had lost its attraction for me, so how could I attract others? As long as I was not living my own life but was borne on the waves of some other life—as long as

I believed that life had a meaning, though one I could not express—the reflection of life in poetry and art of all kinds afforded me pleasure: it was pleasant to look at life in the mirror of art. But when I began to seek the meaning of life and felt the necessity of living my own life, that mirror became for me unnecessary, superfluous, ridiculous. or painful. I could no longer soothe myself with what I now saw in the mirror, namely, that my position was stupid and desperate. It was all very well to enjoy the sight when in the depth of my soul I believed that my life had a meaning. Then the play of lights—comic, tragic, touching, beautiful, and terrible—in life amused me. No sweetness of honey could be sweet to me when I saw the dragon and saw the mice gnawing away my support.

Nor was that all. Had I simply understood that life had no meaning I could have borne it quietly, knowing that that was my lot. But I could not satisfy myself with that. Had I been like a man living in a wood from which he knows there is no exit, I could have lived; but I was like one lost in a wood who, horrified at having lost his way, rushes about wishing to find the road. He knows that each step he takes confuses him more and more, but still he cannot help rushing about.

It was indeed terrible. And to rid myself of the terror I wished to kill myself. I experienced terror at what awaited me—knew that that terror was even worse than the position I was in, but still I could not patiently await the end. However convincing the argument might be that in any case some vessel in my heart would give way, or something would burst and all would be over, I could not patiently await that end. The horror of darkness was too great, and I wished to free myself from it as quickly as possible by noose or bullet. That was the feeling which drew me most strongly towards suicide.

V

"But perhaps I have overlooked something, or misunderstood something?" I said to myself several times. "It cannot be that this condition of despair is natural to man!" And I sought for an explanation of these problems in all the branches of knowledge acquired by men. I sought painfully and long, not from idle curiosity or listlessly, but painfully and persistently day and night—sought as a perishing man seeks for safety—and I found nothing.

I sought in all the sciences, but far from finding what I wanted, became convinced that all who like myself had sought in knowledge for the meaning of life had found nothing. And not only had they found nothing, but they had plainly acknowledged that the very thing which made me despair—namely the senselessness of life—is the one indubitable thing man can know.

I sought everywhere; and thanks to a life spent in learning, and thanks also to my relations with the scholarly world, I had access to scientists and scholars in all branches of knowledge, and they readily showed me all their knowledge, not only in books but also in conversation, so that I had at my disposal all that science has to say on this question of life.

I was long unable to believe that it gives no other reply to life's questions than that which it actually does give. It long seemed to me, when I saw the important and serious air with which science announces its conclusions which have nothing in common with the real questions of human life, that there was something I had not understood. I long was timid before science, and it seemed to me that the lack of conformity between the answers and my questions arose not by the fault of science but from my ignorance, but the matter was for me not a game or an amusement but one of life and death, and I was involuntarily brought to the conviction that my questions were the only legitimate ones, forming the basis of all knowledge, and that I with my questions was not to blame, but science if it pretends to reply to those questions.

My question—that which at the age of fifty brought me to the verge of suicide—was the simplest of questions, lying in the soul of every man from the foolish child to the wisest elder: it was a question without an answer to which one cannot live, as I had found by experience. It was: "What will come of what I am doing today or shall do tomorrow? What will come of my whole life?"

Differently expressed, the question is: "Why should I live, why wish for anything, or do anything?" It can also be expressed thus: "Is there any meaning in my life that the inevitable death awaiting me does not destroy?"

To this one question, variously expressed, I sought an answer in science. And I found that in relation to that question all human knowledge is divided as it were into two opposite hemispheres at the ends of which are two poles: the one a negative and the other a positive; but that neither at the one nor the other pole is there an answer to life's questions.

The one series of sciences seems not to recognize the question, but replies clearly and exactly to its own independent questions: that is the series of experimental sciences, and at the extreme end of it stands mathematics. The other series of sciences recognizes the question, but does not answer it; that is the series of abstract sciences, and at the extreme end of it stands metaphysics.

From early youth I had been interested in the abstract sciences, but later the mathematical and natural sciences attracted me, and until I put my question definitely to myself, until that question had itself grown up within me urgently demanding a decision, I contented myself with those counterfeit answers which science gives.

Now in the experimental sphere I said to myself: "Everything develops and differentiates itself, moving towards complexity and perfection, and there are laws directing this movement. You are a part of the whole. Having learnt as far as possible the whole, and having learnt the law of evolution, you will understand also your place in the whole and will know yourself." Ashamed as I am to confess it, there was a time when I seemed satisfied with that. It was just the time when I was myself becoming more complex and was developing. My muscles were growing and strengthening, my memory was being enriched, my capacity to think and understand was increasing, I was growing and developing; and feeling this growth in myself it was natural for me to think that such was the universal law in which I should find the solution of the question of my life. But a time came when the growth within me ceased. I felt that I was not developing, but fading, my muscles were weakening, my teeth falling out, and I saw that the law not only did not explain anything to me, but that there never had been or could be such a law, and that I had taken for a law what I had found in myself at a certain period of my life. I regarded the definition of that law more strictly. and it became clear to me that there could be no law of endless development; it became clear that to say, "in infinite space and time everything develops, becomes more perfect and more complex, is differentiated", is to say nothing at all. These are all words with no meaning, for in the infinite there is neither complex nor simple, neither forward nor backward, nor better or worse.

Above all, my personal question, "What am I with my desires?" remained quite unanswered. And I understood that those sciences are very interesting and attractive, but that they are exact and clear in inverse proportion to their applicability to the question of life: the less their applicability to the question of life, the more exact and clear they are, while the more they try to reply to the question of life, the more obscure and unattractive they become. If one turns to the division of sciences which attempt to reply to the questions of life—to physiology, psychology, biology, sociology—one encounters an appalling poverty of thought, the greatest obscurity, a quite unjustifiable pretension to solve irrelevant question, and a continual contradiction of each authority by others and even by himself. If one turns to the branches of science which are not concerned with the solution of the questions of life, but which reply to their own special scientific questions, one is enraptured by the power of man's mind, but one knows in advance that they give no reply to life's questions. Those sciences simply ignore life's questions. They say: "To the question of what you are and why you live we have no reply, and are not occupied with that; but if you want to know the laws of light, of chemical combinations, the laws of development of organisms, if you want to know the laws of bodies and their form, and the relation of numbers and quantities, if you want to know the laws of your mind, to all that we have clear, exact and unquestionable replies."

In general the relation of the experimental sciences to life's question may be expressed thus: Question: "Why do I live?" Answer: "In infinite space, in infinite time, infinitely small particles change their forms in infinite complexity, and when you have understood the laws of those mutations of form you will understand why you live on the earth."

Then in the sphere of abstract science I said to myself: "All humanity lives and develops on the basis of spiritual principles and ideals which guide it. Those ideals are expressed in religions, in sciences, in arts, in forms of government. Those ideals become more and more elevated, and humanity advances to its highest welfare. I am part of humanity, and therefore my vocation is to forward the recognition and the realization of the ideals of humanity." And at the time of my weak-mindedness I was satisfied with that; but as soon as the question of life presented itself clearly to me, those theories immediately crumbled away. Not to speak of the unscrupulous obscurity with which those sciences announce conclusions formed on the study of a small part of mankind as general conclusions; not to speak of the mutual contradictions of different adherents of this view as to what are the ideals of humanity; the strangeness, not to say stupidity, of the theory consists in the fact that in order to reply to the question facing each man: "What am I?" or "Why do I live?" or "What must I do?" one has first to decide the question: "What is the life of the whole?" (which is to him unknown and of which he is acquainted with one tiny part in one minute period of time). To understand what he is, one man must first understand all this mysterious humanity, consisting of people such as himself who do not understand one another.

I have to confess that there was a time when I believed this. It was the time when I had my own favourite ideals justifying my own caprices, and I was trying to devise a theory which would allow one to consider my caprices as the law of humanity. But as soon as the question of life arose in my soul in full clearness that reply at once flew to dust. And I understood that as in the experimental sciences there are real sciences, and semi-sciences which try to give answers to questions beyond their competence, so in this sphere there is a whole series of most diffused sciences which try to reply to irrelevant questions. Semi-sciences of that kind, the juridical and the social-historical, endeavour to solve the questions of a man's life by pretending to decide, each in its own way, the question of the life of all humanity.

But as in the sphere of man's experimental knowledge one who sincerely inquires how he is to live cannot be satisfied with the reply—"Study in endless space the mutations, infinite in time and in complexity, of innumerable atoms, and then you will understand your life"—so also a sincere man cannot be satisfied with the reply: "Study the whole life of humanity of which we cannot know either the beginning or the end, of which we do not even know a small part, and then you will understand your own life." And like the experimental semi-sciences, so these other semi-sciences are the more filled with obscurities, inexactitudes, stupidities, and contradictions, the further they diverge from the real problems. The problem of experimental science is the sequence of cause and effect in material phenomena. It is only necessary for experimental science to introduce the question of a final cause for it to become nonsensical. The problem of abstract science is the recognition of the primordial essence of life. It is only necessary to introduce the investigation of consequential phenomena (such as social and historical phenomena) and it also becomes nonsensical.

Experimental science only then gives positive knowledge and displays the greatness of the human mind when it does not introduce into its investigations the question of an ultimate cause. And, on the contrary, abstract science is only then science and displays the greatness of the human mind when it puts quite aside questions relating to the consequential causes of phenomena and regards man solely in relation to an ultimate cause. Such in this realm of science—forming the pole of the sphere—is metaphysics or philosophy. That science states the question clearly: "What am I, and what is the universe? And why do I exist, and why does the universe exist?" And since it has existed it has always replied in the same way. Whether the philosopher calls the essence of life existing within me, and in all that exists, by the name of "idea", or "substance", or "spirit", or "will", he says one and the same thing: that this essence exists and that I am of that same essence; but why it is he does not know, and does not say, if he is an exact thinker. I ask: "Why should this essence exist? What results from the fact that it is and will be?" . . . And philosophy not merely does not reply, but is itself only asking that question. And if it is real philosophy all its labour lies merely in trying to put that question clearly. And if it keeps firmly to its task it cannot reply to the question otherwise than thus: "What am I, and what is the universe?" "All and nothing"; and to the question "Why?" by "I do not know".

So that however I may turn these replies of philosophy, I can never obtain anything like an answer—and not because, as in the clear experimental sphere, the reply does not relate to my question, but because here, though all the mental work is directed just to my question, there is no answer, but instead of an answer one gets the same question, only in a complex form.

VI

In my search for answers to life's questions I experienced just what is felt by a man lost in a forest.

He reaches a glade, climbs a tree, and clearly sees the limitless distance, but sees that his home is not and cannot be there; then he goes into the dark wood and sees the darkness, but there also his home is not.

So I wandered that wood of human knowledge, amid the gleams of mathematical and experimental science which showed me clear horizons but in a direction where there could be no home, and also amid the darkness of the abstract sciences where I was immersed in deeper gloom the further I went, and where I finally convinced myself that there was, and could be, no exit.

Yielding myself to the bright side of knowledge, I understood that I was only diverting my gaze from the question. However alluringly clear those horizons which opened out before me might be, however alluring it might be to immerse oneself in the limitless expanse of those sciences, I already understood that the clearer they were the less they met my need and the less they applied to my question.

"I know," said I to myself, "what science so persistently tries to discover, and along that road there is no reply to the question as to the meaning of my life." In the abstract sphere I understood that notwithstanding the fact, or just because of the fact, that the direct aim of science is to reply to my question, there is no reply but that which I have myself already given: "What is the meaning of my life?" "There is none." Or: "What will come of my life?" "Nothing." Or: "Why does everything exist that exists, and why do I exist?" "Because it exists."

Inquiring for one region of human knowledge, I received an innumerable quantity of exact replies concerning matters about which I had not asked: about the chemical constituents of the stars, about the movement of the sun towards the constellation Hercules, about the origin of species and of man, about the forms of infinitely minute imponderable particles of ether; but in this sphere of knowledge the only answer to my question, "What is the meaning of my life?" was: "You are what you call your 'life'; you are a transitory, casual cohesion of particles. The mutual interactions and changes of these particles produce in you what you call your 'life'. That cohesion will last some time; afterwards the interaction of these particles will cease and what you call 'life' will cease, and so will all your questions. You are an accidentally united little lump of some-thing, that little lump ferments. The little lump calls that fermenting its 'life'. The lump will disintegrate and there will be an end of the fermenting and of all the questions." So answers the clear side of science and cannot answer otherwise if it strictly follows its principles.

From such a reply one sees that the reply does not answer the question. I want to know the meaning of my life, but that it is a fragment of the infinite, far from giving it a mean-ing destroys its every possible meaning. The obscure compromises which that side of experimental exact science makes with abstract science when it says that the meaning of life consists in development and in cooperation with development, owing to their inexactness and obscurity cannot be considered as replies.

The other side of science—the abstract side—when it holds strictly to its principles, replying directly to the question, always replies, and in all ages has replied, in one and the same way: "The world is something infinite and incomprehensible part of that incomprehensible 'all'." Again I exclude all those compromises between abstract and experimental sciences which supply the whole ballast of the semi-sciences called juridi-cal, political, and historical. In those semi-sciences the conception of development and progress is again wrongly introduced, only with this difference, that there it was the development of everything while here it is the development of the life of mankind. The error is there as before: development and progress in infinity can have no aim or direction, and, as far as my question is concerned, no answer is given.

In truly abstract science, namely in genuine philosophy—not in that which Schopenhauer calls "professorial philosophy" which serves only to classify all existing phenomena in new philosophic categories and to call them by new names—where the philosopher does not lose sight of the essential question, the reply is always one and the same—the reply given by Socrates, Schopenhauer, Solomon, and Buddha.

"We approach truth only inasmuch as we depart from life", said Socrates when preparing for death. "For what do we, who love truth, strive after in life? To free ourselves from the body, and from all the evil that is caused by the life of the body! If so, then how can we fail to be glad when death comes to us?

"The wise man seeks death all his life and therefore death is not terrible to him."

And Schopenhauer says:

"Having recognized the inmost essence of the world as will, and all its phenomena—from the unconscious working of the obscure forces of Nature up to the completely conscious action of man—as only the objectivity of that will, we shall in no way avoid the conclusion that together with the voluntary renunciation and self-destruction of the will all those phenomena also disappear, that constant striving and effort without aim or rest on all the stages of objectivity in which and through which the world exists; the diversity of successive forms will disappear, and together with the form all the manifestations of will, with its most universal forms, space and time, and finally its most fundamental form—subject and object. Without will there is no concept and no world. Before us, certainly, nothing remains. But what resists this transition into annihilation, our nature, is only that same wish to live—Wille zum Leben—which forms ourselves as well as our world. That we are so afraid of annihilation or, what is the same thing, that we so wish to live, merely means that we are ourselves nothing else but this desire to live, and know nothing but it. And so what remains after the complete annihilation of the will, for us who are so full of the will, is, of course, nothing; but on the other hand, for those in whom the will has turned and renounced itself, this so real world of ours with all its suns and milky way is nothing."

"Vanity of vanities", says Solomon—"vanity of vanities—all is vanity. What profit hath a man of all his labor which he taketh under the sun? One generation passeth away, and another generation commeth: but the earth abideth for ever.... The thing that hath been, is that which shall be; and that which is done is that which shall be done: and there is no new thing under the sun. Is there anything whereof it may be said, See, this is new? it hath been already of old time, which was before us, there is no remembrance of former things; neither shall there be any remembrance of things that are to come with those that shall come after. I the Preacher was King over Israel in Jerusalem. And I gave my heart to seek and search out by wisdom concerning all that is done under heaven: this sore travail hath God given to the sons of man to be exercised therewith. I have seen all the works that are done under the sun; and behold, all is vanity and vexation of spirit. . . . I communed with my own heart, saying, Lo, I am come to great estate, and have gotten more wisdom than all they that have been before me over Jerusalem: yea, my heart hath great experience of wisdom and knowledge. And I gave my heart to know wisdom, and to know madness and folly: I perceived that this also is vexation of spirit. For in much wisdom is much grief: and he that increaseth knowledge increaseth sorrow.

"I said in my heart, Go to now, I will prove thee with mirth, therefore enjoy pleasure: and behold this also is vanity. I said of laughter, It is mad: and of mirth, What doeth it? I sought in my heart how to cheer my flesh with wine, and while my heart was guided by wisdom, to lay hold on folly, till I might see what it was good for the sons of men that they should do under heaven the number of the days of their life. I made me great works; I builded me houses; I planted me vineyards; I made me gardens and orchards, and I planted trees in them of all kinds of fruits: I made me pools of water, to water therefrom the forest where trees were reared: I got me servants and maidens, and had servants born in my house; also I had great possessions of herds and flocks above all that were before me in Jerusalem: I gathered me also silver and gold and the peculiar treasure from kings and from the provinces: I got me men singers and women singers; and the delights of the sons of men, as musical instruments and all that of all sorts. So I was great, and increased more than all that were before me in Jerusalem: also my wisdom re-mained with me. And whatever mine eyes desired I kept not from them. I withheld not my heart from any joy. . . . Then I looked on all the works that my hands had wrought, and on the labour that I had laboured to do: and, behold, all was vanity and vexation of spirit, and there was no profit from them under the sun. And I turned myself to behold wisdom, and madness, and folly. . . . But I perceived that one even happeneth to them all. Then said I in my heart, As it happeneth to the fool, so it happeneth even to me, and why was I then more wise? then I said in my heart, that this also is vanity. For there is no remembrance of the wise more than of the fool for ever; seeing that which now is in the days to come shall all be forgotten. And how dieth the wise man? as the fool. Therefore I hated life; because the work that is wrought under the sun is grievous unto me: for all is vanity and vexation of spirit. Yea, I hated all my labour which I had taken under the sun: seeing that I must leave it unto the man that shall be after me. . . . For what hath man of all his labour, and of the vexation of his heart, wherein he hath laboured under the sun? For all his days are sorrows, and his travail grief; yea, even in the night his heart taketh no rest, this is also vanity. Man is not blessed with security that he should eat and drink and cheer his soul from his own labour. . . . All things come alike to all: there is one event to the righteous and to the wicked; to the good and to the evil; to the clean and to the unclean; to him that sacrificeth and to him that sacrificeth not; as is the good, so is the sinner; and he that sweareth, as he that feareth an oath. This is an evil in all that is done under the sun, that there is one event unto all; yea, also the heart of the sons of men is full of evil, and madness is in their heart while they live, and after that they go to the dead. For him that is among the living there is hope: for a living dog is better than a dead lion. For the living know that they shall die: but the dead know not any thing, neither have they any more a reward; for the memory of them is forgotten. Also their love, and their hatred, and their envy, is now perished; neither have they any more a portion for ever in anything that is done under the sun."

So said Solomon, or whoever wrote those words.[7]

And this is what the Indian wisdom tells:

Sakya Muni, a young, happy prince, from whom the existence of sickness, old age, and death had been hidden, went out to drive and saw a terrible old man, toothless and slobbering. The prince, from whom till then old age had been concealed, was amazed, and asked his driver what it was, and how that man had come to such a wretched and disgusting condition, and when he learnt that this was the common fate of all men, that the same thing inevitably awaited him—the young prince—he could not continue his drive, but gave orders to go home, that he might consider this fact. So he shut himself up alone and considered it, and he probably devised some consolation for himself, for he subsequently again went out to drive, feeling merry and happy. But this time he saw a sick man. He saw an emaciated, livid, trembling man with dim eyes. The prince, from whom sickness had been concealed, stopped and asked what this was. And when he learnt that this was sickness, to which all men are liable, and that he himself—a healthy and happy prince—might himself fall ill tomorrow, he again was in no mood to enjoy himself but gave orders to drive home, and again sought some solace, and probably found it, for he drove out a third time for pleasure. But this third time he saw another new sight: he saw men carrying something. 'What is that?' 'A dead man.' 'What does dead mean?' asked the prince. He was told that to become dead means to become like that man. The prince approached the corpse, uncovered it, and looked at it. 'What will happen to him now?' asked the prince. He was told that the corpse would be buried in the ground. 'Why?' 'Because he will certainly not return to life, and will only produce a stench and worms.' 'And is that the fate of all men? Will the same thing happen to me? Will they bury me, and shall I cause a stench and be eaten by worms?' 'Yes.' 'Home! I shall not drive out for pleasure, and never will so drive out again!'

---

7   Tolstoy's version differs slightly in a few places from our own Authorized or Revised version. I have followed his text, for in a letter to Fee, quoted on p. 18, vol. ii, of my "Life of Tolstoy," he says that 'The Authorized English version [of Ecclesiastes] is bad.'—A.M.

And Sakya Muni could find no consolation in life, and decided that life is the greatest of evils; and he devoted all the strength of his soul to free himself from it, and to free others; and to do this so that, even after death, life shall not be renewed any more but be completely destroyed at its very roots. So speaks all the wisdom of India.

These are the direct replies that human wisdom gives when it replies to life's question.

"The life of the body is an evil and a lie. Therefore the destruction of the life of the body is a blessing, and we should desire it," says Socrates.

"Life is that which should not be—an evil; and the passage into Nothingness is the only good in life," says Schopenhauer.

"All that is in the world—folly and wisdom and riches and poverty and mirth and grief—is vanity and emptiness. Man dies and nothing is left of him. And that is stupid," says Solomon.

"To live in the consciousness of the inevitability of suffering, of becoming enfeebled, of old age and of death, is impossible—we must free ourselves from life, from all possible life," says Buddha.

And what these strong minds said has been said and thought and felt by millions upon millions of people like them. And I have thought it and felt it.

So my wandering among the sciences, far from freeing me from my despair, only strengthened it. One kind of knowledge did not reply to life's question, the other kind replied directly confirming my despair, indicating not that the result at which I had arrived was the fruit of error or of a diseased state of my mind, but on the contrary that I had thought correctly, and that my thoughts coincided with the conclusions of the most powerful of human minds.

It is no good deceiving oneself. It is all—vanity! Happy is he who has not been born: death is better than life, and one must free oneself from life.

VII

Not finding an explanation in science I began to seek for it in life, hoping to find it among the people around me. And I began to observe how the people around me—people like myself—lived, and what their attitude was to this question which had brought me to despair.

And this is what I found among people who were in the same position as myself as regards education and manner of life.

I found that for people of my circle there were four ways out of the terrible position in which we are all placed.

The first was that of ignorance. It consists in not knowing, not understanding, that life is an evil and an absurdity. People of this sort—chiefly women, or very young or very dull people—have not yet understood that question of life which presented itself to Schopenhauer, Solomon, and Buddha. They see neither the dragon that awaits them nor the mice gnawing the shrub by which they are hanging, and they lick the drops of honey. But they lick those drops of honey only for a while: something will turn their attention to the dragon and the mice, and there will be an end to their licking. From them I had nothing to learn—one cannot cease to know what one does know.

The second way out is epicureanism. It consists, while knowing the hopelessness of life, in making use meanwhile of the advantages one has, disregarding the dragon and the mice, and licking the honey in the best way, especially if there is much of it within reach. Solomon expresses this way out thus: "Then I commended mirth, because a man hath no better thing under the sun, than to eat, and to drink, and to be merry: and that this should accompany him in his labour the days of his life, which God giveth him under the sun.

"Therefore eat thy bread with joy and drink thy wine with a merry heart. . . . Live joyfully with the wife whom thou lovest all the days of the life of thy vanity. . . . for this is thy portion in life and in thy labours which thou takest under the sun. . . . Whatsoever thy hand findeth to do, do it with thy might, for there is not work, nor device, nor knowledge, nor wisdom, in the grave, whither thou goest."

That is the way in which the majority of people of our circle make life possible for themselves. Their circumstances furnish them with more of welfare than of hardship, and their moral dullness makes it possible for them to forget that the advantage of their position is accidental, and that not everyone can have a thousand wives and palaces like Solomon, that for everyone who has a thousand wives there are a thousand without a wife, and that for each palace there are a thousand people who have to build it in the sweat of their brows; and that the accident that has today made me a Solomon may tomorrow make me a Solomon's slave. The dullness of these people's imagination enables them to forget the things that gave Buddha no peace—the inevitability of sickness, old age, and death, which today or tomorrow will destroy all these pleasures.

So think and feel the majority of people of our day and our manner of life. The fact that some of these people declare the dullness of their thoughts and imaginations to be a philosophy, which they call Positive, does not remove them, in my opinion, from the ranks of those who, to avoid seeing the question, lick the honey. I could not imitate these people; not having their dullness of imagination I could not artificially produce it in myself. I could not tear my eyes from the mice and the dragon, as no vital man can after he has once seen them.

The third escape is that of strength and energy. It consists in destroying life, when one has understood that it is an evil and an absurdity. A few exceptionally strong and consistent people act so. Having understood the stupidity of the joke that has been played on them, and having understood that it is better to be dead than to be alive, and that it is best of all not to exist, they act accordingly and promptly end this stupid joke, since there are means: a rope round one's neck, water, a knife to stick into one's heart, or the trains on the railways; and the number of those of our circle who act in this way becomes greater and greater, and for the most part they act so at the best time of their life, when the strength of their mind is in full bloom and few habits degrading to the mind have as yet been acquired.

I saw that this was the worthiest way of escape and I wished to adopt it.

The fourth way out is that of weakness. It consists in seeing the truth of the situation and yet clinging to life, knowing in advance that nothing can come of it. People of this kind know that death is better than life, but not having the strength to act rationally—to end the deception quickly and kill themselves—they seem to wait for something. This is the escape of weakness, for if I know what is best and it is within my power, why not yield to what is best? . . . I found myself in that category.

So people of my class evade the terrible contradiction in four ways. Strain my attention as I would, I saw no way except those four. One way was not to understand that life is senseless, vanity, and an evil, and that it is better not to live. I could not help knowing this, and when I once knew it could not shut my eyes to it; the second way was to use life such as it is without thinking of the future. And I could not do that. I, like Sakya Muni, could not ride out hunting when I knew that old age, suffering, and death exist. My imagination was too vivid. Nor could I rejoice in the momentary accidents that for an instant threw pleasure to my lot. The third way, having understood that life is evil and stupid, was to end it by killing oneself. I understood that, but somehow still did not kill myself. The fourth way was to live like Solomon and Schopenhauer—knowing that life is a stupid joke played upon us, and still to go on living, washing oneself, dressing, dining, talking, and even writing books. This was to me repulsive and tormenting, but I remained in that position.

I see now that if I did not kill myself it was due to some dim consciousness of the invalidity of my thoughts. However convincing and indubitable appeared to me the sequence of my thoughts and of those of the wise that have brought us to the admission of the senselessness of life, there remained in me a vague doubt of the justice of my conclusion.

It was like this: I, my reason, have acknowledged that life is senseless. If there is nothing higher than reason (and there is not: nothing can prove that there is), then reason is the creator of life for me. If reason did not exist there would be for me no life. How can reason deny life when it is the creator of life? Or to put it the other way: were there no life, my reason would not exist; therefore reason is life's son. Life is all. Reason is its fruit yet reason rejects life itself! I felt that there was something wrong here.

Life is a senseless evil, that is certain, said I to myself. Yet I have lived and am still living, and all mankind lived and lives. How is that? Why does it live, when it is possible not to live? Is it that only I and Schopenhauer are wise enough to understand the senselessness and evil of life?

The reasoning showing the vanity of life is not so difficult, and has long been familiar to the very simplest folk; yet they have lived and still live. How is it they all live and never think of doubting the reasonableness of life?

My knowledge, confirmed by the wisdom of the sages, has shown me that everything on earth—organic and inorganic—is all most cleverly arranged—only my own position is stupid, and those fools—the enormous masses of people—know nothing about how everything organic and inorganic in the world is arranged; but they live, and it seems to them that their life is very wisely arranged! . . .

And it struck me: "But what if there is something I do not yet know? Ignorance behaves just in that way. Ignorance always says just what I am saying. When it does not know something, it says that what it does not know is stupid. Indeed, it appears that there is a whole humanity that lived and lives as if it understood the meaning of its life, for without understanding it could not live; but I say that all this life is senseless and that I cannot live.

"Nothing prevents our denying life by suicide, well then, kill yourself, and you won't discuss. If life displeases you, kill yourself! You live, and cannot understand the meaning of life—then finish it, and do not fool about in life, saying and writing that you do not understand it. You have come into good company where people are contented and know what they are doing; if you find it dull and repulsive—go away!"

Indeed, what are we who are convinced of the necessity of suicide yet do not decide to commit it, but the weakest, most inconsistent, and to put it plainly, the stupidest of men, fussing about with our own stupidity as a fool fusses about with a painted hussy? For our wisdom, however indubitable it may be, has not given us the knowledge of the meaning of our life. But all mankind who sustain life—millions of them—do not doubt the meaning of life.

Indeed, from the most distant time of which I know anything, when life began, people have lived knowing the argument about the vanity of life which has shown me its sense-lessness, and yet they lived attributing some meaning to it.

From the time when any life began among men they had that meaning of life, and they led that life which has descended to me. All that is in me and around me, all, corpo-real and incorporeal, is the fruit of their knowledge of life. Those very instruments of thought with which I consider this life and condemn it were all devised not by me but by them. I myself was born, taught, and brought up thanks to them. They dug out the iron, taught us to cut down the forests, tamed the cows and horses, taught us to sow corn and to live together, organized our life, and taught me to think and speak. And I, their product, fed, supplied with drink, taught by them, thinking with their thoughts and words, have argued that they are an absurdity! "There is something wrong," said I to myself. "I have blundered somewhere." But it was a long time before I could find out where the mistake was.

VIII

All these doubts, which I am now able to express more or less systematically, I could not then have expressed. I then only felt that however logically inevitable were my conclusions concerning the vanity of life, confirmed as they were by the greatest thinkers, there was something not right about them. Whether it was in the reasoning itself or in the statement of the question I did not know—I only felt that the conclusion was rationally convincing, but that that was insufficient. All these conclusions could not so convince me as to make me do what followed from my reasoning, that is to say, kill myself. And I should have told an untruth had I, without killing myself, said that reason had brought me to the point I had reached. Reason worked, but something else was also working which I can only call a consciousness of life. A force was working which compelled me to turn my attention to this and not to that; and it was this force which extricated me from my desperate situation and turned my mind in quite another direction. This force compelled me to turn my attention to the fact that I and a few hundred similar people are not the whole of mankind, and that I did not yet know the life of mankind.

Looking at the narrow circle of my equals, I saw only people who had not understood the question, or who had understood it and drowned it in life's intoxication, or had understood it and ended their lives, or had understood it and yet from weakness were living out their desperate life. And I saw no others. It seemed to me that that narrow circle of rich, learned, and leisured people to which I belonged formed the whole of humanity, and that those milliards of others who have lived and are living were cattle of some sort—not real people.

Strange, incredibly incomprehensible as it now seems to me that I could, while reasoning about life, overlook the whole life of mankind that surrounded me on all sides; that I could to such a degree blunder so absurdly as to think that my life, and Solomon's and Schopenhauer's, is the real, normal life, and that the life of the milliards is a circumstance undeserving of attention—strange as this now is to me, I see that so it was. In the delusion of my pride of intellect it seemed to me so indubitable that I and Solomon and Schopenhauer had stated the question so truly and exactly that nothing else was possible—so indubitable did it seem that all those milliards consisted of men who had not yet arrived at an apprehension of all the profundity of the question—that I sought for the meaning of my life without it once occurring to me to ask: "But what meaning is and has been given to their lives by all the milliards of common folk who live and have lived in the world?"

I long lived in this state of lunacy, which, in fact if not in words, is particularly characteristic of us very liberal and learned people. But thanks either to the strange physical affection I have for the real labouring people, which compelled me to understand them and to see that they are not so stupid as we suppose, or thanks to the sincerity of my conviction that I could know nothing beyond the fact that the best I could do was to hang myself, at any rate I instinctively felt that if I wished to live and understand the meaning of life, I must seek this meaning not among those who have lost it and wish to kill themselves, but among those milliards of the past and the present who make life and who support the burden of their own lives and of ours also. And I considered the enormous masses of those simple, unlearned, and poor people who have lived and are living and I saw something quite different. I saw that, with rare exceptions, all those milliards who have lived and are living do not fit into my divisions, and that I could not class them as not understanding the question, for they themselves state it and reply to it with extraordinary clearness. Nor could I consider them epicureans, for their life consists more of privations and sufferings than of enjoyments. Still less could I consider them as irrationally dragging on a meaningless existence, for every act of their life, as well as death itself, is explained by them. To kill themselves they consider the greatest evil. It appeared that all mankind had a knowledge, unacknowledged and despised by me, of the meaning of life. It appeared that reasonable knowledge does not give the meaning of life, but excludes life: while the meaning attributed to life by milliards of people, by all humanity, rests on some despised pseudo-knowledge.

Rational knowledge presented by the learned and wise, denies the meaning of life, but the enormous masses of men, the whole of mankind receive that meaning in irrational knowledge. And that irrational knowledge is faith, that very thing which I could not but reject. It is God, One in Three; the creation in six days; the devils and angels, and all the rest that I cannot accept as long as I retain my reason.

My position was terrible. I knew I could find nothing along the path of reasonable knowledge except a denial of life; and there—in faith—was nothing but a denial of reason, which was yet more impossible for me than a denial of life. From rational knowledge it appeared that life is an evil, people know this and it is in their power to end life; yet they lived and still live, and I myself live, though I have long known that life is senseless and an evil. By faith it appears that in order to understand the meaning of life I must renounce my reason, the very thing for which alone a meaning is required.

IX

A contradiction arose from which there were two exits. Either that which I called reason was not so rational as I supposed, or that which seemed to me irrational was not so irrational as I supposed. And I began to verify the line of argument of my rational knowledge.

Verifying the line of argument of rational knowledge I found it quite correct. The conclusion that life is nothing was inevitable; but I noticed a mistake. The mistake lay in this, that my reasoning was not in accord with the question I had put. The question was: "Why should I live, that is to say, what real, permanent result will come out of my illusory transitory life—what meaning has my finite existence in this infinite world?" And to reply to that question I had studied life.

The solution of all the possible questions of life could evidently not satisfy me, for my question, simple as it at first appeared, included a demand for an explanation of the finite in terms of the infinite, and vice versa.

I asked: "What is the meaning of my life, beyond time, cause, and space?" And I replied to quite another question: "What is the meaning of my life within time, cause, and space?" With the result that, after long efforts of thought, the answer I reached was: "None."

In my reasonings I constantly compared (nor could I do otherwise) the finite with the finite, and the infinite with the infinite; but for that reason I reached the inevitable result: force is force, matter is matter, will is will, the infinite is the infinite, nothing is nothing—and that was all that could result.

It was something like what happens in mathematics, when thinking to solve an equation, we find we are working on an identity, the line of reasoning is correct, but results in the answer that a equals a, or x equals x, 0 equals 0, the same thing happened with my reasoning in relation to the question of the meaning of my life. The replies given by all science to that question only result in—identity.

And really, strictly scientific knowledge—that knowledge which begins, as Descartes's did, with complete doubt about everything—rejects all knowledge admitted on faith and builds everything afresh on the laws of reason and experience, and cannot give any other reply to the question of life than that which I obtained: an indefinite reply. Only at first had it seemed to me that knowledge had given a positive reply—the reply of Schopenhauer: that life has no meaning and is an evil. But on examining the matter I understood that the reply is not positive, it was only my feeling that so expressed it. Strictly expressed, as it is by the Brahmins and by Solomon and Schopenhauer, the reply is merely indefinite, or an identity: 0 equals 0, life is nothing. So that philosophic knowledge denies nothing, but only replies that the question cannot be solved by it—that for it the solution remains indefinite.

Having understood this, I understood that it was not possible to seek in rational knowledge for a reply to my question, and that the reply given by rational knowledge is a mere indication that a reply can only be obtained by a different statement of the question and only when the relation of the finite to the infinite is included in the question. And I understood that, however irrational and distorted might be the replies given by faith, they have this advantage, that they introduce into every answer a relation between the finite and the infinite, without which there can be no solution.

In whatever way I stated the question, that relation appeared in the answer. How am I to live?—According to the law of God. What real result will come of my life?—Eternal torment or eternal bliss. What meaning has life that death does not destroy?—Union with the eternal God: heaven.

So that besides rational knowledge, which had seemed to me the only knowledge, I was inevitably brought to acknowledge that all live humanity has another irrational knowledge—faith which makes it possible to live. Faith still remained to me as irrational as it was before, but I could not but admit that it alone gives mankind a reply to the questions of life, and that consequently it makes life possible. Reasonable knowledge had brought me to acknowledge that life is senseless—my life had come to a halt and I wished to destroy myself. Looking around on the whole of mankind I saw that people live and declare that they know the meaning of life. I looked at myself—I had lived as long as I knew a meaning of life and had made life possible.

Looking again at people of other lands, at my contemporaries and at their predecessors, I saw the same thing. Where there is life, there since man began faith has made life possible for him, and the chief outline of that faith is everywhere and always identical.

Whatever the faith may be, and whatever answers it may give, and to whomsoever it gives them, every such answer gives to the finite existence of man an infinite meaning, a meaning not destroyed by sufferings, deprivations, or death. This means that only in faith can we find for life a meaning and a possibility. What, then, is this faith? And I understood that faith is not merely "the evidence of things not seen", etc., and is not a revelation (that defines only one of the indications of faith) is not the relation of man to God (one has first to define faith and then God, and not define faith through God); it is not only agreement with what has been told one (as faith is most usually supposed to be), but faith is a knowledge of the meaning of human life in consequence of which man does not destroy himself but lives. Faith is the strength of life. If a man lives he believes in something. If he did not believe that one must live for something, he would not live. If he does not see and recognize the illusory nature of the finite, he believes in the finite; if he understands the illusory nature of the finite, he must believe in the infinite. Without faith he cannot live.

And I recalled the whole course of my mental labour and was horrified. It was now clear to me that for man to be able to live he must either not see the infinite, or have such an explanation of the meaning of life as will connect the finite with the infinite. Such an explanation I had had; but as long as I believed in the finite I did not need the explanation, and I began to verify it by reason. And in the light of reason the whole of my former explanation flew to atoms. But a time came when I ceased to believe in the finite. And then I began to build up on rational foundations, out of what I knew, an explanation which would give a meaning to life; but nothing could I build. Together with the best human intellects I reached the result that 0 equals 0, and was much astonished at that conclusion, though nothing else could have resulted.

What was I doing when I sought an answer in the experimental sciences? I wished to know why I live, and for this purpose studied all that is outside me. Evidently I might learn much, but nothing of what I needed.

What was I doing when I sought an answer in philosophical knowledge? I was studying the thoughts of those who had found themselves in the same position as I, lacking a reply to the question "why do I live?" Evidently I could learn nothing but what I knew myself, namely that nothing can be known.

What am I?—A part of the infinite. In those few words lies the whole problem.

Is it possible that humanity has only put that question to itself since yesterday? And can no one before me have set himself that question—a question so simple, and one that springs to the tongue of every wise child?

Surely that question has been asked since man began; and naturally for the solution of that question since man began it has been equally insufficient to compare the finite with the finite and the infinite with the infinite, and since man began the relation of the finite to the infinite has been sought out and expressed.

All these conceptions in which the finite has been adjusted to the infinite and a meaning found for life—the conception of God, of will, of goodness—we submit to logical examination. And all those conceptions fail to stand reason's criticism.

Were it not so terrible it would be ludicrous with what pride and self-satisfaction we, like children, pull the watch to pieces, take out the spring, make a toy of it, and are then surprised that the watch does not go.

A solution of the contradiction between the finite and the infinite, and such a reply to the question of life as will make it possible to live, is necessary and precious. And that is the only solution which we find everywhere, always, and among all peoples: a solution descending from times in which we lose sight of the life of man, a solution so difficult that we can compose nothing like it—and this solution we light-heartedly destroy in order again to set the same question, which is natural to everyone and to which we have no answer.

The conception of an infinite god, the divinity of the soul, the connection of human affairs with God, the unity and existence of the soul, man's conception of moral goodness and evil—are conceptions formulated in the hidden infinity of human thought, they are those conceptions without which neither life nor I should exist; yet rejecting all that labour of the whole of humanity, I wished to remake it afresh myself and in my own manner.

I did not then think like that, but the germs of these thoughts were already in me. I understood, in the first place, that my position with Schopenhauer and Solomon, notwithstanding our wisdom, was stupid: we see that life is an evil and yet continue to live. That is evidently stupid, for if life is senseless and I am so fond of what is reasonable, it should be destroyed, and then there would be no one to challenge it. Secondly, I understood that all one's reasonings turned in a vicious circle like a wheel out of gear with its pinion. However much and however well we may reason we cannot obtain a reply to the question; and 0 will always equal 0, and therefore our path is probably erroneous. Thirdly, I began to understand that in the replies given by faith is stored up the deepest human wisdom and that I had no right to deny them on the ground of reason, and that those answers are the only ones which reply to life's question.

X

I understood this, but it made matters no better for me. I was now ready to accept any faith if only it did not demand of me a direct denial of reason—which would be a falsehood. And I studied Buddhism and Mohammedanism from books, and most of all I studied Christianity both from books and from the people around me.

Naturally I first of all turned to the orthodox of my circle, to people who were learned: to Church theologians, monks, to theologians of the newest shade, and even to Evangelicals who profess salvation by belief in the Redemption. And I seized on these believers and questioned them as to their beliefs and their understanding of the meaning of life.

But though I made all possible concessions, and avoided all disputes, I could not accept the faith of these people. I saw that what they gave out as their faith did not explain the meaning of life but obscured it, and that they themselves affirm their belief not to answer that question of life which brought me to faith, but for some other aims alien to me.

I remember the painful feeling of fear of being thrown back into my former state of despair, after the hope I often experienced in my intercourse with these people.

The more fully they explained to me their doctrines, the more clearly did I perceive their error and realized that my hope of finding in their belief an explanation of the meaning of life was vain.

It was not that in their doctrines they mixed many unnecessary and unreasonable things with the Christian truths that had always been near to me: that was not what repelled me. I was repelled by the fact that these people's lives were like my own, with only this difference—that such a life did not correspond to the principles they expounded in their teachings. I clearly felt that they deceived themselves and that they, like myself found no other meaning in life than to live while life lasts, taking all one's hands can seize. I saw this because if they had had a meaning which destroyed the fear of loss, suffering, and death, they would not have feared these things. But they, these believers of our circle, just like myself, living in sufficiency and superfluity, tried to increase or preserve them, feared privations, suffering, and death, and just like myself and all of us unbelievers, lived to satisfy their desires, and lived just as badly, if not worse, than the unbelievers.

No arguments could convince me of the truth of their faith. Only deeds which showed that they saw a meaning in life making what was so dreadful to me—poverty, sickness, and death—not dreadful to them, could convince me. And such deeds I did not see among the various believers in our circle. On the contrary, I saw such deeds done[8] by people of our circle who were the most unbelieving, but never by our so-called believers.

And I understood that the belief of these people was not the faith I sought, and that their faith is not a real faith but an epicurean consolation in life.

I understood that that faith may perhaps serve, if not for a consolation at least for some distraction for a repentant Solomon on his death-bed, but it cannot serve for the great majority of mankind, who are called on not to amuse themselves while consuming the labour of others but to create life.

For all humanity to be able to live, and continue to live attributing a meaning to life, they, those milliards, must have a different, a real, knowledge of faith. Indeed, it was not the fact that we, with Solomon and Schopenhauer, did not kill ourselves that convinced me of the existence of faith, but the fact that those milliards of people have lived and are living, and have borne Solomon and us on the current of their lives.

And I began to draw near to the believers among the poor, simple, unlettered folk: pilgrims, monks, sectarians, and peasants. The faith of these common people was the same Christian faith as was professed by the pseudo-believers of our circle. Among them, too, I found a great deal of superstition mixed with the Christian truths; but the difference was that the superstitions of the believers of our circle were quite unnecessary to them and were not in conformity with their lives, being merely a kind of epicurean diversion;

---

8   This passage is noteworthy as being one of the few references made by Tolstoy at this period to the revolutionary or "Back-to-the-People" movement, in which many young men and women were risking and sacrificing home, property, and life itself from motives which had much in common with his own perception that the upper layers of Society are parasitic and prey on the vitals of the people who support them.—A.M.

but the superstitions of the believers among the labouring masses conformed so with their lives that it was impossible to imagine them to oneself without those superstitions, which were a necessary condition of their life, the whole life of believers in our circle was a contradiction of their faith, but the whole life of the working-folk believers was a confirmation of the meaning of life which their faith gave them. And I began to look well into the life and faith of these people, and the more I considered it the more I became convinced that they have a real faith which is a necessity to them and alone gives their life a meaning and makes it possible for them to live. In contrast with what I had seen in our circle—where life without faith is possible and where hardly one in a thousand acknowledges himself to be a believer—among them there is hardly one unbeliever in a thousand. In contrast with what I had seen in our circle, where the whole of life is passed in idleness, amusement, and dissatisfaction, I saw that the whole life of these people was passed in heavy labour, and that they were content with life. In contradistinction to the way in which people of our circle oppose fate and complain of it on account of deprivations and sufferings, these people accepted illness and sorrow without any perplexity or opposition, and with a quiet and firm conviction that all is good. In contradistinction to us, who the wiser we are the less we understand the meaning of life, and see some evil irony in the fact that we suffer and die, these folk live and suffer, and they approach death and suffering with tranquillity and in most cases gladly. In contrast to the fact that a tranquil death, a death without horror and despair, is a very rare exception in our circle, a troubled, rebellious, and unhappy death is the rarest exception among the people, and such people, lacking all that for us and for Solomon is the only good of life and yet experiencing the greatest happiness, are a great multitude. I looked more widely around me. I considered the life of the enormous mass of the people in the past and the present. And of such people, understanding the meaning of life and able to live and to die, I saw not two or three, or tens, but hundreds, thousands, and millions, and they all—endlessly different in their manners, minds, education, and position, as they were—all alike, in complete contrast to my ignorance, knew the meaning of life and death, laboured quietly, endured deprivations and sufferings, and lived and died seeing therein not vanity but good.

And I learnt to love these people. The more I came to know their life, the life of those who are living and of others who are dead of whom I read and heard, the more I loved them and the easier it became for me to live. So I went on for about two years, and a change took place in me which had long been preparing and the promise of which had always been in me. It came about that the life of our circle, the rich and learned, not merely became distasteful to me, but lost all meaning in my eyes. All our actions, discussions, science and art, presented itself to me in a new light. I understood that it is all merely self-indulgence, and to find a meaning in it is impossible; while the life of the whole labouring people, the whole of mankind who produce life, appeared to me in its true significance. I understood that that is life itself, and that the meaning given to that life is true: and I accepted it.

XI

And remembering how those very beliefs had repelled me and had seemed meaningless when professed by people whose lives conflicted with them, and how these same beliefs attracted me and seemed reasonable when I saw that people lived in accord with them, I understood why I had then rejected those beliefs and found them meaningless, yet now accepted them and found them full of meaning. I understood that I had erred, and why I erred. I had erred not so much because I thought incorrectly as because I lived badly. I understood that it was not an error in my thought that had hid truth from me as much as my life itself in the exceptional conditions of epicurean gratification of desires in which I passed it. I understood that my question as to what my life is, and the answer—and evil—was quite correct. The only mistake was that the answer referred only to my life, while I had referred it to life in general. I asked myself what my life is, and got the reply: An evil and an absurdity, and really my life—a life of indulgence of desires—was senseless and evil, and therefore the reply, "Life is evil and an absurdity", referred only to my life, but not to human life in general. I understood the truth which I afterwards found in the Gospels, "that men loved darkness rather than the light, for their works were evil. For everyone that doeth ill hateth the light, and cometh not to the light, lest his works should be reproved." I perceived that to understand the meaning of life it is necessary first that life should not be meaningless and evil, then we can apply reason to explain it. I understood why I had so long wandered round so evident a truth, and that if one is to think and speak of the life of mankind, one must think and speak of that life and not of the life of some of life's parasites. That truth was always as true as that two and two are four, but I had not acknowledged it, because on admitting two and two to be four I had also to admit that I was bad; and to feel myself to be good was for me more important and necessary than for two and two to be four. I came to love good people, hated myself, and confessed the truth. Now all became clear to me.

What if an executioner passing his whole life in torturing people and cutting off their heads, or a hopeless drunkard, or a madman settled for life in a dark room which he has fouled and imagines that he would perish if he left—what if he asked himself: "What is life?" Evidently he could not other reply to that question than that life is the greatest evil, and the madman's answer would be perfectly correct, but only as applied to himself. What if I am such a madman? What if all we rich and leisured people are such madmen? and I understood that we really are such madmen. I at any rate was certainly such.

And indeed a bird is so made that it must fly, collect food, and build a nest, and when I see that a bird does this I have pleasure in its joy. A goat, a hare, and a wolf are so made that they must feed themselves, and must breed and feed their family, and when they do so I feel firmly assured that they are happy and that their life is a reasonable one, then what should a man do? He too should produce his living as the animals do, but with this difference, that he will perish if he does it alone; he must obtain it not for himself but for all. And when he does that, I have a firm assurance that he is happy and that his life is reasonable. But what had I done during the whole thirty years of my responsible life? Far from producing sustenance for all, I did not even produce it for myself. I lived as a parasite, and on asking myself, what is the use of my life? I got the reply: "No use." If the meaning of human life lies in supporting it, how could I—who for thirty years had been engaged not on supporting life but on destroying it in myself and in others—how could I obtain any other answer than that my life was senseless and an evil?... It was both senseless and evil.

The life of the world endures by someone's will—by the life of the whole world and by our lives someone fulfills his purpose. To hope to understand the meaning of that will one must first perform it by doing what is wanted of us. But if I will not do what is wanted of me, I shall never understand what is wanted of me, and still less what is wanted of us all and of the whole world.

If a naked, hungry beggar has been taken from the cross-roads, brought into a building belonging to a beautiful establishment, fed, supplied with drink, and obliged to move a handle up and down, evidently, before discussing why he was taken, why he should move the handle, and whether the whole establishment is reasonably arranged—the begger should first of all move the handle. If he moves the handle he will understand that it works a pump, that the pump draws water and that the water irrigates the garden beds; then he will be taken from the pumping station to another place where he will gather fruits and will enter into the joy of his master, and, passing from lower to higher work, will understand more and more of the arrangements of the establishment, and taking part in it will never think of asking why he is there, and will certainly not reproach the master.

So those who do his will, the simple, unlearned working folk, whom we regard as cattle, do not reproach the master; but we, the wise, eat the master's food but do not do what the master wishes, and instead of doing it sit in a circle and discuss: "Why should that handle be moved? Isn't it stupid?" So we have decided. We have decided that the master is stupid, or does not exist, and that we are wise, only we feel that we are quite useless and that we must somehow do away with ourselves.

XII

The consciousness of the error in reasonable knowledge helped me to free myself from the temptation of idle ratiocination, the conviction that knowledge of truth can only be found by living led me to doubt the rightness of my life; but I was saved only by the fact that I was able to tear myself from my exclusiveness and to see the real life of the plain working people, and to understand that it alone is real life. I understood that if I wish to understand life and its meaning, I must not live the life of a parasite, but must live a real life, and—taking the meaning given to live by real humanity and merging myself in that life—verify it.

During that time this is what happened to me. During that whole year, when I was asking myself almost every moment whether I should not end matters with a noose or a bullet—all that time, together with the course of thought and observation about which I have spoken, my heart was oppressed with a painful feeling, which I can only describe as a search for God.

I say that that search for God was not reasoning, but a feeling, because that search proceeded not from the course of my thoughts—it was even directly contrary to them—but proceeded from the heart. It was a feeling of fear, orphanage, isolation in a strange land, and a hope of help from someone.

Though I was quite convinced of the impossibility of proving the existence of a Deity (Kant had shown, and I quite understood him, that it could not be proved), I yet sought for God, hoped that I should find Him, and from old habit addressed prayers to that which I sought but had not found. I went over in my mind the arguments of Kant and Schopenhauer showing the impossibility of proving the existence of a God, and I began to verify those arguments and to refute them. Cause, said I to myself, is not a category of thought such as are Time and Space. If I exist, there must be some cause for it, and a cause of causes. And that first cause of all is what men have called "God". And I paused on that thought, and tried with all my being to recognize the presence of that cause. And as soon as I acknowledged that there is a force in whose power I am, I at once felt that I could live. But I asked myself: What is that cause, that force? How am I to think of it? What are my relations to that which I call "God"? And only the familiar replies occurred to me: "He is the Creator and Preserver." This reply did not satisfy me, and I felt I was losing within me what I needed for my life. I became terrified and began to pray to Him whom I sought, that He should help me. But the more I prayed the more apparent it became to me that He did not hear me, and that there was no one to whom to address myself. And with despair in my heart that there is no God at all, I said: "Lord, have mercy, save me! Lord, teach me!" But no one had mercy on me, and I felt that my life was coming to a standstill.

But again and again, from various sides, I returned to the same conclusion that I could not have come into the world without any cause or reason or meaning; I could not be such a fledgling fallen from its nest as I felt myself to be. Or, granting that I be such, lying on my back crying in the high grass, even then I cry because I know that a mother has borne me within her, has hatched me, warmed me, fed me, and loved me. Where is she—that mother? If I have been deserted, who has deserted me? I cannot hide from myself that someone bored me, loving me. Who was that someone? Again "God"? He knows and sees my searching, my despair, and my struggle."

"He exists," said I to myself. And I had only for an instant to admit that, and at once life rose within me, and I felt the possibility and joy of being. But again, from the admission of the existence of a God I went on to seek my relation with Him; and again I imagined that God—our Creator in Three Persons who sent His Son, the Saviour—and again that God, detached from the world and from me, melted like a block of ice, melted before my eyes, and again nothing remained, and again the spring of life dried up within me, and I despaired and felt that I had nothing to do but to kill myself. And the worst of all was, that I felt I could not do it.

Not twice or three times, but tens and hundreds of times, I reached those conditions, first of joy and animation, and then of despair and consciousness of the impossibility of living.

I remember that it was in early spring: I was alone in the wood listening to its sounds. I listened and thought ever of the same thing, as I had constantly done during those last three years. I was again seeking God.

"Very well, there is no God," said I to myself; "there is no one who is not my imagination but a reality like my whole life. He does not exist, and no miracles can prove His existence, because the miracles would be my imagination, besides being irrational.

"But my perception of God, of Him whom I seek," I asked myself, "where has that perception come from?" And again at this thought the glad waves of life rose within me. All that was around me came to life and received a meaning. But my joy did not last long. My mind continued its work.

"The conception of God is not God," said I to myself. "The conception is what takes place within me. The conception of God is something I can evoke or can refrain from evoking in myself. That is not what I seek. I seek that without which there can be no life." And again all around me and within me began to die, and again I wished to kill myself.

But then I turned my gaze upon myself, on what went on within me, and I remembered all those cessations of life and reanimations that recurred within me hundreds of times. I remembered that I only lived at those times when I believed in God. As it was before, so it was now; I need only be aware of God to live; I need only forget Him, or disbelieve Him, and I died.

What is this animation and dying? I do not live when I lose belief in the existence of God. I should long ago have killed myself had I not had a dim hope of finding Him. I live, really live, only when I feel Him and seek Him. "What more do you seek?" exclaimed a voice within me. "This is He. He is that without which one cannot live. To know God and to live is one and the same thing. God is life." "Live seeking God, and then you will not live without God." And more than ever before, all within me and around me lit up, and the light did not again abandon me.

And I was saved from suicide. When and how this change occurred I could not say. As imperceptibly and gradually the force of life in me had been destroyed and I had reached the impossibility of living, a cessation of life and the necessity of suicide, so impercep-tibly and gradually did that force of life return to me. And strange to say the strength of life which returned to me was not new, but quite old—the same that had borne me along in my earliest days.

I quite returned to what belonged to my earliest childhood and youth. I returned to the belief in that Will which produced me and desires something of me. I returned to the belief that the chief and only aim of my life is to be better, i.e., to live in accord with that Will, and I returned to the belief that I can find the expression of that Will in what humanity, in the distant past hidden from, has produced for its guidance: that is to say, I returned to a belief in God, in moral perfection, and in a tradition transmitting the meaning of life. There was only this difference, that then all this was accepted uncon-sciously, while now I knew that without it I could not live.

What happened to me was something like this: I was put into a boat (I do not remember when) and pushed off from an unknown shore, shown the direction of the opposite shore, had oars put into my unpractised hands, and was left alone. I rowed as best I could and moved forward; but the further I advanced towards the middle of the stream the more rapid grew the current bearing me away from my goal and the more frequently did I encounter others, like myself, borne away by the stream. There were a few rowers who continued to row, there were others who had abandoned their oars; there were large boats and immense vessels full of people. Some struggled against the current, oth-ers yielded to it. And the further I went the more, seeing the progress down the current of all those who were adrift, I forgot the direction given me. In the very centre of the stream, amid the crowd of boats and vessels which were being borne downstream, I quite lost my direction and abandoned my oars. Around me on all sides, with mirth and rejoicing, people with sails and oars were borne down the stream, assuring me and each other that no other direction was possible. And I believed them and floated with them. And I was carried far; so far that I heard the roar of the rapids in which I must be shattered, and I saw boats shattered in them. And I recollected myself. I was long unable to understand what had happened to me. I saw before me nothing but destruc-tion, towards which I was rushing and which I feared. I saw no safety anywhere and did not know what to do; but, looking back, I perceived innumerable boats which unceas-ingly and strenuously pushed across the stream, and I remembered about the shore, the oars, and the direction, and began to pull back upwards against the stream and towards the shore.

That shore was God; that direction was tradition; the oars were the freedom given me to pull for the shore and unite with God. And so the force of life was renewed in me and I again began to live.

XIII

I turned from the life of our circle, acknowledging that ours is not life but a simulation of life—that the conditions of superfluity in which we live deprive us of the possibility of understanding life, and that in order to understand life I must understand not an exceptional life such as our who are parasites on life, but the life of the simple labouring folk—those who make life—and the meaning which they attribute to it. The simplest labouring people around me were the Russian people, and I turned to them and to the meaning of life which they give. That meaning, if one can put it into words, was as follows: Every man has come into this world by the will of God. And God has so made man that every man can destroy his soul or save it. The aim of man in life is to save his soul, and to save his soul he must live "godly" and to live "godly" he must renounce all the pleasures of life, must labour, humble himself, suffer, and be merciful. That meaning the people obtain from the whole teaching of faith transmitted to them by their pastors and by the traditions that live among the people. This meaning was clear to me and near to my heart. But together with this meaning of the popular faith of our non-sectarian folk, among whom I live, much was inseparably bound up that revolted me and seemed to me inexplicable: sacraments, Church services, fasts, and the adoration of relics and icons. The people cannot separate the one from the other, nor could I. And strange as much of what entered into the faith of these people was to me, I accepted everything, and attended the services, knelt morning and evening in prayer, fasted, and prepared to receive the Eucharist: and at first my reason did not resist anything. The very things that had formerly seemed to me impossible did not now evoke in me any opposition.

My relations to faith before and after were quite different. Formerly life itself seemed to me full of meaning and faith presented itself as the arbitrary assertion of propositions to me quite unnecessary, unreasonable, and disconnected from life. I then asked myself what meaning those propositions had and, convinced that they had none, I rejected them. Now on the contrary I knew firmly that my life otherwise has, and can have, no meaning, and the articles of faith were far from presenting themselves to me as unnecessary—on the contrary I had been led by indubitable experience to the conviction that only these propositions presented by faith give life a meaning, formerly I looked on them as on some quite unnecessary gibberish, but now, if I did not understand them, I yet knew that they had a meaning, and I said to myself that I must learn to understand them.

I argued as follows, telling myself that the knowledge of faith flows, like all humanity with its reason, from a mysterious source. That source is God, the origin both of the human body and the human reason. As my body has descended to me from God, so also has my reason and my understanding of life, and consequently the various stages of the development of that understanding of life cannot be false. All that people sincerely believe in must be true; it may be differently expressed but it cannot be a lie, and therefore if it presents itself to me as a lie, that only means that I have not understood it. Furthermore I said to myself, the essence of every faith consists in its giving life a meaning which death does not destroy. Naturally for a faith to be able to reply to the questions of a king dying in luxury, of an old slave tormented by overwork, of an unreasoning child, of a wise old man, of a half-witted old woman, of a young and happy wife, of a youth tormented by passions, of all people in the most varied conditions of life and education—if there is one reply to the one eternal question of life: "Why do I live and what will result from my life?"—the reply, though one in its essence, must be endlessly varied in its presentation; and the more it is one, the more true and profound it is, the more strange and deformed must it naturally appear in its attempted expression, conformably to the education and position of each person. But this argument, justifying in my eyes the queerness of much on the ritual side of religion, did not suffice to allow me in the one great affair of life—religion—to do things which seemed to me questionable. With all my soul I wished to be in a position to mingle with the people, fulfilling the ritual side of their religion; but I could not do it. I felt but I should lie to myself and mock at what was sacred to me, were I to do so. At this point, however, our new Russian theological writers came to my rescue.

According to the explanation these theologians gave, the fundamental dogma of our faith is the infallibility of the Church. From the admission of that dogma follows inevitably the truth of all that is professed by the Church. The Church as an assembly of true believers united by love and therefore possessed of true knowledge became the basis of my belief I told myself that divine truth cannot be accessible to a separate individual; it is revealed only to the whole assembly of people united by love. To attain truth one must not separate, and in order not to separate one must love and must endure things one may not agree with.

Truth reveals itself to love, and if you do not submit to the rites of the Church you transgress against love; and by transgressing against love you deprive yourself of the possibility of recognizing the truth. I did not then see the sophistry contained in this argument. I did not see that union in love may give the greatest love, but certainly cannot give us divine truth expressed in the definite words of the Nicene Creed. I also did not perceive that love cannot make a certain expression of truth an obligatory condition of union. I did not then see these mistakes in the argument and thanks to it was able to accept and perform all the rites of the Orthodox Church without understanding most of them. I then tried with all strength of my soul to avoid all arguments and contradictions, and tried to explain as reasonably as possible the Church statements I encountered.

When fulfilling the rites of the Church I humbled my reason and submitted to the tradition possessed by all humanity. I united myself with my forefathers: the father, mother, and grandparents I loved. They and all my predecessors believed and lived, and they produced me. I united myself also with the missions of the common people whom

I respected. Moreover, those actions had nothing bad in themselves ("bad" I considered the indulgence of one's desires). When rising early for Church services I knew I was doing well, if only because I was sacrificing my bodily ease to humble my mental pride, for the sake of union with my ancestors and contemporaries, and for the sake of finding the meaning of life. It was the same with my preparations to receive Communion, and with the daily reading of prayers with genuflections, and also with the observance of all the fasts. However insignificant these sacrifices might be I made them for the sake of something good. I fasted, prepared for Communion, and observed the fixed hours of prayer at home and in church. During Church service I attended to every word, and gave them a meaning whenever I could. In the Mass the most important words for me were: "Let us love one another in conformity!" The further words, "In unity we believe in the Father, the Son, and Holy Ghost", I passed by, because I could not understand them.

XIV

It was then so necessary for me to believe in order to live that I unconsciously concealed from myself the contradictions and obscurities of theology, but this reading of meanings into the rites had its limits. If the chief words in the prayer for the Emperor became more and more clear to me, if I found some explanation for the words "and remembering our Sovereign Most-Holy Mother of God and all the Saints, ourselves and one another, we give our whole life to Christ our God", if I explained to myself the frequent repetition of prayers for the Tsar and his relations by the fact that they are more exposed to temptations than other people and therefore are more in need of being prayed for—the prayers about subduing our enemies and evil under our feet (even if one tried to say that sin was the enemy prayed against), these and other prayers, such as the "cherubic song" and the whole sacrament of oblation, or "the chosen Warriors", etc.—quite two-thirds of all the services—either remained completely incomprehensible or, when I forced an explanation into them, made me feel that I was lying, thereby quite destroying my relation to God and depriving me of all possibility of belief.

I felt the same about the celebration of the chief holidays. To remember the Sabbath, that is to devote one day to God, was something I could understand. But the chief holiday was in commemoration of the Resurrection, the reality of which I could not picture to myself or understand. And that name of "Resurrection" was also given the weekly holiday.[9] And on those days the Sacrament of the Eucharist was administered, which was quite unintelligible to me. The rest of the twelve great holidays, except Christmas, commemorated miracles—the things I tried not to think about in order not to deny: the Ascension, Pentecost, Epiphany, the Feast of the Intercession of the Holy Virgin, etc. At the celebration of these holidays, feeling that importance was being attributed to the very things that to me presented a negative importance, I either devised tranquillizing explanations or shut my eyes in order not to see what tempted me.

---

9   In Russia Sunday was called Resurrection-day.—A.M.

Most of all this happened to me when taking part in the most usual Sacraments, which are considered the most important: baptism and communion. There I encountered not incomprehensible but fully comprehensible doings: doings which seemed to me to lead into temptation, and I was in a dilemma—whether to lie or to reject them.

Never shall I forget the painful feeling I experienced the day I received the Eucharist for the first time after many years. The service, confession, and prayers were quite intelligible and produced in me a glad consciousness that the meaning of life was being revealed to me. The Communion itself I explained as an act performed in remembrance of Christ, and indicating a purification from sin and the full acceptance of Christ's teaching. If that explanation was artificial I did not notice its artificiality: so happy was I at humbling and abasing myself before the priest—a simple, timid country clergyman—turning all the dirt out of my soul and confessing my vices, so glad was I to merge in thought with the humility of the fathers who wrote the prayers of the office, so glad was I of union with all who have believed and now believe, that I did not notice the artificiality of my explanation. But when I approached the altar gates, and the priest made me say that I believed that what I was about to swallow was truly flesh and blood, I felt a pain in my heart: it was not merely a false note, it was a cruel demand made by someone or other who evidently had never known what faith is.

I now permit myself to say that it was a cruel demand, but I did not then think so: only it was indescribably painful to me. I was no longer in the position in which I had been in youth when I thought all in life was clear; I had indeed come to faith because, apart from faith, I had found nothing, certainly nothing, except destruction; therefore to throw away that faith was impossible and I submitted. And I found in my soul a feeling which helped me to endure it. This was the feeling of self-abasement and humility. I humbled myself, swallowed that flesh and blood without any blasphemous feelings and with a wish to believe. But the blow had been struck and, knowing what awaited me, I could not go a second time.

I continued to fulfil the rites of the Church and still believed that the doctrine I was following contained the truth, when something happened to me which I now understand but which then seemed strange.

I was listening to the conversation of an illiterate peasant, a pilgrim, about God, faith, life, and salvation, when a knowledge of faith revealed itself to me. I drew near to the people, listening to their opinions of life and faith, and I understood the truth more and more. So also was it when I read the Lives of Holy men, which became my favourite books. Putting aside the miracles and regarding them as fables illustrating thoughts, this reading revealed to me life's meaning. There were the lives of Makarius the Great, the story of Buddha, there were the words of St. John Chrysostom, and there were the stories of the traveller in the well, the monk who found some gold, and of Peter the publican. There were stories of the martyrs, all announcing that death does not exclude life, and there were the stories of ignorant, stupid men, who knew nothing of the teaching of the Church but who yet were saved.

But as soon as I met learned believers or took up their books, doubt of myself, dissatisfaction, and exasperated disputation were roused within me, and I felt that the more I entered into the meaning of these men's speech, the more I went astray from truth and approached an abyss.

XV

How often I envied the peasants their illiteracy and lack of learning! Those statements in the creeds which to me were evident absurdities, for them contained nothing false; they could accept them and could believe in the truth—the truth I believed in. Only to me, unhappy man, was it clear that with truth falsehood was interwoven by finest threads, and that I could not accept it in that form.

So I lived for about three years. At first, when I was only slightly associated with truth as a catechumen and was only scenting out what seemed to me clearest, these encounters struck me less. When I did not understand anything, I said, "It is my fault, I am sinful"; but the more I became imbued with the truths I was learning, the more they became the basis of my life, the more oppressive and the more painful became these encounters and the sharper became the line between what I do not understand because I am not able to understand it, and what cannot be understood except by lying to oneself.

In spite of my doubts and sufferings I still clung to the Orthodox Church. But questions of life arose which had to be decided; and the decision of these questions by the Church—contrary to the very bases of the belief by which I lived—obliged me at last to renounce communion with Orthodoxy as impossible. These questions were: first the relation of the Orthodox Eastern Church to other Churches to the Catholics and to the so-called sectarians. At that time, in consequence of my interest in religion, I came into touch with believers of various faiths: Catholics, protestants, Old-Believers, Molokans,[10] and others. And I met among them many men of lofty morals who were truly religious. I wished to be a brother to them. And what happened? That teaching which promised to unite all in one faith and love—that very teaching, in the person of its best representatives, told me that these men were all living a lie; that what gave them their power of life was a temptation of the devil; and that we alone possess the only possible truth. And I saw that all who do not profess an identical faith with themselves are considered by the Orthodox to be heretics, just as the Catholics and others consider the Orthodox to be heretics. And I saw that the Orthodox (though they try to hide this) regard with hostility all who do not express their faith by the same external symbols

---

10   A sect that rejects sacraments and ritual.

and words as themselves; and this is naturally so; first, because the assertion that you are in falsehood and I am in truth, is the most cruel thing one man can say to another; and secondly, because a man loving his children and brothers cannot help being hostile to those who wish to pervert his children and brothers to a false belief. And that hostility is increased in proportion to one's greater knowledge of theology. And to me who considered that truth lay in union by love, it became self-evident that theology was itself destroying what it ought to produce.

This offence is so obvious to us educated people who have lived in countries where various religions are professed and have seen the contempt, self assurance, and invincible contradiction with which Catholics behave to the Orthodox Greeks and to the Protestants, and the Orthodox to Catholics and Protestants, and the Protestants to the two others, and the similar attitude of Old-Believers, Pashkovites (Russian Evangelicals), Shakers, and all religions—that the very obviousness of the temptation at first perplexes us. One says to oneself: it is impossible that it is so simple and that people do not see that if two assertions are mutually contradictory, then neither of them has the sole truth which faith should possess. There is something else here, there must be some explanation. I thought there was, and sought that explanation and read all I could on the subject, and consulted all whom I could. And no one gave me any explanation, except the one which causes the Sumsky Hussars to consider the Sumsky Hussars the best regiment in the world, and the Yellow Uhlans to consider that the best regiment in the world is the Yellow Uhlans. The ecclesiastics of all the different creeds, through their best representatives, told me nothing but that they believed themselves to have the truth and the others to be in error, and that all they could do was to pray for them. I went to archimandrites, bishops, elders, monks of the strictest orders, and asked them; but none of them made any attempt to explain the matter to me except one man, who explained it all and explained it so that I never asked any one any more about it. I said that for every unbeliever turning to a belief (and all our young generation are in a position to do so) the question that presents itself first is, why is truth not in Lutheranism nor in Catholicism, but in Orthodoxy? Educated in the high school he cannot help knowing what the peasants do not know—that the Protestants and Catholics equally affirm that their faith is the only true one. Historical evidence, twisted by each religion in its own favour, is insufficient. Is it not possible, said I, to understand the teaching in a loftier way, so that from its height the differences should disappear, as they do for one who believes truly? Can we not go further along a path like the one we are following with the Old-Believers? They emphasize the fact that they have a differently shaped cross and different alleluias and a different procession round the altar. We reply: You believe in the Nicene Creed, in the seven sacraments, and so do we. Let us hold to that, and in other matters do as you please. We have united with them by placing the essentials of faith above the unessentials. Now with the Catholics can we not say: You believe in so and so and in so and so, which are the chief things, and as for the Filioque clause and the Pope—do as you please. Can we not say the same to the Protestants, uniting with them in what is most important?

My interlocutor agreed with my thoughts, but told me that such conceptions would bring reproach to the spiritual authorities for deserting the faith of our forefathers, and this would produce a schism; and the vocation of the spiritual authorities is to safeguard in all its purity the Greco-Russian Orthodox faith inherited from our forefathers.

And I understood it all. I am seeking a faith, the power of life; and they are seeking the best way to fulfil in the eyes of men certain human obligations, and fulfilling these human affairs they fulfil them in a human way. However much they may talk of their pity for their erring brethren, and of addressing prayers for them to the throne of the Almighty—to carry out human purposes violence is necessary, and it has always been applied and is and will be applied. If of two religions each considers itself true and the other false, then men desiring to attract others to the truth will preach their own doctrine. And if a false teaching is preached to the inexperienced sons of their Church— which as the truth—then that Church cannot but burn the books and remove the man who is misleading its sons. What is to be done with a sectarian—burning, in the opinion of the Orthodox, with the fire of false doctrine—who in the most important affair of life, in faith, misleads the sons of the Church? What can be done with him except to cut off his head or to incarcerate him? Under the Tsar Alexis Mikhaylovich people were burned at the stake, that is to say, the severest method of punishment of the time was applied, and in our day also the severest method of punishment is applied—detention in solitary confinement.[11]

The second relation of the Church to a question of life was with regard to war and executions.

At that time Russia was at war. And Russians, in the name of Christian love, began to kill their fellow men. It was impossible not to think about this, and not to see that killing is an evil repugnant to the first principles of any faith. Yet prayers were said in the churches for the success of our arms, and the teachers of the Faith acknowledged killing to be an act resulting from the Faith. And besides the murders during the war, I saw, during the disturbances which followed the war, Church dignitaries and teachers and monks of the lesser and stricter orders who approved the killing of helpless, erring youths. And I took note of all that is done by men who profess Christianity, and I was horrified.

XVI

And I ceased to doubt, and became fully convinced that not all was true in the religion I had joined. Formerly I should have said that it was all false, but I could not say so now.

---

11   At the time this was written capital punishment was considered to be abolished in Russia.—A.M.

The whole of the people possessed a knowledge of the truth, for otherwise they could not have lived. Moreover, that knowledge was accessible to me, for I had felt it and had lived by it. But I no longer doubted that there was also falsehood in it. And all that had previously repelled me now presented itself vividly before me. And though I saw that among the peasants there was a smaller admixture of the lies that repelled me than among the representatives of the Church, I still saw that in the people's belief also falsehood was mingled with the truth.

But where did the truth and where did the falsehood come from? Both the falsehood and the truth were contained in the so-called holy tradition and in the Scriptures. Both the falsehood and the truth had been handed down by what is called the Church.

And whether I liked or not, I was brought to the study and investigation of these writings and traditions—which till now I had been so afraid to investigate.

And I turned to the examination of that same theology which I had once rejected with such contempt as unnecessary. Formerly it seemed to me a series of unnecessary absurdities, when on all sides I was surrounded by manifestations of life which seemed to me clear and full of sense; now I should have been glad to throw away what would not enter a healthy head, but I had nowhere to turn to. On this teaching religious doctrine rests, or at least with it the only knowledge of the meaning of life that I have found is inseparably connected.

However wild it may seem to my firm old mind, it was the only hope of salvation. It had to be carefully, attentively examined in order to understand it, and not even to understand it as I understand the propositions of science: I do not seek that, nor can I seek it, knowing the special character of religious knowledge. I shall not seek the explanation of everything. I know that the explanation of everything, like the commencement of everything, must be concealed in infinity. But I wish to understand in a way which will bring me to what is inevitably inexplicable. I wish to recognize anything that is inexplicable as being so not because the demands of my reason are wrong (they are right, and apart from them I can understand nothing), but because I recognize the limits of my intellect. I wish to understand in such a way that everything that is inexplicable shall present itself to me as being necessarily inexplicable, and not as being something I am under an arbitrary obligation to believe.

That there is truth in the teaching is to me indubitable, but it is also certain that there is falsehood in it, and I must find what is true and what is false, and must disentangle the one from the other. I am setting to work upon this task. What of falsehood I have found in the teaching and what I have found of truth, and to what conclusions I came, will form the following parts of this work, which if it be worth it and if anyone wants it, will probably some day be printed somewhere.

1879.

The foregoing was written by me some three years ago, and will be printed.

Now a few days ago, when revising it and returning to the line of thought and to the feelings I had when I was living through it all, I had a dream. This dream expressed in condensed form all that I had experienced and described, and I think therefore that, for those who have understood me, a description of this dream will refresh and elucidate and unify what has been set forth at such length in the foregoing pages. The dream was this:

I saw that I was lying on a bed. I was neither comfortable nor uncomfortable: I was lying on my back. But I began to consider how, and on what, I was lying—a question which had not till then occurred to me. And observing my bed, I saw I was lying on plaited string supports attached to its sides: my feet were resting on one such support, my calves on another, and my legs felt uncomfortable. I seemed to know that those supports were moveable, and with a movement of my foot I pushed away the furthest of them at my feet—it seemed to me that it would be more comfortable so. But I pushed it away too far and wished to reach it again with my foot, and that movement caused the next support under my calves to slip away also, so that my legs hung in the air. I made a movement with my whole body to adjust myself, fully convinced that I could do so at once; but the movement caused the other supports under me to slip and to become entangled, and I saw that matters were going quite wrong: the whole of the lower part of my body slipped and hung down, though my feet did not reach the ground. I was holding on only by the upper part of my back, and not only did it become uncomfortable but I was even frightened. And then only did I ask myself about something that had not before occurred to me. I asked myself: Where am I and what am I lying on? And I began to look around and first of all to look down in the direction which my body was hanging and whither I felt I must soon fall. I looked down and did not believe my eyes. I was not only at a height comparable to the height of the highest towers or mountains, but at a height such as I could never have imagined.

I could not even make out whether I saw anything there below, in that bottomless abyss over which I was hanging and whither I was being drawn. My heart contracted, and I experienced horror. To look thither was terrible. If I looked thither I felt that I should at once slip from the last support and perish. And I did not look. But not to look was still worse, for I thought of what would happen to me directly I fell from the last support. And I felt that from fear I was losing my last supports, and that my back was slowly slipping lower and lower. Another moment and I should drop off. And then it occurred to me that this cannot be real. It is a dream. Wake up! I try to arouse myself but cannot do so. What am I to do? What am I to do? I ask myself, and look upwards. Above, there is also an infinite space. I look into the immensity of sky and try to forget about the immensity below, and I really do forget it. The immensity below repels and frightens me; the immensity above attracts and strengthens me. I am still supported above the abyss by the last supports that have not yet slipped from under me; I know that I am hanging, but I look only upwards and my fear passes. As happens in dreams, a voice says: "Notice this, this is it!" And I look more and more into the infinite above me and feel that I am becoming calm. I remember all that has happened, and remember how it all happened; how I moved my legs, how I hung down, how frightened I was, and how I was saved from fear by looking upwards. And I ask myself: Well, and now am I not hanging just the same? And I do not so much look round as experience with my whole body the point of support on which I am held. I see that I no longer hang as if about to fall, but am firmly held. I ask myself how I am held: I feel about, look round, and see that under me, under the middle of my body, there is one support, and that when I look upwards I lie on it in the position of securest balance, and that it alone gave me support before. And then, as happens in dreams, I imagined the mechanism by means of which I was held; a very natural intelligible, and sure means, though to one awake that mechanism has no sense. I was even surprised in my dream that I had not understood it sooner. It appeared that at my head there was a pillar, and the security of that slender pillar was undoubted though there was nothing to support it. From the pillar a loop hung very ingeniously and yet simply, and if one lay with the middle of one's body in that loop and looked up, there could be no question of falling. This was all clear to me, and I was glad and tranquil. And it seemed as if someone said to me: "See that you remember."

And I awoke.

1882.

Friedrich Nietzsche

Introduction to *On the Genealogy of Morals*, Preface
Ki Joo Choi and Anthony Sciglitano

Friedrich Nietzsche, born near Leipzig, Germany, on the birth date of the German Prussian Friedrich Wilhelm IV in 1844, belonged to a family of prominent Lutheran ministers in Germany. He studied theology and primarily philology (the study of biblical and linguistic origins) at the University of Bonn and Leipzig, and then, at the very young age of twenty-four, was appointed as professor at the University of Basel in Switzerland. Although he would write some significant philosophical texts during his time at Basel (such as *The Birth of Tragedy,* 1872), his more well-known texts were written after leaving Basel due to some very serious medical ailments. It is suspected that he died from a form of syphilis.

Although his many works in philosophy were not well-received during the mature years of his career and life, the impact they had in various fields of human life after his death have been tremendous. He is often referred to as one of the intellectual fathers of postmodern thought, and sometimes atheism—given his provocative denunciations of religion, particularly Christianity and Judaism, as you will see in our readings. This rejection of Christianity is perhaps ironic given that he comes from such a long line of Lutheran pastors! But it is important to note that his rejection of Christianity was also a rejection of many aspects of ancient Greek thought such as Plato's, as well as some of the leading philosophical schools of his time.

The reading from Nietzsche comes from his *On the Genealogy of Morals,* completed in 1887. The first selection from *Genealogy* is the book's Preface. The Preface maps out Nietzsche's intentions and procedures of the book. For those unfamiliar with Nietzsche's writings, *Genealogy* will be a challenging text to read—it may very well be one of the more difficult texts of the course. His writing style is unique and his use of language can make his meaning rather opaque. Thus, this Reading Guide is intended to map out the basic structure of the argument of the text.

We will first focus our attention on the Preface. It is worth noting that *Genealogy* is a follow-up, according to Nietzsche, to his text *Beyond Good and Evil* (1886) and a "response" to his friend Paul Rée's book *The Origin of the Moral Sensations* (1887)—see the Preface. More specifically, his response is really a criticism of Rée's book, which reflects his larger criticism of those he refers to as "English psychologists," the British utilitarian philosophers, among others. The criticism is primarily that they are not sufficiently "historical" in their "genealogies" of morality, leading them to erroneous moral conclusions.

With that in mind, we need to ask what Nietzsche's aims are in the book. What is he up to in the text?

1. We can begin with his title. Nietzsche calls his book a "genealogy" of morals. We probably understand what a genealogy is with respect to our family; what might it mean with respect to morals? Nietzsche gives us some helpful clues. He remarks early in his Preface that the subject of his "polemic" is the "*origin* of our moral prejudices" (Preface, #2). A little bit later, he tells us that his quest is to better understand "where good and evil originated" and thus who we really are. This leads him to ask the following questions: "Under what conditions did man devise these value judgments good and evil? And what value do they themselves possess? Have they hitherto hindered or furthered human prosperity? Are they a sign of distress, of impoverishment, of the degeneration of life? Or is there revealed in them, on the contrary, the plenitude, force, and will of life, its courage, certainty, future?" These questions, according to Nietzsche, are his "a priori." Pay special attention to the last two questions as they express what might be considered Nietzsche's criteria for any view of morality.

   So, a genealogy has to do with origins, and Nietzsche's genealogy has to do with the origins of human morality. A genealogy traces family relations, and Nietzsche's genealogy of morals will trace the relations of different moral ideas such as "good," "right," "just," and their opposites. Equally important are the words *polemic* and *prejudices*. Do you think that Plato, Paul, Augustine, Anselm, Maimonides, Ibn Rushd, or Thomas Aquinas would think of their positions as "prejudices"? Do you think of moral views as prejudices? What effect does Nietzsche's posing the question in this form have rhetorically? He also calls his essay a "polemic." The word *polemic* comes from the Greek word *polemikos*, which means "hostile" or "warlike." What views do you think Nietzsche is waging metaphorical war against?

2. We can now get more specific. Nietzsche wants to investigate major questions in his text:

   a. Why do we reflexively take "the unegoistic" as having "value-in-itself"? In other words, why do we typically think that "unegoism" or a form of *selfless love* is the primary or central moral value?

   b. Has our commitment to the value of unegoism been corrosive—or dangerous—to European culture and to human life?

3. For Nietzsche, the answer to question (b) is yes! But why? Why is unegoism so wrongheaded? According to Nietzsche, we need to examine what he refers to as the "value of these [unegoistic] values," which refers to question (a). When we do so, according to Nietzsche, we will see that the notions of good and evil are "a danger, a seduction, a poison, a narcotic, through which the present was possibly living at the expense of the future." Pay close attention to this line in the Preface!!! Here, you may want to stop and revisit what he announces as his "a priori," what we previously called his moral criteria.

Note: *It is absolutely critical that you notice how Nietzsche characterizes the value of unegoism or selfless love. He says it is dangerous and poisonous, a kind of illicit drug—something that makes life worse rather than better. To our modern ears, this surely sounds rather odd!—yes, no? As you read the Preface, ask yourself why for Nietzsche unegoism is dangerous and problematic. And, more important-ly, if unegoism or selfless love (such as charity, compassion, mercy, empathy, etc.) is dangerous, then what alternative value ought to guide human life? Shouldn't unegoism be at the heart of human life, of human morality? Nietzsche does not think so. Why? Then what is the alternative? What do you think about the proposi-tion that unegoism or selfless love is dangerous? What are your initial reactions to this proposition?*

ON THE GENEALOGY OF MORALS
Preface

1

We are unknown to ourselves, we men of knowledge—and with good reason. We have never sought ourselves—how could it happen that we should ever *find* ourselves? It has rightly been said: "Where your treasure is, there will your heart be also";[1] our treasure is where the beehives of our knowledge are. We are constantly making for them, being by nature winged creatures and honey gatherers of the spirit; there is one thing alone we really care about from the heart—"bringing something home." Whatever else there is in life, so-called "experiences"—which of us has sufficient earthiness for them? Or sufficient time? Present experience has, I am afraid always found us "absent-minded": we cannot give our hearts to it—not even our ears! Rather, as one divinely preoccupied and immersed in himself into whose ear the bell has just boomed with all its strength the twelve beats of noon suddenly starts up and asks himself: "what really was that which just struck?" so we sometimes rub our ears *afterward* and ask, utterly surprised and disconcerted, "what really was that which we have just experienced?" and moreover: "who *are* we really?" and, afterward as aforesaid, count the twelve trembling bell-strokes of our experience, our life, our *being*—and alas! miscount them—So we are necessarily strangers to ourselves, we do not comprehend ourselves, we *have* to misunderstand ourselves, for us the law "Each is furthest from himself" applies to all eternity—we are not "men of knowledge" with respect to ourselves.

2

My ideas on *origin* of our moral prejudices—for this is the subject of this polemic—received their first, brief, and provisional expression in the collection of aphorisms that bears the title *Human, All-Too-Human: A Book for Free Spirits.* This book was begun in Sorrento during a winter when it was given to me to pause as a wanderer pauses and look back across the broad and dangerous country my spirit had traversed up to that time. This was in the winter of 1876–77; the ideas themselves are older. They were already in essentials the same ideas that I take up again in the present treatises—let us hope the long interval has done them good, that they have become riper, dearer, stronger, more perfect! *That* I still cleave to them today, however, that they have become in the meantime more and more firmly attached to one another, indeed entwined and interlaced

---

1 Matthew 6:12.

with one another, strengthens my joyful assurance that they might have arisen in me from the first not as isolated, capricious, or sporadic things but from a common root, from a *fundamental will* of knowledge, pointing imperiously into the depths, speaking more and more precisely, demanding greater and greater precision. For this alone is fitting for a philosopher. We have no right to *isolated* acts of any kind: we may not make isolated errors or hit upon isolated truths. Rather do our ideas, our values, our yeas and nays, our ifs and buts, grow out of us with the necessity with which a tree bears fruit—related and each with an affinity to each, and evidence of *one* will, *one* health, *one* soil, *one* sun.—Whether *you* like them, these fruits of ours?—But what is that to the trees! What is that to *us*, to us philosophers!

3

Because of a scruple peculiar to me that I am loth to admit to—for it is concerned with *morality*, with all that has hitherto been celebrated on earth as morality—a scruple that entered my life so early, so uninvited, so irresistibly, so much in conflict with my environment, age, precedents, and descent that I might almost have the right to call it my *"a priori"*—my curiosity as well as my suspicions were bound to halt quite soon at the question of where our good and evil really *originated*. In fact, the problem of the origin of evil pursued me even as a boy of thirteen: at an age in which you have "half childish trifles, half God in your heart,"[2] I devoted to it my first childish literary trifle, my first philosophical effort—and as for the "solution" of the problem I posed at that time, well, I gave the honor to God, as was only fair, and made him the *father* of evil. Was *that* what my *"a priori"* demanded of me? that new immoral, or at least unmoralistic *"a priori"* and the alas! so anti-Kantian, enigmatic "categorical imperative" which spoke through it and to which I have since listened more and more closely, and not merely listened?

Fortunately I learned early to separate theological prejudice from moral prejudice and ceased to look for the origin of evil *behind* the world. A certain amount of historical and philological schooling, together with an inborn fastidiousness of taste in respect to psychological questions in general, soon transformed my problem into another one: under what conditions did man devise these value judgments good and evil? *and what value do they themselves possess?* Have they hitherto hindered or furthered human prosperity? Are they a sign of distress, of impoverishment, of the degeneration of life? Or is there revealed in them, on the contrary, the plenitude, force, and will of life, its courage, certainty, future?

Thereupon I discovered and ventured divers answers; I distinguished between ages, peoples, degrees of rank among individuals; I departmentalized my problem; out of my answers there grew new questions, inquiries, conjectures, probabilities—until at length I had a country of my own, a soil of my own, an entire discrete, thriving, flourishing

---

2   Goethe's *Faust*, lines 3781f.

world, like a secret garden the existence of which no one suspected.—Oh how *fortunate* we are, we men of knowledge, provided only that we know how to keep silent long enough!

4

The first impulse to publish something of my hypotheses concerning the origin of morality was given me by a clear, tidy, and shrewd—also precocious—little book in which I encountered distinctly for the first time an upside-down and perverse species of genealogical hypothesis, the genuinely *English* type, that attracted me with that power of attraction which everything contrary, everything antipodal possesses. The title of the little book was *The Origin of the Moral Sensations;* its author Dr. Paul Rée; the year in which it appeared 1877. Perhaps I have never read anything to which I would have said to myself No, proposition by proposition, conclusion by conclusion, to the extent that I did to this book: yet quite without ill-humor or impatience. In the abovementioned work, on which I was then engaged, I made opportune and inopportune reference to the propositions of that book, not in order to refute them—what have I to do with refutations!—but, as becomes a positive spirit, to replace the improbable with the more probable, possibly one error with another. It was then, as I have said, that I advanced for the first time those genealogical hypotheses to which this treatise is devoted—ineptly, as I should be the last to deny, still constrained, still lacking my own language for my own things and with much backsliding and vacillation. One should compare in particular what I say in *Human, All-Too-Human*, section 45, on the twofold prehistory of good and evil (namely, in the sphere of the noble and in that of the slaves); likewise, section 136, on the value and origin of the morality of asceticism; likewise, sections 96 and 99 and volume II, section 89, on the "morality of mores," that much older and more primitive species of morality which differs *toto caelo*[3] from the altruistic mode of evaluation (in which Dr. Rée, like all English moral genealogists, sees moral evaluation *as such*); likewise, section 92, *The Wanderer*, section 26, and *Dawn*, section 112, on the origin of justice as an agreement between two approximately equal powers (equality as the presupposition of all compacts, consequently of all law); likewise *The Wanderer*, sections 22 and 33, on the origin of punishment, of which the aim of intimidation is neither the essence nor the source (as Dr. Rée thinks—it is rather only introduced, under certain definite circumstances, and always as an incidental, as something added).[4]

---

3   Diametrically: literally, by the whole heavens.

4   Nietzsche always gives page references to the first editions. I have substituted section numbers, which are the same in all editions and translations; and in an appendix most of the sections cited are offered in my translations.
For Nietzsche's relation to Rée, see Rudolph Binion, *Frau Lou*, Princeton, N.J., Princeton University Press, 1968.

5

Even then my real concern was something much more important than hypothesis-mongering, whether my own or other people's, on the origin of morality (or more precisely: the latter concerned me solely for the sake of a goal to which it was only one means among many). What was at stake was the *value* of morality—and over this I had to come to terms almost exclusively with my great teacher Schopenhauer, to whom that book of mine, the passion and the concealed contradiction of that book, addressed itself as if to a contemporary (—for that book, too, was a "polemic"). What was especially at stake was the value of the "unegoistic," the instincts of pity, self-abnegation, self-sacrifice, which Schopenhauer had gilded, deified, and projected into a beyond for so long that at last they became for him "value-in-itself," on the basis of which he *said No* to life and to himself. But it was against precisely *these* instincts that there spoke from me an ever more fundamental mistrust, an ever more corrosive skepticism! It was precisely here that I saw the *great* danger to mankind, its sublimest enticement and seduction—but to what? to nothingness?—it was precisely here that I saw the beginning of the end, the dead stop, a retrospective weariness, the will turning *against* life, the tender and sorrowful signs of the ultimate illness: I understood the ever spreading morality of pity that had seized even on philosophers and made them ill, as the most sinister symptom of a European culture that had itself become sinister, perhaps as it by-pass to a new Buddhism? to a Buddhism for Europeans? to—*nihilism*?

For this overestimation of and predilection for pity on the part of modern philosophers is something new: hitherto philosophers have been at one as to the *worthlessness* of pity. I name only Plato, Spinoza, La Rochefoucauld and Kant—four spirits as different from one another as possible, but united in one thing: in their low estimation of pity.

6

This problem of the *value* of pity and of the morality of pity (—I am opposed to the pernicious modern effeminacy of feeling—) seems at first to be merely something detached, an isolated question mark; but whoever sticks with it and *learns* how to ask questions here will experience what I experienced—a tremendous new prospect opens up for him, a new possibility comes over him like a vertigo, every kind of mistrust, suspicion, fear leaps up, his belief in morality, in all morality, falters—finally a new demand becomes audible. Let us articulate this *new demand:* we need a *critique* of moral values, *the value of these values themselves must first be called in question*—and for that there is needed knowledge of the conditions and circumstances in which they grew, under which they evolved and changed (morality as consequence, as symptom, as mask, as tartufferie, as illness, as misunderstanding; but also morality as cause, as remedy, as stimulant, as restraint, as poison), a knowledge of a kind that has never yet existed or even been desired. One has taken the *value* of these "values" as given, as factual, as beyond all question; one has hitherto never doubted or hesitated in the slightest degree in supposing "the good man" to be of greater value than "the evil man," of greater value in the sense of further-ing the advancement and prosperity of man in general (the future of man included). But what if the reverse were true? What if a symptom of regression were inherent in the "good," likewise a danger, a seduction, a poison, a narcotic, through which the present was possibly living *at the expense of the future*? Perhaps more comfortably, less danger-ously, but at the same time in a meaner style, more basely?—So that precisely morality would be to blame if the *highest power and splendor* actually possible to the type man was never in fact attained? So that precisely morality was the danger of dangers?

7

Let it suffice that, after this prospect had opened up before me, I had reasons to look about me for scholarly, bold, and industrious comrades (I am still looking). The project is to traverse with quite novel questions, and as though with new eyes, the enormous, distant, and so well hidden land of morality—of morality that has actually existed, ac-tually been lived; and does this not mean virtually to *discover* this land for the first time?

If I considered in this connection the abovementioned Dr. Rée, among others, it was because I had no doubt that the very nature of his inquiries would compel him to adopt a better method for reaching answers. Have I deceived myself in this? My desire, at any rate, was to point out to so sharp and disinterested an eye as his a better direction in which to look, in the direction of an actual *history of morality*, and to warn him in time against gazing around haphazardly in the blue after the English fashion. For it must be obvious which color is a hundred times more vital for a genealogist of morals than blue: namely *gray*, that is, what is documented, what can actually be confirmed and has actually existed, in short the entire long hieroglyphic record, so hard to decipher, of the moral past of mankind!

This was unknown to Dr. Rée; but he had read Darwin—so that in his hypotheses, and after a fashion that is at least entertaining, the Darwinian beast and the ultramodern unassuming moral milksop who "no longer bites" politely link hands, the latter wearing an expression of a certain goodnatured and refined indolence, with which is mingled even a grain of pessimism and weariness, as if all these things—the problems of moral-ity—were really not worth taking quite so seriously. But to me, on the contrary, there seems to be nothing *more* worth taking seriously, among the rewards for it being that some day one will perhaps be allowed to take them *cheerfully*. For cheerfulness—or in my own language *gay science*—is a reward: the reward of a long, brave, industrious, and subterranean seriousness, of which, to be sure, not everyone is capable. But on the day we can say with all our hearts, "Onwards! our old morality too is part *of the comedy*!" we shall have discovered a new complication and possibility for the Dionysian drama of "The Destiny of the Soul"—and one can wager that the grand old eternal comic poet of our existence will be quick to make use of it!

8

If this book is incomprehensible to anyone and jars on his ears, the fault, it seems to me, is not necessarily mine. It is clear enough, assuming, as I do assume, that one has first read my earlier writings and has not spared some trouble in doing so: for they are, indeed, not easy to penetrate.[5] Regarding my *Zarathustra*, for example, I do not allow that anyone knows that book who has not at some time been profoundly wounded and at some time profoundly delighted by every word in it; for only then may he enjoy the privilege of reverentially sharing in the halcyon element out of which that book was born and in its sunlight clarity, remoteness, breadth, and certainty. In other cases, people find difficulty with the aphoristic form: this arises from the fact that today this form is *not taken seriously enough*. An aphorism, properly stamped and molded, has not been "deciphered" when it has simply been read; rather, one has then to begin its *exegesis*, for which is required an art of exegesis. I have offered in the third essay of the present book an example of what I regard as "exegesis" in such a case—an aphorism is prefixed to this essay, the essay itself is a commentary on it. To be sure, one thing is necessary above all if one is to practice reading as an *art* in this way, something that has been unlearned most thoroughly nowadays—and therefore it will be some time before my writings are "readable"—something for which one has almost to be a cow and in any case *not* a "modern man"; *rumination*

Sils-Maria, Upper Engadine,

July 1887

---

5   See also the end of Nietzsche's Preface to the new edition of *The Dawn*, written the fall of 1886: "...to read *well*, that means reading slowly, deeply, with consideration and caution . . ." The last four words do not adequately render *rück und vorsichtig*, which can also mean, looking backward and forward—i.e., with a regard for the context, including also the writer's earlier and later works. Cf. *Beyond Good and Evil*, my note on section 250.

Yet Arthur Danto voices a very common assumption when he says on the first page of the first chapter of his *Nietzsche as Philosopher* (New York, Macmillan, 1965): "No one of them [i.e., Nietzsche's books] presupposes an acquaintance with any other ... his writings may be read in pretty much any order, without this greatly impeding the comprehension of his ideas." This is as wrong as Danto's claim on the same page that "it would be difficult even for a close reader to tell the difference between those works he [Nietzsche] saw through the press [e.g., the *Genealogy*] and those [sic] pieced together by his editors [i.e., *The Will to Power*]." Indeed, Danto, like most readers, approaches Nietzsche as if "any given aphorism or essay might as easily have been placed in one volume as in another"; he bases his discussions on short snippets, torn from their context, and frequently omits phrases without indicating that he has done so; and he does not bother to consider all or most of the passages that are relevant to the topics he discusses.

This is one of the few books in English that deal with Nietzsche as a philosopher, and Danto's standing as a philosopher inspires confidence; but his account of Nietzsche's moral and epistemological ideas unfortunately depends on this untenable approach. See also the first footnote to the second essay, below.

Introduction to *On the Genealogy of Morals*, First Essay
Ki Joo Choi

The challenge of making sense of Nietzsche's argument against the value of unegoism comes into full light in this required reading from *Genealogy*, First Essay. His argument is not a straightforward argument and may not look like an argument at all to many of us. It is perhaps, then, better to approach First Essay as a kind of narrative. That is, in order to show why he thinks we should call into question the significance of unegoism as a central, foundational moral value, his strategy is to tell a story of how the moral value of unegoism became such an integral part of contemporary human life. He feels the need to tell this story because he thinks that too many of us *immediately assume, without question,* that selfless love (or compassion, charity, empathy) are values to be pursued and acquired (don't we all for the most part assume that to be a *good person involves being charitable*, compassionate, loving, etc.?—who would question that?). Nietzsche, therefore, thinks that if we can come to a better understanding of why we automatically assume the value of selfless love, then we can better understand why we *should not* give unegoism the kind of reverence and respect that we do. Our task for this reading is to investigate and assess the story Nietzsche tells, but to do that we need to first see what this story is.

The Narrative Structure of First Essay

1. Where did the concept of "good" (as rooted in unegoism) originate? For Nietzsche, this is a difficult question given that unegoism has become a habitual belief.

2. "Good" as unegoism originates from a struggle between *two* "classes" of beings, according to Nietzsche:

   a. The knights-nobles-aristocrats (see First Essay, #7, and pay close attention to the words Nietzsche employs to describe these people: *physicality, abundance, health, hunting, adventure, war games, joyful activity*)

   b. The priests or the slaves (see First Essay, #7, and pay close attention to the words Nietzsche employs to describe the priests or the slaves: *impotent, the wretched, the poor*)

3. Notice here that Nietzsche is trying to undermine our general assumptions that anyone who talks about people being "good" necessarily means the same things we do. This is one of the critical points that Nietzsche is making. He wants us to see that words are used in larger contexts of meaning, and if we do not look at those cultural contexts, we are liable to assume everyone means what we mean when we use moral terms. He thinks this leads to complete misunderstandings. More specifically, Nietzsche thinks that his age assumes that the ancient Greeks used "good" and "right" as moral terms that apply equally to people as people. But as we saw when

we discussed the Homeric view in chapter 1, this is not the case. The "goodness" or the "virtue" of a particular person depended not upon that person doing the right thing in our sense, but upon him or her correctly performing a socially given or class-based role. What is interesting to note is that Nietzsche thinks that Judaism and Christianity truly offer something radically new in history, but that this is not a good thing! On his view, Jews and Christians stage a kind of slave revolt against noble moral values.

4. According to Nietzsche, the priests or the slaves revolted against the knightly-noble-aristocratic peoples. He refers to this revolt as the "slave revolt"—and to the extent that this revolt was successful, Nietzsche suggests that the displacement of the nobles led to the rise of the kind of moral values championed by the slaves or the priestly peoples. What values did the slaves or priests hold?—Unegoism was the central moral value! According to Nietzsche, the priests, insofar as they were "slaves" to the nobles, were oppressed and downtrodden; they were the "poor." But when slaves/priests revolted successfully against the nobles, the slaves "inverted" the moral and social order, that is, the slaves/priests demeaned the characteristics of the nobles and elevated their own slave/priestly characteristics. The value of unegoism (and thus the notion of goodness as centered on selfless love) comes directly from the elevation of the priests or slaves to power. Observe also that Nietzsche thinks that the priests/slaves include Jews and Christians. Thus, when Nietzsche calls attention to the problem of unegoism in *Genealogy*, he is calling attention to the "problem" of Judaism and Christianity. (Christianity is merely a different form of Judaism in Nietzsche's eyes.)

5. Note Nietzsche's comments in First Essay, #16, the paragraphs on "Rome versus Judea." He thinks that one concrete historical example of the slaves revolting and displacing the nobles is the case of Rome versus Judea. He asks: Who now occupies the heart of what was once the mighty Roman Empire? The answer to this question he thinks is obvious and it indicates that the nobles have certainly been displaced by the slaves/priests and their morality.

6. Pay careful attention to how Nietzsche describes the consequence of the slave revolt and thus the ascendency of the priests/slaves and their morality rooted in unegoism. He claims that this turn of events has made us weak, "weary or afraid of man." Recall again the criteria for morality that we noticed in his Preface: "Are they a sign of distress, of impoverishment, of the degeneration of life? Or is there revealed in them, on the contrary, the plenitude, force, and will of life, its courage, certainty, future?" How does the morality of the slaves, that is, compassion and unegoism, fare in Nietzsche's view when measured against these criteria?

7. If we are to be less like the priests/slaves, then that means we must be more like the nobles once again. But what does that mean? In First Essay, #11, Nietzsche hints that for the noble, goodness is not based on some commitment to unegoism but rather emerges "spontaneously out of himself." This is a critical passage in First Essay. Study it carefully and try to discern what this might mean. What does it mean to be a noble? What does it mean to be a kind of person whose notion of goodness emerges "spontaneously out of himself?"

8. Contrast Nietzsche's conception of the noble with the priest or slave. Unlike the noble, Nietzsche claims that the priest/slave lives according to "*ressentiment*" or through a kind of resentment. See First Essay 1, #10, in particular; note how Nietzsche describes people who live according to *ressentiment*: They love "secret hiding places, secret paths, back doors." Here, Nietzsche indicates the primary problem with the *ressentiment* of slave morality; *ressentiment* gives birth to values by turning outward (by responding to an "external world" or "other") rather than turning inward into the self. Thus, *ressentiment* indicates the *reactive* quality of slave morality; moral values for the slaves are always responses rather than spontaneous. *So, the slaves or priests believe in unegoism as the primary moral value because it is in reaction to their previous masters, the nobles*. The nobles, however, lived life not by reacting to something or someone else, but rather lived life spontaneously.

As you read First Essay with this reading guide in hand, consider the following questions:

1. Does Nietzsche accurately describe the Christian meaning of love? He thinks that it is simply a kind of unegoism (supported by "*ressentiment*"). Is that all there is to say about Christian love? And, do you think he is correct to conclude that Christian love makes human persons weak? Do you think he is correct to suggest that Christian love prevents human flourishing and creativity? It may help you to recall your reading of Paul's First Letter to the Corinthians to work toward a substantial answer here. More broadly, do you think he paints a fair picture of religion? Do you think that religion simply makes life uninteresting, boring, and uncreative? Is religion the kind of threat to human life and progress that Nietzsche suggests?

2. Is Nietzsche's alternative to slave/priest morality (and, thus, by implication Christian morality) compelling? That is, what do you think of Nietzsche's advocacy of the noble ideal. What do you think it means to live as a noble, one whose notion of goodness emerges spontaneously out of oneself? Do you think that this kind of life makes sense—do you think this kind of life is a possibility, realistic? What would be the moral and social consequences of embracing the noble ideal, as Nietzsche conceives of it?

3.   In rejecting the priestly notion of unegoism and embracing the noble ideal,
     do you think Nietzsche believes in an *objective* notion of morality? Is there
     such a thing as objective truth (truth with a capital T!) for Nietzsche? Or, is
     truth, for Nietzsche, simply a function of power? More specifically, is truth
     merely something you create through your own individual imagination and
     creative capacities? If so, then what might be the social and moral implica-
     tions of such a notion of truth?

ON THE GENEALOGY OF MORALS
First Essay

"Good and Evil," "Good and Bad"

1

These English psychologists, whom one has also to thank for the only attempts hitherto to arrive at a history of the origin of morality—they themselves are no easy riddle; I confess that, as living riddles, they even possess one essential advantage over their books—*they are interesting*! These English psychologists—what do they really want? One always discovers them voluntarily or involuntarily at the same task, namely at dragging the *partie honteuse*[6] of our inner world into the foreground and seeking the truly effective and directing agent, that which has been decisive in its evolution, in just that place where the intellectual pride of man would least *desire* to find it (in the *vis inertiae*[7] of habit, for example, or in forgetfulness, or in a blind and chance mechanistic hooking-together of ideas, or in something purely passive, automatic reflexive, molecular, and thoroughly stupid)—what is it really that always drives these psychologists in just *this* direction? Is it a secret, malicious, vulgar, perhaps self-deceiving instinct for belittling man? Or possibly a pessimistic suspicion, the mistrustfulness of disappointed idealists grown spiteful and gloomy? Or a petty subterranean hostility and rancor toward Christianity (and Plato) that has perhaps not even crossed the threshold of consciousness? Or even a lascivious taste for the grotesque, the painfully paradoxical, the questionable and absurd in existence? Or finally—something of each of them, a little vulgarity, a little gloominess, a little anti-Christianity, a little itching and need for spice?

But I am told they are simply old, cold, and tedious frogs, creeping around men and into men as if in their own proper element, that is, in a *swamp*. I rebel at that idea; more, I do not believe it; and if one may be allowed to hope where one does not know, then I hope from my heart they may be the reverse of this—that these investigators and microscopists of the soul may be fundamentally brave, proud, and magnanimous animals, who know how to keep their hearts as well as their sufferings in bounds and have trained themselves to sacrifice all desirability to truth, *every* truth, even plain, harsh, ugly, repellent, unChristian, immoral truth.—For such truths do exist.

---

6   Shame.
7   Inertia.

2

All respect then for the good spirits that may rule in these historians of morality! But it is, unhappily, certain that the *historical spirit* itself is lacking in them, that precisely all the good spirits of history itself have left them in the lurch! As is the hallowed custom with philosophers, the thinking of all of them is *by nature* unhistorical; there is no doubt about that. The way they have bungled their moral genealogy comes to light at the very beginning, where the task is to investigate the origin of the concept and judgment "good." "Originally"—so they decree— "one approved unegoistic actions and called them good from the point of view of those to whom they were done, that is to say, those to whom they were *useful*; later one *forgot* how this approval originated and, simply because unegoistic actions were always *habitually* praised as good, one also felt them to be good—as if they were something good in themselves." One sees straightaway that this primary derivation already contains all the typical traits of the idiosyncrasy of the English psychologists—we have "utility," "forgetting," "habit," and finally "error," all as the basis of an evaluation of which the higher man has hitherto been proud as though it were a kind of prerogative of man as such. This pride *has* to be humbled, this evaluation disvalued: has that end been achieved?

Now it is plain to me, first of all, that in this theory the source of the concept "good" has been sought and established in the wrong place: the judgment "good" did *not* originate with those to whom "goodness" was shown! Rather it was "the good" themselves, that is to say, the noble, powerful, high-stationed and high-minded, who felt and established themselves and their actions as good, that is, of the first rank, in contradistinction to all the low, low-minded, common and plebeian. It was out of this *pathos of distance*[8] that they first seized the right to create values and to coin names for values: what had they to do with utility! The viewpoint of utility is as remote and inappropriate as it possibly could be in face of such a burning eruption of the highest rank-ordering, rank-defining value judgments: for here feeling has attained the antithesis of that low degree of warmth which any calculating prudence, any calculus of utility, presupposes—and not for once only, not for an exceptional hour, but for good. The pathos of nobility and distance, as aforesaid, the protracted and domineering fundamental total feeling on the part of a higher ruling order in relation to a lower order, to a "below"—*that* is the origin of the antithesis "good" and "bad." The lordly right of giving names extends so far that one should allow oneself to conceive the origin of language itself as an expression of power on the part of the rulers: they say "this *is* this and this," they seal every thing and event with a sound and, as it were, take possession of it.) It follows from this origin that the word "good" was definitely *not* linked from the first and by necessity to "unegoistic" actions, as the superstition of these genealogists of morality would have it. Rather it was only when aristocratic value judgments *declined* that the whole antithesis

---

8   Ct. *Beyond Good and Evil*, section 257.

"egoistic" "unegoistic" obtruded itself more and more on the human conscience—it is, to speak in my own language the *herd instinct* that through this antithesis at last gets its word (and its *words*) in. And even then it was a long time before that instinct attained such dominion that moral evaluation was actually stuck and halted at this antithesis (as, for example, is the case in contemporary Europe: the prejudice that takes "moral," "unegoistic," "désintéressé" as concepts of equivalent value already rules today with the force of a "fixed idea" and brain-sickness).

4

The signpost to the *right* road was for me the question: what was the real etymological significance of the designations for "good" coined in the various languages? I found they all led back to the *same conceptual transformation*—that everywhere "noble," "aristocratic" in the social sense, is the basic concept from which "good" in the sense of "with aristocratic soul," "noble," "with a soul of a high order," "with a privileged soul" necessarily developed: a development which always runs parallel with that other in which "common," "plebeian," "low" are finally transformed into the concept "bad." The most convincing example of the latter is the German word *schlecht* [bad] itself: which is identical with *schlicht* [plain, simple]—compare *schlechtweg* [plainly], *schlechterdings*, [simply]—and originally designated the plain, the common man, as yet with no inculpatory implication and simply in contradistinction to the nobility. About the time of the Thirty Years' War, late enough therefore, this meaning changed into the one now customary.[9]

With regard to a moral genealogy this seems to me a *fundamental* insight; that it has been arrived at so late is the fault of the retarding influence exercised by the democratic prejudice in the modern world toward all questions of origin. And this is so even in the apparently quite objective domain of natural science and physiology, as I shall merely hint here. But what mischief this prejudice is capable of doing, especially to morality and history, once it has been unbridled to the point of hatred is shown by the notorious case of Buckle;[10] here the *plebeianism* of the modern spirit, which is of English origin, erupted once again on its native soil, as violently as a mud volcano and with that salty, noisy, vulgar eloquence with which all volcanos have spoken hitherto.—

5

With regard to *our* problem, which may on good grounds be called a *quiet* problem and one which fastidiously directs itself to few ears, it is of no small interest to ascertain that through those words and roots which designate "good" there frequently still shines the most important nuance by virtue of which the noble felt themselves to be men of

---

9   Cf. *Dawn*, section 231, included in the present volume.

10   Henry Thomas Buckle (1821–1862), English historian, is known chiefly for his *History of Civilization* (1857ff.).
      The suggestion in the text is developed more fully in section 876 of *The Will to Power*.

a higher rank. Granted that, in the majority of cases, they designate themselves simply by their superiority in power (as "the powerful," "the masters," "the commanders") or by the most clearly visible signs of this superiority, for example, as "the rich," "the possessors" (this is the meaning of *arya*; and of corresponding words in Iranian and Slavic). But they also do it by a *typical character trait*: and this is the case that concerns us here. They call themselves, for instance, *"the truthful"*; this is so above all of the Greek nobility, whose mouthpiece is the Megarian poet Theognis.[11] The root of the word coined for this, *esthlos*,[12] signifies one who is, who possesses reality, who is actual, who is true; then, with a subjective turn, the true as the truthful in this phase of conceptual transformation it becomes a slogan and catchword of the nobility and passes over entirely into the sense of "noble," as distinct from the *lying* common man, which is what Theognis takes him to be and how he describes him—until finally, after the decline of the nobility, the word is left to designate nobility of soul and becomes as it were ripe and sweet. In the word *kakos*,[13] as in *deilos*[14] (the plebeian in contradistinction to the *agathos*[15]), cowardice is emphasized: this perhaps gives an indication in which direction one should seek the etymological origin of *agathos*, which is susceptible of several interpretations. The Latin *malus*[16] (beside which I set *melas*[17]) may designate the common man as the

---

11   Nietzsche's first publication, in 1867 when he was still a student at the University of Leipzig, was article in a leading classical journal, *Rheinisches Museum*, on the history of the collection of the maxims of Theognis ("Zur Geschichte der Theognideischen Spruchsammlung"). Theognis of Megara lived in the sixth century B.C.

12   Greek: good, brave. Readers who are not classical philologists may wonder as they read this section how well taken Nietzsche's points about the Greeks are. In this connection one could obviously cite a vast literature, but in this brief commentary it will be sufficient to quote Professor Gerald F. Else's monumental study *Aristotle's Poetics: The Argument* (Cambridge, Mass., Harvard University Press, 1957), a work equally notable for its patient and thorough scholarship and its spirited defense of some controversial interpretations. On the points at issue here, Else's comments are not, I think, controversial; and that is the reason for citing them here.

"The dichotomy is mostly taken for granted in Homer: there are not many occasions when the heaven-wide gulf between heroes and commoners even has to be mentioned.[30] [30Still, one finds 'good' (*esthloi*) and 'bad' (*kakoi*) explicitly contrasted a fair number of times: B366, Z489, I319,...] In the . . . seventh and sixth centuries, on the other hand, the antithesis grows common. . . . Greek thinking begins with and for a long time holds to the proposition that mankind is divided into 'good' and 'bad,' and these terms are quite as much social, political, and economic as they are moral. . . . The dichotomy is absolute and exclusive for a simple reason: it began as the aristocrats' view of society and reflects their idea of the gulf between themselves and the 'others.' In the minds of a comparatively small and close-knit group like the Greek aristocracy there are only two kinds of people, 'we' and 'they'; and of course 'we' are the good people, the proper, decent, good-looking, right-thinking ones, while 'they' are the rascals, the poltroons, the good-for-nothings. . . . Aristotle knew and sympathized with this older aristocratic, 'practical' ideal, not as superior to the contemplative, but at least as next best to it" (p. 75).

13   Greek: bad, ugly, ill-born, mean, craven.

14   Greek: cowardly, worthless, vile, wretched.

15   Greek: good, well-born, gentle, brave, capable.

16   Bad.

17   Greek: black, dark.

dark-colored, above all as the black-haired man ("*hic niger est*[18]—"), as the pre-Aryan occupant of the soil at Italy who was distinguished most obviously from the blond, that is Aryan, conqueror race by his color; Gaelic, at any rate, offers us a precisely similar case—*fin* (for example in the name *Fin-Gal*), the distinguishing word for nobility, finally for the good, noble, pure, originally meant the blond-headed, in contradistinction to the dark, black-haired aboriginal inhabitants.

The Celts, by the way, were definitely a blond race; it is wrong to associate traces of an essentially dark-haired people which appear on the more careful ethnographical maps of Germany with any sort of Celtic origin or blood-mixture, as Virchow[19] still does: it is rather the *pre-Aryan* people of Germany who emerge in these places. (The same is true of virtually all Europe: the suppressed race has gradually recovered the upper hand again, in coloring, shortness of skull, perhaps even in the intellectual and social instincts: who can say whether modern democracy, even more modern anarchism and especially that inclination for "*commune*," for the most primitive form of society, which is now shared by all the socialists of Europe, does not signify in the main a tremendous *counterattack*—and that the conqueror and *master race*,[20] the Aryan, is not succumbing physiologically, too?

I believe I may venture to interpret the Latin *bonus*[21] as "the warrior," provided I am right in tracing *bonus* back to an earlier *duonus*[22] (compare *bellum = duellum = duenlum*, which seems to me to contain *duonus*). Therefore *bonus* as the man of strife, of dissention (*duo*), as the man of war: one sees what constituted the "goodness" of a man in ancient Rome. Our German *gut* [good] even: does it not signify "the godlike," the man of "godlike race"? And is it not identical with the popular (originally noble) name of the Goths? The grounds for this conjecture cannot be dealt with here.—

6

To this rule that a concept denoting political superiority always resolves itself into a concept denoting superiority of soul it is not necessarily an exception (although it provides occasions for exceptions) when the highest caste is at the same time the *priestly* caste and therefore emphasizes in its total description of itself a predicate that calls to mind

---

18   Quoted from Horace's *Satires*, I.4, line 85: "He that backbites an absent friend ... and cannot keep secrets, is black, Roman, beware!" *Niger*, originally "black," also came to mean unlucky and, as in this quotation, wicked. Conversely, *candidus* means white, bright, beautiful, pure, guileless, candid, honest, happy, fortunate. And in *Satires*, I.5, 41, Horace speaks of "the whitest souls earth ever bore" (*animae qualis neque candidiores terra tulit*).

19   Rudolf Virchow (1821–1902) was one of the greatest German pathologists, as well as a liberal politician, a member of the German Reichstag (parliament), and an opponent of Bismarck.

20   For a detailed discussion both of this concept and of Nietzsche's attitude toward the Jews and anti-Semitism see Kaufmann's *Nietzsche*, Chapter 10: "The Master-Race."

21   Good.

22   Listed in Harper's Latin Dictionary as the old form of *bonus*, with the comment: "for *duonus*, cf. *bellum*." And *duellum* is identified as an early and poetic form of *bellum* (war).

its priestly function. It is then, for example, that "pure" and "impure" confront one another for the first time as designations of station; and here too there evolves a "good" and a "bad" in a sense no longer referring to station. One should be warned, moreover, against taking these concepts "pure" and "impure" too ponderously or broadly, not to say symbolically: all the concepts of ancient man were rather at first incredibly uncouth, coarse, external, narrow, straightforward, and altogether *unsymbolical* in meaning to a degree that we can scarcely conceive. The "pure one" is from the beginning merely a man who washes himself, who forbids himself certain foods that produce skin ailments, who does not sleep with the dirty women of the lower strata, who has an aversion to blood—no more, hardly more! On the other hand, to be sure, it is clear from the whole nature of an essentially priestly aristocracy why antithetical valuations could in precisely this instance soon become dangerously deepened, sharpened, and internalized; and indeed they finally tore chasms between man and man that a very Achilles of a free spirit would not venture to leap without a shudder. There is from the first something *unhealthy* in such priestly aristocracies and in the habits ruling in them which turn them away from action and alternate between brooding and emotional explosions, habits which seem to have as their almost invariable consequence that intestinal morbidity and neurasthenia which has afflicted priests at all times; but as to that which they themselves devised as a remedy for this morbidity—must one not assert that it has ultimately proved itself a hundred times more dangerous in its effects than the sickness it was supposed to cure? Mankind itself is still ill with the effects of this priestly naïveté in medicine! Think, for example, of certain forms of diet (abstinence from meat), of fasting, of sexual continence, of flight "into the wilderness" (the Weir Mitchell isolation cure[23]—without, to be sure, the subsequent fattening and over-feeding which constitute the most effective remedy for the hysteria induced by the ascetic ideal): add to these the entire anti-sensualistic metaphysic of the priests that makes men indolent and overrefined, their auto-hypnosis in the manner of fakirs and Brahmins—Brahma used in the shape of a glass knob and a fixed idea—and finally the only-too-comprehensible satiety with all this, together with the radical cure for it, *nothingness* (or God—the desire for a *unio mystica* with God is the desire of the Buddhist for nothingness, Nirvana—and no more!). For with the priests *everything* becomes more dangerous, not only cures and remedies, but also arrogance, revenge, acuteness, profligacy, love, lust to rule, virtue, disease—but it is only fair to add that it was on the soil of this *essentially dangerous* form of human existence, the priestly form, that man first became *an interesting animal*, that only here did the human soul in a higher sense acquire *depth* and become *evil*—and these are the two basic respects in which man has hitherto been superior to other beasts!

---

23   The cure developed by Dr. Silas Weir Mitchell (1829–1914, American) consisted primarily in isolation, confinement to bed, dieting, and massage.

7

One will have divined already how easily the priestly mode of valuation can branch off from the knightly-aristocratic and then develop into its opposite; this is particularly likely when the priestly caste and the warrior caste are in jealous opposition to one another and are unwilling to come to terms. The knightly-aristocratic value judgments presupposed a powerful physicality, a flourishing, abundant, even overflowing health, together with that which serves to preserve it: war, adventure, hunting, dancing, war games, and in general all that involves vigorous, free, joyful activity. The priestly-noble mode of valuation presupposes, as we have seen, other things: it is disadvantageous for it when it comes to war! As is well known. the priests are the *most evil enemies*—but why? Because they are the most impotent. It is because of their impotence that in them hatred grows to monstrous and uncanny proportions, to the most spiritual and poisonous kind of hatred. The truly great haters in world history have always been priests; likewise the most ingenious[24] haters: other kinds of spirit[25] hardly come into consideration when compared with the spirit of priestly vengefulness. Human history would be altogether too stupid a thing without the spirit that the impotent have introduced into it—let us take at once the most notable example. All that has been done on earth against "the noble," "the powerful," "the masters," "the rulers," fades into nothing compared with what the *Jews* have done against them; the Jews, that priestly people, who in opposing their enemies and conquerors were ultimately satisfied with nothing less than a radical revaluation of their enemies' values, that is to say, an act of the most *spiritual revenge*. For this alone was appropriate to a priestly people, the people embodying the most deeply repressed[26] priestly vengefulness. It was the Jews who, with awe-inspiring consistency, dared to invert the aristocratic value-equation (good = noble = powerful = beautiful = happy = beloved of God) and to hang on to this inversion with their teeth, the teeth of the most abysmal hatred (the hatred of impotence), saying "the wretched alone are the good; the poor, impotent, lowly alone are the good; the suffering, deprived, sick, ugly alone are pious, alone are blessed by God, blessedness is for them alone—and you, the powerful and noble, are on the contrary the evil, the cruel, the lustful, the insatiable, the godless to all eternity; and you shall be in all eternity the unblessed, accursed, and damned!"... One knows *who* inherited this Jewish revaluation... In connection with the tremendous and immeasurably fateful initiative provided by the Jews through this most fundamental of all declarations of war, I recall the proposition I arrived at on a previous occasion (*Beyond Good and Evil* section 195)[27]—that with the Jews there begins *the slave revolt in morality*: that revolt which has a history of two thousand years behind it and which we no longer see because it—has been victorious.

---

24   *Geistreich.*

25   *Geist.*

26   *Zurückgetretensten.*

27   See my commentary on that section in *Beyond Good and Evil* (New York, Vintage Books, 1966), section 195, note 11.

8

But you do not comprehend this? You are incapable of seeing something that required two thousand years to achieve victory?—There is nothing to wonder at in that: all *protracted* things are hard to see, to see whole. *That,* however, is what has happened: from the trunk of that tree of vengefulness and hatred, Jewish hatred—the profoundest and sublimest kind of hatred, capable of creating ideals and reversing values, the like of which has never existed on earth before—there grew something equally incomparable, a *new love,* the profoundest and sublimest kind of love—and from what other trunk could it have grown?

One should not imagine it grew up as the denial of that thirst for revenge, as the opposite of Jewish hatred! No, the reverse is true! That love grew out of it as its crown, as its triumphant crown spreading itself farther and farther into the purest brightness and sunlight, driven as it were into the domain of light and the heights in pursuit of the goals of that hatred—victory, spoil, and seduction—by the same impulse that drove the roots of that hatred deeper and deeper and more and more covetously into all that was profound and evil. This Jesus of Nazareth, the incarnate gospel of love, this "Redeemer" who brought blessedness and victory to the poor, the sick, and the sinners was he not this seduction in its most uncanny and irresistible form, a seduction and bypath to precisely those *Jewish* values and new ideals? Did Israel not attain the ultimate goal of its sublime vengefulness precisely through the bypath of this "Redeemer," this ostensible opponent and disintegrator of Israel? Was it not part of the secret black art of truly *grand* politics of revenge, of a farseeing, subterranean, slowly advancing, and premeditated revenge, that Israel must itself deny the real instrument of its revenge before all the world as a mortal enemy and nail it to the cross, so that "all the world," namely all the opponents of Israel, could unhesitatingly swallow just this bait? And could spiritual subtlety imagine any *more dangerous* bait than this? Anything to equal the enticing, intoxicating, overwhelming, and undermining power of that symbol of the "holy cross," that ghastly paradox of a "God on the cross," that mystery of an unimaginable ultimate cruelty and self-crucifixion of God for the *salvation of man*?

What is certain, at least, is that *sub hoc signo*[28] Israel, with its vengefulness and revaluation of all values, has hitherto triumphed again and again over all other ideals, over all *nobler* ideals.—

9

"But why are you talking about *nobler* ideals! Let us stick to the facts: the people have won—or 'the slaves' or 'the mob' or 'the herd' or whatever you like to call them—if this has happened through the Jews, very well! in that case no people ever had a more

---

28   Under this sign.

world-historic mission. 'The masters' have been disposed of; the morality of the common man has won. One may conceive of this victory as at the same time a blood-poisoning (it has mixed the races together)—I shan't contradict; but this in-toxication has undoubtedly been *successful*. The 'redemption' of the human race (from 'the masters,' that is) is going forward; everything is visibly becoming Judaized, Christianized, mob-ized (what do the words matter!). The progress of this poison through the entire body of mankind seems irresistible, its pace and tempo may from now on even grow slower, subtler, less audible, more cautious—there is plenty of time.—To this end, does the church today still have any *necessary* role to play? Does it still have the right to exist? Or could one do without it? *Quaeritur.*²⁹ It seems to hinder rather than hasten this progress. But perhaps that is its usefulness.—Certainly it has, over the years, become something crude and boorish, something repellent to a more delicate intellect, to a truly modern taste. Ought it not to become at least a little more refined?—Today it alienates rather than seduces. —Which of us would be a free spirit if the church did not exist? It is the church, and not its poison, that repels us.—Apart from the church, we, too, love the poison.—"

This is the epilogue of a "free spirit" to my speech; an honest animal, as he has abundantly revealed, and a democrat, moreover; he had been listening to me till then and could not endure to listen to my silence. For at this point I have much to be silent about.

10

The slave revolt in morality begins when *ressentiment*³⁰ itself becomes creative and gives birth to values: the *ressentiment* of natures that are denied the true reaction, that of deeds, and compensate themselves with an imaginary revenge. While every noble morality develops from a triumphant affirmation of itself, slave morality from the outset says No to what is "outside," what is "different," what is "not itself"; and *this* No is its creative deed. This inversion of the value-positing eye—this *need* to direct one's view outward instead of back to oneself—is of the essence of *ressentiment*: in order to exist, slave morality always first needs a hostile external world; it needs, physiologically speaking, external stimuli in order to act at all —its action is fundamentally reaction.

The reverse is the case with the noble mode of valuation: it acts and grows spontaneously, it seeks its opposite only so as to affirm itself more gratefully and triumphantly— its negative concept to "low," "common," "bad" is only a subsequently invented pale, contrasting image in relation to its positive basic concept—filled with life and passion through and through—"we noble ones, we good, beautiful, happy ones!" When the noble mode of valuation blunders and sins against reality, it does so in respect to the sphere with which it is *not* sufficiently familiar, against a real knowledge of which it has indeed inflexibly guarded itself: in some circumstances it misunderstands the sphere it

---

29   One asks.
30   Resentment. The term is discussed above, in section 3 of the Introduction.

despises, that of the common man, of the lower orders; on the other hand, one should remember that, even supposing that the affect of contempt, of looking down from a superior height, *falsifies* the image of that which it despises, it will at any rate still be a much less serious falsification than that perpetrated on its opponent—in *effigie* of course—by the submerged hatred, the vengefulness of the impotent. There is indeed too much carelessness, too much taking lightly, too much looking away and impatience involved in contempt, even too much joyfulness, for it to be able to transform its object into a real caricature and monster.

One should not overlook the almost benevolent nuances that the Greek nobility, for example, bestows on all the words it employs to distinguish the lower orders from itself; how they are continuously mingled and sweetened with a kind of pity, consideration, and forbearance, so that finally almost all the words referring to the common man have remained as expressions signifying "unhappy," "pitiable" (campore *deilos*,[31] *deilaios*,[32] *poneros*,[33] *mochtheros*,[34] the last two of which properly designate the common man as work-slave and beast of burden)—and how on the other hand "bad," "low," "unhappy" have never ceased to sound to the Greek ear as one note with a tone-color in which "unhappy" preponderates: this as an inheritance from the ancient nobler aristocratic mode of evaluation, which does not belie itself even in its contempt (—philologists should recall the sense in which *oïzyros*,[35] *anolbos*,[36] *tlēmōn*,[37] *dystychein*,[38] *xymphora*[39] are employed). The "well-born" *felt* themselves to be the "happy"; they did not have to establish their happiness artificially by examining their enemies, or to persuade themselves, deceive themselves, that they were happy (as all men of *ressentiment* are in the habit of doing); and they likewise knew, as rounded men replete with energy and therefore *necessarily* active, that happiness should not be sundered from action—being active was with them necessarily a part of happiness (whence *eu prattein*[40] takes its origin)—all very much the opposite of "happiness" at the level of the impotent, the oppressed, and those in whom poisonous and inimical feelings are festering, with whom it appears as essentially narcotic, drug, rest, peace, "sabbath," slackening of tension and relaxing of limbs, in short *passively.*

---

31 All of the footnoted words in this section are Greek. The first four mean wretched, but each has a separate note to suggest some of its other connotations. *Deilos:* cowardly, worthless, vile.

32 Paltry.

33 Oppressed by toils, good for nothing, worthless, knavish, base, cowardly.

34 Suffering, hardship, knavish.

35 Woeful, miserable, toilsome; wretch.

36 Unblest, wretched, luckless, poor.

37 Wretched, miserable.

38 To be unlucky, unfortunate.

39 Misfortune.

40 To do well in the sense of faring well.

While the noble man lives in trust and openness with himself (*gennaios*[41] "of noble descent" underlines the nuance "upright" and probably also "naïve"), the man of *ressentiment* is neither upright nor naïve nor honest and straightforward with himself. His soul *squints*; his spirit loves hiding places, secret paths and back doors, everything covert entices him as *his* world, *his* security, *his* refreshment; he understands how to keep silent, how not to forget, how to wait, how to be provisionally self-deprecating and humble. A race of such men of *ressentiment* is bound to become eventually *cleverer* than any noble race; it will also honor cleverness to a far greater degree: namely, as a condition of existence of the first importance; while with noble men cleverness can easily acquire a subtle flavor of luxury and subtlety—for here it is far less essential than the perfect functioning of the regulating *unconscious* instincts or even than a certain imprudence, perhaps a bold recklessness whether in the face of danger or of the enemy, or that enthusiastic impulsiveness in anger, love, reverence, gratitude, and revenge by which noble souls have at all times recognized one another. *Ressentiment* itself, if it should appear in the noble man, consummates and exhausts itself in an immediate reaction, and therefore does not *poison*: on the other hand, it fails to appear at all on countless occasions on which it inevitably appears in the weak and impotent.

To be incapable of taking one's enemies, one's accidents, even one's misdeeds seriously for very long—that is the sign of strong, full natures in whom there is an excess of the power to form, to mold, to recuperate and to forget (a good example of this in modern times is Mirabeau,[42] who had no memory for insults and vile actions done him and was unable to forgive simply because he—forgot). Such a man shakes off with a *single* shrug many vermin that eat deep into others; here alone genuine "love of one's enemies" is possible—supposing it to be possible at all on earth. How much reverence has a noble man for his enemies!—and such reverence is a bridge to love.—For he desires his enemy for himself, as his mark of distinction; he can endure no other enemy than one in whom there is nothing to despise and *very much* to honor! In contrast to this, picture "the enemy" as the man of *ressentiment* conceives him—and here precisely is his deed, his creation: he has conceived "the evil enemy," "*the Evil One,*" and this in fact is his basic concept, from which he then evolves, as an afterthought and pendant, a "good one"—himself!

11

This, then, is quite the contrary of what the noble man does, who conceives the basic concept "good" in advance and spontaneously out of himself and only then creates for himself an idea of "bad"! This "bad" of noble origin and that "evil" out of the cauldron of unsatisfied hatred—the former an after-production, a side issue, a contrasting

---

41   High-born, noble, high-minded.
42   Honoré Gabriel Riqueti, Comte de Mirabeau (1749–1791), was a celebrated French Revolutionary statesman and writer.

shade, the latter on the contrary the original thing, the beginning, the distinctive *deed* in the conception of a slave morality—how different these words "bad" and "evil" are, although they are both apparently the opposite of the same concept "good." But it is *not* the same concept "good": one should ask rather precisely *who* is "evil" in the sense of the morality of *ressentiment*. The answer, in all strictness, is: *precisely* the "good man" of the other morality, precisely the noble, powerful man, the ruler, but dyed in another color, interpreted in another fashion, seen in another way by the venomous eye of *ressentiment*.

Here there is one thing we shall be the last to deny: he who knows these "good men" only as enemies knows only *evil enemies*, and the same men who are held so sternly in check *interpares*[43] by custom, respect, usage, gratitude, and even more by mutual suspicion and jealousy, and who on the other hand in their relations with one another show themselves so resourceful in consideration, self-control, delicacy, loyalty, pride, and friendship—once they go outside, where the strange, the *stranger* is found, they are not much better than uncaged beasts of prey. There they savor a freedom from all social constraints, they compensate themselves in the wilderness for the tension engendered by protracted confinement and enclosure within the peace of society, they go *back* to the innocent conscience of the beast of prey, as triumphant monsters who perhaps emerge from a disgusting[44] procession of murder, arson, rape, and torture, exhilarated and undisturbed of soul, as if it were no more than a student's prank, convinced they have provided the poets with a lot more material for song and praise. One cannot fail to see at the bottom of all these noble races the beast of prey, the splendid *blond beast*[45]

---

43   Among equals.

44   *Scheusslichen.*

45   This is the first appearance in Nietzsche's writings of the notorious "blond beast." It is encountered twice more in the present section; a variant appears in section 17 of the second essay; and then the *blonde Bestie* appears once more in *Twilight*, "The 'Improvers' of Mankind." section 2 (*Portable Nietzsche*, p. 502). That is all. For a detailed discussion of these passages see Kaufmann's *Nietzsche*, Chapter 7, section III: "…The 'blond beast' is not a racial concept and does not refer to the 'Nordic race' of which the Nazis later made so much. Nietzsche specifically refers to Arabs and Japanese…—and the 'blondness' presumably refers to the beast, the lion."

Francis Golffing, in his free translation, of the *Genealogy*, deletes the blond beast three times out of four; only where it appears the second time in the original text, he has "the blond Teutonic beast." This helps to corroborate the myth that the blondness refers to the Teutons. Without the image of the lion, however, we lose not only some of Nietzsche's poetry as well as any chance to understand one of his best known coinages; we also lose an echo of the crucial first chapter of *Zarathustra*, where the lion represents the second stage in "The Three Metamorphoses" of the spirit—above the obedient camel but below the creative child (*Portable Nietzsche*, pp. 138f.),

Arthur Danto has suggested that if lions were black and Nietzsche had written "Black Beast," the expression would "provide support for African instead of German nationalists" (*Nietzsche as Philosopher*, New York, Macmillan, 1965, p. 170). Panthers *are* black and magnificent animals, but anyone calling Negroes black beasts and associating them with "a disgusting procession of murder, arson, rape, and torture," adding that "the animal has to get out again and go back to the wilderness," and then going on to speak of their hair-raising cheerfulness and profound joy in all destruction," would scarcely be taken to "provide support for… nationalists." On the contrary, he would be taken for a highly prejudiced critic of the Negro.

No other German writer of comparable stature has been a more extreme critic of German nationalism than Nietzsche. For all that, it is plain that in this section he sought to describe the behavior of the ancient Greeks and Romans, the Goths and the vandals, not that of nineteenth-century Germans.

prowling about avidly in search of spoil and victory; this hidden core needs to erupt from time to time, the animal has to get out again and go back to the wilderness: the Roman, Arabian, Germanic, Japanese nobility, the Homeric heroes, the Scandinavian Vikings—they all shared this need.

It is the noble races that have left behind them the concept "barbarian" wherever they have gone; even their highest culture betrays a consciousness of it and even a pride in it (for example, when Pericles says to his Athenians in his famous funeral oration "our boldness has gained access to every land and sea, everywhere raising imperishable monuments to its goodness *and wickedness*"). This "boldness" of noble races, mad, absurd, and sudden in its expression, the incalculability, even incredibility of their undertakings—Pericles specially commends the *rhathymia*[46] of the Athenians—their indifference to and contempt for security, body, life, comfort, their hair-raising[47] cheerfulness and pro-found joy in all destruction, in all the voluptuousness of victory and cruelty—all this came together, in the minds of those who suffered from it, in the image of the "barbarian," the "evil enemy," perhaps as the "Goths," the "Vandals." The deep and icy mistrust the German still arouses today whenever he gets into a position of power is an echo of that inextinguishable horror with which Europe observed for centuries that raging of the blond Germanic beast (although between the old Germanic tribes and us Germans there exists hardly a conceptual relationship, let alone one of blood).

I once drew attention to the dilemma in which Hesiod found himself when he concocted his succession of cultural epochs and sought to express them in terms of gold, silver, and bronze: he knew no way of handling the contradiction presented by the glorious but at the same time terrible and violent world of Homer except by dividing one epoch into two epochs, which he then placed one behind the other—first the epoch of the heroes and demigods of Troy and Thebes, the form in which that world had survived in the memory of the noble races who were those heroes' true descendants; then the bronze epoch, the form in which that same world appeared to the descendants of the downtrodden, pillaged, mistreated, abducted, enslaved: an epoch of bronze, as aforesaid, hard, cold, cruel, devoid of feeling or conscience, destructive and bloody.

Supposing that what is at any rate believed to be the "truth" really is true, and the *meaning of all culture* is the reduction of the beast of prey "man" to a tame and civilized animal, a *domestic animal*, then one would undoubtedly have to regard all those instincts of reaction and *ressentiment* through whose aid the noble races and their ideals were finally confounded and overthrown as the actual *instruments of culture*, which is not to

---

46   Thucydides, 2.39. In *A Historical Commentary on Thucydides,* vol. II (Oxford, Clarendon Press, 1956; corrected imprint of 1966), p. 118, A. W. Comme comments on this word: "in its original sense, 'ease of mind,' 'without anxiety'... But ease of mind can in certain circumstances become carelessness, remissness, frivolity: Demosthenes often accused the Athenians of *rhathymia* ..."

47   *Entsetzliche.*

say that the bearers of these instincts themselves represent culture. Rather is the reverse not merely probable—no! today it is *palpable*! These bearers of the oppressive instincts that thirst for reprisal, the descendants of every kind of European and non-European slavery, and especially of the entire pre-Aryan populace—they represent the *regression* of mankind! These "instruments of culture" are a disgrace to man and rather an accusation and counterargument against "culture" in general! One may be quite justified in continuing to fear the blond beast at the core of all noble races and in being on one's guard against it: but who would not a hundred times sooner fear where one can also admire than *not* fear but be permanently condemned to the repellent sight of the ill-constituted, dwarfed, atrophied, and poisoned?[48] And is that not *our* fate? What today constitutes *our* antipathy to "man"?—for we *suffer* from man, beyond doubt.

Not fear; rather that we no longer have anything left to fear in man; that the maggot[49] "man" is swarming in the foreground; that the "tame man," the hopelessly mediocre and insipid[50] man, has already learned to feel himself as the goal and zenith, as the meaning of history, as "higher man"—that he has indeed a certain right to feel thus, insofar as he feels himself elevated above the surfeit of ill-constituted, sickly, weary and exhausted people of which Europe is beginning to stink today, as something at least relatively well-constituted, at least still capable of living, at least affirming life.

12

At this point I cannot suppress a sigh and a last hope. What is it that I especially find utterly unendurable? That I cannot cope with, that makes me choke and faint? Bad air! Bad air! The approach of some ill-constituted thing; that I have to smell the entrails of some ill-constituted soul!

How much one is able to endure: distress, want, bad weather, sickness, toil, solitude. Fundamentally one can cope with everything else, born as one is to a subterranean life of struggle; one emerges again and again into the light, one experiences again and again one's golden hour of victory—and then one stands forth as one was born, unbreakable, tensed, ready for new, even harder, remoter things, like a bow that distress only serves to draw tauter.

But grant me from time to time—if there are divine goddesses in the realm beyond good and evil—grant me the sight, but *one* glance of something perfect, wholly achieved, happy, mighty, triumphant, something still capable of arousing fear! Of a man who

---

48   If the present section is not clear enough to any reader, he might turn to *Zarathustra's* contrast of the *overman* and the *last man* (Prologue, sections 1–5) and, for good measure, read also the first chapter or two of Part One. Then he will surely see how Aldous Huxley's *Brave New World* and George Orwell's *1984*—but especially the former—are developments of Nietzsche's theme. Huxley, in his novel, uses Shakespeare as a foil; Nietzsche, in the passage above, Homer.

49   *Gewürm* suggests wormlike animals; *wimmelt* can mean swarm or crawl but is particularly associated with maggots—in a cheese, for example.

50   *Unerquicklich.*

justifies *man*, of a complementary and redeeming lucky hit on the part of man for the sake of which one may still *believe in man*!

For this is how things are: the diminution and leveling of European man constitutes *our* greatest danger, for the sight of him makes us weary.—We can see nothing today that wants to grow greater, we suspect that things will continue to go down, down, to become thinner, more good-natured, more prudent, more comfortable, more mediocre, more indifferent, more Chinese, more Christian—there is no doubt that man is getting "better" all the time.

Here precisely is what has become a fatality for Europe—together with the fear of man we have also lost our love of him, our reverence for him, our hopes for him, even the will to him. The sight of man now makes us weary—what is nihilism today if it is not *that*?—We are weary of *man*.

13

But let us return: the problem of the *other* origin of the "good," of the good as conceived by the man of *ressentiment*, demands its solution.

That lambs dislike great birds of prey does not seem strange: only it gives no ground for reproaching these birds of prey for bearing off little lambs. And if the lambs say among themselves: "these birds of prey are evil, and whoever is least like a bird of prey, but rather its opposite, a lamb—would he not be good?" there is no reason to find fault with this institution of an ideal, except perhaps that the birds of prey might view it a little ironically and say: "*we* don't dislike them at all, these good little lambs; we even love them: nothing is more tasty than a tender lamb."

To demand of strength that it should *not* express itself as strength, that it should *not* be a desire to overcome, a desire to throw down, a desire to become master, a thirst for enemies and resistances and triumphs, is just as absurd as to demand of weakness that it should express itself as strength. A quantum of force is equivalent to a quantum of drive, will, effect—more, it is nothing other than precisely this very driving, willing, effecting, and only owing to the seduction of language (and of the fundamental errors of reason that are petrified in it) which conceives and misconceives all effects as conditioned by something that causes effects, by a "subject," can it appear otherwise. For just as the popular mind separates the lightning from its flash and takes the latter for an *action*, for the operation of a subject called lightning, so popular morality also separates strength from expressions of strength, as if there were a neutral substratum behind the strong man, which was *free* to express strength or not to do so. But there is no such substratum; there is no "being" behind doing, effecting, becoming; "the doer" is merely a fiction added to the deed—the deed is everything. The popular mind in fact doubles the deed; when it sees the lightning flash, it is the deed of a deed: it posits the same event first as cause and then a second time as its effect. Scientists do no better when they say "force moves," "force causes," and the like—all its coolness, its freedom from emotion notwithstanding, our entire science still lies under the misleading influence of language and has not disposed of that little changeling, the "subject" (the atom, for example, is such a changeling, as is the Kantian "thing-in-itself"); no wonder if the submerged, darkly glowering emotions of vengefulness and hatred exploit this belief for their own ends and in fact maintain no belief more ardently than the belief that *the strong man is free* to be weak and the bird of prey to be a lamb—for thus they gain the right to make the bird of prey *accountable* for being a bird of prey.

When the oppressed, downtrodden, outraged exhort one another with the vengeful cunning of impotence: "let us be different from the evil, namely good! And he is good who does not outrage, who harms nobody, who does not attack, who does not requite, who leaves revenge to God, who keeps himself hidden as we do, who avoids evil and desires little from life, like us, the patient, humble, and just"—this, listened to calmly and without previous bias, really amounts to no more than: "we weak ones are, after all, weak; it would be good if we did nothing *for which we are not strong enough*"; but this dry matter of fact, this prudence of the lowest order which even insects possess (posing as dead, when in great danger, so as not to do "too much"), has, thanks to the counterfeit and self-deception of impotence, clad itself in the ostentatious garb of the virtue of quiet, calm resignation, just as if the weakness of the weak—that is to say, their *essence*, their effects, their sole ineluctable, irremovable reality—were a voluntary achievement, willed, chosen, a *deed*, a *meritorious act*. This type of man *needs* to believe in a neutral independent "subject," prompted by an instinct for self-preservation and self-affirmation in which every lie is sanctified. The subject (or, to use a more popular expression, the *soul*) has perhaps been believed in hitherto more firmly than anything else on earth because it makes possible to the majority of mortals, the weak and oppressed of every kind, the sublime self-deception that interprets weakness as freedom, and their being thus-and-thus as a *merit*.

14

Would anyone like to take a look into the secret of how *ideals are made* on earth? Who has the courage?—Very well! Here is a point we can see through into this dark workshop. But wait a moment or two, Mr. Rash and Curious: your eyes must first get used to this false iridescent light.—All right! Now speak! What is going on down there? Say what you see, man of the most perilous kind of inquisitiveness—now I am the one who is listening.—

—"I see nothing, but I hear the more. There is a soft, wary, malignant muttering and whispering coming from all the corners and nooks. It seems to me one is lying; a saccharine sweetness clings to every sound. Weakness is being lied into something *meritorious*, no doubt of it—so it is just as you said"—

—Go on!

—"and impotence which does not requite into 'goodness of heart'; anxious lowliness into 'humility': subjection to those one hates into 'obedience' (that is, to one of whom they say he commands this subjection—they call him God). The inoffensiveness of the weak man, even the cowardice of which he has so much, his lingering at the door, his being ineluctably compelled to wait, here acquire flattering names, such as 'patience,' and are even called virtue itself; his inability for revenge is called unwillingness to revenge, perhaps even forgiveness ('for *they* know not what they do—we alone know what *they* do!'). They also speak of 'loving one's enemies'—and sweat as they do so."

—Go on!

—"They are miserable, no doubt of it, all these mutterers and nook counterfeiters, although they crouch warmly together—but they tell me their misery is a sign of being chosen by God; one beats the dogs one likes best; perhaps this misery is also a preparation, a testing, a schooling, perhaps it is even more—something that will one day be made good and recompensed with interest, with huge payments of gold, no! of happiness. This they call 'bliss.'"

—Go on!

—"Now they give me to understand that they are not merely better than the mighty, the lords of the earth whose spittle they have to lick (*not* from fear, not at all from fear! but because God has commanded them to obey the authorities)[51]—that they are not merely better but are also 'better off,' or at least will be better off someday. But enough! enough! I can't take any more. Bad air! Bad air! This workshop where *ideals are manufactured*—it seems to me it stinks of so many lies."

—No! Wait a moment! You have said nothing yet of the masterpiece of these black magicians, who make whiteness, milk, and innocence of every blackness—haven't you noticed their perfection of refinement, their boldest, subtlest, most ingenious, most mendacious artistic stroke? Attend to them! These cellar rodents full of vengefulness and hatred—what have they made of revenge and hatred? Have you heard these words uttered? If you trusted simply to their words, would you suspect you were among men of *ressentiment*? . . .

—"I understand; I'll open my ears again (oh! oh! oh! and *close* my nose). Now I can really hear what they have been saying all along: 'We good men—*we are the just*'—what they desire they call, not retaliation, but 'the triumph of *justice*'; what they hate is not their enemy, no! they hate 'injustice,' they hate 'godlessness'; what they believe in and hope for is not the hope of revenge, the intoxication of sweet revenge (—'sweeter than

---

51   Allusion to Romans 13:1–2.

honey' Homer called it), but the victory of God, of the *just* God, over the godless; what there is left for them to love on earth is not their brothers in hatred but their 'brothers in love,' as they put it, all the good and just on earth."

—And what do they call that which serves to console them for all the suffering of life—*their* phantasmagoria of anticipated future bliss?

—"What? Do I hear aright? They call that 'the Last Judgment,' the coming of *their* kingdom, of the 'Kingdom of God'—meanwhile, however, they live 'in faith,' 'in love,' 'in hope.'"

—Enough! Enough!

16

Let us conclude. The two *opposing* values "good and bad," "good and evil" have been engaged in a fearful struggle on earth for thousands of years; and though the latter value has certainly been on top for a long time, there are still places where the struggle is as yet undecided. One might even say that it has risen ever higher and thus become more and more profound and spiritual: so that today there is perhaps no more decisive mark of a "*higher nature*," a more spiritual nature, than that of being divided in this sense and a genuine battleground of these opposed values.[52]

The symbol of this struggle, inscribed in letters legible across all human history, is "Rome against Judea, Judea against Rome":—there has hitherto been no greater event than *this* struggle, *this* question, *this* deadly contradiction. Rome felt the Jew to be something like anti-nature itself, its antipodal monstrosity as it were: in Rome the Jew stood "*convicted* of hatred for the whole human race"; and rightly, provided one has a right to link the salvation and future of the human race with the unconditional dominance of aristocratic values, Roman values.

How, on the other hand, did the Jews feel about Rome? A thousand signs tell us; but it suffices to recall the Apocalypse of John, the most wanton of all literary outbursts that vengefulness has on its conscience. (One should not underestimate the profound consistency of the Christian instinct when it signed this book of hate with the name of the disciple of love, the same disciple to whom it attributed that amorous-enthusiastic Gospel: there is a piece of truth in this, however much literary counterfeiting might have been required to produce it.) For the Romans were the strong and noble, and nobody stronger and nobler has yet existed on earth or even been dreamed of: every remnant of them, every inscription gives delight, if only one divines *what* it was that was

---

52   This remark which recalls *Beyond Good and Evil*, section 200, is entirely in keeping with the way in which the contrast of master and slave morality is introduced in *Beyond Good and Evil*, section 260; and it ought not to be overlooked. It sheds a good deal of light not only on this contrast but also on Nietzsche's *amor fati* his love of fate. Those who ignore all this material are bound completely to misunderstand Nietzsche's moral philosophy.

there at work. The Jews, on the contrary, were the priestly nation of *ressentiment par excellence*, in whom there dwelt an unequaled popular-moral genius: one only has to compare similarly gifted nations—the Chinese or the Germans, for instance—with the Jews, to sense which is of the first and which of the fifth rank.[53]

Which of them has won *for the present*, Rome or Judea? But there can be no doubt: consider to whom one bows down in Rome itself today, as if they were the epitome of all the highest values—and not only in Rome but over almost half the earth, everywhere that man has become tame or desires to become tame: *three Jews*, as is known, and *one Jewess* (Jesus of Nazareth, the fisherman Peter, the rug weaver Paul, and the mother of the aforementioned Jesus, named Mary). This is very remarkable: Rome has been defeated beyond all doubt.

There was, to be sure, in the Renaissance an uncanny and glittering reawakening of the classical ideal, of the noble mode of evaluating all things; Rome itself, oppressed by the new superimposed Judaized Rome that presented the aspect of an ecumenical synagogue and was called the "church," stirred like one awakened from seeming death: but Judea immediately triumphed again, thanks to that thoroughly plebeian (German and English) *ressentiment* movement called the Reformation, and to that which was bound to arise from it, the restoration of the church—the restoration too of the ancient sepulchral repose of classical Rome.

With the French Revolution, Judea once again triumphed over the classical ideal, and this time in an even more profound and decisive sense: the last political noblesse in Europe, that of the *French* seventeenth and eighteenth century, collapsed beneath the popular instincts of *ressentiment*—greater rejoicing, more uproarious enthusiasm had never been heard on earth! To be sure, in the midst of it there occurred the most tremendous, the most unexpected thing: the ideal of antiquity itself stepped *incarnate* and in unheard-of splendor before the eyes and conscience of mankind—and once again, in opposition to the mendacious slogan of *ressentiment*, "supreme rights of the majority," in opposition to the will to the lowering, the abasement, the leveling and the decline and twilight of mankind, there sounded stronger, simpler, and more insistently than ever the terrible and rapturous counterslogan "supreme rights of the few"! Like a last signpost to the *other* path, Napoleon appeared, the most isolated and late-born man there has ever been, and in him the problem of the *noble ideal as such* made flesh—one might well ponder *what* kind of problem it is: Napoleon, this synthesis of the *inhuman* and *superhuman*.

---

53   Having said things that can easily be misconstrued as grist to the mill of the German anti-Semites, Nietzsche goes out of his way, as usual, to express his admiration for the Jews and his disdain for the Germans.

D
LIBERALISM AND ITS CRITICS

John Locke

Editor's Introduction
Anthony Sciglitano

John Locke was born in Somerset, England, and attended some of the best schools, including Oxford, available at the time. He studied both philosophy and medicine there, and then later taught at Oxford from the age of twenty to thirty-four. Locke wrote during a time of great turmoil in Europe at large, and in England specifically. The unity of Western Europe under the Catholic Church dissolved during the Reformation of the sixteenth century. Great violence, including the Thirty Years War (1618–1648), occurred between different factions of Europe for the greater part of two centuries. This violence is often loosely labeled the "religious wars," as Protestants of various kinds and Catholics shed each others' blood over religious views and their desire to control territory. Today, however, this view of sixteenth and seventeenth century violence is hotly debated, as other historians point out that Protestants[i] sometimes fought other Protestants, while Catholics sometimes fought Catholics. An alternative explanation for the violence of these centuries is that the birth-pangs of the nation state required the elimination of all allegiances beyond or apart from the state itself, that is, allegiances to a church that is beyond the control of a particular state or to organizations such as different guilds. Many historians will see some mix of causes. In any event, it was certainly a tumultuous time that begged for a new formulation of the role of government as older models no longer fit the needs of developing states.

One view of government was that monarchs were designated by God to rule by divine right. This view was supported by, for instance, Robert Filmer (1588–1653), who would make the view of the monarch or "sovereign" the equivalent of law. On this view, the law equals what the monarch declares and there is no higher authority to be had. It is against this view that John Locke wrote his *First Treatise of Government*. His *Second Treatise* offers an alternative view of government. Here, Locke outlines why he believes people form themselves into societies, why they create central governing bodies, what makes up the limits of government, the legitimacy of the rule of law as opposed to the absolute rule of a monarch, the origins of property rights, and the legitimacy of economic inequality. The excerpts you will read are from the *Second Treatise*. Locke's writing was greatly appreciated and discussed in the American colonies; in fact, he was one of the principal writers of *The Fundamental Constitutions of Carolina* in 1669. We can only note briefly here that Locke was a controversial figure. In his own time, he took part in conspiracies to overthrow King Charles II and King James II of England and was a major proponent of the Glorious Revolution (1688). On the one hand, he appears to outline a theory of rights that protects individuals from tyranny and argues against slavery; on the other hand, he was

---

i   I am using the imprecise *Protestant* here for convenience's sake, but know that in the sixteenth century, this term designated Lutheran princes who "protested" the Second Diet [meeting] of Speyer in 1529. In fact, there is no one protestant movement, but a collection of groups united in their rejection of the Catholic Church but divided among themselves on issues such as relation to the state, the nature of Eucharist, the proper form of church organization, and so on.

an investor in the British slave trade and can be viewed as a defender of the rights of the propertied class against those without property or rights.

As you read the excerpts from John Locke's *Second Treatise on Government*, be sure to attend to the following issues:

1. How does Locke describe the state of nature? What is the difference between license and liberty?

2. What reasons does Locke give for the formation of society and government? For Locke, what are the pursuits of human beings that government ought to protect?

3. What does Locke think justifies private ownership or property? What counts as property, according to Locke?

4. How does Locke believe inequality with respect to ownership originates? Does he think this inequality is justified? Why or why not?

5. According to Locke, does this inequality occur through violent or peaceful means?

6. The book of Genesis begins with a story of Adam and Eve living peacefully in the Garden of Eden. In chapter 2, Adam and Eve disobey the divine prohibition on eating the fruit, and are cast out. By chapter 3, and especially by chapter 11, we read of terrible antagonisms, alienations, and disruptions of human relationships to God, one another, and the land. Do you see any parallels to Locke's discussion of the state of nature and the state of war in his *Second Treatise*?

SECOND TREATISE OF GOVERNMENT (Selection)

From *Second Treatise of Government, by John Locke*, ed. By C.B. Macpherson. Hackett Publishing Company, Indianapolis, IN 1980. Used with permission.

1. "Political power then, I take to be a right of making laws with penalties of death and consequently all less penalties, for the regulating and preserving of property... and all this only for the public good" (§3).

2. "To understand political power right, and derive it from its original, we must consider, what state all men are naturally in, and that is, a state of perfect freedom to order their actions, and dispose of their possessions and persons, as they think fit within the bounds of the law of nature, without asking leave or depending upon the will of any other man" (§4).

3. "But though this be a state of liberty yet it is not a state of license...The state of nature has a law to govern it, which obliges every one: and reason, which is that law, teaches all mankind that being all equal and independent, no one ought to harm another in his life, health, liberty, or possessions. Every one, as he is bound to preserve himself... so by the like reason, when his own preservation comes not in competition, ought he, as much as he can, to preserve the rest of mankind" (§6).

4. "Though the earth, and all inferior creatures, be common to all men, yet every man has a property in his own person; this nobody has any right to but himself. The labour of his body, and the work of his hands, we may say, are properly his. Whatsoever then he removes out of the state that nature hath provided, and left it in, he hath mixed his labour with, and joined to it something that is his own, and thereby makes it his property. It being by him removed from the common state nature hath placed it in, it hath by this labour something annexed to it, that excludes the common right of other men: for this labour being the unquestionable property of the labourer, no man but he can have a right to what that is once joined to, at least where there is enough, and as good, left in common for others" (§26).

5. "He that is nourished by the acorns he picked up under an oak, or the apples he gathered from the trees in the wood, has certainly appropriated them to himself. Nobody can deny but the nourishment is his. I ask then, when did they begin to be his? when he digested? or when he eat? or when he boiled? or when he brought them home? or when he picked them up? and it is plain, if the first gathering made them not his, nothing else could. That labour put a distinction between them and common: that added something to them more than nature, the common mother of all, had done; and so they became his private right. And will anyone say, he had no right to those acorns or apples, he thus appropriated, because he had not the consent of all mankind to make them his? Was it a robbery thus to assume to himself what belonged to all in common? If such a consent as that was necessary, man

had starved, notwithstanding the plenty God had given him. We see in commons, which remain so by compact, that it is the taking any part of what is common, and removing it out of the state nature leaves it in, which begins the property; without which the common is of no use. And the taking of this or that part, does not depend on the express consent of all the commoners. Thus the grass my horse has bit; the turfs my servant has cut; and the ore I have digged in any place, where I have a right to them in common with others, become my property, without the assignation or consent of anybody. The labour that was mine, removing them out of that common state they were in, hath fixed my property in them" (§28).

6. "It will perhaps be objected to this, that if gathering the acorns, or other fruits of the earth, &c. makes a right to them, then anyone may ingross as much as he will. To which I answer, Not so. The same law of nature, that does by this means give us property, does also bound that property too. God has given us all things richly, 1 Tim. vi. 12. is the voice of reason confirmed by inspiration. But how far has he given it us? To enjoy. As much as any one can make use of to any advantage of life before it spoils, so much he may by his Labour fix a property in: whatever is beyond this, is more than his share, and belongs to others. Nothing was made by God for man to spoil or destroy. And thus, considering the plenty of natural provisions there was a long time in the world, and the few spenders; and to how small a part of that provision the industry of one man could extend itself, and ingross it to the prejudice of others; especially keeping within the bounds, set by reason, of what might serve for his use; there could be then little room for quarrels or contentions about property so established" (§31).

7. "But the chief matter of property being now not the fruits of the earth, and the beasts that subsist on it, but the earth itself; as that which takes in and carries with it all the rest; I think it is plain, that property in that too is acquired as the former. As much land as a man tills, plants, improves, cultivates, and can use the product of, so much is his property. He by his labour does, as it were, inclose it from the common. Nor will it invalidate his right, to say everybody else has an equal title to it; and therefore he cannot appropriate, he cannot inclose, without the consent of all his fellow-commoners, all mankind. God, when he gave the world in common to all mankind, commanded man also to labour, and the penury of his condition required it of him. God and his reason commanded him to subdue the earth, i.e. improve it for the benefit of life, and therein lay out something upon it that was his own, his labour. He that in obedience to this command of God, subdued, tilled and sowed any part of it, thereby annexed to it something that was his property, which another had no title to, nor could without injury take from him" (§32).

8. "...it is plain that men have agreed to a disproportionate and unequal possession of the earth, they having by a tacit and voluntary consent, found out a way how a man

may fairly possess more land than he himself can use the product of, by receiving in exchange for the overplus gold and silver, which may be hoarded up without injury to anyone... This partage of things in an inequality of private possessions, men have made practicable out of the bounds of society, and without compact, only by putting a value on gold and silver, and tacitly agreeing in the use of money: for in governments, the laws regulate the right of property..." (§50).

9. "If man in the state of nature be so free, if he be absolute lord of his own person and possessions, equal to the greatest, and subject to no body, why will he part with his freedom? To which it is obvious to answer, that though in the state of nature he hath such a right, yet the enjoyment of it is very uncertain, and constantly exposed to the invasion of others: for all being kings as much as he, every man his equal, and the greater part no strict observers of equity and justice, the enjoyment of the property he has in this state is very unsafe, very unsecure. This makes him willing to quit a condition, which, however free, is full of fears and continual dangers: and it is not without reason, that he seeks out, and is willing to join in society with others, for the mutual preservation of their lives, liberties and estates, which I call by the general name property" (§123).

10. "The great chief end, therefore, of men's uniting into commonwealths, and putting themselves under government, is the preservation of their property" (§124).

Jean-Jacques Rousseau

Introduction
Roseanne Mirabella

Jean-Jacques Rousseau, one of the most influential thinkers of the Enlightenment Era, was born in Geneva in 1712. He was reared and educated primarily by his father, as his mother died a few days after his birth. When his father was forced to leave Switzerland to avoid imprisonment, the boy was sent to live with an uncle in nearby Bossey and was sent to a boarding school outside Geneva. This experience resulted in his lifelong love of the rural life. Upon his return to Geneva, he was apprenticed to an engraver, who was violent and mistreated him. Rousseau ran away with nothing but the shirt on his back. He traveled to Turin, [Italy], where he converted to Catholicism and briefly entered the seminary to study for the priesthood. After this didn't work out, he served briefly as a shopkeeper, tutor, and music copyist. During this time, Rousseau began to familiarize himself with the works of the major Enlightenment authors.

On a walk from Paris to Vincennes (a journey of two leagues or about a two-hour walk), Rousseau came upon a newspaper announcement for an essay contest sponsored by the Academy of Dijon: "Has the progress of sciences and arts contributed to corrupt or purify morals?" Rousseau won first prize with his essay, "The Discourse on the Arts and Sciences," in which he wrote: "Our souls have become corrupted to the extent that our sciences and our arts have advanced towards perfection. Will someone say that this is a misfortune peculiar to our age? No, gentlemen. The evils brought about by our vain curiosity are as old as the world." In short, in his discourse he argues that a consequence of the luxuries brought about by civil society is "the dissolution of morals." This is important for us to understand, as the ideas expressed here by Rousseau form the beginning of his philosophy about the nature of people in civilized society and in the state of nature: Society has a corrupting influence on people, and as society advances, individual morals become more corrupted. In this work, Rousseau introduces his idea of the natural goodness of people. His understanding seems to be in contrast to that of John Locke and Thomas Hobbes.

Recall that, for Locke, in the state of nature, all people are basically free and also in a state of equality. In this state, people have the right to life, liberty, and property. People come together in communities to preserve the rights that are naturally theirs in the state of nature, "for their mutual preservation of their lives, liberties and estates." Thus, people willingly join the society for the preservation of these basic rights. Without the state, the property and liberty that is one's right would be uncertain and "constantly exposed to the invasion of others."

If you are familiar with the philosophy of Thomas Hobbes, you recognize that he has a much more negative view, though still a self-interested view, of life in the state of nature. He wrote: "Without a common power to keep them all in awe, they are in a condition which is called war . . . no arts; no letters; no society; and which is worst of all, continual fear and danger of violent death; and the life of man, solitary, poor, nasty, brutish, and short." In short, without the state, people would live in a condition of uncertainty about the future and civilization would not thrive. This contrasts with Rousseau's notion that civilized society is what brings about the corruption of individuals and a decline in morals.

During the cultural movement of the Enlightenment Era, human progress was to be made through advances in science and the application of reason (rather than faith) to life's big questions. In his rejection of scientific advances and their corrupting influences on individual character, Rousseau proposed a more "romantic" view of the human experience, emphasizing the naturalness and goodness of people living the simple life. Rousseau is considered by many to be the father of Romanticism. These thinkers sought to put the human emotions and feelings back into the equation when the emphasis on science and reason seemed to be pushing them out.

The excerpt below is from the "Discourse on the Origin of Inequality," which Rousseau wrote in response to yet another Academy contest posing the question: "What is the origin of inequality among men, and is it authorized by the natural law?" Although he did not win this contest, the essay he wrote became widely read and discussed. This piece first introduced Rousseau's terms *amour de soi* and *amour propre*. By understanding his use of these terms, we can begin to understand his moral philosophy.

In the state of nature, which exists prior to the organized community or a civil society, individuals have a form of self-love based on self-preservation, *amour de soi*. For Rousseau, within "the state of nature, being that in which the care for our own preservation is the least prejudicial to that of others, was consequently the best calculated to promote peace, and the most suitable for mankind." In contrast to the state of nature understood by Hobbes, in which the life of the individual is "nasty, brutish and short," Rousseau posits that in the state of nature, humans are naturally good. Rather than "do to others as you would have them do to you," which for Hobbes resulted in a violent state of nature, Rousseau suggests that this maxim is much more useful in the natural state of "do good to yourself with as little evil as possible to others."

Moral or political inequality, Rousseau maintains, results from life *within* civilized society. This inequality begins when humans embrace a new form of love, *amour propre*, a form of self-love or self-esteem that depends upon the opinion of others, opinions that can be formed only by comparison with others. Inequality among people can be traced back to the establishment of private property:

> The first man who, having enclosed a piece of ground, bethought himself of saying *This is mine*, and found people simple enough to believe him, was the real founder of civil society. From how many crimes, wars and murders, from how many horrors and misfortunes might not any one have saved mankind, by pulling up the stakes, or filling up the ditch, and crying to his fellows, "Beware of listening to this impostor; you are undone if you once forget that the fruits of the earth belong to us all, and the earth itself to nobody." But there is great probability that things had then already come to such a pitch that they could no

longer continue as they were; for the idea of property depends on many prior ideas, which could only be acquired successively, and cannot have been formed all at once in the human mind.

This new form of love identified by Rousseau as *amour propre* promotes jealousy through comparison, discord among previously peaceful neighbors, and the release of the passions driving "crime, war and murders." Rousseau romanticizes about a simpler, purer life, a peasant's existence, in which inequality was related to biological differences among people not from artificially created legal constructs. For Rousseau, permanent inequality among people and a decline in individual character and moral virtues can be traced to the establishment of private property and the establishment of laws to protect property rights.

DISCOURSE ON THE ORIGIN AND FOUNDATIONS OF INEQUALITY AMONG MEN (Selection)

From *Discourse on the Origin of Inequality Among Men* by Jean Jacques Rousseau, translated by Helena Rosenblatt. Copyright © 2010 by Bedford/St. Martin's, an imprint of Macmillan Learning. Used by permission of the publisher.

1. I conceive of two sorts of inequality in the human Species: one, which I call natural or Physical, because it is established by Nature and consists in the difference of ages, health, Bodily strengths, and qualities of Mind or Soul; the other, which may be called moral or Political inequality, because it depends upon a sort of convention and is established, or at least authorized, by the consent of Men. The latter consists in the different Privileges that some men enjoy to the prejudice of others, such as to be richer, more honored, more Powerful than they, or even to make themselves obeyed by them.

2. The Philosophers who have examined the foundations of society have all felt the necessity of going back to the state of Nature, but none of them has reached it. Some have not hesitated to attribute to Man in that state the notion of the Just and Unjust without troubling themselves to show that he had to have that notion or even that it was useful to him. Others have spoken of the Natural Right that everyone has to preserve what belongs to him, without explaining what they meant by belong. Still others, giving the stronger authority over the weaker from the first, have forthwith made Government arise, without thinking of the time that must have elapsed before the meaning of the words "authority" and "government" could exist among Men. All of them, finally, speaking continually of need, avarice, oppression, desires, and pride, have carried over to the state of Nature ideas they had acquired in society: they spoke about savage man and they described Civil man.

3. Every animal has ideas, since it has senses; it even combines its ideas up to a certain point, and in this regard man differs from a Beast only in degree. Some Philosophers have even suggested that there is more difference between a given man and another than between a given man and a given beast. Therefore it is not so much understanding which constitutes the distinction of man among the animals as it is his being a free agent. Nature commands every animal, and the Beast obeys. Man feels the same impetus, but he realizes that he is free to acquiesce or resist; and it is above all in the consciousness of this freedom that the spirituality of his soul is shown. For Physics explains in some way the mechanism of the senses and the formation of ideas; but in the power of willing, or rather of choosing, and in the sentiment of this power are found only purely spiritual acts about which the Laws of Mechanics explain nothing.

4. Above all, let us not conclude with Hobbes that because man has no idea of good-
    ness he is naturally evil; that he is vicious because he does not know virtue; that he
    always refuses his fellows services he does not believe he owes them; nor that, by
    virtue of the right he reasonably claims to things he needs, he foolishly imagines
    himself to be the sole proprietor of the whole Universe. Hobbes saw very clearly
    the defect of all modern definitions of Natural right; but the consequences he
    draws from his own definition show that he takes it in a sense which is no less false.
    Reasoning upon the principles he establishes, this Author ought to have said that
    since the state of Nature is that in which care of our self-preservation is the least
    prejudicial to the self-preservation of others, that state was consequently the best
    suited to Peace and the most appropriate for the Human Race. He says precisely
    the opposite, because of having improperly included in the Savage man's care of
    self-preservation the need to satisfy a multitude of passions which are the product
    of Society and which have made Laws *necessary*.

5. It is very certain, therefore, that pity is a natural feeling which, moderating in each
    individual the activity of love of oneself, contributes to the mutual preservation of
    the entire species. It carries us without reflection to the aid of those whom we see
    suffer; in the state of Nature, it takes the place of Laws, morals, and virtue, with
    the advantage that no one is tempted to disobey its gentle voice; it will deter every
    robust Savage from robbing a weak child or an infirm old man of his hard-won
    subsistence if he himself hopes to be able to find his own elsewhere. Instead of that
    sublime maxim of reasoned justice, *Do unto others as you would have them do unto
    you*, it inspires all Men with this other maxim of natural goodness, much less per-
    fect but perhaps more useful than the preceding one: *Do what is good for you with
    the least possible harm to others*. In a word, it is in this Natural feeling, rather than in
    subtle arguments that we must seek the cause of the repugnance every man would
    feel in doing evil, even independently of the maxims of education. Although it may
    behoove Socrates and Minds of his stamp to acquire virtue through reason, the
    human Race would have perished long ago if its presentation had depended only
    on the reasoning of its members.

6. The first person who, having fenced off a plot of ground, took it into his head to say
    this is mine and found people simple enough to believe him, was the true founder
    of civil society. What crimes, wars, murders what miseries and horrors would the
    human Race have been spared by someone who, uprooting the stakes or filling in
    the ditch, had shouted to his fellows: Beware of listening to this impostor; you
    are lost if you forget that the fruits belong to all and the Earth to no one! But it
    is very likely that by then things had already come to the point where they could
    no longer remain as they were. For this idea of property, depending on many prior
    ideas which could only have arisen successively, was not conceived all at once in the

human mind. It was necessary to make much progress, to acquire much industry and enlightenment, and to transmit and augment them from age to age, before arriving at this last stage of the state of Nature. Therefore let us start further back in time and attempt to assemble from a single point of view this slow succession of events and knowledge in their most natural order.

7. Everything begins to change its appearance. Men who until this time wandered in the Woods, having adopted a more fixed settlement, slowly come together, unite into different bands, and finally form in each country a particular Nation, unified by morals and character, not by Regulations and Laws but by the same kind of life and foods and by the common influence of Climate. A permanent proximity cannot fail to engender at length some contact between different families. Young people of different sexes live in neighboring Huts; the passing intercourse demanded by Nature soon leads to another kind no less sweet and more permanent through mutual frequentation. People grow accustomed to consider different objects and to make comparisons; imperceptibly they acquire ideas of merit and beauty which produce sentiments of preference. By dint of seeing one another, they can no longer do without seeing one another again. A tender and gentle sentiment is gradually introduced into the soul and at the least obstacle becomes an impetuous fury. Jealousy awakens with love; Discord triumphs and the gentlest of the passions receives sacrifices of human blood.

8. From the cultivation of land, its division necessarily followed; and from property once recognized, the first rules of justice. For in order to give everyone what is his, it is necessary that everyone can have something; moreover, as men began to look to the future and as they all saw themselves with some goods to lose, there was not one of them who did not have to fear reprisals against himself for wrongs he might do to another. This origin is all the more natural as it is impossible to conceive of the idea of property arising from anything except manual labor; because one cannot see what man can add other than his own labor, in order to appropriate things he has not made. It is labor alone which, giving the Cultivator a right to the product of the land he has tilled, gives him a right to the soil as a consequence, at least until the harvest, and thus from year to year; which, creating continuous possession, is easily transformed into property. When the Ancients, says Grotius, gave Ceres the epithet of legislatrix, and gave the name of Thesmaphories to a festival celebrated in her honor, they thereby made it clear that the division of lands produced a new kind of right: that is, the right of property, different from the one which results from natural Law.

9. Things in this state could have remained equal if talents had been equal, and if, for example, the use of iron and the consumption of foodstuffs had always been exactly balanced. But this proportion, which nothing maintained, was soon broken;

the stronger did more work; the cleverer turned his to better advantage; the more ingenious found ways to shorten his labor; the Farmer had greater need of iron or the blacksmith greater need of wheat; and working equally, the one, earned a great deal while the other barely had enough to live. Thus does natural inequality imperceptibly manifest itself along with contrived inequality; and thus do the differences among men, developed by those of circumstances, become more perceptible, more permanent in their effects begin to have a proportionate influence over the fate of individuals.

10. It is not possible that men should not at last have reflected upon such a miserable situation and upon the calamities overwhelming them. The rich above all must have soon felt how disadvantageous to them was a perpetual war in which they alone paid all the costs, and in which the risk of life was common to all while the risk of goods was theirs alone. Moreover, whatever pretext they might give for their usurpations, they were well aware that these were established only on a precarious and abusive right, and that having been acquired only by force, force could take them away without their having grounds for complaint. Even those enriched by industry alone could hardly base their property upon better titles. In vain might they say: But I built this wall; I earned this field by my labor. Who gave you its dimensions, they might be answered, and by virtue of what do you presume to be paid at our expense for work we did not impose on you? Do you not know that a multitude of your brethren die or suffer from need of what you have in excess, and that you needed express and unanimous consent of the human Race to appropriate for yourself anything from common subsistence that exceeded your own? Destitute of valid reasons to justify himself and of sufficient forces to defend himself; easily crushing an individual, but himself crushed by groups of bandits; alone against enemies united by the common hope of plunder, the rich, pressed by necessity, finally conceived the most deliberate project that ever entered the human mind. It was to use in his favor the very forces of those who attacked him, to make his defenders out of his adversaries, inspire them with other maxims, and give them other institutions which were as favorable to him as natural Right was adverse.

11. To this end, after having shown his neighbors the horror of a situation that made them all take up arms against one another, that made their possessions as burdensome as their needs, and in which no one found security in either poverty or wealth, he easily invented specious reasons to lead them to his goal. "Let us unite," he says to them, "to protect the weak from oppression, restrain the ambitious, and secure for everyone the possession of what belongs to him. Let us institute regulations of Justice and peace to which all are obliged to conform, which make an exception of no one, and which compensate in some way for the caprices of fortune by equally subjecting the powerful and the weak to mutual duties. In a

word, instead of turning our forces against ourselves, let us gather them into one supreme power which governs us according to wise Laws, protects and defends all the members of the association, repulses common enemies, and maintains us in an eternal concord."

12. Such was, or must have been, the origin of Society and Laws, which gave new fetters to the weak and new forces to the rich, destroyed natural freedom for all time, established forever the Law of property and inequality, changed a clever usurpation into an irrevocable right, and for the profit of a few ambitious men henceforth subjected the whole human Race to work, servitude, and misery. It is easily seen how the establishment of a single Society made that of all the others indispensable and how, to stand up to the united forces, it was necessary to unite in turn. Societies, multiplying or spreading rapidly, soon covered the entire surface of the earth; and it was no longer possible to find a single corner in the universe where one could free oneself from the yoke and withdraw one's head from the sword, often ill-guided, that every man saw perpetually hanging over his head. Civil right having thus become the common rule of Citizens, the Law of Nature no longer operated except between the various Societies, where, under the name Right of nations it was tempered by some tacit conventions in order to make intercourse possible and to take the place of natural commiseration which losing between one Society and another nearly all the force it had between one man and another, no longer dwells in any but a few great Cosmopolitan Souls, who surmount the imaginary barriers that separate peoples and who, following the example of the sovereign being who created them, include the whole human Race in their benevolence.

13. I have tried to set forth the origin and progress of inequality, the establishment and abuse of political Societies, insofar as these things can be deduced from the Nature of man by the light of reason alone, and independently of the sacred Dogmas which give to Sovereign authority the Sanction of Divine Right. It follows from this exposition that inequality, being almost null in the state of Nature, draws its force and growth from the development of our faculties and the progress of the human Mind, and finally becomes stable and legitimate by the establishment of property and Laws. It follows, further, that moral inequality, authorized by positive right alone, is contrary to Natural Right whenever it is not combined in the same proportion with Physical inequality: a distinction which sufficiently determines what one ought to think in this regard of the sort of inequality that reigns among all civilized Peoples; since it is manifestly against the Law of Nature, in whatever manner it is defined, that a child command an old man, an imbecile lead a wise man and a handful of men be glutted with superfluities while the starving multitude lacks necessities.

Karl Marx

Introduction
John Ranieri

Without question, the *Manifesto of the Communist Party* is the most well-known of the writings of Karl Marx (1818–1883) and Friedrich Engels (1820–1895). However, this does not mean that it is the most typical expression of their thought or that it represents a definitive statement of their views. The *Manifesto* needs to be read, not as a final formulation of the worldview of Engels or Marx, but as a response to a particular historical situation. We also need to take seriously the document's own self-description as a "manifesto"; in other words, that this is not a treatise or a systematic presentation of communism. Rather, it is a proclamation, meant to state in provocative, non-technical language, the self-understanding and aims of the communist movement. In writing it, Engels and Marx were interested in addressing their contemporary situation and how it came to be the way it was.

This was a period of social and political unrest in much of Western Europe, with several revolutionary uprisings taking place during 1848. Both the beneficial and distressing effects of the Industrial Revolution were being felt. In England, in particular, the wealth of society as a whole was increasing dramatically, but this was accompanied by tremendous upheaval and dislocation of workers. Traditional rural agricultural ways of life were disrupted, and people crowded into cities looking for work. Cities at the time were not equipped to handle this huge influx, and living conditions among the working poor were often appalling. In fact, Engels' first major work was a study called *Condition of the Working Class in England*. In some places workers began to organize and protest. In 1836, a group of radical German workers living in Paris formed a secret association called "League of the Just." In 1847, they changed their name to the "Communist League," and asked Marx and Engels (who had recently become members) to draft a manifesto. The *Communist Manifesto* was originally published in February 1848 in London; in June of the same year it was published in Paris shortly before the outbreak of revolution there. We should be careful, though, about assuming any causal relationship. It is more accurate to say that the *Manifesto* *reflected* the unrest among much of the Western European working classes; it did not create it. At the time of its publication, Marx and Engels were leaders with the German communist movement, but their influence at the time did not extend much beyond that. In fact, it would take a decades-long struggle among various European workers' movements before communism as understood by Marx and Engels became the dominant form of European socialism.

Part of the significance of the *Manifesto* is that it moved the communists from being a secret association without a clearly thought out plan or theory to a movement with definite aims and a more sophisticated analysis of social and historical evolution. Although much of earlier socialism had been quite strong in its criticism of the failings of capitalism, this criticism tended to be moralistic in tone, with socialism embodying the forces of good and capitalism depicted as the embodiment of evil. The workers' movement lacked a comprehensive and specific analysis of social and economic processes. That changed with

Engels and Marx. Whether we agree with their analyses or not, these were serious, sophisticated thinkers who produced between them an extensive body of work that claimed to give a "scientific" interpretation of social, economic, political, and historical development.

In order to appreciate the *Manifesto*, it is important to understand some of the assumptions about human behavior that underpin the claims made by Marx and Engels. Fundamental to Marx's philosophical anthropology is the notion that what is distinctively human about human beings is our ability to interact with the natural world and to transform it by our labor activity. For Marx, human labor ought to be an expression of human creativity, through which we "humanize" nature and bend it to serve human needs. Thus, Marx's philosophy, despite its sometimes dense theoretical language, is primarily concerned with human *activity*, or to use a fancier philosophical term, with *praxis*. This attitude is pithily expressed in one of Marx's *Theses on Feuerbach*: "The philosophers have only *interpreted* the world, in various ways; the point is, however, to *change* it."

With this in mind, we can begin to appreciate Marx's critique of life under capitalism. The key here is his understanding of alienation. Since Marx identifies the human person with his/her creative labor activity, anything that comes between or separates that activity from a person is seen as deeply alienating and dehumanizing. This is precisely what he and Engels believed happened to workers in the capitalist system. Under capitalism, human labor was understood to be a commodity to be bought and sold just like any other commodity necessary to produce certain goods. The owners of the means of production (referred to as the bourgeoisie in the *Manifesto*) purchased the labor power of the workers (the proletariat) by paying them a wage. As with any other commodity, wages are based upon what it costs to maintain a worker in existence. When there is an oversupply of workers, wages go down and workers compete against one another for the existing jobs. In addition, whatever the workers produce does not belong to them but to the employer, who then sells the product to make a profit. This alienation of labor and product results in a situation in which the misery of workers continually increases. Describing the effects of alienation, Marx observes how:

> Labor is external to the worker, i.e., it does not belong to his essential being; that in his work, therefore, he does not affirm himself but denies himself, does not feel content but unhappy, does not develop freely his physical and mental energy but mortifies his body and ruins his mind. The worker therefore only feels himself outside his work, and in his work feels outside himself. . . . His labor is therefore not voluntary but coerced; it is forced labor. . . . Its alien character emerges clearly in the fact that as soon as no physical or other compulsion exists, labour is shunned like the plague. . . . Lastly, the external character of labour for the worker appears in the face that it is not his own, but someone else's, that it does not belong to him, that in it he belongs, not to himself, but to another. . . . *Private property* is thus the product, the result, the necessary consequence, of alienated labor, of

the external relation of the worker to nature and to himself (*Economic and Philosophic Manuscripts* of 1844)

Marx and Engels believed that the capitalist system (just like every other economic, social, and political system before it) would eventually bring about its own demise. Marx summed up the reasons why in the following passage:

> The general result at which I arrived . . . can be briefly formulated as follows: In the social production of their life, men enter into definite relations that are indispensable and independent of their will, relations of production which correspond to a definite stage of development of their material productive forces. The sum total of these relations of production constitutes the economic structure of society, the real foundation, on which rises a legal and political superstructure and to which correspond definite forms of social consciousness. The mode of production of material life conditions the social, political and intellectual life process in general. It is not the consciousness of men that determines their being, but, on the contrary, their social being that determines their consciousness. At a certain stage of their development, the material productive forces of society come in conflict with the existing relations of production, or—what is but a legal expression for the same thing—with the property relations within which they have been at work hitherto. From forms of development of the productive forces these relations turn into their fetters. Then begins an epoch of social revolution. (*A Contribution to the Critique of Political Economy*, 1859)

What Marx means here is that every society, civilization, and historical epoch exemplifies some "mode of production"—which is a brief way of describing the various historically determined ways of organizing economic life. For example, bourgeois society embodies a capitalist mode of production, whereas medieval society was an example of a feudal mode of production. Instead of bourgeoisie and proletarians, the medieval world had nobility and serfs who reflected the particular economic basis and structure of the time. A "mode of production" consists of two main elements: the "forces of production" (referred to as "productive forces" in the previous passage) and the "relations of production." The forces of production comprise the material resources available in a given society. This includes natural resources such as minerals, land, water, and so on; however, it also refers to the available human resources such as the character of the population, the skills they possess, and the techniques they can bring to bear in their work. By comparison, the relations of productions are (according to Professor of Economics Robert Heilbroner) "the social arrangements that direct the forces of production and that allocate its output." These include institutions of power and hierarchy embodied in social classes. For Marx and Engels, social classes are largely defined by their relationship to the productive, distributive process, and the relationship between classes is often antagonistic. It is the playing out of the relationships and tensions between the forces and relations of production that constitutes history. Existing relations of production allow for the development of the forces of production. In turn, these developed forces create new economic conditions that threaten the existing relations of production. For example, in late eighteenth century and early nineteenth century England, improvements in agriculture (forces of production) led to a situation in which fewer workers were required to produce food for the nation. The growth of technology to make textiles also meant that land previously farmed for raising food could be used to graze sheep to provide wool. This resulted in the freeing (or expulsion) of agricultural workers from the land, and led many to seek work in factories in cities. A new class of industrial laborers (the proletariat) was thereby brought into existence, accompanied by new relations of production (between bourgeoisie and proletarians). Marx and Engels predicted that the relentless desire for profit would drive the bourgeoisie to bring about changes in which the living conditions of the proletariat would become intolerable. Once again the development of forces of production would have led to a situation in which the existing relations of production would be shattered-in this case, as the proletarians seized political power and ownership of the means of production.

It is important to emphasize that neither the forces nor the relations of production should be understood in narrowly economic terms. Marx and Engels were both of the view that the social, political, religious, and cultural realms all interact with—and are in turn affected by—the economic realm. Note the following passage from Engels on this point:

> According to the materialist conception of history, the *ultimately* determining element in history is the production and reproduction of real life. More than this neither Marx nor I have ever asserted. Hence if anybody wishes to twist this into saying that the economic element is the *only* determining one, he transforms that proposition into a meaningless, abstract, senseless phrase. The economic situation is the basis, but the various elements of the superstructure: political forms of the class struggle and its results . . . political, juristic, philosophical theories, religious views and their further development into systems of dogmas, all also exercise their influence upon the course of the historical struggles, and in many cases preponderate in determining their *form*. Marx and I are partly to blame for the fact that the younger people sometimes lay more stress on the economic side than is due to it. We had to emphasize the main principle vis-à-vis our adversaries, who denied it, and we had not always the time, the place, or the opportunity to allow the other elements involved in the interaction to come into their rights. (Letters on Historical Materialism)

This means that economic motives do not necessarily dominate non-economic concerns, nor do economic activities directly dictate what people think. What Marx and Engels sought to emphasize was the ways in which the economic base sets *limits* on what can happen in the social, political, and cultural realm. Because they thought this insight had been underappreciated by previous thinkers, they were determined to highlight it, even at the risk of exaggeration.

There is a sense in which the *Manifesto* takes these insights and presents them in narrative form. It tells the story of the class struggles that brought human history to the point in time in which it is written, and it confidently predicts where history is heading. The story, as told by Marx and Engels, is a powerful one that has come to exert tremendous influence. Today we may tend to read it in light of the dissolution of the Soviet Union, and thereby conclude that the document is of interest only as a historical artifact whose ideas have been once and for all proven wrong. However, such a judgment would be hasty. Soviet communism represents but one development in the history of Marxism; it is certainly not the only way to apply the teachings of the *Manifesto*. During their own lifetimes both Marx and Engels were aware of ways in which the predictions contained in the *Manifesto* had not occurred as they expected, and the two authors admitted that their vision for society would have to be adapted to changing circumstances. In admitting this, they were not abandoning their previous convictions, but applying them to new situations. In reading the *Manifesto* today it will be well to keep this in mind. Rather than dismiss the document as a relic of the past, we might consider ways in which its insights are applicable in our current circumstances.

MANIFESTO OF THE COMMUNIST PARTY

From "Manifesto of the Communist Party," English translation by Samuel Moore, published in 1888.

A spectre is haunting Europe—the spectre of Communism. All the Powers of old Europe have entered into a holy alliance to exorcise this spectre: Pope and Czar, Metternich and Guizot, French Radicals and German police spies.

Where is the party in opposition that has not been decried as Communistic by its opponents in power? Where the Opposition that has not hurled back the branding reproach of Communism, against the more advanced opposition parties, as well as against its reactionary adversaries?

Two things result from this fact:

I.   Communism is already acknowledged by all European Powers to be itself a Power.

II. It is high time that Communists should openly, in the face of the whole world, publish their views, their aims, their tendencies, and meet this nursery tale of the Spectre of Communism with a Manifesto of the party itself.

To this end, Communists of various nationalities have assembled in London, and sketched the following Manifesto, to be published in the English, French, German, Italian, Flemish and Danish languages.

I. Bourgeois and Proletarians[1]

The history of all hitherto existing society[2] is the history of class struggles.

Freeman and slave, patrician and plebeian, lord and serf, guild-master[3] and journeyman, in a word, oppressor and oppressed, stood in constant opposition to one another, carried on an uninterrupted, now hidden, now open fight, a fight that each time ended, either in a revolutionary re-constitution of society at large, or in the common ruin of the contending classes.

---

1   By bourgeoisie is meant the class of modern Capitalists, owners of the means of social production and employers of wage labour. By proletariat, the class of modern wage-labourers who, having no means of production of their own, are reduced to selling their labour power in order to live. [*Note by Engels to the English edition of 1888.*]

2   That is, all *written* history. In 1847, the pre-history of society, the social organisation existing previous to recorded history, was all but unknown. Since then, Haxthausen discovered common ownership of land in Russia, Maurer proved it to be the social foundation from which all Teutonic races started in history, and by and by village communities were found to be, or to have been the primitive form of society everywhere from India to Ireland. The inner organisation of this primitive Communistic society was laid bare, in its typical form, by Morgan's crowning discovery of the true nature of the *gens* and its relation to the *tribe*. With the dissolution of these primeval communities society begins to be differentiated into separate and finally antagonistic classes. I have attempted to retrace this process of dissolution in: "Der Ursprung der Familie, des Privateigenthums und des Staats" [*The Origin of the Family, Private Property and the State*], 2nd edition, Stuttgart 1886. [*Note by Engels to the English edition of 1888.*]

3   Guild-master, that is, a full member of a guild, a master within, not a head of a guild. [*Note by Engels to the English edition of 1888.*]

In the earlier epochs of history, we find almost everywhere a complicated arrangement of society into various orders, a manifold gradation of social rank. In ancient Rome we have patricians, knights, plebeians, slaves; in the Middle Ages, feudal lords, vassals, guild-masters, journeymen, apprentices, serfs; in almost all of these classes, again, subordinate gradations.

The modern bourgeois society that has sprouted from the ruins of feudal society has not done away with class antagonisms. It has but established new classes, new conditions of oppression, new forms of struggle in place of the old ones.

Our epoch, the epoch of the bourgeoisie, possesses, however, this distinctive feature: it has simplified the class antagonisms. Society as a whole is more and more splitting up into two great hostile camps, into two great classes directly facing each other: Bourgeoisie and proletariat.

From the serfs of the Middle Ages sprang the chartered burghers of the earliest towns. From these burgesses the first elements of the bourgeoisie were developed.

The discovery of America, the rounding of the Cape, opened up fresh ground for the rising bourgeoisie. The East-Indian and Chinese markets, the colonisation of America, trade with the colonies, the increase in the means of exchange and in commodities generally, gave to commerce, to navigation, to industry, an impulse never before known, and thereby, to the revolutionary element in the tottering feudal society, a rapid development.

The feudal system of industry, under which industrial production was monopolised by closed guilds, now no longer sufficed for the growing wants of the new markets. The manufacturing system took its place. The guild-masters were pushed on one side by the manufacturing middle class; division of labour between the different corporate guilds vanished in the face of division of labour in each single workshop.

Meantime the markets kept ever growing, the demand ever rising. Even manufacture no longer sufficed. Thereupon, steam and machinery revolutionised industrial production. The place of manufacture was taken by the giant, Modern Industry, the place the industrial middle class, by industrial millionaires, the leaders of whole industrial armies, the modern bourgeois.

Modern industry has established the world market, for which the discovery of America paved the way. This market has given an immense development to commerce, to navigation, to communication by land. This development has, in its turn, reacted on the extension of industry; and in proportion as industry, commerce, navigation, railways extended, in the same proportion the bourgeoisie developed, increased its capital, and pushed into the background every class handed down from the Middle Ages.

We see, therefore, how the modern bourgeoisie is itself the product of a long course of development, of a series of revolutions in the modes of production and of exchange.

Each step in the development of the bourgeoisie was accompanied by a corresponding political advance of that class. An oppressed class under the sway of the feudal nobility, an armed and self-governing association in the medieval commune;[4] here independent urban republic (as in Italy and Germany), there taxable "third estate" of the monarchy (as in France), afterwards, in the period of manufacture proper, serving either the semi-feudal or the absolute monarchy as a counterpoise against the nobility, and, in fact, cornerstone of the great monarchies in general, the bourgeoisie has at last, since the establishment of Modern Industry and of the world market, conquered for itself, in the modern representative State, exclusive political sway. The executive of the modern State is but a committee for managing the common affairs of the whole bourgeoisie.

The bourgeoisie, historically, has played a most revolutionary part.

The bourgeoisie, wherever it has got the upper hand, has put an end of all feudal, patri-archal, idyllic relations. It has pitilessly torn asunder the motley feudal ties that bound man to his "natural superiors", and has left remaining no other nexus between man and man than naked self-interest, than callous "cash payment". It has drowned the most heavenly ecstasies of religious fervour, of chivalrous enthusiasm, of philistine sentimen-talism, in the icy water of egotistical calculation. It has resolved personal worth into exchange value, and in place of the numberless indefeasible chartered freedoms, has set up that single, unconscionable freedom—Free Trade. In one word, for exploitation, veiled by religious and political illusions, it has substituted naked, shameless, direct, brutal exploitation.

The bourgeoisie has stripped of its halo every occupation hitherto honoured and looked up to with reverent awe. It has converted the physician, the lawyer, the priest, the poet, the man of science, into its paid wage-labourers.

The bourgeoisie has torn away from the family its sentimental veil, and has reduced the family relation to a mere money relation.

The bourgeoisie has disclosed how it came to pass that the brutal display of vigour in the Middle Ages, which Reactionists so much admire, found its fitting complement in the most slothful indolence. It has been the first to shew what man's activity can bring about. It has accomplished wonders far surpassing Egyptian pyramids, Roman

---

4   "Commune" was the name taken, in France, by the nascent towns even before they had conquered from their feudal lords and masters local self-government and political rights as the "Third Estate". Generally speaking, for the economical development of the bourgeoisie, England is here taken as the typical country; for its political development, France. [*Note by Engels to the English edition of 1888.*]

This was the name given their urban communities by the townsmen of Italy and France, after they had purchased or wrested their initial rights of self-government from their feudal lords. [*Note by Engels to the German edition of 1890.*]

aqueducts, and Gothic cathedrals; it has conducted expeditions that put in the shade all former Exoduses of nations and crusades.

The bourgeoisie cannot exist without constantly revolutionising the instruments of production, and thereby the relations of production, and with them the whole relations of society. Conservation of the old modes of production in unaltered form, was, on the contrary, the first condition of existence for all earlier industrial classes. Constant revolutionising of production, uninterrupted disturbance of all social conditions, everlasting uncertainty and agitation distinguish the bourgeois epoch from all earlier ones. All fixed, fast-frozen relations, with their train of ancient and venerable prejudices and opinions are swept away, all new-formed ones become antiquated before they can ossify. All that is solid melts into air, all that is holy is profaned, and man is at last compelled to face with sober senses, his real conditions of life, and his relations with his kind.

The need of a constantly expanding market for its products chases the bourgeoisie over the whole surface of the globe. It must nestle everywhere, settle everywhere, establish connexions everywhere.

The bourgeoisie has through its exploitation of the world market given a cosmopolitan character to production and consumption in every country. To the great chagrin of Reactionists, it has drawn from under the feet of industry the national ground on which it stood. All old-established national industries have been destroyed or are daily being destroyed. They are dislodged by new industries, whose introduction becomes a life and death question for all civilised nations, by industries that no longer work up indigenous raw material, but raw material drawn from the remotest zones; industries whose products are consumed, not only at home, but in every quarter of the globe. In place of the old wants, satisfied by the productions of the country we find new wants, requiring for their satisfaction the products of distant lands and climes. In place of the old local and national seclusion and self-sufficiency, we have intercourse in every direction, universal inter-dependence of nations. And as in material, so also in intellectual production. The intellectual creations of individual nations become common property. National one-sidedness and narrow-mindedness become more and more impossible, and from the numerous national and local literatures, there arises a world literature.

The bourgeoisie, by the rapid improvement of all instruments of production, by the immensely facilitated means of communication, draws all, even the most barbarian, nations into civilisation. The cheap prices of its commodities are the heavy artillery with which it batters down all Chinese walls, with which it forces the barbarians' intensely obstinate hatred of foreigners to capitulate. It compels all nations, on pain of extinction, to adopt the bourgeois mode of production; it compels them to introduce what it calls civilisation into their midst, *i.e.*, to become bourgeois themselves. In one word, it creates a world after its own image.

The bourgeoisie has subjected the country to the rule of the towns. It has created enormous cities, has greatly increased the urban population as compared with the rural, and has thus rescued a considerable part of the population from the idiocy of rural life. Just as it has made the country dependent on the towns, so it has made barbarian and semi-barbarian countries dependent on the civilised ones, nations of peasants on nations of bourgeois, the East on the West.

The bourgeoisie keeps more and more doing away with the scattered state of the population, of the means of production, and of property. It has agglomerated population, centralised means of production, and has concentrated property in a few hands. The necessary consequence of this was political centralisation. Independent, or but loosely connected, provinces with separate interests, laws, governments and systems of taxation, became lumped together into one nation, with one government, one code of laws, one national class-interest, one frontier and one customs-tariff.

The bourgeoisie, during its rule of scarce one hundred years, has created more massive and more colossal productive forces than have all preceding generations together. Subjection of Nature's forces to man, machinery, application of chemistry to industry and agriculture, steam-navigation, railways, electric telegraphs, clearing of whole continents for cultivation, canalisation of rivers, whole populations conjured out of the ground—what earlier century had even a presentiment that such productive forces slumbered in the lap of social labour?

We see then: the means of production and of exchange, on whose foundation the bourgeoisie built itself up, were generated in feudal society. At a certain stage in the development of these means of production and of exchange, the conditions under which feudal society produced and exchanged, the feudal organisation of agriculture and manufacturing industry, in one word, the feudal relations of property became no longer compatible with the already developed productive forces; they became so many fetters. They had to be burst asunder; they were burst asunder.

Into their place stepped free competition, accompanied by a social and political constitution adapted to it, and by the economical and political sway of the bourgeois class.

A similar movement is going on before our own eyes. Modern bourgeois society with its relations of production, of exchange and of property, a society that has conjured up such gigantic means of production and of exchange, is like the sorcerer, who is no longer able to control the powers of the nether world whom he has called up by his spells. For many a decade past the history of industry and commerce is but the history of the revolt of modern productive forces against modern conditions of production, against the property relations that are the conditions for the existence of the bourgeoisie and of its rule. It is enough to mention the commercial crises that by their periodical return put on its trial, each time more threateningly, the existence of the entire bourgeois society.

In these crises a great part not only of the existing products, but also of the previously created productive forces, are periodically destroyed. In these crises there breaks out an epidemic that, in all earlier epochs, would have seemed an absurdity—the epidemic of overproduction. Society suddenly finds itself put back into a state of momentary barbarism; it appears as if a famine, a universal war of devastation had cut off the supply of every means of subsistence; industry and commerce seem to be destroyed; and why? Because there is too much civilisation, too much means of subsistence, too much industry, too much commerce. The productive forces at the disposal of society no longer tend to further the development of the conditions of bourgeois property; on the contrary, they have become too powerful for these conditions, by which they are fettered, and so soon as they overcome these fetters, they bring disorder into the whole of bourgeois society, endanger the existence of bourgeois property. The conditions of bourgeois society are too narrow to comprise the wealth created by them. And how does the bourgeoisie get over these crises? On the one hand by enforced destruction of a mass of productive forces; on the other, by the conquest of new markets, and by the more thorough exploitation of the old ones. That is to say, by paving the way for more extensive and more destructive crises, and by diminishing the means whereby crises are prevented.

The weapons with which the bourgeoisie felled feudalism to the ground are now turned against the bourgeoisie itself.

But not only has the bourgeoisie forged the weapons that bring death to itself; it has also called into existence the men who are to wield those weapons—the modern working class—the proletarians.

In proportion as the bourgeoisie, *i.e.*, capital, is developed, in the same proportion is the proletariat, the modern working class, developed—a class of labourers, who live only so long as they find work, and who find work only so long as their labour increases capital. These labourers, who must sell themselves piecemeal, are a commodity, like every other article of commerce, and are consequently exposed to all the vicissitudes of competition, to all the fluctuations of the market.

Owing to the extensive use of machinery and to division of labour, the work of the proletarians has lost all individual character, and, consequently, all charm for the workman. He becomes an appendage of the machine, and it is only the most simple, most monotonous, and most easily acquired knack, that is required of him. Hence, the cost of production of a workman is restricted, almost entirely, to the means of subsistence that he requires for his maintenance, and for the propagation of his race. But the price of a commodity, and therefore also of labour,* is equal to its cost of production. In

---

*   Subsequently Marx pointed out that the worker does not sell his labour but his labour power. See in this connexion Engels's introduction to Marx's *Wage Labour and Capital*, 1891, in K. Marx and F. Engels, *Selected Works*, Eng. ed., Vol. I, Moscow 1951. pp. 66–73.-Ed.

proportion, therefore, as the repulsiveness of the work increases, the wage decreases. Nay more, in proportion as the use of machinery and division of labour increases, in the same proportion the burden of toil also increases, whether by prolongation of the working hours, by increase of the work exacted in a given time or by increased speed of the machinery, etc.

Modern industry has converted the little workshop of the patriarchal master into the great factory of the industrial capitalist. Masses of labourers, crowded into the factory, are organised like soldiers. As privates of the industrial army they are placed under the command of a perfect hierarchy of officers and sergeants. Not only are they slaves of the bourgeois class, and of the bourgeois State; they are daily and hourly enslaved by the machine, by the over-looker, and, above all, by the individual bourgeois manufacturer himself. The more openly this despotism proclaims gain to be its end and aim, the more petty, the more hateful and the more embittering it is.

The less the skill and exertion of strength implied in manual labour, in other words, the more modern industry becomes developed, the more is the labour of men superseded by that of women. Differences of age and sex have no longer any distinctive social validity for the working class. All are instruments of labour, more or less expensive to use, according to their age and sex.

No sooner is the exploitation of the labourer by the manufacturer, so far, at an end, that he receives his wages in cash, than he is set upon by the other portions of the bourgeoisie, the land-lord, the shopkeeper, the pawnbroker, etc.

The lower strata of the middle class—the small tradespeople, shopkeepers, and retired tradesmen generally, the handicraftsmen and peasants—all these sink gradually into the proletariat, partly because their diminutive capital does not suffice for the scale on which Modern Industry is carried on, and is swamped in the competition with the large capitalists, partly because their specialized skill is rendered worthless by new methods of production. Thus the proletariat is recruited from all classes of the population.

The proletariat goes through various stages of development. With its birth begins its struggle with the bourgeoisie. At first the contest is carried on by individual labourers, then by the work people of a factory, then by the operatives of one trade, in one locality, against the individual bourgeois who directly exploits them. They direct their attacks not against the bourgeois conditions of production, but against the instruments of production themselves; they destroy imported wares that compete with their labour, they smash to pieces machinery, they set factories ablaze, they seek to restore by force the vanished status of the workman of the Middle Ages.

At this stage the labourers still form an incoherent mass scattered over the whole country, and broken up by their mutual competition. If anywhere they unite to form more compact bodies, this is not yet the consequence of their own active union, but of the union of the bourgeoisie, which class, in order to attain its own political ends, is compelled to set the whole proletariat in motion, and is moreover yet, for a time, able to do so. At this stage, therefore, the proletarians do not fight their enemies, but the enemies of their enemies, the remnants of absolute monarchy, the landowners, the non-industrial bourgeois, the petty bourgeoisie. Thus the whole historical movement is concentrated in the hands of the bourgeoisie; every victory so obtained is a victory for the bourgeoisie.

But with the development of industry the proletariat not only increases in number; it becomes concentrated in greater masses, its strength grows, and it feels that strength more. The various interests and conditions of life within the ranks of the proletariat are more and more equalised, in proportion as machinery obliterates all distinctions of labour, and nearly everywhere reduces wages to the same low level. The growing competition among the bourgeois, and the resulting commercial crises, make the wages of the workers ever more fluctuating. The unceasing improvement of machinery, ever more rapidly developing, makes their livelihood more and more precarious; the collisions between individual workmen and individual bourgeois take more and more the character of collisions between two classes. Thereupon the workers begin to form combinations (Trades' Unions) against the Bourgeois; they club together in order to keep up the rate of wages; they found permanent associations in order to make provision beforehand for these occasional revolts. Here and there the contest breaks out into riots.

Now and then the workers are victorious, but only for a time. The real fruit of their battles lies, not in the immediate result, but in the ever expanding union of the workers. This union is helped on by the improved means of communication that are created by modern industry and that place the workers of different localities in contact with one another. It was just this contact that was needed to centralise the numerous local struggles, all of the same character, into one national struggle between classes. But every class struggle is a political struggle. And that union, to attain which the burghers of the Middle Ages, with their miserable highways, required centuries, the modern proletarians, thanks to railways, achieve in a few years.

This organisation of the proletarians into a class, and consequently into a political parry, is continually being upset again by the competition between the workers themselves. But it ever rises up again, stronger, firmer, mightier. It compels legislative recognition of particular interests of the workers, by taking advantage of the divisions among the bourgeoisie itself. Thus the ten-hours' bill in England was carried.

Altogether collisions between the classes of the old society further, in many ways, the course of development of the proletariat. The bourgeoisie finds itself involved in a constant battle. At first with the aristocracy; later on, with those portions of the bourgeoisie itself, whose interests have become antagonistic to the progress of industry; at all times, with the bourgeoisie of foreign countries. In all these battles it sees itself compelled to appeal to the proletariat, to ask for its help, and thus, to drag it into the political arena. The bourgeoisie itself, therefore, supplies the proletariat with its own elements of political and general education, in other words, it furnishes the proletariat with Weapons for fighting the bourgeoisie.

Further, as we have already seen, entire sections of the ruling classes are, by the advance of industry, precipitated into the proletariat, or are at least threatened in their conditions of existence. These also supply the proletariat with fresh elements of enlightenment and progress.

Finally, in times when the class struggle nears the decisive hour, the process of dissolution going on within the ruling class, in fact within the whole range of old society, assumes such a violent, glaring character that a small section of the ruling class cuts itself adrift, and joins the revolutionary class, the class that holds the future in its hands. Just as, therefore, at an earlier period, a section of the nobility went over to the bourgeoisie, so now a portion of the bourgeoisie goes over to the proletariat, and in particular, a portion of the bourgeois ideologists, who have raised themselves to the level of comprehending theoretically the historical movement as a whole.

Of all the classes that stand face to face with the bourgeoisie today, the proletariat alone is a really revolutionary class. The other classes decay and finally disappear in the face of modern industry; the proletariat is its special and essential product.

The lower middle class, the small manufacturer, the shopkeeper, the artisan, the peasant, all these fight against the bourgeoisie, to save from extinction their existence as fractions of the middle class. They are therefore not revolutionary, but conservative. Nay more, they are reactionary, for they try to roll back the wheel of history. If by chance they are revolutionary, they are so only in view of their impending transfer into the proletariat, they thus defend not their present, but their future interests, they desert their own standpoint to place themselves at that of the proletariat.

The "dangerous class", the social scum, that passively rotting mass thrown off by the lowest layers of old society, may, here and there, be swept into the movement by a proletarian revolution; its conditions of life, however, prepare it far more for the part of a bribed tool of reactionary intrigue.

In the conditions of the proletariat, those of old society at large are already virtually swamped. The proletarian is without property; his relation to his wife and children has no longer anything in common with the bourgeois family relations; modern industrial labour, modern subjection to capital, the same in England as in France, in America as in Germany, has stripped him of every trace of national character. Law, morality, religion, are to him so many bourgeois prejudices, behind which lurk in ambush just as many bourgeois interests.

All the preceding classes that got the upper hand, sought to fortify their already acquired status by subjecting society at large to their conditions of appropriation. The proletarians cannot become masters of the productive forces of society, except by abolishing their own previous mode of appropriation, and thereby also every other previous mode of appropriation. They have nothing of their own to secure and to fortify; their mission is to destroy all previous securities for, and insurances of, individual property.

All previous historical movements were movements of minorities, or in the interest of minorities. The proletarian movement is the self-conscious, independent movement of the immense majority in the interest of the immense majority. The proletariat, the lowest stratum of our present society, cannot stir, cannot raise itself up, without the whole superincumbent strata of official society being sprung into the air.

Though not in substance, yet in form, the struggle of the proletariat with the bourgeoisie is at first a national struggle. The proletariat of each country must, of course, first of all settle matters with its own bourgeoisie.

In depicting the most general phases of the development of the proletariat, we traced the more or less veiled civil war, raging within existing society, up to the point where that war breaks out into open revolution, and where the violent overthrow of the bourgeoisie lays the foundation for the sway of the proletariat.

Hitherto, every form of society has been based, as we have already seen, on the antagonism of oppressing and oppressed classes. But in order to oppress a class, certain conditions must be assured to it under which it can, at least, continue its slavish existence. The serf, in the period of serfdom, raised himself to membership in the commune, just as the petty bourgeois, under the yoke of feudal absolutism, managed to develop into a bourgeois. The modern labourer, on the contrary, instead of rising with the progress of industry, sinks deeper and deeper below the conditions of existence of his own class. He becomes a pauper, and pauperism develops more rapidly than population and wealth. And here it becomes evident, that the bourgeoisie is unfit any longer to be the ruling class in society, and to impose its conditions of existence upon society as an over-riding law. It is unfit to rule because it is incompetent to assure an existence to its slave within his slavery, because it cannot help letting him sink into such a state, that it has to feed him, instead of being fed by him. Society can no longer live under this bourgeoisie, in other words, its existence is no longer compatible with society.

The essential condition for the existence, and for the sway of the bourgeois class, is the formation and augmentation of capital; the condition for capital is wage labour. Wage labour rests exclusively on competition between the labourers. The advance of industry, whose involuntary promoter is the bourgeoisie, replaces the isolation of the labourers, due to competition, by their revolutionary combination, due to association. The development of Modern Industry, therefore, cuts from under its feet the very foundation on which the bourgeoisie produces and appropriates products. What the bourgeoisie, therefore, produces, above all, is its own grave-diggers. Its fall and the victory of the proletariat are equally inevitable.

II. Proletarians and Communists

In what relation do the Communists stand to the proletarians as a whole?

The Communists do not form a separate party opposed to other working-class parties.

They have no interests separate and apart from those of the proletariat as a whole.

They do not set up any sectarian principles of their own, by which to shape and mould the proletarian movement.

The Communists are distinguished from the other working-class parties by this only: 1. In the national struggles of the proletarians of the different countries, they point out and bring to the front the common interests of the entire proletariat, independently of all nationality. 2. In the various stages of development which the struggle of the working class against the bourgeoisie has to pass through, they always and everywhere represent the interests of the movement as a whole.

The Communists, therefore, are on the one hand, practically, the most advanced and resolute section of the working-class parties of every country, that section which pushes forward all others; on the other hand, theoretically, they have over the great mass of the proletariat the advantage of clearly understanding the line of march, the conditions, and the ultimate general results of the proletarian movement.

The immediate aim of the Communists is the same as that of all the other proletarian parties: formation of the proletariat into a class, overthrow of the bourgeois supremacy, conquest of political power by the proletariat.

The theoretical conclusions or the Communists are in no way based on ideas or principles that have been invented, or discovered, by this or that would-be universal reformer.

They merely express, in general terms, actual relations springing from an existing class struggle, from a historical movement going on under our very eyes. The abolition of existing property relations is not at all a distinctive feature of Communism.

All property relations in the past have continually been subject to historical change consequent upon the change in historical conditions.

The French Revolution, for example, abolished feudal property in favour of bourgeois property.

The distinguishing feature of Communism is not the abolition of property generally, but the abolition of bourgeois property. But modern bourgeois private property is the final and most complete expression of the system of producing and appropriating products, that is based on class antagonisms, on the exploitation of the many by the few.

In this sense, the theory of the Communists may be summed up in the single sentence: Abolition of private property.

We Communists have been reproached with the desire of abolishing the right of personally acquiring property as the fruit of a man's own labour, which property is alleged to be the ground work of all personal freedom, activity and independence.

Hard-won, self-acquired, self-earned property! Do you mean the property of the petty artisan and of the small peasant, a form of property that preceded the bourgeois form? There is no need to abolish that; the development of industry has to a great extent already destroyed it, and is still destroying it daily.

Or do you mean modern bourgeois private property?

But does wage labour create any property for the labourer? Not a bit. It creates capital, *i.e.*, that kind of property which exploits wage labour, and which cannot increase except upon condition of begetting a new supply of wage labour for fresh exploitation. Property, in its present form, is based on the antagonism of capital and wage labour. Let us examine both sides of this antagonism.

To be a capitalist, is to have not only a purely personal, but a social *status* in production. Capital is a collective product, and only by the united action of many members, nay, in the last resort, only by the united action of all members of society, can it be set in motion.

Capital is, therefore, not a personal, it is a social power.

When, therefore, capital is converted into common property, into the property of all members of society, personal property is not thereby transformed into social property. It is only the social character of the property that is changed. It loses its class character.

Let us now take wage labour.

The average price of wage labour is the minimum wage, *i.e.*, that quantum of the means of subsistence, which is absolutely requisite to keep the labourer in bare existence as a labourer. What, therefore, the wage-labourer appropriates by means of his labour, merely suffices to prolong and reproduce a bare existence. We by no means intend to abolish this personal appropriation of the products of labour, an appropriation that is made for the maintenance and reproduction of human life, and that leaves no surplus wherewith to command the labour of others. All that we want to do away with is the miserable character of this appropriation, under which the labourer lives merely to increase capital, and is allowed to live only in so far as the interest of the ruling class requires it.

In bourgeois society, living labour is but a means to increase accumulated labour. In Communist society, accumulated labour is but a means to widen, to enrich, to promote the existence of the labourer.

In bourgeois society, therefore, the past dominates the present; in Communist society, the present dominates the past. In bourgeois society capital is independent and has individuality, while the living person is dependent and has no individuality.

And the abolition of this state of things is called by the bourgeois, abolition of individuality and freedom! And rightly so. The abolition of bourgeois individuality, bourgeois independence, and bourgeois freedom is undoubtedly aimed at.

By freedom is meant, under the present bourgeois conditions of production, free trade, free selling and buying.

But if selling and buying disappears, free selling and buying disappears also. This talk about free selling and buying, and all the other "brave words" of our bourgeoisie about freedom in general, have a meaning, if any, only in contrast with restricted selling and buying, with the fettered traders of the Middle Ages, but have no meaning when opposed to the Communistic abolition of buying and selling, of the bourgeois conditions of production, and of the bourgeoisie itself

You are horrified at our intending to do away with private property. But in your existing society, private property is already done away with for nine-tenths of the population: its existence for few is solely due to its non-existence in the hands of those nine-tenths. You reproach us, therefore, with intending to do away with a form of property, the necessary condition for whose existence is, the non-existence of any property for the immense majority of society.

In one word, you reproach us with intending to do away with your property. Precisely so; that is just what we intend.

From the moment when labour can no longer be converted into capital, money, or rent, into a social power capable of being monopolised, *i.e.*, from the moment when individual property can no longer be transformed into bourgeois property, into capital, from that moment, you say, individuality vanishes.

You must, therefore, confess that by "individual" you mean no other person than the bourgeois, than the middle-class owner of property. This person must, indeed, be swept out of the way, and made impossible.

Communism deprives no man of the power to appropriate the products of society; all that it does is to deprive him of the power to subjugate the labour of others by means of such appropriation.

It has been objected that upon the abolition of private property all work will cease, and universal laziness will overtake us.

According to this, bourgeois society ought long ago to have gone to the dogs through sheer idleness; for those of its members who work, acquire nothing, and those who acquire anything, do not work. The whole of this objection is but another expression of the tautology: that there can no longer be any wage labour when there is no longer any capital.

All objections urged against the Communistic mode of producing and appropriating material products, have, in the same way, been urged against the Communistic modes of producing and appropriating intellectual products. Just as, to the bourgeois, the disappearance of class property is the disappearance of production itself, so the disappearance of class culture is to him identical with the disappearance of all culture.

That culture, the loss of which he laments, is, for the enormous majority, a mere training to act as a machine.

But don't wrangle with us so long as you apply, to our intended abolition of bourgeois property, the standard of your bourgeois notions of freedom, culture, law, &c. Your very ideas are but the outgrowth of the conditions of your bourgeois production and bourgeois property, just as your jurisprudence is but the will of your class made into a law for all, a will, whose essential character and direction are determined by the economical conditions of existence of your class.

The selfish misconception that induces you to transform into eternal laws of nature and of reason, the social forms springing from your present mode of production and form of property—historical relations that rise and disappear in the progress of production—this misconception you share with every ruling class that has preceded you. What you see clearly in the case of ancient property, what you admit in the case of feudal property, you are of course forbidden to admit in the case of your own bourgeois form of property.

Abolition of the family! Even the most radical flare up at this infamous proposal of the Communists.

On what foundation is the present family, the bourgeois family, based? On capital, on private gain. In its completely developed form this family exists only among the bourgeoisie. But this state of things finds its complement in the practical absence of the family among the proletarians, and in public prostitution.

The bourgeois family will vanish as a matter of course when its complement vanishes, and both will vanish with the vanishing of capital.

Do you charge us with wanting to stop the exploitation of children by their parents? To this crime we plead guilty.

But, you will say, we destroy the most hallowed of relations, when we replace home education by social.

And your education! Is not that also social, and determined by the social conditions under which you educate, by the intervention, direct or indirect, of society, by means of schools, &c? The Communists have not invented the intervention of society in education; they do but seek to alter the character of that intervention, and to rescue education from the influence of the ruling class.

The bourgeois clap-trap about the family and education, about the hallowed co-relation of parent and child, becomes all the more disgusting, the more, by the action of Modern Industry, all family ties among the proletarians are torn asunder, and their children transformed into simple articles of commerce and instruments of labour.

But you Communists would introduce community of women, screams the whole bourgeoisie in chorus.

The bourgeois sees in his wife a mere instrument of production. He hears that the instruments of production are to be exploited in common, and, naturally, can come to no other conclusion than that the lot of being common to all will likewise fall to the women.

He has not even a suspicion that the real point aimed at is to do away with the status of women as mere instruments of production.

For the rest, nothing is more ridiculous than the virtuous indignation of our bourgeois at the community of women which, they pretend, is to be openly and officially established by the Communists. The Communists have no need to introduce community of women; it has existed almost from time immemorial.

Our bourgeois? not content with having the wives and daughters of their proletarians at their disposal, not to speak of common prostitutes, take the greatest pleasure in seducing each other's wives.

Bourgeois marriage is in reality a system of wives in common and thus, at the most, what the Communists might possibly be reproached with, is that they desire to introduce, in substitution for a hypocritically concealed, an openly legalised, community of women. For the rest, it is self-evident that the abolition of the present system of production must bring with it the abolition of the community of women springing from that system, *i.e.*, of prostitution both public and private.

The Communists are further reproached with desiring to abolish countries and nationality.

The working men have no country. We cannot take from them what they have not got. Since the proletariat must first of all acquire political supremacy, must rise to be the leading class of the nation, must constitute itself *the* nation, it is, so far, itself national, though not in the bourgeois sense of the word.

National differences and antagonisms between peoples are daily more and more vanishing, owing to the development of the bourgeoisie, to freedom of commerce, to the world market, to uniformity in the mode of production and in the conditions of life corresponding thereto.

The supremacy of the proletariat will cause them to vanish still faster. United action, of the leading civilised countries at least, is one of the first conditions for the emancipation of the proletariat.

In proportion as the exploitation of one individual by another is put an end to, the exploitation of one nation by another will also be put an end to. In proportion as the antagonism between classes within the nation vanishes, the hostility of one nation to another will come to an end.

The charges against Communism made from a religious, a philosophical, and, generally, from an ideological standpoint, are not deserving of serious examination.

Does it require deep intuition to comprehend that man's ideas, views and conceptions, in one word, man's consciousness, changes with every change in the conditions of his material existence, in his social relations and in his social life?

What else does the history of ideas prove, than that intellectual production changes its character in proportion as material production is changed? The ruling ideas of each age have ever been the ideas of its ruling class.

When people speak of ideas that revolutionise society, they do but express the fact, that within the old society, the elements of a new one have been created, and that the dissolution of the old ideas keeps even pace with the dissolution of the old conditions of existence.

When the ancient world was in its last throes, the ancient religions were overcome by Christianity. When Christian ideas succumbed in the 18th century to rationalist ideas, feudal society fought its death battle with the then revolutionary bourgeoisie. The ideas of religious liberty and freedom of conscience, merely gave expression to the sway of free competition within the domain of knowledge.

"Undoubtedly," it will be said, "religious; moral, philosophical and juridical ideas have been modified in the course of historical development. But religion, morality, philosophy, political science, and law, constantly survived this change."

"There are, besides, eternal truths, such as Freedom, Justice, etc., that are common to all states of society. But communism abolishes eternal truths, it abolishes all religion, and all morality, instead of constituting them on a new basis; it therefore acts in contradiction to all past historical experience."

What does this accusation reduce itself to? The history of all past society has consisted in the development of class antagonisms, antagonisms that assumed different forms at different epochs.

But whatever form they may have taken, one fact is common to all past ages, *viz.*, the exploitation of one part of society by the other. No wonder, then, that the social consciousness of past ages, despite all the multiplicity and variety it displays, moves within certain common forms, or general ideas, which cannot completely vanish except with the total disappearance of class antagonisms.

The Communist revolution is the most radical rupture with traditional property relations; no wonder that its development involves the most radical rupture with traditional ideas.

But let us have done with the bourgeois objections to Communism.

We have seen above, that the first step in the revolution by the working class, is to raise the proletariat to the position of ruling class, to win the battle of democracy.

The proletariat will use its political supremacy to wrest, by degrees, all capital from the bourgeoisie, to centralise all instruments of production in the hands of the State, *i.e.*, of the proletariat organised as the ruling class; and to increase the total of productive forces as rapidly as possible.

Of course, in the beginning, this cannot be effected except by means of despotic inroads on the rights of property, and on the conditions of bourgeois production; by means of measures, therefore, which appear economically insufficient and untenable, but which, in the course of the movement, outstrip themselves, necessitate further inroads upon the old social order, and are unavoidable as a means of entirely revolutionising the mode of production.

These measures will of course be different in different countries.

Nevertheless in the most advanced countries, the following will be pretty generally applicable:

1. Abolition of property in land and application of all rents of land to public purposes.

2. A heavy progressive or graduated income tax.

3. Abolition of all right of inheritance.

4. Confiscation of the property of all emigrants and rebels.

5. Centralisation of credit in the hands of the State, by means of a national bank with State capital and an exclusive monopoly.

6. Centralisation of the means of communication and transport in the hands of the State.

7. Extension of factories and instruments of production owned by the State; the bringing into cultivation of waste-lands, and the improvement of the soil generally in accordance with a common plan.

8. Equal liability of all to labour. Establishment of industrial armies, especially for agriculture.

9. Combination of agriculture with manufacturing industries; gradual abolition of the distinction between town and country, by a more equable distribution of the population over the country.

10. Free education for all children in public schools. Abolition of children's factory labour in its present form. Combination of education with industrial production, &c., &c.

When, in the course of development, class distinctions have disappeared, and all production has been concentrated in the hands of a vast association of the whole nation, the public power will lose its political character. Political power, properly so called, is merely the organised power of one class for oppressing another. If the proletariat during its contest with the bourgeoisie is compelled, by the force of circumstances, to organise itself as a class, if, by means of a revolution, it makes itself the ruling class, and, as such, sweeps away by force the old conditions of production, then it will, along with these conditions, have swept away the conditions for the existence of class antagonisms and of classes generally, and will thereby have abolished its own supremacy as a class.

In place of the old bourgeois society, with its classes and class antagonisms, we shall have an association, in which the free development of each is the condition for the free development of all.

John Henry Newman

Introduction
Richard Liddy

This sermon was written by John Henry Newman in 1841 while he was a young clergyman at the University of Oxford.

Newman was born in London in 1801, the son of a banker. As a young man, he read many of the "free-thinkers" or secular writers of the day: Voltaire, David Hume, Thomas Payne. These writers represented the anti-traditional spirit of the Enlightenment with its many scientific discoveries. Such discoveries were felt to be inaugurating a new age in which scientific progress would destroy narrow religious allegiances. However, as a young man Newman experienced a religious conversion. Later he would say that he was more certain that God touched him and led him as a young man "than that I have hands and feet."

The upshot of Newman's conversion was a life dedicated to spiritual growth and study—especially the study of ancient Christianity and its implications for its encounter with modern culture. In his thirties he was the central figure in what came to be known as "the Oxford movement" in the Church of England, that is, the effort to recall the Church to its ancient roots and sacramental/spiritual life. Eventually, in 1845 Newman converted to Roman Catholicism. He once wrote: "Catholics did not make me a Catholic, the Fathers made me a Catholic"—meaning the ancient Christian writers.

Newman was a fluent English stylist. James Joyce considered him the preeminent prose writer in the English language. In addition to his many sermons, Newman wrote *The Idea of a University*, the classic work on the meaning of a university education; *Apologia pro vita sua*, on his conversion to Catholicism; and *The Grammar of Assent*, on how we make judgments strong enough to support decisive action.

The present sermon, written before his conversion to Catholicism, was given in St. Mary's Church in Oxford. Newman was considered at the time the outstanding preacher in England and his sermons were attended by large groups of undergraduates. Newman's preaching at St. Mary's became legendary and many descriptions were written of it, the most famous being Matthew Arnold's evocation of "the charm of that spiritual apparition, gliding in the dim afternoon light through the aisles of St. Mary's, rising into the pulpit, and then, in the most entrancing of voices, breaking the silence with words and thoughts which were a religious music,—subtle, sweet, mournful."

In general, Newman contrasts an attitude open to belief with the modern rationalist attitude of doubting everything. Newman felt it was far better to be open to believing everything—and then letting go of what was not worthy of belief—rather than beginning with a skeptical attitude.

In this sermon, Newman contrasts bigotry, a narrow adherence to a partial vision of things, with faith, an openness of heart and mind to divine guidance. Eventually faith can lead to wisdom, an overall viewpoint rooted in faith. The sermon itself is an illustration of wisdom.

At their announcement of his death in 1890, the *Times of London* wrote that whether or not the Church of Rome canonizes him, Cardinal Newman will be canonized in the hearts of his countrymen. The first step toward formal canonization—and perhaps declaring Newman a "Doctor of the Church"—was for Pope Benedict XVI to beatify him in 2010 in Birmingham, England, where he lived for the latter part of his life.

Newman's writings need to be read slowly and carefully. One might particularly reflect on the relevance of Newman's sermon to the cultural situation of Christianity today.

SERMON XIV.

WISDOM, AS CONTRASTED WITH FAITH AND WITH BIGOTRY

Preached on Whit-Tuesday, 1841.

Sermons, Chiefly on the Theory of Religious Belief, Preached before the University of Oxford by John Henry Newman, B.D. Second Edition, 1844.

1 COR. ii. 15.

> *"He that is spiritual judgeth all things, yet he himself is judged of no man."*

The gift to which this high characteristic is ascribed by the Apostle, is Christian Wisdom, and the Giver is God the Holy Ghost. "We speak wisdom," he says, shortly before the text, "among them that are perfect, yet not the wisdom of this world... but we speak the wisdom of God in a mystery, even the hidden wisdom." And after making mention of the heavenly truths which Wisdom contemplates, he adds: "God hath revealed them unto us by His Spirit... we have received, not the spirit of the world, but the Spirit which is of God."

In a former verse St. Paul contrasts this divine Wisdom with Faith. "My speech and my preaching was not with enticing words of man's wisdom, but in demonstration of the Spirit and of power, that your faith should not stand in the wisdom of men, but in the power of God. Howbeit, we speak wisdom among them that are perfect." Faith, then, and Wisdom, are distinct, or even opposite gifts. Wisdom belongs to the perfect, and more especially to preachers of the Gospel; and Faith is the elementary grace which is required of all, especially of hearers. The two are introduced again in a later chapter of the same Epistle: "To one is given by the Spirit the word of Wisdom, to another the word of Knowledge by the same Spirit, to another Faith by the same Spirit." Such are the two gifts which will be found to lie at the beginning and at the end of our new life, both intellectual in their nature, and both divinely imparted; Faith being an exercise of the Reason, so spontaneous, unconscious, and unargumentative, as to seem at first sight even to have a moral origin, and Wisdom being that orderly and mature development of thought, which in earthly language goes by the name of science and philosophy.

In like manner, in the Services of this sacred Season, both these spiritual gifts are intimated, and both referred to the same heavenly source. The Collect virtually speaks of Faith, when it makes mention of Almighty God's "teaching the hearts of His faithful people by the sending to them the light of His Holy Spirit;" and of the Wisdom of the perfect, when it prays God, that "by the same Spirit" we may "have a right judgment in all things."

Again, in the Gospel for Whitsunday, the gift of Wisdom is surely implied in Christ's promise, that the Comforter should teach the Apostles "all things," and "bring all things to their remembrance whatsoever He had said unto them;" and in St. Paul's exhortation, which we read yesterday, "In malice be children, but in understanding be men." Again, a cultivation of the reasoning faculty, near akin to Philosophy or Wisdom, is surely implied in the precepts, of which we have heard, or shall hear, from the same Apostle and St. John to-day, about "proving all things," and "holding fast that which is good," and about "trying the spirits whether they are of God."

Again, other parts of our Whitsun Services speak of exercises of Reason more akin to Faith, as being independent of processes of investigation or discussion. In Sunday's Gospel our Lord tells us, "He that loveth Me shall be loved of My Father, and I will love him, and will manifest Myself to him...If a man love Me, he will keep My words, and My Father will love him, and We will come unto him, and make Our abode with him." This manifestation is doubtless made to us through our natural faculties; but who will maintain that even so far as it is addressed to our Reason, it comes to us in forms of argument? Again, in the Gospel for yesterday, "He that doeth truth cometh to the light," and on the contrary, "Light is come into the world, and men loved darkness rather than light, because their deeds were evil; for every one that doeth evil hateth the light." Men do not choose light or darkness without Reason, but by an instinctive Reason, which is prior to argument and proof. And in the Gospel for to-day, "The sheep hear His voice, and He calleth His own sheep by name, and leadeth them out. The sheep follow Him, for they know His voice, and a stranger will they not follow, for they know not the voice of strangers." The sheep could not tell *how* they knew the Good Shepherd; they had not analyzed their own impressions or cleared the grounds of their knowledge, yet doubtless grounds there were: they, however, acted spontaneously on a loving Faith.

In proceeding, then, as I shall now do, to inquire into the nature of Christian Wisdom, as a habit or faculty of mind distinct from Faith, the mature fruit of Reason, and nearly answering to what is meant by Philosophy, it must not be supposed that I am denying its spiritual nature or its divine origin. Almighty God influences us and works in us, through our minds, not without them or in spite of them; as at the fall we did not become other beings than what we had been, but forfeited gifts which had been added to us on our creation, so under the Gospel we do not lose any part of the nature in which we are born, but regain what we have lost. We are what we were, and something more. And what is true of God's dealings with our minds generally, is true in particular as regards our reasoning powers. His grace does not supersede, but uses them, and renews them by using. We gain Truth by reasoning, whether implicit or explicit, in a state of nature; we gain it in the same way in a state of grace. Both Faith and Wisdom, the elementary and the perfecting gift of the Holy Spirit, are intellectual habits, and involve the exercise of Reason, and may be examined and defined as any other power of the mind, and are subject to perversion and error, and may be fortified by rules, just as if they were not instruments in the hands of the Most High. It is no derogation, then, from the divine origin of Christian Wisdom, to treat it in its human aspect, to show what it consists in, and what are its counterfeits and perversions; to determine, for instance, that it is much the same as Philosophy, and that its perversions are such as love of system, theorizing, fancifulness, dogmatism, and bigotry,—as we shall be led to do. And now to enter upon our subject.

The words philosophy, a philosophical spirit, enlargement or expansion of mind, enlightened ideas, a wise and comprehensive view of things, and the like, are, I need hardly say, of frequent occurrence in the literature of this day, and are taken to mean very much the same thing. That they are always used with a definite meaning, or with any meaning at all, will be maintained by no one; that so many persons, and many of them men of great ability, should use them absolutely with no meaning whatever, and yet should lay such stress and rest so much upon them, is, on the other hand, not to be supposed. Yet their meaning certainly requires drawing out and illustrating. Perhaps it will be best ascertained by setting down some cases, which are commonly understood, or will be claimed, as instances of this process of mental growth or enlargement; in the sense in which the words are at present used.

I suppose that, when a person whose experience has hitherto been confined to our own calm and unpretending scenery, goes for the first time into parts where physical nature puts on her wilder and more awful forms, whether at home or abroad, as especially into mountainous districts,—or when one who has ever lived in a quiet village comes for the first time to a great metropolis,—he will have a sensation of mental enlargement, as having gained a range of thoughts to which he was before a stranger.

Again, the view of the heavens, which the telescope opens upon us, fills and possesses the mind, and is called an enlargement, whatever is meant by the term.

Again, the sight of an assemblage of beasts of prey and other foreign animals, their strangeness and startling novelty, the originality (if I may use the term,) and mysteriousness of their forms, and gestures, and habits, and their variety and independence of one another, expand the mind, not with out its own consciousness; as if knowledge were a real opening, and as if an addition to the external objects presented before it were an addition to its inward powers.

Hence physical science, generally, in all its departments, as bringing before us the exuberant riches, the active principles, yet the orderly course of the universe, is often set forth even as the only true philosophy, and will be allowed by all persons to have a certain power of elevating and exciting the mind, and yet to exercise a tranquillizing influence upon it.

Again, the knowledge of history, and again, the knowledge of books generally—in a word, what is meant by education, is commonly said to enlighten and enlarge the mind, whereas ignorance is felt to involve a narrow range and a feeble exercise of its powers.

Again, what is called seeing the world, entering into active life, going into society, travelling, acquaintance with the various classes of the community, coming into contact with the principles and modes of thought of separate parties, interests, or nations, their opinions, views, aims, habits, and manners, their religious creeds and forms of worship,—all this exerts a perceptible effect upon the mind, which it is impossible to mistake, be it good or be it bad, and which is popularly called its enlargement or enlightenment.

Again, when a person for the first time hears the arguments and speculations of unbelievers, and feels what a very novel light they cast upon what he has hitherto accounted most sacred, it cannot be denied, that, unless he is shocked and closes his ears and heart to them, he will have a sense of expansion and elevation.

Again, sin brings with it its own enlargement of mind, which Eve was tempted to covet, and of which she made proof. This, perhaps, in the instance of some sins, to which the young are especially tempted, is their great attraction and their great recompense. They excite the curiosity of the innocent, and they intoxicate the imagination of their miserable victims, whose eyes seem opened upon a new world, from which they look back upon their state of innocence with a sort of pity and contempt, as if it were below the dignity of men.

On the other hand, religion has its own enlargement. It is often remarked of uneducated persons, who hitherto have lived without seriousness, that on their turning to God, looking into themselves, regulating their hearts, reforming their conduct, and studying the inspired Word, they seem to become, in point of intellect, different beings from what they were before. Before, they took things as they came, and thought no more of one thing than of another. But now every event has a meaning; they form their own estimate of whatever occurs; they recollect times and seasons; and the world, instead of being like the stream which the countryman gazed on, ever in motion and never in progress, is a various and complicated drama, with parts and with an object.

Again, those who, being used to nothing better than the divinity of what is historically known as the non-conformist school,—or, again, of the latitudinarian,—are introduced to the theology of the early Church, will often have a vivid sense of enlargement, and will feel they have gained something, as becoming aware of the existence of doctrines, opinions, trains of thought, principles, aims, to which hitherto they have been strangers.

And again, such works as treat of the Ministry of the Prophets under the various divine Dispensations, of its nature and characteristics, why it was instituted and what it has effected; the matter, the order, the growth of its disclosures; the views of divine Providence, of the divine counsels and attributes which it was the means of suggesting; and its contrast with the pretences to prophetical knowledge which the world furnishes in mere political partisans or popular fortune-tellers; such treatises, as all will admit, may fitly be said to enlarge the mind.

Once more, such works as Bishop Butler's Analogy, which carry on the characteristic lineaments of the Gospel Dispensation into the visible course of things, and, as it were, root its doctrines into nature and society, not only present before the mind a large view of the matters handled, but will be commonly said, and surely, as all will feel, with a true meaning, to enlarge the mind itself which is put in possession of them.

These instances show beyond all question that what is called Philosophy, Wisdom, or Enlargement of mind, has some intimate dependence upon the acquisition of Knowledge; and Scripture seems to say the same thing. "God gave Solomon," says the inspired writer, "wisdom and understanding, exceeding much, and largeness of heart even as the sand that is on the sea shore . . . . And he spake three thousand proverbs, and his songs were a thousand and five. And he spake of trees, from the cedar-tree that is in Lebanon, even unto the hyssop that springeth out of the wall. He spake also of beasts and of fowl, and of creeping things and of fishes." And again, when the Queen of Sheba came, "Solomon told her all her questions; there was not any thing hid from the king, which he told her not." And in like manner St. Paul, after speaking of the Wisdom of the perfect, calls it a revelation, a knowledge, of the things of God, such as the natural man "discerneth" not. And in another Epistle, evidently speaking of the same Wisdom, he prays that his brethren may be given to "comprehend with all saints what is the breadth and length and depth and height, and to know the love of Christ which passeth knowledge, that they might be filled with all the fulness of God."

However, a very little consideration will make it plain also, that knowledge itself, though a condition of the mind's enlargement, yet, whatever be its range, is not that very thing which enlarges it. Rather the foregoing instances show that this enlargement consists in the *comparison* of the subjects of knowledge one with another. We feel ourselves to be ranging freely, when we not only learn something, but also refer it to what we knew before. It is not the mere addition to our knowledge which is the enlargement, but the change of place, the movement onwards, of that moral centre, to which what we know and what we have been acquiring, the whole mass of our knowledge, as it were, gravitates. And therefore a philosophical cast of thought, or a comprehensive mind, or wisdom in conduct or policy, implies a connected view of the old with the new; an insight into the bearing and influence of each part upon every other; without which there is no whole, and could be no centre. It is the knowledge, not only of things, but of their mutual relations. It is organized, and therefore living knowledge.

A number of instances might readily be supplied in which knowledge is found apart from this analytical treatment of the matter of it, and in which it is never associated with Philosophy, or considered to open, enlarge, and enlighten the mind.

For instance, a great memory is never made synonymous with Wisdom, any more than a dictionary would be called a treatise. There are men who contemplate things both in the mass and individually, but not correlatively, who accumulate facts without forming judgments, who are satisfied with deep learning or extensive information. They may be linguists, antiquarians, annalists, biographers, or naturalists; but, whatever their merits, which are often very great, they have no claim to be considered philosophers.

To the same class belong persons, in other respects very different, who have seen much of the world, and of the men who, in their own day, have played a conspicuous part in it, who are full of information, curious and entertaining, about men and things, but who, having lived under the influence of no very clear or settled principles, speak of every one and everything as mere facts of history, not attempting to illustrate opinions, measures, aims, or policy,—not discussing or teaching, but conversing.

Or take, what is again a very different instance, the case of persons of little intellect, and no education, who perhaps have seen much of foreign countries, and who receive in a passive, otiose, unfruitful way, the various facts which are forced upon them. Seafaring men, for example, range from one end of the earth to the other; but the multiplicity of phenomena which they have encountered, forms no harmonious and consistent picture upon their imagination; they, as it were, see the tapestry of human life on the wrong side of it. They sleep, and they rise up, and they find themselves now in Europe, now in Asia; they see visions of great cities and wild regions; they are in the marts of commerce, or amid the islands of the ocean; they gaze on the Andes, or they are ice-bound; and nothing which meets them carries them on to any idea beyond itself. Nothing has a meaning, nothing has a history, nothing has relations. Everything stands by itself, and comes and goes in its turn, like the shifting sights of a show, leaving the beholder where he was. Or, again, under other circumstances, everything seems to such persons strange, monstrous, miraculous, and awful; as in fable, to Ulysses and his companions in their wanderings.

Or, again, the censure often passed on what is called undigested reading, shows us that knowledge without system is not Philosophy. Students who store themselves so amply with literature or science, that no room is left for determining the respective relations which exist between their acquisitions, one by one, are rather said to load their minds than to enlarge them.

Scepticism, in religious matters, affords another instance in point. Those who deliberately refuse to form a judgment upon the most momentous of all subjects; who are content to pass through life in ignorance, why it is given, or by whom, or to what it leads; and who bear to be without tests of truth and error in conduct, without rule and measure for the principles, persons, and events, which they encounter daily,—these men, though they often claim, will not by any Christian be granted, the name of philosophers.

All this is more than enough to show that some analytical process, some sort of systematizing, some insight into the mutual relation of things, is essential to that enlargement of mind or philosophical temper, which is commonly attributed to the acquisition of knowledge. In other words, Philosophy is Reason exercised upon Knowledge; for, from the nature of the case, where the facts are given, as is here supposed, Reason is synonymous with analysis, having no office beyond that of ascertaining the relations existing between them. Reason is the power of proceeding to new ideas by means of given ones. Where but one main idea is given, it can employ itself in developing this into its consequences. Thus, from scanty data, it often draws out a whole system, each part with its ascertained relations, collateral or lineal, towards the rest, and all consistent together, because all derived from one and the same origin. And should means be found of ascertaining directly some of the facts which it has been deducing by this abstract process, then their coincidence with its *á priori* judgments will serve to prove the accuracy of its deductions.

Where, however, the facts or doctrines in question are all known from the first, there, instead of advancing from idea to idea, Reason does but connect fact with fact; instead of discovering, it does but analyze; and what was, in the former case, the tracing out of inferences, becomes a laying down of relations.

Philosophy, then, is Reason exercised upon Knowledge; or the Knowledge not merely of things in general, but of things in their relations to one another. It is the power of referring everything to its true place in the universal system,—of understanding the various aspects of each of its parts,—of comprehending the exact value of each,—of tracing each backwards to its beginning, and forward to its end,—of anticipating the separate tendencies of each, and their respective checks or counteractions; and thus of accounting for anomalies, answering objections, supplying deficiencies, making allowance for errors, and meeting emergencies. It never views any part or the extended subject-matter of knowledge, without recollecting that it is but a part, or without the associations which spring from this recollection. It makes everything lead to everything else; it communicates the image of the whole body to every separate member, till the whole becomes in imagination like a spirit, everywhere pervading and penetrating its component parts, and giving them their one definite meaning. Just as our bodily organs, when mentioned, recall to mind their function in the body, as the word creation suggests the idea of a Creator, as subjects that of a sovereign, so in the mind of a philosopher, the elements of the physical and moral world, sciences, arts, pursuits, ranks, offices, events, opinions, individualities, are all viewed, not in themselves, but as relative terms, suggesting a multitude of correlatives, and gradually, by successive combinations, converging one and all to their true centre. Men, whose minds are possessed by some one object, take exaggerated views of its importance, are feverish in their pursuit of it, and are startled or downcast on finding obstacles in the way of it; they are ever in alarm or in transport; and they, on the contrary, who have no firm grasp of principles, are perplexed and lose their way every fresh step they take. They do not know what to think or say of new phenomena which meet them, of whatever kind; they have no view, as it may be called, concerning persons, or occurrences, or facts, which come upon them suddenly; they cannot form a judgment, or determine on a course of action; and they ask the opinion or advice of others as a relief to their minds. But Philosophy cannot be partial, cannot be exclusive, cannot be impetuous, cannot be surprised, cannot fear, cannot lose its balance, cannot be at a loss, cannot but be patient, collected, and majestically calm, because it discerns the whole in each part, the end in each beginning, the worth of each interruption, the measure of each delay, because it always knows where it is, and how its path lies from one point to another. There are men who, when in difficulties, by the force of genius, originate at the moment vast ideas or dazzling projects; who, under the impulse of excitement, are able to cast a light, almost as if from inspiration, on a subject or course of action which comes before them; who have a sudden presence of mind equal to any emergency, rising with the occasion, and an undaunted heroic bearing, and an energy and keenness, which is but sharpened by opposition. Faith is a gift analogous to this thus far, that it acts promptly and boldly on the occasion, on slender evidence, as if guessing and reaching forward to the truth, amid darkness or confusion; but such is not the Wisdom of the perfect. It is the clear, calm, accurate vision, and comprehension of the whole course, the whole work of God; and though there is none who has it in its fulness but He who "searcheth all things, yea, the deep things of" the Creator, yet "by that Spirit" they are, in a measure, "revealed unto us." And thus, according to that measure, is the text fulfilled, that "he that is spiritual judgeth all things, yet he himself is judged by no man." Others understand him not, master not his ideas, fail to combine, harmonize, or make consistent, those distinct views and principles which come to him from the Infinite Light, and are inspirations of the breath of God. He, on the contrary, compasses others, and locates them, and anticipates their acts, and fathoms their thoughts, for, in the Apostle's language, he "hath the mind of Christ," and all things are his, "whether Paul, or Apollos, or Cephas, or the world, or life, or death, or things present, or things to come." Such is the marvellousness of the Pentecostal gift, wherein we "have an unction from the Holy One, and know all things."

Now, this view of the nature of Philosophy leads to the following remark: that, whereas no arguments in favour of religion are of much account but such as rest on a philosophical basis, Evidences of Religion, as they are called, which are truly such, must consist mainly in such investigations into the relation of idea to idea, and developments of system, as have been described, if Philosophy lie in these abstract exercises of Reason. Such, for instance, is the argument from analogy, or from the structure of prophecy, or from the needs of human nature and the fulness of time; or from the Catholic Church. From which it follows, first, that what may be called the rhetorical or forensic Evidences,—I mean those which are content with the proof of certain facts, motives, and the like, such as, that a certain miracle must have taken place, or a certain prophecy must have been both written before, and fulfilled in, a certain event; these, whatever their merits, which I have no wish to disparage, are not philosophical. And next, it follows that Evidences in general are not the essential groundwork of Faith, but its reward; since Wisdom is the last gift of the Spirit, and Faith the first.

In the foregoing observations I have, in fact, been showing,—in prosecution of a line of thought to which I have before now drawn attention,—what is the true office, and what the legitimate bounds of those abstract exercises of Reason which may best be described by the name of systematizing. They are in their highest and most honourable place, when they are employed upon the vast field of Knowledge, not conjecturing unknown truths, but comparing, adjusting, connecting, explaining facts and doctrines ascertained. Such a use of Reason is Philosophy; such employment was it to which the reason of Newton dedicated itself; and the reason of Butler; and the reason of those ancient Catholic Divines, nay, in their measure, of those illustrious thinkers of the middle ages, who have treated of the Christian faith on system, Athanasius, Augustine, Aquinas. But where the exercise of Reason much outstrips our Knowledge; where Knowledge is limited, and Reason active; where ascertained truths are scanty, and courses of thought abound; there indulgence of system is unsafe, and may be dangerous. In such cases there is much need of wariness, jealousy of self, and habitual dread of presumption, paradox, and unreality, to preserve our deductions within the bounds of sobriety, and our guesses from assuming the character of discoveries. System, which is the very soul, or, to speak more precisely, the formal cause of Philosophy, when exercised upon adequate knowledge, does but make, or tend to make, theorists, dogmatists, philosophists, and sectarians, when or so far as Knowledge is limited or incomplete.

This statement, which will not be questioned, perhaps, in the abstract, requires to be illustrated in detail, and that at a length inconsistent with my present limits. At the risk, however, of exceeding them, I will attempt so much as this,—to show that Faith, distinct as it is from argument, discussion, investigation, philosophy, nay, from Reason altogether, in the popular sense of the word, is at the same time perfectly distinct also from narrowness of mind in all its shapes, though sometimes accidentally connected with it in particular instances. I am led to give attention to this point from its connection with subjects, of which I have already treated on former occasions.

It is as if a law of the human mind, ever to do things in one and the same way. It is not various in its modes of action, except by an effort; but, if left to itself, it becomes almost mechanical, as a matter of course. Its doing a thing in a certain way today, is the cause of its doing it in the same way tomorrow. The order of the day perpetuates itself. This is, in fact, only saying that habits arise out of acts, and that character is inseparable from our moral nature. Not only do our features and make remain the same day after day, but we speak in the same tone, adopt the same phrases and turns of thought, fall into the same expressions of countenance, and walk with the same gait as yesterday. And, besides, we have an instinctive love of order and arrangement; we think and act by rule, not only unconsciously, but of set purpose. Method approves itself to us, and aids us in various ways, and to a certain point is pleasant, and in some respects absolutely necessary. Even sceptics cannot proceed without elementary principles, though they would fain dispense with every yoke and bond. Even the uneducated have their own rude modes of classifying, not the less really such, because fantastic or absurd; children too, amid their awe at all that meets them, yet in their own thoughts unconsciously subject these wonders to a law. Poets, while they disown philosophy, frame an ideal system of their own; and naturalists invent, if they do not find, orders and genera, to assist the memory. Latitudinarians, again, while they profess charity towards all doctrines, nevertheless count it heresy to oppose the principle of latitude. Those who condemn persecution for religious opinions, in self-defence, persecute those who advocate it. Few of those who maintain that the exercise of private judgment upon Scripture leads to the attainment of Gospel truth, can tolerate the Socinian and Pelagian, who in their own inquiries have taken pains to conform to this rule. Thus, what is invidiously called dogmatism and system, in one shape or other, in one degree or another, is, I may say, necessary to the human mind; we cannot reason, feel, or act, without it; it forms the stamina of thought, which, when it is removed, languishes, and droops. Sooner than dispense with principles, the mind will take them at the hand of others, will put up with such as are faulty or uncertain;—and thus much Wisdom, Bigotry, and Faith, have in common. Principle is the life of them all; but Wisdom is the application of adequate principles to the state of things as we find them, Bigotry is the application of inadequate or narrow principles, while Faith is the maintenance of principles, without caring to apply or adjust them. Thus they differ; and this distinction will serve to enable us to contrast Bigotry and Faith with Wisdom, as I proposed.

Now, certainly, Faith may be confused with Bigotry, dogmatism, positiveness, and kindred habits of mind, on several plausible grounds; for, what is Faith but a reaching forth after truth amid darkness, upon the warrant of certain antecedent notions or spontaneous feelings? It is a presumption about matters of fact, upon principle rather than on knowledge; and what is Bigotry also but this? And, further still, its grounds being thus conjectural, what does it issue in? in the absolute acceptance of a certain message or doctrine as divine; that is, it starts from probabilities, yet it ends in peremptory statements, if so be, mysterious, or at least beyond experience. It believes an informant amid doubt, yet accepts his information without doubt. Such is the *primá facie* resemblance between two habits of mind, which nevertheless are as little to be confused as the Apostles with their Jewish persecutors, as a few words may suffice to show.

Now, in the first place, though Faith be a presumption of facts under defective knowledge, yet, be it observed, it is altogether a practical principle. It judges and decides because it cannot help doing so, for the sake of the man himself, who exercises it, not in the way of opinion, not as aiming at abstract truth, not as teaching some theory or view. It is the act of a mind feeling that it is its duty any how, under its particular circumstances, to judge and to act, whether its light be greater or less, and wishing to make the most of that light and acting for the best. Its knowledge, then, though defective, is not insufficient for the purpose for which it uses it, for this plain reason, because (such is God's will) it has no more. The servant who hid his Lord's money was punished; and we, since we did not make our circumstances, but were placed in them, shall be judged, not by them, but by our use of them. A view of duty, such as this, may lead us to wrong acts, but not to act wrongly. Christians have sometimes inflicted death from a zeal not according to knowledge; and sometimes they have been eager for the toleration of heresy from an ill-instructed charity. Under such circumstances a man's error may be more acceptable to God than his truth; for his truth, it may be, but evidences clearness of intellect, whereas his error proceeds from conscientiousness; though whence it proceeds, and what it evidences, in a particular case, must be left to the Searcher of hearts.

Faith, then, though a presumption, has this peculiarity, that it is exercised under a sense of personal responsibility. It is when our presumptions take a wide range, when they affect to be systematical and philosophical, when they are indulged in matters of speculation, not of conduct, not in reference to self but to others, then it is that they deserve the name of bigotry and dogmatism. For in such a case we make a wrong use of such light as is given us, and mistake what is "a lantern unto our feet" for the sun in the heavens.

Again, it is true that Faith as well as Bigotry maintains dogmatic statements which go beyond its knowledge. It uses words, phrases, propositions, it accepts doctrines and practices, which it but partially understands, or not at all. Now, so far indeed as these statements do not relate to matters of this world, but to heavenly things, of course they are no evidence of Bigotry. As the widest experience of life would not tend to remove the mysteriousness of the doctrine of the Holy Trinity, so even the narrowest does not deprive us of the right of asserting it. Much knowledge and little knowledge leave us very much as we were, in a matter of this kind. But the case is very different when positions are in question of a social or moral character, which claim to be rules or maxims for political combination or conduct, for the well-being of the world, or for the guidance of public opinion. Yet many such positions Faith certainly does accept; and thus it seems to place the persons who act upon it in the very position of the bigoted, theoretical, and unreal; who use words beyond their depth, or avow sentiments to which they have no right, or enunciate general principles on defective knowledge. Questions, for instance, about the theory of government, national duties, the establishment of Religion, its relations to the State, the treatment of the poor, and the nature of the Christian

Church: these and other such, may, it cannot be denied, be peremptorily settled, on religious grounds, by persons whose qualifications are manifestly unequal to so great an undertaking, who have not the knowledge, penetration, subtlety, calmness, or experience, which are a claim upon our attention, and who in consequence are, at first sight, to say the least, very like bigots and partisans.

Now that Faith may run into Bigotry, or may be mixed with Bigotry in matter of fact in this instance or that, of course I do not deny; at the same time the two habits of mind, whatever be their resemblance, differ in their dogmatism, in this:—Bigotry professes to understand what it maintains, though it does not; it argues and infers, it disowns Faith, and makes a show of Reason instead of it. It persists, not in abandoning argument, but in arguing only in one way. It takes up, not a religious, but a philosophical position; it lays claim to Wisdom, whereas Faith from the first makes men willing, with the Apostle, to be fools for Christ's sake. Faith sets out with putting reasoning aside as out of place, and proposes instead simple obedience to a revealed command. Its disciples represent that they are neither statesmen nor philosophers; that they are not developing principles or evolving systems; that their ultimate end is not persuasion, popularity, or success; that they are but doing God's will, and desiring His glory. They profess a sincere belief that certain views which engage their minds come from God; that they know well that they are beyond them; that they are not able to enter into them, or to apply them as others may do; that, understanding them but partially themselves, they are not sanguine about impressing them on others; that a divine blessing alone can carry them forward; that they look for it; that they feel that God will maintain His own cause; that *that* belongs to Him, not to them[1]; that if their cause is God's cause, it will be blessed, in His time and way; that if it be not, it will come to nought; that they securely wait the issue; that they leave it to the generation to come; that they can bear to seem to fail, but cannot bear to be "disobedient to a heavenly vision;" that they think that God has taught them and put a word in their mouths; that they speak to acquit their own souls; that they protest, in order to be on the side of God's host, of the glorious company of the Apostles, the goodly fellowship of the Prophets, the noble army of Martyrs, in order to be separate from the congregation of His enemies. "Blessed is the man that hath not walked in the counsel of the ungodly, nor stood in the way of sinners, and hath not sat in the seat of the scornful." They desire to gain this blessedness; and though they have not the capacity of mind to embrace, nor the keenness to penetrate and analyze the contents of this vast world, nor the comprehensive faculty which resolves all things into their true principles, and connects them in one system, though they can neither answer objections made to their doctrines, nor say for certain whither they are leading them, yet profess them they can and must. Embrace them they can, and go out, not knowing whither they go. Faith, at least, they may have; Wisdom, if so be, they have not; but

---

1   Dan. iii. 17, 18.

Faith fits them to be the instruments and organs, the voice and the hands and the feet of Him who is invisible, the Divine Wisdom in the Church,—who knows what they know not, understands their words, for they are His own, and directs their efforts to His own issues, though they see them not, because they dutifully place themselves upon His path. This is what they will be found to profess; and their state is that of the multitude of Christians in every age, nay even in the Apostolic, when, for all the supernatural illumination of such as St. Paul, "God chose the foolish things of the world to confound the wise, and the weak things of the world to confound the things which were mighty, and base things of the world, and things which were despised, yea and things which were not, to bring to nought things that were, that no flesh should glory in His presence."

Such a view of things is not of a nature to be affected by what is external to it. It did not grow out of knowledge, and an increase or loss of knowledge cannot touch it. The revolution of kingdoms, the rise or the fall of parties, the growth of society, the discoveries of science, leave it as they found it. On God's word does it depend; that word alone can alter it. And thus we are introduced to a distinct peculiarity of Faith; for considering that Almighty God often speaks, nay is ever speaking in one way or another, if we would watch for His voice, Faith, while it is so stable, is necessarily a principle of mental growth also, in an especial way; according, that is, as God sees fit to employ it. "I will stand upon my watch," says the prophet, "and set me upon the tower, and will watch to see what He will say unto me;" and, though since Christ came, no new revelation has been given, yet much even in the latter days has been added in the way of explaining and applying what was given, once for all. As the world around varies, so varies also, not the principles of the doctrine of Christ, but the outward shape and colour which they assume. And as Wisdom only can apply or dispense the Truth in a change of circumstances, so Faith alone is able to accept it as one and the same under all its forms. And thus Faith is ever the means of learning something new, and in this respect differs from Bigotry, which has no element of advance in it, and is under a practical persuasion that it has nothing to learn. To the narrow-minded and the bigoted the history of the Church for eighteen centuries is unintelligible and useless; but where there is Faith, it is full of sacred principles, ever the same in substance, ever varying in accidentals, and is a continual lesson of "the manifold Wisdom of God."

Moreover, though Faith has not the gift of tracing out and connecting one thing with another, which Wisdom has, and Bigotry professes to have, but is an isolated act of Reason upon any matter in hand, as it comes; yet on this very account it has as wide a range as Wisdom, and a far wider one than can belong to any narrow principle or partial theory, and is able to take discursive views, though not systematic. There is no subject which Faith working by Love may not include in its province, on which it may not have a judgment, and to which it may not do justice, though it views each point by itself, and not as portions of a whole. Hence, unable as Faith is to analyze its grounds, or to show the consistency of one of its judgments with another, yet every one of these has its own place, and corresponds to some doctrine or precept in the philosophical system of the Gospel, for they are all the instincts of a pure mind, which steps forward truly and boldly, and is never at fault. Whatever be the subject-matter and the point in question, sacred or profane, Faith has a true view of it, and Wisdom can have no more; nor does it become truer because it is held in connexion with other opinions, or less true because it is not. And thus, whereas Faith is the characteristic gift of all Christians, a peasant may take the same view of human affairs in detail as a philosopher; and we are often perplexed whether to say that such persons are intellectually gifted or not. They have clear and distinct opinions; they know what they are saying; they have something to say about any subject; they do not confuse points of primary with those of secondary importance; they never contradict themselves: on the other hand they are not aware that there is anything extraordinary about their judgment; they do not connect any two judgments together; they do not recognize any common principles running through them; they forget the opinions they have expressed with the occasion; they cannot defend themselves; they are easily confused and silenced; and, if they set themselves to reason, they use arguments which appear to be faulty, as being but types and shadows of those which they really feel, and attempts to analyze that vast system of thought which is their life, but not their instrument.

It is the peculiarity, then, of Faith, that it forms its judgment under a sense of duty and responsibility, with a view to personal conduct, according to revealed directions, with a confession of ignorance, with a carelessness about consequences, in a teachable and humble spirit, yet upon a range of subjects which Philosophy itself cannot surpass. In all these respects it is contrasted with Bigotry. Men of narrow minds, far from confessing ignorance and maintaining Truth mainly as a duty, profess, as I observed just now, to understand the subjects which they take up and the principles which they apply to them. They do not see difficulties. They consider that they hold their doctrines, whatever they are, at least as much upon Reason as upon Faith; and they expect to be able to argue others into a belief of them, and are impatient when they cannot. They consider that the premises with which they start just prove the conclusions which they draw, and nothing else. They think that their own views are exactly fitted to solve all the facts which are to be accounted for, to satisfy all objections, and to moderate and arbitrate between all parties. They conceive that they profess just *the* truth which makes all things easy. They have their one idea or their favourite notion, which occurs to them on every occasion. They have their one or two topics, which they are continually obtruding, with a sort of pedantry, being unable to discuss, in a natural unconstrained way, or to let their thoughts take their course, in the confidence that they will come safe home at the last. Perhaps they have discovered, as they think, the leading idea, or simple view, or sum and substance of the Gospel; and they insist upon this or that isolated tenet, selected by themselves or by others not better qualified, to the disparagement of the rest of the revealed scheme. They have, moreover, clear and decisive explanations always ready of the sacred mysteries of Faith; they may deny those mysteries or retain them, but in either case they think their own to be the rational view and the natural explanation of them, and all minds feeble or warped or disordered which do not acknowledge this. They profess that the inspired writers were precisely of their particular creed, be it a creed of to-day, or yesterday, or of a hundred years since; and they do not shrink from appealing to the common sense of mankind at large to decide this point. Then their proof of doctrines is as meagre as their statement of them. They are ready with the very places of Scripture,—one, two, or three,—where it is to be found; they profess to say just what each passage and verse means, what it cannot mean, and what it must mean. To see in it less than they see is, in their judgment, to explain away; to see more, is to gloss over. To proceed to other parts of Scripture than those which they happen to select, is, they think, superfluous, since they have already adduced the very arguments sufficient for a clear proof; and if so, why go beyond them? And again, they have their own terms and names for every thing; and these must not be touched any more than the things which they stand for. Words of party or politics, of recent date and unsatisfactory origin, are as much a portion of the Truth in their eyes, as if they were the voice of Scripture or of Holy Church. And they have their forms, ordinances, and usages, which are as sacred to them as the very Sacraments given us from heaven.

Narrow minds have no power of throwing themselves into the minds of others. They have stiffened in one position, as limbs of the body subjected to confinement, or as our organs of speech, which after a while cannot learn new tones and inflections. They have already parcelled out to their own satisfaction the whole world of knowledge; they have drawn their lines, and formed their classes, and given to each opinion, argument, principle, and party, its own locality; they profess to know where to find every thing; and they cannot learn any other disposition. They are vexed at new principles of arrangement, and grow giddy amid cross divisions; and, even if they make the effort, cannot master them. They think that any one truth excludes another which is distinct from it, and that every opinion is contrary to their own opinions which is not included in them. They cannot separate words from their own ideas, and ideas from their own associations; and if they attain any new view of a subject, it is but for a moment. They catch it one moment, and let it go the next; and then impute to subtlety in it, or obscurity in its expression, what really arises from their own want of elasticity or vigour. And when they attempt to describe it in their own language, their nearest approximation to it is a mistake; not from any purpose to be unjust, but because they are expressing the ideas of another mind, as it were, in translation.

It is scarcely necessary to observe upon the misconceptions which such persons form of foreign habits of thought, or again of ancient faith or philosophy; and the more so, because they are unsuspicious of their own deficiency. Thus we hear the Greek Fathers, for instance, sometimes called Arminians, and St. Augustine Calvinistic; and that not analogously, but as if each party really answered to the title given it. And again an inquiry is made whether Christians in those early days held this or that point of doctrine, which may be in repute in particular sects or schools now; as, for instance, whether they upheld the union of Church and State, or the doctrine of assurance. It is plain that to answer in the affirmative or negative would be to misrepresent them; yet the persons in question do not contemplate more than such an absolute alternative.

Nor is it only in censure and opposition that narrowness of view is shown; it lies quite as often in approval and partisanship. None are so easily deceived by others as they who are pre-occupied with their own notions. They are soon persuaded that another agrees with them, if he disagrees with their opponents. They resolve his ideas into their own, and, whatever words he may use to clear his meaning, even the most distinct and forcible, these fail to convey to them any new view, or to open to them his mind.

Again, if those principles are narrow which claim to interpret and subject the whole world of knowledge, without being adequate to the task, one of the most striking characteristics of such principles will be the helplessness which they exhibit, when new materials or fields of thought are opened upon them. True philosophy admits of being carried out to any extent; it is its very test that no knowledge can be submitted to it with which it is not commensurate, and which it cannot annex to its territory. But the theory of the narrow or bigoted has already run out within short limits, and a vast and anxious region lies beyond, unoccupied and in rebellion. Their "bed is shorter than that a man can stretch himself on it; and the covering narrower, than that he can wrap himself in it." And then what is to be done with these unreclaimed wastes?—the exploring of them must in consequence be forbidden, or even their existence denied. Thus, in the present day, there are new sciences, especially physical, which we all look at with anxiety, feeling that our views, as we at present hold them, are unequal to them, yet feeling also that no truth can really exist external to Christianity. Another striking proof of narrowness of mind among us, may be drawn from the alteration of feeling with which we often regard members of this or that communion, before we know them and after. If our theory and our view of facts agreed together, they could not lead to opposite impressions about the same matters. And another instance occurs daily: true Catholicity is commensurate with the wants of the human mind; but persons are often to be found who are surprised that they cannot persuade all men to follow them, and cannot destroy dissent, by preaching a portion of the Divine system, instead of the whole of it.

Under these circumstances, it is not wonderful that persons of narrow views are often perplexed, and sometimes startled and unsettled, by the difficulties of their position. What they did not know, or what they knew but had not weighed, suddenly presses upon their notice. Then they become impatient that they cannot make their proofs clear, and try to make a forcible riddance of objections. They look about for new arguments, and put violence on Scripture or on history. They show a secret misgiving about the truth of their principles, by shrinking from the appearance of defeat, or from occasional doubt within. They become alarmists, and they forget that the issue of all things, and the success of their own cause, (if it be what they think it,) is sealed and secured by Divine promise; and sometimes, in this conflict between broad fact and narrow principle, the hard material breaks their tools; they are obliged to give up their principles. A state of uncertainty and distress follows, and, in the end, perhaps, bigotry is supplanted by general scepticism. They who thought their own ideas could measure all things, end in thinking that even a Divine Oracle is unequal to the task.

In these remarks, it will be observed that I have been contrasting Faith and Bigotry as habits of mind entirely distinct from each other. They are so; but it must not be forgotten, as indeed I have already observed, that, though distinct in themselves, they may and do exist together in the same person. No one so imbued with a loving Faith but has somewhat, perhaps, of Bigotry to unlearn; no one so narrow-minded, and full of self, but is influenced, it is to be hoped, in his degree, by the spirit of Faith. Let us ever make it our prayer and our endeavour, that we may know the whole counsel of God, and grow unto the measure of the stature of the fulness of Christ; that all prejudice, and self-confidence, and hollowness, and unreality, and positiveness, and partisanship, may be put away from us under the light of Wisdom, and the fire of Faith and Love; till we see things as God sees them, with the judgment of His Spirit, and according to the mind of Christ.

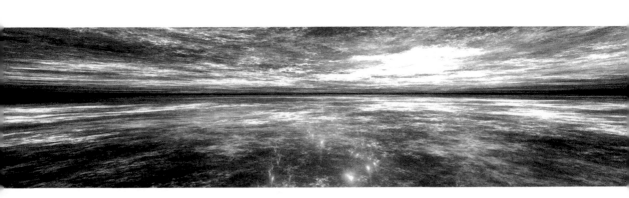

John Courtney Murray

Introduction
Ki Joo Choi

The Jesuit priest and moral theologian John Courtney Murray (1904–1967), a native of New York City, was a leading figure in twentieth-century church-state discussions in the United States. He studied at Boston College and the Gregorian University in Rome, and is widely credited for securing passage of the groundbreaking Vatican II document *Dignitatis Humanae Personae*, which is commonly referred to as "The Declaration on Religious Freedom" (1965).

Murray's intellectual work paved the way, theologically speaking, for greater Catholic engagement and participation in American public life. His defense of religious freedom from a Catholic perspective underscored his larger project of bridging Catholic thought and American democratic discourse. *TIME* magazine's decision to feature Murray on its December 12, 1960, cover validated Murray's position as one of the great public intellectuals in modern U.S. history.

The following selection from Father Murray's "The Doctrine Lives: The Eternal Return of the Natural Law" is an outstanding example of Murray's efforts to show how religious belief can serve as an indispensible source for the advancement of democratic governance and public life.

Following the spirit of Vatican II's *Gaudium et Spes*, Murray believed in the importance of certain kinds of political and social institutions for human flourishing. For Murray, liberal democracy was a significant and unique contribution to the advancement of human well-being. Therefore, it was also the responsibility of Catholics to support and participate in its development and vitality. This responsibility entailed, Murray argued, offering Christian theological and philosophical evaluations and insights on political, social, and civil questions.

As you will see from the following excerpt from Murray's "The Doctrine Lives: The Eternal Return of the Natural Law," Murray proposes that traditional Christian reflections on the *natural law* offer a more surefooted and constructive conceptual foundation for democratic communities than conceptions of the law of nature offered by various Enlightenment philosophies, particularly John Locke's version of it. It is important to emphasize that in criticizing Locke's law of nature and its hypothetical "state of nature" premise, Murray is not rejecting constitutionalism, the notion of rights, and related political ideas. Instead, Murray wonders whether such liberal-Enlightenment political concepts can flourish if their conceptual foundation centers on the notion of the law of nature.

Murray's text begins with a critique of Locke's formulation of the law of nature. For Murray, Locke provides a questionable understanding of human nature on three counts: (1) its rationalism, (2) its individualism, and (3) its nominalism. What are these three critiques of Locke's understanding of human nature (and, by implication, Locke's conception of the law of nature)? Murray thinks that the logical consequence of Locke's rationalism, individualism, and nominalism is the conception of the state proposed by French *philosophes*. What are Murray's concerns with this French conception of the state, and how does he link it to Locke's conception of the law of nature? Note his discussion of power and the state and the role of (or lack of) civic associations (or what is often referred to as the concept of subsidiarity—he will refer to this concept more specifically in his concluding reflections).

Though Murray's critique of Locke's law of nature might suggest that Murray is suspicious of liberal ideals of rights, limited government, and liberty, a careful reading suggests otherwise. Note how he refers to Charles Darwin and Karl Marx as ways of showing that the individualism of Locke's law of nature, for instance, is conceptually untenable! But Murray's larger point is to show that Locke's law of nature, despite its conceptual flaws, served an important political function *for Locke's time*. Given Locke's particular historical circumstance, his conception of the law of nature served as a useful political weapon for the ends of liberty and constitutionalism against profligate monarchy. With that in mind, Murray thinks that these liberal ends can be better served *today* with a more surefooted, coherent conceptual scheme—not Locke's law of nature, but what he refers to as *natural law doctrine* (the idea of the natural law as advanced by Thomas Aquinas).

Be sure to grasp why Murray thinks that Thomistic natural law theory is more adequate for the advancement of liberal ideals in *today's* world. How does Thomistic natural law respond to the problems of rationalism, individualism, and nominalism in the Lockean-liberal concept of the law of nature?

Murray also gives us a more specific discussion of Thomistic natural law doctrine. Pay careful attention to the characteristics of Thomistic natural law. As you do so, study how each characteristic contrasts with the premises of Locke's conception of the law of nature. Murray attempts to show that the doctrine of the natural law entails a form of moral reasoning that is different from the kind of moral reasoning advanced in Locke's conception of the law of nature. It is important to note the differences between these forms of rationality.

Finally, pay careful attention to the political ramifications of Thomistic natural law. Murray outlines two sets of principles that indicate the positive political benefits of Thomistic natural law. What are these principles, and how do they advance the liberal ideals of politics (e.g., limited government, human rights, and liberty)?

WE HOLD THESE TRUTHS
The Law of Nature
John Courtney Murray

Reprinted from *We Hold These Truths: Catholic Reflections on the American Proposition*, by John Courtney Murray. © 2005, pp. 273–300, by permission of Rowman & Littlefield Publishers.

Everybody knows that in the eighteenth century the "law of nature" and the "law of reason" were phrases to conjure with. With his usual engaging cynicism, that in this case does not veil the truth, the late Carl L. Becker described the phenomenon and the climate of opinion, set by Cartesian philosophy and Newtonian physics, that made it possible. To justify what one considered desirable, socially or personally, one appealed in those days to the "law of nature," as today one appeals to "democracy," always with fervor, if not always with good sense. This was true not only in France of the *philosophes*, but to a lesser degree even in America. Mr. Carl Van Doren in *The Great Rehearsal* recounts how one disturbed New Englander objected to the two-year senatorial term proposed by the Constitutional Convention, on the ground that a one-year term was a "dictate of the law of nature"; spring comes once a year, and so should a batch of new Senators.

If it is difficult for us today to share this enthusiasm for the law of nature, it is still more difficult for us to grasp the pivotal concept on which the seventeenth- and eighteenth-century theory of the law of nature depended—the concept of the "state of nature." Yet this was a concept that had all the power of a myth. It found its literary immortalizations, familiar to us all, in Defoe's *Robinson Crusoe* (1719) and Rousseau's *Émile* (1762). And its prominence in the philosophical and political literature of the time is a well-known fact.

This "state of nature" was a purely imaginary construct possible only to the eighteenth-century reason; it was an imaginary state that was nevertheless supposed theoretically to have existed. It depicted what man was and how he lived antecedently to the formation of all human communities and to the establishment of all the laws and customs of social life. The value of the concept was functional. It was a methodological postulate, an abstraction posited as the starting point for a theory of the law of nature; for in the state of nature man was ruled only by the law of nature, and consequently in this state the law of nature could be discovered in all its abstract purity. The further function of the state of nature was to explain, in conjunction with the theory of the social contract, the genesis of political society, its form, and the relative rights of government and citizen.

The state of nature was, of course, a purely formal concept; one could fill it with whatever content one wished, make it pregnant of whatever political consequences one fancied. Here, however, we may confine ourselves simply to the theory of John Locke; it had the greatest fortune both in the Anglo-Saxon and in the French political world. In Locke's system, the state of nature had the initial essential function of establishing the inalienability of the rights of man, as Locke conceived them. In the state of nature, man appears with complete suddenness as a full-grown individual, a hard little atom in the midst of atoms equally hard, all solitary and self-enclosed, each a sociological monad. The idea of man, therefore, is that of an individual who is "absolute lord of his own person and possessions, equal to the greatest and subject to nobody," as he says in his *Second Essay*. In this absolute lordship, equality, and independence consists the Lockean idea of man's "freedom," a freedom that is natural and therefore inalienable save within the limits of his own free choice. On this free individual rests a single law—the law of nature—with a single precept, that of self-preservation, the preservation of his own life, liberty, and property. This law has only one limitation—the same law as obligatory also on other individuals, who in their equally sovereign independence are likewise bound to preserve themselves. Beyond this duty of self-preservation, but subject to its primal exigencies, the individual has one further duty: "Every one, as he is bound to preserve himself, and not to quit his station willfully, so by the like reason, when his own preservation comes not in competition, ought he as much as he can to preserve the rest of mankind."

This is the Lockean state of nature and law of nature. On it is based, by a process of pure postulation, the inalienability of the rights of the individual to life, liberty, and property, and the limitation of these rights solely by the equal rights of other individuals. The chief difficulty about this state of nature is, of course (as Locke naively admits), the obvious fact that it is "not to be endured." With the optimism characteristic of his age and the inconsistency characteristic of himself, Locke prattles a bit about the "innocent delights" attendant on the "liberty" of the state of nature. But it is difficult to see how a state could be delightful wherein every individual is a sort of little god almighty, whose power to preserve himself is checked only at the point where another little god almighty starts preserving *himself*. At this point, one is more sympathetic with the ruthless logic of Thomas Hobbes, who says forthrightly in his *Leviathan* that the state of nature is a "condition which we call Warre," and that the life of the omnipotent monads, among whom prevails the single law of the right of all to all things, is "solitary, poore, nasty, brutish and short." The first impulse of the law of nature, which is that of self-preservation, is, says Hobbes, that of "getting themselves out of the miserable condition of Warre." Locke puts it more politely: "Thus mankind, notwithstanding all the privileges of the state of Nature, being but in an ill condition while they remain in it, are quickly driven into society."

But how does one get these "absolute lords" into society, under government, subject to limitations on their natural omnipotence? Only by their own free act: "Men being, as has been said, by nature all free, equal, and independent, no one can be put out of this estate and subjected to the political power of another without his own consent." Society is not the product of nature but of artifice. It comes into being by the social contract, by the act of men "agreeing together mutually to enter into one community and make one body politic." Thus Locke establishes his second principle on the same grounds as the first: as the rights of man are inalienable, because man is by nature an omnipotent sociological monad, so for the same reason government must be by the consent of the governed.

Moreover, the motive of the consent, as of the "drive" that gets men into society, is self-interest, self-preservation, and particularly the preservation of what was very dear to Locke's middle-class heart, the preservation of property: "The great and chief end, therefore, of men uniting into commonwealths and putting themselves under government, is the preservation of their property, to which in the state of nature there are many things wanting." Society, paradoxically, is the product of egoism. It is an artificial contrivance to rescue the ego by restraining somewhat its egoism. The essence of social man, as of individual man, is selfishness. Finally, pursuing the same line of thought, Locke comes to his third principle, the limitation of governmental power by the "common good." This common good consists merely in the security of each individual in the possession of his property. That is the end of social life as of individual life; the social end differs from the individual end only quantitatively.

This, briefly, is Locke's theory of the law of nature, as embracing a theory of natural rights and their inalienability, of the origins of political society, and of the functions and limitations of governmental power—all based, as is clear, on an idea of man. The three characteristics of the system are obvious—its rationalism, individualism, nominalism. The law of nature, the rights of man, and the origins of society are not derived from what is "real," from the concrete totality of man's nature as it really is. They are deduced from an abstraction, a fictitious state of nature, a disembodied idea of man that is put forward as "rational" and by that sole title real, whereas it was in effect but a reflex of the socio-philosophical individualism of a superficial age.

This individualism, this atomistic social outlook, is the predominant characteristic of Locke's system. His law of nature is solely a law of individual nature, conceived after the abstract fashion of the rationalist. The premise of Locke's state of nature is a denial that sociality is inherent in the very nature of man, and the assertion that the civil state is adventitious, that man is by nature only a solitary atom, who does not seek in society the necessary condition of his natural perfectibility as man, but only a utilitarian convenience for the fuller protection of his individual self in its individuality. Bentham's utilitarianism is, in fact, but the logical prolongation of Locke's thought. Locke's individualism completely deprives society of any organic character. Society is not organized in ascending forms of sociality that are made necessary by, and radicated in, nature itself, beginning with the family, through the occupational group, and culminating in the "perfect society," the political community as such, the *respublica*.

In Locke's theory all forms of sociality are purely contractual; they have no deeper basis in the nature of man than a shallow "reason" that judges them useful. (Even the church he will allow to be no more than a voluntary association of like-minded people—a concept congenial indeed to a certain wing of Protestantism, but one that an increasing number of Protestants today are finding it difficult to live with.) Against this evacuation of all reality from the notion of society and "social being" the Romantic movement, with its love of the "organic," was a reaction, that in time carried the world to the excesses of the totalitarianisms of race and class.

In England, of course, Locke's individualistic law of nature never had its logical social consequences. There were too many elements of the more human medieval tradition deposited in English institutions, and above all in the English common law, for the inherent consequence of Locke's theory to work itself out; I mean the dissolution of the organic character of the total political relationship and its reduction to the harsh antithesis, individual *versus* state, together with the connected idea of the juridical omnipotence of the state. However, the French enthusiasts who took up his ideas had none of the inhibitions imposed on him by his British common sense, caution, and feeling for tradition. In consequence, his law of nature, when it had passed through their politically irresponsible "reason," results in the complete social atomism of the Constitution of 1791 and the Declaration of the Rights of Man and Citizen. There it appears that there are only two "sovereignties": that of the individual over his private life and that of the state over all forms of social life. There are no autonomous social forms intermediate between the individual and the state. Not only are the traditional *états* dissolved, but it is decreed that "There are no longer *iurandes*, nor corporations of professions, arts and crafts, nor any private humanitarian associations or private schools." (The famous *loi Chapelier* of 1793 carried this atomism to its ultimate absurdity, that produced a reaction; not even the conquering "reason" of the *philosophes* could convince a lot of sensible, provincial Frenchmen that they had only two loyalties—one to themselves as individuals and the other to the state.)

Finally, the individualism of Locke's law of nature results in a complete evacuation of the notion of the "rights" of man. It is quite evident that Locke's state of nature reveals no *ordo juris*, and no rights in any recognizably moral sense. There is simply a pattern of power relationships—the absolute lordship of one individual balanced against the equally absolute lordship of others. Significantly, Locke uses the word "power" more frequently than the word "right" in describing the state of nature. Moreover, what the social contract does, in effect, is simply to transfer this system of power relationships into the civil state, with the sole but significant difference that there is now added to it a "third power," the public power of government. In the naked essence of Locke's thought, government is the arbiter of "right," only in the sense that it is a power to check power. And its use is "right" when behind it is the consent of the community, that is, the consent of the majority, that is, again (in Locke's explanation of majority rule), "the greater force," in which is embodied "the power of the whole."

Again, Locke did not draw all the implications from his theory, but the French did. There was Montesquieu, for instance, with his doctrinaire theory that only power checks power, and that when the checks are adequate the mechanical resultant is freedom (unless, one is inclined to add, it be the situation in which the French to this day seem to delight—the paralysis of power and consequent chaos). Moreover, there was the fourth article of the Declaration of the Rights of Man, wherein the logic of Locke's theory runs out in the statement that the "limits" of individual rights "can be determined only by law," that is, by positive law. Here is the explicit denial of any *ordo juris* antecedent to the state; here is the seed of legal positivism, and the essence of Rousseau's omnipotent democracy, wherein there is complete identification of state and national community, and the consequent subjection of all forms of community life to total state control. The logical outcome of Locke's individualistic law of nature, in its French transcription, was the juridical monism of the successive French Republics. In consequence of the false antithesis, individual *versus* state, all self-governing intermediary social forms with particular ends are destroyed, in order to create "free and equal citizens," who are subject only to one law, the positive law of the state, the exclusively competent law-maker. There is no longer any pluralism of social institutions existent and self-directing by natural or positive divine right (e.g., workers' unions or the Church), antecedent to, or above the state. There is only the monistic unity of the political order, under a legislative that is juridically omnipotent, the source and origin of all right. And to enforce this political unity, by destruction of all possibly competing allegiances, there was a state-fostered political mysticism—the "civil religion" of Rousseau, which was indeed no kind of religion but simply a means to homogeneity in the state. (I have already pointed out in a previous chapter that it was against this type of liberalist individualism—as positing a social and juridical monism and a concept of the juridical omnipotence of the state, both based on the concept of the absolute autonomy of the individual human reason—that: the Catholic Church directed her uncompromising attacks during the nineteenth century, under appeal to the traditional natural law.)

The third characteristic of Locke's system of natural law is its nominalism. Since he was on the one hand an empiricist in epistemology (who denied the power of intelligence to reach anything beyond the individual singular thing), and since on the other hand he wished to talk as a philosopher (using the traditional terms—man, nature, law, right, authority, society, state, etc.), Locke could not be anything but that most decadent of all philosophical things, a nominalist. All these terms to him are mere *flatus vocis*, symbols to which corresponds no metaphysical reality. For instance, society as such, or man as *ens sociale*, signifies nothing real; the terms are symbols indicating a certain amount of material utility that the individual derives from contractual forms of association with other individuals. Similarly, the law of nature is but a nominalist symbol for a collection of particular empowerments considered desirable for the preservation of "property" in the wide Lockean sense. Or again, the "common good" is nothing real in itself, a social good qualitatively distinct from individual goods, but simply a symbol for the quantitative sum of individual goods. Finally, "right" is not a term relating to a moral order deriving from the essence of things; it is simply a symbol flourished to assure the free functioning of self-interest. In the rarefied mental climate of the *philosophes*, as well as in the muzzy mysticism of Rousseau, this purely symbolic value of the phrase, "the rights of man," as a potent form of political incantation, is still more marked.

The Law of Nature as a Political Instrument

What then does one say about this individualistic law of nature in Locke's statement, and the French restatement, of it? What one says depends on whether one regards it as a piece of philosophy or as a political weapon. As a piece of philosophy—that is, as ultimately resting on an idea of man and human society—it hardly needs refutation today. As a matter of fact, the refutation of the system was supplied before the system itself was born; Aristotle himself suggested its substance, even apart from the development of Aristotelian epistemology, ethics, and political philosophy in the Scholastic tradition. However, one need not appeal to thinkers antecedent to Locke; those subsequent to him will do. Darwin, Freud, and Marx are sufficiently his judges in what concerns the pillars of his system. The genuine and true insights that lie at the root of these three latterly proposed systems have destroyed completely the Lockean idea of man, of the state of nature, and of civil society; this, notwithstanding the fact that these true insights are so denatured by their incorporation into falsely monistic systems that in their own context they are themselves false.

Darwin and the principle of continuity in nature dealt a mortal blow to the atomism of post-Reformation anthropology, with its theory of discrete individuals who "happen" suddenly and live "unattached" save in so far as with sovereign freedom they attach themselves. In evolutionary theory, man is solidary, by all that is material in him, with all life. Purified of monistic connotations, the notion is compatible with a central thesis of Christian anthropology, that asserts the law of solidarity for both flesh and spirit; but it is not compatible with Lockean individualism. Again, when Freud fulfilled his promise, "Acheronta movebo," he shattered forever the "angel-mindedness" of the Cartesian man, and the brittle rationalistic optimism founded on it with the aid of eighteenth-century mechanism, which supposed that there were "laws of reason" in human affairs that needed only to be discovered to be acted upon, and likewise (with

Rousseau) supposed that all men would, as has been said, cease to be evil, if only no one tried to compel them to be good. Finally, the Marxist intuition of the reality of the "collective" and its organic character, of the importance of material factors in society, and of the conditions of heteronomy and loss of freedom produced by the individualism of capitalist society, effectively disposed of the empty nominalism and false idealism of the "law of nature" concept of human community based solely on the social contract struck between "absolute lords."

In this day and age, therefore, one need not take with any philosophical seriousness Locke's account of human nature, or his individualistic law of nature, or his simplistic theory of the origins of society; these are all as "dated" as the clothes Locke himself wore. The same remark goes for Rousseau. How "dated" he, and the Declaration of the Rights of Man and Citizen inspired by him, actually are, may be seen, for instance, by a glance at the Italian Constitution of 1948, into whose making went the four currents of the contemporary world—the Christian Democratic, the Liberal (of the Mazzinian tradition), the Socialist, and the Communist. The Second Article will illustrate the difference of spirit: "The Republic recognizes and guarantees the inviolable rights of man, both as an individual and in the social formations in which his personality unfolds itself, and calls for the fulfillment of the duties of political, economic and social solidarity." Neither Locke nor Rousseau could have written that.

At all events, Locke's law of nature did not owe its undeniable success to its philosophical shallowness (though in a philosophically shallow age that was no disadvantage). Its philosophical weakness vanished before its strength as a political weapon in the performance of the political task that at the moment needed to be done. At bottom, the focus of Locke's thought was narrow and practical. He was not searching for a generalized theory that would make society right, but simply for a theory that would make it right for England to have resisted an autocratic king—to have cut off his head (Charles I) or at least dethroned him (James II). He wrote, as he admitted, to justify the "Glorious Revolution" of 1688, and to settle William of Orange on a throne to which his theoretical title was highly dubious. Besides this particular political aim, he had other preoccupations of a practical order that appealed to common sense. He wrote at a time when the common sense of England was weary of the socially sterile enthusiasms of the Civil Wars; when the business community of England stood looking into the long horizons of commercial prosperity opened by colonial expansion and the development of foreign trade; when mercantile influence on government in the interests of property and freedom for commercial enterprise was on the rise; when economic advantage rather than dynastic or religious rivalries was becoming the moving force in the international field. Consequently, Locke was interested in seeing government influenced by the propertied class through the principle of representation; he wanted government by the consent of the landowners and merchants (this, in effect, is what Locke's "consent of the governed" meant). He was further interested in advancing the concept that government's sole function is the guaranteeing of individual liberty (i.e., property, and the freedom to increase it). In a word, his problem was to devise a law of nature that would support a political theory that would in turn support a businessman's commonwealth, a society dominated by bourgeois political influence through the medium of the "watch dog" State whose functions would be reduced to a minimum, especially in the fields of business and trade.

As an instrument for these particular political and politico-economic aims, his theory of the individualistic law of nature was admirably adapted, whatever its philosophical shortcomings. With the last of the Stuarts gone, and a new world opening up, the time was ripe for a new kind of polity; and since Locke was not its prophet but its apologist, he had honor in his own country. Whether his law of nature made philosophical sense or not, the ordinary English property owner did not trouble to ask; it delivered the goods demanded at the moment, and that was enough. I should add, too, that Locke delivered the goods—helped to create a stable and vigorous political community—largely because he restated, and did not quite succeed in denaturing, the great political truths that were the medieval heritage, but that had been obscured in the era of absolutism and the divine right of kings (which, as Kern has pointed out, was not a development but a denial of medieval ideas).

Against the principle of absolutism—the assertion of the irresponsibility of the king and the unlimited scope of his power—Locke asserted (in debased form) the central medieval tradition of the supremacy of law over government, and of government by law which is reason, not will. Against the central point of divine-right theory—that the monarch's right to rule is inalienable and independent of human agency—he asserted (on philosophically indefensible grounds) the medieval principle that sovereignty is "translated" from the people to the ruler, who is responsible to the people in its exercise and holds title to it only as long as he serves their common good. Finally, against absolute centralization of power in the monarch, he asserted (again on false premises) the medieval doctrine of the right of the people to participate in government. In other words, though Locke knew only an artificial law of nature, he asserted in effect the fundamental positions of the natural-law philosophy of the state that had been the creation of greater minds than his, operating at the center of a tradition to whose periphery he himself had moved. These truths, that were not of Locke's own devising, furnished the essential dynamism of his system. Their truth stood up, in spite of Locke's failure to understand and demonstrate it; and this truth gave them their impact on the political conscience of the time. Not even Locke's narrow individualism, his thin rationalism, and his empty nominalism could quite veil their absolute validity as imperatives of a human reason that has a greater and more universal power than was dreamt of in Locke's philosophy.

Locke had great honor also in France. The success of his theory of the law of nature, put into more doctrinaire form by French theorists, might be explained on similar lines. It was congenial to the individualistic and rationalistic mentality of that extraordinarily small group of men whose ideas succeeded in turning France upside down. They were not concerned, as Locke was, with justifying a revolution, but with making one. And they made it in the name of the law of nature. The prime value of the idea lay in its power of destruction. What these men, for a variety of reasons, wanted to do was to destroy the rigid, clumsy, anachronistic, crippling absolutism of the *ancien régime*. What they needed to lay hands on in the first instance was a corrosive, not a constructive, force. And they found it in the theory of the "rights of man" based on the individualistic law of nature.

There is no need here to go into the history of the lengthy, complicated, very bloody revolution that strove to incorporate this theory into political institutions. What I want to note is that the revolution was professedly political. It has been remarked that the political essence of the revolution was in the decision of the Third Estate on June 17, 1789, to set about the making of a constitution quite by itself, apart from the nobles and clergy, and in the subsequent resolution of the Estates General into the National Assembly. This was a political decision—the assumption by "the people" of their right to govern themselves. The problem of the moment was essentially political. And the temper of the time was largely that voiced by Rousseau when he said in his *Confessions*, describing the inspiration of his *Social Contract*. "I had come to see that in the last resort everything depends on politics, and that whatever men may do, no nation will ever be anything but what the nature of its Government may make it." The principle, like most things at the time, is on its head; its reverse is more certainly correct. However, it was the revolutionary principle. And it was allied with the further principle that government will necessarily be good if "the people" run it; for "the people," according to Rousseau, are themselves necessarily good; it is only bad government that makes them bad. If then the "general will" of the people makes the laws, the laws will be right, because the sovereign people is always right.

Thus spake the *Éclaircissement*—as usual, mixing truth with nonsense. And also as usual, the truth derives from the Western political tradition of natural law; the nonsense, from the eighteenth-century philosophoumenon, the law of nature. The agglomeration of both (obviously, along with other causes) made the Revolution. But it was powerful enough to do so (and this is my point) for the reason that the Revolution to be made was political. The determination that existed was that of bringing to an end an era and an order of political privilege (or, in America, that of preventing the rise of such an order). The principle embedded in the political philosophy of St. Thomas Aquinas was having a rebirth under the pressure of arbitrary power on the conscience of the people: "In regard of the good ordering of rulers in a city or nation . . . the first thing [to be observed] is that all should have some share in the government. . . ." And the validity of the reason he gives, on the authority of Aristotle, was again being confirmed: "for in this way the peace of the people is preserved, and all love and cherish such an order, as it is said in the Second Book of the *Politics*" (*Summa Theologia*, II, q. 105, a.1). Locke and Rousseau, in whose angular rationalistic thought there was little room for experience and psychology as sources of political philosophy, were, in fact, carried to popularity by a psychological drive of discontent born of harsh experience. In such times of discontent with the fundamental structures of society, as Laski has pointed out, the gospel of human rights always has a resurgence.

The eighteenth-century gospel, based on the individualistic law of nature, could not at the time fail to be popular. For the primary drive then was toward destruction, and the law of nature concept of human rights was an appropriate dynamism of destruction, precisely because of the philosophical nonsense it enshrined. I mean that its individualistic rationalistic nominalism, precisely because it disregarded the organic character of society, and precisely because its concept of "progress" entailed a complete denial of the past and of the continuity of human effort, was an effective solvent of the corporate institutional structure of society as it then was. It could not (in France, at least) initiate simply a movement of reform; it could only operate as an engine of destruction. In the same way, its rationalistic secularism was effective against the usurping theory of divine right on which sovereignty at the time was based. And its mobilization of the "power of the people," under the nominalist slogan of the "rights of man," was an effective counter-poise to the unendurable centralization of power in king and nobles. This theory, therefore, could ride against the evils of the time with all the force, not only of truth but of error itself. Its theoretic dogmas were, as theories, false; but, as dogmas, powerful. Its exclusive attention to the problem of politics, and its attempt to solve it by violently creating an artificial "equality of citizens" (free, supposedly, as men, because equal as citizens), could end, as it did, only in dictatorship. But at least it could accomplish the social ruin that made dictatorship inevitable. And for the moment, a work of ruin was the immediate objective; for anger was abroad as well as reason, and it was not averse to using "reason" as its instrument.

On the other hand, the theory of natural rights, based on a law of nature, had also a measure of constructive dynamism—this time, not by reason of the philosophical nonsense involved in its theoretical scaffolding, but by reason of the intuition of truth that even the scaffolding could not wholly obscure. By nature all men are, as Bergbohm despairingly said, natural-law jurists. Intuitively they reach the essential imperatives of their own nature and know them to be unthwartably imperative—however much they may subsequently deform them, and destroy their proper bases, by uninformed or prejudiced reflective thought. And just as all men by nature—by the native power of moral intelligence—know that there is a difference between the *iustum naturale* and the *iustum legale* (the one based on natural law, the other on positive law), so, too, they naturally "see" the natural-law truth that "sovereignty is from the people," however much they may then go on falsely to conceptualize this truth. Usually the suffering of injustice is needed to bring the vision, just as immunity from suffering may obscure it. It is, as Pascal said, "the passions that make us think." And in those days the theory of divine right, together with the oppressive weight of the remnants of the feudal system, generated enough passion to make men think—furiously. In their fury, they thought of the truth anciently deposited in the *lex regia* of Justinian's Institutes, and elaborated by the Christian intelligence since the eleventh century.

Being men of the eighteenth century, whose intelligences were by this time very super-ficially Christian, they did not see this truth in its proper setting, the natural law. But they at least dimly glimpsed it: "Sovereignty is from the people; therefore they are not to be ruled save by their consent, and for their common good, by a power subject to law, whose end is justice, which is an order of right." They did not, I say, know that they were looking at natural law; for the law of nature had shut off natural law from their vision. But it was, for all that, natural law that swam before them; and this obscure intuition furnished whatever positive, constructive dynamism there was behind their revolutionary, destructive efforts. So they set about their work of political liberation—the work of incorporating the doctrine of consent into the structures of government, of creating channels of consent, of establishing political institutions whereby the natural-law right of popular participation in government might be made effective. In a word, they brought into almost exclusive focus the problems of representation and suffrage, as the necessary expression of the doctrine of popular sovereignty, which was at the heart of the "principles of '89." Their dominant concern was with the external form of government.

To make a long story short, let it be said that this movement for political liberty through political equality expressed in the equal right of franchise ultimately succeeded; by the last decade of the nineteenth century "the people" were furnished with their political weapon in all the major countries of Western Europe. This was a great fundamental suc-cess indeed, though it is highly improbable that much of it was due to the law-of-nature concept of natural rights that was the theoretical justification of the original political explosion. At all events, by the end of the nineteenth century Rousseau's man, the in-dividual atom, who had been born free and was everywhere in chains, had supposedly struck off his chains with the hammer of natural rights, based on the law of nature. The only remaining difficulty was that the unfortunate fellow found himself still in chains. And by a curious paradox, the new chains were forged by the very doctrine that was supposed to free him. The doctrine of natural rights that in the eighteenth century was the dynamism destructive of political privilege became in the nineteenth century the dynamism constructive of economic privilege. It was the bulwark of Manchesterism and the *laissez-faire* state.

No one need have been surprised at this who understood the empty nominalism of the doctrine. Its inherent ambivalence and susceptibility of opposite consequences had already been manifested. In Locke the state of nature and the individualistic law of nature had been so interpreted as to yield moderately liberalist consequences. But with Hobbes its consequences had been rigorously statist; it had been the justification of the royal absolutism of the Stuarts. The "omnipotent democracy" which Rousseau drew from the doctrine became, with Hegel, a statism that Rousseau would have repudiated. And the individualistic law of nature as evolved by Pufendorf and Thomasius was used to justify the "enlightened despotism" of the Prussian Fredericks and of the Austrian Emperor Joseph II. The law of nature was, in effect, a veritable Pandora's box. There seemed to be a great hope at the bottom of it, but on its opening many winged evils took their flight across the face of Europe.

If one were, in fine, to sum up its political significance, one would have to say, I think, that it was able to destroy an order of political privilege and inaugurate an era of political equality; but it was not able to erect an order of social justice or inaugurate an order of human freedom. The testimony to the fact is the contemporary protest, in the name of "human rights," against the order (if one can call it an order) which is our heritage from the law of nature of the eighteenth and nineteenth centuries. The characteristics of the law of nature—its rationalism, individualism, and nominalism—made it an effective force for dissolution in its time; but today we are not looking for forces of dissolution, but for constructive forces. Similarly, its power as a solvent made it a force for liberty, in the thin and bloodless, individualist and negative nineteenth-century concept of liberty; but today we are looking for liberation and liberty in something better than this purely formal sense. We want liberty with a positive content within an order of liberty of rational design. Rousseau's "man everywhere in chains" is still too largely a fact. Our problem is still that of human freedom, or, in juridical terms, human rights. It is a problem of the definition of freedom, and then, more importantly, its institutionalization.

But the statement of the problem that we have in common with Locke and with the men of Paris and Philadelphia in 1789 has greatly changed. It is now seen to have a social dimension that no longer permits its statement in the old individualistic terms. Its multiple factors are now grasped with a realism that will not suffer its solution in the old nominalistic categories. And its background now has a new depth that the old one-dimensional, rationalistic thought never penetrated. The background is an idea of man in his nature, history, and psychology, that transcends the limited horizons of the rationalist mind. Finally, the growing conviction as to the ultimate impotence of the old attempts to solve the problem of human liberty and social order in purely secularistic positivist terms had created a new openness to the world of metaphysical and religious values. If these alterations in the statement of the problem of freedom and human rights have in fact come about, as I think they have, they will explain the contemporary

Wiederkehr of the ancient natural law of the Greek, Roman, and Christian traditions. Only the old idea is adequate in the face of the new problem. It alone affords the dynamic basis from which to attack the problem of freedom as posited in the "age of order" on whose threshold we stand. And it is such a basis because it is metaphysical in its foundations, because it is asserted within a religious framework, and because it is realist (not nominalist), societal (not individualist), and integrally human (not rationalist) in its outlook on man and society. In other words, the structure of the old idea of natural law follows exactly the structure of the new problem of human liberty.

Natural Law in the New Age

This is the point to which I have been coming. However, I have been so long in coming to it that there is now no time or space to develop it! I shall have to be content with some brief comments on the viral resources inherent in the idea of natural law, that indicate its new validity.

First in importance is its metaphysical character, its secure anchorage in the order of reality—the ultimate order of beings and purposes. As a metaphysical idea, the idea of natural law is timeless, and for that reason timely; for what is timeless is always timely. But it has an added timeliness. An age of order is by definition a time for metaphysical decisions. They are being made all round us. No one escapes making them; one merely escapes making this one rather than that one. Our decisions, unlike those of the eighteenth century, cannot be purely political, because our reflection on the bases of society and the problem of its freedom and its order must be much more profound. And this in turn is so because these problems stand revealed to us in their depths; one cannot any longer, like John Locke, be superficial about them. Our reflection, therefore, on the problem of freedom, human rights, and political order must inevitably carry us to a metaphysical decision in regard of the nature of man. Just as we now know that the written letter of a Bill of Rights is of little value unless there exist the institutional means whereby these rights may have, and be guaranteed, their expression in social action, so also we know—or ought to know—that it is not enough for us to be able to concoct the written letter unless we are likewise able to justify, in terms of ultimates in our own thinking about the nature of man, our assertion that the rights we list are indeed rights and therefore inviolable, and human rights and therefore inalienable. Otherwise we are writing on sand in a time of hurricanes and floods.

There are perhaps four such ultimate decisions open to our making, and each carries with it the acceptance of certain political consequences.

First, one could elect to abide by the old Liberal individualism. At bottom then one would be saying that "natural rights" are simply individual material interests (be they of individuals or social groups or nations), so furnished with an armature by positive law as to be enforceable by the power of government. In this view one would be consenting to a basically atomist concept of society, to its organization in terms of power relationships, to a concept of the state as simply an apparatus of compulsion without the moral function of realizing an order of justice; for in this view there is no order of justice antecedent to positive law or contractual agreements. In a word, one would be accepting yesterday's national and international status quo; for one would be accepting its principles.

Secondly, by an extreme reaction from individualistic Liberalism, wherein the individual as an individual is the sole bearer of rights, one could choose the Marxist concept of human rights as based solely on social function, economic productivity. One would then be saying that all rights are vested in the state, which is the sole determinant of social function. It is the state that is free, and the individual is called simply to share its freedom by pursuing its purposes, which are determined by the laws of dialectical materialism. In this view one would be consenting to the complete socialization of man (his mind and will, as well as his work), within the totalitarian state, all his energies being requisitioned for the realization of a pseudo-order of "justice," which is the triumph of collective man over nature in a classless society that will know no "exploitation of man by man." In this view, as in the foregoing one, one accepts as the ultimate reality the material fact of power—in one case the power of the individual, in the other the power of the collectivity. One bases society and the state on a metaphysic of force (if the phrase be not contradictory).

A third decision, that somehow attempts a mediation between these extreme views, is soliciting adherents today; I mean the theory that its protagonists call "modern evolutionary scientific humanism," but that I shall call "the new rationalism."

It is a rationalism, because its premise is the autonomy of man, who transcends the rest of nature and is transcended by nothing and nobody (at least nothing and nobody knowable). It is new, because (unlike the old rationalism) it maintains (with Spinoza, whom Bowle has pointed to as one of its earliest forerunners) that man is something more than reason. It identifies natural law (though the term is not frequent with it) with "the drive of the whole personality," the totality of the impulses whereby men strive to "live ever more fully." It is new, too, because it abandons the old rationalist passion for deductive argument and for the construction of total patterns, in favor of the new passion for scientific method and the casting up of provisional and partial hypotheses. Finally, it is new because it does not, like eighteenth-century rationalism, conceive nature and its laws, or the rights of man, as static, given once for all, needing only to be "discovered." It adds to the old rationalistic universe the category of time; it supplements the processes of reason with the processes of history and the consequent experience of change and evolution.

Nature, therefore, is an evolving concept, and its law is emergent. It is also wholly immanent; for the new rationalism, like the old, denies to man, his nature, or its law all transcendental reference. The new rationalistic universe, like the old, is anthropocentric; all human values (reason, justice, charity) are man-made, and in consequence all human "rights," which are the juridical expression of these values, look only to man for their creation, realization, and guarantee. Their ultimate metaphysical justification lies in the fact that they have been seen, by experience, to be the contemporaneously necessary "expression of life itself." And for "life itself" one does not seek a metaphysical justification; it is, when lived in its fullness, self-authenticating. In this system, therefore, the theological concept is "fullness of life." As this is the end for the individual (to be realized as best may be in his stage of the evolutionary process), so, too, it is the end for the state. The *ordo juris* is conceived, after the fashion of the modern schools of sociological jurisprudence or realistic jurisprudence, as a pure instrumentality whereby lawmakers and judges, recognizing the human desires that are seeking realization at a given moment in human society, endeavor to satisfy these desires with a minimum of social friction. The ideals of law or of human rights are "received" from the "wants" of the society of the time and place, and any particular *ordo juris* is throughout its whole texture experimental.

Much could be said further to explain, and then to criticize, this subtle and seductive system, so much a product of the contemporary secularist mentality (its basic premise is, of course, secularism, usually accepted from the surrounding climate, not reached as the term of a metaphysical journey—few secularists have ever purposefully journeyed to secularism). I shall say only two things.

First, the new rationalism is at bottom an ethical relativism pure and simple. Its immanentism, its allegiance to scientific method as the sole criterion of truth, its theory of values as emergent in an evolutionary process, alike forbid it the affirmation of any absolute values (that is, as long as its adherents stay within their own system, which, being men and therefore by intrinsic necessity of reason also natural-law jurists, they frequently do not, but rather go on to talk of right, justice, equity, liberty, rationality, etc., investing these concepts with an absoluteness they could not possibly have within the system). Second as an ethical relativism, the new rationalism is vulnerable to all the criticisms that historically have been advanced against that ancient mode of thought, since the time when Socrates first argued against the Sophists and their dissolution of a knowable objective world of truth and value.

Chiefly, there are two objections. The first is that the new rationalism, like all the old ones, is unreasonable—surely something of a serious objection to a philosophy. "You do not," said Socrates to the Sophists, "know yourselves—your own nature, the nature of your reason." The same ignorance, though in more learned form, recurs in the modern heirs of sophistry. Secondly, the new rationalism, like all the old ones, is ruinous of sound political philosophy. "You are," said Socrates to the Sophists, "the enemies of the *polis*, who undermine its *nomoi*, especially its supreme *nomos*, the idea of justice, for whose realization all laws exist."

This objection, of course, will be vehemently repudiated by the new rationalists. They are fond of putting their system forward as the proper ideological basis of democracy; conversely, they say that democracy is the political expression of their philosophy. Its separation of church and state is the expression of their secular humanism. Its freedom of thought and speech are the reflection of their philosophical and ethical relativism. Its respect for human rights creates the atmosphere in which science may further the evolution of man to higher dignities and fuller life. For my part, however, I should maintain that, by a curious but inevitable paradox, the relativism of the new rationalists must find its native political expression in a new and subtle form of state absolutism. The essential dialectic has already been displayed in history. The absolute autonomy of human reason, postulated by the old rationalism, had as its counterpart the juridical omnipotence of the state. And with accidental variations the dialectic will repeat itself: the autonomy of human reason (the denial of its subjection to a higher law not of its own creation) = relativism in regard of human values = absolution in regard of the value and functions of the state. Admittedly, the new Leviathan would not be on the Hobbesian model, but it would be for all that the "Mortal God." And the outwardly humble garments that it would wear—the forms of political democracy—would hardly hide the fact that it was in effect the *divina maiestas*. It would be a long business to explain the workings of this dialectic; let me state the substance in a brief paragraph.

I take it that the political substance of democracy consists in the admission of an order of rights antecedent to the state, the political form of society. These are the rights of the person, the family, the church, the associations men freely form for economic, cultural, social, and religious ends. In the admission of this prior order of rights—inviolable as well by democratic majorities as by absolute monarchs—consists the most distinctive assertion of the service-character of the democratic state. And this service-character is still further enforced by the affirmation, implicit in the admission of the order of human rights, of another order of right also antecedent to the state and regulative of its public action as a state; I mean the order of justice. In other words, the democratic state serves both the ends of the human person (in itself and in its natural forms of social life) and also the ends of justice. As the servant of these ends, it has only a relative value. Now it is precisely this service-character of the state, its relative value, that tends to be undermined by the theories of the new rationalism—by their inherent logic and by the psychology they generate.

Psychologically, it is not without significance that evolutionary scientific humanism should be the favorite creed of our contemporary social engineers, with their instrumental theories of education, law and government. And it seems that their inevitable temptation is to hasten the process of evolution by use of the resources of government, just as it is to advance the cause of scientific humanism by a somewhat less than human application of science. The temptation is enhanced by the circumstance of the contemporary welfare state in the midst of an urbanized and industrialized mass civilization. The "sin" then takes the initial form of a desertion of their own premises. The "socially desirable objectives" are no longer "received" from society itself (as in the theory they should be); rather they are conceived in committee and imposed on society. The humanism ceases to evolve from below, and is directed from above; it remains scientific, and becomes inhuman. This is the psychological dynamism of the system: the state tends to lose its character of servant, and assume that of master. The psychological dynamism would be less destructive were it not in the service of the logic of the system. In the logic of the system is the destruction of all barriers to the expanding competence of the state. For one thing, the new rationalism is far too pale and bloodless a creed to stand against the flushed and full-blooded power of the modern state. For another, it hardly attempts to make a stand; in fact, its ethical relativism destroys the only ground on which a stand can be made—the absoluteness of the order of human rights that stands irremovably outside the sphere of state power, and the absoluteness of the order of justice that stands imperiously above the power of the state.

These then are three possible metaphysical decisions that one can make as a prelude to the construction of the new age. None of them, I think, carries a promise that the age will be one of true order.

There remains the fourth possible decision—the option of natural law in the old traditional sense. Here the decision is genuinely metaphysical; one does not opt for a rationalization of power, but for a metaphysic of right. I say "right" advisedly, not "rights." The natural law does not in the first instance furnish a philosophy of human rights in the sense of subjective immunities and powers to demand. This philosophy is consequent on the initial furnishing of a philosophy of right, justice, law, juridical order, and social order. The reason is that natural-law thinking does not set out, as Locke did, from the abstract, isolated individual, and ask what are his inalienable rights as an individual. Rather, it regards the community as "given" equally with the person. Man is regarded as a member of an order instituted by God, and subject to the laws that make the order an order—laws that derive from the nature of man, which is as essentially social as it is individual. In the natural-law climate of opinion (very different from that set by the "law of nature"), objective law has the primacy over subjective rights. Law is not simply the protection of rights but their source, because it is the foundation of duties.

The Premises of Natural Law

The whole metaphysic involved in the idea of natural law may seem alarmingly complicated; in a sense it is. Natural law supposes a realist epistemology, that asserts the real to be the measure of knowledge, and also asserts the possibility of intelligence reaching the real, i.e., the nature of things—in the case, the nature of man as a unitary and constant concept beneath all individual differences. Secondly, it supposes a metaphysic of nature, especially the idea that nature is a teleological concept, that the "form" of a thing is its "final cause," the goal of its becoming; in the case, that there is a natural inclination in man to become what in nature and destination he is—to achieve the fullness of his own being. Thirdly, it supposes a natural theology, asserting that there is a God, Who is eternal Reason, *Nous*, at the summit of the order of being, Who is the author of all nature, and Who wills that the order of nature be fulfilled in all its purposes, as these are inherent in the natures found in the order. Finally, it supposes a morality, especially the principle that for man, a rational being, the order of nature is not an order of necessity, to be fulfilled blindly, but an order of reason and therefore of freedom. The order of being that confronts his intelligence is an order of "oughtness" for his will; the moral order is a prolongation of the metaphysical order into the dimensions of human freedom.

This sounds frightfully abstract; but it is simply the elaboration by the reflective intelligence of a set of data that are at bottom empirical. Consider, for instance, the contents of the consciousness of a man who is protesting against injustice, let us say, in a case where his own interests are not touched and where the injustice is wrought by technically correct legislation. The contents of his consciously protesting mind would be something like these. He is asserting that there is an idea of justice; that this idea is transcendent to the actually expressed will of the legislator; that it is rooted somehow in the nature of things; that he really *knows* this idea; that it is not made by his judgment but is the measure of his judgment; that this idea is of the kind that ought to be realized in law and action; that its violation is injury, which his mind rejects as unreason; that this unreason is an offense not only against his own intelligence but against God, Who commands justice and forbids injustice.

Actually, this man, who may be no philosopher, is thinking in the categories of natural law and in the sequence of ideas that the natural-law mentality (which is the human mentality) follows. He has an objective idea of the "just" in contrast to the "legal." His theoretical reason perceives the idea as true; his practical reason accepts the truth as good, therefore as law; his will acknowledges the law as normative of action. Moreover, this man will doubtless seek to ally others in his protest, in the conviction that they will think the same as he does. In other words, this man, whether he be protesting against the Taft-Hartley Act or the Nazi genocidal laws, is making in his own way all the metaphysical affirmations that undergird the concept of natural law. In this matter philosophical reflection does not augment the data of common sense. It merely analyzes, penetrates, and organizes them in their full abstractness; this does not, however, remove them from vital contact with their primitive source in experience.

Law Immanent and Transcendent

From the metaphysical premises of natural law follow its two characteristics. It is a law immanent in the nature of man, but transcendent in its reference. It is rational, not rationalist. It is the work of reason, but not of an absolutely autonomous reason. It is immanent in nature in the sense that it consists in the dictates of human reason that are uttered as reason confronts the fundamental moral problems of human existence. These are the problems of what I, simply because I am a man and apart from all other considerations, ought to do or avoid in the basic situations in which I, again simply because I am a man, find myself. My situation is that of a creature before God; that of a "self" possessed of freedom to realize its "self"; that of a man living among other men, possessing what is mine as the other possesses what is his. In the face of these situations, certain imperatives "emerge" (if you like) from human nature. They are the product of its inclinations, as these are recognized by reason to be conformed to my rational nature. And they are formed by reason into dictates that present themselves as demanding obedience. Appearing, as they do, as dictates, these judgments of reason are law. Appearing, as they do, in consequence of an inclination that reason recognizes as authentically human, they are "natural" law.

However, these dictates are not simply emergent in the rationalist sense. Reason does not create its own laws, any more than man creates himself. Man has the laws of his nature given to him, as nature itself is given. By nature he is the image of God, eternal Reason; and so his reason reflects a higher reason; therein consists its rightness and its power to oblige. Above the natural law immanent in man stands the eternal law immanent in God transcendent; and the two laws are in intimate correspondence, as the image is to the exemplar. The eternal law is the Uncreated Reason of God; it appoints an order of nature—an order of beings, each of which carries in its very nature also its end and purposes; and it commands that this order of nature be preserved by the steady pursuit of their ends on the part of all the natures within the order. Every created nature has this eternal law, this transcendent order of reason, imprinted on it by the very fact that it is a nature, a purposeful dynamism striving for the fullness of its own being. In the irrational creation, the immanence of the eternal law is unconscious; the law itself is a law of necessity. But in the rational creature the immanent law is knowable and known; it is a moral law that authoritatively solicits the consent of freedom. St. Thomas, then, defines the natural law as the "rational creature's participation in the eternal law." The participation consists in man's possession of reason, the godlike faculty, whereby man knows himself—his own nature and end—and directs himself freely, in something of divine fashion but under God, to the plenitude of self-realization of his rational and social being.

Evidently, the immanent aspect of natural law relieves it of all taint of tyrannical heteronomy. It is not forcibly imposed as an alien pattern; it is discovered by reason itself as reason explores nature and its order. Moreover, it is well to note that in the discovery there is a necessary and large part reserved to experience, as St. Thomas insists: "What pertains to moral science is known mostly through experience "(*Eth.*, I, 3). The natural law, Rommen points out, "is not in the least some sort of rationalistically deduced, norm-abounding code of immediately evident or logically derived rules that fits every concrete historical situation." Like the whole of the *philosophia perennis*, the doctrine of natural law is orientated toward constant contact with reality and the data of experience. The point was illustrated above, in the chapter on public consensus.

The "man" that it knows is not the Lockean individual, leaping full grown into abstract existence in a "state of nature," but the real man who grows in history, amid changing conditions of social life, acquiring wisdom by the discipline of life itself, in many respects only gradually exploring the potentialities and demands and dignities of his own nature. He knows indeed that there is an order of reason fixed and unalterable in its outlines, that is not at the mercy of his caprice or passion. But he knows, too, that the order of reason is not constructed in geometric fashion, apart from consultation of experience, and the study of "the customs of human life and . . . all juridical and civil matters, such as are the laws and precepts of political life," as St. Thomas puts it. The natural-law philosopher does not indeed speak of a "natural law with a changing content," as do the Neo-Kantians, to whom natural law is a purely formal category, empty of material content until it be filled by positive law and its process of legalizing the realities of a given sociological situation. However, the natural-law philosopher does speak of a "natural law with changing and progressive applications," as the evolution of human life brings to light new necessities in human nature that are struggling for expression and form. Natural law is a force conservative of all acquired human values; it is also a dynamic of progress toward fuller human realization, personal and social. Because it is law, it touches human life with a firm grasp, to give it form; but because it is a living law, it lays upon life no "dead hand," to petrify it into formalism.

In virtue of its immanent aspect, therefore, the natural law constantly admits the possibility of "new orders," as human institutions dissolve to be replaced by others. But in virtue of its transcendent aspect, it always demands that the new orders conform to the order of reason, which is structured by absolute and unalterable first principles.

Natural Law and Politics

In the order of what is called *ius naturae* (natural law in the narrower sense, as regulative of social relationships), there are only two self-evident principles: the maximum, "*Suum cuique*," and the wider principle, "Justice is to be done and injustice avoided." Reason particularizes them, with greater or less evidence, by determining what is "one's own" and what is "just" with the aid of the supreme norm of reference, the rational and social nature of man. The immediate particularizations are the precepts in the "Second Table" of the Decalogue. And the totality of such particularizations go to make up what is called the juridical order, the order of right and justice. This is the order (along with the orders of legal and distributive justice) whose guardianship and sanction is committed to the state. It is also the order that furnishes a moral basis for the positive legislation of the state, a critical norm of the justice of such legislation, and an ideal of justice for the legislator.

This carries us on to the function of natural law in political philosophy—its solution to the eternally crucial problem of the legitimacy of power, its value as a norm for, and its dictates in regard of, the structures and processes of society. The subject is much too immense. Let me say, first, that the initial claim of natural-law doctrine is to make political life part of the moral universe, instead of leaving it to wander as it too long has, like St. Augustine's sinner, *in regione dissimilitudinis*. There are doubtless a considerable number of people not of the Catholic Church who would incline to agree with Pius XII's round statement in *Summi Pontificatus* that the "prime and most profound root of all the evils with which the City is today beset" is a "heedlessness and forgetfulness of natural law." Secretary of State Marshall said practically the same thing, but in contemporary idiom, when he remarked that all our political troubles go back to a neglect or violation of human rights.

For the rest, I shall simply state the major contents of the political ideal as it emerges from natural law.

One set of principles is that which the Carlyles and others have pointed out as having ruled (amid whatever violations) the political life of the Middle Ages. First, there is the supremacy of law, and of law as reason, not will. With this is connected the idea of the ethical nature and function of the state (*regnum* or *imperium* in medieval terminology), and the educative character of its laws as directive of man to "the virtuous life" and not simply protective of particular interests. Secondly, there is the principle that the source of political authority is in the community. Political society as such is natural and necessary to man, but its form is the product of reason and free choice; no ruler has a right to govern that is inalienable and independent of human agency. Thirdly, there is the principle that the authority of the ruler is limited; its scope is only political, and the whole of human life is not absorbed in the polis. The power of the ruler is limited, as it were, from above by the law of justice, from below by systems of private right, and from the sides by the public right of the Church. Fourthly, there is the principle of the contractual nature of the relations between ruler and ruled. The latter are not simply material organized for rule by the *rex legibus solutus*, but human agents who agree to be ruled constitutionally, in accordance with law.

A second set of principles is of later development, as ideas and in their institutional form, although their roots are in the natural-law theories of the Middle Ages.

The first is the principle of subsidiarity. It asserts the organic character of the state—the right to existence and autonomous functioning of various sub-political groups, which unite in the organic unity of the state without losing their own identity or suffering infringement of their own ends or having their functions assumed by the state. These groups include the family, the local community, the professions, the occupational groups, the minority cultural or linguistic groups within the nation, etc. Here on the basis of natural law is the denial of the false French revolutionary antithesis, individual versus state, as the principle of political organization. Here too is the denial of all forms of state totalitarian monism, as well as of Liberalistic atomism that would remove all forms of social or economic life from any measure of political control. This principle is likewise the assertion of the fact that the freedom of the individual is secured at the interior of institutions intermediate between himself and the state (e.g., trade unions) or beyond the state (the church).

The second principle is that of popular sharing in the formation of the collective will, as expressed in legislation or in executive policy. It is a natural-law principle inasmuch as it asserts the dignity of the human person as an active co-participant in the political decisions that concern him, and in the pursuit of the end of the state, the common good. It is also related to all the natural-law principles cited in the first group above. For instance, the idea that law is reason is fortified in legislative assemblies that discuss the reasons for laws. So, too, the other principles are fortified, as is evident.

Conclusion

Here then in briefest compass are some of the resources resident in natural law, that would make it the dynamic of a new "age of order." It does not indeed furnish a detailed blueprint of the order; that is not its function. Nor does it pretend to settle the enormously complicated technical problems, especially in the economic order, that confront us today. It can claim to be only a "skeleton law," to which flesh and blood must be added by that heart of the political process, the rational activity of man, aided by experience and by high professional competence. But today it is perhaps the skeleton that we mostly need, since it is precisely the structural foundations of the political, social, and economic orders that are being most anxiously questioned. In this situation the doctrine of natural law can claim to offer all that is good and valid in competing systems, at the same time that it avoids all that is weak and false in them.

Its concern for the rights of the individual human person is no less than that shown in the school of individualist Liberalism with its "law of nature" theory of rights, at the same time that its sense of the organic character of the community, as the flowering in ascending forms of sociality of the social nature of man, is far greater and more realistic. It can match Marxism in its concern for man as worker and for the just organization of economic society, at the same time that it forbids the absorption of man in matter and its determinisms. Finally, it does not bow to the new rationalism in regard of a sense of history and progress, the emerging potentialities of human nature, the value of experience in settling the forms of social life, the relative primacy in certain respects of the empirical fact over the preconceived theory; at the same time it does not succumb to the doctrinaire relativism, or to the narrowing of the object of human intelligence, that cripple at their root the high aspirations of evolutionary scientific humanism. In a word, the doctrine of natural law offers a more profound metaphysic, a more integral humanism, a fuller rationality, a more complete philosophy of man in his nature and history.

I might say, too, that it furnishes the basis for a firmer faith and a more tranquil, because more reasoned, hope in the future. If there is a law immanent in man—a dynamic, constructive force for rationality in human affairs, that works itself out, because it is a natural law, in spite of contravention by passion and evil and all the corruptions of power—one may with sober reason believe in, and hope for, a future of rational progress. And this belief and hope is strengthened when one considers that this dynamic order of reason in man, that clamors for expression with all the imperiousness of law, has its origin and sanction in an eternal order of reason whose fulfillment is the object of God's majestic will.

E
CONTEMPORARY VOICES

Second Vatican Council

Editor's Introduction
Anthony Sciglitano

Gaudium et Spes (GS) stems from an extraordinary event in twentieth century religious history called the Second Vatican Council (1962–1965). You may have heard about this Council when you read *Nostra Aetate*, also a document of the Second Vatican Council, in your Journey of Transformation course. *Nostra Aetate* addressed the Catholic Church's relation to other great religious traditions. As you probably also learned, Seton Hall's Monsignor John Oesterreicher had a significant role in formulating Catholic teaching on Judaism at the Second Vatican Council and exerted considerable influence on *Nostra Aetate*. He also founded the Institute of Jewish Christian Studies here at Seton Hall in 1953.

The Second Vatican Council is an ecumenical council called by Pope John XXIII in 1959 and completed under Pope Paul VI. An ecumenical council is a meeting of bishops from around the world to address important issues of Church belief and practice. The Council met in Rome, included over two thousand bishops representing over one hundred countries, guests and observers from non-Catholic churches, and more than four hundred theological advisors to the bishops. Of the many themes important to this Council, two are particularly relevant for us here: aggiornamento (or "updating") and solidarity.

Aggiornamento
Since the French Revolution in the late eighteenth century, the Church and modern cultural movements for religious freedom, nationalism, and individualism have at times found themselves at odds. These issues are historically complex. In calling the Council, Pope John XXIII made it clear that this engagement with the modern world was to be a new and more positive one designed to bring joy and offer edification. Of course this more positive engagement did not prohibit critical discernment. In any event, with *Gaudium et Spes (GS)* and other documents of the Council such as *The Declaration on Religious Freedom (Dignitatis Humanae),* the Council strove to open up a new dialogue with modern culture in its personal-ethical, political, economic, and intellectual components. In view of this basic orientation, *Gaudium et Spes* relates fundamental Catholic beliefs to analysis of contemporary issues in all of these different areas of human life. In a key passage, *Gaudium et Spes* speaks of the Church's responsibility of "reading the signs of the times and of interpreting them in the light of the Gospel" (#4). Thus, *Gaudium et Spes* calls for a dialogue between contemporary society and the Church (#92), and an interpretation of contemporary culture in light of the Gospel.

Solidarity
Solidarity is another key theme of the Second Vatican Council generally, and of *Gaudium et Spes* specifically. This is famously captured in the first paragraph of *GS*:

> The joys and hopes, the grief and anguish of the people of our time, especially of those who are poor or afflicted, are the joys and hopes, the grief and anguish of the followers of Christ as well. Nothing that is genuinely human fails to find an echo in their hearts. (#1)

The Council roots this solidarity in the fact that the Christian message of salvation is meant for all people, and not merely for those in the Church itself (#1). It makes sense, then, that they explicitly address the letter to "the whole of humanity" (#2).

Like the readings from Karl Marx and from John Locke, *GS* makes claims regarding what it means to be human, the nature of political society and political rights, the common good, and economic and social justice. *GS* also has a distinct form of organization that it helps to be aware of when reading the document. Let's examine some of this structure for clues as to how to read this document.

We have already noted the Council's emphasis on solidarity with all people in their wonderful and terrible experience on the one hand, and the responsibility to read the signs of the times in light of the Gospel on the other. The Introduction to the document then gives a reading of the signs of the times in broad strokes to be filled out later in the document (#4 to #8, all of Part II). Then, #9 of *GS* contends that the challenges of the modern world reveal underlying aspirations or hopes and a fundamental modern dilemma.

- How does the Council articulate these hopes or aspirations? Does this appear accurate to you?

- What is the fundamental modern dilemma according to the Council?

At the end of the Introduction (#10), the Council speaks of the "dichotomy affecting the modern world" that is "rooted in humanity itself."

- What is this human dichotomy?

- Why might the human situation be described as "dramatic" by the Council?

At the very end of the Introduction, *GS* confesses that Christ is the center and meaning of human history. Notice that the structure of this Introduction, then, moves from a broad and general description of the human situation in the modern world to a confession that Christ is the meaning of history in which all these dilemmas articulated in the first part find their solution. The remainder of the document will take up this claim and try to show why the Church makes it while continuing to take seriously and learn from the experiences of contemporary humanity.

After the Introduction, *GS* is divided into two main parts with many chapter and section divisions. *Part I* first makes a claim that echoes what you have seen before in Paul, Tertullian and Justin, Saint Augustine, and Thomas Aquinas: "Faith casts a new light on everything and makes known the full ideal which God has set for humanity, thus guiding the mind towards solutions that are fully human" (#11). It is because of this view that the Church then goes on in Part I to articulate its basic views of the human person, society, and how the Church's views of these things might be of service to the world at large, not neglecting how the Church also receives genuine goods from the modern world (#44). Theologians call this *theological anthropology*, that is, a view of the human person in light of God's revelation.

- Observe that the first two sections on humanity as the image of God and on sin are rooted directly in Genesis 1–3.

- Attend to the ways in which the original dichotomy that they speak of in the Introduction returns here to be interpreted by Scripture.

- Finally, notice how each chapter begins with human dilemmas, relates these dilemmas to Christian belief, and ends with the claim that the Incarnation, that is, God's Word made flesh in Christ, reveals what it means to be fully human, and thus offers help in resolving some of the problems of the human family (#22, #32, #38, and #45).

Part II of *Gaudium et Spes* relates these basic Christian beliefs and principles to contemporary issues. Each chapter addresses one major issue:

- Chapter I: The Dignity of Marriage and the Family

- Chapter II: Proper Development of Culture

- Chapter III: Economic and Social Life

- Chapter IV: The Political Community

- Chapter V: Fostering of Peace and Establishment of a Community of Nations

Our focus in this reader will be on those sections that relate to political and economic community in relation to the *Manifesto of the Communist Party*, John Locke's *Second Treatise of Government,* and John Courtney Murray's *We Hold These Truths . . .* , that is, in relation to different visions of human nature and of political and economic order. Thus, we include #1 to #45, #63 to #76, and #91 to #93. The first numbers (#1 to #45) lay down basic Catholic principles. The rest of these sections apply these principles to contemporary issues. Also, be aware that you may find you agree with all of the principles, but do not agree with a description of modern culture or with a particular application of a principle. Or, you may find that you agree with a course of action, but for reasons other than the principle that is being applied. In other words, principles and applications are logically independent.

When reading this document, be sure to think about how its discussion of political rights, the nature of the person, the concept of private property, and its view of economic and social justice relate to what you find in John Locke, Karl Marx, and in John Courtney Murray.

GAUDIUM ET SPES
Pastoral Constitution on the Church in the Modern World[1]
(Selections)
7 December, 1965

> Excerpts from documents of the *Second Vatican Council are from Vatican Council II: Constitutions, Decrees, Declarations—The Basic Sixteen Documents*, edited by Austin Flannery, OP, © 1996. Used with permission of Liturgical Press, Collegeville, Minnesota.

Preface[2]

Solidarity of the Church with the Whole Human Family

1. The joys and hopes, the grief and anguish of the people of our time, especially of those who are poor or afflicted, are the joys and hopes, the grief and anguish of the followers of Christ as well. Nothing that is genuinely human fails to find an echo in their hearts. For theirs is a community of people united in Christ and guided by the holy Spirit in their pilgrimage towards the Father's kingdom, bearers of a message of salvation for all of humanity. That is why they cherish a feeling of deep solidarity with the human race and its history.

The Council Addresses All of Humanity

2. Now that the Second Vatican council has studied the mystery of the church more deeply, it addresses not only the daughters and sons of the church and all who call upon the name of Christ, but the whole of humanity as well, and it wishes to set down how it understands the presence and function of the church in the world of today.

The world which the council has in mind is the world of women and men, the entire human family seen in its total environment. It is the world as the theatre of human history, bearing the marks of its travail, its triumphs and failures. It is the world which Christians believe has been created and is sustained by the love of its maker, has fallen

---

1   Although it consists of two parts, the Pastoral Constitution "The Church in the World Today" constitutes an organic unity.

     The Constitution is called "pastoral" because, while resting on doctrinal principles, it sets out the relation of the church to the world and to the people of today. In Part I, therefore, the pastoral emphasis is not overlooked, nor is the doctrinal emphasis overlooked in Part II.

     In Part I the church develops its teaching on humanity, the world it inhabits, and its relationship to women and men. Part II treats at length of various aspects of life and human society today and in particular deals with those questions and problems which seem to have a greater urgency in our day. The result is that in Part II the subject matter which is viewed in the light of doctrinal principles consists of elements, some of which are permanent and some of which are contingent. The Constitution is to be interpreted according to the general norms of theological interpretation, while taking into account, especially in Part II, the changing circumstances which the subject matter, by its very nature, involves.

2   With the exception of Part I, chap. 1 (translated by the late Ambrose McNicholl, O.P., University of St Thomas, Rome), the Constitution was translated by Paul Lennon, O. Carm. It was revised for this edition by AF.

into the slavery of sin but has been freed by Christ, who was crucified and rose again in order to break the stranglehold of the evil one, so that it might be fashioned anew according to God's design and brought to its fulfillment.

An Offer of Service to Humankind

3. Though proud of its discoveries and its power, humanity is often concerned about current developments in the world, about humanity's place and role in the universe, about the meaning of individual and collective endeavor, and finally about the destiny of nature and of humanity. And so the council, as witness and guide to the faith of all of God's people, gathered together by Christ, can find no more eloquent expression of this people's solidarity, respect and love for the whole human family, of which it forms part, than to enter into dialogue with it about all these various problems, throwing the light of the Gospel on them and supplying humanity with the saving resources which the church has received from its founder under the promptings of the holy Spirit. It is the human person that is to be saved, human society which must be renewed. It is the human person, therefore, which is the key to this discussion, each individual human person in her or his totality, body and soul, heart and conscience, mind and will.

This is the reason why this holy synod, in proclaiming humanity's noble destiny and affirming that there exists in it a divine seed, offers the human race the sincere cooperation of the church in fostering a sense of sisterhood and brotherhood to correspond to their destiny. The church is not motivated by earthly ambition but is interested in one thing only—to carry on the work of Christ under the guidance of the holy Spirit, who came into the world to bear witness to the truth,[3] to save and not to judge, to serve and not to be served.[4]

Introduction

The Condition of Humanity in the World Today

Hope and Anguish

4. In every age, the church carries the responsibility of reading the signs of the times and of interpreting them in the light of the Gospel, if it is to carry out its task. In language intelligible to every generation, it should be able to answer the ever recurring questions which people ask about the meaning of this present life and of the life to come, and how one is related to the other. We must be aware of and understand the aspirations, the yearnings, and the often dramatic features of the world in which we live. An outline of some of the more important features of the modern world forms the subject of the following paragraphs.

---

3   See Jn 18:37.
4   See Jn 3:17; Mt 20:28; Mk 10:45.

Ours is a new age of history with profound and rapid changes spreading gradually to all corners of the earth. They are the products of people's intelligence and creative activity, but they recoil upon them, upon their judgments and desires, both individual and collective, upon their ways of thinking and acting in regard to people and things. We are entitled then to speak of a real social and cultural transformation whose repercussions are felt at the religious level also.

A transformation of this kind brings with it the serious problems associated with any crisis of growth. Increase in power is not always accompanied by control of that power for the benefit of humanity. In probing the recesses of their own minds, people often seem more uncertain than ever of themselves: in the gradual and precise unfolding of the laws of social living, they are uncertain about how to plot its course.

In no other age has humanity enjoyed such an abundance of wealth, resources and economic wellbeing; and yet a huge proportion of the people of the world is plagued by hunger and extreme need while countless numbers are totally illiterate. At no time have people had such a keen sense of freedom, only to be faced by new forms of social and psychological slavery. The world is keenly aware of its unity and of mutual interdependence in essential solidarity, but at the same time it is split into bitterly opposing camps. We have not yet seen the last of bitter political, social, and economic hostility, and racial and ideological antagonism, nor are we free from the spectre of a war of total destruction. If there is a growing exchange of ideas, there is still widespread disagreement in competing ideologies about the meaning of the words which express our key concepts. There is lastly a painstaking search for a better material world, without a parallel spiritual advancement.

Small wonder then, that many of our contemporaries are prevented by this complex situation from recognizing permanent values and duly applying them to recent discoveries. As a result, they hover between hope and anxiety and wonder uneasily about the present course of events. It is a situation that challenges and even obliges people to respond.

Deep-seated Changes

5. The spiritual uneasiness of today and the changing structure of life are part of a broader upheaval, whose symptoms are the increasing part played on the intellectual level by the mathematical, natural and human sciences and on the practical level by their repercussions on technology. The scientific mentality has brought about a change in the cultural sphere and on habits of thought, and the progress of technology is now reshaping the face of the earth and has its sights set on the conquest of space.

The human mind is, in a certain sense, increasing its mastery over time—over the past through the insights of history, over the future by foresight and planning. Advances in biology, psychology, and the social sciences not only lead humanity to greater self-awareness, but provide it with the technical means of molding the lives of whole societies as well. At the same time, the human race is giving more and more thought to the forecasting and control of its own population growth.

The accelerated pace of history is such that one can scarcely keep abreast of it. The destiny of the human race is viewed as a complete whole, no longer, as it were, in the particular histories of various peoples: now it merges into a complete whole. And so humankind substitutes a dynamic and more evolutionary concept of nature for a static one, and the result is an immense series of new problems calling for a new endeavor of analysis and synthesis.

Changes in the Social Order

6. As a result, the traditional structure of local communities—family, clan, tribe, village, various groupings and social relationships—is subjected to ever more sweeping changes. Industrialization is on the increase and has raised some nations to a position of affluence, while it radically transfigures ideas and social practices hallowed by centuries. Urbanization too is on the increase, both on account of the expanding number of city dwellers and the spread of an urban way of life into rural settings. New and more effective mass media are contributing to the spread of knowledge and the speedy diffusion far and wide of habits of thought and feeling, setting off chain reactions in their wake. Nor should one underestimate the effect of emigration on those who, for whatever reason, are led to undertake a new way of life. On the whole, the bonds uniting human beings multiply unceasingly, and *socialization* creates yet other bonds, without, however, a corresponding personal development, and truly personal relationships (*personalization*). It is above all in countries with advanced standards of economic and social progress that this evolution is apparent, but it also affects developing nations, who are eager to share in the benefits of industrialization and urbanization. Peoples like these, especially where ancient traditions are still strong, are at the same time conscious of the need to exercise their freedom in a more mature and personal way.

Changes in Attitudes, Morals and Religion

7. A change in attitudes and structures frequently calls accepted values into question. This is true above all of young people who have grown impatient at times and, indeed, rebellious. Conscious of their own importance in the life of society, they aspire to play their part in it all the earlier. Consequently, it frequently happens that parents and teachers find their tasks increasingly difficult.

Traditional institutions, laws and modes of thought and emotion do not always appear to be in harmony with today's world. This has given rise to a serious disruption of patterns and even of norms of behavior.

As regards religion, there is a completely new atmosphere that conditions its practice. On the one hand people are taking a hard look at all magical world-views and prevailing superstitions and are demanding a more personal and active commitment of faith, so that not a few have achieved a lively sense of the divine. On the other hand, greater numbers are falling away from the practice of religion. In the past it was the exception to repudiate God and religion to the point of abandoning them, and then only in individual cases; but nowadays it seems a matter of course to reject them as incompatible with scientific progress and a new kind of humanism. In many places it is not only in philosophical terms that such trends are expressed, there are signs of them in literature, art, the humanities, the interpretation of history and even civil law: all of which is very disturbing to many people.

Imbalances in the World of Today

8. Such rapid and uneven change, coupled with an increasingly keener awareness of existing inequalities make for the creation and aggravation of differences and imbalances.

On the personal level, there often arises an imbalance between a modern practical outlook and a theoretical way of thinking which fails to master and synthesize the sum total of its ideas. Another imbalance occurs between concern for practical effectiveness and the demands of moral conscience; yet another occurs between life in society and the individual's need for reflection and contemplation. A final imbalance takes the form of conflict between the specialization of human activity and a global view of reality.

On the family level there are tensions arising out of demographic, economic and social pressures, out of conflicts between the generations, and out of new social relationships between the sexes.

On the level of race and social class we find tensions between the affluent and the underdeveloped nations; we find them between international bodies set up in the interests of peace and the desire to spread ideologies along with national or bloc expansionism. In the midst of it all stands humanity, at once the author and the victim of mutual distrust, animosity, conflict and woe.

Broader Aspirations of Humankind

9. Meanwhile there is a growing conviction that humanity is able and has the duty to strengthen its mastery over nature and that there is need to establish a political, social, and economic order at the service of humanity, to assert and develop the dignity proper to individuals and to societies.

Great numbers of people are acutely conscious of being deprived of the world's goods through injustice and unfair distribution and are vehemently demanding their share of them. Developing nations, such as the recently independent states, are anxious to share in the political and economic benefits of modern civilization and to play their part freely in the world, but they are hampered by their economic dependence on the rapidly expanding richer nations and the ever widening gap between them. The hungry nations cry out to their affluent neighbors; women claim parity with men in fact as well as of right, where they have not already obtained it; labourers and agricultural workers insist not just on the necessities of life but also on the opportunity to develop by their labor their personal talents and to play their due role in organizing economic, social, political, and cultural life. Now for the first time in history people are not afraid to think that cultural benefits are for all and should be available to everybody.

These claims are but the sign of a deeper and more widespread aspiration. Women and men as individuals and as members of society crave a life that is full, autonomous, and worthy of their nature as human beings; they long to harness for their own welfare the immense resources of the modern world. Among nations there is a growing movement to set up a worldwide community.

In the light of the foregoing factors there appears the dichotomy of a world that is at once powerful and weak, capable of doing what is noble and what is base, disposed to freedom and slavery, progress and decline, amity and hatred. People are becoming conscious that the forces they have unleashed are in their own hands and that it is up to themselves to control them or be enslaved by them. Here lies the modern dilemma.

Humanity's Deeper Questionings

10. The dichotomy affecting the modern world is, in fact, a symptom of the deeper dichotomy that is rooted in humanity itself. It is the meeting point of many conflicting forces. As created beings, people are subject to many limitations, but they feel unlimited in their desires and their sense of being destined for a higher life. They feel the pull of many attractions and are compelled to choose between them and reject some among them. Worse still, feeble and sinful as they are, they often do the very thing they hate and do not do what they want.[5] And so they feel themselves divided, and the result is a host of discords in social life. Many, it is true, fail to see the dramatic nature of this state of affairs in all its clarity for their vision is in fact blurred by materialism, or they are prevented from even thinking about it by the wretchedness of their plight. Others delude themselves that they have found peace in a world-view now fashionable. There are still others whose hopes are set on a genuine and total emancipation of humankind through human effort alone and look forward to some future earthly paradise where all the desires of their hearts will be fulfilled. Nor is it unusual to find people who, having lost faith in life, extol the kind of foolhardiness which would empty life of all significance in itself and invest it with a meaning of their own devising. Nonetheless, in the

---

5   See Rom 7:14 ff.

face of modern developments there is a growing body of people who are asking the most fundamental of all questions or are glimpsing them with a keener insight: What is humanity? What is the meaning of suffering, evil, death, which have not been eliminated by all this progress? What is the purpose of these achievements, purchased at so high a price? What can people contribute to society? What can they expect from it? What happens after this earthly life is ended?

The church believes that Christ, who died and was raised for the sake of all,[6] can show people the way and strengthen them through the Spirit so that they become worthy of their destiny: nor is there given any other name under heaven by which they can be saved[7]. The church likewise believes that the key, the center and the purpose of the whole of human history is to be found in its Lord and Master. It also maintains that beneath all those changes there is much that is unchanging, much that has its ultimate foundation in Christ, who is the same yesterday, and today, and forever.[8] And that is why the council, relying on the inspiration of Christ, the image of the invisible God, the firstborn of all creation,[9] proposes to speak to all people in order to unfold the mystery that is humankind and cooperate in tackling the main problems facing the world today.

Part One

The Church and the Human Vocation

Responding to the Promptings of the Spirit

11. The people of God believes that it is led by the Spirit of the Lord who fills the whole world. Impelled by that faith, they try to discern the true signs of God's presence and purpose in the events, the needs and the desires which it shares with the rest of humanity today. For faith casts a new light on everything and makes known the full ideal which God has set for humanity, thus guiding the mind towards solutions that are fully human.

The council intends first of all to assess by that light those values which are most highly prized today and to relate them to their divine source. For such values are very good, in so far as they stem from the God-given character of the human person. Frequently, however, thanks to the corruption of the human heart, they are disordered and need to be purified.

What does the church think of humanity? What measures are to be recommended for building up society today? What is the ultimate meaning of human activity in the universe? These questions call for answers. From the answers it will be increasingly clear

---

6   See 2 Cor 5:15.

7   See Acts 4:12.

8   See Heb 13:8.

9   See Col 1:15.

that the people of God, and the human race of which it forms part, are of service to each other; and the mission of the church will show itself to be supremely human by the very fact of being religious.

Chapter I

The Dignity of the Human Person

Women and Men in the Image of God

12. Believers and unbelievers agree almost unanimously that all things on earth should be ordained to humanity as to their center and summit.

But what is humanity? People have put forward, and continue to put forward, many views about humanity, views that are divergent and even contradictory. Sometimes they either set it up as the absolute measure of all things, or debase it to the point of despair. Hence humanity's doubt and anguish. The church is keenly sensitive to these difficulties. Enlightened by divine revelation it can offer a solution to them by which the true state of humanity may be described, its weakness explained in such a way that at the same time its dignity and vocation may be perceived in their true light.

For sacred scripture teaches that women and men were created "in the image of God," able to know and love their creator, and set by him over all earthly creatures[10] that they might rule them, and make use of them, while glorifying God.[11] "What are women and men that you are mindful of them, their sons and daughters that you care for them? You have made them little less than angels, and crown them with glory and honor. You have given them dominion over the works of your hands; you have put all things under their feet" (Ps 8:5–8).

But God did not create men and women as solitary beings. From the beginning "male and female God created them" (Gen 1:27). This partnership of man and woman constitutes the first form of communion between people. For by their innermost nature men and women are social beings; and if they do not enter into relationships with others they can neither live nor develop their gifts.

So God, as we read again in the Bible, saw "all the things that he had made, and they were very good" (Gen 1:31).

---

10   See Gen 1:26; Wis 2:23.
11   See Ecclus 17:3–10.

Sin

13. Although set by God in a state of righteousness, men and women, enticed by the evil one, abused their freedom at the very start of history. They raised themselves up against God, and tried to attain their goal apart from him. Although they had known God, they did not glorify him as God, but their senseless hearts were darkened, and they served the creature rather than the creator.[12] What revelation makes known to us is confirmed by our own experience. For when people look into their own hearts they find that they are drawn towards what is wrong and are sunk in many evils which cannot have come from their good creator. Often refusing to acknowledge God as their source, men and women have also upset the relationship which should link them to their final destiny; and at the same time they have broken the right order that should exist within themselves as well as between them and other people and all creatures.

They are therefore divided interiorly. As a result, the entire life of women and men, both individual and social, shows itself to be a struggle, and a dramatic one, between good and evil, between light and darkness. People find that they are unable of themselves to overcome the assaults of evil successfully, so that everyone feels as if in chains. But the Lord himself came to free and strengthen humanity, renewing it inwardly and casting out the "prince of this world" (Jn 12:31), who held it in the bondage of sin.[13] For sin diminished humanity, preventing it from attaining its fulfillment.

Both the high calling and the deep misery which people experience find their final explanation in the light of this revelation.

Humanity's Essential Nature

14. The human person, though made of body and soul, is a unity. In itself, in its very bodily condition, it synthesizes the elements of the material world, which through it are thus brought to their highest perfection and are enabled to raise their voice in spontaneous praise of the creator.[14] For this reason human beings may not despise their bodily life. They are, rather, to regard their bodies as good and to hold them in honor since God has created them and will raise them up on the last day. Nevertheless humanity has been wounded by sin. People find by experience that their bodies are in revolt. Their very dignity therefore requires that they should glorify God in their bodies,[15] and not allow them to serve the evil inclinations of their hearts.

Women and men are not mistaken when they regard themselves as superior to merely bodily creatures and as more than mere particles of nature or nameless units in human

---

12   See Rom 1:21–25.
13   See Jn 8:34.
14   See Dan 3:57–90.
15   See 1 Cor 6:13–20.

society. For by their power to know themselves in the depths of their being they rise above the entire universe of mere objects.[16] When they are drawn to think about their real selves they turn to those deep recesses of their being where God who probes the heart[17] awaits them, and where they themselves decide their own destiny in the sight of God. So when they recognize in themselves a spiritual and immortal soul, this is not an illusion, a product of their imagination, to be explained solely in terms of physical or social causes. On the contrary, they have grasped the profound truth of the matter.

Dignity of the Intellect, of Truth, and of Wisdom

15. Men and women, sharing in the light of the divine mind, rightly affirm that by their intellect they surpass the world of mere things. By diligent use of their talents through the ages they have indeed made progress in the empirical sciences, in technology, and in the liberal arts. In our time, their attempts to search out the secrets of the material universe and to bring it under their control have been extremely successful. Yet they have always looked for, and found truths of a higher order. For their intellect is not confined to the range of what can be observed by the senses. They can, with genuine certainty, reach to realities known only to the mind, even though, as a result of sin, their vision has been clouded and their powers weakened.

Humanity's intellectual nature finds at last its perfection, as it needs to, in wisdom, which gently draws the human mind to look for and to love what is true and good. Endowed with wisdom, women and men are led through visible realities to those which are invisible.

Our age, more than any of the past, needs such wisdom if all humanity's discoveries are to be ennobled through human effort. Indeed the future of the world is in danger unless wiser people are forth coming. It should also be pointed out that many nations which are poorer as far as material goods are concerned, yet richer in wisdom, can be of the greatest advantage to others.

It is by the gift of the holy Spirit that humanity, through faith, comes to contemplate and savor the mystery of God's design.[18]

---

16   The Latin text (*Interioritate enim sua universitatem rerum excedit: ad haec profunda redit, quando convertitur ad cor . . .*) here shows most closely its dependence on the French draft prepared under the direction of Abbé P. Haubtmann. I have had to render the French *interiorité* and the semi-biblical *revertitur ad cor* by paraphrasing. Similarly, in (#15), with regard to the words *ut humaniora fiant* as applied to what humanity has discovered. [Translator].

17   See 1 Kg 16:7; Jer 17:10.

18   See Eccl 17:7–8.

Dignity of Moral Conscience

16. Deep within their consciences men and women discover a law which they have not laid upon themselves and which they must obey. Its voice, ever calling them to love and to do what is good and to avoid evil, tells them inwardly at the right moment: do this, shun that. For they have in their hearts a law inscribed by God. Their dignity rests in observing this law, and by it they will be judged.[19] Their conscience is people's most secret core, and their sanctuary. There they are alone with God whose voice echoes in their depths.[20] By conscience, in a wonderful way, that law is made known which is fulfilled in the love of God and of one's neighbor.[21] Through loyalty to conscience, Christians are joined to others in the search for truth and for the right solution to so many moral problems which arise both in the life of individuals and from social relationships. Hence, the more a correct conscience prevails, the more do persons and groups turn aside from blind choice and endeavor to conform to the objective standards of moral conduct. Yet it often happens that conscience goes astray through ignorance which it is unable to avoid, without thereby losing its dignity. This cannot be said of the person who takes little trouble to find out what is true and good, or when conscience is gradually almost blinded through the habit of committing sin.

The Excellence of Freedom

17. It is, however, only in freedom that people can turn themselves towards what is good. The people of our time prize freedom very highly and strive eagerly for it. In this they are right. Yet they often cherish it improperly, as if it gave them leave to do anything they like, even when it is evil. But genuine freedom is an exceptional sign of the image of God in humanity. For God willed that men and women should "be left free to make their own decisions"[22] so that they might of their own accord seek their creator and freely attain their full and blessed perfection by cleaving to God. Their dignity therefore requires them to act out of conscious and free choice, as moved and drawn in a personal way from within, and not by their own blind impulses or by external constraint. People gain such dignity when, freeing themselves of all slavery to the passions, they press forward towards their goal by freely choosing what is good, and, by their diligence and skill, effectively secure for themselves the means suited to this end. Since human freedom has been weakened by sin it is only by the help of God's grace that people can properly orientate their actions towards God. Before the judgment seat of God everybody will have to give an account of their life, according as they have done either good or evil.[23]

---

19 See Rom 2:14–16.
20 See Pius XII, radio message on rightly forming the Christian conscience in youth, 23 March 1952: AAS 44(1952), p. 271.
21 See Mt 22:37–40; Gal 5:14
22 See Eccl 15:14.
23 See 2 Cor 5:10.

The Mystery of Death

18. It is when faced with death that the enigma of the human condition is most evident. People are tormented not only by pain and by the gradual diminution of their bodily powers but also, and even more, by the dread of forever ceasing to be. But a deep instinct leads them rightly to shrink from and to reject the utter ruin and total loss of their personality. Because they bear in themselves the seed of eternity, which cannot be reduced to mere matter, they rebel against death. All the helps made available by technology, however useful they may be, cannot set their anguished minds at rest. They may prolong their lifespan; but this does not satisfy their heartfelt longing, one that can never be stifled, for an after-life.

While the imagination is at a loss before the mystery of death, the church, taught by divine revelation, declares that God has created people in view of a blessed destiny that lies beyond the boundaries of earthly misery. Moreover, the christian faith teaches that bodily death, from which people would have been immune had humanity not sinned,[24] will be overcome when that wholeness which they lost through their own fault will be given once again to them by the almighty and merciful Savior. For God has called men and women, and still calls them, to attach themselves with all their being to him in sharing forever a life that is divine and free from all decay. Christ won this victory when he rose to life, for by his death he freed women and men from death.[25] Faith, therefore, with its solidly based teaching, provides thoughtful people with an answer to their anxious queries about their future lot. At the same time it makes them capable of being united in Christ with their loved ones who have already died, and gives hope that they have found true life with God.

Kinds of Atheism and Its Causes

19. Human dignity rests above all on the fact that humanity is called to communion with God. The invitation to converse with God is addressed to men and women as soon as they are born. For if people exist it is because God has created them through love, and through love continues to keep them in existence. They cannot live fully in the truth unless they freely acknowledge that love and entrust themselves to their creator. Many, however, of our contemporaries either do not at all perceive, or else explicitly reject, this intimate and vital relationship with God. Atheism must therefore be regarded as one of the most serious problems of our time, and one that deserves more thorough treatment.

The word atheism is used to signify things that differ considerably from one another. Some people expressly deny the existence of God. Others maintain that people cannot make any assertion whatsoever about God. Still others admit only such methods

---

24   See Wis 1:13; 2:23–24; Rom 5:21; 6:23; Jas 1:15.

25   See 1 Cor 15:56–57.

of investigation as would make it seem quite meaningless to ask questions about God. Many, trespassing beyond the boundaries of the positive sciences, either contend that everything can be explained by the reasoning process used in such sciences, or, on the contrary, hold that there is no such thing as absolute truth. With others it is their exaggerated idea of humanity that causes their faith to languish; they are more prone, it would seem, to affirm humanity than to deny God. Yet others have such a faulty notion of God that when they disown this product of their imagination their denial has no reference to the God of the Gospels. There are also those who never enquire about God; religion never seems to trouble or interest them at all, nor do they see why they should bother about it. Not infrequently atheism is born from a violent protest against the evil in the world, or from the fact that certain human ideals are wrongfully invested with such an absolute character as to be taken for God. Modern civilization itself, though not of its very nature but because it is too engrossed in the concerns of this world, can often make it harder to approach God.

Without doubt those, who wilfully try to drive God from their heart and to avoid all questions about religion, not following the dictates of their conscience, are not free from blame. But believers themselves often share some responsibility for this situation. For, in general, atheism is not present in people's minds from the beginning. It springs from various causes, among which must be included a critical reaction against religions and, in some places, against the christian religion in particular. Believers can thus have more than a little to do with the rise of atheism. To the extent that they are careless about their instruction in the faith, or present its teaching falsely, or even fail in their religious, moral, or social life, they must be said to conceal rather than to reveal the true nature of God and of religion.

Systematic Atheism

20. Modern atheism often takes a systematic form. There are a number of reasons for this, among them an insistence on human autonomy so great as to put obstacles in the way of any degree of dependence on God. For those who profess atheism of this kind freedom means that humanity constitutes its own end and is the sole maker, in total control, of its own history. They claim that this outlook cannot be reconciled with the assertion of a Lord who is author and end of all things, or that at least it makes such an affirmation altogether unnecessary. The sense of power which modern technical progress produces in people may encourage this outlook.

One form of modern atheism which should not be ignored is that which looks to people's economic and social emancipation for their liberation. It holds that religion, of its very nature, frustrates such emancipation by investing people's hopes in a future life, thus both deceiving them and discouraging them from working for a better form of life on earth. That is why those who hold such views, wherever they gain control of the state, violently attack religion, and in order to spread atheism, especially in the education of young people, make use of all the means by which the civil authority can bring pressure to bear on its subjects.

The Attitude of the Church Towards Atheism

21. The church, faithful to its obligations both to God and humanity, cannot cease, as in the past,[26] to deplore, sadly yet with the utmost firmness, those harmful teachings and ways of acting which are in conflict with reason and with common human experience, and which cast humanity down from the noble state to which it is born. It tries nevertheless to seek out the secret motives which lead the atheistic mind to deny God. Well knowing how important are the problems raised by atheism, and urged by its love for everyone, it considers that these motives deserve an earnest and more thorough scrutiny.

The church holds that to acknowledge God is in no way to diminish human dignity, since such dignity is grounded and brought to perfection in God. Women and men have in fact been placed in the world by God, who created them as intelligent and free beings; but over and above this they are called as daughters and sons to intimacy with God and to share in his happiness. It further teaches that hope in a life to come does not take away from the importance of the duties of this life on earth but rather adds to it by giving new motives for fulfilling those duties. When, on the other hand, people are deprived of this divine support and without hope of eternal life their dignity is deeply impaired, as may so often be seen today. The problems of life and death, of guilt and of suffering, remain unsolved, so that people are frequently thrown into despair.

Meanwhile, everybody remains a question to themselves, one that is dimly perceived and left unanswered. For there are times, especially in the major events of life, when nobody can altogether escape from such self-questioning. God alone, who calls people to deeper thought and to more humble probing, can fully and with complete certainty supply an answer to this questioning.

Atheism must be countered both by properly presenting true teaching and by the full and complete life of the church and of its members. For it is the function of the church to render God the Father and his incarnate Son present and as it were visible, while ceaselessly renewing and purifying itself[27] under the guidance of the holy Spirit.[28] This

---

26   See Pius XI, Encyclical *Divini Redemptoris*, 19 March 1937: AAS 29 (1937), pp. 65–106; Pius XII, Encyclical *Ad Apostolorum Principes*, 29 June 1958: AAS 50 (1958), pp. 601–14; John XXIII, Encyclial *Mater et Magistra*, 15 May 1961: AAS 53 (1961), pp. 451–3; Paul VI, Encyclical *Ecclesiam Suam*, 6 August 1964: AAS 56 (1964), pp. 651–3.

27   Grammatically the text could read: by ceaselessly renewing and purifying herself. But this would imply that the church makes God present only when she renews herself. The text, in trying to be short, mixes two ideas, that of the presence of God in the world through the church, and that of a presence made more visible and striking through a renewal of christian life. [Translator].

28   See Vatican Council II, Dogmatic Constitution on the Church, *Lumen gentium,* ch. 1, n. 8.

is brought about chiefly by the witness of a living and mature faith, one namely that is so well formed that it can see difficulties clearly and overcome them. Many martyrs have borne, and continue to bear, a splendid witness to this faith. This faith should show its fruitfulness by penetrating the entire life, even the worldly activities, of those who believe, and by urging them to be loving and just, especially towards those in need. Lastly, what does most to show God's presence clearly is the familial love of the faithful who, being all of one mind and spirit, work together for the faith of the Gospel[29] and present themselves as a sign of unity.

Although the church altogether rejects atheism, it nevertheless sincerely proclaims that all men and women, those who believe as well as those who do not, should help to establish right order in this world where all live together. This certainly cannot be done without a dialogue that is sincere and prudent. The church therefore deplores the discrimination between believers and unbelievers which some civil authorities unjustly practise, in defiance of the fundamental rights of the human person. It demands effective freedom for the faithful to be allowed to build up God's temple in this world also. It courteously invites atheists to weigh the merits of the Gospel of Christ with an open mind.

For the church knows full well that its message is in harmony with the most secret desires of the human heart, since it champions the dignity of humanity's calling, giving hope once more to those who already despair of their higher destiny. Its message, far from diminishing humanity helps people to develop themselves by bestowing light, life, and freedom. Apart from this message nothing is able to satisfy the human heart: "You have made us for yourself, O Lord, and our heart is restless until it rest in you."[30]

Christ the New Man

22. In reality it is only in the mystery of the Word made flesh that the mystery of humanity truly becomes clear. For Adam, the first man, was a type of him who was to come,[31] Christ the Lord. Christ the new Adam, in the very revelation of the mystery of the Father and of his love, fully reveals humanity to itself and brings to light its very high calling. It is no wonder, then, that all the truths mentioned so far should find in him their source and their most perfect embodiment.

He who is the "image of the invisible God" (Col 1:15),[32] is himself the perfect man who has restored in the children of Adam that likeness to God which had been disfigured ever since the first sin. Human nature, by the very fact that it was assumed, not

---

29   See Phil 1:27.
30   St Augustine, *Confessions* 1, 1: PL 32, 661.
31   See Rom 5:14. See Tertullian, *De carnis resurrectione*, 6: "For in all the form which was moulded in the clay, Christ was in his thoughts as the man who was to be.": PL 2, 802 (848); CSEL, 47, p. 33, lines 12–13.
32   See 2 Cor 4:4.

absorbed, in him, has been raised in us also to a dignity beyond compare.[33] For, by his incarnation, he, the Son of God, has in a certain way united himself with each individual. He worked with human hands, he thought with a human mind. He acted with a human will,[34] and with a human heart he loved. Born of the Virgin Mary, he has truly been made one of us, like to us in all things except sin.[35]

As an innocent lamb he merited life for us by his blood which he freely shed. In him God reconciled us to himself and to one another,[36] freeing us from the bondage of the devil and of sin, so that each one of us could say with the apostle: the Son of God "loved me and gave himself for me" (Gal 2:20). By suffering for us he not only gave us an example so that we might follow in his footsteps,[37] but he also opened up a way. If we follow this path, life and death are made holy and acquire a new meaning.

Conformed to the image of the Son who is the firstborn of many brothers and sisters,[38] Christians receive the "first fruits of the Spirit" (Rom 8:23) by which they are able to fulfill the new law of love.[39] By this Spirit, who is the "pledge of our inheritance" (Eph 1:14), the entire person is inwardly renewed, even to the "redemption of the body" (Rom 8:23). "If the Spirit of him who raised Jesus from the dead dwells in you, God who raised Christ Jesus from the dead will give life to your mortal bodies also through his Spirit who dwells in you" (Rom 8:11).[40] The Christian is certainly bound both by need and by duty to struggle with evil through many afflictions and to suffer death; but, as one who has been made a partner in the paschal mystery, and as one who has been configured to the death of Christ, will go forward, strengthened by hope, to the resurrection.[41]

All this holds true not only for Christians but also for all people of good will in whose hearts grace is active invisibly.[42] For since Christ died for everyone,[43] and since all are in fact called to one and the same destiny, which is divine, we must hold that the holy Spirit offers to all the possibility of being made partners, in a way known to God, in the paschal mystery.

---

33   See council of Constantinople II, can. 7; "Neither was God the Word changed into the nature of flesh, nor his flesh changed into the nature of the word.": Denz. 219 (428); see also council Constantinople III: "For as his all-holy and immaculate ensouled flesh was not destroyed *(theothesia ouk anerethé)* by being deified, but persisted in its own state and sphere.": Denz. 291 (556), see council Chalcedon: "Recognized in two natures, without confusion, without change, without division, without separation.": Denz. 291 (302).

34   See council of Constantinople III: "So also his human will was not destroyed by being deified, but was rather preserved.": Denz. 291 (556).

35   See Heb 4:15.

36   See 2 Cor 5:18–19; Col 1:20–22.

37   See 1 Pet 2:21; Mt 16:24; Lk 14:27.

38   See Rom 8:29; Col 1:18.

39   See Rom 8:1–11.

40   See 2 Cor 4:14.

41   See Phil 3:10, Rom 8:17.

42   See Vatican Council II Constitution on the Church, *Lumen gentium*, n. 16.

43   See Rom 8:32.

Such is the nature and the greatness of the mystery of humankind as enlightened for the faithful by the christian revelation. It is therefore through Christ, and in Christ, that light is thrown on the mystery of suffering and death which, apart from his Gospel, overwhelms us. Christ has risen again, destroying death by his death, and has given life abundantly to us[44] so that, becoming sons in the Son, we may cry out in the Spirit: Abba, Father![45]

Chapter II

The Human Community

The Council's Intention

23. One of the most striking features of today's world, and one due in no small, measure to modern technical progress, is the very great increase in mutual interdependence between people. Genuine sororal and fraternal dialogue is not advanced by progress of this sort, however, but takes place at a deeper level in a community of persons which calls for mutual respect for each one's full spiritual dignity. Christian revelation greatly fosters the establishment of such communion and at the same time promotes deeper understanding of the laws of social living which the creator has inscribed in people's spiritual and moral nature.

Some recent pronouncements of the church's teaching authority have dealt at length with christian teaching on human society.[46] The council therefore, proposes to repeat only a few of the more important truths and to outline the basis of these truths in the light of revelation. Later, it will deal with some of their implications which have special importance for our day.

Communitarian Nature of the Human Vocation: God's Design

24. God, who has a parent's care for all of us, desired that all men and women should form one family and deal with each other as brothers and sisters. All, in fact, are destined to the very same end, namely God himself, since they have been created in the likeness of God, who "made from one every nation of humankind who live on all the face of the earth" (Acts 17:26). Love of God and of one's neighbor, then, is the first and greatest commandment. Scripture teaches us that love of God cannot be separated from love of one's neighbor: "Any other commandment [is] summed up in this sentence: 'You shall love your neighbor as yourself...' therefore love is the fulfilling of the law" (Rom 13:9–10; see 1 Jn 4:20). It goes without saying that this is a matter of the

---

44 See *Byzantine Easter Liturgy.*
45 See Rom 8:15 and Gal 4:6; see also 1 Jn 3:1.
46 See John XXIII, Encyclical *Mater et Magistra*, 15 May 1961: AAS 53 (1961), pp. 401–64, and Encyclical *Pacem in Terris*, 11 April 1963: AAS 55 (1963), pp. 257–304; Paul VI, *Encyclical Ecclesiam* Suam, 6 August 1964: AAS 56 (1964), pp. 609–59.

utmost importance to people who are coming to rely more and more on each other and to a world which is becoming more unified every day.

Furthermore, the Lord Jesus, when praying to the Father "that they may all be one... even as we are one" (Jn 17:21–22), has opened up new horizons closed to human reason by indicating that there is a certain similarity between the union existing among the divine persons and the union of God's children in truth and love. It follows, then, that if human beings are the only creatures on earth that God has wanted for their own sake, they can fully discover their true selves only in sincere self-giving.[47]

Person and Society: Interdependence

25. The fact that human beings are social by nature indicates that the betterment of the person and the improvement of society depend on each other. Insofar as humanity by its very nature stands completely in need of life in society,[48] it is and it ought to be the beginning, the subject and the object of every social organization. Life in society is not something accessory to humanity: through their dealings with others, through mutual service, and through fraternal and sororal dialogue, men and women develop all their talents and become able to rise to their destiny.

Among the social ties necessary for humanity's development, some correspond more immediately to our innermost nature—the family, for instance, and the political community; others are freely chosen. Nowadays, for various reasons, mutual relationships and interdependence increase from day to day and give rise to a variety of associations and organizations, both public and private. Socialization, as it is called, is not without its dangers, but it brings with it many advantages for the strengthening and betterment of human qualities and for the protection of human rights.[49]

On the one hand, in fulfilling their calling, including their religious calling, men and women are greatly helped by life in society, on the other hand, however, it cannot be denied that they are often turned away from the good and towards evil by the social environment in which they live and in which they have been immersed since their birth. Without doubt frequent upheavals in the social order are in part the result of economic, political, and social tensions. But at a deeper level they come from selfishness and pride, two things which contaminate the atmosphere of society as well. As it is, human beings are prone to evil, but whenever they are confronted with an environment where the effects of sin are to be found, they are exposed to further inducements to sin, which can be overcome only by unremitting effort with the help of grace.

---

47   See Lk 17:33.
48   See St Thomas Aquinas, *I Ethic.*, Lect. 1.
49   See John XXIII, Encyclical. *Mater et Magistra* 15 May 1961: AAS 53 (1961); p. 418. See also Pius XI, Encyclical *Quadragesimo Anno,* 15 May 1931: AAS 23 (1931), p. 222 ff.

The Common Good

26. Because of the increasingly close interdependence which is gradually extending to the entire world, we are today witnessing an extension of the role of the common good, which is the sum total of social conditions which allow people, either as groups or as individuals, to reach their fulfillment more fully and more easily. The resulting rights and obligations are consequently the concern of the entire human race. Every group must take into account the needs and legitimate aspirations of every other group, and even those of the human family as a whole.[50]

At the same time, however, there is a growing awareness of the sublime dignity of human persons, who stand above all things and whose rights and duties are universal and inviolable. They ought, therefore, to have ready access to all that is necessary for living a genuinely human life: for example, food, clothing, housing, the right freely to choose their state of life and set up a family, the right to education, work, to their good name, to respect, to proper knowledge, the right to act according to the dictates of conscience and to safeguard their privacy, and rightful freedom, including freedom of religion.

The social order and its development must constantly yield to the good of the person, since the order of things must be subordinate to the order of persons and not the other way around, as the Lord suggested when he said that the Sabbath was made for men and women and not men and women for the Sabbath.[51] The social order requires constant improvement: it must be founded in truth, built on justice, and enlivened by love: it should grow in freedom towards a more humane equilibrium.[52] If these objectives are to be attained there will first have to be a renewal of attitudes and far-reaching social changes.

The Spirit of God, who, with wonderful providence, directs the course of time and renews the face of the earth, assists at this development. The ferment of the Gospel has aroused and continues to arouse in human hearts an unquenchable thirst for human dignity.

Respect for the Human Person

27. Coming to topics which are practical and of some urgency, the council lays stress on respect for the human person: everybody should look upon his or her neighbor (without any exception) as another self, bearing in mind especially their neighbor's life and the means needed for a dignified way of life,[53] lest they follow the example of the rich man who ignored Lazarus, who was poor.[54]

---

50 See John XXIII, Encyclical *Mater et Magistra*: AAS 53 (1961), p. 417.
51 Mk 2:27.
52 See John XXIII, Encyclical *Pacem in Terris*: AAS 55 (1963), p. 266.
53 See Jas 2:15–16.
54 See Lk 16:19–31.

Today, there is an inescapable duty to make ourselves the neighbor of every individual, without exception, and to take positive steps to help a neighbor whom we encounter, whether that neighbor be an elderly person abandoned by everyone, a foreign worker who suffers the injustice of being despised, a refugee, an illegitimate child wrongly suffering for a sin of which the child is innocent, or a starving human being who awakens our conscience by calling to mind the words of Christ: "As you did it to one of the least of these my brothers or sisters, you did it to me" (Mt 25:40).

The varieties of crime are numerous: all offenses against life itself, such as murder, genocide, abortion, euthanasia and willful suicide; all violations of the integrity of the human person, such as mutilation, physical and mental torture, undue psychological pressures; all offenses against human dignity, such as subhuman living conditions, arbitrary imprisonment, deportation, slavery, prostitution, the selling of women and children, degrading working conditions where people are treated as mere tools for profit rather than free and responsible persons: all these and the like are criminal: they poison civilization; and they debase the perpetrators more than the victims and militate against the honor of the creator.

Respect and Love for Enemies

28. Those also have a claim on our respect and charity who think and act differently from us in social, political, and religious matters. In fact, the more deeply, through courtesy and love, we come to understand their ways of thinking, the more easily will we be able to enter into dialogue with them.

Love and courtesy of this kind should not, of course, make us indifferent to truth and goodness. Love, in fact, impels the followers of Christ to proclaim to everyone the truth which saves. But we must distinguish between the error (which must always be rejected) and the people in error, who never lose their dignity as persons even though they flounder amid false or inadequate religious ideas.[55] God, who alone is the judge and the searcher of hearts, forbids us to pass judgment on the inner guilt of others.[56]

The teaching of Christ even demands that we forgive injury,[57] and the precept of love, which is the commandment of the New Law, includes all our enemies: "You have heard that it was said, 'You shall love your neighbor and hate your enemy.' But I say to you, love your enemies, do good to them that hate you; and pray for those who persecute and calumniate you" (Mt 5:43–44).

---

55   See John XXIII, Encyclical *Pacem in Terris*: AAS 55 (1963), pp. 299 and 300.

56   See Lk 6:37–38; Mt 7:1–2; Rom 2:1–11, 14:10–12

57   See Mt 5:43–47.

Essential Equality of All: Social Justice

29. All women and men are endowed with a rational soul and are created in God's image; they have the same nature and origin and, being redeemed by Christ they enjoy the same divine calling and destiny; there is here a basic equality between all and it must be accorded ever greater recognition.

Undoubtedly not all people are alike as regards physical capacity and intellectual and moral powers. But any kind of social or cultural discrimination in basic personal rights on the grounds of sex, race, color, social conditions, language or religion, must be curbed and eradicated as incompatible with God's design. It is deeply to be deplored that these basic personal rights are not yet being respected everywhere, as is the case with women who are denied the chance freely to choose a husband, or a state of life, or to have access to the same educational and cultural benefits as are available to men.

Furthermore, while there are just differences between people, their equal dignity as persons demands that we strive for fairer and more humane conditions. Excessive economic and social disparity between individuals and peoples of the one human race is a source of scandal and militates against social justice, equity, human dignity, as well as social and international peace.

It is for public and private organizations to be at the service of the dignity and destiny of humanity; let them spare no effort to banish every vestige of social and political slavery and to safeguard basic human rights under every political system. And even if it takes a considerable time to arrive at the desired goal, these organizations should gradually align themselves with spiritual realities, which are the most sublime of all.

Need to Transcend an Individualistic Morality

30. The pace of change is so far-reaching and rapid nowadays that it is imperative that no one, out of indifference to the course of events or because of inertia, would indulge in a merely individualistic morality. The best way to fulfil one's obligations of justice and love is to contribute to the common good according to one's means and the needs of others, and also to promote and help public and private organizations devoted to bettering the conditions of life. There are people who profess noble sentiments and who in practice, however, are carelessly indifferent to the needs of society. There are many in various countries who make light of social laws and directives and are not ashamed to resort to fraud and cheating to avoid paying just taxes and fulfilling other social obligations. There are others who neglect the norms of social conduct such as those regulating public hygiene and speed limits, forgetting that they are endangering their own lives and the lives of others by their carelessness.

All must consider it their sacred duty to count social obligations among their chief duties today and observe them as such. For the more closely the world comes together, the more widely do people's obligations transcend particular groups and extend to the whole world. This will be realized only if individuals and groups practise moral and social virtues and foster them in social living. Then, under the necessary help of divine grace, there will arise a generation of new women and men, the molders of a new humanity.

Responsibility and Participation

31. To help individuals to carry out more carefully their obligations in conscience towards themselves and towards the various groups to which they belong, they must be carefully educated to a higher degree of culture through the employment of the immense resources available today to the human race. Above all, we must undertake the training of youth from all social backgrounds if we are to produce the kind of men and women so urgently needed today, men and women who not only are highly cultured but are generous in spirit as well.

But this sense of responsibility will not be achieved unless people are so circumstanced that they are aware of their dignity and are capable of responding to their calling in the service of God and of humanity. For freedom is often crippled by extreme destitution, just as it can wither in an ivory-tower isolation brought on by overindulgence in the good things of life. It can, however, be strengthened by accepting the inevitable constraints of social life, by undertaking the manifold demands of human relationships, and by service to the community at large.

All should therefore be encouraged to play their part in communal enterprises. One must pay tribute to those nations whose systems permit the largest possible number of the citizens to take part in public life in a climate of genuine freedom. At the same time one must bear in mind the concrete circumstances of each nation and the need for strong public authority. However, if all citizens are to be persuaded to take part in the activities of the various groups which make up the social body, such groups must offer sufficient motivation to attract them and dispose them to serve their fellow men and women. One is right in thinking that the future of humanity rests with people who are capable of providing the generations to come with reasons for living and for hope.

The Word Made Flesh and Human Solidarity

32. Just as God did not create people to live as individuals but to come together in the formation of social unity, so he "willed to make women and men holy and to save them, not as individuals without any bond between them, but rather to make them into a people who might acknowledge him and serve him in holiness."[58] From the beginning of the history of salvation, God chose certain people as members of a given community, not as individuals, and revealed his plan to them, calling them "his people" (Ex 3:7–12) and making a covenant on Mount Sinai with them.[59]

This communitarian character is perfected and fulfilled in the work of Jesus Christ, for the Word made flesh willed to take his place in human society. He was present at the wedding feast at Cana, he visited the house of Zacchaeus, he sat down with publicans and sinners. In revealing the Father's love and humanity's sublime calling, he made use of the most ordinary things of social life and illustrated his words with expressions and imagery from everyday life. He sanctified those human ties, above all family ties, which are the basis of social structures. He willingly observed the laws of his country and chose to lead the life of an ordinary craftsman of his time and place.

In his preaching he clearly described an obligation on the part of the daughters and sons of God to treat each other as sisters and brothers. In his prayer he asked that all his followers should be one. As the redeemer of all of humanity he delivered himself up to death for the sake of all: "No one has greater love than this, to lay down one's life for one's friends" (Jn 15:13). His command to the apostles was to preach the Gospel to all nations in order that the human race would become the family of God, in which love would be the fullness of the law.

As the firstborn of many, and by the gift of his Spirit, he established, after his death and resurrection, a new communion of sisters and brothers among all who received him in faith and love; this is the communion of his own body, the church, in which all as members one of the other would render mutual service in the measure of the different gifts bestowed on each.

This solidarity must be constantly increased until that day when it will be brought to fulfillment; on that day humanity, saved by grace, will offer perfect glory to God as the family beloved of God and of Christ their brother.

---

58   Vatican Council II, Dogmatic Constitution on the Church, *Lumen gentium*, ch 2, n. 9.
59   See Ex 24:1–8.

Chapter III

Humanity's Activity in the Universe

The Problem

33. Humanity has always tried to develop its life by its own effort and ingenuity. Nowadays, it has extended and continues to extend its mastery over nearly all spheres of nature with the help of science and technology. Thanks, above all, to an increase in all kinds of interchange between nations the human family is gradually coming to recognize itself and constitute itself as one single community world-wide. As a result, it now produces by its own enterprise many things which in former times it expected would come largely from heavenly powers.

In the face of this immense enterprise now involving the whole human race people face many worrying questions. What is the meaning and value of this feverish activity? How ought all of these things be used? To what goal is all this individual and collective enterprise heading? The church is guardian of the deposit of God's word and draws religious and moral principles from it, but it does not always have a ready answer to every question. Still, it is eager to associate the light of revelation with the experience of humanity in trying to clarify the course upon which it has recently entered.

Value of Human Activity

34. Individual and collective activity, that monumental effort of humanity through the centuries to improve living conditions, in itself presents no problem to believers, it corresponds to the plan of God. Men and women were created in God's image and were commanded to conquer the earth with all it contains and to rule the world in justice and holiness:[60] they were to acknowledge God as maker of all things and refer themselves and the totality of creation to him, so that with all things subject to God, the divine name would be glorified through all the earth.[61]

This holds good also for our daily work. When men and women provide for themselves and their families in such a way as to be of service to the community as well, they can rightly look upon their work as a prolongation of the work of the creator, a service to other men and women, and their personal contribution to the fulfilment in history of the divine plan.[62]

---

60   See Gen 1:26–27; 9:2–3; Wis 9:2–3.

61   See Ps 8:7 and 10.

62   See John XXIII, Encyclical *Pacem in Terris*: AAS 55 (1963), p. 297.

Far from thinking that what human enterprise and ability have achieved is opposed to God's power as if the rational creature is a rival to the creator, Christians are convinced that the achievements of the human race are a sign of God's greatness and the fulfilment of his mysterious design. The more the power of men and women increases the greater is their responsibility as individuals and as members of the community. There is no question, then, of the christian message inhibiting them from building up the world or making them disinterested in the good of others: on the contrary it makes it a matter of stricter obligation.[63]

Regulation of Human Activity

35. Human activity is for the benefit of human beings, proceeding from them as it does. When they work, not only do they transform matter and society, they also perfect themselves. They learn, develop their faculties, emerging from and transcending themselves. Rightly understood, this kind of growth is more precious than any kind of wealth that can be amassed. People are of greater value for what they are than for what they have.[64] Technical progress is of less value than advances towards greater justice, wider kinship and a more humane social environment. Technical progress may supply the material for human advance but it is powerless to achieve it.

Here then is the norm for human activity—to harmonize with the authentic interests of the human race, in accordance with God's will and design, and to enable people as individuals and as members of society to pursue and fulfil their total vocation.

Rightful Autonomy of Earthly Affairs

36. Many of our contemporaries seem to fear that a close association between human activity and religion will endanger the autonomy of humanity, of organizations and of science. If by the autonomy of earthly affairs is meant the gradual discovery, utilization and ordering of the laws and values of matter and society, then the demand for autonomy is perfectly in order: it is at once the claim of humankind today and the desire of the creator. By the very nature of creation, material being is endowed with its own stability, truth and excellence, its own order and laws. These, as the methods proper to every science and technique must be respected. Consequently, methodical research in all branches of knowledge, provided it is carried out in a truly scientific manner and does not override moral laws, can never conflict with the faith, because the things of the world and the things of faith derive from the same God.[65] The humble and persevering investigators of the secrets of nature are being led, as it were, by the hand of God, even

---

63   See *Message to all men and women*, issued by the Fathers at the beginning of Vatican Council II, October 1962: AAS 54 (1962), p. 823.

64   See Paul VI, Allocution to the Diplomatic Corps, 7 January 1965: AAS 57 (1965), p. 232.

65   See Vatican Council I, Dogmatic Constitution on the Catholic Faith, *Dei Filius,* ch. 3: Denz. 1785–1786 (3004–3005).

unawares, for it is God, the conserver of all things, who made them what they are. We cannot but deplore certain attitudes, not unknown among Christians, deriving from a short-sighted view of the rightful autonomy of science; they have occasioned conflict and controversy and have misled many into opposing faith and science.[66]

However, if by the term "the autonomy of earthly affairs" is meant that material being does not depend on God and that humanity can use it as if it had no relation to its creator, then the falsity of such a claim will be obvious to anyone who believes in God. Without a creator there can be no creature. In any case, believers, no matter what their religion, have always recognized the voice and the revelation of God in the language of creatures. Besides, once God is forgotten, the creature itself is left in darkness.

Human Activity Infected by Sin

37. Sacred scripture teaches humankind what has also been confirmed by centuries of experience, namely, that the great advantages of human progress bring with them grave temptations: the hierarchy of values has been disordered, good and evil intermingle, and every person and group are interested only in their own affairs, not in those of others. So it is that the earth has not yet become the scene of true amity; rather, humanity's growing power now threatens to put an end to the human race itself.

The whole of human history has been the story of dour combat with the powers of evil, stretching, as our Lord tells us,[67] from the very dawn of history until the last day. Finding themselves in the battlefield, men and women have to struggle to do what is right, and it is at great cost to themselves, and aided by God's grace, that they succeed in achieving their own inner integrity. Hence the church of Christ, trusting in the design of the creator and accepting that progress can contribute to humanity's true happiness, still feels called upon to echo the words of the apostle: "Do not be conformed to this world" (Rom 12:2). "World" here means a spirit of vanity and malice whereby human activity from being ordered to the service of God and humanity is reduced to being an instrument of sin.

To the question of how this unhappy situation can be overcome, Christians reply that all these human activities, which are daily endangered by pride and inordinate self love, must be purified and perfected by the cross and resurrection of Christ. Redeemed by Christ and made a new creature by the holy Spirit, a person can, and indeed must, love the things which God has created: it is from God that they have been received, and it is as coming from God's hand that they are seen and revered. Thanks are owed to the divine benefactor for all these things; they are used and enjoyed in a spirit of poverty and freedom: thus a person is brought to a true possession of the world, as having nothing

---

66   See Pius Paschini, *Vita e opere di Galileo Galilei,* 2 vol., Vatican City, 1964.
67   See Mt 24:13; 13:24–30 and 36–43.

yet possessing everything:[68] "All are yours; and you are Christ's; and Christ is God's" (1 Cor 2:22–23).

Human Activity: Its Fulfillment in the Paschal Mystery

38. The Word of God, through whom all things were made, became man and dwelt among us,[69] a perfect man, he entered world history, taking that history into himself and recapitulating it.[70] He reveals to us that "God is love" (1 Jn 4:8) and at the same time teaches that the fundamental law of human perfection, and consequently of the transformation of the world, is the new commandment of love. He assures those who trust in the charity of God that the way of love is open to all and that the effort to establish a universal communion will not be in vain.

This love is not something reserved for important matters, but must be exercised above all in the ordinary circumstances of daily life. Christ's example in dying for us sinners[71] teaches us that we must carry the cross, which the flesh and the world inflict on the shoulders of any who seek after peace and justice. Constituted Lord by his resurrection and given all authority in heaven and on earth,[72] Christ is now at work in human hearts by the power of his Spirit; not only does he arouse in them a desire for the world to come but he quickens, purifies, and strengthens the generous aspirations of humanity to make life more humane and conquer the earth for this purpose. The gifts of the Spirit are manifold: some are called to testify openly to humanity's yearning for its heavenly home and to keep the awareness of it vividly before people's minds; others are called to dedicate themselves to the service of people on earth and in this way to prepare the way for the kingdom of heaven. But the Spirit makes all of them free, ready to put aside love of self and assume earthly resources into human life, stretching out towards that future day when humanity itself will become an offering accepted by God.[73]

Christ left to his followers a pledge of this hope and food for the journey in the sacrament of faith, in which natural elements, the fruits of human cultivation, are changed into his glorified Body and Blood, as a supper of brotherly and sisterly communion and a foretaste of the heavenly banquet.

39. We do not know the moment of the consummation of the earth and of humanity[74] nor the way the universe will be transformed. The form of this world, distorted by sin, is passing away[75] and we are taught that God is preparing a new dwelling and a new earth

---

68 See 2 Cor 6:10.
69 See Jn 1:3 and 14.
70 See Eph 1:10.
71 See Jn 3:16; Rom 5:8–10.
72 See Acts 2:36; Mt 28:18.
73 See Rom 15:16.
74 See. Acts 1:7.
75 See I Cor 7:31; St Irenaeus *Adversus Haereses*, V, 36, 1: PG 7, 1222.

in which righteousness dwells,[76] whose happiness will fill and surpass all the desires of peace arising in human hearts.[77] Then death will have been conquered, the daughters and sons of God will be raised in Christ and what was sown in weakness and dishonor will become incorruptible;[78] charity and its works will remain[79] and all of creation, which God made for humanity, will be set free from its bondage to decay.[80]

We have been warned, of course, that it profits us nothing if we gain the whole world and lose or forfeit ourselves.[81] Far from diminishing our concern to develop this earth, the expectation of a new earth should spur us on, for it is here that the body of a new human family grows, foreshadowing in some way the age which is to come. That is why, although we must be careful to distinguish earthly progress clearly from the increase of the kingdom of Christ, such progress is of vital concern to the Kingdom of God, insofar as it can contribute to the better ordering of human society.[82]

When we have spread on earth the fruits of our nature and our enterprise—human dignity, sisterly and brotherly communion, and freedom—according to the command of the Lord and in his Spirit, we will find them once again, cleansed this time from the stain of sin, illuminated and transfigured, when Christ presents to his Father an eternal and universal kingdom "of truth and life, a kingdom of holiness and grace, a kingdom of justice, love and peace."[83] Here on earth the kingdom is mysteriously present; when the Lord comes it will enter into its perfection.

Chapter IV

Role of the Church in the Modern World

Mutual Relationship of Church and World

40. All we have said up to now about the dignity of the human person, the community of men and women, and the deep significance of human activity, provides a basis for discussing the relationship between the church and the world and the dialogue between them.[84] The council now intends to consider the presence of the church in the world, and its life and activity there, in the light of what it has already declared about the mystery of the church.

---

76   See 2 Cor 5:2; 2 Pet 3:13.
77   See 1 Cor 2:9; Apoc 21:4–5.
78   See 1 Cor 15:42 and 53.
79   See 1 Cor 13:8; 3:14.
80   See Rom 8:19–21.
81   See Lk 9:25.
82   See Pius XI, Encyclical *Quadragesimo Anno*: AAS 23 (1931), p. 207.
83   Preface for the Feast of Christ the King.
84   Paul VI Encyclical *Ecclesiam Suam*, III: AAS 56 (1964), pp. 637–659.

Proceeding from the love of the eternal Father,[85] the church was founded by Christ in time and gathered into one by the holy Spirit.[86] It has a saving and eschatological purpose which can be fully attained only in the next life. But it is now present here on earth and is composed of women and men; they, the members of the earthly city, are called to form the family of the children of God even in this present history of human-kind and to increase it continually until the Lord comes. Made one in view of heavenly benefits and enriched by them, this family has been "constituted and organized as a society in the present world"[87] by Christ and "provided with means adapted to its vis-ible and social union."[88] Thus the church, at once "a visible organization and a spiritual community,"[89] travels the same journey as all of humanity and shares the same earthly lot with the world: it is to be a leaven and, as it were, the soul of human society in its renewal by Christ[90] and transformation into the family of God.

That the earthly and the heavenly city penetrate one another is a fact open only to the eyes of faith; moreover, it will remain the mystery of human history, which will be ha-rassed by sin until the perfect revelation of the splendor of the children of God. In pursuing its own salvific purpose not only does the church communicate divine life to humanity but in a certain sense it casts the reflected light of that divine life over all the earth, notably in the way it heals and elevates the dignity of the human person, in the way it consolidates society, and endows people's daily activity with a deeper sense and meaning. The church, then, believes that through each of its members and its commu-nity as a whole it can help to make the human family and its history still more human.

Furthermore, the Catholic Church deeply appreciates what other Christian churches and ecclesial communities have contributed and are contributing cooperatively to the realization of this aim. Similarly, it is convinced that there is a great variety of help that it can receive from the world in preparing the ground for the Gospel, both from indi-viduals and from society as a whole, by their talents and activity. The council will now outline some general principles for the proper fostering of mutual exchange and help in matters which are in some way common to the church and the world.

What the Church Offers to Individuals

41. Contemporary women and men are in process of developing their personality and of increasingly discovering and affirming their rights. The church is entrusted with the task of manifesting to them the mystery of God, who is their final destiny; in doing so it

---

85   See Tit 3:4: 'philantropia.'
86   See Eph 1:3, 5–6, 13–14, 23.
87   Vatican Council II, Dogmatic Constitution on the Church, *Lumen gentium*, ch, 1, n. 8.
88   Ibid., ch. 2, n. 9.
89   Ibid., ch. 1, n. 8.
90   Ibid., ch. 4, 38.

discloses to them the meaning of their own existence, the innermost truth about themselves. The church knows well that God alone, whom it serves, can satisfy the deepest cravings of the human heart, for it can never be fully content with the world and what it has to offer. The church also realizes that men and women are continually being aroused by the Spirit of God and that they will never be utterly indifferent to religion—a fact confirmed by the experience of past ages and by a variety of evidence today. For people will always be keen to know, if only in a general way, what is the meaning of their life, their activity, their death. The very presence of the church recalls these problems to their minds. The most perfect answer to these questions is to be found in God alone, who created women and men in his own image and redeemed them from sin; and this answer is given in the revelation in Christ his Son who became man. To follow Christ the perfect human is to become more human oneself.

By this faith the church can keep the dignity of human nature out of the reach of changing opinions which, for example, either devalue the human body or glorify it. There is no human law so well fitted to safeguard the personal dignity and human freedom as is the Gospel which Christ entrusted to the church; for the Gospel announces and proclaims the freedom of the daughters and sons of God, it rejects all bondage resulting from sin,[91] it scrupulously respects the dignity of conscience and its freedom of choice, it never ceases to encourage the employment of human talents in the service of God and humanity, and, finally, it commends everyone to the charity of all.[92] This is nothing other than the basic law of the christian dispensation. The fact that it is the same God who is at once saviour and creator, Lord of human history and of the history of salvation, does not mean that this divine order deprives creation, and humanity in particular, of their rightful autonomy; on the contrary, it restores and strengthens its dignity.

In virtue of the Gospel entrusted to it, the church proclaims human rights; it acknowledges and holds in high esteem the dynamic approach of today which is fostering these rights all over the world. But this approach needs to be animated by the spirit of the Gospel and preserved from all traces of false autonomy. For there is a temptation to feel that our personal rights are fully maintained only when we are free from every restriction of divine law. But this is the way leading to the extinction of human dignity, not its preservation.

What the Church Offers to Society

42. The union of the human family is greatly consolidated and perfected by the unity which Christ established among the sons and daughters of God.[93] Christ did not bequeath to the church a mission in the political, economic, or social order: the purpose

---

91   See Rom 8:14–17.
92   See Mt 22:39.
93   See Vatican Council II, Dogmatic Constitution on the Church, *Lumen gentium*, ch. 2, n. 9.

he assigned to it was religious.[94] But this religious mission can be the source of commitment, direction, and vigor to establish and consolidate the human community according to the law of God. In fact, the church is able, indeed it is obliged, if times and circumstances require it, to initiate action for the benefit of everyone, especially of those in need, such as works of mercy and the like.

The church, moreover, acknowledges the good to be found in the social dynamism of today, especially in progress towards unity, healthy socialization, and civil and economic cooperation. The encouragement of unity is in harmony with the deepest nature of the church's mission, for it is "a sacrament—a sign and instrument, that is, of communion with God and of the unity of the entire human race."[95] It shows to the world that social and exterior union comes from a union of hearts and minds, from the faith and love by which its own indissoluble unity has been founded in the holy Spirit. The impact which the church can have on modern society is due to an effective living of faith and love, not to any external power exercised by purely human means.

By its nature and mission the church is universal in that it is not committed to any one culture or to any political, economic or social system. Hence, it can be a very close bond between the various communities of people and nations, provided they trust the church and guarantee it true freedom to carry out its mission. With this in view the church calls upon its members and upon all people to put aside, in the family spirit of the children of God, all conflict between nations and races and to build up the internal strength of just human associations.

Whatever truth, goodness, and justice is to be found in past or present human institutions is held in high esteem by the council. In addition, the council declares that the church wants to help and foster these institutions insofar as this depends on it and is compatible with its mission. The church desires nothing more ardently than that it should develop in freedom in the service of all, under any regime which recognizes the basic rights of the person and the family, and the requirements of the common good.

What the Church Offers to Human Activity Through Its Members

43. The council exhorts Christians, as citizens of both cities, to perform their duties faithfully in the spirit of the Gospel. It is a mistake to think that, because we have here no lasting city, but seek the city which is to come,[96] we are entitled to evade our earthly responsibilities; this is to forget that because of our faith we are all the more bound to fulfil these responsibilities according to each one's vocation.[97] But it is no less mistaken

---

94 See Pius XII, Allocution to Historians and Artists, 9 March 1956: AAS 48 (1956), p. 212.

95 Vatican Council II, Dogmatic Constitution on the Church, *Lumen gentium*, ch. 1, n. 1.

96 See Heb 13:14.

97 See 2 Th 3:6–13; Eph 4:28.

to think that we may immerse ourselves in earthly activities as if these latter were utterly foreign to religion, and religion were nothing more than the fulfilment of acts of worship and the observance of a few moral obligations. One of the gravest errors of our time is the dichotomy between the faith which many profess and their day-to-day conduct. As far back as the Old Testament the prophets vehemently denounced this scandal, [98] and in the New Testament Christ himself even more forcibly threatened it with severe punishment.[99] Let there, then, be no such pernicious opposition between professional and social activity on the one hand and religious life on the other. Christians who shirk their temporal duties shirk their duties towards his neighbor, neglect God himself, and endanger their eternal salvation. Let Christians follow the example of Christ who worked as a craftsman; let them be proud of the opportunity to carry out their earthly activity in such a way as to integrate human, domestic, professional, scientific and technical enterprises with religious values, under whose supreme direction all things are ordered to the glory of God.

It is to the laity, though not exclusively to them, that secular duties and activity properly belong. When therefore, as citizens of the world, they are engaged in any activity either individually or collectively, they will not be satisfied with meeting the minimum legal requirements but will strive to become truly proficient in that sphere. They will gladly cooperate with others working towards the same objectives. Let them be aware of what their faith demands of them in these matters and derive strength from it; let them not hesitate to take the initiative at the opportune moment and put their findings into effect. It is their task to cultivate a properly informed conscience and to impress the divine law on the affairs of the earthly city. For guidance and spiritual strength let them turn to the clergy; but let them realize that their pastors will not always be so expert as to have a ready answer to every problem, even every grave problem, that arises; this is not the role of the clergy: it is rather the task of lay people to shoulder their responsibilities under the guidance of christian wisdom and with careful attention to the teaching authority of the church.[100]

Very often their christian vision will suggest a certain solution in some given situation. Yet it happens rather frequently, and legitimately so, that some of the faithful, with no less sincerity, will see the problem quite differently. Now if one or other of the proposed solutions is readily perceived by many to be closely connected with the message of the Gospel, they ought to remember that in those cases no one is permitted to identify the authority of the church exclusively with his or her own opinion. Let them, then, try to

---

98   See Is 58:1–12.
99   See Mt 23:3–33; Mk 7:10–13.
100   See John XXIII, Encyclical *Mater et Magistra*, IV: AAS 53 (1961), pp. 456–7: see 1: AAS Loc. cit., pp. 407, 410–411.

guide each other by sincere dialogue in a spirit of mutual charity and with a genuine concern for the common good above all.

The laity are called to participate actively in the entire life of the church; not only are they to animate the world with the spirit of Christianity, they are to be witnesses to Christ in all circumstances and at the very heart of the human community.

The task of directing the church of God has been entrusted to bishops and they, with their priests, are to preach the message of Christ in such a way that the light of the Gospel will shine on all activities of the faithful. Let all pastors of souls bear in mind that by their daily behavior and concerns[101] they are presenting the face of the church to the world and that people judge from that the power and truth of the christian message. By their words and example and in union with religious and with the faithful, let them show that the church with all its gifts is, by its presence alone, an inexhaustible source of all those virtues of which the modern world stands most in need. Let them prepare themselves by careful study to meet to enter into dialogue with the world and with people of all shades of opinion: let them have in their hearts above all these words of the council: "Since the human race today is tending more and more towards civil, economic and social unity, it is all the more necessary that priests should unite their efforts and combine their resources under the leadership of the bishops and the Supreme Pontiff and thus eliminate division and dissension in every shape or form, so that all humanity may be led into the unity of the family of God."[102]

By the power of the holy Spirit the church is the faithful spouse of the Lord and will never fail to be a sign of salvation in the world; but it is by no means unaware that down through the centuries there have been among its members,[103] both clerical and lay, some who were disloyal to the Spirit of God. Today as well, the church is not blind to the discrepancy between the message it proclaims and the human weakness of those to whom the Gospel has been entrusted. Whatever is history's judgment on these shortcomings, we cannot ignore them and we must combat them assiduously, lest they hinder the spread of the Gospel. The church also realizes how much it needs the maturing influence of centuries of past experience in order to work out its relationship to the world. Guided by the holy Spirit the church ceaselessly exhorts her children "to purification and renewal so that the sign of Christ may shine more brightly over the face of the church."[104]

---

101 Vatican Council II, Dogmatic Constitution on the Church, *Lumen gentium*, ch. 3, n. 28.

102 Ibid., n. 28.

103 See St Ambrose, *De virginitate*, ch. VIII, n. 48: PL 16, 278.

104 Vatican Council II, Dogmatic Constitution on the Church, *Lumen gentium*, ch. 2, n. 15.

What the Church Receives from the Modern World

44. Just as it is in the world's interest to acknowledge the church as a social reality and a driving force in history, so too the church is not unaware how much it has profited from the history and development of humankind. It profits from the experience of past ages, from the progress of the sciences, and from the riches hidden in various cultures, through which greater light is thrown on human nature and new avenues to truth are opened up. The church learned early in its history to express the christian message in the concepts and languages of different peoples and tried to clarify it in the light of the wisdom of their philosophers: it was an attempt to adapt the Gospel to the understanding of all and the requirements of the learned, insofar as this could be done. Indeed, this kind of adaptation and preaching of the revealed word must ever be the law of all evangelization. In this way it is possible to create in every country the possibility of expressing the message of Christ in suitable terms and to foster vital contact and exchange between the church and different cultures.[105] Nowadays when things change so rapidly and thought patterns differ so widely, the church needs to step up this exchange by calling upon the help of people who are living in the world, who are expert in its organizations and its forms of training, and who understand its mentality, in the case of believers and non believers alike. With the help of the holy Spirit, it is the task of the whole people of God, particularly of its pastors and theologians, to listen to and distinguish the many voices of our times and to interpret them in the light of God's word, in order that the revealed truth may be more deeply penetrated, better understood, and more suitably presented.

The church has a visible social structure, which is a sign of its unity in Christ: as such it can be enriched, and it is being enriched, by the evolution of social life, not as if something were missing in the constitution which Christ gave the church, but in order to understand this constitution more deeply, express it better, and adapt it more successfully to our times. The church acknowledges gratefully that, both as a whole and in its individual sons and daughters, it has been helped in various ways by people of all classes and conditions. Whoever contributes to the development of the human community on the level of family, culture, economic and social life, and national and international politics, according to the plan of God, is also contributing in no small way to the community of the church insofar as it depends on things outside itself. The church itself also recognizes that it has benefited and is still benefiting from the opposition of its enemies and persecutors.[106]

---

105   Vatican Council II, Dogmatic Constitution on the Church, *Lumen gentium*, ch. 2, n. 13.

106   Justin, *Dialogus cum Tryphone* ch. 110: PG 6, 729: ed. Otto, 1897, pp. 391–393: "...for the more such persecutions are inflicted upon us, the greater the number of others who will become devout believers in the name of Jesus." See Tertullian, *Apologeticus*, ch. 50, 13: Corpus Christ. ser. Iat. l, p. 171: "We become even more numerous when you mow us down, for the blood of Christians is a seed!" See Vatican council II, Dogmatic Constitution on the Church, *Lumen gentium*, ch. 2, n. 9.

Christ: Alpha and Omega

45. Whether it aids the world or whether it benefits from it, the church has but one sole purpose—that the kingdom of God may come and the salvation of the human race may be accomplished. Every benefit the people of God can confer on humanity during its earthly pilgrimage is rooted in the church's being "the universal sacrament of salvation,"[107] at once manifesting and actualizing the mystery of God's love for humanity.

The Word of God, through whom all things were made, was made flesh, so that as a perfect man he could save all women and men and sum up all things in himself. The Lord is the goal of human history, the focal point of the desires of history and civilization, the center of humanity, the joy of all hearts, and the fulfillment of all aspirations.[108] It is he whom the Father raised from the dead, exalted and placed at his right hand, constituting him judge of the living and the dead. Animated and drawn together in his Spirit we press onwards on our journey towards the consummation of history which fully corresponds to the plan of his love: "to unite all things in him, things in heaven and things on earth" (Eph 1:10).

The Lord himself said: "See, I am coming soon, my reward is with me, to repay according to everyone's work, I am the alpha and the omega, the first and the last, the beginning and the end" (Apoc 22:12–13).

CHAPTER III

Economic and Social Life

Some Characteristics of Economic Life Today

63. In the sphere of economics and social life, too, the dignity and vocation of the human person as well as the welfare of society as a whole have to be respected and fostered; for people are the source, the focus and the aim of all economic and social life.

Like all other areas of social life, the economy of today is marked by humanity's growing dominion over nature, by closer and more developed relationships between individuals, groups and peoples, and by the frequency of state intervention. At the same time increased efficiency in production and improved methods of distribution, of productivity and services have rendered the economy an instrument capable of meeting the increasing needs of the human family.

---

107   Vatican Council II, Dogmatic Constitution on the Church, *Lumen gentium*, ch. 7, n. 28.
108   See Paul VI, Allocution, Feb. 1965.

But the picture is not without its disturbing elements. Many people, especially in economically advanced areas, seem to be dominated by economics; almost all of their personal and social lives are permeated with a kind of economic mentality, and this is true of nations that favor a collective economy as well as of other nations. At the very time when economic progress, provided it is directed and organized in a reasonable and human way, could do so much to reduce social inequalities, it serves all too often only to aggravate them; in some places it even leads to a decline in the situation of the underprivileged and to contempt for the poor. In the midst of huge numbers deprived of the bare necessities of life there are some who live in riches and squander their wealth; and this happens in less developed areas as well. Luxury and misery exist side by side. While a few individuals enjoy almost unlimited freedom of choice, the vast majority have no chance whatever of exercising personal initiative and responsibility, and quite often have to live and work in conditions unworthy of human beings.

Similar economic and social imbalances exist between those engaged in agriculture, industry, and the service industries, and even between different areas of the same country. The growing contrast between the economically more advanced countries and others could well endanger world peace.

Our contemporaries are daily becoming more keenly aware of these discrepancies because they are thoroughly convinced, that this unhappy state of affairs can and should be rectified by the greater technical and economic resources available in the world today. To achieve this, considerable reform in economic and social life is required along with a universal change of mentality and of attitude. It was for this reason that the church in the course of centuries has worked out in the light of the Gospel principles of justice and equity demanded by right reason for individual and social life and also for international relations. The council now intends to reiterate these principles in accordance with the situation of the world today and will outline certain guidelines, particularly with reference to the requirements of economic development.[109]

Section 1: Economic Development

Economic Development in the Service of Humanity

64. Today, more than ever before, there is an increase in the production of agricultural and industrial goods and in the number of services available, and this is as it should be in view of the population expansion and growing human needs. Therefore we must encourage technical progress and the spirit of enterprise, the wish to create and improve

---

109   Pius XII, Message, 23 March 1952: AA 44 (1952), p. 273; John XXIII, Allocution to the Italian Catholic Workers Association, 1 May 1959: AA 51 (1959), p. 358.

new enterprises, and we must promote adaptation of the means of production and all serious efforts by people engaged in production—in other words everything which contributes to economic progress. The ultimate and basic purpose of economic production does not consist merely in producing more goods, nor in profit or prestige; economic production is meant to be at the service of humanity in its totality, taking into account people's material needs and the requirements of their intellectual, moral, spiritual, and religious life; it is intended to benefit all individuals and groups of people of whatever race or from whatever part of the world. Therefore, economic activity is to be carried out in accordance with techniques and methods belonging to the moral order,[110] so that God's design for humanity may be carried out.[111]

Economic Development Under Man's Direction

65. Economic development must remain under the people's control; it is not to be left to the judgment of a few individuals or groups possessing too much economic power, nor to the political community alone, nor to a few powerful nations. It is only right that, in matters of general interest, as many people as possible, and, in international relations, all nations, should participate in decision making. It is likewise necessary that the voluntary initiatives of individuals and of free associations should be integrated with state enterprises and organized suitably and harmoniously. Nor should development be left to the almost mechanical evolution of economic activity nor to the decision of public authority. Hence we must denounce as false those doctrines which stand in the way of all reform on the pretext of a false notion of freedom, as well as those which subordinate the basic rights of individuals and of groups to the collective organization of production.[112]

All citizens should remember that they have the right and the duty to contribute according to their ability to the progress of their own community and that this must be recognized by the civil authority. Above all in economically underdeveloped areas, where there is urgent need to exploit all available resources, the common good is seriously endangered by those who hoard their resources unproductively and by those who, apart from the personal right to emigrate, deprive their community of much needed material and spiritual assistance.

---

110 Pius XI, Encyclical *Quadragesimo Anno: AA* 23 (1931), p. 190 ff.; Pius XII, Message, 23 March 1952: AA 44 (1952), p. 276 ff.; John XXIII, Encyclical *Mater et Magistra:* AA 53 (1961), p. 450; Vatican Council II, Decree on the Mass Media, *Inter Mirifica*, ch. 1, n. 6.

111 See Mt 16:26; Lk 16:1–31; Col 3:17.

112 See Leo XIII, Encyclical *Libertas Praestantissimum*, 20 June 1888: AAS 20 (1887–1888), p. 597 ff.; Pius XI, Encyclical *Quadragesimo Anno:* AAS 23 (1931), p. 191 ff.; Pius XI, Encyclical *Divini Redemptoris: AAS* 29 (1937), p. 65 ff.; Pius XII, Christmas Message, 1941: AAS 34 (1942), p. 10 ff.; John XXIII, Encyclical *Mater et Magistra:* AAS 53 (1961). pp. 401–464.

An End to Excessive Economic and Social Differences

66. To meet the requirements of justice and equity, every effort must be made, while respecting the rights of individuals and national characteristics, to put an end as soon as possible to the immense economic inequalities which exist in the world, which increase daily and which go hand and hand with individual and social discrimination. Likewise in many areas, in view of the special difficulties of production and marketing in agriculture, rural people must be helped to improve methods of production and marketing, to introduce necessary developments and innovations, and to receive a fair return for their products, lest, as often happens, they remain second-class citizens. Farmers themselves, especially young farmers, ought to set about improving their professional skills, without which the advancement of farming is impossible.[113]

Justice and equity also demand that the sort of mobility which is a necessary feature of developing economies should not be allowed to jeopardize the livelihood of individuals and their families. Every kind of discrimination in wages and working conditions should be avoided in regard to workers who come from other countries or areas and contribute by their work to the economic development of a people or a region. Furthermore, no one, especially public authorities, should treat such workers simply as mere instruments of production, but as persons; they should help them to bring their families with them and to obtain decent housing conditions, and they should try to integrate them into the social life of the country or area to which they have come. However, employment should be found for them so far as possible in their own countries.

Nowadays, when an economy is undergoing change, with the introduction of new forms of industrialization, such as automation, for example, care must be taken to ensure that there is sufficient suitable employment available; opportunities for appropriate technical and professional training should be provided, and safeguards should be put in place to protect the livelihood and human dignity of those who through age or ill health are seriously disadvantaged.

Section 2:
Some Principles Governing Economic and Social Life as a Whole

Work, Working Conditions, Leisure

67. Human work which is carried out in the production and exchange of goods or in the provision of economic services, surpasses all other elements of economic life, which are only its instruments.

---

113   For the problem of agriculture see especially John XXIII, Encyclical *Mater et Magistra:* AAS 53 (1961), p. 341 ff.

Human work, whether it is done independently or as an employee, proceeds from the human person, who as it were puts a personal seal on the things of nature and reduces them to her or his will. By their work people ordinarily provide for themselves and their family, associate with others as their brothers and sisters, and serve them; they can exercise genuine charity and be partners in the work of bringing God's creation to perfection. Moreover, we believe by faith that through the homage of work offered to God humanity is associated with the redemptive work of Jesus Christ, whose labor with his hands at Nazareth greatly added to the dignity of work. This is the source of every person's duty to work loyally as well as of their right to work; moreover, it is the duty of society to see to it that, in the prevailing circumstances, all citizens have the opportunity of finding employment. Finally, remuneration for work should guarantee to individuals the capacity to provide a dignified livelihood for themselves and their family on the material, social, cultural and spiritual level corresponding to their roles and productivity, having regard to the relevant economic factors in their employment, and the common good.[114]

Since economic activity is, for the most part, the fruit of the collaboration of many, it is unjust and inhuman to organize and direct it in such a way that some of the workers are exploited. But it frequently happens, even today, that workers are almost enslaved by the work they do. So-called laws of economics are no excuse for this. The entire process of productive work, then, must be accommodated to the needs of the human person and the nature of his or her life, with special attention to domestic life, that of mothers of families in particular, always taking sex and age into account. Workers should have the opportunity to develop their talents and their personalities in the very exercise of their work. While devoting their time and energy to the performance of their work with a due sense of responsibility, they should nevertheless be allowed sufficient rest and leisure to cultivate their family, cultural, social and religious life. And they should be given the opportunity to develop those energies and talents, which perhaps are little utilised in their professional work.

Co-Responsibility in Enterprise and in the Economic System as a Whole; Labor Disputes

68. It is persons who associate together in business enterprises, people who are free and autonomous, who have been created in the image of God. Therefore, while taking into account the role of every person concerned—owners, employers, management, and employees—and without diminishing the requisite executive unity, the active participation

---

114   See Leo XIII, Encyclical *Rerum Novarum:* AA 23 (1890–1891), pp. 649–662; Pius XI, Encyclical *Quadragesimo Anno:* AA 23 (1931), p. 200; Pius XI, Encyclical *Divini Redemptoris:* AA 29 (1937), p. 92; Pius XII, Christmas Message, 1942: AA 35 (1943) p. 20; Pius XII, Radio Message to Spanish workers, 11 March 1951: AA 43 (1951), p. 215; John XXIII, Encyclical *Mater et Magistra:* AA 53 (1961), p. 419.

of everybody in administration is to be encouraged.[115] More often, however, decisions concerning economic and social conditions are made not so much within the business itself as by institutions at a higher level, and since it is on these that the future of the employees and their children depends, the employees ought to have a say in decision-making, either in person or through their representatives.

Among the fundamental rights of the individual must be numbered the right of workers to form truly representative unions which contribute to the proper structuring of economic life, and also the right to play their part in the activities of such associations without risk of reprisal. Thanks to such organized participation, along with progressive economic and social education, there will be a growing awareness among all people of their role and their responsibility, and according to the capacity and aptitudes of each one, they will feel that they have an active part to play in the whole task of economic and social development and in the achievement of the common good as a whole.

In the event of economic-social disputes all should strive to arrive at peaceful settlements. The first step is to engage in sincere discussion between all sides; but the strike remains even in today's conditions, a necessary, although an ultimate, instrument for the defence of workers' rights and the satisfaction of their lawful aspirations. As soon as possible, however, avenues should be explored to resume negotiations and effect reconciliation.

Earthly Goods Destined for All

69. God destined the earth and all it contains for all people and nations so that all created things would be shared fairly by all humankind under the guidance of justice tempered by charity.[116] No matter how property is structured in different countries, adapted to their lawful institutions according to various and changing circumstances, we must never lose sight of this universal destination of earthly goods. In their use of things people should regard the external goods they lawfully possess as not just their own but common to others as well, in the sense that they can benefit others as well as themselves.[117] Therefore everyone has the right to possess a sufficient amount of the earth's goods for themselves and their family. This has been the opinion of the Fathers and Doctors of the church, who taught that people are bound to come to the aid of the

---

115   See John XXIII, Encyclical *Mater et Magistra:* AA 53 (1961), pp. 408, 424, 427; the word "curatione" used in the original text is taken from the Latin version of the Encyclical *Quadragesimo Anno:* AA 23 (1931), p. 199. For the evolution of the question see also: Pius XII, Allocution, 3 June 1950: AA 42 (1950), pp. 484–8; Paul VI, Allocution, 8 June 1964: AA 56 (1964), pp. 574–9.

116   See Pius XII, Encyclical *Sertum Laetitiae:* AAS 31 (1939), p. 642; John XXIII, Consistorial Allocution: AA 52 (1960), pp. 5–11; John XXIII, Encyclical *Mater et Magistra:* MS 53 (1961), p. 411.

117   See St Thomas Aquinas, *Summa Theologiae,* II–II, q. 32, a. 5 ad 2; ibid., q.66, a.2; see the explanation in Leo XIII, Encyclical *Rerum Novarum:* AA 23 (1890–1891), p. 651; see also Pius XII, Allocution, 1 June 1941: AA 33 (1941), p. 199; Pius XII, Christmas Message, 1954: AAS 47 (1955), p. 27.

poor and to do so not merely out of their superfluous goods.[118] Persons in extreme necessity are entitled to take what they need from the riches of others,[119] Faced with a world today where so many people are suffering from want, the council asks individuals and governments to remember the saying of the Fathers: "Feed the people dying of hunger, because if you do not feed them you are killing them,"[120] and it urges them according to their ability to share and dispose of their goods to help others, above all by giving them aid which will enable them to help and develop themselves.

In economically less developed societies, it often happens that the common destination of goods is partly achieved by a system of community customs and traditions which guarantee a minimum of necessities to each one. Certain customs must not be considered sacrosanct if they no longer correspond to modern needs; on the other hand one should not rashly do away with respectable customs which, if they are brought up to date, can still be very useful. In the same way, in economically advanced countries the common destination of goods is achieved through a system of social institutions dealing with insurance and security. Family and social services, especially those providing for culture and education, should be further developed. In setting up these different organizations care must be taken to prevent the citizens from slipping into a kind of passivity vis-à-vis society, or of irresponsibility in their duty, or of a refusal to do their fair share.

Investment and Money

70. Investment in its turn should be directed to providing employment and ensuring sufficient income for the people of today and of the future. Those responsible for investment and the planning of the economy—individuals, associations, public authorities—must keep these objectives in mind; they must show themselves to be aware of their serious obligation, on the one hand, to ensure that the necessities for living a decent life

---

118   See St Basil, *Hom. in illud Lucae "Destruam horrea mea,"* n. 2: PG 31, 263; Lactantius, *Divinarum Institutionum,* bk. V on justice: PL 6, 565 B; St Augustine, *In Ioann. Ev.,* tr. 50, n. 6: PL 35, 1760; St Augustine, *Enarratio in Ps. CXLVII,* 12: PL 37,1922; St Gregory the Great, *Homiliae in Ev.,* hom. 20: PL 76, 1165; St Gregory the Great, *Regulae Pastoralis liber,* part III, c. 21: PL 77, 87; St Bonaventure, *In 111 Sent.,* d. 33, dub. 1 (ed. Quaracchi III, 728); St Bonaventure, In IV Sent., d. 15, p. 11, a. 2, q. 1 (ed. cit IV, 371 b) q. de superfluo (ms. Assisi, Bibl, commun. 186, ff. 112a–l13a); St Albert the Great, In 111 Sent., d. 33, a. 3, sol. 1 (ed. Borgnet XXVIII, 611); St Albert the Great, In IV Sent., d. 15, a. 16 (ed. cit. XXIX, 494–497). As regards the determination of what is superfluous today see John XXIII, Radio-Television Message, 11 Sept. 1962: AA 54 (1962), p. 682: "It is the duty of everyone, the compelling duty of Christians, to calculate what is superfluous by the measure of the needs of others and to see to it that the administration and distribution of created goods be utilized for the advantage of all."

119   In this case the old principle holds good: "In extreme necessity all goods are common, that is, they are to be shared." On the other hand for the scope, the extension, and the way this principle is to be applied in the text, besides accepted modern authors, see St Thomas Aquinas, *Summa Theologiae,* II–II, q. 66, a. 7. Clearly, for the correct application of the principle all the moral conditions required must be fulfilled.

120   See Gratian, *Decretum,* c. 21, dist. LXXXVI: ed. Friedberg I, 302. This axiom is found already in PL 54, 591a and PL 56, 1132b; see *Antonianum,* 27 (1952), 349–366.

are available to individuals and to the community as a whole, and, on the other hand, to provide for the future and strike a rightful balance between the needs of present-day consumption, individual and collective, and the requirements of investment for future generations. Always they must keep before their eyes the pressing needs of underdeveloped countries and areas. In fiscal matters they must be careful not to do harm to their own country, or to any other. Care must also be taken that economically weak countries do not unjustly suffer loss from a change in the value of money.

Ownership, Private Property, Large Estates

71. Property and other forms of private ownership of external goods contribute to self-expression and provide people with the opportunity of exercising a role in society and in the economy; it is very important, then, to facilitate access to some ownership of external goods on the part of individuals and communities.

Private property or some form of ownership of external goods affords each person an indispensable zone for personal and family autonomy and ought to be considered an extension of human freedom. Further, in encouraging the exercise of responsibility it provides one of the conditions for civil liberty.[121] Nowadays the forms of such ownership or property are varied and are becoming more diversified with time. In spite of the social security, the rights, and the services guaranteed by society, all these forms of ownership remain a source of security which must not be underestimated. And this applies not only to ownership of material goods but also to the possession of professional skills.

The right to private ownership is not opposed to the various forms of public ownership. But the transfer of goods from private to public ownership may be undertaken only by competent authority, in accordance with the demands and within the limits of the common good, and it must be accompanied by adequate compensation. Furthermore, the state has the duty to prevent people from abusing their private property to the detriment of the common good.[122] By its nature private property has a social dimension which is based on the law of the common destination of earthly goods.[123] Whenever the social aspect is forgotten, ownership can often become the object of greed and a source of serious disorder, and its opponents easily find a pretext for calling the right itself into question.

---

121   See Leo XII, Encyclical *Rerum Novarum*: AAS 23 (1890–1891), pp. 643–6; Pius XI, Encyclical *Quadragesimo Anno*: AAS 23 (1931), p. 191; Pius XII, Radio Message, 1 June 1941: AAS 33 (1941), p. 199; Pius XII, Christmas Message, 1942: MS 35 (1943), p. 17; Pius XII, Radio Message, I Sept. 1944: AA 36 (1944), p. 253; John XXIII, Encyclical *Mater et Magistra:* AAS 53 (1961), pp. 428ff.

122   See Pius XI, Encyclical *Quadragesimo Anno:* AA 23 (1931), p. 214; John XXIII, Encyclical *Mater et Magistra:* AA 53 (1961), p. 429.

123   See Pius XII, Radio message for Pentecost 1941: AAS 44 (1941), p. 199 John XXIII, Encyclical *Mater et Magistra*: AAS 53 (1961), p. 430.

In several economically under-developed areas there exist large, and sometimes very large, rural estates which are either very little cultivated or are left uncultivated as speculative ventures, while the majority of the population are landless or have very small holdings and at the same time it is obvious that there is a pressing need to increase agricultural production. Not infrequently those who are hired as labourers or who farm a portion of the land as tenants receive a wage or income unworthy of a human being; they are deprived of decent living conditions and are exploited by entrepeneurs. They lack all sense of security and live in such a state of personal dependence that almost all chance of exercising initiative and responsibility is closed to them and they are denied any cultural advancement or participation in social and political life. Reforms are called for in these different situations; incomes must be raised, working conditions improved, security in employment assured, and personal incentives to work encouraged; insufficiently cultivated estates should be divided up and given to those who will be able to make them productive. When this happens the necessary resources and equipment must be supplied, especially educational facilities and proper cooperative organizations. However, when the common good calls for expropriation, compensation must be made and is to be calculated according to equity with all circumstances taken into account.

Economic and Social Activity and the Kingdom of Christ

72. Christians engaged actively in modern economic and social progress and in the struggle for justice and charity must be convinced that they have much to contribute to the prosperity of humanity and to world peace. Let them, as individuals and as a group, give a shining example to others. Endowed with the skill and experience so absolutely necessary for them, let them preserve a proper sense of values in their earthly activity in loyalty to Christ and his Gospel, in order that their lives, individual as well as social, may be inspired by the spirit of the Beatitudes, and in particular by the spirit of poverty.

All who in obedience to Christ seek first the kingdom of God will derive from it a stronger and purer motivation for helping all their brothers and sisters and for accomplishing the task of justice under the inspiration of charity.[124]

---

124   For the right use of goods according to the teaching of the New Testament see Lk 3:11; 10:30 ff.; 11:41; Mk 8:36, 12:29–31; 1 Pet 5:3; Jas 5:1–6; 1 Tim 6:8; Eph 4:28; 2.Cor 8:13 f.; 1 Jn 3:17–18.

Chapter IV

The Political Community

Modern Public Life

73. In our times profound transformations are to be noticed in the structure and institutions of nations; they are the accompaniment of cultural, economic, and social development. These transformations exercise a deep influence on political life, particularly as regards the rights and duties of the individual, in the exercise of civil liberty and in the achievement of the common good; and they affect the organization of the relations of citizens with each other and with the state.

A clearer awareness of human dignity has given rise in various parts of the world to a movement to establish a politico-juridical order which will provide better protection for the rights of women and men in public life—the right of free assembly and association for example, the right to express one's opinions and to profess one's religion privately and publicly. The guarantee of the rights of the person is, indeed, a necessary condition for citizens, individually and collectively, to play an active part in public life and administration.

Linked with cultural, economic, and social progress there is a growing desire among many to assume greater responsibilities in the organization of political life. Many people are becoming more willing to ensure that the rights of minority groups in their country are safeguarded, without overlooking the duties of these minorities towards the political community; there is also an increase in tolerance for others who differ in opinion and religion; at the same time wider cooperation is taking place to enable all citizens, and not just a few privileged individuals, to exercise their rights effectively as persons.

People condemn those political systems which flourish in some parts of the world and which diminish civil and religious liberty, make many people the victims of political passions and crimes, cease to exercise authority in the interests of the common good, but rather in the interests of a particular faction or of the government.

There is no better way to establish political life on a truly human basis than by encouraging an interior sense of justice, of good will and of service to the common good, and by consolidating people's basic convictions as to the true nature of the political community and the aim, proper exercise, and the limits of public authority.

Nature and Purpose of the Political Community

74. Individuals, families, and the various groups which make up the civil community, are aware of their inability to achieve a truly human life by their own unaided efforts; they see the need for a wider community where each one will make a specific contribution

to an even broader implementation of the common good.[125] For this reason they set up various forms of political communities. The political community, then, exists for the common good: this is its full justification and meaning and the source of its specific and basic right to exist. The common good embraces the sum total of all those conditions of social life which enable individuals, families, and organizations to achieve complete and effective fulfillment.[126]

The people who go to make up the political community are many and varied; quite rightly, then, they may have widely differing points of view. Therefore, lest the political community be jeopardized because all individuals follow their own opinion, an authority is needed to guide the energies of all towards the common good—not mechanically or despotically, but by acting above all as a moral force based on freedom and a sense of responsibility. It is clear that the political community and public authority are based on human nature, and therefore that they need to belong to an order established by God; nevertheless, the choice of the political regime and the appointment of rulers are left to the free decision of the citizens.[127]

It follows that political authority, either within the political community as such or through organizations representing the state, must be exercised within the limits of the moral order and directed towards the common good, understood in the dynamic sense of the term, according to the juridical order legitimately established or due to be established. Citizens, then, are bound in conscience to obey.[128] Accordingly, the responsibility, the status, and the importance of the rulers of a state are clear.

When citizens are being oppressed by a public authority which oversteps its competence, they should not refuse whatever is objectively demanded of them by the common good; but it is legitimate for them to defend their own rights and those of their fellow citizens against abuses of this authority within the limits of the natural law and the law of the Gospel.

The concrete forms of structure and organization of public authority adopted in political communities will vary according to people's differing characters and historical developments; but their aim should always be the formation of human persons who are cultured, peace-loving, and well disposed towards all, to the benefit of the whole human race.

---

125   See John XXIII, Encyclical *Mater et Magistra*: AAS 53 (1961), p. 417.
126   See John XXIII, ibid.
127   See Rom 13:1–5.
128   See Rom 13:5.

Participation by All in Public Life

75. It is fully in accord with human nature that politico-juridical structures be devised which will increasingly and without discrimination provide all citizens with effective opportunities to play a free, active part in the establishment of the juridical founda- tions of the political community, in the administration of public affairs, in determining the aims and the terms of reference of public bodies, and in the election of political leaders.[129] All citizens ought to be aware of their right and duty to promote the common good by casting their votes. The church praises and esteems those who devote them- selves to the public good and who take upon themselves the burdens of public office in order to be of service.

If the citizens' cooperation and their sense of responsibility are to produce the favorable results expected of them in the normal course of public life, a system of positive law is required which provides for a suitable division of the functions and organs of public authority and an effective and independent protection of citizens' rights. The rights of all individuals, families, and organizations and their practical implementation must be acknowledged, protected, and fostered,[130] together with the public duties binding on all citizens. Among these duties, it is worth mentioning the obligation to render to the state whatever material and personal services are required for the common good. Governments should take care not to put obstacles in the way of family cultural or so- cial groups, or of organizations and intermediate institutions, nor to hinder their lawful and constructive activity; rather, they should eagerly seek to promote such orderly activ- ity. Citizens, on the other hand, either individually or in association, should take care not to vest too much power in public authority nor to make untimely and exaggerated demands for favors and subsidies, lessening in this way the responsible role of individu- als, families, and social groups.

The growing complexity of modern situations makes it necessary for public authority to intervene more frequently in social, cultural and economic matters in order to achieve conditions more favorable to the free and effective pursuit by citizens and groups of the advancement of people's total well-being. The understanding of the relationship between socialization[131] and personal autonomy and progress will vary according to different areas and the development of peoples. However, if restrictions are imposed temporarily for the common good on the exercise of human rights, these restrictions are to be lifted as soon as possible after the situation has changed. In any case it is inhuman for public authority to fall back on totalitarian methods or dictatorship which violate the rights of persons or social groups.

---

129   See Pius XII, Christmas Message 1942: AAS 35 (1043), pp. 9–24; Christmas Message 1944: AAS 37 (1945), pp. 11–17, John XXIII, Encyclical *Pacem in Terris*: AAS 55 (1963), pp. 263, 271, 277, 278.

130   See Pius XII, Radio Message, 1 June 1941: AAS (1941), p. 200; John XXIII, Encyclical *Pacem in Terris*: AAS 55 (1963), pp. 273–274.

131   See John XXIII, Encyclical *Mater et Magistra*: AAS 53 (1961), p. 415–418.

Citizens should cultivate a generous and loyal spirit of patriotism, but without narrow-mindedness, so that they will always keep in mind the welfare of the entire human family which is formed into one by various kinds of links between races, peoples, and nations.

Christians must be conscious of their specific and proper role in the political community; they should be a shining example by their sense of responsibility and their dedication to the common good; they should show in practice how authority can be reconciled with freedom, personal initiative with solidarity and the needs of the social framework as a whole, and the advantages of unity with the benefits of diversity. They should recognize the legitimacy of differing points of view on the organization of worldly affairs and should show respect for the individual citizens and groups who defend their opinions by legitimate means. Political parties, for their part, must support whatever in their opinion is conducive to the common good. but must never put their own interests before the common good.

So that all citizens will be able to play their part in political affairs, civil and political education is vitally necessary for the population as a whole and for young people in particular, and must be diligently attended to. Those with a talent for the difficult yet noble art of politics,[132] or whose talents in this matter can be developed, should prepare themselves for it, and, setting aside their own convenience and material interests, they should engage in political activity. They must combat injustice and oppression, arbitrary domination and intolerance by individuals or political parties, and they must do so with integrity and wisdom. They must dedicate themselves to the welfare of all in a spirit of sincerity and fairness, of love and of the courage demanded by political life.

The Political Community and the Church

76. It is very important, especially in a pluralist society, to have a proper understanding of the relationship between the political community and the church, and to distinguish clearly between the activities of Christians, acting individually or collectively in their own name as citizens guided by the dictates of a christian conscience, and what they do together with their pastors in the name of the church.

The church, by reason of her role and competence, is not identified with any political community nor is it tied to any political system. It is at once the sign and the safeguard of the transcendental dimension of the human person.

The political community and the church are autonomous and independent of each other in their own fields. They are both at the service of the personal and social vocation of the same individuals, though under different titles. Their service will be more

---

132   See Pius XI, Allocution to the Directors of the Catholic University Federation: *Discorsi di Pio XI* ed. Bertetto, Torino, vol. 1 (1960) p. 743.

efficient and beneficial to all if both institutions develop better cooperation according to the circumstances of place and time. For humanity's horizons are not confined to the temporal order; living in human history they retain the fullness of their eternal calling. The church, for its part, being founded on the love of the Redeemer, contributes towards the spread of justice and charity among nations and in the nations themselves. By preaching the truths of the Gospel and clarifying all sectors of human activity through its teaching and the witness of its members, the church respects and encourages the political freedom and responsibility of the citizens.

Since the apostles, their successors with their helpers have been given the task of proclaiming Christ, Savior of the world, to women and men, they rely in their apostolate on the power of God, who often shows forth the force of the Gospel in the weakness of its witnesses. Those who devote themselves to the ministry of God's word should employ the ways and means which are suited to the Gospel, which differ in many respects from those obtaining in the earthly city.

Nevertheless, there are close links between the things of earth and those things in the human condition which transcend the world, and the church utilizes temporal realities as often as its mission requires it. But it does not pin its hopes on privileges accorded to it by civil authority; indeed, it will give up the exercise of certain legitimate rights whenever it becomes clear that their use will compromise the sincerity of its witness, or whenever new circumstances call for a different approach. But at all times and in all places, the church should be genuinely free to preach the faith, to proclaim its teaching about society, to carry out its task among people without hindrance, and to pass moral judgments even in matters relating to politics, whenever the fundamental human rights or the salvation of souls requires it. The means, the only means, it may use are those which are in accord with the Gospel and the welfare of humanity according to the diversity of times and circumstances.

With loyalty to the Gospel in the fulfillment of its mission in the world, the church, whose duty it is to foster and elevate all that is true, all that is good, and all that is beautiful in the human community,[133] consolidates peace between peoples for the glory of God.[134]

Conclusion

Role of Individual Christians and of Local Churches
91. Drawn from the treasury of the church's teachings, the proposals of this council are intended for all people, whether they believe in God or whether they do not explicitly acknowledge God; they are intended to help them to a keener awareness of their own

---

133   See Vatican Council II, Dogmatic Constitution on the Church, *Lumen gentium*, n. 13.
134   See Lk 2:14.

destiny, to fashion a world better suited to the surpassing dignity of humanity to strive for a more deeply rooted sense of universal sisterhood and brotherhood, and to meet the pressing appeals of our times with a generous and common effort of love.

Faced with the wide variety of situations and forms of human culture in the world, this conciliar program is deliberately general on many points; indeed, while the teaching presented is that already accepted in the church, it will have to be pursued further and amplified because it often deals with matters which are subject to continual development. Still, we have based our proposals on the word of God and the spirit of the Gospel. Hence we entertain the hope that many of our suggestions will succeed in effectively assisting all people, especially after they have been adapted to different nations and mentalities and put into practice by the faithful under the direction of their pastors.

Dialogue

92. In virtue of its mission to enlighten the whole world with the message of the Gospel and to gather together in one spirit all women and men of every nation, race and culture, the church shows itself as a sign of that amity which renders possible sincere dialogue and strengthens it.

Such a mission requires us first of all to create in the church itself mutual esteem, reverence and harmony, and to acknowledge all legitimate diversity; in this way all who constitute the one people of God will be able to engage in ever more fruitful dialogue, whether they are pastors or other members of the faithful. For the ties which unite the faithful together are stronger than those which separate them: let there be unity in what is necessary, freedom in what is doubtful, and charity in everything.[135]

At the same time our thoughts go out to those brothers and sisters and those communities who are not yet living in full communion with us; yet we are united by our worship of the Father, the Son, and the holy Spirit and the bonds of love. We are also mindful that the unity of Christians is today awaited and desired by many non-believers. For the more this unity is realized in truth and charity under the powerful impulse of the holy Spirit, the more will it be a harbinger of unity and peace throughout the whole world. Let us, then, join our forces, in ways more suitable and effective today for achieving this lofty goal, and let us pattern ourselves daily more and more after the spirit of the Gospel and work together in a spirit of brotherhood and sisterhood to serve the human family which has been called to become in Christ Jesus the family of the children of God.

Our thoughts also go out to all who acknowledge God and who preserve precious religious and human elements in their traditions; it is our hope that frank dialogue will spur us all on to receive the impulses of the Spirit with fidelity and act upon them with alacrity.

---

135   See John XXIII, Encyclical *Ad Petri Cathedram*, 29 June 1959: AAS 55 (1959), p. 513.

For our part, our eagerness for such dialogue, conducted with appropriate discretion and leading to truth by way of love alone, excludes nobody; we would like to include those who respect outstanding human values without realizing who the author of those values is, as well as those who oppose the church and persecute it in various ways. Since God the Father is the beginning and the end of all things, we are all called to be brothers and sisters; we ought to work together without violence and without deceit to build up the world in a spirit of genuine peace.

A World to Be Built Up and Brought to Fulfillment

93. Mindful of the words of the Lord: "By this all will know that you are my disciples, if you have love for one another" (Jn. 13:35), Christians can yearn for nothing more ardently than to serve the people of this age successfully with increasing generosity. Holding loyally to the Gospel, enriched by its resources, and joining forces with all who love and practice justice, they have shouldered a weighty task here on earth and they must render an account of it to him who will judge all people on the last day. Not everyone who says "Lord, Lord," will enter the kingdom of heaven, but those who do the will of the Father[136] and who courageously set to work. It is the Father's will that we should recognize Christ our brother in the persons of all men and women and should love them with an active love, in word and in deed, thus bearing witness to the truth; and it is his will that we should share with others the mystery of his heavenly love. In this way people all over the world will awaken to a lively hope, the gift of the holy Spirit, that they will one day be admitted to the haven of surpassing peace and happiness in their homeland radiant with the glory of the Lord.

"Now to him who by the power at work within us is able to do far more abundantly than all that we ask or think, to him be glory in the church and in Christ Jesus to all generations, for ever and ever. Amen" (Eph 3:20–21).

---

136   See Mt 7:21.

Marilynne Robinson

Introduction
Mary Balkun

Best known as an award-winning novelist (*Home, Gilead*), Marilynne Robinson also is a provocative essayist. The first piece in *The Death of Adam: Essays on Modern Thought* (1998)—a collection Robinson has described as "contrarian in method and spirit"—"Darwinism" is an excellent example of Robinson's willingness to take on a difficult contemporary issue. In this case, the way that some interpretations of Darwin's theories about adaptation of species and competition for survival have become a rationale for inhumane behavior. Starting with the example of market capitalism—which she claims to have spawned Darwinism, and which many treat today as if it were a "natural force" to be accepted without question—Robinson sets the stage for a discussion of progressivism, competition, and religion.

When reading this essay, we first must understand that Robinson is distinguishing between "evolution, the change that occurs in organisms over time, and Darwinism, the interpretation of this phenomenon." She rightly points to the way in which Darwin's theories about evolution and natural selection have been used and abused in an effort to justify inhumane behaviors such as colonialism, the extermination of races/peoples, and the primacy of the biggest and strongest. According to Robinson, just as economics requires "conscious choice and control, the making of moral and ethical judgments," so does the application of a scientific theory such as Darwin's.

Robinson covers a wide variety of ideas in this piece, but her primary focus is on the ethical dimensions of Darwinist thought, and particularly its relation to religion and faith-informed attitudes toward the weak, the poor, and the less "fit." As she acknowledges, "The debate between Darwinism and religion is and has always been very strange." She continues later:

> The modern fable is that science exposed religion as a delusion and
> more or less supplanted it. But science cannot serve in the place of
> religion because it cannot generate an ethics or a morality. It can give
> us no reason to prefer a child to a dog, or to choose honorable poverty
> over fraudulent wealth. It can give us no grounds for preferring what
> is excellent to what is sensationalistic. And this is more or less where
> we are now.

Although this is not to displace science with religion or vice versa, it suggests that each has its place and its function.

As you read, pay attention to the way Robinson questions premises on all sides. For example, while she clearly takes issue with Darwinism—at one point describing it as "a chilling doctrine"— she is equally critical of religious hypocrisy.

Using the rhetorical device of thesis/antithesis, Robinson argues:

> The defenders of "religion" have made religion seem foolish
> while rendering it mute in the face of a prolonged and highly
> effective assault on the poor. The defenders of "science"
> have imputed objectivity and rigor to an account of reality
> whose origins and consequences are indisputably economic,
> social, and political.

Finally, Robinson is concerned with the conflation of the inhuman and the human that she attributes to Darwinist thought, and the ethical results of that position. In this essay, she repeatedly gives priority to "mind"—to our ability to judge and discriminate—as the distinguishing characteristic of humans. It is mind, for Robinson, that leads to ethics and religion. Our ability to go beyond the facts of existence—even if those facts describe a schema that can seem harsh in the extreme—and to make choices is what ultimately, for Robinson, makes us most human.

DARWINISM

American culture has entered a period in which atavism looks to us for all the world like progress. The stripping away of humane constraints to liberate great "natural" forces, such as capital flow or the (*soi-disant*) free market, has acquired such heady momentum that no one even pauses to wonder whether such forces are indeed particularly "natural." The use of the word implies a tendentious distinction. Billions of dollars can vanish into the ether under the fingers of a bad young man with a dark stare, yet economics is to be regarded as if it were lawful and ineluctable as gravity. If the arcane, rootless, disruptive phenomenon we call global economics is natural, then surely anything else is, too.

Rivers flow to the sea—this fact implies no obligation on our part to abet them in it, to eliminate meanders and flood plains. If economics were natural in this sense, presumably moderating, stabilizing mechanisms would be intrinsic to its systems. But economics is simply human traffic in what people make and do and value and need, or think they need, a kind of epitome of civilization. It is the wealth of nations, and also their fraudulence and malice and vainglory. It is no more reliably benign or rational than any other human undertaking. That is to say, it requires conscious choice and control, the making of moral and ethical judgments.

Primitive, sometimes called classical, economics has long lived symbiotically with Darwinism, which sprang from it. Darwinists have always claimed that they were simple scientists, pursuing truth even in the face of outrage and rejection, even at the cost of dispelling myths upon which weaker souls preferred to remain dependent. It seems fair to allow that Darwinism might have evolved long enough on its own to have become another species of thought than the one in which it had its origins, though nature provides no analogy for change of that kind. Yet we find the recrudescence of primitive economics occurring alongside a new prominence of Darwinism. We find them separately and together encouraging faith in the value of self-interest and raw competition. Furthermore, we find in them certain peculiar assumptions which are incompatible with their claims to being objective, freestanding systems. One is progressivism, which is implied everywhere in primitive economics, and denied everywhere in contemporary Darwinism.

The idea of progress implies a judgment of value. We are to believe the world will be better if people are forced into severe and continuous competition. If they work themselves weary making a part for a gadget assembled on the other side of the earth, in fear of the loss of their livelihoods, the world will be better for it. If economic forces recombine and shed these workers for cheaper ones, the world will be still better. In what sense, better? To ask is to refuse to accept the supposedly inevitable, to deny the all-overriding reality of self-interest and raw competition, which will certainly overwhelm us if we allow ourselves some sentimental dream of a humane collective life. This economics implies progress and has no progress to show.

Contemporary Darwinism shuns the suggestion that the workings of natural selection are progressive, perhaps in resistance to the old error of assuming that humankind is the masterpiece of evolution. To do so would be to discover special value in peculiarly human attributes, to suggest, for example, that mind is something toward which evolution might have tended. That would be to legitimize the works of the mind, its most characteristic intuitions, concerning, for example, ethics and religion. Yet we are told by Darwinists to celebrate the wondrous works of natural selection, the tangled bank. Its authority must be received, its truth made the measure of all truth, because heaven and earth are full of its glory. To claim creation as the signature act of whatever power one prefers is clearly to overstep the bounds of scientific discourse. The intention is to demonstrate that there are emotional satisfactions in this worldview, which is at least to acknowledge the claims of one distinctively human longing. Characteristically, however, Darwinists, like primitive economists, assume that what is humane—I use the word here, unexceptionably, as I believe, to mean whatever arises from the desire to mitigate competition and to put aside self-interest—is unnatural, and therefore wrong.

The debate between Darwinism and religion is and has always been very strange. I wish to make a distinction here between evolution, the change that occurs in organisms over time, and Darwinism, the interpretation of this phenomenon which claims to refute religion and to imply a personal and social ethic which is, not coincidentally, antithetical to the assumptions imposed and authorized by Judaeo-Christianity. Darwin's theory was published in 1859, two years before the inauguration of Abraham Lincoln. His achievement would be impressive if even a tiny core of scientific insight survived such an explosion of new understanding of the nature of things as has occurred in the last century and a half. It is important to remember, however, that evolution as I have defined it was observed and noted even in antiquity. In 1850 Alfred Tennyson had published in *Memoriam*, the long poem in which he ponders the dark implications of an evolutionary origin of man and creation, and arrives at a reconciliation of this theory with a new understanding of divine providence. In 1852 Matthew Arnold published "Empedocles on Etna," in which evolution is represented as exposing religion as mere human illusion. The tendency to confuse Darwin with Prometheus obscures the fact that his ideas, too, have an ancestry, and an evolution, and, most certainly, a genus.

What, precisely, this theory called Darwinism really is, is itself an interesting question. The popular shorthand version of it is "the survival of the fittest." This is a phrase coined by the so-called Social Darwinist, Herbert Spencer, in work published before the appearance of the *Origin of Species* and adopted—with acknowledgment of Spencer as the source—in later editions of Darwin's book. There is an apparent tautology in the phrase. Since Darwinian (and, of course, Spenserian) fitness is proved by survival, one could as well call the principle at work "the survival of survivors." This is not, strictly speaking, tautological, if the point is to bless things as they are, insofar as they are a matter of life and death. (The words "competition" and "struggle" are grossly euphemistic, since what is being described in Thomas Malthus's *Essay on the Principle of Population* [1798], the winnowing that inspired Darwin, was the withholding of very meager sustenance from those who would die without it. Nothing more heroic was called for than closing one's hand, or turning one's back, both of them familiar and congenial exercises in Darwin's time, and both of them what Spencer was commending when he coined this phrase.)

If we are to take this notion of natural selection as a chaste, objectively functioning scientific principle, however, the issue of tautology is not so easily resolved. Since those who are alive tend to make up the majority of any population, one cannot really be surprised to find their traits predominant, and their offspring relatively numerous. At the same time, one cannot be sure that they have not found the broad path to extinction, like so many creatures before them, doomed by traits that cannot at this moment be called incompatible with their survival, given the fact of their survival. In other words, the theory understood in these terms is notably weak in its ability to generalize, describe or predict. Life forms do change, and there is orderliness in their existence over time, notably in the phenomenon of species, whose origins Darwin did not, in fact, explain, or even claim to have explained. That the drifting of the forms of life corresponds in significant ways to the drift of the content or configurations of their genetic endowment is not a fact whose meaning is self-evident. The change to be observed is change, not necessarily refinement or complication, and not even adaptation, because it is often maladaptive. In *The Descent of Man*, Darwin notes, "Natural Selection acts only tentatively." Behold the great Law that governs nature.

It appears to me that the conjunction which allowed evolution to flourish as Darwinism was the appropriation of certain canards about animal breeding for the purpose of social criticism, together with a weariness in European civilization with Christianity, which did cavil, if anything did, at the extraordinary cruelty of industrial and colonial civilization. Malthus wrote his *Essay on the Principle of Population* to demonstrate the harmful consequences of intervening between the poor and their death by starvation. In his *Autobiography*, Darwin says:

> [In 1838] I happened to read for amusement Malthus on *Population*, and being well prepared to appreciate the struggle for existence which everywhere goes on from long-continued observation of the habits of animals and plants, it at once struck me that under these circumstances favorable variations would tend to be preserved, and unfavorable ones to he destroyed. The result of this would be the formation of new species. Here, then, I had at last got a theory by which to work...

It would appear he made Malthus's grim thesis, that alleviation of misery only results in greater misery, darker still by concluding that those who die deserve to, as the embodiments of unfavorable "variations." In *The Descent of Man* he treats human fecklessness as atavism, and perhaps that is part of what he means here. But as a consequence of the progressive character of change brought about by the process of destruction he describes as occurring within and between populations, survival is always a function of *relative* fitness. There is no such thing as intrinsic worth. No value inheres in whatever is destroyed, or destructible. In *Origin of Species* he says:

> In each well-stocked country natural selection acts through the competition of the inhabitants, and consequently leads to success in the battle for life, only in accordance with the standard of that particular country. Hence the inhabitants of one country, generally the smaller one, often yield to the inhabitants of another and generally the larger country. For in the larger country there will have existed more individuals and more diversified forms, and the competition will have been severer, and thus the standard of perfection will have been rendered higher.

Those who have wondered how it can be that larger countries so consistently dominate smaller ones will find their answer here—bigger countries have better people in them. Insights like this one must have sweetened the pill of Darwinism considerably for those among the British who felt any doubts about the glory of Empire. Especially to be noted is the progressivist spin Darwin puts on Malthus. A more populous country implies for him one in which there is more severe attrition, therefore a more highly evolved people. That is to say, success depends not on numbers but on the severity of competition that is the presumed consequence of large population. Brutal conditions at home legitimize domination abroad. Surely this is the worst of all possible worlds. But my point here is that the idea of progressive evolution through natural selection occurred to Darwin as a consequence of reading about endemic starvation in the populations of wealthy countries. He elaborated it into a theory of national aggression.

If Darwin retreated, in one context or another, from the assertion that there is in fact such a thing as progress in evolution among the plants and animals, he nevertheless consistently assumed that human beings were "perfected" by the struggle for survival. In *The Descent of Man* he makes quite clear what form this progress takes. He says:

> At some future period, not very distant as measured by centuries, the civilized races of man will almost certainly exterminate, and replace, the savage races throughout the world. At the same time the anthropomorphous apes . . . will no doubt be exterminated. The break between man and his nearest allies will then be wider, for it will intervene between man in a more civilized state, as we may hope, even than the Caucasian, and some ape as low as a baboon, instead of as now between the negro or Australian and the gorilla.

Darwin speaks frequently about higher and lower races of man, and he also says that there is little difference in mind or temperament among the races of men. Mind is not a consideration for him, so this causes him no embarrassment. It is true of Darwinism in general that the human mind, and those of its creatures which are not compatible with the Darwinist world-view, are discounted as anomaly or delusion. Elsewhere Darwin remarks, with striking obduracy, "If man had not been his own classifier, he would never have thought of founding a separate order for his own reception." The fact that we alone are capable of describing order in nature is not a significant distinction in his view, but instead a source of error, even though the human brain is taxonomically singular, and should therefore set us apart if our sciences and civilizations did not. Darwin freely concedes to the savages (as to the ants) courage and loyalty and affection. He describes an anthropologist's overhearing African mothers teaching their children to love the truth. These things do not affect the confidence with which he assigns them to the condition of inferiority, which for him is proved by their liability to extermination by the civilized races.

In his useful book, *Darwinian Impacts: An Introduction to the Darwinian Revolution* (1980), D.R. Oldroyd, defending the phrase "survival of the fittest" from the charge that it is tautological, proposes that the reader "consider a simple case of natural selection arising from the struggle for existence." It is the "struggle" that led to the extermination of the native people of Tasmania by European settlers in the nineteenth century. "One group (to their lasting *moral*, but not biological shame) survived; another group failed to survive. Surely it is perfectly clear that this may be explained in terms of some criterion of fitness (say the possession of fire-arms) that is quite separate from the *contingent* fact that the Europeans *did* survive. Thus we can readily see this example as an empirical exemplification of the principle of natural selection or the survival of the fittest." He goes on to discuss the change in coloration of the English peppered moth, omitting to provide the list of contributions made by Anglo-Tasmanians to global well-being which might assuage our doubts about the persuasive force of this simple case, this systematic destruction of unarmed people. Darwinism is, intrinsically, a chilling doctrine.

Rejection of religion was abroad in Europe in the nineteenth century, just as evolution was. Ludwig Feuerbach and Friedrich Nietzsche are two noted debunkers who flourished in Darwin's lifetime, and Karl Marx is another. Marx, the gentlest of them, said, "*Religious* suffering is at the same time an expression of real suffering and a *protest* against real suffering. Religion is the sigh of the oppressed creature, the sentiment of a heartless world, and the soul of soulless conditions. It is the *opium* of the people." Whether the protest against suffering makes suffering harder to relieve, as he argues, or simply makes it harder to ignore, weariness with the sigh of the oppressed creature is easy to document in the thought of the time, and the mode or avenue of such sentiment was religion.

Whether Darwin himself intended to debunk religion is not a matter of importance, since he was perceived to have done so by those who embraced his views. His theory, as science, is irrelevant to the question of the truth of religion. It is only as an inversion of Christian ethicalism that it truly engages religion. And in those terms it is appropriately the subject of challenge from any humane perspective, religious or other. Insofar as ethical implications are claimed for it, it is not science, yet historically it has sheltered under the immunities granted to science. The churches generally have accepted the idea of evolution with great and understandable calm. The God of Abraham, Isaac, and Jacob, or of Luther, Calvin, and Ignatius of Loyola, or of Dietrich Bonhoeffer, Simone Weil, and Martin Luther King, is no Watchmaker. To find him at the end of even the longest chain of being or causality would be to discover that he was a thing (however majestic) among things. Not God, in other words. Daniel Dennett's *Darwin's Dangerous Idea* (1995) declares from its irksomely alliterative title onward that the complex of assertions I have described as Darwinism is vigorously alive. Dennett asks, "If God created and designed all these wonderful things, who created God? Supergod? And who created Supergod? Supersupergod? Or did God create himself? Was it hard work? Did it take time?" This is my point precisely. It is manifestly not consistent with the nature of God to be accessible to description in such terms. Even Dennett, who appears to have no meaningful acquaintance with religious thought, is clearly aware that to speak of God in this way is absurd.

If one looks at the creation narrative in Genesis one finds no Watchmaker, as the Darwinists would have us believe, but a God who stands outside his creation, and calls it into being by, in effect, willing its existence. This terse account does as little to invoke the model of a human artisan as it could do. The creation and blessing of everything, from light to the great sea creatures to whatever creeps on the earth, is done in the same formulaic terms. It all has the same origin, and it is all good. There is no suggestion of hierarchy in the order in which things come into being any more than in the language that names them, with the exception of man/woman, who are made in God's image and given dominion over the rest of creation.

The narrative stabilizes essential theological assertions, first of all, that God is not embodied in any part of creation. He is not light, nor is he the sun, as the gods of other ancient peoples were thought to be. He is in no sense limited or local. He is not the force of good or order struggling against forces of evil or chaos, but the sole creator of a creation that is in whole and in part "very good." There are no loci of special holiness, humanity aside, and nothing evil or alarming or unclean. The sun and moon are simply "lights" and the markers of days and seasons. The alternation of day and night are not the endless recurrence of a terrifying primal struggle but the frame of a great order, identified by the repeated reference to evening and morning with the ordering of creation itself. All these things articulate a vision of being which is sharply distinct from those expressed in competing ancient cosmogonies. The narrative, with its refrain, tells off the days in a week, and culminates in the Sabbath, which is, therefore, as fundamental a reality as creation itself. It is as if God's rest were the crown of his work. This is a very powerful statement of the value of the Sabbath, so essential to the life of the Jews, and it seems to me it probably accounts for the fact of the narrative's describing creation as the business of a week.

Certainly this cosmogony describes a natural order which is freestanding and complete, with rainfall and seasons established, as well as the fecundity of all living things. In *Human, All Too Human*, Nietzsche says:

> In the imagination of religious people all nature is a summary of the actions of conscious and voluntary creatures, an enormous complex or *arbitrariness*. No conclusion may be drawn with regard to everything that is outside of us, that anything will *be* so and so, *must* be so and so; the approximately sure, reliable are we,—man is the *rule*, nature is *irregularity*—

This statement is wrong, point for point, as a characterization of the world of the Genesis cosmogony, which is not in the least degree animistic or demon-haunted or dependent for its functioning on divine intervention. If ancient people had consciously set out to articulate a worldview congenial to science, it is hard to imagine how, in the terms available to them, they could have done better. And in fact, Judeo-Christian culture has been uniquely hospitable to science.

But the point to be stressed is that religious people—by definition, I would say—do not look for proof of the existence of God, or understand God in a way that makes his existence liable to proof or disproof. It is naive to talk about proof in that way, which is why Darwinists need not apologize for their failure to prove the existence of the process of natural selection, which they freely concede they have not done. That attempts at proofs of God's existence have been made from time to time, under the influence of the prestige of Aristotle, or of early science, does not mean that religious belief has sought or depended on that kind of affirmation, as any reader of theology is well aware. Faith is called faith for a reason. Darwinism is another faith—a loyalty to a vision of the nature of things despite its inaccessibility to demonstration.

The Creationist position has long been owned by the Religious Right and the Darwinist position by the Irreligious Right. The differences between these camps are intractable because they are meaningless. People who insist that the sacredness of Scripture depends on belief in creation in a literal six days seem never to insist on a literal reading of "to him who asks, give," or "sell what you have and give the money to the poor." In fact, their politics and economics align themselves quite precisely with those of their adversaries, who yearn to disburden themselves of the weak, and to unshackle the great creative forces of competition. The defenders of "religion" have made religion seem foolish while rendering it mute in the face of a prolonged and highly effective assault on the poor. The defenders of "science" have imputed objectivity and rigor to an account of reality whose origins and consequences are indisputably economic, social, and political.

Creationism is the best thing that could have happened to Darwinism, the caricature of religion that has seemed to justify Darwinist contempt for the whole of religion. Creationism has tended to obscure the fact that religion—precisely as the hope of the powerless and the mitigator of the abuse of the weak—has indeed come under determined attack by people who have claimed the authority of science, and that Darwin's work was quite rightly seized upon by antireligionists who had other fish to fry than the mere demystification of cosmogony. I am speaking, as I know it is rude to do, of the Social Darwinists, the eugenicists, the Imperialists, the Scientific Socialists who showed such firmness in reshaping civilization in Eastern Europe, China, Cambodia, and elsewhere, and, yes, of the Nazis. Darwin influenced the nationalist writer Heinrich von Treitschke and the biologist Ernst Haeckel, who influenced Hitler and also the milieu in which he flourished.

If there is felt to be a missing link between Darwinism and these distinctive phenomena of modern history, it is because we pretend that only Darwin's most presentable book would have had circulation and impact. Reading *The Descent of Man*, one finds Darwin the obsessive taxonomist marveling that Hindus, who are apparently so unlike Europeans, are in fact also Aryans, while Jews, who look just like Europeans, are in fact Asiatics. This sort of language is a reminder of the kind of thinking that was going on in Europe at that time, which Darwin's cheerful interest in the extermination of races, and his insistence on ranking races in terms of their nearness to the apes, could only have abetted.

Daniel Dennett alludes delicately to the sources and history of Darwin's thesis. He says, "The grim Malthusian vision of his social and political forces that could act to check human overpopulation may have strongly flavored Darwin's thinking (and undoubtedly has flavored the shallow political attacks of many an anti-Darwinian) [Shallow! Gentle reader, is this sufficient? Is this fair?], but the idea Darwin needed from Malthus is purely logical. It has nothing at all to do with political ideology, and can be expressed in very abstract and general terms." The idea Darwin took from Malthus was of a continuous cull. Darwin's understanding of the phenomenon was neither abstract nor general. The economic and social programs which claim the authority of Darwin have tended to apply this idea, in one way or another, to human society, in a manner he himself might well have approved, considering that he discovered it in its application to human society. The notion that this idea could have "nothing at all to do with political ideology," presumably because it is "purely logical," is the thinking of a true fundamentalist. Dennett seems unaware that zealots of every sort find every one of their tenets purely logical. Discussing the ongoing Malthusian "crunch," which means that only some organisms in a population will leave progeny, Dennett says:

> Will it be a fair lottery, in which every organism has an equal chance of being among the few that reproduce? In a political context, this is where invidious themes enter, about power, privilege, injustice, treachery, class warfare, and the like, but we can elevate the observation from its political birthplace and consider in the abstract, as Darwin did, what would—must happen in nature.

This language is evasive, and also misleading. As we have seen, if by nature we are to understand the nonhuman world, that is by no means the only setting in which Darwin saw his principle at work. If, as Darwin argues, the human and nonhuman worlds are continuous and of a kind, then Dennett implies a distinction that is in fact meaningless. Since Dennett insists that an ethic is to be derived from Darwinism, our concern is not properly with what happens in nature—since, in any case, it *must* happen—but with the interactions among people in society, concerning which choice is possible. I think we all know that we cannot look to nature for a model, unless we are able to find equity in predation, as, in this century particularly, certain people have in fact claimed to do.

The notion of "fitness" is not now and never has been value neutral. The model is basically physical viability, or as the political economists used to say, physical efficiency. In *The Descent of Man*, Darwin says:

> With savages, the weak in body or mind are soon eliminated; and those that survive commonly exhibit a vigorous state of health. We civilized men, on the other hand, do our utmost to check the process of elimination; we build asylums for the imbecile, the maimed, and the sick; we institute poor laws; and our medical men exert their utmost skill to save the life of everyone to the last moment. There is reason to believe that vaccination has preserved thousands who from a weak constitution would formerly have succumbed to smallpox. Thus the weak members of civilized society propagate their kind. No one who has attended to the breeding of domestic animals will doubt that this must be highly injurious to the race of man. It is surprising how soon a want of care, or care wrongly directed, leads to the degeneration of a domestic race; but excepting in the case of man himself, hardly anyone is so ignorant as to allow his worst animals to breed.

This is pure Malthus. So is the demurral: "[We could not] check our sympathy, even at the urging of hard reason, without deterioration in the noblest part of our nature . . . . We must therefore bear the undoubtedly bad effects of the weak surviving and propagating their kind . . . ," None of this is abstract or general or innocent of political history or implication. *The Descent of Man* (1871) is a late work which seems to be largely ignored by Darwinists now. The persistence of Malthusian influence in such explicit form indicates not only the power but also the meaning of its influence in Darwin's thinking.

And of course its relevance is clearer when Darwin has turned his gaze, as Malthus did, to human society.

It does bear mentioning in this context that the full title of his first book is *On the Origin of Species by Means of Natural Selection, or the Preservation of Favoured Races in the Struggle for Life*. However generously this title is interpreted, clearly it does not assume that biological systems evolve by chance and not design, as Darwin is always said to have done. It clearly implies that whatever is right, and—even less tenably—that whatever is the product of raw struggle, and—still less tenably—that there is a teleology behind it all, one which favors and preserves. Darwinists seem unable to refrain from theology, as the supplanters of it. The old God may have let the rain fall on the just and the unjust alike, but this new god is more implacable in his judgments, and very straightforward, killing off those who die, to state the matter baldly. What need of this theology except to imply that there is wisdom and blessing and meaning in "selection," which the phenomenon itself does not by any means imply? If the temperature on earth rose or fell by five degrees, this same god would curse where he had cherished and love what he had despised, which is only to say that natural selection must indeed be thought of as blind, from the preserving and favoring point of view, if consistency is to be respected at all.

Surely we must assume that a biosphere generated out of any circumstances able to sustain life is as good as any other, that if we make a desert of this planet, for example, and the god of survival turns his countenance upon the lurkers and scuttlers who emerge as fittest, under the new regime, we can have no grounds for saying that things have changed for the worse or for the better, in Darwinist terms. In other words, absent teleology, there are no grounds for saying that survival means anything more or other than survival. Darwinists praise complexity and variety as consequences of evolution, though the success of single-celled animals would seem to raise questions. I am sure we all admire ostriches, but to call a Darwinist creation good because it is credited with providing them is simply another version of the old argument from design, proving in this use of it not the existence of God but the appropriateness of making a judgment of value: that natural selection, whose existence is to be assumed, is splendid and beneficent, and therefore to be embraced.

I am aware that many Darwinists do not argue that the complexity of organisms is a mark of progress in evolution, yet the idea is implicit in their model of adaptation. It is difficult to read about an amoeba, or for that matter a hydrogen atom, without beginning to doubt the usefulness of the word "simplicity." Rather, the universe itself seems to have evolved so far beyond simplicity, before there was any planet Earth or any sun to rise on it, that the only question is, how will complexity be manifest? Shut up in a cell or a spore, it is clearly still complexity. In other words, there is something archaic in the Darwinist assumption that there was anything simple to begin from, and that complexity was knocked together out of accident and circumstance, as a secondary quality of life. And it is consistent with this same archaism that its model for interaction among creatures is simpler than anything to be found anywhere in experimentally accessible nature. In considering how a black hole might lose mass, the simplest account is to be preferred, no doubt. But this is simplicity of a very rarefied kind. We are of one substance with these roaring phenomena our mathematics stumbles in describing.

In any case, the passage from *The Descent of Man* quoted above, which undertakes to account for the physical superiority of the savages, suggests extraordinary limits to Darwin's powers of observation and reflection. If it was true, so far into the era of the contact of savages and Europeans, that the health of the former was still comparatively good, it was true despite the disasters of invasion and colonization and slavery and the near and actual extinctions on this continent and elsewhere brought about by the introduction of European diseases. Darwin notes these effects of the contact of civilized and savage at length in other contexts. He is remarkably inconsistent. He assumes elsewhere, as I have noted, that it is the high rate of attrition within nations that makes them successful in their "struggles" with the less-favored races.

And if it was true that savages throve relatively well it was because they did not live in their own filth in vast conurbations, did not breathe air heavy with brown coal smoke, did not expose themselves to lead or mercury or phosphorus poisoning, did not hold torches to the feet of children to force them to crawl up narrow chimneys or set five-year-olds to work in factories or brickyards, did not sell one another opium tonic to hush the crying of babies. Malthus pondered at length the fact that the mass of the population of Europe, and especially Britain, lived continuously in a state of near starvation. There were two instances of outright famine in Ireland, an agricultural country, in the first half of Darwin's century. In neither case did any crop fail but potatoes, the staple food of the poor, who were virtually the whole of the population. Vastly more than adequate food to end the famine was exported for sale by nonresident landowners while death by starvation swept over the country. Relief was given only to those who had eaten the potatoes they would have put aside to plant a new crop, so the famine went on and on. No doubt the fittest survived, scrawnier for the experience, and not terribly presentable by comparison with the savages. Darwin is simply repeating a commonplace in finding benevolence the villain in the matter of European "degeneracy." History does not at all support the idea that benevolence was ever an important enough phenomenon to have done measurable harm, if, for the sake of argument, we concede it that power.

That human beings should be thought of as better or worse animals, and human well-being as a product of culling, is a willful exclusion of context, which seems to me to have remained as a stable feature of Darwinist thought. There is a worldview implicit in the theory which is too small and rigid to accommodate anything remotely like the world. This is no doubt true in part because acknowledging the complexity of the subject would amount to acknowledging the difficulty of demonstrating the usefulness of the theory. Those best suited to survive do no doubt survive in their descendants, all things being equal, as they rarely are. The point is that, in the matter of interpretation, judicious and dispassionate consideration of all factors would be required to establish with certainty why an organism seems to be successful in evolutionary terms in any specific case. While Darwin argues, in one context, that traits such as generosity and self-sacrifice enhance group survival, though not the survival of the individual organism, in others he clearly sees these same traits as defeating the process of selection at the level of the social group. In the first instance he wishes to prove that such motives and emotions are biologically based and analogous with those of animals because they promote survival, and in the second to argue that their effect is contrary to the workings of nature because it prevents the elimination of the weak or defective. His conclusions seem merely opportunistic. Contemporary Darwinism appears generally to discount group survival as a factor in the operations of natural selection.

Darwinism is harsh and crude in its practical consequences, in a degree that sets it apart from all other respectable scientific hypotheses; not coincidentally, it had its origins in polemics against the poor, and against the irksome burden of extending charity to them—a burden laid on the back of Europe by Christianity. The Judeo-Christian ethic of charity derives from the assertion that human beings are made in the image of God, that is, that reverence is owed to human beings simply as such, and also that their misery or neglect or destruction is not, for God, a matter of indifference, or of merely compassionate interest, but is something in the nature of sacrilege. Granting that the standards of conduct implied by this assertion have rarely been acknowledged, let alone met, a standard is not diminished or discredited by the fact that it is seldom or never realized, and, especially, a religious imperative is not less powerful in its claims on any individual even if the whole world excepting him or her is of one mind in ignoring it and always has been. To be free of God the Creator is to be free of the religious ethic implied in the Genesis narrative of Creation. Charity was the shadow of a gesture toward acknowledging the obligations of human beings to one another, thus conceived. It was a burden under which people never stopped chafing, witness this unfathomably rich country now contriving new means daily to impoverish the poor among us.

Darwinism always concerns itself with behavior, as the expression of the biological imperatives of organisms. Though, historically, it is truer to say that this feature of the theory arose from rather than that it ended in a critique of traditional ethical systems, Darwinism is still offered routinely as a source of objective scientific insight on questions like the nature of human motivation and the possibility of altruism. As I have said, the views of contemporary adherents on these matters are darker than Darwin's own. The theory has been accommodated to Mendelian genetics, yielding the insight that it is not personal but genetic survival for which the organism strives, a refinement which does not escape the tautology implicit in the popular version of the theory, but does add a little complexity to the myth of the battle of each against all, which, however it may thrill sophomores, cannot account for the existence of social behavior in animals. The redefinition of survival enlarges the theater of possible selfish behavior. "Selfish" is a word apologists use without hesitation or embarrassment, because they remain committed to the old project of transforming values, and therefore still insist on using ethically weighted language in inappropriate contexts. It is no more "selfish" for an organism to abide by its nature, whatever that is, than for an atom to appropriate an electron. Certainly finding selfishness in a gene is an act of mind which rather resembles finding wrath in thunder.

In any case, the slightly expanded definition of selfishness is not without problems. This would be a somewhat sweeter world than the one we have if it were true among human beings, at least, that the flourishing of kin and offspring were nearer our hearts than any other interest. As it is, I propose that since this hypothesis cannot survive the evidence to be gathered from reading any newspaper, it ought not to be allowed too great an influence in the formation of social policy. Anecdotal evidence is of the highest order of relevance—evidence gathered inductively would be a better phrase, if the mass of relevant data were not infinitely great, therefore peculiarly vulnerable to misinterpretation as a result of the design of specific inquiries or of bias in the observer, and therefore not really deserving of a more dignified name than anecdote. Studies that proceed by excluding variables are of no use in discovering patterns that signify adaptation to the complexities of the natural order. In zoos we can learn little more than that animals experience boredom and depression.

Observations of human behavior can only be meaningful if they are made in real-world conditions, with an understanding of all factors at play in every instance, and on a scale great enough to allow for every sort of deviation of individuals and groups, and their circumstances, from what might be appropriately described as a norm. To do this would be impossible, of course. But surely science cannot extrapolate with authority from evidence which is only what happens to be available, especially when its appropriateness as evidence is very doubtful. Cats and dogs are quite closely related, but a lifetime of studying dogs would not qualify anyone to speak with authority on the ways of cats. So with the whole earthly bestiary which has been recruited to the purposes of the proper study of mankind.

I fell to pondering Darwinism while reading an essay by Robert Wright in *Time*, in an issue of the magazine that featured Bill Moyers's televised discussions of the Book of Genesis. Wright's essay, titled "Science and Original Sin," delivers the "verdict of science" on human nature, while generously allowing that the biblical view is not entirely misguided. I would never wish to suggest that Wright speaks for science, a word he uses synonymously with Darwinism. His essay is mired in logical problems virtually sentence by sentence. But its appearance in a major mass publication, offered as an antidote, apparently, lest we be misled by the respectful attention paid to Genesis into forgetting that science had displaced its fables with Fact and Truth, indicates the persisting importance of the theory, and the form in which it has its life among the general literate public.

The essay is full of Darwinian eccentricities. Wright says, "Such impulses as compassion, empathy, generosity, gratitude and remorse are genetically based. Strange as it may sound, these impulses, with their checks on raw selfishness, helped our ancestors survive and pass their genes to future generations." To whom on earth would this sound strange except to other Darwinists? Most human beings live collaboratively and have done so for millennia. But Darwinists insist that "selfishness" is uniquely the trait rewarded by genetic survival. So while Wright does concede a biological basis to the traits we call humane and civilized, he puts them in a different category from the more primary traits (in his view) of selfishness and competition. It is not at all clear to me how some biologically based survival mechanisms have priority over others. Wright goes on to say, as Darwinists do, that we are kind to our kin, those custodians of our genetic immortality. "This finickiness gives our 'moral' sentiments a naturally seamy underside. Beneath familial love, for example, is malice toward our relatives' rivals." So our beguiling attributes can be reduced to the little meanness that governs all. It seems inevitable that, over time, doctrines and worldviews would recruit those to whom they make sense, who would therefore, generation after generation, and given the tendency of creatures to herd with their kind, become less and less capable of assuming a posture of critical distance. I cannot report from my own experience and observation that the malice he describes underlies family love. There is a tendency to consider, as he does in this case, pathological behavior as the laying bare of impulses that are in fact universal, so that any quantity of data can be refuted by a single example of behavior that would seem to illustrate his point. This kind of thinking makes all experience that contradicts its assumptions into the product of illusion or self-deception. A splendid way to win every argument.

The idea of illusion is very important to Darwinian thinking, and I am at a loss to understand how it can function legitimately in a Darwinist context. It is often used to reinterpret behavior to make it consistent with the assumptions of the observer. Wright says that when we send money to help victims of a famine on another continent, our "equipment of reciprocal altruism . . . . is being 'fooled' by electronic technology into (unconsciously) thinking that the victims of famine are right next door and might someday reciprocate." Well, perhaps. This may be truer of Wright's equipment than of mine. The elaboration of this nonsensical machinery, whose function, I would suggest, is not the behavioral one of converting selfishness into generosity but the rhetorical one of converting generosity into selfishness, looks to me like anything but science. If behavior is genetically based, then the only insight one can have into the content of the genes that govern behavior is in manifest behavior, which, like it or not, includes generosity.

Wright does make one very valuable point. He says, "There remains one basic, unbridgeable divergence between religious doctrine and Darwinism: according to Genesis, nature is in essence benign... Only when man fell to temptation did the natural world receive a coating of evil. But according to Darwinism, the evil in nature lies at its very roots, instilled by its creator, natural selection. After all, natural selection is chronic competition untrammeled by moral rules. Heedless selfishness and wanton predation are traits likely to endure. If these things are sins, then the roots of sin lie at the origin—not just of humankind but of life." In the degree that we have persuaded ourselves of the truth of this peculiar "science," we have lost a demiparadise, in which there was a knowledge of good as well as of evil. I do not intend this as a defense of religion. I do not share the common assumption that religion is always in need of defending. What is needed here is a defense of Darwinism.

Why generosity and morality, whose ordinary, commonplace utility need hardly be defended, should be given secondary and probationary status is a question I think is best answered in terms of the history of Darwinism, or of the kind of thinking of which it is one manifestation. Utility, after all, should be a synonym for benefit, from the point of view of promoting survival. And behaviors should be looked at indifferently for their survival value, not screened to assure that they satisfy the narrowest definition of self-seeking before they can be regarded as natural and real. The rejection of religion by Darwinism is in essence a rejection of Christian ethicalism, which is declared to be "false" in terms of a rhetoric that pointedly precludes or disallows it. This is manifestly illogical.

Daniel Dennett quotes Friedrich Nietzsche frequently and with admiration as a writer with a profound understanding of Darwinist thinking and its implications. He deals with the problem of the historical consequences of Nietzsche's work by remarking that he "indulged in prose so overheated that it no doubt serves him right that his legion of devotees has included a disreputable gaggle of unspeakable and uncomprehending Nazis." Elsewhere he says, combining optimism with understatement, "fortunately few find [Nietzsche's idea of a will to power] attractive today." The following is a passage from Nietzsche's *Ecce Homo*:

> Let us look a century ahead, let us suppose that my *attentat* on two millennia of anti-nature and the violation of man succeeds. That party of life which takes in hand the greatest of all tasks, the higher breeding of humanity, together with the remorseless destruction of all degenerate and parasitic elements, will again make possible on earth that *superfluity of life* out of which the dionysian condition must

again proceed. I promise a tragic *age*: the supreme art in the affirmation of life, tragedy, will be reborn when mankind has behind it the consciousness of the harshest
but most necessary wars *without suffering from it—*

Nietzsche's many defenders always scold as naive the suggestion that he should be taken
to mean what he says, that he is not just being "overheated." What is most striking to me
is the profound similarity between this language and Darwin's in *The Descent of Man*.
Not that Nietzsche had to know Darwin's work directly. I do not wish to blame Darwin
for Nietzsche, and there is no need to. This passage is entirely conventional except for
the detail of heroizing the unpoetic business of breeding and, especially, culling.

One Nazi who was surely comprehending, and who still seems to be highly reputable—
I use the term "Nazi" in the strict sense, to mean a member of the Nazi Party in the time
of Hitler and an active supporter of his regime—is the Darwinian biologist Konrad
Lorenz. In 1943 Lorenz wrote about the decline of humans in civilization: "In a very
short time the degenerative types, thanks to their larger reproductive rates and their
coarser competitive methods toward the fellow members of the species, pervade the
Volk and the state and lead to their downfall, for the same biological reasons that the
likewise 'asocial' cells of a cancerous growth destroy the structure of the cellular state."
In 1940 he wrote: "From the very beginning the Nordic movement has been emotion-
ally opposed to this 'domestication' of humankind, all its ideals are such as would be
destroyed by the biological consequences of civilization and domestication I have discussed." In 1973 he wrote:

> It is one of the many dilemmas into which mankind has maneuvered itself that
> here again, what humane feelings demand for the individual is in opposition to the
> interests of mankind as a whole. Our sympathy with the asocial defective, whose
> inferiority might be caused just as well by irreversible injury in early infancy as
> by hereditary defects, endangers the security of the nondefective. In speaking of
> human beings, even the words 'inferior' or 'valuable' cannot be used without arous-
> ing the suspicion that one is advocating the gas chamber.

How true. I quote Lorenz only to illustrate that his views can be derived from Darwin
or from Nietzsche with equal plausibility. The fact that these ideas are fully within the
intellectual range of the average blowhard is very far from exculpating their distinguished proponents.

The "two millennia of anti-nature" of which Nietzsche speaks is the Christian era.
They are to be undone through "remorseless destruction," making up for time lost,
presumably, to the practice of mercy while that myth held sway. I hope for the sake
of Christianity that it was indeed a constraint on cruelty, on balance. Certainly it
was often enough a pretext for it. The thing to note here is that it is not the failure of
Christianity but its success, in terms of its own highest values, for which it is despised.

And it is despised because it is "anti-nature," that is, it has fostered degeneracy and parasitism. The antireligious animus is directed at a "falseness" which inhibits the instinct of cruelty. It is another expression of the belief—for which no proof is imaginable—that human goodness is not natural, and therefore is neither beneficial, nor, if the truth were known, even truly good. This is the impetus of the attack on religion; the rejection of the belief, encoded in the terms of myth, that goodness is not only present in creation but is the essence of it. This attack is an impulse of fierce, fastidious aversion directed at humankind, which alone is capable of "degeneracy."

Let us, as a thought experiment, imagine that all those disreputable Nazis who admired Nietzsche were not uncomprehending after all; that, being culturally and historically closer to Nietzsche than Daniel Dennett, and intimate with his language, they were actually the better interpreters. Let us say that they found in passages like the one quoted above an imperative to act as the agents of nature and to effect the splendid restoration foreseen by Nietzsche. The result was, of course, a hideous crime, which issued in so many kinds of catastrophe that we will never see the end of them. History would then have demonstrated, certainly, the superior naturalness of the very values Nietzsche so passionately derides, if naturalness can be taken to imply consistency with the survival of nature. Perhaps we ought not to be treating these questions of value as if they were purely theoretical, but should instead consider drawing tentative conclusions from experience and observation.

Surely it is useful to note affinity. Dennett remarks of Darwin's contemporary and supporter Herbert Spencer that he was responsible for "an odious misapplication of Darwinian thinking in defense of political doctrines that range from callous to heinous." Why do these innocent scientific ideas veer so predictably toward ugliness and evil? I would suggest they do so because they systematically disallow the legitimacy of benign, or for that matter merely neutral, motives and behavior. They are not designed to arrive at any other result. Dennett notes, in his circuitous way, that Darwin did not disavow Spencer, publicly or privately. He interprets this as a regrettable omission. But since Spencer's odious views were already in print while Darwin was still at work on *Origin of Species*, it seems appropriate to consider the implications of the very great probability that influence in fact went from Spencer to Darwin.

Then there is Sigmund Freud, a good Darwinist who has had as much to do with shaping the modern soul as any one man. Himself a compulsive mythologizer, he rejected the myths of Judeo-Christianity, and replaced them with his own luridly dismal accounts of primal cannibalism and so on. In keeping with the absurdity of this strain of intellectual history, this great debunker insists the events he sets at the beginning of human civilization actually happened. In *Civilization and Its Discontents* he says of religion, "Its technique consists in depressing the value of life and distorting the picture of the real world in a delusional manner—which presupposes an intimidation of the intelligence. At this price, by forcibly fixing them in a state of psychical infantilism and by drawing them into a mass-delusion, religion succeeds in sparing many people an individual neurosis. But hardly anything more." It is characteristic of Freud to personify abstractions and to attribute to them motive and strategy. I know of no one else but Hesiod who is so inclined to this way of thinking.

In any case Freud restates the commonplace that religion is delusional, that it is external to the "real world"—though clearly very actively employed in it. And how does this un-deluded scientist view the world? Well, "the ego detaches itself from the external world. Or, to put it more correctly, originally the ego includes everything, later it separates off an external world from itself. Our present ego-feeling is, therefore, only shrunken residue of a much more inclusive—indeed, an all-embracing—feeling which corresponded to a more intimate bond between the ego and the world around it." This is the "oceanic feeling" he associates with religion, his version of Wordsworthian clouds of glory. He is expounding romanticism with the poles reversed, so that maturity as "shrunken residue" is a condition superior to the "intimate bond between the ego and the world." Clearly in his own terms it is arbitrary to call one sense of things truer than the other, though it might have seemed daring, and therefore true, in a culture weary of romanticism.

As for the sentimental joy associated with feeling a bond with the world, the Freudian psyche has no place for it. "The program of becoming happy, which the pleasure principle imposes on us, cannot be fulfilled," though we must try. "Happiness, in the reduced sense in which we recognize it as possible, is a problem of the economics of the individual's libido." I will not pause here over the absolute awfullness of this language, a machinery of imposition and imprecision worthy of a Kafka story. I wish only to point out the utter asociality of the self in the Freudian world. Presumably the existence of others is implied in the concept "libido." The Freudian psyche operates under the constraints and imperatives now to be found in the Darwinist's "selfish gene," with the difference that the psyche has no interest in genetic survival. In *The Future of an Illusion*, Freud ridicules the idea that one might love one's neighbor as oneself, a commandment Jesus quotes from Leviticus, on the grounds that it is contrary to human nature. This is the great peculiarity of this school of thought, that it wishes to make an ethic of what it presents as an inevitability, when, if inevitability were a factor, no ethic would be needed.

Freud's star has dimmed, at last. But his theories were propagated so widely for so long, with so great a degree of certainty of their value, that they survive the demise of his reputation and flourish among us as received truths. They are remarkably meager and charmless. Their lack of scientific foundation, their *prima facie* implausibility, and their profound impact on modern thought, prove together that we can in fact choose myths which will function for us as myths, that is, that will express visions of reality which form values and behavior. This thought is more frightening than reassuring, though if Freud had not been able to adapt the great influence of Darwin and Nietzsche to his purposes, and if they had not themselves been codifiers of widely held attitudes, Freudian theories would never have achieved the status of myth. Since we do in fact have some power of choice, however, what in the world could have moved us to choose anything so graceless and ugly! Darwinians to this day watch for murder in baboon colonies. Altruism was thought to have been sighted among the penguins, but a study of the question found that they did indeed reliably feed their own offspring and not others, so the shimmering possibility of altruism slipped out of our beaks, as it were, and into the arctic waters of the biological imperatives common to humankind and penguins. Surely there was some wisdom in the old story that we are exceptional among the creatures. George Williams, honored among the Darwinists, wonders briefly in his book *Adaptation and Natural Selection* what function there could be for human "cerebral hypertrophy." Obviously it serves to allow us to learn our limitations from the penguins.

Ironically, Darwin, Nietzsche, and Freud have all benefited from a myth of origins. Even now, the idea that they astonished a world of settled belief with brave new insight, and that they dispelled the gloom of an unvalued present life by turning their piercing gaze resolutely to Truth and Nature, makes giants of them—and, more regrettably, makes history a suitable backdrop for this opera, at whatever loss to verisimilitude. In 1932 Albert Einstein wrote an open letter to Sigmund Freud titled "Why War?" In it he asked:

> Is it possible to control man's mental evolution so as to make him proof against the psychoses of hate and destructiveness? Here I am thinking by no means of the so-called uncultured masses. Experience proves that it is rather the so-called "Intelligentzia" that is most apt to yield to these disastrous collective suggestions, since the intellectual has no direct contact with life in the raw, but encounters it in its easiest synthetic form—upon the printed page.

Freud replied:

> We have been guilty of the heresy of attributing the origin of conscience to this diversion inwards of aggressiveness. You will notice that it is by no means a trivial matter if this process is carried too far: it is positively unhealthy. On the other hand if these forces are turned to destruction in the external world, the organism will be relieved and the effect must be beneficial. This would serve as a biological justification for all the ugly and dangerous impulses against which we are struggling. It must be admitted that they stand nearer to Nature than does our resistance to them for which an explanation also needs to be found.

Freud took his heresy from Nietzsche. This account of the origins of conscience was at the center of Nietzsche's theory of the "transvaluation of values," by which the noble types who ruled mankind were made to accept constraints on their behavior by the craftiness of priests. Nietzsche says "*conscience…is the instinct of cruelty turned backwards after it can no longer discharge itself outwards. Cruelty here brought to light for the first time as one of the oldest substrata of culture and one that can least be thought away.*" Freud is quoting back to Einstein one of those books which Einstein blames for propagating "disastrous collective suggestions." He is refusing, also, Einstein's characterization of the cult of hate and destructiveness as psychotic—the "organism" will benefit from the release of these impulses upon the "external" world. (It is eerie how alien from the self the world is for Freud.) Pathology is the consequence of the *restraining* of these impulses. They in themselves are natural and biologically justified.

Note that Freud speaks of humankind as an "organism" on which conscience is artificially imposed. This implies that whatever conscience might tell us about obligations to others, or respect for them, is unnatural and also at odds with our own well-being. History had proved, and was about to prove again, that the well-being of human organisms is not served by the unrestrained release of aggression. It is as if Freud truly were not persuaded of the reality of the external world, as if he did not understand the simple fact that aggression is followed by retaliation in the great majority of cases. And when it is not, it still impoverishes the world, on which, oceanic feelings aside, one does indeed depend for what traditionalists would call the good things in life. As realists would point out, one depends on it for life itself.

It is bizarre in the circumstances, with the horrors of World War I a recent memory and the Nazi era under way, that Freud would consider the attempt to resist hatred and destructiveness to be as much in need of explanation as the desire to act on them. To say the least, this strongly implies a refusal to find value in human life. Note that Freud refers the question to study, to explanation, not to common experience or common sense or common decency. He is telling Einstein that the "Intelligentzia" are indeed the appropriate arbiters of these great questions, no doubt because human beings are misled by such artificial phenomena as conscience. Einstein's query and Freud's reply make the politics of this "science" very clear. Utter moral passivity, and a presumption in favor of aggressive violence, together with an almost perfect lack of imagination for the reality of other "organisms"—who can doubt that Pericles proceeded from other assumptions?

It is a persistent characteristic of the school of thought called Darwinism to resist finding a biological basis for true social behavior, that is, behavior designed to exploit the benefits and satisfactions of attending to collective well-being, of valuing others irrespective of issues of survival. But then the grievance against civilization from which the theory sprang was precisely that it has prevented survival from being a pressing consideration for many people most of the time. All the forms in which this freedom has been celebrated, all the arts and sciences and philanthropies, are only possible because civilization is intrinsically sociable and collaborative. And human beings everywhere create civilizations. The prophet Zechariah, in his vision of Jerusalem restored, says, "Old men and old women shall again sit in the streets of Jerusalem, each with staff in hand for very age. And the streets of the city shall be full of boys and girls playing in its streets." This fine, plain peace and human loveliness are the things we are learning not to hope for.

For old Adam, that near-angel whose name means Earth, Darwinists have substituted a creature who shares essential attributes with whatever beast has been recently observed behaving shabbily in the state of nature. Genesis tries to describe human exceptionalism, and Darwinism tries to discount it. Since Malthus, to go back no farther, the impulse has been vigorously present to desacralize humankind by making it appropriately the prey of unmitigated struggle. This desacralization—fully as absolute with respect to predator as to prey—has required the disengagement of conscience, among other things. It has required the grand-scale disparagement of the traits that distinguish us from the animals—and the Darwinists take the darkest possible view of the animals. What has been rejected is the *complexity* of the Genesis account, in favor of a simplicity so extreme it cannot—by design, perhaps—deal with that second term in the Biblical view of humankind, our destiny, that is, the consequences of our actions. It is an impressive insight, in a narrative so very ancient as the Genesis account of the Fall, that the fate of Adam is presented as the fate of the whole living world. I have heard people comfort themselves with the thought of the perdurability of cockroaches, a fact which does not confute the general truth of the view that our species is very apt to put an end to life on this planet.

Surely *this* makes us exceptional among the animals. Surely this complicates the idea that we are biologically driven by the imperatives of genetic survival. Surely it also complicates the idea that competition and aggression serve the ends of genetic survival in our case, at least. Perhaps our unique moral capacities were designed to compensate for our singular power to do harm—clearly some corrective has been needed. There is a mad cheerfulness in Darwinism, *a laissez-faire, enrichissiez-vous* kind of optimism that persists with absolutely no reference to history or experience. So we find Freud, in the smoldering ashes of Europe, ready to study the question of why the impulses of hatred and destructiveness should be restrained. We have Robert Wright finding hope for a future Eden of human self-transcendence in the appearance of Buddha (born 563 B.C.E.) and Jesus (born 4 B.C.E.). If the rate of appearance of salvific figures were to have continued without deceleration, there would have been three more by now—which is only to say I find this a frail hope. We have Daniel Dennett and Stephen Jay Gould offering hymns to the new Darwinist vision, as if there were anything the least bit new about it.

Evolution has been debated in America for most of this century in the unfortunate terms of the Scopes trial, in which the State of Tennessee asserted its right to forbid the teaching of Darwinism in the public schools. William Jennings Bryan, lawyer for the prosecution, wrote a concluding statement to the Scopes trial jury, which he did not deliver and which was published after his death. It is an interesting document, a moment worth pondering in the transvaluation of American values. Bryan, a former secretary of state, was a pacifist, an anti-Imperialist and a progressive, and a rapturous Presbyterian. He was a graduate of Illinois College and a product of the near Utopian culture of idealism and social reform established in the Middle West in the decades before the Civil War. Religious passion was a great impetus to enlightened reform in that culture, which sprang directly from the Second Great Awakening, and which appealed freely to the Bible to give authority and urgency to its causes. He is described as a populist, which implies some pandering to the mob, but his speeches express a high-mindedness that, especially by present standards, is positively ethereal. To understand the tone of them, it is necessary to remember that his tradition of "fundamentalism" had behind it abolitionism, the higher education of women, and the creation of the public school system. There is sadness in Bryan's tone, a kind of casting about that suggests an awareness of the fact that the ethos of reform was dying out, that after almost a hundred years the old biblical language of justice and mercy was finally losing its power.

Bryan won his case, insisting on the right of a Christian populace not to subsidize the teaching of an inimical doctrine. The problems of this approach are obvious, but he was mortally ill and weary and might have done better under other circumstances. His was a Pyrrhic victory if there ever was one, bringing down a torrent of journalistic ridicule that is usually said to have killed him, and appearing to close, from the point of view of intelligent people, an issue that was then and is now very much in need of meaningful consideration. This is not altogether his fault. His argument, putting aside its appeal to religious majoritarianism, anticipates questions Einstein would raise in his letter to Freud a few years later. These are real questions, not to be dismissed by the invocation of science, and not to be ignored because they were posed in terms that seem archaic to us now.

Bryan makes no distinction between evolution and Darwinism, the philosophical or ethical system that has claimed to be implied by evolution. Perhaps the distinction is not important to him because he is a biblical literalist who insists on the truth of the six-day creation. It requires a little effort, that being the case, to remember that his attack on Darwinism came from the *left*, from the side of pacifism and reform. His argument against Darwinism is essentially political (though he does note that the origin of species was not accounted for, or the theory of natural selection demonstrated). Like Einstein, he associated war with the enthusiasms of the intelligentsia, specifically with the huge influence of Friedrich Nietzsche in the universities. We are all familiar with the anomaly of the success of Fascism in the most cultured countries of Europe, with the anomaly of the high percentage of Ph.D.'s in the SS, and with the startling zeal of learned men in pursuing scientific activities of one sort and another meant to affirm the Nazi worldview. Without wishing to seem to descend to shallow rationalism, I propose that there might in fact be a reason for all this—that Einstein, and also Bryan, may have had a point.

Clarence Darrow, the defense attorney in the Scopes trial, had, the previous year, defended Leopold and Loeb, two young men found guilty of the gratuitous murder of a child. Bryan quotes Darrow's arguments in extenuation of the crime. They are rather bizarre, but so were the times. Leopold, he said, as a young university student, had misread Nietzsche, while Loeb was the victim of hereditary criminality, passed down to him by an unknown ancestor. Darrow was eager to concede the brilliance of Nietzsche, although he read to the court passages "almost taken at random" which he felt were liable to such misreading as his "impressionable, visionary, dreamy" client had made of them. He said, "There is not any university in the world where the professor is not familiar with Nietzsche, not one... If this boy is to blame for this, where did he get it? Is there any blame attached because somebody took Nietzsche's philosophy seriously and fashioned his life upon it? . . . Your Honor, it is hardly fair to hang a nineteen-year-old boy for the philosophy that was taught him at the university." Darrow hastened to assure the court that he did not blame the philosopher, the professors, or the university.

This is very murky business. Of course it is the duty of a lawyer to make the best defense he can of his clients, and the problem must have been especially difficult in this notorious case, where the accused were gifted and privileged and the crime was without motive in any ordinary sense. Bryan used Darrow's defense of Leopold to argue that schools and universities should not have books in them that might corrupt "the souls entrusted to them." This is clearly the wrong conclusion to draw, though, of course, perfectly consistent with the prosecution of Scopes. But Bryan asks a question that seems, from the perspective of subsequent history, hauntingly prescient "[W]ould the State be blameless if it permitted the universities under its control to be turned into training schools for murderers?" This is a very extreme, almost preposterous question, and yet among the most cultured people in Europe something very like this happened. It was not unforeseen—the "disastrous collective suggestions" of which Einstein spoke flourished among the intelligentsia.

Then what to conclude? What magic is there about the word "modern" that makes us assume what we think has no effect on what we do? Bryan wrote, "Science has made war so hellish that civilization was about to commit suicide; and now we are told that newly discovered instruments of destruction will make the cruelties of the late war seem trivial in comparison with the cruelties of wars that may come in the future." This being true, how could a cult of war recruit many thousands of intelligent people? And how can we now, when the fragility of the planet is every day more obvious, be giving ourselves over to an ethic of competition and self-seeking, a sort of socioeconomic snake handling, where faith in a theory makes us contemptuous of very obvious perils? And where does this theory get its seemingly unlimited power over our *moral* imaginations, when it can rationalize stealing candy from babies—or, a more contemporary illustration, stealing medical care or schooling from babies—as readily as any bolder act; Why does it have the stature of science and the chic of iconoclasm and the vigor of novelty when it is, *pace* Nietzsche, only mythified, respectablized resentment, with a long, dark history behind it?

The strain in Western civilization that is expressed in Malthus/Darwin/Nietzsche/Freud has no place in it for the cult of the soul, that old Jacob lamed and blessed in a long night of struggle. There is a passionate encounter with the cruelty of the world at the center of Judeo-Christian experience. So far as we can tell, only we among the creatures can even form the thought that the world is cruel. We are the species most inclined to adapt the environment to ourselves, so perhaps noting the difference between what is and what, from a human point of view, ought to be, is simply a function of our nature, a recognition of the fact that we have choices, that we can improvise. If, as the Darwinists assure us, there is only the natural world, then nothing can be alien to it, and our arrangements, however extravagantly they depart from the ways of other creatures, can never he called unnatural. It is certainly one of the oddest features of a school of thought that denies human exceptionalism as its first premise that it finds so much of human behavior contrary to nature—and objectionable on those grounds. Such an idea can only have survived as part of a self-declared scientific worldview because it allows the making of value judgments, the oldest project of this line of thought. If life had only such meaning as arose from within it, then people could practice philanthropy and give themselves over to mystical visions and harden themselves to their own interests and passions without fear of rebuke. The persistent use of the idea of unnaturalness by people who insist there is only nature suggests that their model of reality is too constricted to permit even its own elaboration. This is true because it is first of all—as premise, not as conclusion—a rejection of things demonstrably present in the world, for example, human fellow-feeling. The idea of the antinatural, of decadence and priestly imposition, gives Darwinism its character as a cause.

This school of thought—ordinarily referred to as modern thought—tells us nothing more urgently than that we are wrong about ourselves. We are to believe we are the dupes of the very reactions that make us judges of circumstance, and that make us free in relation to it. Obviously, if we must act in our own interest, crudely understood, we have few real options, but if we act from a sense of justice, or from tact or compassionate imagination, then we put the impress of our own sense of things on the external world. If this is another version of the will to power, it is in any case the kind of power that religion, and civilization in its highest forms, has always sought to confer. If this is another version of self-interest, it is also a proof of the fact that the definition of that term is very broad indeed, classically friendly to paradox—"It is more blessed to give than to receive," for example, or "it is in dying we live." This does not by any means imply the moral equality of every act that can be construed as rewarding to the one who carries it out, without reference to its consequences. Nor does it imply that apparently selfless conduct is in fact merely less honest than straightforward selfishness. It means that there are rewards in experience for generosity, probably because it serves the collective well-being, but probably also because it is appropriate to our singular dignity as creatures who can act freely, outside the tedious limits of our own interests.

I am sure I would risk offending if I were to say outright that modern thought is a failed project. Still, clearly it partakes as much of error as the worst thinking it has displaced. Daniel Dennett scolds Judeo-Christianity for Genesis 1:28, in which humankind is given dominion over all the earth, as if it licensed depredation. Notions of this kind go unchallenged now because the Bible is so little known. In the recapitulation of creation that occurs after the waters have receded in the narrative of the Flood (Genesis 9:1–4), people are told, as if for the first time, that they may eat the flesh of animals. It would appear the Edenic regime was meant to be rather mild. And of course the most reassuring images of the lordliness of God in both Testaments describe him as a shepherd. Over against this we have Darwin and Nietzsche with their talk of extermination.

If it is objected—and there would be grounds for alarm if it were not objected—that the passages I have quoted above from Darwin and Nietzsche are misread by those who take issue with them, their defenders must make some little effort to be fair to the context of Genesis. It may be true historically that people have justified brutal misuse of nature on the authority of Genesis 1:28, but it is surely true that they have taken a high hand against the whole of creation on the pretext offered them by "the survival of the fittest" or "the will to power." The verse in Genesis 9 that permits the eating of animals is followed by a verse that forbids the shedding of human blood, pointedly invoking the protection of the divine image. This is the human exceptionalism which Dennett and the whole tribe of Darwinians reject as if on a moral scruple. But its effect is to *limit* violence, not to authorize it.

In nothing is the retrograde character of modern thought more apparent. These ancients are never guilty of the parochialism of suggesting that any ambiguity surrounds the word "human," or that there is any doubt about human consanguinity, though such notions would be forgivable in a people surrounded by tribes and nations with which their relations were often desperately hostile. To say this is to grant what is clearly true, that they often failed to live up to their own most dearly held beliefs. This can be looked at from another side, however. They were loyal over many centuries to standards by which they themselves (though less, no doubt, than humankind in general) were found guilty and wanting. This is a burden they could have put down. It is the burden Western civilization has put down, in the degree that it has rejected the assertion of human uniqueness. Darwin's response to objections to the idea of kinship with monkeys was, better a monkey than a Fuegian, a naked savage.

History is a nightmare, generally speaking, and the effect of religion, where its authority has been claimed, has been horrific as well as benign. Even in saying this, however, we are judging history in terms religion has supplied. The proof of this is that, in the twentieth century, "scientific" policies of extermination, undertaken in the case of Stalin to purge society of parasitic or degenerate or recalcitrant elements, and in the case of Hitler to purge it of the weak or defective or, racially speaking, marginally human, have taken horror to new extremes. Their scale and relentlessness have been owed to the disarming of moral response by theories authorized by the word "science," which, quite inappropriately, has been used as if it meant "truth." Surely it is fair to say that science is to the "science" that inspired exterminations as Christianity is to the "Christianity" that inspired Crusades. In both cases the human genius for finding pretexts seized upon the most prestigious institution of the culture and appropriated a great part of its language and resources and legitimacy. In the case of religion, the best and the worst of it have been discredited together. In the case of science, neither has been discredited. The failure in both instances to distinguish best from worst means that both science and religion are effectively lost to us in terms of disciplining or enlarging our thinking.

These are not the worst consequences, however. The modern fable is that science exposed religion as a delusion and more or less supplanted it. But science cannot serve in the place of religion because it cannot generate an ethics or a morality. It can give us no reason to prefer a child to a dog, or to choose honorable poverty over fraudulent wealth. It can give us no grounds for preferring what is excellent to what is sensationalistic. And this is more or less where we are now.

"Worship" means the assigning or acknowledging of worth. Language, in its wisdom, understands this to be a function of creative, imaginative behavior. The suffix "-ship" is kin to the word "shape." It is no wonder that the major arts in virtually every civilization have centered around religion. Darwin, always eager to find analogues and therefore inferred origins for human behavior among the animals, said that, to a dog, his master is a god. But this is to speak of religion as if it were mere credulous awe in the face of an apparently greater power and wisdom, as if there were only natural religion, only the Watchmaker. The relationship between creation and discovery—as Greek sculpture, for example, might be said to have discovered the human form, or mathematics might be said to have discovered the universe—is wholly disallowed in this comparison.

Religion is inconceivable because it draws on the human mind in ways for which nature, as understood by Darwinists, offers no way of accounting. Collaboratively, people articulate perceptions of value and meaning and worth, which are perhaps right and wrong, that is, profoundly insightful, or else self-interested or delusional, at about the rate of the best science. We tend to forget the long respect paid to the Piltdown man, a hoax whose plausibility arose from the fact that it seemed to confirm Darwinist evolutionary theory. We forget that it is only fairly recently that the continents have been known to drift. Until very recently the biomass of the sea at middle and great depths has been fantastically underestimated, and the mass and impact of microbial life in the earth has been virtually unreckoned. We know almost nothing about the biology of the air, that great medium of migration for infectious agents, among other things. The wonderful Big Bang is beset with problems. In other words, our best information about the planet has been full of enormous lacunae, and is, and will be. Every grand venture at understanding is hypothesis, not so different from metaphysics. Daniel Dennett attributes the brilliance of J. S. Bach to the fortuitous accumulation of favorable adaptations in his nervous system. Bach, of all people, is not to be imagined without a distinctive, highly elaborated conception of God, and life in a culture that invoked the idea of God by means of music. That is why his work is profound, rather than merely very clever. And it is profound. It is not about illusion, it is not about superstition or denial or human vainglory or the peculiarities of one sensorium.

We try now to establish value in economic terms, lacking better, and this has no doubt contributed to the bluntly mercenary character of contemporary culture. But economic value is extraordinarily slippery. Buying cheap and selling dear is the essence of profit making. The consumer is forever investing in ephemera, cars or watches that are made into symbols of prosperity, and are therefore desirable because they are expensive. So people spend a great deal of money for the advantages of being perceived to have spent a great deal of money. These advantages are diminished continuously by the change of styles either toward or away from the thing they have bought, which make it either commonplace or passé.

Or manufacture is taken from a setting in which adults work for reasonable wages and there are meaningful protections of the environment, and moved into a setting where children work for meager wages and the environment is desolated. This creates poverty among workers in both settings and destroys the wealth that is represented in a wholesome environment—toxins in the air or the water are great destroyers of wealth. So economic value is created at the cost of the economic value of workers who are made unable to figure as consumers, and of resources that are made unsuitable for any use. A few people may get rich, but the transaction altogether is a loss, perhaps a staggering loss. A global economy organized on these principles will be full of poor, sick, dispirited people, and shoddy goods, since they will be cheapened to suit the dwindling prosperity of the workforce, who are also the buying public. An objective accounting of value would find disaster here. Humane limits to the exploitation of people would solve the problem, but they would also interfere with competition, which is the great law of nature, supposedly, and which therefore functions as a value, because "science" has supplanted religion.

How much misery and premature death (most of it out of sight, granted) do we agree to when we accept this new economic order: Is it in any way an advance on colonialism:

Do we imagine, as the colonialists sometimes did, that we are bringing benefits of civilization to the far reaches of the world? Are we not in fact decivilizing ourselves as we decivilize them? Why is there no outcry? Is it because we have cast off the delusion of human sanctity? I think we should study our silence for insight into other momentous silences in recent history.

This is not the worst of it. Now that the mystery of motive is solved—there are only self-seeking and aggression, and the illusions that conceal them from us—there is no place left for the soul, or even the self. Moral behavior has little real meaning, and inwardness, in the traditional sense, is not necessary or possible. We use analysts and therapists to discover the content of our experience. Equivalent trauma is assumed to produce more or less equivalent manifestations in every case, so there is little use for the mind, the orderer and reconciler, the artist of the interior world. Whatever it has made will only be pulled apart. The old mystery of subjectivity is dispelled; individuality is a pointless complication of a very straightforward organic life. Our hypertrophic brain, that prodigal indulgence, that house of many mansions, with its stores, and competences, and all its deep terrors and very rich pleasures, which was so long believed to be the essence of our lives, and a claim on one another's sympathy and courtesy and attention, is going the way of every part of collective life that was addressed to it—religion, art, dignity, graciousness. Philosophy, ethics, politics, properly so called. It is a thing that bears reflecting upon, how much was destroyed, when modern thought declared the death of Adam.

Simone Weil

Introduction
Nancy Enright

Simone Weil was born in 1909 in Paris and attended the Ecole Normale Super-ieure, where she excelled as a scholar. Her first published work was *Gravity and Grace*. Gustave Thibon, in his introduction to the fifteenth anniversary edition of this text, tells of his first meeting with Weil, through an introduction from a mu-tual friend, Reverend Father Perrin, a Dominican, to whom Weil wrote another of her works, *Letter to a Priest*. Thibon took in Weil while she worked for a time in the country despite her high-level training in philosophy. Weil believed in the sacramental value of manual, physical work. She also felt a deep sympathy for the plight of the working class. She worked for a time in factories, as well as doing farm work. She worked diligently in the vineyards until her health caused her to return to Marseille, France, where she lived with her parents for a while until they all left for the United States.

For Weil, everything, work included, was part of the loving plan of God. A Jew by birth, she grew up in a family without strong religious beliefs but developed a deep interest in philosophy and politics. She was particularly interested in the thoughts of Pascal, especially the *Pensees*, her favorite book. As a secular intel-lectual, she gradually felt drawn to Christianity, and Catholicism in particular. She experienced moments of mysticism, including an encounter with Christ after reading George Herbert's religious poem "Love III." She described reading and re-reading the poem as a kind of prayer, though she did not typically pray at that point in her life. She wrote to Fr. Perrin, "Christ himself came down and took possession of me." However, she believed that she could not submit to the rite of Baptism, for reasons that she outlined in her *Letter to a Priest*.

Some sense of Weil's generosity of spirit is shown in her giving half of her food rations to the poor and tutoring poor children after her hard day's labor in the vineyard. She died in London in 1943.

REFLECTIONS ON THE RIGHT USE OF SCHOOL STUDIES WITH A VIEW TO THE LOVE OF GOD

The key to a Christian conception of studies is the realization that prayer consists of attention. It is the orientation of all the attention of which the soul is capable toward God. The quality of the attention counts for much in the quality of the prayer. Warmth of heart cannot make up for it.

The highest part of the attention only makes contact with God, when prayer is intense and pure enough for such a contact to be established; but the whole attention is turned toward God.

Of course school exercises only develop a lower kind of attention. Nevertheless, they are extremely effective in increasing the power of attention that will be available at the time of prayer, on condition that they are carried out with a view to this purpose and this purpose alone.

Although people seem to be unaware of it today, the development of the faculty of attention forms the real object and almost the sole interest of studies. Most school tasks have a certain intrinsic interest as well, but such an interest is secondary. All tasks that really call upon the power of attention are interesting for the same reason and to an almost equal degree.

School children and students who love God should never say: "For my part I like mathematics"; "I like French"; "I like Greek." They should learn to like all these subjects, because all of them develop that faculty of attention which, directed toward God, is the very substance of prayer.

If we have no aptitude or natural taste for geometry, this does not mean that our faculty for attention will not be developed by wrestling with a problem or studying a theorem. On the contrary it is almost an advantage.

It does not even matter much whether we succeed in finding the solution or understanding the proof, although it is important to try really hard to do so. Never in any case whatever is a genuine effort of the attention wasted. It always has its effect on the spiritual plane and in consequence on the lower one of the intelligence, for all spiritual light lightens the mind.

If we concentrate our attention on trying to solve a problem of geometry, and if at the end of an hour we are no nearer to doing so than at the beginning, we have nevertheless been making progress each minute of that hour in another more mysterious dimension. Without our knowing or feeling it, this apparently barren effort has brought more light into the soul. The result will one day be discovered in prayer. Moreover, it may very likely be felt in some department of the intelligence in no way connected with mathematics. Perhaps he who made the unsuccessful effort will one day be able to grasp the beauty of a line of Racine more vividly on account of it. But it is certain that this effort will bear its fruit in prayer. There is no doubt whatever about that.

Certainties of this kind are experimental. But if we do not believe in them before experiencing them, if at least we do not behave as though we believed in them, we shall never have the experience that leads to such certainties. There is a kind of contradiction here. Above a given level this is the case with all useful knowledge concerning spiritual progress. If we do not regulate our conduct by it before having proved it, if we do not hold on to it for a long time by faith alone, a faith at first stormy and without light, we shall never transform it into certainty. Faith is the indispensable condition.

The best support for faith is the guarantee that if we ask our Father for bread, he does not give us a stone. Quite apart from explicit religious belief, every time that a human being succeeds in making an effort of attention with the sole idea of increasing his grasp of truth, he acquires a greater aptitude for grasping it, even if his effort produces no visible fruit. An Eskimo story explains the origin of light as follows: "In the eternal darkness, the crow, unable to find any food, longed for light, and the earth was illumined." If there is a real desire, if the thing desired is really light, the desire for light produces it. There is a real desire when there is an effort of attention. It is really light that is desired if all other incentives are absent. Even if our efforts of attention seem for years to be producing no result, one day a light that is in exact proportion to them will flood the soul. Every effort adds a little gold to a treasure no power on earth can take away. The useless efforts made by the Cure d'Arcy, for long and painful years, in his attempt to learn Latin bore fruit in the marvelous discernment that enabled him to see the very soul of his penitents behind their words and even their silences.

Students must therefore work without any wish to gain good marks, to pass examinations, to win school successes; without any reference to their natural abilities and tastes; applying themselves equally to all their tasks, with the idea that each one will help to form in them the habit of that attention which is the substance of prayer. When we set out to do a piece of work, it is necessary to wish to do it correctly, because such a wish is indispensable in any true effort. Underlying this immediate objective, however, our deep purpose should aim solely at increasing the power of attention with a view to prayer; as, when we write, we draw the shape of the letter on paper, not with a view to the shape, but with a view to the idea we want to express. To make this the sole and exclusive purpose of our studies is the first condition to be observed if we are to put them to the right use.

The second condition is to take great pains to examine squarely and to contemplate attentively and slowly each school task in which we have failed, seeing how unpleasing and second rate it is, without seeking any excuse or overlooking any mistake or any of our tutor's corrections, trying to get down to the origin of each fault. There is a great temptation to do the opposite, to give a sideways glance at the corrected exercise if it is bad and to hide it forthwith.

Most of us do this nearly always. We have to withstand this temptation. Incidentally, moreover, nothing is more necessary for academic success, because, despite all our efforts, we work without making much progress when we refuse to give our attention to the faults we have made and our tutor's corrections.

Above all it is thus that we can acquire the virtue of humility, and that is a far more precious treasure than all academic progress. From this point of view it is perhaps even more useful to contemplate our stupidity than our sin. Consciousness of sin gives us the feeling that we are evil, and a kind of pride sometimes finds a place in it. When we force ourselves to fix the gaze, not only of our eyes but of our souls, upon a school exercise in which we have failed through sheer stupidity, a sense of our mediocrity is borne in upon us with irresistible evidence. No knowledge is more to be desired. If we can arrive at knowing this truth with all our souls we shall be well established on the right foundation.

If these two conditions are perfectly carried out there is no doubt that school studies are quite as good a road to sanctity as any other.

To carry out the second, it is enough to wish to do so. This is not the case with the first. In order really to pay attention, it is necessary to know how to set about it.

Most often attention is confused with a land of muscular effort. If one says to one's pupils: "Now you must pay attention," one sees them contracting their brows, holding their breath, stiffening their muscles. If after two minutes they are asked what they have been paying attention to, they cannot reply. They have been concentrating on nothing. They have not been paying attention. They have been contracting their muscles.

We often expend this kind of muscular effort on our studies. As it ends by making us tired, we have the impression that we have been working. That is an illusion. Tiredness has nothing to do with work. Work itself is the useful effort, whether it is tiring or not. This kind of muscular effort in work is entirely barren, even if it is made with the best of intentions. Good intentions in such cases are among those that pave the way to hell. Studies conducted in such a way can sometimes succeed academically from the point of view of gaining marks and passing examinations, but that is in spite of the effort and thanks to natural gifts; moreover such studies are never of any use.

Will power, the kind that, if need be, makes us set our teeth and endure suffering, is the principal weapon of the apprentice engaged in manual work. But, contrary to the usual belief, it has practically no place in study. The intelligence can only be led by desire. For there to be desire, there must be pleasure and joy in the work. The intelligence only grows and bears fruit in joy. The joy of learning is as indispensable in study as breathing is in running. Where it is lacking there are no real students, but only poor caricatures of apprentices who, at the end of their apprenticeship, will not even have a trade.

It is the part played by joy in our studies that makes of them a preparation for spiritual life, for desire directed toward God is the only power capable of raising the soul. Or rather, it is God alone who comes down and possesses the soul, but desire alone draws God down. He only comes to those who ask him to come; and he cannot refuse to come to those who implore him long, often, and ardently.

Attention is an effort, the greatest of all efforts perhaps, but it is a negative effort. Of itself, it does not involve tiredness. When we become tired, attention is scarcely possible any more, unless we have already had a good deal of practice. It is better to stop working altogether, to seek some relaxation, and then a little later to return to the task; we have to press on and loosen up alternately, just as we breathe in and out.

Twenty minutes of concentrated, untried attention is infinitely better than three hours of the kind of frowning application that leads us to say with a sense of duty done: "I have worked well!"

But, in spite of all appearances, it is also far more difficult. Something in our soul has a far more violent repugnance for true attention than the flesh has for bodily fatigue. This something is much more closely connected with evil than is the flesh. That is why every time that we really concentrate our attention, we destroy the evil in ourselves. If we concentrate with this intention, a quarter of an hour of attention is better than a great many good works.

Attention consists of suspending our thought, leaving it detached, empty, and ready to be penetrated by the object; it means holding in our minds, within reach of this thought, but on a lower level and not in contact with it, the diverse knowledge we have acquired which we are forced to make use of. Our thought should be in relation to all particular and already formulated thoughts, as a man on a mountain who, as he looks forward, sees also below him, without actually looking at them, a great many forests and plains. Above all our thought should be empty, waiting, not seeking anything, but ready to receive in its naked truth the object that is to penetrate it.

All wrong translations, all absurdities in geometry problems, all clumsiness of style, and all faulty connection of ideas in compositions and essays, all such things are due to the fact that thought has seized upon some idea too hastily, and being thus prematurely blocked, is not open to the truth. The cause is always that we have wanted to be too active; we have wanted to carry out a search. This can be proved every time, for every fault, if we trace it to its root. There is no better exercise than such a tracing down of our faults, for this truth is one to be believed only when we have experienced it hundreds and thousands of times. This is the way with all essential truths.

We do not obtain the most precious gifts by going in search of them but by waiting for them. Man cannot discover them by his own powers, and if he sets out to seek for them he will find in their place counterfeits of which he will be unable to discern the falsity.

The solution of a geometry problem does not in itself constitute a precious gift, but the same law applies to it because it is the image of something precious. Being a little fragment of particular truth, it is a pure image of the unique, eternal, and living Truth, the very Truth that once in a human voice declared: "I am the Truth."

Every school exercise, thought of in this way, is like a sacrament.

In every school exercise there is a special way of waiting upon truth, setting our hearts upon it, yet not allowing ourselves to go out in search of it. There is a way of giving our attention to the data of a problem in geometry without trying to find the solution or to the words of a Latin or Greek text without trying to arrive at the meaning, a way of waiting, when we are writing, for the right word to come of itself at the end of our pen, while we merely reject all inadequate words.

Our first duty toward school children and students is to make known this method to them, not only in a general way but in the particular form that bears on each exercise. It is not only the duty of those who teach them but also of their spiritual guides. Moreover the latter should bring out in a brilliantly clear light the correspondence between the attitude of the intelligence in each one of these exercises and the position of the soul, which, with its lamp well filled with oil, awaits the Bridegroom's coming with confidence and desire. May each loving adolescent, as he works at his Latin prose, hope through this prose to come a little nearer to the instant when he will really be the slave—faithfully waiting while the master is absent, watching and listening—ready to open the door to him as soon as he knocks. The master will then make his slave sit down and himself serve him with meat.

Only this waiting, this attention, can move the master to treat his slave with such amazing tenderness. When the slave has worn himself out in the fields, his master says on his return, "Prepare my meal, and wait upon me." And he considers the servant who only does what he is told to do to be unprofitable. To be sure in the realm of action we have to do all that is demanded of us, no matter what effort, weariness, and suffering it may cost, for he who disobeys does not love; but after that we are only unprofitable servants, Such service is a condition of love, but it is not enough. What forces the master to make himself the slave of his slave, and to love him, has nothing to do with all that. Still less is it the result of a search the servant might have been bold enough to undertake on his own initiative. It is only watching, waiting, attention.

Happy then are those who pass their adolescence and youth in developing this power of attention. No doubt they are no nearer to goodness than their brothers working in fields and factories. They are near in a different way. Peasants and workmen possess a nearness to God of incomparable savor which is found in the depths of poverty, in the absence of social consideration and in the endurance of long-drawn-out sufferings. If, however, we consider the occupations in themselves, studies are nearer to God because of the attention which is their soul. Whoever goes through years of study without developing this attention within himself has lost a great treasure.

Not only does the love of God have attention for its substance; the love of our neighbor, which we know to be the same love, is made of this same substance. Those who are unhappy have no need for anything in this world but people capable of giving them their attention. The capacity to give one's attention to a sufferer is a very rare and difficult thing; it is almost a miracle; it is a miracle. Nearly all those who think they have this capacity do not possess it. Warmth of heart, impulsiveness, pity are not enough.

In the first legend of the Grail, it is said that the Grail (the miraculous vessel* that satisfies all hunger by virtue of the consecrated Host) belongs to the first comer who asks the guardian of the vessel, a king three-quarters paralyzed by the most painful wound, "What are you going through?"

The love of our neighbor in all its fullness simply means being able to say to him: "What are you going through?" It is a recognition that the sufferer exists, not only as a unit in a collection, or a specimen from the social category labelled "unfortunate," but as a man, exactly like us, who was one day stamped with a special mark by affliction. For this reason it is enough, but it is indispensable, to know how to look at him in a certain way.

This way of looking is first of all attentive. The soul empties itself of all its own contents in order to receive into itself the being it is looking at, just as he is, in all his truth.

Only he who is capable of attention can do this.

So it comes about that, paradoxical as it may seem, a Latin prose or a geometry problem, even though they are done wrong, may be of great service one day, provided we devote the right kind of effort to them. Should the occasion arise, they can one day make us better able to give someone in affliction exactly the help required to save him, at the supreme moment of his need.

---

* According to some legends the Grail was made of a single stone, in color like an emerald.

For an adolescent, capable of grasping this truth and generous enough to desire this fruit above all others, studies could have their fullest spiritual effect, quite apart from any particular religious belief.

Academic work is one of those fields containing a pearl so precious that it is worthwhile to sell all our possessions, keeping nothing for ourselves, in order to be able to acquire it.